# Learning VBScript

# Learning VBScript

## Paul Lomax

# O'REILLY®

*Beijing · Cambridge · Farnham · Köln · Paris · Sebastopol · Taipei · Tokyo*

**Learning VBScript**
by Paul Lomax

Published by O'Reilly & Associates, Inc., 101 Morris Street, Sebastopol, CA 95472.

**Editor:** Ron Petrusha

**Production Editor:** Nicole Gipson Arigo

**Printing History:**

      July 1997:         First Edition.

ISBN: 1-56592-247-6

# Table of Contents

# *Preface*

The rate of change in computing in general, and of the Web in particular, continues to increase. The reduced development and distribution times afforded by the Internet have turned what was once a gradual learning process into a frenzy of activity just to keep up to date with developments. Web pages, once a medium for plain text and graphics, are now becoming containers for complex applications, even becoming applications in their own right.

The move towards the goal of a seamless desktop and web—where the source of the data, even the source of the application itself, is immaterial—is forcing changes upon two distinct sets of developers. First, there are those people coming from a desktop programming environment who have had little exposure to creating web-based content. To them, the web page metaphor is largely an unfamiliar concept, but they now find they must extend their programming skills to include the creation of dynamic client-side and server-side applications through the use of a scripting language. Second, there are the people responsible for creating web sites, web pages, and web content, many of whom had their first experience of programming with the HTML tag. They are now being forced down a road that requires them to acquire new and unfamiliar programming skills in order to keep abreast of the latest technology.

The latest technology to which I refer is Microsoft's Active Content. A family of technologies that can be used to add spice to a web page, it can recreate a desktop application within a web page, improve the look, feel, and functionality of HTML pages, and even control the browser itself.

Whatever your needs, an Active Content solution is achieved by means of a wide variety of controls, components, and objects, at both the client and the server, all of which are standalone programs, and all of which need to be controlled and marshaled into a single coherent application. This coherence and organization is achieved by a common thread that runs through all of Microsoft's Active Content or ActiveX technologies: VBScript. VBScript is the glue that binds ActiveX controls to web pages, binds ActiveX components to the web server, and interfaces the browser with HTML controls. A prerequisite for creating a successful Active Content web application is therefore a thorough knowledge of VBScript.

VBScript is set to do for the Web what Visual Basic did for the Windows desktop—it allows almost anyone to quickly and easily create professional results, without having to invest months of time in learning a new and complex language. Using VBScript, desktop developers can leverage their current knowledge to speed the development process, while those new to scripting and programming will find that the easy-to-understand syntax of VBScript allows them to progress quickly from creating a simple "Hello, World" type of application to building useful, meaningful, and, above all, robust applications.

## The Book's Audience

This book has been written to reflect the needs of the three diverse groups who now find that a knowledge of scripting in general, and of VBScript in particular, is needed for their web development work:

1. Web content providers and HTML authors with little or no programming experience, who are looking to VBScript as an accessible tool with which to start programming. If you belong to this group, VBScript's simple and logical syntax will enable you to produce pleasing results quickly and without the frustrations often associated with other programming languages. *Learning VBScript* takes you through the process of creating web applications and programs using VBScript in a structured and methodical way, allowing you to build on your skills as you progress.

2. Visual Basic developers who are using or planning to use VBScript as their tool of choice for web page and Intranet development. If you are a VB programmer, you'll find that *Learning VBScript* is an essential part of your reference collection. Author Paul Lomax and editor Ron Petrusha have drawn on many years of VB experience, coupled with an intimate knowledge of VBScript and web application development, to point out the subtle yet essential differences between VBScript and VB, thus smoothing the transition from developing desktop client/server applications to developing web-browser-based Intranet applications. *Learning VBScript* will show you how to leverage your VB experience to best effect, using the HTML page and the HTML Layout Control as your canvas, rather than the VB Form. The importance of being able to create VB-type applications in a web environment should not be underestimated as the corporate world embraces the Intranet.

3. Last, and certainly not least, hobbyists wishing to keep up with the latest developments on the Web and in programming in general. If that describes you, you are advised to use *Learning VBScript* as your springboard for coming to grips with the challenging new world of ActiveX and Active Scripting, technologies that will continue to grow in prominence and importance, both on the Web and on the Windows desktop in the months and years to come.

# Organization of This Book

The book contains seventeen chapters and six appendixes.

The first two chapters are introductory in character. That is, they attempt to position VBScript as a tool for developing client-side web applications, both among the various components of the Visual Basic family and among the various technologies and strategies that are available today for developing Internet and Intranet applications.

Chapter 1, *Introduction*, examines the development of the Web and its evolution to the point at which scripting languages like VBScript are needed. It continues this theme by looking at the needs of the Web, and in particular the need for dynamic web documents, which can help alleviate the problem of Internet bandwidth. This chapter also discusses the differences between client-side processing and server-side processing, gives an overview of the components of client-side processing, and wraps up with a look at what can be achieved using VBScript.

Chapter 2, *What Is VBScript?*, provides an overview of where VBScript fits into the Visual Basic family, as well as a high-level look at how VBScript works. It also explains how, through the use of OLE Automation, Active Scripting will soon be commonplace outside of the web browser. Finally, the differences between VBScript and JavaScript are discussed.

The following two chapters offer an introduction to the language elements and the syntax of VBScript. If you're new to programming, you'll certainly want to read these chapters carefully. If you already know VB, you'll want to focus on the chapters' treatment of the differences between VB and VBScript.

Chapter 3, *Getting Started*, offers an in-depth explanation of the `<SCRIPT>` tag and the various ways in which you can invoke scripts in your web pages. This chapter provides extensive coverage of the basics needed to start writing programs in VBScript. For example, it covers such topics as variables and constants, scope, VBScript's variant data type and its data subtypes, and converting data from one subtype to another.

Chapter 4, *Program Flow and Structure*, provides extensive coverage of VBScript control statements, including decision-making statements like `If...Then`, and looping statements like `For...Next`.

The next two chapters introduce the MSIE object model, as the book takes you from working with the VBScript language to using the elements of the language to create web pages and web applications. Through the access that it gives you to the browser's object model, VBScript becomes a powerful tool that you can use to control the behavior of the browser, building solid, professional web pages in the process.

Chapter 5, *Controlling the Browser*, shows how you can use VBScript to add functionality to your web pages using the MSIE Scripting Object Model. A thorough examination of its Objects, Properties, Methods, and Events leads you through each subject with complete examples and helpful undocumented hints and tips.

Chapter 6, *The Element Object and HTML Intrinsic Controls*, continues the documentation on the MSIE Object Model by concentrating on the Element Object, which allows your script to manipulate the HTML Intrinsic Controls that you use to create HTML Forms.

The next two chapters focus on adding ActiveX controls to your applications, and on using two integrated tools, the ActiveX Control Pad and the HTML Layout Control, that are readily available to help you work with ActiveX controls.

Chapter 7, *Using the ActiveX Control Pad*, provides documentation and examples for using the `<OBJECT>` tag, and an extensive look at the ActiveX Control Pad, an essential tool for creating ActiveX HTML pages. The chapter also covers downloading and installing the ActiveX Control Pad, and provides examples using the Script Wizard. It also discusses Microsoft's little-known ACList utility.

Chapter 8, *The HTML Layout Control*, examines how you can use the HTML Layout Control to create state-of-the-art web pages to give the look and feel of a Windows desktop application. The chapter provides documentation on the HTML Layout Control Toolbox, and provides a complete example that shows how to create an HTML Layout.

The remainder of the book focuses on a variety of techniques that you can use to enhance your web pages and add spice to your web applications.

Chapter 9, *An HTML Layout Common Menu Object*, is a tutorial example reinforcing the importance of the Layout Control, by showing how the Layout Control can be used to create common objects. It also introduces you to the concept of creating reusable components that can appear in multiple web pages. The chapter takes you though creating a Menu Bar and adding the Menu Bar to a series of HTML documents.

Chapter 10, *Date and Time in VBScript*, provides extensive documentation and examples for the rich set of date and time functions in VBScript. It shows you how to perform such operations as checking the validity of a date, returning the client machine's date and time, splitting up the date and time into their components, performing calculations with dates and times, and reformatting date expressions. The chapter also provides two complete examples that you may find particularly useful: a cookie example, and a countdown example.

Chapter 11, *Describing Your Hyperlinks*, examines the various means by which you can improve the way your web page communicates with your visitors. Its examples show how to include link descriptions using HTML intrinsic objects, the status bar, and the ActiveX Label control.

Chapter 12, *Image Maps Made Easy*, is a tutorial chapter taking you through the steps to create a VBScript image map application. It examines the screen coordinate scheme, shows how to define a clickable image map, and takes you through creating an image map script.

Chapter 13, *Building Dynamic HTML Pages*, reviews the Document object methods, then details building a document on download to the browser, shows you how to add variables to a web page at download, and demonstrates the linchpin of dynamic web documents: creating a new web page entirely from a script.

Chapter 14, *Form Input Validation*, starts with an investigation of working with object references, then goes on to detail the VBScript data validation functions, focusing on string manipulation functions and formatting data. This chapter also discusses the pros and cons of various techniques for *timing* data validation, which allows you to build web pages that provide valid data but are as unobtrusive as possible to their users.

Chapter 15, *Error Handling and Debugging*, offers a thorough examination of the various debugging techniques you can use with VBScript. It discusses debugging, handling syntax errors and logical errors, and using the Microsoft Script Debugger. The section on error handling takes you through the *Err* object, and demonstrates how to create an error handler for a scripted application. The chapter also shows you many helpful techniques for building robust applications, by detailing common problem areas and how to avoid them.

Chapter 16, *The VBScript Shopping Cart*, takes you step by step through the creation of a complete, highly functional, client-side shopping cart application.

Chapter 17, *Handling Other Browsers*, demonstrates and investigates the various options for creating scripted web pages that can be used with browsers other than Microsoft Internet Explorer. The discussion includes methods for determining the type of browser used to view your web pages, techniques for creating multibrowser enhanced pages, and a description of the NCompass ScriptActive plug-in for Navigator.

Appendix A, *VBScript 1.0 Language Quick Reference*, details the keywords you will find in the first release of VBScript.

Appendix B, *VBScript Version 2*, details the keywords that support client-side programming in VBScript Version 2.0.

Appendix C, *VBScript 2.0 Intrinsic Constants*, details the new constants introduced in VBScript Version 2.0.

Appendix D, *ActiveX Controls Quick Reference*, is designed purely as a "memory jogger." It lists the events, methods, and properties of each of the standard ActiveX controls.

Appendix E, *Active Server Pages*, provides a high-level overview of scripting with VBScript at the server using the new Active Server Pages technology.

Appendix F, *The Learning VBScript CD-ROM*, details how to use the CD-ROM accompanying *Learning VBScript*.

## *Conventions in This Book*

Throughout this book, we've used the following typographic conventions:

`Constant width`
> Constant width indicates a language construct such as an HTML tag or attribute, or a VBScript statement (like `For` or `Set`) data type. Code fragments and code examples appear exclusively in constant width text. In syntax statements, text in constant width indicates such language elements as the function's or procedure's name and any invariable elements required by the syntax.

*Italic*
> Italic in command syntax indicates parameter names. Italicized words in the text also represent variable and parameter names, as well as VBScript intrinsic and user-defined functions. System elements like filenames are also italicized.

**VBS 2.0** VBScript 2.0
> Recently, Microsoft has released a new version of VBScript, VBScript 2. We've used the VBScript 2 icon shown here to help you identify those language features that apply exclusively to the new version. Since many browsers will probably continue to support only Version 1.0 of VBScript for a while, you'll have to decide the degree to which you want to make use of the new features of VBScript 2 in your web pages.

# Obtaining Updated Information

All sample programs presented in the book, as well as the software discussed in the book, are included on the accompanying CD-ROM; for details, see Appendix F, *The Learning VBScript CD-ROM*. Updates to the material contained in the book, along with other developments, are available from our web site at *http://www.ora.com/publishing/windows*.

# Acknowledgments

First and foremost, my heartiest thanks go to an outstanding editor, Ron Petrusha, who has helped to shape this book into a work of which I am extremely proud. I can honestly say that the book you see before you owes an awful lot to Ron, not only for his having had faith in me originally to entrust its creation to me, but for his attention to detail, his striving for excellence, and his vision for the book. At the same time, he's allowed me as the author the leeway to express ideas and concepts in my own style—may I venture to say, the hallmark of an O'Reilly book.

My thanks also go to Tim O'Reilly and Frank Willison at O'Reilly & Associates for giving me the opportunity to write for O'Reilly & Associates, and for their continuing and unfailing support. Troy Mott provided the organizing skills that helped move this book along from conception to completion. I look forward to our future projects together.

Thanks also to the staff at O'Reilly & Associates. Nicole Gipson Arigo was the production editor and project manager. Jane Ellin and Nancy Kotary performed quality control checks. Seth Maislin wrote the index. Mike Sierra worked with the tools to create the book. Chris Reilley and Robert Romano fine-tuned the figures. Nancy Priest designed the interior book layout, and Edie Freedman designed the front cover.

Of course, a project of this depth cannot be undertaken without the support of one's family, as always my strength and motivation—Deb, Russel, and Victoria.

# 1

# Introduction

VBScript—Visual Basic Scripting Edition—is a subset of the popular Microsoft Visual Basic programming language. Microsoft has introduced VBScript as a language for programming documents displayed by World Wide Web browsers, and has designed it to be lightweight, fast, and safe. With VBScript, you have at your disposal a simple and straightforward language that you can use to author powerful web pages and applications.

You can use VBScript to dynamically generate web pages, validate form data, and even write games for the Web. You can turn your web pages and web sites into the sort of exciting and dynamic places that people using the Net will want to return to again and again. What's more, all of this can be achieved by including VBScript code within your HTML pages without either referring back to the server or involving you in writing complex server-side scripts and programs.

While VBScript brings the power and flexibility of a programming language to web documents, it is surprisingly accessible at the same time. If you've programmed in Visual Basic before, you'll quickly find yourself at home with the familiar syntax and style of VBScript. If VBScript is your first taste of Visual Basic programming, you'll be pleasantly surprised at how quickly you can master it to achieve professional results. You will be producing active scripting quickly and easily.

But why would you want to bother? After all, aren't the techniques for designing today's web pages good enough?

## The Need for VBScript

When it was first established, the Internet service that we now call the World Wide Web was nothing more than a repository for huge amounts of data and documents. The original HTML specification provided the mechanism for presenting that data. It was designed for page layout and text formatting, and handled those tasks easily and elegantly. It is easy to learn and use, and is very forgiving—if it doesn't recognize a tag, it simply ignores it. The HTML file is downloaded to the browser as simple ASCII text, rather than as binary data that has the potential to transmit viruses.

Given the simplicity of the HTML specification and the fact that web documents were primarily textual, the original needs of web page designers were much less complex than the needs of today's new webmasters. The major challenge of web design was to present the reader with text in a readable form, maybe combined with some data displayed in a tabular format. So web pages were simple documents—a flat textual medium—the only life in them being that which a skillful writer could breath in.

Because they were primarily concerned with handling text, the first generation of web browsers were actually command-based, and were very different from the graphical browsers that we're accustomed to using today. Many early users of the Web didn't even have a browser, but instead used their telnet utility (*telnet* is a console mode terminal emulation utility) to connect to a public access browser, which they could then use to "surf" the Web. Figure 1-1, which displays the opening portion of a session using the public access browser at *info.cern.ch*, makes it  clear that this early rendition of the World Wide Web was virtually a text-only service. In fact, as the Linx browser shown in Figure 1-2 illustrates, these types of browser are actually still around today, although they're used by only a very small number of netizens.

Since its original appearance as a text-only medium, the Web has undergone a very rapid evolution that has transformed it into the Internet's multimedia service. This in turn has been responsible for its emergence as the most popular and fastest growing of the many services available on the Internet. In fact, the massive growth of the Web has attracted users with high expectations—expectations not just of the quality of information available on the Web, but also of the quality of its presentation. And the HTML specification, as well as the content of web pages, has undergone an equally dramatic change. Tags were added to allow the inclusion of graphics. Through its support for forms, the later HTML specification also provided a method for inputting data and then having the browser submit this data to the server. Recent innovations have included the introduction of a number of new HTML tags to improve the formatting of web pages; we can now add tables to our pages, split the browser screen to show more than one page at a time by using frames, and even enhance the background of our page with a nice graphic.

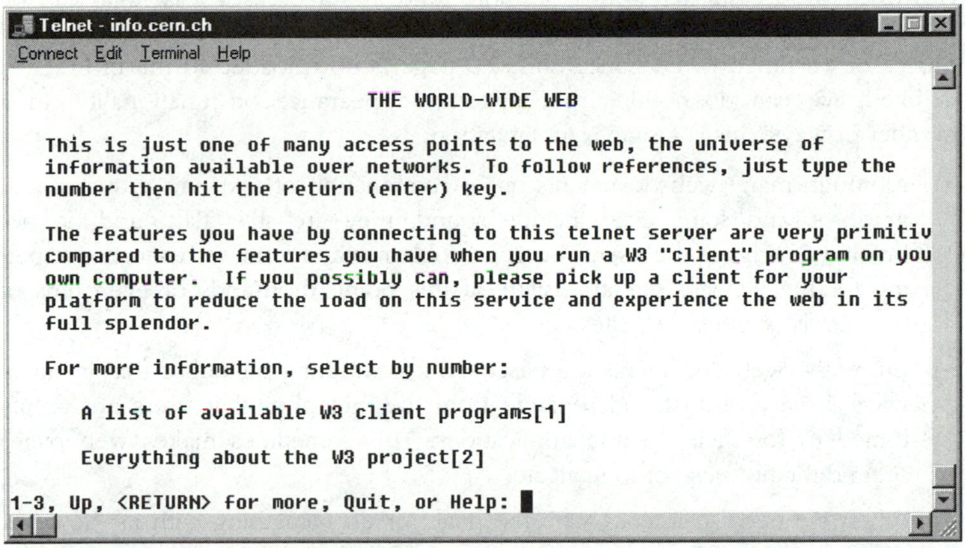

*Figure 1-1. The Web as seen by the public access browser at info.cern.ch*

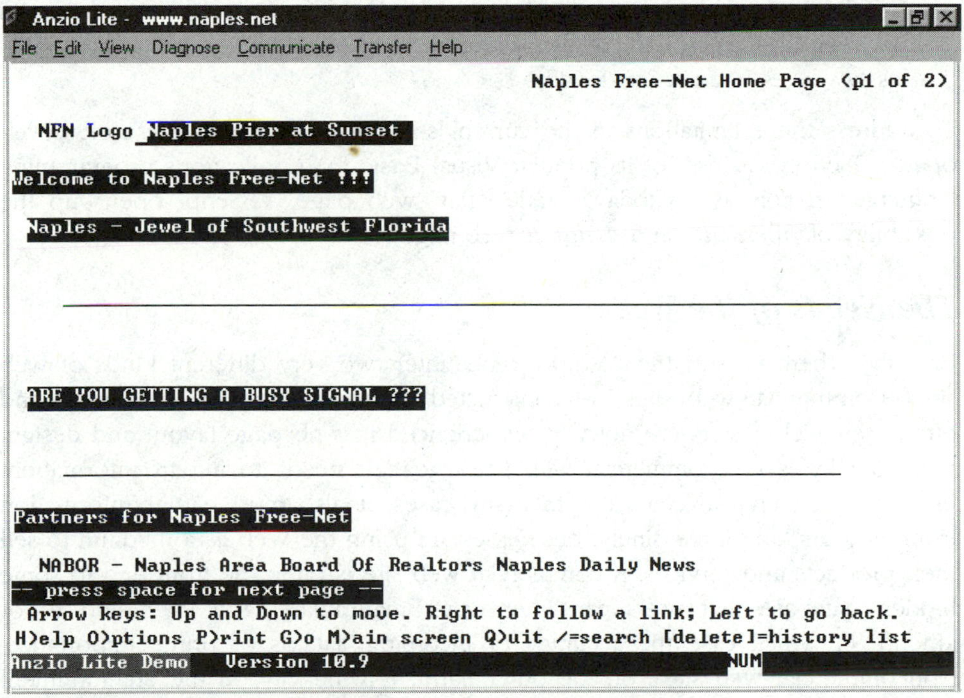

*Figure 1-2. A Linx browser, used through the Anzio Telnet software*

However, we are still left with little more (and in some cases less) than can be achieved by opening a well-designed document created by a graphical word processor on our own PC. Once our web page is downloaded to the browser, it is fixed; we can do nothing to change its appearance or functionality. In a number of ways, this is a significant limitation:

- Although many web documents use a combination of text, image maps, and graphics, and some even include sound, they are still "flat," and do not involve or engage the user. This is a problem when your web site is competing for the viewer's attention with, at this point, thousands or even tens of thousands of other web sites.

- Currently, web documents are based on a computing metaphor that in many ways is very distinct and separate from the metaphor that users are accustomed to for their desktop applications. This sometimes makes web pages seem difficult to use or to navigate.

- When we need to interact with the page, or do something with it—however trivial—another page must be called from the server, leading to poor performance and often to frustration on the part of the user.

- Because incorporating interactivity into a web document relies on exchanges between the browser and a web server, the current model of web usage needlessly wastes Internet bandwidth.

To address these limitations in the current state of web pages, Microsoft developed VBScript, a subset of its popular Visual Basic for Applications programming language. In contrast to today's static, "flat" web page, VBScript opens up the possibility of *interactive* and *dynamic* web pages.

## The Needs of the Web

Broadly, when we surf the Web, we encounter two very different kinds of web sites. Commercial web sites are constructed to do business in some way, and often their webmasters are not very experienced in web page layout and design. Functionality is the commercial web site's goal. It needs to impart information, usually of a technical character; in many cases, it also must gather information from its users, and increasingly, businesses are using the Web as a medium to sell their products and services. A commercial web site is often the front end to some hidden database that users can interrogate, manipulate, and even add to or amend, in which case the accuracy of incoming data is of prime importance. Noncommercial web sites, on the other hand, rely heavily on the entertainment experience gained by the visitor. It is no surprise that noncommercial sites tend to be the leaders when it comes to the latest innovations on the Web. Many users of the Web (myself included) see innovative sites as entertainment, and many netizens spend their time surfing around the Web to find cool graphics, animations, Java applets, etc., etc. Good webmasters will spend hours just surfing the Net, gaining inspiration, or just plain copying things that they see in their travels.

Although these commercial and noncommercial web sites are constructed for very different purposes, they nevertheless must have something in common in order to attract the attention of users surfing the Web:

- In order to help visitors gain the maximum benefit from the site, they must be easy to use.

- They must be fast. We've all had the experience of web pages that seem to take forever to download. At one point or another, each of us has almost certainly stopped a web page from downloading or completely abandoned a web site because it was too slow.

- They must present information in a way that gives it some added value. Whether a web site is commercial or not, it cannot limit itself to presenting the bare information; all web sites require some functional or aesthetic "enticement" that makes the user want to revisit the site.

Thus, independently of the goal or content of the web site, it is becoming increasingly important to create attractive, polished, professional-looking, interactive web pages. If you want your web site to be noticed in a world in which there are tens of thousands of web sites competing for the attention of individual users, it is no longer sufficient to provide significant content. The content also has to be presented in a way that is as well designed and attractive as possible.

To see how VBScript can be used as a tool for creating well-designed, attractive, user-friendly web pages, let's look at a fairly representative example of a conventional web site. Then, let's revisit the same web site after it's had a quick face-lift. The Web Wonder Spices Company has included a recipes page within its web site. The main page for the recipes, which is shown in Figure 1-3, welcomes the user to the recipes page and lists this month's recipes. The company is hoping that its web page (as well as its line of spices) will appeal to users of the Web who, because they're so busy surfing, have little time to cook and shop. As you can see, the main recipes page is much like thousands of other index pages: it contains a list of hyperlinks, along with brief descriptions.

Let's approach this recipes page from a busy user's point of view. You decide that coq-au-vin sounds tasty, so you click on its hyperlink. Then you wait until you're shown the page with the coq-au-vin recipe. You look at the page, but discover that actually preparing coq-au-vin involves two rather unfortunate requirements:

- It's going to take you two hours to cook and prepare, but you've only got 30 minutes.

- You need a chicken, which you don't have.

So you click back to the main page, and either look at a new recipe or leave Web Wonder Spices' web site. We've all had similar experiences, almost every time we surf, of clicking back and forth to find the information that suits our needs. Half our time is spent waiting for pages that we almost instantly dismiss.

*Figure 1-3. The Web Wonder Spices recipes page before its makeover*

Using a spoonful of redesign and a dash of VBScript, lets see what we can cook up for the new Web Wonder Spices recipes main page. The result is shown in Figure 1-4. Users can now select the recipe that's right for them without leaving the main page; once a particular dish has been selected, the user can click on the hyperlink to get detailed cooking instructions. As Figure 1-4 shows, icons have been added for Cooking Time, Calories, and Main Ingredients. By passing the mouse over these icons, the user is instantly shown the cooking time, number of calories, and list of ingredients on the right-hand side of the page. By utilizing VBScript's ability to create documents on the fly, we can construct the right-hand portion of the main recipes page at the browser without having to refer back to the server.

Most of the makeover centers around the VBScript *MouseMove* event, which is linked to the icons. You will use *MouseMove* regularly when you start to program in VBScript. The right-hand side of the page uses the new borderless frames tag—introduced with Microsoft Internet Explorer 3.0—to give the appearance of a single page, when in fact the Ingredients page is a totally separate document. You can see from a code sample from this example, which is shown in Figure 1-5, how the seemingly complex problem of displaying individual items of information about a recipe without querying the web site's server can be solved easily using VBScript.

*Figure 1-4. The Web Wonder Spices recipes page after its makeover*

## The Need for Interactive or Dynamic Web Documents

We've emphasized the importance of interactive web pages. And no doubt you've heard that, by using VBScript or ActiveX components or JavaScript or Java applets, you can create these interactive web pages. In fact, "interactive" seems to be a major new buzzword for webmasters. But just what do we mean by interactive? In the context of a web page, *interactivity* is the functional physical relationship between the user and the document that allows the user in some way to produce an effect on the document. To a certain extent, it can be argued that the vast majority of web documents are already interactive: we can interact with them by clicking on a hyperlink, which causes a new document to load. This,

```
recipe2.htm - Notepad                                                    _ ₽ X
File   Edit   Search   Help

Sub Cals2_MouseMove(s,b,x,y)
    parent.valuepage.document.valueform.calval.value = 3000
    parent.valuepage.document.valueform.cooktime.value = ""
End Sub

Sub Cals3_MouseMove(s,b,x,y)
    parent.valuepage.document.valueform.calval.value = 750
    parent.valuepage.document.valueform.cooktime.value = ""
End Sub

Sub ingre1_MouseMove(s,b,x,y)
    Parent.ingredientspage.Document.Open
    Parent.ingredientspage.Document.Write "<HTML><BODY BGCOLOR=white>"
    Parent.ingredientspage.Document.Write "<CENTER><FONT FACE=ARIAL SIZE=2>"
    Parent.ingredientspage.Document.Write "<H3>Ingredients for Coq-Au-Vin</H3>"
    Parent.ingredientspage.Document.Write "2 tsp Garlic<BR>"
    Parent.ingredientspage.Document.Write "1 Big Chicken<BR>"
    Parent.ingredientspage.Document.Write "10 Carrots<BR>"
    Parent.ingredientspage.Document.Write "1 Onion<BR>"
    Parent.ingredientspage.Document.Write "2 Pints Red Wine<BR>"
    Parent.ingredientspage.Document.Write "1 Potato<BR>"
    Parent.ingredientspage.Document.Write "1pkt Herbs de Provence"
    Parent.ingredientspage.Document.Write "</HTML>"
    Parent.ingredientspage.Document.Close
End Sub
```

*Figure 1-5. A section of the VBScript code used in the Web Wonder Spices page*

however, is only a limited form of interaction; what we cannot do with HTML in its current state is to change or affect the existing document itself. By clicking on a hyperlink, we simply instruct the browser to load a different document. We therefore need to interact with, or in some way to *cause a change* in, the current document without recreating the page; this is, in short, a dynamic document. Once we can interact with a dynamic document, we can enable documents to act more like the Windows programs that we are used to working with.

Think for a moment about the Windows programs you use all the time. One of the major benefits of Windows is its common user interface. By following a set pattern of interface guidelines, software publishers allow us to quickly learn their product, leaving us free to concentrate on the particular features of the product, rather than on how to interface with them. Menu items tend to be in the same place; to open an application file, we select the Open option on the File menu. Most keyboard shortcuts are the same regardless of the application we use; for example, we know that by pressing F1, we can get instant online help. Such familiar interface objects as toolbars, status bars, and icons help to guide us in using the software.

Internet applications, on the other hand, adhere to no such standardized guide-lines for interface design, which forces users to spend (or to waste) time learning how to navigate their way around, and how to use each site they visit. With VBScript, however, web documents and web sites can appear and behave more like the Windows programs that we use on our desktops. When that happens, we'll see people adapting quickly from their desktop programs to their Internet browser, and we'll in fact be taking the first steps toward seamlessly integrating Internet applications with the rest of the programs that we use daily. A medium that is familiar is easier to use, will be used more readily and learned more quickly, and will allow users to gain more from the experience. Interactive or dynamic documents give users the feeling that they are an integral part of the experience, rather than just onlookers or viewers, like a television audience. To achieve a truly interactive or dynamic web environment, users need to have a degree of control over the document; it is immaterial whether or not the users are aware that they have this control.

To illustrate this point, let's look at a simple example that shows how we can greatly improve the functionality and interactivity of a web site by allowing the user to "passively" control the document. XYZ Web Furniture sells furniture over the Internet. They have two main products: the Easy Relax Sofa, and the Comfy Sofa.

In the past, producing an order form for these two items posed something of a problem, since the Easy Relax sofa is available in green, red, yellow, and floral patterns, but the Comfy Sofa is only available in blue, brown, white, or striped patterns. When the original order form was designed, XYZ's webmaster had two options: He could include all colors for both products, along with some textual explanation indicating which colors or patterns are available for which model of sofa. In this case, though, the selection process has the potential of confusing the user and can create orders that can't be processed. Alternately, he could ask the user to select the product first, submit the request to the server, and use that information to return a second form that includes only those colors available for the particular product selected by the user. This wastes the user's time, interrupts the buyer's thought processes, involves server-side programming, and wastes the Internet's bandwidth. The original order form is shown in Figure 1-6.

While both of these alternatives leave much to be desired, the ideal solution to this web design problem is for a decision process to be carried out at the browser: if the user selects the Easy Relax Sofa, only those fabric colors available for the Easy Relax should be shown; if the user selects the Comfy Sofa, only the fabric colors for it should be shown. Utilizing client-side processing in this way allows users to continue immediately with the important process of choosing the product, without having their thought pattern interrupted or the process of selecting their new sofa delayed. In fact, users may even be unaware of the changes that have taken place within the order form. Moreover, this is more than

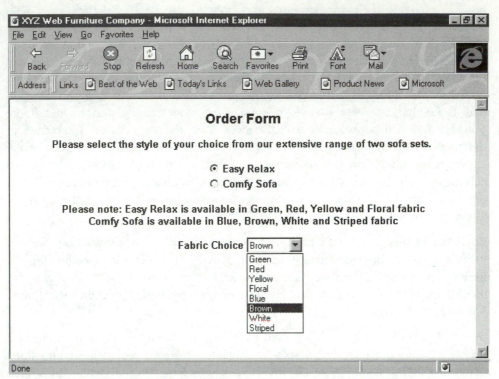

*Figure 1-6. XYZ Web Furniture's original, potentially confusing, order form*

altruistic interface design—it materially benefits XYZ Web Furniture, since the company will always receive orders that it can process. VBScript is able to handle this otherwise complex design problem in a way that is quick, seamless, and simple. The results are shown in Figure 1-7.

It's also important to emphasize that this implementation of the order form using VBScript is very easy to maintain. You can see from the fragment of the VBScript code used in this example (shown in Figure 1-8) that, while the operation of the page may appear complex, the underlying code itself is very straightforward. So adding additional products, or adding and removing fabric colors and patterns, requires only a few minutes' worth of coding, rather than an extensive redesign of the page.

## Performance and Internet Bandwidth

As computer users, we've grown accustomed to using highly sophisticated graphical programs, usually in the Windows or Macintosh environments. For example, we're used to being presented with a Word document that contains an embedded Excel spreadsheet. Not only can we view this spreadsheet data from within Word, but we can also amend it, in the process automatically changing the underlying

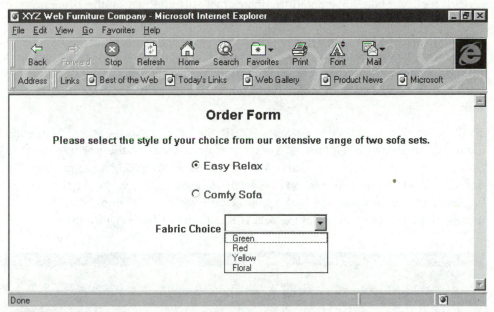

*Figure 1-7. The order form redesigned using ActiveX controls and VBScript*

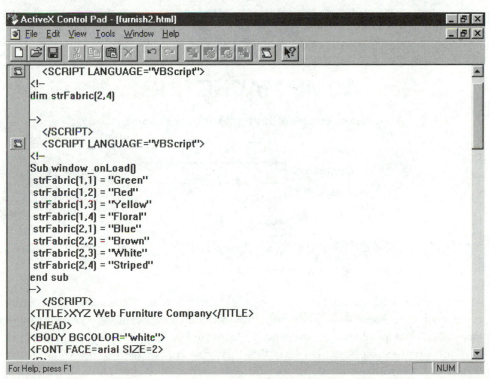

*Figure 1-8. VBScript code fragment from XYZ Web Furniture's new order form*

spreadsheet. We take for granted the interactivity afforded us by the programs we use every day. Yet when we access the Internet, we are presented with a document that, should we have the option to "interact" with it, requires us to instruct the browser to go back to the server to retrieve another document or an updated version of the current document. Therefore, browsing the Internet is often a slow process (especially via a modem connection), and frequently a frustrating one as well.

To illustrate this, let's look at a simple HTML input form, like the Acme Marketing inquiry form shown in Figure 1-9. Let's say that, as users of the site, we need to obtain some information on Acme Marketing's new WebWidget. After filling in our details in the text boxes on the form in Figure 1-9, we press the Submit button, and the browser sends the information we gave it along with the field names to the server specified in the `ACTION` attribute of the `<FORM>` tag.

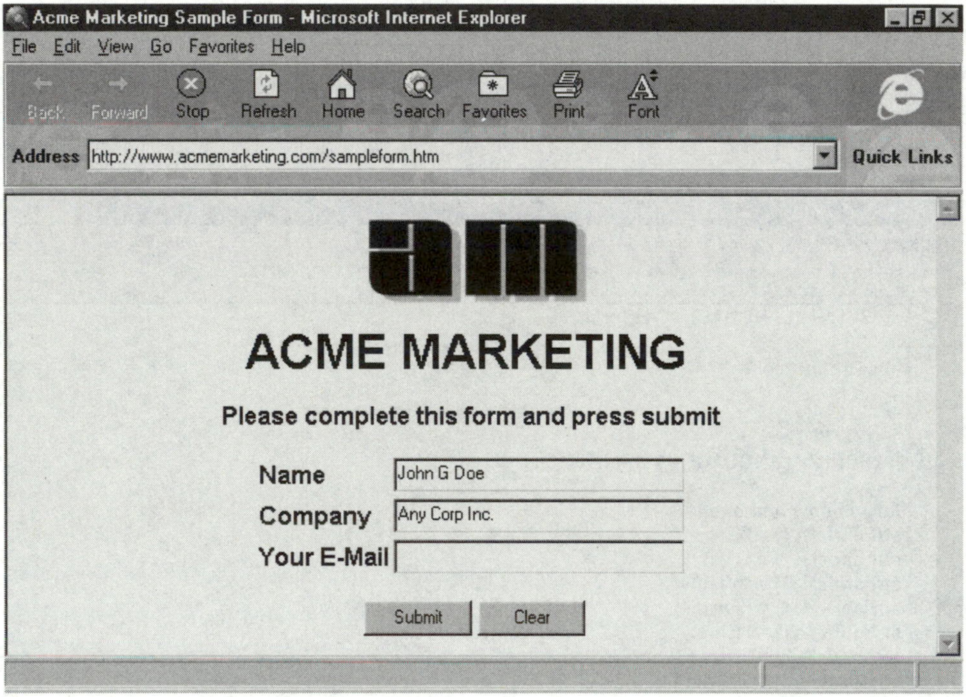

*Figure 1-9. Acme Marketing's inquiry form*

At the server end, Acme Marketing has a program that checks the data before processing it further. Most commonly, this program is a Common Gateway Interface (CGI) script that is automatically activated when the server receives a particular request message. Let's say that this program is called *CHECKITOUT.CGI*. When the appropriate message and our data arrive at Acme Marketing's server, *CHECKITOUT.CGI* springs into life.

The program checks the data submitted to it and finds that we've forgotten to enter our email address, so *CHECKITOUT.CGI* sends back another document to us, this time the brand-new page shown in Figure 1-10 that says, "Sorry, you didn't enter your email address—please press Back on your browser and re-submit the form." So it's back to the form, where we enter the email address we forgot, before resubmitting the form data.

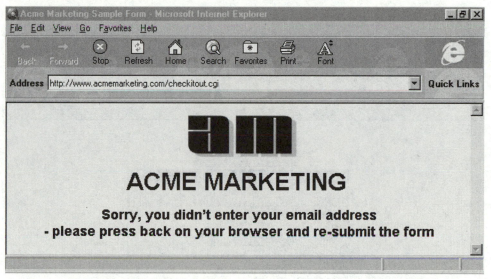

*Figure 1-10. Acme Marketing's failure page*

Even on a fast connection to the Acme Marketing server, we could wait some time for the message that we had omitted our email address to reach us. On a more complex form that perhaps didn't make clear which information was required and which was optional, we might have to go through this process several times before either getting fed up and leaving the site, or successfully submitting the data.

Apart from the time we waste sending data back and forth across the Web, there is another consideration, which tends to escape most users and webmasters. As web usage grows, billions and millions of billions more bytes are being sent around the Web, which has the effect of slowing down the overall "system." We should all be concerned about conservation of what is known as bandwidth—the available physical resources for transmitting data. Wherever possible, we should look to limit the amount of data being transmitted back and forth.

So let's imagine for a moment the above form example implemented much differently. Let's add some interactivity to the document. Now, when we press Submit, instead of sending data back to the server for checking, the document checks the data itself. If an errant piece of data is found (or is not found, as the case may be), a message box like the one shown in Figure 1-11 is displayed immediately, to inform us of our misdoings and allow us to make changes without further ado. Only when all the data is in order does the browser send it to the server. Moving data validation from the server to the client in this way saves the user a good deal of time, possibly prevents Acme Marketing from losing a user, lessens the load on the Acme Marketing server, and saves the net's bandwidth.

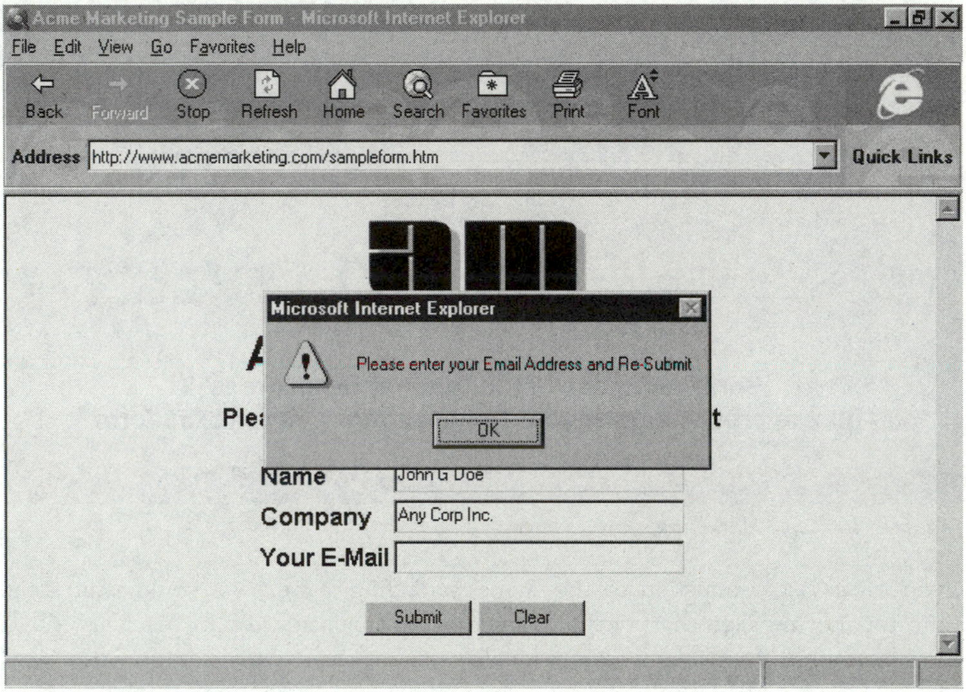

*Figure 1-11. Acme Marketing's form verified at the browser using VBScript*

This is just a simple example. But imagine the millions of bytes that could be saved from going around the net needlessly if this type of interactive document were commonplace. An interface of this type is also much more pleasurable to use, and closely resembles the functionality of many of the Windows programs we use every day.

Increasingly, web sites need to canvas information from the user, if only to help heighten the visitor's experience when using that site in the future. Your web site must perform this function quickly, with as little effort on the user's part as possible, and must make efficient use of Internet resources. Only then will your site be able to compete with the tens of thousands of other web sites vying for web users' time and attention. Producing fast, efficient web applications can only be achieved by dispensing with needless references back to the server. This requires web pages that perform functions (that is, web pages that are really short programs rather than documents in the conventional sense), that offer a high degree of self-containment, and that allow the decision-making process to occur at the client side rather than at the server.

## Client-Side Processing Versus Server-Side Processing

In a network environment such as the World Wide Web, we refer to the two main parties as the client and the server (see Figure 1-12). You have probably seen many magazines talk endlessly about client-server computing or client-server environments. The *client* quite simply is the browser that you use to access the Web. The *server* is the computer that stores the web documents, graphic images, and other resources that make up a web site. In its simplest form, the browser—or client—sends a message to the web server requesting a particular document. The server receives the request and in return sends the HTML file back to the browser, where it is interpreted and shown as a web document.

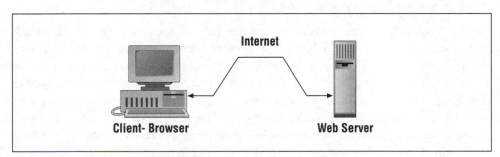

*Figure 1-12. A simplified Internet client-server configuration*

### What is client-side processing?

As we saw in the earlier Acme Marketing form example, there are many instances in which a certain amount of processing is required for a particular web application to function correctly. For example, a programmatic process is required to determine if all the fields on the form have been entered correctly (as in our earlier example), or to identify the part of an image map on which the user has clicked.

*Client-side processing* refers to this type of processing, or decision making, being carried out by the browser, as Figure 1-13 illustrates. It means that the browser has been enabled to interpret the instructions that would usually be sent to the server. In fact, we can think of a browser that supports client-side processing as consisting of an interface (the part we see) and processing software (the part we don't see). The browser interface still has to send a message or messages, but it

sends them internally to another part of the overall browser software; this part—
the processing part—sends messages and data back to the interface, which then
displays the resulting output.

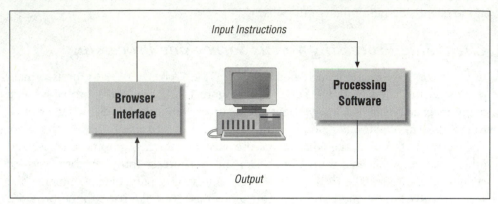

*Figure 1-13. Client-side processing*

### What is server-side processing?

Would you believe that server-side processing is the converse of client-side
processing? Good. It is exactly that. *Server-side processing* means that the server,
via its software, makes decisions based on information supplied to it from the
client or browser, as Figure 1-14 illustrates. Messages in the form of instructions
and data are transmitted across the Internet from the client machine. The web
server then runs the appropriate software. The resulting data and output are then
transmitted back from the server across the Internet to the client machine, where
the result is interpreted and displayed by the browser.

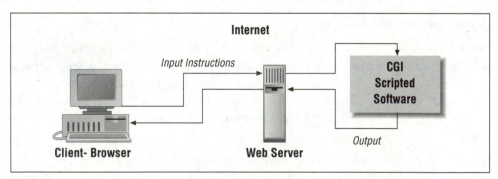

*Figure 1-14. Server-side processing*

At the moment, the vast majority of processing is carried out at the server, using
CGI programs and programs written in scripting languages, such as the ubiquitous
Perl or the increasingly popular PHP/FI. Until the advent of client-side scripting

languages such as JavaScript and VBScript, the only way to perform many of the tasks and decision-making processes, as well as to create web pages "on the fly," was to write a program that resides and runs on the web server.

### What are the benefits of client-side processing?

The operation of both server-side and client-side processing requires some type of input from the browser; this can take the form of instructions or of software messages generated by the browser in response to an event, such as the user clicking a button or a hyperlink. In server-side processing, these instructions must be transmitted across the Web, to activate a script or program residing on the server. This is obviously costly in terms of time, resources, and, as we mentioned earlier, bandwidth. A main benefit of client-side processing is therefore time saved, which means much faster applications. A user clicks the Submit button on our form, for example, and is instantly told that he or she did not complete the form correctly; there is no need to wait for that information to come back from the server. But although saving time, thus producing faster Internet applications, is a very important benefit, it is by no means the only one that client-side processing offers.

When we activate a program or script that is located on the server, we set in motion what can be a very complex process, a process that uses memory and processor resources on the server. Now imagine a busy web server, a server that perhaps is host to many people's web pages and many different companies' web sites, the majority of which use CGI scripts. The load placed on such a server during busy periods is amazing. If only a small part of the processing that usually occurs on the server were transferred to the users' computers, we could dramatically reduce the overall load placed on the web server. We would thus free up valuable resources, and in turn make vital tasks, such as page requests, that much faster.

# The Components of Client-Side Processing

So, how are we going to achieve interactivity and dynamism in our web documents? What are the individual pieces that are needed to embark on this new and exciting course toward a seamless, high-performance web/desktop interface?

## The Browser (MSIE 3.0)

The ability to implement client-side processing depends, first of all, on the web browser. It is the browser that interprets the current HTML code that we download from a web site, and displays the results as a visually pleasing document (we hope). We therefore need an enhanced browser that will interpret a wider range

## *What Client-Side Processing Can't Do*

Although client-side processing can replace some of the functions performed by CGI scripts and applications, it is not intended to be a complete replacement for server-side processing. VBScript makes it possible to transfer some of the functions traditionally performed on the server to the client, because, whereas the client was "dumb" in the past, a scripting language makes it become "smart." But there are still many functions that cannot be handled directly at the browser, and that continue to rely on server-side processing—either by a CGI application or by a server-side script such as VBScript and Active Server Pages. For example, updating or accessing the records within a database can only be done at the server. Forwarding of form data is also handled better at the server. It has even been argued that data validation, although it is best carried out on the client, should also be duplicated on the server, since users can create their own local, modified copies of remote HTML documents containing forms that they can submit to the server.

of commands to allow the rendering of far more sophisticated web pages. We then need a way of coding these extended commands within the HTML document in a way that allows fast download times—a coding method that can be readily understood and learned by the very large number of people who author their own HTML pages, and one that does not compromise the security of the Internet.

We have already witnessed the birth of a new generation of browser from Netscape that interprets JavaScript and Java applets (more on these later). Microsoft's Internet Explorer 3.0 (MSIE3.0) has continued along this avenue of web development and support for client-side scripting. MSIE3.0 can interpret HTML code, JavaScript, Java applets, ActiveX components, and VBScript. The combined power of the latter two, in particular, is the bedrock of Microsoft's' further advance into the Internet market, and the means by which this book will show you how to turn web documents into desktop applications and embed desktop applications in web documents.

To ensure that a high percentage of web users take advantage of the new technology, Microsoft has made the MSIE3.0 web browser freely available, and at the time of writing, Microsoft has no plans to charge for MSIE3.0. It can be obtained from their web site, *http://www.microsoft.com/ie/*, and installed as follows:

1. Download the self-extracting archive file into a temporary directory.

2. Locate the downloaded file using the Windows Explorer, and double-click to extract the file's contents. The setup program will run automatically after the contents of the file have been expanded.

Microsoft also has announced plans to include Microsoft Internet Explorer as an integral part of the Windows operating system. Such wide and free availability will undoubtedly boost Microsoft's share of the browser market, and consequently, the usage and acceptance of VBScript and ActiveX components.

## A Scripting Language (VBScript)

VBScript is the tool you will use to bring client-side processing to your web pages and applications. VBScript is a text-based, interpreted language that is downloaded to the browser within the HTML stream. Once at the browser, the VBScript program is compiled by the VBScript engine within the browser and placed into memory, where it then waits to be executed. The VBScript engine is actually an OLE automation server, integrated with the browser via Microsoft's new ActiveX OLE scripting interface. In the next chapter, we'll see how this allows other scripting languages to be used with MSIE3.0 and also offers the potential for other applications to make use of VBScript.

At present, VBScript is only available through MSIE3.0, although VBScript applications can also run on Netscape browsers by using third-party add-ons. If the user's browser on the computer that is displaying an HTML page is not VBScript-enabled, and it encounters a web page that includes VBScript, one of two things might happen, depending on the age of the browser. First, if the browser is quite old, the VBScript code may be translated as pure text and shown on the page. To prevent this, Microsoft recommends that the <SCRIPT>...</SCRIPT> construct, which is used to mark the beginning and end of a script's code, be embedded within the HTML comment tags <!-- and -->; we'll explore this in greater detail in Chapter 3, *Getting Started*. Second, and most likely, the script may be ignored, and the program contained within the <SCRIPT> tag will simply be consigned to the garbage dump area of the browser's memory.

If you have MSIE3.0, you already "have" VBScript. There's no need to rush down to your local software store to buy a copy of VBScript; it is a system component that is installed by the MSIE installation program. And unlike many other programming languages, you can't "see" the VBScript product. VBScript has no integrated development environment (IDE), which means that it has no project manager, no debugger, and no text editor. You write VBScript code directly into the HTML document using either your favorite HTML editor or Notepad text editor. When MSIE encounters your VBScript code, it automatically handles the process of calling the VBScript engine to execute your program.

In this book, we will concentrate on VBScript, or, to give it its official name, Visual Basic Scripting Edition. We will show the differences between VBScript and JavaScript, we will investigate how to implement the new ActiveX components using VBScript, and above all we will give you a good grounding and understanding of VBScript, to arm you with the confidence to tackle more and more complex web applications and documents.

## ActiveX Controls

An ActiveX control is in reality an OCX control, like the ones that are used in almost every 32-bit Windows program (and, if you're a Visual Basic 4.0 programmer, like the ones that you use all the time in constructing your applications). ActiveX controls are "slimmed down" versions of OCX controls that allow faster download across the Web, but it is also possible to use standard OCX custom controls in a web page using VBScript. ActiveX controls allow us to add to and extend the functionality of our web applications in almost the same way that Java applets have enhanced the Netscape browser. The main difference is that ActiveX controls are more closely related to the Windows 95 environment and to the Microsoft philosophy as a whole. We will therefore see ActiveX controls coming onto the market that will give us, at the very least, subsets of common Windows 95 controls and applications.

This is best demonstrated with a simple example. The web page shown in Figure 1-15 uses the now common tabbed notebook metaphor. The control used in this example is actually the same control that is used in hundreds of different Windows programs. The screen has been split horizontally into two frames using normal HTML tags, with the addition of the new MSIE3.0 HTML extension for borderless frames. In the top frame is a page written in VBScript that contains the relevant code to call and use the ActiveX tab control. Clicking on the tabs changes the pages in the bottom section of the screen. It may interest you to know that it actually took longer to type in the text for the sample pages than it did to produce the VBScript program for controlling the tab. Almost the entire VBScript code for this application is shown in Figure 1-16.

But what happens if you load a page like this that contains an ActiveX control that isn't currently installed on your computer? If the browser cannot find the specified control on the computer, it automatically downloads the control from the location specified in the VBScript program. This location can be the same server that the HTML page came from, or it can be a totally unrelated location, perhaps a third-party "controls pool." Once the control is downloaded to your machine, it is registered with Windows and is available for use with other pages and applications. In Chapter 9, *An HTML Layout Common Menu Object*, where we discuss adding ActiveX controls to your VBScript pages, we'll look in more depth at downloading ActiveX controls across the Internet, and at the potential security risks this involves.

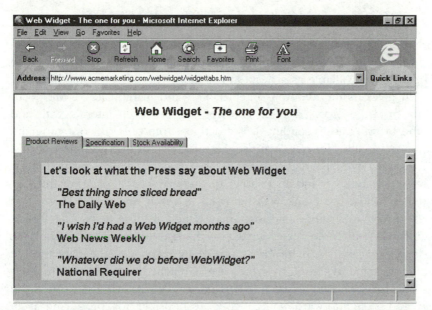

*Figure 1-15. Using an ActiveX control on a web page to give that "Windows" application feel*

```
webwidget.alx - Notepad

File   Edit   Search   Help

<SCRIPT LANGUAGE="vbscript">
<!--
Dim pagearray(3)
 pagearray(0) = "widget3.htm"
 pagearray(1) = "widget4.htm"
 pagearray(2) = "widget5.htm"

Sub TabStrip1_Click(ByVal Index)
    Top.frames(1).location.href=pagearray(Index)
end sub
-->
</SCRIPT>
<DIV BACKGROUND="#ffffff" STYLE="LAYOUT:FIXED;WIDTH:477pt;HEIGHT:272pt;">
    <OBJECT ID="TabStrip1"
      CLASSID="CLSID:EAE50EB0-4A62-11CE-BED6-00AA00611080" STYLE="TOP:20pt;LEF
        <PARAM NAME="ListIndex" VALUE="2">
        <PARAM NAME="BackColor" VALUE="16777215">
        <PARAM NAME="Size" VALUE="16581;882">
        <PARAM NAME="Items" VALUE="Product Reviews;Specification;Stock Availal
        <PARAM NAME="TipStrings" VALUE="What the press think of Web Widget;Al
        <PARAM NAME="Names" VALUE="Tab1;Tab2;Tab3;">
        <PARAM NAME="NewVersion" VALUE="-1">
        <PARAM NAME="TabsAllocated" VALUE="3">
        <PARAM NAME="Tags" VALUE=";;;">
        <PARAM NAME="TabData" VALUE="3">
        <PARAM NAME="Accelerator" VALUE="P;S;t;">
```

*Figure 1-16. VBScript code to produce the tab control document*

# *What Can Be Achieved Using VBScript?*

VBScript brings professional programming techniques to HTML web documents. With VBScript, we can create documents and applications that previously could only have been made available as a desktop program written with something like Visual Basic. It gives us the ability to interact with and manipulate HTML documents directly from the browser. With VBScript, we can even interact with and manipulate the browser itself, sending it instructions from our VBScript program, and pulling in its variables for our own use. Let's look at a quick example of this. Figure 1-17 shows a web page that displays the date on which this particular HTML file was last modified, and also shows the *referrer* of this page, or the URL of the document whose hyperlink was followed to reach this page. As you are probably well aware, it is impossible to display either of these items of information with standard HTML (unless, of course, you "hardcode" them into your HTML document, in which case you're probably not really displaying the date the file was last modified or the hyperlink by which it was reached). Instead, HTML intermixed with VBScript was used to produce this page. You can see a portion of the very simple and straightforward source code responsible for producing it in Figure 1-18.

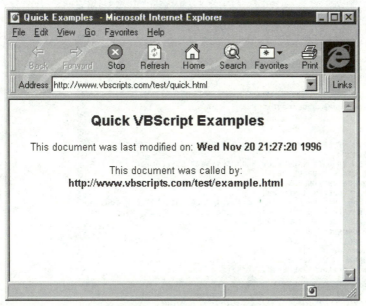

*Figure 1-17. Using VBScript to get information from the browser*

Above all, VBScript brings to us true client-side processing, so let's briefly look at some of the main uses of VBScript:

- Reference and manipulate document objects

- Reference and manipulate the browser

- Reference the contents of another loaded document or documents

- Create a document "on the fly" from the browser

- Store, reference, and manipulate data input by the user

- Store, reference, and manipulate data downloaded from the server

- Perform calculations on data

- Display messages to the user

- Access cookies easily

- Reference and manipulate a wide range of "add-on" components, both ActiveX controls and Java applets

- Display two-dimensional HTML

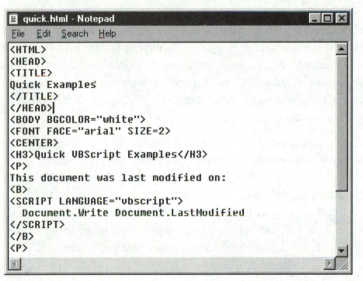

*Figure 1-18. VBScript and HTML source code for the example in Figure 1-17*

## Reference and Manipulate Document Objects

Document objects, or, to give them their correct title, intrinsic HTML objects, are the display objects we currently use time and again in our HTML code, usually within the <INPUT> tag, to create forms. VBScript gives us the ability to access the properties of these objects (for example, to determine the value typed into an input text box by the user). Not only do we have access to these properties, we can also use VBScript to set the values of these properties. For example, we could set the value of an HTML text box to a particular value—perhaps to the current date and time on the client machine—as the page loads.

With normal HTML code, you can set the **VALUE** attribute of a text box just as easily. But unless you build your HTML source code from a script on the server (using an older technology like server-side includes, or a newer one like server-side VBScript with Active Server Pages), any value must be "hardcoded" into your HTML document. For instance, to continue with our date and time example, you could include the following line in your HTML document so that your web page displays the date and time:

```
<INPUT  TYPE=text NAME=txtTime VALUE="2/3/97 12:01:00 PM">
```

But unless you update your page immediately before each user accesses it, the date and time displayed when a user's browser displays the page is going to become increasingly inaccurate. Rather than using hardcoded HTML, you could instead use CGI to transmit the current date and time to display on a client machine. This is, however, the time on the server machine, and not the time on the client machine; in some cases (on slow Internet connections, in periods of heavy traffic, and, of course, in cases where the Internet server is in a different time zone than the client), the web page ends up displaying a date and time that may be more or less inaccurate. And a basic problem is that, whether you hardcode the date and time into your HTML document or whether you generate it "dynamically" through a CGI application, once the page is displayed, the value of the date and time becomes fixed.

How does VBScript help with some simple task like displaying the date and time? VBScript not only supports the standard document objects, it also allows us to attach events to these objects. To put this another way, when the user or another part of our program interacts in some way with a particular object, like a command button, the browser can automatically run a particular routine within our program. For example, if the user clicks on a certain button or moves away from a text box, an "event" is fired that causes a particular routine to execute.

The HTML code in Example 1-1 illustrates how easy it is to display the current date and time on the client machine when the document is loaded. It also allows the user to update the date and time by pressing the Update Time button.

*Example 1-1. Using VBScript to Display the Date and Time*

```
<HTML>
<HEAD>
<TITLE>Date/Time Example</TITLE>
</HEAD>

<BODY>
<CENTER>
```

*Example 1-1. Using VBScript to Display the Date and Time (continued)*

```
<H3> Welcome to my Web page! </H3>
<FORM NAME="frmMyForm">
    <INPUT TYPE=text  NAME="timeinfo">
    <INPUT TYPE=button VALUE="Update Time" NAME="btnTime">
</FORM>

<SCRIPT LANGUAGE="vbscript">
    frmMyForm.timeinfo.value = Now

    Sub btnTime_OnClick
        frmMyForm.timeinfo.value = Now
    End Sub
</SCRIPT>

</BODY>
</HTML>
```

# Reference and Manipulate the Browser

To VBScript, the browser itself is an object; in fact, it is several objects, all of which have properties. Using VBScript, you can control things such as the browser's history list and its status bar. You have tight control over how frames are handled within the browser window. You can check and reset the location or the URL, and automatically navigate to another page or even another web site. Let's say an application has one main document and two secondary documents, and that which of the two secondary documents you load depends on a combination of responses from the user to the primary document (much more complex than simply clicking on a hyperlink). Automatically handling that decision process and retrieving the chosen document is an ideal job for VBScript. You can also call other VBScript programs in other frames and windows within the browser, and even open new browser windows at will, while controlling the appearance of the window at the same time. Chapter 5, *Controlling the Browser*, and Chapter 6, *The Element Object and HTML Intrinsic Controls*, provide an in-depth look at the objects exposed by the browser.

Example 1-2 contains a very simple script that controls the browser's status bar. When the user clicks the Click Me button, a VBScript routine generates a random number. If its value is less than .5, the text "Here's some text in the status bar" appears in the status bar; if its value is greater than .5, any text in the status bar is removed.

*Example 1-2. Using VBScript to Control the Status Bar*

```
<HTML>
<HEAD>
<SCRIPT LANGUAGE="vbscript">
 Randomize
```

*Example 1-2. Using VBScript to Control the Status Bar (continued)*

```
Sub cmdButton1_OnClick
    dblNumber = Rnd()
    If dblNumber <= .5 Then
        Status = "Here's some text in the status bar."
    Else
        Status = ""
    End If
End Sub
</SCRIPT>
</HEAD>
<BODY BGCOLOR="white">
<CENTER>
<INPUT TYPE="button" NAME="cmdButton1" VALUE="Click Me">
</CENTER>
</BODY>
</HTML>
```

## Reference the Contents of Another Loaded Document or Documents

Many of us use frames in our web pages and applications. Implemented correctly, frames enhance the experience of a web site by creating a presentation that is more pleasing to the eye, and by making navigation easier. Using VBScript, we can reference the document in one frame from a document in a different frame, or from the document that created the frameset.

Figure 1-19 shows two documents loaded into two frames, named `LeftFrame` and `RightFrame`. The VBScript code linked to the button in `LeftFrame` actually retrieves a value located in a form embedded in `RightFrame`. The relatively simple code from `LeftFrame` is shown in Figure 1-20.

As you can see from the code in Figure 1-20, we can also reference the frame itself. This allows us, for example, to have a VBScript in one frame that decides which page the browser needs to load in another frame, based upon some input from the user. We can even reference another VBScript program in another frame.

## Create a Document from the Browser "on the Fly"

Using VBScript, we can create a complete new page from the browser without referring back to the server. In fact, this is one of the most valuable assets that VBScript gives us. In theory (although it's somewhat impractical), we could have our entire web site contained in a single document, and then have all of our web pages built on the fly by the browser, based on the users' specifications, needs, and preferences. This is the ultimate in client-side processing.

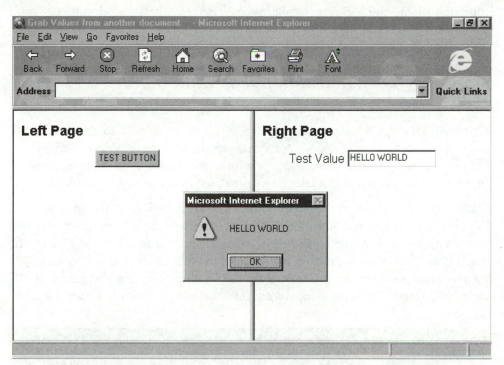

*Figure 1-19. Using VBScript to retrieve a value in another document*

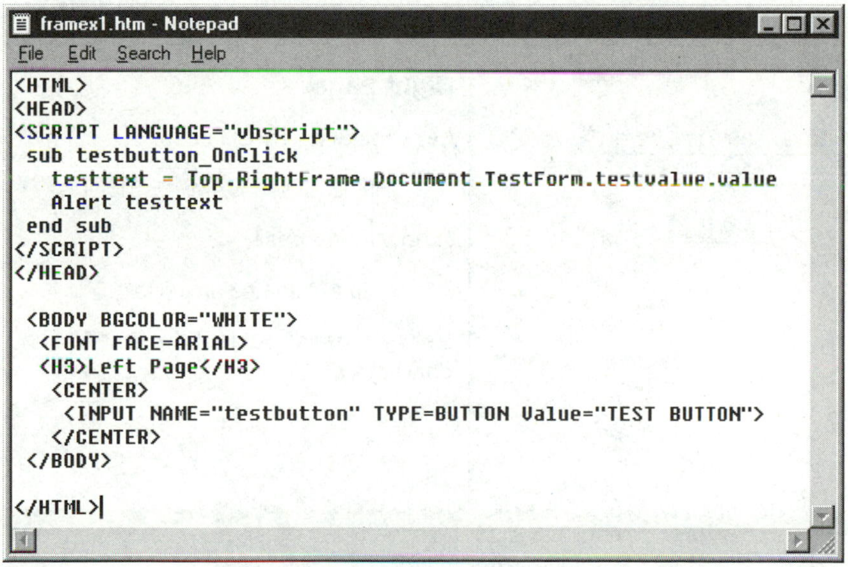

```
framex1.htm - Notepad
File  Edit  Search  Help
<HTML>
<HEAD>
<SCRIPT LANGUAGE="vbscript">
 sub testbutton_OnClick
   testtext = Top.RightFrame.Document.TestForm.testvalue.value
   Alert testtext
 end sub
</SCRIPT>
</HEAD>

 <BODY BGCOLOR="WHITE">
  <FONT FACE=ARIAL>
  <H3>Left Page</H3>
   <CENTER>
    <INPUT NAME="testbutton" TYPE=BUTTON Value="TEST BUTTON">
   </CENTER>
 </BODY>

</HTML>
```

*Figure 1-20.  The code used in Figure 1-19*

Although there are several examples of creating dynamic documents with VBScript throughout this book, Chapter 13, *Building Dynamic HTML Pages*, provides a comprehensive insight into the *Document.Write* method.

## Store, Reference, and Manipulate Data Input by the User

Although VBScript does not currently allow us to store data to the user's disk (with the exception of cookies), we can store data in memory. For example, as the user enters data in a form, VBScript allows us to retrieve this data and store it in arrays or variables that can later be manipulated in some way by our script.

Figure 1-21 shows how we can extract the data input by a user and manipulate it in some way before sending it to the server. The left frame contains a text box and a command button. Sample text is entered into the text box, and when the user clicks the button, the text is manipulated by the VBScript program and—just for this example—a page is generated by the VBScript program and placed in the right-hand frame. The code snippet from this example is shown in Figure 1-22.

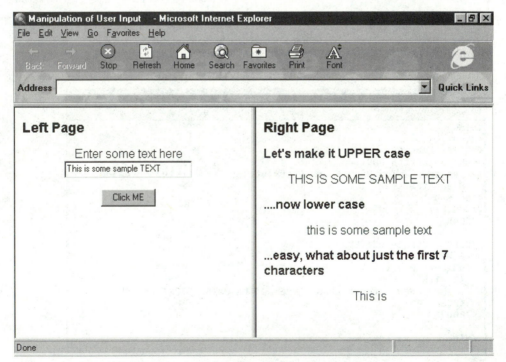

*Figure 1-21. Using VBScript to manipulate user input*

```
manipulate1.htm - Notepad                                    _ □ ×
File   Edit   Search   Help
<HTML>
<HEAD>
 <SCRIPT LANGUAGE="vbscript">
  Sub DoItNow_OnClick
   Top.RightFrame.Document.Open
    Top.RightFrame.Document.Write "<HTML><BODY BGCOLOR=white><FONT FACE=ARIAL
    Top.RightFrame.Document.Write "<H3>Right Page</H3><P>"
    Top.RightFrame.Document.Write "<H4>Let's make it UPPER case</H4><CENTER>"
     txtTheEntry = UCase(Self.Document.frmTest.txtEntry.Value)
    Top.RightFrame.Document.Write txtTheEntry
    Top.RightFrame.Document.Write "</CENTER><H4>....now lower case</H4><CENTE
     txtTheEntry = LCase(Self.Document.frmTest.txtEntry.Value)
    Top.RightFrame.Document.Write txtTheEntry
    Top.RightFrame.Document.Write "</CENTER><H4>...easy, what about just the
     txtTheEntry = Left(Self.Document.frmTest.txtEntry.Value,7)
    Top.RightFrame.Document.Write txtTheEntry
    Top.RightFrame.Document.Write "</CENTER></BODY></HTML>"
   Top.RightFrame.Document.Close
  End Sub
 </SCRIPT>
</HEAD>

 <BODY BGCOLOR="white">
  <FONT FACE="Arial">
<H3>Left Page</H3>
<P>
```

*Figure 1-22. VBScript code to manipulate user input*

## Store, Reference, and Manipulate Data Downloaded from the Server

Let's say we have a fixed data set we wish to include in our page. We can hard code this data set into the HTML page using an array variable. VBScript will then automatically load this data into the memory of the client machine. We can then directly reference this data, again based on input from the user. Another method of implementing this data set is to create our initial page using a server-side script to include data in our page based on the request from the client, in very much the same way as most search engines operate. But with the inclusion of VBScript, we can manipulate this data further once the page has been downloaded to the client browser. In Figure 1-23, for example, data are hardcoded into the HTML page, although it could just as easily be added by a server-side script. The user selects a product from a drop-down list box and enters the quantity required. When the user clicks the Calculate button, the price of the product is accessed from the data array, and a simple calculation is performed to determine the total cost.

The complete source code for the example shown in Figure 1-23 appears in Example 1-3. Don't worry about the ins and outs of the code at this stage. It is

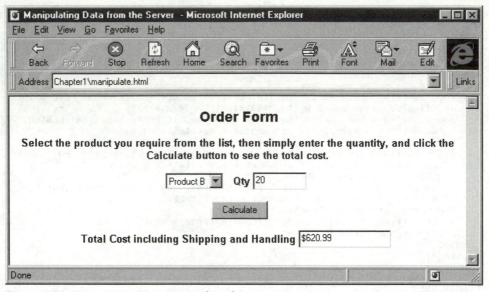

*Figure 1-23. Using VBScript to manipulate data*

shown here purely to illustrate how quickly and easily you can perform programmatic tasks at the browser. And as you can see, the majority of code for this
example is in fact good old HTML!

*Example 1-3. HTML Source with VBScript for Figure 1-23*

```
<HTML>
<HEAD>
<TITLE>
Manipulating Data from the Server
</TITLE>
<SCRIPT LANGUAGE="vbscript">
    OPTION EXPLICIT
    Dim dblPrices(2)
    Dim dblShipping

    dblPrices(0) = 25.95
    dblPrices(1) = 30.50
    dblPrices(2) = 50.55
    dblShipping = 10.99

Sub cmdCalc_OnClick
    Dim intSelected
    Dim dblTotal
    Dim dblTot

    intSelected = frmForm1.cboProducts.SelectedIndex
    dblTot = dblPrices(intSelected) * frmForm1.txtQty.Value
    dblTot = dblTot + dblShipping
```

*Example 1-3. HTML Source with VBScript for Figure 1-23 (continued)*

```
    frmForm1.txtTotal.Value = "$" & dblTot
End Sub

</SCRIPT>
</HEAD>
<BODY BGCOLOR="white">
<FONT FACE="arial" SIZE=2><B>
<CENTER>
<H3>Order Form</H3>
<P>
Select the product you require from the list, then
simply enter the quantity, and click the Calculate
button to see the total cost.
</P>
<FORM NAME="frmForm1">
<SELECT NAME="cboProducts">
<OPTION>Product A
<OPTION>Product B
<OPTION>Product C
</SELECT>
  Qty
<INPUT TYPE="text" NAME="txtQty" SIZE=10>
<P>
<INPUT TYPE="button" NAME="cmdCalc" VALUE="Calculate">
<P>
Total Cost including Shipping and Handling
<INPUT TYPE="text" NAME="txtTotal">
</FORM>
</BODY>
</HTML>
```

## Perform Calculations on Data

Once we have captured data either from the server or as a result of user input, using VBScript to perform calculations on this data is very straightforward, as Figure 1-23 and the HTML source code in Example 1-3 illustrate. Whether a simple calculation or a series of complex calculations is required, VBScript gives us control over form data. VBScript provides a rich assortment of built-in functions for numerical operations, and also allows calculations to be performed on dates and times.

## Display Messages to the User

One way we can interact with the user is to display a simple message box, or alert box, like the ones we've seen in earlier examples. Messages such as these quickly and easily guide users of our web site or page.

Messages that our program displays do not necessarily have to be fixed; they can be built dynamically, based on the values of program variables. For example, a message box linked to an input form could include the user's name, for that personal touch ("Hey Paul, you didn't enter your Zip Code!"). The techniques for doing this are covered in Chapter 15, *Error Handling and Debugging*.

## Easy Access to Cookies

Cookies (I still don't know why they're called cookies) allow us to store information on the client's machine. The main use of cookies is to store and retrieve data that helps to personalize the web page. For example, we could check to see if a visitor to our site has one of our cookies. If not, we can ask him to complete a simple questionnaire. In the future, when he returns to the site, we can retrieve this information. This allows our web page, for example, to display a banner saying, "Hi Paul, welcome back! We haven't seen you for 6 days." (Yes, we can store the date he last visited us, too.) We could also store the filenames of pages that interest him, and possibly highlight those pages that have changed since his last visit.

There has been much confusion in the past as to how to read or set the value of cookies, or how to "bake a cookie"... seriously!! But VBScript has a very simple and straightforward method of reading and writing cookies, which we will explore in detail in Chapter 5, *Controlling the Browser*.

## Reference and Manipulate a Wide Range of "Add-on" Components—Both ActiveX Controls and Java Applets

The OCX third-party market spawned by Visual Basic will no doubt be mirrored by a plethora of third-party add-ons for use in web pages using VBScript. Using ActiveX components in VBScripted web documents will change the face of the Web, giving us interfaces that look, act, and feel more like the standard windows interface we are all used to. This is not to say that web documents will become "boring" and uniform. On the contrary, the availability of ActiveX components will be a source of further creativity and inspiration. The ingenuity of webmasters and web programmers—who currently have a very limited toolbox—has already shown that the next generation of web pages will be even more fun to look at and use.

We'll discuss ActiveX controls and Java applets in much more depth in a later chapter, and Chapter 9, provides an example that shows how you can add ActiveX controls to your web pages. For now, it's sufficient to realize that the combination of VBScript and ActiveX controls is the backbone of all Microsoft's current and future software architecture plans, and not just those for the Web. In fact, Microsoft Internet Explorer 3.0 itself is mainly the result of cleverly weaving together two ActiveX controls.

## Two-Dimensional HTML

In standard HTML, precisely positioning objects on a page can sometimes be quite challenging; positioning objects on top of one another, so that they wholly or partially overlap, is impossible. In contrast, 2D HTML is a new development that allows us to create web pages in which various controls and objects are able to overlap. While new to HTML, this feature has become so standard a part of visual programming environments that it's simply taken for granted. VBScript and ActiveX controls make it possible, since these controls have properties (such as `TOP`, which determines the distance from the top of the page to the top of the control, and `LEFT` which determines the distance from the left-hand side of the page to the left-hand side of the control) that can be used to position objects precisely on web pages. Chapter 8, *The HTML Layout Control*, details how to use and implement 2D HTML.

## Server-Side VBScript

So far, in listing the types of tasks that VBScript has been developed to handle, we've focused exclusively on client-side VBScript—that is, on web pages on the client's browser. However, VBScript is also now the preferred language to control pages transmitted by Microsoft Internet Information Server (IIS). Scripts can be written directly within the HTML page to be run at the server, and only their results will be visible to the person calling the page from the browser. You can use server-side VBScript as the glue to interface with components or other services running on the server, such as a SQL Server database. You can also use server-side VBScript to process incoming form data from a web page and to transmit a page on the fly that is sent back to the client. The combination of server-side and client-side VBScript together gives you complete control over your web applications.

Server-side scripting using VBScript is a whole subject on its own, and is really beyond the scope of this book. However, Appendix E, *Active Server Pages*, introduces you to some of the basic concepts of writing scripts for the IIS.

# Summary

VBScript can bring our web pages to life. It allows us to incorporate the same objects that we take for granted in the Windows programs we use every day into our web pages, and to control their behavior and appearance by setting their properties. Not only can we access a web page and make changes to it, we can interact with the browser too. We can have control over the browser, the environment, and web documents as never before, and those who can effectively manipulate this control will have a recipe for success. We can empower the users of our web sites to use our web sites in ways that we have only dreamed of until now.

In short, if you're using VBScript, you should let your imagination run wild. What we have seen so far is just a taste of what VBScript can do. The really neat thing about any programming language is that it allows programmers to express their creativity and to realize their imaginations.

The diversity of applications, and the sheer number of web sites and webmasters, will undoubtedly lead to an explosion of imaginative implementations of VBScript web sites and pages. We are entering a very exciting time for the World Wide Web, which is in truth still in its infancy. We're like the kid who's just learned to read. From this point onwards a whole new world of wondrous discoveries is within our grasp.

# 2

# What Is VBScript?

In the last chapter, we focused on the relationship of VBScript to HTML and to the previous "state of the art" in producing web pages. In this chapter, we'll continue to introduce you to VBScript, although from a somewhat different point of view. Here, we'll examine how VBScript works, and assess the relationship between VBScript and a variety of Microsoft technologies and products. The foremost of these is the Visual Basic programming language family itself; if you're one of the millions of Visual Basic programmers, you'll be particularly interested in this discussion. The chapter also covers ActiveX Scripting and OLE Automation, which allow VBScript to be used not only with a web browser, but with other applications too. We'll also explore some other issues, such as the relationship between VBScript and JavaScript and the behavior of VBScript under various browsers, such as Microsoft Internet Explorer and Netscape Navigator.

## VBScript and the Visual Basic Family

As Figure 2-1 shows, VBScript is not an entirely new product. Instead, it is part of the Visual Basic programming language family, along with the various editions of Visual Basic (specifically, Visual Basic, Standard Edition; Visual Basic, Professional Edition; and Visual Basic, Enterprise Edition) and Visual Basic for Applications.

*Figure 2-1. The Visual Basic family*

## *Visual Basic*

When Windows 3.0 was first released, in May 1990, acceptance of the product by endusers was immediate and overwhelming. Software for Windows, though, was very slow in coming; in fact, only within the last several years has Windows software reached the kind of critical mass that has allowed it to more or less completely supplant DOS software. The reason for this delay was that, although using Windows was very easy, developing utilities and applications for Windows was extremely challenging. Producing a Windows application required that the programmer use one of a small number of available tools (primarily a C or assembly language product, combined with Microsoft's Windows Software Development Kit), and that he or she have a good sense of how Windows as a system operates. As a result, producing even a trivial program (like one that displays "Hello World!" in a standard window) requires several pages of code.

In 1991, Microsoft released the first version of Visual Basic. This was significant not only because the product proved to be enormously successful, but also because, for the first time, developing Windows applications ceased to be the exclusive preserve of an elite number of C and C++ programmers. Instead, users with little or no programming experience, and with little or no knowledge of the intricacies of Windows' internal operation and of Windows programming, were able to use Visual Basic to produce high-quality Windows applications.

In part, Visual Basic was and is successful because the Visual Basic language, with its readable and logical syntax, is easy to learn and use. As its name suggests, Visual Basic is a specific implementation of the BASIC language. The direct predecessor to Visual Basic was Microsoft's QuickBasic or QBasic; in fact, many of the language constructs used in Visual Basic have changed little, if at all, since the early days of BASIC. For example, the following tiny piece of BASIC code adds the current value of the variable $x$ to the variable $y$ ten times:

```
y = 3
For x = 1 To 10
    y = y + x
Next x
```

As another example, the following piece of code makes a decision: if the value of the variable $x$ is ten, then do something; otherwise, do something else.

```
If x = 10 Then
    y = 3
Else
    y = 4
End If
```

But while the BASIC language had a reputation for accessibility and ease of use, at the same time it was considered unsuitable for "serious" applications. So the simplicity of the language alone does not account for Visual Basic's enormous popularity. Of greater importance were the new features that Visual Basic offered the programmer, above all its support for objects. "Objects" here doesn't refer to the objects used in object-oriented programming (although version 4.0 of Visual Basic can support object-oriented programming); instead, it refers to Visual Basic's support for creating and manipulating such common Windows interface objects as windows, text boxes, drop-down list boxes, option buttons, etc.

This support for objects means, above all, that Visual Basic supports the drag-and-drop placement of objects. This contrasts with a language like C, which requires each interface object to be defined, positioned, and painted in a program's source code. Visual Basic replaced the hundreds of lines of code needed to create common interface objects, in even a very simple C program, with a toolbox containing a variety of interface objects. So to create a text box, for instance, the programmer simply had to click the text box icon in the toolbox, drag the new text box to its position on the Visual Basic form (or window), and release the mouse button.

In addition to making it easy to create and position interface objects, Visual Basic gave the programmer an easy way both to get and to set their properties (like the background color of a form, or the text contained within a text box object), even when the program was running. For example:

```
If x = 10 Then
    Text1.Text = "hello world"
End If
```

In the above example, under a certain set of circumstances—if $x$ equals 10—the Text property (that is, the text that the text box contains) of the text box named Text1 will change to "hello world." Properties can also be read into a program by placing the property's name on the right side of the assignment statement:

```
y = Text1.Text
```

This copies whatever text is in the text box named Text1 to the variable $y$.

Today, the Visual Basic success story speaks for itself. Literally millions of people develop programs using Visual Basic, and a whole industry has grown up to support them. Visual Basic has gained the respect and recognition of many professional programmers who otherwise regard BASIC as nothing more than an amateur "toy." Because of the ease and speed with which applications could be built using Visual Basic, the term *rapid application development* (RAD) environment was coined to describe Visual Basic and a number of other programming tools that have been released since Visual Basic's initial appearance. And while the easy-to-use integrated development environment of Visual Basic allows application developers to concentrate their energies on the creative aspects of programming, rather than the technical aspects of Windows operation, Visual Basic also provides an "open" development environment that can be readily extended through its support for OLE, for ActiveX (or .OCX) controls, and for calls to external dynamic link libraries (like the Win32 API).

## Visual Basic for Applications

Visual Basic for Applications (VBA) followed on the original success of Visual Basic. A subset of Visual Basic, VBA was launched to provide an integrated programming language for the Microsoft Office suite. VBA is now widely used in commercial organizations to produce customized applications in Excel, Word, Project, and Access.

In itself, VBA doesn't have an integrated development environment; instead, it uses an application that is hosting VBA, like Microsoft Excel. VBA programs can be created in much the same way as the application's native macros are, but VBA supports many more and refined features, thus allowing complex custom applications to be created from the Microsoft Office programs.

## VBScript

In many respects, Internet programming today is not unlike Windows programming five years ago: the Internet has become popular among users, but it is difficult to develop Internet applications. While most Internet "programmers" are using HTML to create simple web pages, developing complete Internet applications often requires a good sense of how Internet protocols work, as well as access to some high-end development tools, like Microsoft Visual C++ and a Windows sockets library. Now, in the same way that Visual Basic revolutionized Windows application programming, VBScript promises to bring Internet application development to those whose only experience of Internet "programming" is authoring HTML pages. This will allow web authors to take a familiar medium—a normal HTML document—and, by including Visual Basic commands, procedures, and functions within it, to develop some fairly powerful Internet applications.

VBScript is a strict subset of VBA, which ensures that VBScript is and will remain compatible with the entire range of Microsoft Office and BackOffice products. This is worth emphasizing, especially for those who are concerned with the development of intranet applications. The intranet is really a new name (and a slightly new form) for the client-server systems that so many corporate developers have been rushing to build for the last several years. Most of these systems rely very heavily on Microsoft products—like SQL Server, Microsoft Access, or Microsoft Excel—for their existence. When adapting this client-server technology into intranet applications that operate through a browser, it therefore makes sense to use a Microsoft product as the enabling tool as well. This gives you as near to a guarantee as you can get that you won't suddenly find that the individual components of your application have become incompatible with one another.

Since Internet applications, by their very nature, are client-server applications, it is appropriate that VBScript can be used as a programming language either on the client (that is, the script executes on the browser) or on the server (that is, the script is executed by the web server, and its output is sent as HTML to the browser).

VBScript has also been designed to be a safe language to use for Internet scripting when it is running on the client. Microsoft has left out of VBScript the parts of VBA that could prove harmful to the client machine. These include the ability to open and to write to files on the client machine, and to interact with the host machine's operating system. Not only is this type of safety important for reducing or even eliminating damage done by a malicious webmaster, but also I'm sure that none of us wants hundreds or even thousands of angry netizens beating down our doors because our web page inadvertently deleted critical files! Another notable feature absent from VBScript is the ability to create and manipulate a user interface (aside from its inclusion of functions to display pop-up message boxes). All client-side VBScript interfacing with the "outside world" must be done via the HTML document, or by using any OLE, ActiveX, or Java controls present.

---

### VBScript 2.0

VBScript Version 2.0 was released at the end of 1996, and extends the capabilities of VBScript. The new version's features include some neat string manipulation functions and several new objects. It also allows you to check which version and build of scripting engine is being used. Because of space considerations, the standard *Format* function, which is used to produce formatted output, was left out of the original version of VBScript; VBScript 2.0 addresses this limitation by adding four new "lite" format functions to allow the formatting of numbers, percentages, dates and times, and currencies. Finally, several new intrinsic constants have also been added to the language in Version 2.0.

To get the benefits of VBScript 2.0, you must download and install the new .DLL files that make up version 2.0 of VBScript, all of which are freely available from the Microsoft web site (*http://www.microsoft.com/vbscript*). Throughout this book, the **VBS 2.0** icon denotes that the keyword being discussed is only available in Version 2.0 of VBScript.

For more information, see Appendix B, *VBScript Version 2*.

Although this book focuses on using VBScript for client-side programming, VBScript is the same programming language whether it is running on the client or running on the server. However, although the core language is the same, the requirements of security are completely different. In particular, there is (hopefully) no need to protect the server system from malicious scripts. Consequently, objects provided to VBScript applications by the web server (which are discussed in Appendix E, *Active Server Pages*) allow you to interact with the file system and to create instances of objects within your VBScript code, something that carries far too many risks to be allowed in client-side VBScript.

## How Does VBScript Work?

VBScript is an interpreted language that is downloaded as ASCII text within the HTML stream. Once it is received by the browser, it is automatically compiled using the VBScript language engine. The engine is fired up when the browser comes across the `<SCRIPT>` HTML tag, and everything between `<SCRIPT>`, the begin script tag, and `</SCRIPT>`, the end script tag, is passed to the engine.

Here's a simple script:

```
<SCRIPT LANGUAGE="vbscript">
Sub btnMyButton_OnClick
    myvar = Document.frmMyForm.txtMyText1.value
    Document.frmMyForm.txtMyText2.value = myvar
End Sub
</SCRIPT>
```

This script is automatically executed whenever the user clicks on an HTML command button named *btnMyButton*. It simply copies the value from a text box named *txtMyText1* in frmMyForm to another text box named *txtMyText2* on the same form.

---

### VB Programmer's Note

The names of events for HTML intrinsic controls—that is, the standard HTML controls that are defined by the `<INPUT>` tag—differ slightly from those you are used to in Visual Basic. For example, the HTML command button's click event is named OnClick. ActiveX controls have the same event names as Visual Basic controls. For a detailed list of HTML intrinsic control events, methods, and properties, see Chapter 6, *The Element Object and HTML Intrinsic Controls*. The events, methods, and properties of ActiveX controls are listed in Appendix D, *ActiveX Controls Quick Reference*.

The script is compiled once on download, and the resulting program is stored within an area of memory allocated by the browser. Individual portions of code can then be called, or executed, in a variety of ways:

- As various messages or events (like clicks of a button on a web page, as in the previous example) are generated from the browser window, the relevant section of the VBScript program—if you have defined one—is called and runs automatically. In the code fragment just given, for instance, clicking on the button named btnMyButton causes the onClick event to fire, which in turn causes the onClick event procedure to be executed, if one is present in the application's VBScript code.

- Sections of a program can be run by calling them from another part of the program. In your VBScript code, you can define functions that receive one or more optional values from the part of the program that calls the function, perform some predefined calculations or operations, and then return a result to the part of the program that sent the values. You can also define subroutines, which are similar to functions except that they don't return a value to the part of the program that calls them. The following code fragment, for instance, illustrates a function call:

```
<SCRIPT LANGUAGE="vbscript">

Function mycalc(ByVal x, ByVal y)
    mycalc = (x + y) * 3
End Function

Sub btnMyButton_OnClick
    myvar = Document.frmMyForm.txtMyText1.value
    anothervar = Document.frmMyForm.txtMyText2.value
    Document.frmMyForm.txtMyText3.value = mycalc(cint(myvar),
cint(anothervar))
End Sub

</SCRIPT>
```

---

## Handling Data in HTML Forms

HTML forms always return string values. Therefore, note the use of the VB-Script *CInt* function to convert the string values to integers before calling the *mycalc* function, in our second sample code fragment.

---

Here, when the user clicks on a button named btnMyButton, the numeric values contained in two text boxes are stored to the variables *myvar* and *anothervar*. These are then passed as arguments to the *mycalc* function, which adds the two numbers together, triples them, and returns this new value. (In VBScript, a function returns the value stored to the variable whose name is the same as that of the function.) Finally, when the *btnMyButton_OnClick* event procedure receives this value back from the *mycalc* function, it places it in a third text box.

Notice that these two sample code fragments make use of variables, or names that we assign to values that can change. In many programming languages, individual variables are defined as belonging to particular data types. String variables, for instance, are used to hold character strings, while long integer variables are used to hold integers. In contrast, VBScript supports only a single data type, called a Variant, which can handle whatever kind of data you assign to it. This frees you from having to worry about the data types of the variables that you use.

## *The Four Object Classes of VBScript*

Very much as Visual Basic's power was due to its amalgamation of the simplicity of the Basic language with the ease of access to Windows interface objects, VBScript combines the simplicity of Basic with ease of access to Internet objects. In particular, VBScript works with four distinct classes of objects:

- Intrinsic HTML objects
- Browser objects
- ActiveX components and Java applets
- VBScript language engine objects

VBScript allows you to manipulate each of these objects in your code. This means that you have access to both their properties (the values of various settings, or what they are) and their methods (what they do).

### *Intrinsic HTML objects*

First and foremost, VBScript uses the everyday objects, known as intrinsic HTML objects, that you place in an HTML form or document. Accessing them from VBScript code is illustrated in Example 2-1. The program simply copies the text from the first text box into a second text box when the user clicks on a button.

*Example 2-1. Using intrinsic HTML objects*

```
<HTML>
<HEAD>
<TITLE>My First VBScript</TITLE>
<!--
********************************
*           test1.htm          *
* Simple demonstration of how  *
* VBScript interacts with      *
```

*Example 2-1. Using intrinsic HTML objects (continued)*

```
* intrinsic HTML Objects     *
******************************
-->

<SCRIPT LANGUAGE="vbscript">

 Sub btnMyButton_OnClick
    myvar = frmMyForm.txtMyText1.value
    frmMyForm.txtMyText2.value = myvar
 End Sub

</SCRIPT>

</HEAD>

<BODY BGCOLOR="white">
<CENTER>
<H1>TESTING</H1>
 <FORM NAME="frmMyForm">
  <INPUT type="text" name="txtMyText1" value="Hello World">
  <INPUT type="text" name="txtMyText2">
  <INPUT type="button" name="btnMyButton" value="Click Me!">
 </FORM>
</CENTER>

</BODY>
</HTML>
```

You are most likely very familiar with the objects loaded using the `<INPUT>` tag. The particular interface object to be loaded is defined by the `TYPE=` attribute of the `<INPUT>` tag, or, in the case of a drop-down list box, by the `<SELECT>` tag. MSIE 3.0 supports the intrinsic HTML objects listed in Table 2-1. A VBScript program can access any of these objects by referring to its name, which is assigned by the `NAME=` attribute of the `<INPUT>` tag. Note in the code in Example 2-1 that the form is also assigned a name by using the `NAME=` attribute of the `<FORM>` tag. If you have experience using HTML to create forms, you're probably accustomed to giving text input boxes names, which, in a client/server application that relies on server-side processing, are transferred to the server along with their values. It's unlikely, though, that you've assigned both the form and the button a name before. Assigning the form a name is necessary if you want your VBScript code to work with any of the objects contained within the form. Since a form is a kind of container that holds particular interface objects, you must refer to the form before you can access the objects that it contains. Similarly, if you want to customize the behavior of a button in some way, you must assign a name to it so that VBScript is able to identify it. Note also that, since this form isn't being forwarded to the server, the `ACTION=` and `METHOD=` attributes have been intentionally omitted from the `<FORM>` tag.

*Table 2-1. Standard Intrinsic HTML Objects*

| Type attribute | Object description |
|---|---|
| button, reset, submit | command button |
| checkbox | check box |
| <SELECT> | drop-down combo box |
| radio | option button |
| text, password, textarea, hidden | text box |

### Browser objects

Microsoft Internet Explorer itself consists of a relatively small (38K) executable file, *IEXPLORE.EXE*, that relies on a number of OLE server components for the bulk of its operation. This means that the properties and methods (that is, the values of some internal settings that are exposed by an object, as well as some of its routines) of these OLE objects, which are listed in Table 2-2, can be accessed by VBScript. Most commonly, you'll find yourself using a combination of the Internet Explorer Document object and Intrinsic HTML objects, as Example 2-2 demonstrates.

*Table 2-2. MSIE Objects Accessible from VBScript Code*

| Object | Description |
|---|---|
| Anchor | A read-only array containing the anchor text in an HTML document |
| Document | The HTML document currently displayed by MSIE |
| Element | The intrinsic HTML controls (that is, the standard HTML form input elements) and ActiveX controls that are available in a document |
| Form | A form in the current HTML document |
| Link | A read-only array of links appearing in an HTML document |
| History | The browser's history list |
| Location | The current URL |
| Navigator | Application properties of the Netscape Navigator browser |
| Window | The MSIE window |

*Example 2-2. Using Internet Explorer Objects*

```
<HTML>
<HEAD>
<TITLE>My Second VBScript</TITLE>
<!--
*******************************
*          test2.htm          *
* Simple demonstration of how  *
```

*Example 2-2. Using Internet Explorer Objects (continued)*

```
* VBScript interacts with the   *
* Internet Explorer Objects     *
*           * AND *         *
* Intrinsic HTML Objects        *
********************************
-->

<SCRIPT LANGUAGE="vbscript">

 Sub btnMyButton_OnClick
     myvar = Document.frmMyForm.txtMyText1.value
     Document.frmMyForm.txtMyText2.value = myvar
 End Sub

</SCRIPT>

</HEAD>

<BODY BGCOLOR="#FFFFFF">
<CENTER>
<H1>TESTING</H1>
 <FORM NAME="frmMyForm">
  <INPUT type="text" name="txtMyText1" value="Hello World">
  <INPUT type="text" name="txtMyText2">
  <INPUT type="button" name="btnMyButton" value="Click Me!">
 </FORM>
</CENTER>

</BODY>

</HTML>
```

The code in Example 2-2 is very similar to the code in Example 2-1. In fact, at first glance, the two may appear to be identical except for their descriptions (and in fact, it took longer to edit the comment in Example 2-2 than the actual script itself). But if you look at the script more carefully, you'll notice that, whereas Example 2-1 referred to one of the form's text boxes as `frmMy-Form.txtMyText1.value`, Example 2-2 now references the text box as an object that belongs to the *Document* object (since it refers to it as `Document.frmMy-Form.txtMyText1.value`). In doing this, it uses the browser's object model to navigate a path from the document displayed in the browser window to the HTML form, then to the HTML text box control. It then retrieves the value stored to the text box's *Value* property—that is to say, the text that appears in the text box. Note that a dot (or period) is used to separate the object references and the property name from each other. We'll discuss the MSIE object model in greater detail in Chapter 5, *Controlling the Browser* and in Chapter 6, *The Element Object and HTML Intrinsic Controls.*

### ActiveX components and Java applets

The third class of object that VBScript works with is add-on components defined in your HTML code using the `<OBJECT>` tag. These are objects, such as ActiveX components and Java applets, that you add to the page or to your application to extend its functionality or aesthetic appeal. For instance, the following text from an HTML document adds an ActiveX tree view control to a web page:

```
<DIV STYLE="LAYOUT:FIXED;WIDTH:240pt;HEIGHT:180pt;">
    <OBJECT ID="TreeView1"
     CLASSID="CLSID:0713E8A2-850A-101B-AFC0-4210102A8DA7">
        <PARAM NAME="Appearance" VALUE="1">
        <PARAM NAME="ImageList" VALUE="">
        <PARAM NAME="Style" VALUE="7">
    </OBJECT>
</DIV>
```

Don't worry about the rather incomprehensible syntax (e.g., the CLSID attribute) needed to define an ActiveX control. By the time we get to using add-on objects such as ActiveX controls or Java applets, you'll understand the nuts of bolts of it (and anyway, we'll be using the ActiveX Control Pad, which does all this for you!).

### VBScript language engine objects

Finally, VBScript uses objects from the VBScript engine itself. Version 1.0 of VBScript had only one object, the *Err* object. Version 2.0 introduced several more built-in objects, some of which are only available when running VBScript on the server. Table 2-3 details the language engine objects supported by VBScript.

*Table 2-3. VBScript Language Engine Objects*

| Object | Version | Usage |
| --- | --- | --- |
| Err | 1.0 | Client and server |
| Dictionary | 2.0 | Client and server |
| FileSystem | 2.0 | Server only |
| TextStream | 2.0 | Server only |

The *Err* object in VBScript, the most commonly used of the objects made accessible by the language engine, is virtually identical to the Visual Basic *Err* object. The following brief example shows how we can obtain the Description property of an error, then display this to the user in an alert box:

```
strMyString = Err.Description
Alert strMyString
```

## OLE Automation & ActiveX Scripting

In order for your VBScript code to access these objects, though, two major require-ments must be met:

- The browser must be capable of recognizing the `<SCRIPT>` tag.
- More importantly, the browser must have access to the VBScript engine.

As we saw earlier, at the time of writing, only Microsoft Internet Explorer starting with Version 3.0 has the built-in capability to handle VBScript. It does this through its OLE automation interface.

OLE automation involves an application exposing its properties (that is, some indi-vidual items of data that it is using) and methods (that is, executable code that it makes accessible) to other applications, through a set of standard interfaces, in a way that allows the exposed application to be manipulated by the other applica-tion. As an example of an OLE automation application, let's look at Microsoft Internet Explorer. MSIE exposes some of its properties, such as its current URL or the text that appears in its status bar. Other applications that can take advantage of OLE, like VBScript, can ask for and in some cases change the value of those properties.

You can almost imagine the "conversation"...

Q: *VBScript: Hey, you, Explorer.*

A: Explorer: Yeah, wadda you want?

Q: *VBScript: Where are we?*

A: Explorer: *http://www.somewhere.com*

Q: *VBScript: OK, let's go to http://www.anotherplace.com*

A: Explorer: OK, hang on tight.

Microsoft Internet Explorer relies on a specification termed ActiveX Scripting to interface with VBScript. ActiveX Scripting is actually a general specification that deals with connecting a host (an application that parses the script's code) to a scripting engine (the component capable of interpreting and executing the script), in order to process a script read by the host by means of OLE automation, as Figure 2-2 illustrates.

The generality of the ActiveX Scripting specification leads to several very inter-esting possibilities. First, if you were to build an OLE application (any OLE application) in a way that conforms to the ActiveX Scripting specification, then anyone could use VBScript to interface with or manipulate your application. Currently, Microsoft will allow you to use VBScript in this way free of royalties,

*Figure 2-2. The Microsoft Internet Explorer model of the ActiveX scripting interface*

provided that you acknowledge the use of their technology in your copyright information. An application that can be controlled by a scripting language in this way is termed an ActiveX scripting host; this is illustrated in Figure 2-3.

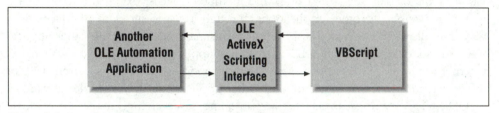

*Figure 2-3. Interfacing VBScript to another (host) application by using ActiveX Scripting*

Second, any other scripting engine that also conforms to the ActiveX Scripting Specification can be used with MSIE without requiring any add-ons, plug-ins, bolt-tos, or amendments to Explorer. Hence, Microsoft's implementation of JavaScript can interface with Internet Explorer just as VBScript can, as Figure 2-4 shows. Similarly, other languages—like Perl, for instance—can be used as scripting languages for Internet Explorer, provided that they support the OLE interfaces required by the ActiveX Scripting specification.

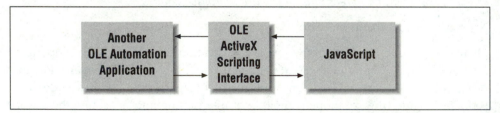

*Figure 2-4. Using another scripting engine with Internet Explorer courtesy of ActiveX Scripting*

Since the scripting engine is a separate OLE component that is not actually a part of the MSIE executable file, you may be wondering how MSIE is able to identify and locate the scripting engine that it is to use to compile and execute a particular script. The answer is that it uses the LANGUAGE attribute of the <SCRIPT> tag, along with the Windows registry*. If you're interested in the technical details of the process, the `LANGUAGE` attribute indicates the name of the scripting language; its value is a *programmatic identifier*, and it corresponds to the name of a subkey of the registry's top-level HKEY_CLASSES_ROOT key. So if the complete script tag reads `<SCRIPT LANGUAGE="vbscript">`, MSIE does the following to identify the scripting engine:

- It begins by opening `HKEY_CLASSES_ROOT\vbscript` key in the registry.

- It then attempts to open the subkey that is called `HKEY_CLASSES_ROOT\vbscript\OLEScript`. The `OLEScript` subkey serves as a flag to indicate that the programmatic identifier (i.e., "vbscript") identifies a valid ActiveX scripting engine.

- It opens the `HKEY_CLASSES_ROOT\vbscript\CLSID` subkey and retrieves its default value, which is the VBScript language engine's *class identifier*. (A class identifier is a globally unique, 64-byte value that identifies an OLE server component.)

- Once it's found the class identifier, it can find the name and location of the VBScript language engine by opening the class identifier's subkey in HKEY_CLASSES_ROOT\CLSID.

Incidentally, instead of specifying `LANGUAGE="vbscript"` in the <SCRIPT> tag, it is also possible to abbreviate it to `LANGUAGE="vbs"`. This abbreviation works because "vbs" is also a programmatic identifier in the registry that MSIE can use to look up information about the VBScript language engine.

# VBScript Beyond the Browser

As you've just seen, because VBScript follows the ActiveX Scripting specification, any application that provides an ActiveX Scripting "socket" will be able to use VBScript. This opens up a world of possibilities. Furthermore, because Microsoft is allowing developers to include VBScript with their applications royalty-free, the chances are that we will soon see many applications coming onto the market that make use of VBScript.

If the desktop and Internet revolution continues along its present path, we could see current desktop applications replaced by a series of components, some of which will be common components, and some of which will be unique to the application. But all will be "tacked" together using VBScript. And all this with platform independence, too. Imagine for a moment that, sitting in front of your

---

* For a discussion of such topics as the organization of the registry and the use of programmatic identifiers to distinguish OLE components, see *Inside the Windows 95 Registry*, by Ron Petrusha, published by O'Reilly & Associates.

favorite PC or Mac, you click the Microsoft Excel icon; immediately the shell of the very latest version of Excel (which you rent from Microsoft) downloads from the nearest (or fastest) Microsoft applications server into your desktop window (which used to be called a browser). As you choose various functions from menu options on the Excel shell, a check is made to ensure that the latest component to perform the task is registered on your machine. If it isn't, the latest component is downloaded automatically. Behind the scenes, the code that is gluing all these components together is VBScript. This hypothetical example, by the way, is almost with us now. As you visit a web site containing ActiveX controls and components, the browser checks to see if you have the correct OCX files registered on your system. If you do, your browser uses them; if not, the control will be downloaded to your browser. This is merely a natural progression from what we currently find behind the scenes in the Windows environment, where many common files (like dynamic link libraries and OCX controls) are used by a wide variety of applications.

Another place where we will start to see more use of VBScript is on the web server itself. Microsoft has recently launched Visual Interdev, a high end web site development tool that allows you to take full advantage of Active Server Pages, which, among other things, allows you to write VBScript to be used on an ActiveX web server like Microsoft Internet Information Server or the Personal Web Server for Windows 95. Microsoft is also hoping that VBScript will be used by hardware and software vendors as a batch-automation language, so we could see VBScript popping up in all sorts of strange places. In fact, VBScript is the batch-automation or programming language for Outlook 1.0, Microsoft's new work-group application product that is included with Microsoft Office 97. All of this makes VBScript a great language to learn both for web pages now, and for who knows what in the future.

## VBScript Versus JavaScript

Before we compare VBScript to JavaScript, let's clarify one thing: JavaScript is not Java, nor is it a subset of Java. Java is a compiled code, which manifests itself on the Web as an applet. Java is a compact, fast implementation (it was originally designed for programming electronic household appliances). Both Java and JavaScript are developed from C++, but there are major differences both in the languages and implementation.

JavaScript was designed by Netscape and was originally known as LiveScript. Netscape renamed the language JavaScript when it licensed the Java name from Sun following the huge media hype surrounding Java. However, the JavaScript that you will find in the Internet Explorer is Microsoft's own implementation, known as JScript, which is built from scratch by Microsoft.

JavaScript and VBScript are both inline text-based scripts that are downloaded in the HTML document. Both are interpreted by the browser, and both enable the developer to create dynamic web applications. At least in the period immediately after the official release of VBScript, JavaScript will have an advantage over VBScript, since Netscape, which currently has the largest share of the browser market, does not directly support VBScript in its browser, Netscape Navigator. This could also be the very same reason why VBScript may steal a march on Java-Script. Anyone sticking relentlessly to JavaScript will have to guess what Netscape will do, what changes they may make to the implementation. Not so with VBScript; as we have seen, VBScript is a subset of VBA, which means that it will always remain compatible with VBA and with the Microsoft products that make use of it.

Let's look at a very simple example HTML form using both JavaScript and VBScript. In both examples, the user simply enters text in the top text box and clicks on the Click Me button; the script copies the text contained in the top text box to the bottom text box. The JavaScript version appears in Example 2-3, while the VBScript version is shown in Example 2-4.

*Example 2-3. JavaScript Version of a Simple Script*

```
<HTML>
<BODY BGCOLOR="white">

<SCRIPT LANGUAGE="javascript">
  function DoAScript()
  {
      var myValue;
      myValue= document.myForm.myTextA.value;
      document.myForm.myTextB.value = myValue;
  }
</SCRIPT>

 <FORM NAME=myForm>
  <INPUT TYPE=text NAME=myTextA><BR>
  <INPUT TYPE=text NAME=myTextB><BR>
  <INPUT TYPE=button NAME=myButton Value="Click Me" OnClick=DoAScript()>
 </FORM>
</BODY>
</HTML>
```

*Example 2-4. VBScript Version of a Simple Script*

```
<HTML>
<BODY BGCOLOR="white">

<SCRIPT LANGUAGE="vbscript">
  Sub DoAScript
      Dim myValue
      myValue = document.myForm.myTextA.value
```

*Example 2-4. VBScript Version of a Simple Script (continued)*

```
        document.myForm.myTextB.value = myValue
   End Sub
</SCRIPT>

 <FORM NAME=myForm>
  <INPUT TYPE=text NAME=myTextA><BR>
  <INPUT TYPE=text NAME=myTextB><BR>
  <INPUT TYPE=button NAME=myButton Value="Click Me" OnClick=DoAScript()>
 </FORM>
</BODY>
</HTML>
```

There are very few differences, as you can see. The `Sub...End Sub` construct does not exist in JavaScript, so VBScript has a `Sub` (a routine within a program that does not return a value) and a `Function` (a routine within a program that returns a value) construct, but JavaScript only has a `function` construct. Also, in JavaScript, unlike VBScript, function names are case sensitive. If you try to set the value of the `OnClick` attribute to *DoaScript()*, you will generate an error. There are also other minor differences, many of which reflect the two quite distinct ancestries of the languages from which the two scripting languages were derived, C and BASIC.

Although you can interface ActiveX controls with JavaScript by using the ActiveX Control Pad, it's somewhat clunky and not as intuitive as the VBScript/ActiveX interface, which is a huge plus for VBScript. With so many thousands of well-developed, mature ActiveX controls already in the marketplace, the use of these add-on controls within web pages is bound to be as popular as it was when we knew them as .VBX and .OCX controls. The ability to implement a particular control quickly and easily is what made VB and custom controls a hit with programmers around the world, regardless of their level of skill. And a direct parallel can be drawn today with ActiveX and VBScript.

As you have seen, JavaScript and VBScript are very much the same, in that they "address the same space." In fact, it is possible to include both JavaScript and VBScript within the same HTML page. However, which procedure will be called? Let's find out by amalgamating the two applications that we developed earlier into the same HTML document; we'll leave the procedure name (*DoAScript*) the same. A web page that combines the scripts appears in Example 2-5.

*Example 2-5. Web Page with Both JavaScript and VBScript*

```
<HTML>
<BODY BGCOLOR="white">

<SCRIPT LANGUAGE="vbscript">
  Sub DoAScript
```

*Example 2-5. Web Page with Both JavaScript and VBScript (continued)*

```
      Alert document.myForm.myTextA.value
  End Sub
</SCRIPT>

<SCRIPT LANGUAGE="javascript">
  function DoAScript()
  {
      var myValue;
      myValue = document.myForm.myTextA.value;
      document.forms[0].myTextB.value = myValue;
  }
</SCRIPT>

 <FORM NAME=myForm>
  <INPUT TYPE=text NAME=myTextA><BR>
  <INPUT TYPE=text NAME=myTextB><BR>
  <INPUT TYPE=button NAME=myButton Value="Click Me" OnClick=DoAScript()>
 </FORM>
</BODY>
</HTML>
```

---

*WARNING*    It is not a good idea to have two functions with the same name written in two different languages on the same HTML page. We've duplicated procedure names in Example 2-5 purely to prove a point. As they say, "Don't try this at home!!"

---

So that we can see which procedure fired (or even whether both fired), the VBScript procedure has been amended and will now show an alert box that contains the text typed into the upper text box, whereas the JavaScript function copies the text from the upper text box into the lower text box. According to Microsoft's VBScript documentation, only the last referenced procedure or method of the two should be activated. In our example, this means that the JavaScript function should execute, since it's defined after the VBScript function. However, when the user clicks on the command button in Example 2-5, the VBScript procedure is fired. If we swap the two procedures around, the JavaScript procedure is run. (Incidentally, this page can be run without error on a Netscape Navigator from version 2.x onwards; only the JavaScript procedure runs regardless of where it is in relation to its VBScript counterpart.)

Notice that, in Example 2-5, we've used the LANGUAGE= attribute in the two <SCRIPT> tags to indicate which scripting language we've embedded in our HTML document. The LANGUAGE attribute, however, is optional; if it is not supplied along with the <SCRIPT> tag, any browser that executes the script will attempt to compile the script using its "default" scripting language. This absence of the LANGUAGE attribute is something that you're likely to encounter very frequently in HTML pages that take advantage of scripting; until recently, only JavaScript existed, making the optional attribute seem superfluous. Now take a look at the JavaScript in Example 2-6. Note that the `LANGUAGE` attribute of the `<SCRIPT>` tag is missing.

*Example 2-6. A Script Without a LANGUAGE= Attribute*

```
<HTML>
<BODY BGCOLOR="white">

<SCRIPT>
  function DoAScript()
  {
      var myValue = document.myForm.myTextA.value;
      document.forms[0].myTextB.value = myValue;
  }
</SCRIPT>

 <FORM NAME=myForm>
  <INPUT TYPE=text NAME=myTextA><BR>
  <INPUT TYPE=text NAME=myTextB><BR>
  <INPUT TYPE=button NAME=myButton Value="Click Me" OnClick=DoAScript()>
 </FORM>
</BODY>
</HTML>
```

When the user clicks on the Click Me button, MSIE executes the *DoAScript* function using JavaScript, indicating that JavaScript, and not VBScript, is MSIE's default scripting language. (We can tell that JavaScript, rather than VBScript, executed the *DoAScript* function, since VBScript does not support the curly braces that are used in JavaScript [as well as in C and C++] to delimit a block of code.) While this may seem surprising, there are some clear reasons for this choice. As a scripting language, VBScript is a late arrival; JavaScript was the first of the scripting languages. Microsoft, however, is concerned not only with popularizing VBScript, but also with making MSIE a superior browser—that is, one that is capable of displaying the widest range of HTML pages in the best way possible. At this point, though, most web pages that use JavaScript do not indicate that the scripting language used is JavaScript. Because it was the first Internet scripting language (and because no other scripting language may have been available when the page was written), they simply assume that the JavaScript engine will compile and execute the code. So in order for MSIE to remain compatible with these web pages, Microsoft wisely chose to make JavaScript the default scripting language for MSIE. This makes it particularly important, when you use the `<SCRIPT>` tag, to mark the beginning of your VBScript code to include the `LANGUAGE` attribute; otherwise, your code will be executed using the JavaScript language engine.

# *VBScript and Netscape Navigator*

As you saw earlier, MSIE has the ability to use different scripting languages that conform to the ActiveX Scripting Specification. Therefore, MSIE3.0 allows you to use VBScript and JavaScript. As an OLE application, it can interface with ActiveX components and Java applets, thus allowing the user of MSIE3.0 the fullest and broadest web surfing experience.

Netscape Navigator is also an OLE application. However, since it does not conform to the ActiveX Scripting Specification, it cannot interpret VBScript, nor does it have a built-in interface for ActiveX objects. Instead, Netscape Navigator can be extended through its OLE "plug-ins" interface. As you can see from Figure 2-5, it is possible to use both VBScript and ActiveX components with Netscape Navigator via a third-party adapter. One such adapter, or Netscape plug-in, is called NCompass, and is available from the NCompass web site at *http://www.ncompasslabs.com.* For a detailed look at using VBScript with other browsers, see Chapter 17, *Handling Other Browsers.*

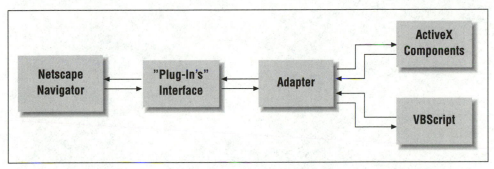

*Figure 2-5. Using ActiveX and VBScript with Netscape Navigator*

# *Summary*

VBScript, as you have seen in this chapter, is an important language to learn now, but it will be even more vital in time to come. More and more ActiveX controls will be used as the Web continues to develop, and the glue that holds these controls together is VBScript.

To get a clear picture of this, imagine that you've included an ActiveX text box control on your web page. You interface with the control from the web page by entering text into it. But once the text has been entered, what are you going to do with it? Regardless of what you want to happen to the text, you need a way of accessing the text programmatically and passing it on to another control or function for further processing—and that's why you need VBScript. It is VBScript that gets hold of the text and passes it to another control, or to a function, or to the server. Without VBScript, ActiveX controls just sit on the page looking pretty!!

The move toward component software started long before Microsoft discovered the Internet, but the Net has accelerated that development, not just for Microsoft, but for the whole software industry. Everyone is now developing applications with at least one, if not both, eyes on the Internet, and (more importantly in terms of profit) on the intranet. Again, many of the componentized applications that you will see launched over the coming months will allow you to interface them using some form of active scripting.

# 3

# *Getting Started*

VBScript is easy to learn and to use. The syntax is straightforward, and you can achieve professional and effective and worthwhile results quickly. At the same time, though, VBScript is a programming language, and to get the most from it, you must be able to write programs.

This chapter is aimed at giving you a grounding in VBScript by providing you with a primer on the basics of Basic. It shows you how to start constructing your VBScript programs and how to include them in your HTML pages. You'll soon find out for yourself that there is no magic or mystique to the VBScript language; just follow a few straightforward rules, and in no time at all you will be amazing yourself, and possibly your clients, with the quality of the work you are producing.

## *The <SCRIPT> Tag*

The `<SCRIPT>` tag is a recent addition to the HTML specification. It allows scripts to be written inline with the rest of your HTML document, and indicates where the embedded scripting code begins. It also indicates the scripting language, and therefore serves to identify which particular scripting engine should be responsible for handling the code. As with nearly all HTML tags, there is the `</SCRIPT>` end tag to close the script.

### *<SCRIPT> Attributes*

The `<SCRIPT>` tag has two main attributes, `LANGUAGE` and `RUNAT`, both of which are optional. There are also two additional attributes, `SCRIPT FOR` and `EVENT`, which give the `<SCRIPT>` tag a specialized meaning.

LANGUAGE is used to specify to the browser which scripting language engine is to compile and interpret the code contained within the script tags. In order to indicate that a script should be handled by the VBScript language engine, either of the following two forms of the <SCRIPT> tag is acceptable:

```
<SCRIPT LANGUAGE="vbscript">

<SCRIPT LANGUAGE="vbs">
```

RUNAT is used to indicate where the script should be executed. By default, scripts run on the browser. However, the value of the RUNAT attribute can be set to "server" so that all scripts defined by a particular <SCRIPT> tag will be interpreted as Active Server Pages scripts that execute on the server. This means that a script defined by the tag

```
<SCRIPT LANGUAGE="vbscript">
```

runs on the browser, but the script

```
<SCRIPT LANGUAGE="vbscript" RUNAT="server">
```

runs on the server. For details, see Appendix E, *Active Server Pages*.

Unless otherwise stated, HTML tags or elements and attributes are *not* case sensitive. Therefore, it would be legal to include the following <SCRIPT> tag in an HTML document:

```
<script language="VBSCRIPT">
```

As we saw earlier, the language attribute is actually optional. However, if you do not specify the language, MSIE3.0 will, by default, treat the script as though it were JavaScript, and use the JavaScript language engine when compiling and executing it.

## *Where to Place <SCRIPT>*

The <SCRIPT> tag can be placed anywhere within the <HEAD> or <BODY> sections of an HTML document. There's also no limitation on the number of <SCRIPT> sections you can place within an HTML file; you can have as many combinations of <SCRIPT> </SCRIPT> as you want. You may choose to bundle all your procedures together into one large <SCRIPT> section and place this at the end of the BODY section, out of the way of the main HTML coding, or you can quite easily split the procedures into their own <SCRIPT> sections, placing them near to or directly after the HTML elements they refer to (or are called from). The three models or templates that appear in Examples 3-1 through 3-3 show where you can place the <SCRIPT> tag within your HTML document.

*Example 3-1. Using a Single <SCRIPT> Section as Part of the <HEAD> Section*

```
<HTML>
  <HEAD>
```

*Example 3-1. Using a Single <SCRIPT> Section as Part of the <HEAD> Section (continued)*

```
    <SCRIPT LANGUAGE="vbscript">
     various scripted procedures
    </SCRIPT>
  </HEAD>
<BODY>
various html coding, etc.
</BODY>
</HTML>
```

*Example 3-2. Using a Single <SCRIPT> Section at the End of the <BODY> Section*

```
<HTML>
  <HEAD>
  </HEAD>
<BODY>
 various html coding, etc.
  <SCRIPT LANGUAGE="vbscript">
   various scripted procedures
  </SCRIPT>
</BODY>
</HTML>
```

*Example 3-3. Using Multiple <SCRIPT> Sections Within the <BODY> Section*

```
<HTML>
  <HEAD>
  </HEAD>
<BODY>
 various html coding, etc.
  <SCRIPT LANGUAGE="vbscript">
   various scripted procedures
  </SCRIPT>
VARIOUS HTML CODING etc
  <SCRIPT LANGUAGE="vbscript">
   various scripted procedures
  </SCRIPT>
various html coding etc
  <SCRIPT LANGUAGE="vbscript">
   various scripted procedures
  </SCRIPT>
</BODY>
</HTML>
```

# Using <!-- --> with <SCRIPT>

Although it's certainly not mandatory, Microsoft recommends that you "comment out" the contents of the <SCRIPT> section by using the two HTML comment tags <!-- and -->. This prevents older browsers that do not recognize the <SCRIPT> tag from interpreting the script as plain text and displaying it on the HTML page, as illustrated in Figure 3-1.

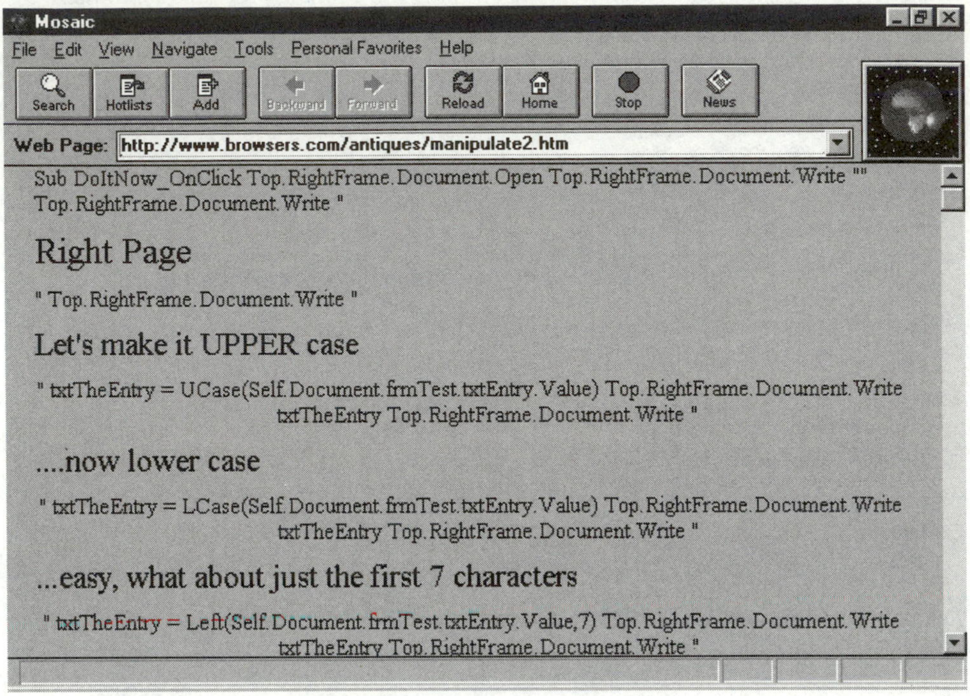

*Figure 3-1. An older browser displaying uncommented script as text*

The comment tags `<!--` and `-->` must be placed within the `<SCRIPT>` tags, as the following code fragment shows:

```
<SCRIPT LANGUAGE="vbscript">
<!--
  Sub DoAScript
     .......
  End Sub
-->
</SCRIPT>
```

Otherwise, the `<SCRIPT>` tags themselves will be ignored by all browsers. Since browsers are expected to overlook tags that they don't understand, older browsers will skip over the `<SCRIPT>` tag. But since they don't "know" that the `<SCRIPT>` tag marks the beginning of executable content, rather than of display-able text, they'll display the text unless the comment tags are present. On the other hand, browsers that support the `<SCRIPT>` tag use the scripting engine to interpret all text between the `<SCRIPT>` and `</SCRIPT>` tags. The HTML comment tags are ignored by the script engine, so that it only "sees" the actual code. However, any additional comment tags, or any comment tags in any other position within the `<SCRIPT>` and `</SCRIPT>` tags, are interpreted as script, and generate a syntax error. This means that if you need to add comments to your code, you don't use the HTML comment tags; use either REM or a single quotation mark, ', at the start of the line.

### VBScript with <SCRIPT FOR>

Strictly speaking, FOR is an attribute of the <SCRIPT> tag. However, I like to consider <SCRIPT> and <SCRIPT FOR> separately, since they are used somewhat differently. <SCRIPT FOR> is used to enclose the script for a single event belonging to a single object or control, whereas <SCRIPT> can contain numerous functions, procedures, events, etc. You can see this clearly in the full <SCRIPT FOR> tag. Unlike all the other <SCRIPT> tags you have seen thus far, this line attaches its script to a specific event of a specific control:

```
<SCRIPT FOR="myButton" EVENT="onClick" LANGUAGE="vbscript">
```

The FOR attribute specifies which control (usually an intrinsic HTML object) the code is to be attached to, and the EVENT attribute tells the scripting engine when the script has to be run. (In Chapter 6, *The Element Object and HTML Intrinsic Controls*, we'll delve deeper into the events available to you for each of the intrinsic HTML objects.) Example 3-4 demonstrates the use of <SCRIPT FOR>.

*Example 3-4. Using the <SCRIPT FOR> Tag*

```
<HTML>
 <BODY BGCOLOR="white">
   <FORM NAME="myForm">
     <INPUT TYPE=text NAME="myText">
     <INPUT TYPE=button NAME="myButton">
        <SCRIPT FOR="myButton" EVENT="onClick" LANGUAGE="vbscript">
          alert Document.myForm.myText.Value
        </SCRIPT>
   </FORM>
 </BODY>
</HTML>
```

As you can see from Example 3-4, the VBScript Sub...End Sub construct is not required, since the event and object have been specified in the <SCRIPT FOR> tag, and the script itself consists of a complete procedure. If you attempt to use the Sub...End Sub construct, the VBScript compiler displays an error message. This means, incidentally, that the procedure defined by the <SCRIPT FOR> tag does not have a name; consequently, it cannot be called from any other part of a VBScript program. Also note that, to improve readability, it is usual to place a <SCRIPT FOR> construct directly after the object to which it relates.

## Invoking Scripts

Let's look now at how we're going to instruct the browser to run our script when we need it. VBScript and HTML provide four main ways of invoking a script.

## Calling Scripts Implicitly

The first method for invoking a script, which uses the `Sub...End Sub` construct to define a procedure that is to be executed whenever some event occurs, is very similar to the event procedures of Visual Basic, and those of you who have a background in VB will probably feel most at home with it. It's constructed purely in VBScript by using the object or control name and event, separated by an underscore, as part of the *Sub* procedure declaration, like this:

```
Sub MyButton_OnClick
```

The procedure is run whenever the specified event—in this case *OnClick*—is fired by the specified object—*MyButton* in our example—being clicked. The scripting engine has previously compiled the code at the time it was downloaded, and it basically maintains a log of which events and which objects have procedures attached to them. As the message—in this case, that *MyButton* has been clicked—passes through this log, the engine knows which part of the code to run.

The brief HTML page shown in Example 3-5 indicates how to call a script implicitly by defining an event procedure. When the user clicks on the command button, the VBScript engine executes the *MyButton_OnClick* procedure, which displays a message box containing the string "Hello World."

*Example 3-5. A Procedure that is Called Implicitly*

```
<HTML>
  <HEAD>
   <SCRIPT LANGUAGE="vbscript">
     Sub MyButton_OnClick
         Alert "Hello World"
     End Sub
   </SCRIPT>
  </HEAD>

  <BODY BGCOLOR="white">
    <FORM>
     <INPUT TYPE="Button" NAME="myButton">
    </FORM>
  </BODY>
</HTML>
```

In Example 3-5, note that the HTML code that is responsible for defining the intrinsic HTML control myButton is identical to HTML code in cases in which no script is attached. That makes this method the easiest to use if you're adding script to existing web pages, since it requires you to make very few changes to your existing HTML code.

Basically, this method of invoking a script by attaching it to a particular event is the same as attaching a script to an event on a particular control by using the `<SCRIPT FOR>` tag; see "VBScript with <SCRIPT FOR>" earlier in this chapter.

## Calling Scripts Directly from HTML Elements

The second method of calling a script, which will probably appeal to those of you with JavaScript experience, specifies the procedure name as part of the HTML object definition, as in the following definMyButtonition of an intrinsic HTML command button:

```
<INPUT TYPE="button" NAME="myButton"  OnClick="myScript"
LANGUAGE="vbscript">
```

This method is particularly useful if you need to call the same procedure from more than one object, as the HTML page in Example 3-6 shows. In this example, when the user clicks on either of two intrinsic HTML command buttons, the myScript procedure, which displays a message box containing the string "Hello World", is invoked.

*Example 3-6. Calling the Same Script Procedure from More Than One HTML Intrinsic Control*

```
<HTML>
 <HEAD>
  <SCRIPT LANGUAGE="vbscript">
   Sub myScript
       Alert "Hello World"
   End Sub
  </SCRIPT>
 </HEAD>

  <BODY BGCOLOR="white">
    <FORM>
     <INPUT TYPE=button NAME="cmdButton1" OnClick="myScript"
          LANGUAGE="vbscript">
     <INPUT TYPE=button NAME="cmdButton2" OnClick="myScript"
          LANGUAGE="vbscript">
    </FORM>
  </BODY>
</HTML>
```

## Automatically Invoking a Script When a Page Is Loaded

The third method of invoking a script is to have the VBScript engine execute it automatically when a page is loaded. This startup script, which is ideal for performing any initialization that is needed for a web page, is executed just once, when the page is first displayed, immediately after the script engine compiles the page's script. (It is also executed again, of course, if the user selects the browser's Refresh option.)

Typically, most VBScript code that appears between the `<SCRIPT>` and `</SCRIPT>` tags appears in procedures (which are indicated by the `Sub...End Sub` construct) and functions (which are indicated by the `Function...End Function` construct). In order to be executed, these routines have to be called either explicitly (i.e., they have to be called by name from a procedure invoked in one of the four ways discussed here) or implicitly. However, it is also possible to include *inline code*, or code at the *script level*, after the `<SCRIPT>` tag. This is VBScript code that does not appear within a particular procedure or subroutine, and that is automatically executed when the form is first loaded. Example 3-7 contains inline code that is invoked when a document is first loaded.

*Example 3-7. Automatically Executing Inline Code*

```
<HTML>
   <BODY BGCOLOR="white">
   <SCRIPT LANGUAGE="vbscript">
      Document.Write "<CENTER><H3>My Web Page</H3>"
      Alert "Welcome to my web page!"
   </SCRIPT>
   </BODY>
</HTML>
```

So, now that you know how to include a script into your HTML document, and how it will be called into action, it's time to start looking at the main language elements that will allow you to write professional and robust scripts for your VBScript pages.

---

### Inline Code and Form_Load

If you're a Visual Basic programmer, you'll notice that inline code, or the script level, corresponds closely to the *Form_Load* event procedure of a Visual Basic form. There are, however, two major differences. The first is that the script level is also used to define public variables and constants; when used for that purpose, it corresponds to a code module or to a Visual Basic form's declarations section. The second is that, whereas *Form_Load* is a formal procedure in Visual Basic, inline code in VBScript is not.

---

## Calling a Procedure from Another Procedure

The fourth and final way to execute a VBScript procedure is to call it from another VBScript procedure. Exactly how you call it depends on the type of procedure (procedures consist of subroutines, functions, and event handlers) you are calling. You'll find an in-depth explanation of how to use them in Chapter 4, *Program Flow and Structure*, but for now, Example 3-8 provides one quick illustration of how you can execute one procedure from within another. When the user clicks on the Click Me button, the *myButton_OnClick* event procedure is executed automatically. It in turn invokes another procedure, named *doAlertMessage*, and passes the string "Hello World" to it as a parameter. So *doAlertMsg*, which simply displays an the string "Hello World" in an alert box, is called by the *myButton_OnClick* procedure.

*Example 3-8. Executing One Script from Within Another*

```
<HTML>
 <HEAD>
  <SCRIPT LANGUAGE="vbscript">
    Sub myButton_OnClick
        Call doAlertMessage("Hello World")
    End Sub

    Sub doAlertMessage(Msg)
        Alert Msg
    End Sub
  </SCRIPT>
 </HEAD>
<BODY BGCOLOR="white">
   <CENTER>
      <INPUT TYPE="button" NAME="myButton" VALUE="Click Me">
   </CENTER>
</BODY>
</HTML>
```

# Some Scripting Basics

Before you get into the fundamentals of the VBScript language, here are a few basic points to remember about VBScript:

1. **VBScript is case-insensitive**. Like HTML in general, and unlike JavaScript, VBScript is not case-sensitive. This applies to all script elements—function names, variable names, statements, etc. However you choose to write your code, if the syntax and spelling are correct, the language engine will understand it. For example:

   ```
   ...
   Dim myVar
   MyvAR = tRiM(RIGHT(x, 4))
   ...
   ```

   If the VBScript engine were to execute this code fragment, it would correctly interpret *myVar* and *MyvAR* as a single variable, despite the difference in case between its two occurrences. Similarly, the VBScript language engine success-fully handles the *tRiM* function, despite its unconventional mixture of upper and lower case.

2. **No restriction on whitespace**. Very much as you can use any combination of upper and lower case within a language element (like a statement, a function, or a variable name), you can use any amount of "whitespace" (that is, space characters) to separate language elements from one another. Not that I'm saying you should add extra spaces to your code just for the sake of adding it. But when you're trying to track down an elusive bug, at least you'll know that the few extra spaces you've added within a code line to improve its read-ability are not the culprit! So, for example, the following lines of code would not produce an error:

```
...
myLongNameVar = somevalue
myVar         = anothervalue
...
```

3. **Commenting VBScript code**. When you need to add a comment to your code, you have the choice of using either the **Rem** statement or a single quotation mark, as the following two lines of code illustrate:

```
Rem This is a code comment
' So is this
```

However, if you use the **Rem** statement to add a comment at the end of a line that contains some code, you must use a colon prior to the **Rem** keyword. The single quotation mark does not require a colon in this way. For example:

```
If x = 10 Then : Rem This is my comment
If x = 10 Then 'This is my comment
```

One further point about comments within scripts: When you are commenting inline scripts (that is, scripts that are written directly within an <INPUT> tag) using VBScript code, use **Rem** instead of the ' character. You can use ' in <SCRIPT> blocks.

4. **Keeping code lines short**. VBScript has inherited a very useful little tool from VBA and VB4: the line continuation character. It enables you to write code that spans several lines (and is therefore much easier to read) but is treated by the language engine as a single code line. The line continuation character is simply an underscore character, _, which is placed after a single space at the end of a line. The following line is then read by the VBScript engine as though the three lines were one. The following code fragment, for example, is seen by the VBScript language engine as a single line of code:

```
If myFirstVariable = 1 And _
   mySecondVariable = 2 And _
   myThirdVariable = 3 Then
      ...
```

### VB Programmer's Note

Whereas in VB4 you are restricted to using no more than nine line continuation characters within a single line of code, in VBScript there appears to be no such limit, or at least the limit is much greater. I've tested a line of code containing 40 continuation characters (just to see if it would break!), and the script still compiled and ran normally.

# VBScript Data Types: The Many Faces of the Variant

Unlike Visual Basic and Visual Basic for Applications, VBScript has only one main data type, called a *variant*. A variant is a very special data type, though, since it can contain many different types of data, and can automatically select the most appropriate data type for the particular context in which it is being used. A simplified view of a variant is that it can hold both string data (that is, characters) and numerical data; however, internally it is much more complex, which permits it to hold a wide range of different numeric types.

## Variant Data Subtypes

While the only data type recognized by VBScript is the variant, any item of variant data belongs to a particular subtype. Let's look in depth at the range of *subtypes*— or the different types of data—that a variant can hold:

- **Empty.** The Empty subtype is automatically assigned to new variables when you declare them, but before you explicitly assign a value to them. For instance, in the code fragment

```
Dim var1, var2
var2 = 0
```

the subtype of **var1** is Empty, whereas **var2** is only Empty for the brief period of time between the execution of the **Dim** statement on the first line, which declares a variable (it is discussed later in this chapter in "Declaring Variables and Constants"), and the assignment statement on the second line. In addition, a variable's subtype is Empty if it has been explicitly assigned a value of Empty, as in the following code fragment:

```
Dim var1
var1 = Empty
```

- **Null.** Null is a special data subtype that is used to indicate that a variable does not contain any valid data. Usually, a variable is assigned a Null value to indicate that an error condition exists. In order for its subtype to be Null, a variable must have a Null value assigned to it explicitly, as in the following line of code:

```
var1 = NULL
```

A Null value also results from any operation in which the value of one or more of the expressions is Null, as the following code fragment shows:

```
dim myVarOne, myVarTwo, myVarThree 'At this stage all three variables
                                   'are EMPTY
myVarOne = 9
myVarTwo=NULL                      'We have now made this variable NULL
myVarThree = myVarOne + myVarTwo   'The result will therefore be NULL
```

- **Boolean**. The Boolean subtype is used to indicate the presence of logical data that can contain either of two values, True or False. The keywords True and False are constants (if you're not sure what a constant is, see "Declaring Variables and Constants" later in this chapter) that are predefined in VBScript, so you can make use of them in your code when you want to assign a value to a Boolean variable, as the following code fragment shows:

```
var1 = True
var2 = False
```

Many of the object properties you will come across later, when we start to investigate ActiveX controls, have possible values of True or False. In addition, within programs, Boolean variables often serve as flags to control program flow, as the following example shows:

```
If myBool = False Then
  myVar = 4
  myBool = True
Else
  myVar = 5
  myBool = False
End If
```

Note that this example toggles (or reverses) the value of *myBool* within the `If...Else...End If` construct.

- **Byte**. A byte is the smallest numeric subtype available in VBScript. One byte (8 binary bits) can represent 256 integer numbers, ranging from 0 to 255 in decimal, or from 00 to FF in hexadecimal. Because only one byte is used to hold the number, there is no room for the "sign," and so only positive numbers can be held in a Byte data type. Attempting to assign a negative number or a number greater than 255 to byte data results in a run-time error.

- **Integer**. An integer is a whole number that Visual Basic uses two bytes of, or 16 bits, to store in memory. Since one bit is used to represent the sign (either positive or negative), the value of integer data can range from –32,768 to

32,767. Attempting to assign a value outside this range results in a run-time error.

- **Long**. A Long is a signed integer that Visual Basic stores in four bytes, or 32 bits, of memory. This allows it to hold a far greater range of negative or positive numbers; the value of a long integer variable can range from −2,147,483,648 to 2,147,483,647.

- **Single**. The three numeric data types that we've examined so far are all integers; that is, they're unable to represent fractional numbers or decimal places. To do this requires a floating-point data subtype, two of which are available in VBScript. The first is Single, which is an abbreviation for single-precision. Because of the large numbers involved, we are forced here to specify the ranges as exponential numbers. There are two ranges, one for negative values and one for positive values. A negative single-precision value can range from −3.402823E38 to −1.401298E–45, while the range of a positive single-precision value is 1.401298E–45 to 3.402823E38.

- **Double**. The Double subtype indicates a double-precision floating-point number; basically, it's the industrial strength version of the Single data subtype. Its value can range from −1.79769313486232E308 to −4.94065645841247E–324 for negative values, and from 4.94065645841247E–324 to 1.79769313486232E-308 for positive values.

- **Date/Time**. The Date subtype contains a specially formatted number that represents the date or time. If the number holds a date value, the earliest date that can be represented is January 1, 100, and taking the view that our web sites will be around for a long time, the furthest into the future that we can go is December 31, 9999. We will look in detail at Dates and Times in Chapter 10, *Date and Time in VBScript*.

- **Currency**. The Currency subtype, which is new to VBScript Version 2.0, provides a special numeric format for storing monetary values.

- **String**. Probably one of the most commonly used data types is the String. The VBScript String subtype can contain virtually an unlimited number of characters—the limit is somewhere in the neighborhood of two billion. The String subtype used in VBScript is a variable-length data type, so you don't have to worry about specifying how much memory to allocate to the variable, as you do in some programming languages. VBScript includes many useful intrinsic functions for handling and manipulating string data; we'll examine them in Chapter 14, *Form Input Validation*.

- **Object**. This data subtype contains a reference to an object. The object can be an OLE automation object, such as an ActiveX component, or it can be one of the HTML intrinsic objects.

- **Error.** The Error subtype is used to store an error number. Error numbers are generated automatically by VBScript, and can then be used by your error handling routine. Error handling routines are discussed in Chapter 15, *Error Handling and Debugging*.

So what does all this mean to the VBScript programmer? Above all, it means simplicity: as with any well-designed system, the variant is complex, but not complicated. That is to say, the interface—the part that you deal with—is straightforward, yet behind the scenes the variant data type does some incredibly complex things. That means you don't have to concern yourself with juggling code to ensure that data types are not mismatched, as Example 3-9 shows.

*Example 3-9. The Power of the Variant Data Type*

```
<HTML>
 <HEAD>
  <SCRIPT LANGUAGE="vbscript">
   Sub cmdMyButton_OnClick
       Dim Var1, Var2
       Var1 = 1
       Var2 = 50000000.2658
       Var1 = Var1 + Var2
       Document.myForm.txtText1.Value = Var1
   End Sub
  </SCRIPT>
 </HEAD>

<BODY BGCOLOR="white">
  <FORM NAME="myForm">
   <INPUT TYPE="text" NAME="txtText1">
   <INPUT TYPE="button" NAME="cmdMyButton" VALUE = "Click Me">
  </FORM>
 </BODY>
</HTML>
```

When the user clicks on the Click Me button, the *cmdMyButton_OnClick* event procedure executes. It begins by using the `Dim` statement to declare two variables. Next, it assigns the integer value 1 to the first variable, *Var1*. Just to make things interesting, it assigns a large, double-precision number, 50,000,000.2658, to the second variable, *Var2*. Then the routine adds the two variables together and stores their result to the integer variable, *Var1*. As you may recall from the overview of data subtypes, the value assigned to an integer cannot exceed 32,767, nor can it include any digits to the left of the decimal. Yet, our script does not generate a compiler error because of this. So in the process of performing the calculation, the VBScript engine converts *Var1* to a double-precision number. In most other programming languages, this task would have to be performed by the programmer.

If you modify the VBScript code in Example 3-9 to try different values for *Var1* and *Var2*, you'll find that the only time the variant cannot handle the conversion occurs when one of the expressions is a string data subtype—i.e., you can't add 100 to "Hello" and expect a valid result. When this happens, the VBScript engine displays a "Type mismatch" error, which indicates that one of the items of data was of the wrong subtype, and the engine was unable to convert it. This raises a good point, though: in a numeric operation, it is possible, especially if the data are input by the user, that one or more of the variables is a string data subtype. How would you be able to know this in advance, before VBScript stops executing your script and displays an error message?

## Determining the Variant Subtype

Having the variant data type take care of all your data typing is all well and good, but what happens when you need to know exactly what type of data is stored to a variable? VBScript provides two easy-to-use functions, *VarType*, which returns a number that indicates the type of data stored to a variable, and *TypeName*, a new function in VBScript 2.0, which returns the name of the data type.

### VarType

The syntax of *VarType* is

```
VarType(variablename)
```

where **variablename** is the name of the variable whose subtype you want to determine. You can provide the name of only a single variable at a time. Table 3-1 details the possible values returned by *VarType* and the data subtypes that they represent. For purposes of reference, Table 3-1 also lists the VBScript 2.0 constants that you can use in your code to compare with the values returned by the *VarType* function. For details, see "Intrinsic Constants" later in this chapter.

*Table 3-1. The Values Returned by the VarType Function*

| Value | Data Subtype | VBScript 2.0 Constant |
|-------|--------------|-----------------------|
| 0 | Empty | vbEmpty |
| 1 | Null | vbNull |
| 2 | Integer | vbInteger |
| 3 | Long Integer | vbLong |
| 4 | Single | vbSingle |
| 5 | Double | vbDouble |
| 6 | Currency | vbCurrency |
| 7 | Date | vbDate |
| 8 | String | vbString |

*Table 3-1. The Values Returned by the VarType Function (continued)*

| Value | Data Subtype | VBScript 2.0 Constant |
|---|---|---|
| 9 | OLE Automation Object | vbObject |
| 10 | Error | vbError |
| 11 | Boolean | vbBoolean |
| 12 | Array of Variant | vbVariant |
| 13 | Data Access Object | vbDataObject |
| 17 | Byte | vbByte |
| 8192 | Array | vbArray |

Before we go on to see how you use *VarType* within a script, we should quickly note the value returned by *VarType* if it detects an array. Actually, the function never returns 8192, as shown in Table 3-1. 8192 is only a base line figure that indicates the presence of an array. In fact, when passed an array, *VarType* always returns 8204, or 8192 + 12 (indicating an array of variants). This is in contradiction to the VBScript documentation, which indicates that the value returned by *VarType* when given an array differs depending on the underlying data subtype of the array. The example used in the VBScript documentation is that of an array of integer subtypes that is said to return 8194, or 8192 + 2 (indicating integer variants). But this is not the case; because VBScript can only create variant arrays, the return value can only be 8204.

Example 3-10 provides a simple example of the *VarType* function. When the user clicks on the Click Me button, the *MyButton_OnClick* procedure executes. It assigns a value of 9 to the `MyVal` variable and calls the *VarType* function, passing to it `MyVal` as a parameter. The value returned by the function, 2, is then displayed in a message box; this indicates that `MyVal` is a variant integer.

*Example 3-10. The VarType Function*

```
<HTML>
 <HEAD>
  <SCRIPT LANGUAGE="vbscript">
   Sub MyButton_OnClick
       Dim MyVal
       MyVal = 9
       Alert VarType(MyVal)
   End Sub
  </SCRIPT>
 </HEAD>

 <BODY BGCOLOR="white">
  <FORM NAME="frmMyForm">
    <INPUT TYPE="button" NAME="MyButton" VALUE="Click Me">
  </FORM>
 </BODY>
</HTML>
```

Try modifying this code by assigning various numbers and strings to *MyVal*. You'll find that you can enter a very large integer for *MyVal* and the code will return 3 for Long, or you can enter a word or string (enclosed in quotation marks) and the code will return 8. You can even enter a number in quotation marks and it will return 8, indicating a String subtype.

Which brings us neatly onto a problem with HTML text boxes. The code in Example 3-11 is very similar to Example 3-10, except that the user enters a value into an intrinsic HTML text box control, and the *MyButton_OnClick* procedure retrieves it and passes it to the *VarType* function. Note that, regardless of the value that you enter into the text box, the result is always 8, the code for a String subtype. This indicates that, if we retrieve a value from an HTML intrinsic control, it is always a variant string.

*Example 3-11. Retrieving the Contents of an Intrinsic HTML Text Box Control*

```
<HTML>
 <HEAD>
  <SCRIPT LANGUAGE="vbscript">
   Sub MyButton_OnClick
    Alert VarType(Document.frmMyForm.txtText1.Value)
   End Sub
  </SCRIPT>
 </HEAD>

 <BODY BGCOLOR="white">
  <FORM NAME="frmMyForm">
    <INPUT TYPE="text" NAME="txtText1"><BR>
    <INPUT TYPE="button" NAME="MyButton" VALUE="Click Me">
  </FORM>
 </BODY>
</HTML>
```

But what happens when we encounter a situation like the one shown in Example 3-12, where we want to retrieve two numbers entered by the user into two HTML text boxes and add them together? Try entering the number 9 in the first text box and 7 in the second. When you click on the Click Me button, the result shown in the message box is 97, instead of the correct answer, which is 16. That has happened because both the numbers that you entered were treated as strings, and when our script "added" them, it concatenated them into one single string. This is exactly the same as if you type "Hello" into one box and "World" into the other; when your script concatenates them, the result is "HelloWorld."

*Example 3-12. Unsuccessfully Adding Contents of Two Intrinsic HTML Text Boxes*

```
<HTML>
 <HEAD>
  <SCRIPT LANGUAGE="vbscript">
   Sub MyButton_OnClick
```

*Example 3-12. Unsuccessfully Adding Contents of Two Intrinsic HTML Text Boxes (continued)*

```
      Dim MyInt
      MyInt = Document.frmMyForm.txtText1.Value +
               _Document.frmMyForm.txtText2.Value
      Alert MyInt
   End Sub
  </SCRIPT>
 </HEAD>

<BODY BGCOLOR="white">
 <FORM NAME="frmMyForm">
    <INPUT TYPE="text" NAME="txtText1"><BR>
    <INPUT TYPE="text" NAME="txtText2"><BR>
    <INPUT TYPE="button" NAME="MyButton" VALUE=Click Me">
 </FORM>
 </BODY>
</HTML>
```

So if you specify a value within your script code, the scripting engine assigns the correct subtype to it. But if the value comes from the HTML form, it is always a string. So how are we going to add values together that come from an HTML form? We must first convert the strings into numbers, a topic discussed in the section "Converting from One Data Subtype to Another" later in this chapter.

## TypeName

The *TypeName* function allows you to write more readable, self-documenting code, by returning the actual data subtype name rather than the more abstract data subtype number. The syntax for *TypeName* is:

```
    result = TypeName(variable)
```

As with its older brother, *TypeName* is read-only, which means that you can use it to determine the subtype of a variable, but you can't use it to explicitly set the type of a variable; to do this, you must use the conversion functions discussed in the next section. Table 3-2 shows the string that the *TypeName* function returns for each data subtype.

*Table 3-2. Strings Returned by the TypeName Function*

| Return Value | Data Subtype |
|---|---|
| \<object type\> | Actual type name of an object |
| Boolean | Boolean value: True or False |
| Byte | Byte value |
| Currency | Currency value |
| Date | Date or time value |
| Decimal | Decimal (single-precision) value |
| Double | Double-precision floating-point value |

*Table 3-2. Strings Returned by the TypeName Function (continued)*

| Return Value | Data Subtype |
| --- | --- |
| Empty | Uninitialized |
| Error | Error |
| Integer | Integer value |
| Long | Long integer value |
| Nothing | Object variable that doesn't yet refer to an object instance |
| Null | No valid data |
| Object | Generic object |
| Single | Single-precision floating-point value |
| String | Character string value |
| Variant() | Variant array |
| Unknown | Unknown object type |

Of interest in Table 3-2 is the Variant Array subtype, which, as you saw in the discussion of *VarType*, has special significance, since it is always returned along with some other value. In fact—although this is not documented—when you pass the name of an array to *TypeName*, even an array that you have forced to be a certain data type by using the conversion functions, the return value is always "Variant()". I suppose you could take this to mean, "I know it's an array, but I'm not sure what data type it's holding." Unfortunately there's no clear answer as to what data subtype lurks within your array.

As for making your code more readable and easier to maintain, just look at this snippet:

```
If TypeName(x) = "Double" Then
```

Now you've no excuse for getting those nasty "type mismatch" errors!

Example 3-13 illustrates the use of *TypeName*. (Don't forget that you need VBScript 2.0 installed to use *TypeName* and to try out this example.) When you type something into the text box and press the What Type? Button, an alert box indicates whether you entered a string, a date, or a number. You may notice, though, that it always identifies (or perhaps misidentifies) numbers as data of subtype Double. That's because our script uses the *CDbl* function to arbitrarily convert a numeric string entered into the text box to a variable of subtype Double. For details on converting data from one subtype to another, see the following section.

*Example 3-13. The TypeName Function*

```
<HTML>
<HEAD>
<SCRIPT LANGUAGE="vbscript">
```

*Example 3-13. The TypeName Function (continued)*

```
Sub cmdButton1_OnClick
    Dim x

    If IsDate(frmForm1.txtText1.Value) Then
        x = CDate(frmForm1.txtText1.Value)
    ElseIf IsNumeric(frmForm1.txtText1.Value) Then
        x = CDbl(frmForm1.txtText1.Value)
    ElseIf frmForm1.txtText1.Value > "" Then
        x = Trim(frmForm1.txtText1.Value)
    End If

    Alert TypeName(x)

End Sub
</SCRIPT>
</HEAD>
<BODY BGCOLOR="white">
<FONT FACE="arial">
<CENTER>
<H3>TypeName()</H3>
<BR><BR>
<FORM NAME="frmForm1">
<INPUT TYPE="text" NAME="txtText1"><BR><BR>
<INPUT TYPE="button" NAME="cmdButton1" VALUE="What Type?">
</FORM>
</CENTER>
</BODY>
</HTML>
```

## *Converting from One Data Subtype to Another*

VBScript provides us with a range of built-in conversion functions that are simple and quick to use. The syntax for each is basically the same. For example,

```
CBool(variablename)
```

where *variablename* is either the name of a variable, a constant, or an expression (like **x – y**) that evaluates to a particular variant subtype. Regardless of the particular function you use, the data subtype being converted is immaterial; what matters is the subtype to which you want to convert a particular value. The conversion functions supported by VBScript are:

- *CBool.* Converts *variablename* to a Boolean data subtype. *variablename* can contain any numeric data subtype or any string capable of being converted into a number. If *variablename* is 0 or "0", *CBool* returns **False**; otherwise, it returns **True** (–1).

- *CByte.* Converts *variablename* to a Byte data subtype. *variablename* can contain any numeric data or string data capable of conversion into a number that is greater than or equal to 0 and less than or equal to 255. If *variable-*

*name* is out of range, VBScript displays an Overflow error message. If *variablename* is a floating-point number, it is rounded to the nearest integer before being converted to byte data.

- *CDate*. Converts *variablename* to a Date/Time data subtype. *CDate* accepts numeric data and string data that appears to be a date, converting them to the correct format for the machine. The date is returned in the format specified by the locale information on the client computer. For example, on a machine set to the American date format `mm/dd/yy`, if you enter the British date format `dd/mm/yy` in a text box and then use the *CDate* function on the contents of the text box, *CDate* will convert it to the American `mm/dd/yy` format.

- *CCur*. Converts *variablename* to a Currency data subtype. *CCur* accepts any numeric or string data that can be expressed as a currency value. The function recognizes the decimal and thousands separators based on locale information on the client computer. It, as well as the Currency variant subtype, is recognized by VBScript 2.0 only.

- *CDbl*. Converts *variablename* to a double-precision data subtype. The function accepts any numeric data within the limits of the Double data subtype or any string data that can be converted to a number within the range of the Double data subtype.

- *CInt*. Converts *variablename* to an Integer data subtype. *CInt* accepts any numeric data within the limits of the Integer data subtype, or any string data that can be converted to a number within the limits of the Integer data subtype.

- *CLng*. Converts *variablename* to a Long data subtype. The function accepts any numeric data within the limits of the Long Integer data subtype, or any string data that can be converted to a number whose value lies within the range of a Long Integer.

- *CSng*. Converts *variablename* to a Single data subtype. The function accepts any numeric data within the limits of the Single data subtype, or any string data that can be converted to a number within the range of the Single data subtype.

- *CStr*. Converts *variablename* to a String data subtype. *CStr* accepts any kind of data.

I have provided a very simple data type conversion application on the CD-ROM, called *CONVERSIONS.HTM*. Enter data in the top text box, and click any of the buttons to find out what the converted output looks like. This allows you to test the limitations of each conversion function and data type.

Now that we know about the data conversion functions, we can correct the error that occurred in Example 3-12 when we attempted to add the contents of two intrinsic HTML text box controls. All we have to do is to convert the string in each text box to an integer by using the *CInt* function. The corrected version of the program is shown in Example 3-14.

*Example 3-14. Adding the Contents of Two Intrinsic HTML Text Boxes*

```
<HTML>
 <HEAD>
  <SCRIPT LANGUAGE="vbscript">
   Sub MyButton_OnClick
    Dim MyInt
     MyInt = CInt(Document.frmMyForm.txtText1.Value) +
             _CInt(Document.frmMyForm.txtText2.Value)
     Alert MyInt
   End Sub
  </SCRIPT>
 </HEAD>

 <BODY BGCOLOR="white">
  <FORM NAME="frmMyForm">
    <INPUT TYPE="text" NAME="txtText1"><BR>
    <INPUT TYPE="text" NAME="txtText2"><BR>
    <INPUT TYPE="button" NAME="MyButton" VALUE="Click Me">
  </FORM>
 </BODY>
</HTML>
```

The script in Example 3-14 assumes that the values entered into the text boxes fall within the numeric limits of the integer data subtype. In a "real" application, if we did need an integer value, we would have to verify the input data or to test the data before attempting to convert it, in order to ensure that we could convert it to an integer without generating a run-time error. This problem is examined in greater depth in Chapter 14. But for now, play around with the script in Example 3-14. See what happens if you enter a really large number into one of the text boxes, and try changing the script to use other conversion functions.

So now that you know what data types VBScript can handle, you know all there is to know about the variant data type, the chameleon of the programming world. You know how to find out how the variant is handling your data, and you can convert from one subtype to another. Let's now look at how you're going to use these data types and data within a script.

# *Variables and Constants*

With all this data flying around inside your script, you need some way to keep track of it. In reality, the data you are using—whether it is data you create as part of the program, or data that is entered by the user—is held somewhere in the computer's memory. Think of the nightmare you'd have trying to keep track of just which memory location your particular piece of data was occupying (completely ignoring the possibility that its memory location might change while the program executes). Those nice people who write the software we use to create our programs and scripts solved this problem a long time ago by giving us variables and constants.

## *What Is a Variable?*

A variable is a placeholder or recognizable name for a memory location. This location is of no consequence to us; all we have to do is remember the name. When we use the name, the script engine will go to the correct memory location and either retrieve the data stored there or change the data, depending upon our instructions. It is important therefore to learn the rules for naming variables:

- Variable names can be no more than 255 characters in length. Variable names tend to become pretty unreadable after about 20 characters anyhow, which then defeats the purpose of having longer variable names.

- The name must be unique within the scope in which it is being used. Don't worry too much about scope; we'll go through that a little later. Just briefly for now, remember not to use the same name for more than one variable in the same procedure—it makes sense, really.

- The variable name must start with an alphabetic character. *2myVar* is illegal, but *myVar2* is good.

- Variable names cannot include either a period (.) or a space ( ). If you need to split up the variable name in some way to improve its readability, use the underscore character, like this: *This_Is_My_First_Variable*.

- You cannot use *reserved words*, sometimes called *keywords*; these language elements, which include function names, statement names, and intrinsic constant names, are part of the VBScript language.

Variable names within VBScript are not case sensitive, so *myvar* is the same as *MyVar*. You may have noticed in the examples so far (and if you haven't, go back and take a look) that I've used a combination of lower case and upper case, with the first few letters usually in lower case, for my variable names, like *myVar*. This improves readability, but is also a good habit to form; you'll see why when we get to naming conventions.

So, variables can either be a simple single character like:

```
x = 10
y = "Hello World"
```

or they can be descriptive, like this:

```
myNewVariable = 10
myStringVariable = "Hello World"
```

Variables are so called because their value can change throughout their lifetime in your script. But you may have a requirement for a variable that isn't variable at all, whose value remains the same throughout your script. Guess what they're called!

## *What Is a Constant?*

Constants perform a similar function as variables, in that they are a symbolic replacement for an item of data in memory. The difference is that a constant keeps the same value throughout its lifetime. Values are assigned to constants using the same method used for variables, and can contain the same range of data subtypes. In most respects, therefore, a constant is the same as a variable. In fact, it could be described as a variable that isn't variable! But because confusion can arise as to whether you are dealing with a constant or a variable within the script, it is safest to use a different naming convention for constants. The accepted method of denoting a constant is to use all capitals for the name. In this case, the use of underscores improves their readability and is highly recommended. The following, for instance, are two examples of constants:

```
MY_NEW_CONSTANT = 54
MY_STRING_CONSTANT = "Hello World"
```

It is also wise when writing scripts within an HTML document to use constant names made up of more than one word linked with underscores, as shown above. This sets them apart visually from HTML elements, which are capitalized by loose convention.

In VBScript Version 1.0, there is no built-in method for declaring a constant (i.e., a named value that cannot be changed). This means that, although you could select a variable to serve as a "constant," its value could in fact be modified, either deliberately or inadvertently. However, VBScript 2.0 allows you to use the `Const` declaration, which is familiar to VB programmers. A constant, which in VBScript 2.0 is declared as follows:

```
Const MYCONSTANT = 10
```

cannot have its value changed throughout the life of the program. If your script does mistakenly attempt to modify its value, MSIE displays an "Illegal Assignment" error message. You will know therefore—using the above example—that whenever you use `MYCONSTANT` in your script, you are sure to be using the value 10.

*WARNING*    Like the constant declaration in VB, `Const` in VBScript cannot be used to assign nonconstant values or the values returned by VBScript functions. This means that a statement like the following:

```
Const NUMCONSTANT = myVar 'Invalid
```

is invalid, since it attempts to assign the value of a variable to a constant. Unfortunately, it also means that the statements

```
Const CARRIAGE_RETURN = Chr(13) 'Invalid
Const CARRIAGE_RETURN = Chr(10) 'Invalid
```

which are handy to use to define a carriage return character, are invalid, since they rely on the value returned by the VBScript *Chr* function. Finally, unlike VB or VBA, VBScript does not allow you to use any value that includes an operator in defining a constant. For example, the following declaration, which is valid in VB, generates a syntax error in VBScript:

```
Const ADDED_CONST = 4 + 1 'Invalid
```

## Intrinsic Constants `VBS 2.0`

In addition to allowing you to define your own constants using the `Const` keyword, VBScript 2.0 includes a number of built-in or intrinsic constants whose values are predefined by VBScript. Along with saving you from having to define these values as constants, the major advantage of using intrinsic constants is that they enhance the readability of your code. So, for instance, instead of having to write code like this:

```
If myObject.ForeColor = &hFFFF Then
```

you can write:

```
If myObject.ForeColor = vbYellow Then
```

Intrinsic constants are available for the following:

- Color
- Comparison
- Date/Time
- Date Format
- File Input/Output (server-side scripting only)
- Message Box
- Object Error
- String
- Tristate
- VarType

Appendix C, *VBScript 2.0 Intrinsic Constants*, contains a complete listing of the built-in constants, along with their meanings and values.

## Declaring Variables and Constants

Unlike many other programming languages, VBScript allows the implicit declaration of variables. This means that, as soon as you use a variable or constant name within your script, VBScript does all the necessary work of allocating memory space, etc., and the variable is considered to be declared. However, it is good programming practice to explicitly declare any variables and constants you want to use at the start of the procedure or script by using the `Dim` statement. Its syntax is:

```
Dim Variable_Or_Constant_Name
```

If you have a number of variables to declare, you can do this on the same line by separating them with commas, as in the following `Dim` statement:

```
Dim intRefNo, intAnyVar
```

As you start to write more and more complex scripts, you can reduce the number of bugs by referring back to the `Dim` statements to check the spelling of the variables you are using. Many a bug has been found to be a simple typo of a variable name. Try the code in Example 3-15 exactly as it's written (including the deliberate mistake). Enter a number into the top text box, then click on the Click Me button.

*Example 3-15. A Typo in a Variable Name*

```
<HTML>
<HEAD>
<SCRIPT LANGUAGE="vbscript">
 Sub cmdButton1_OnClick
   Dim intPartQty
   intPartQty = 200 + CInt(Document.Form1.txtText1.Value)
   Document.Form1.txtText2.Value = intPatQty
 End Sub
</SCRIPT>

</HEAD>

<BODY BGCOLOR="white">
 <FORM NAME="Form1">
  <INPUT TYPE="text" NAME="txtText1"><BR>
  <INPUT TYPE="text" NAME="txtText2"><BR>
  <INPUT TYPE="button" NAME="cmdButton1" VALUE="Click Me">
 </FORM>
</BODY>
</HTML>
```

You may be surprised that, when you load this page and run the script, it doesn't produce an error. Instead, it appears to do nothing at all. In fact, the script has run, and it has put the value of *intPatQty* into the txtText2 text box. However, the value that we wanted to store to the txtText2 text box is in a variable called *intPartQty*, a different variable altogether. VBScript has kindly created a new variable for us, called *intPatQty*, and assigned it a value of Empty. In a simple script like this, it doesn't take long to find that we've mistyped one of the references to *intPartQty*, but in a more complex script, it could take quite a while to track down the elusive cause of our problem. As you can see, even using the `Dim` statement does not guarantee that we won't make an error with variable names. However, there is a way to instruct VBScript to help us out here.

## Option Explicit

Make a very slight amendment to the script shown in Example 3-15: add the words `OPTION EXPLICIT` on a line directly after the `<SCRIPT>` tag. Run the script again, with the mistake still there. Now, instead of getting a useless empty text box that gives us no clue as to why our script didn't work, we get the error message "Variable is undefined." We now know what we are looking for: the message tells us that we haven't declared a variable, and gives us the line number on which the error occurred. Even in a complex script, it usually takes only a couple of seconds to find and correct the bug.

Using `OPTION EXPLICIT` is good programming practice. It forces us to declare all variables and constants with `Dim`, and, should we make an error in the script, makes it easier to find.

## Array Variables

The types of variables we have dealt with so far have contained single values, or, to give them their correct title, *scalar variables*. But there are many occasions when you need to assign a range of values to a single variable. This type of variable is called an *array*. Arrays allow us to store a range of values in memory, each of which can be accessed quickly and efficiently by referring to its position within the array. You can think of an array as a very simple database of values. Arrays can hold the full range of data subtypes.

Before we look at the types of arrays we have at our disposal, let's quickly cover some of the terminology used when talking about arrays. Creating an array is called *dimensioning* (i.e., defining its size). The individual data items within the array are known as *elements*, and the reference number we use to access these elements is known as an *index*. The lowest and highest index numbers are known as *bounds* or *boundaries*. There are four main types of arrays: arrays can be either fixed or dynamic, one-dimensional or multidimensional.

Note for VB Programmers

Because VBScript uses the Variant data type, it is possible to create
an array of mixed subtypes. Try this quick example:

```
<HTML>
<HEAD>
 <SCRIPT LANGUAGE="vbscript">
   Dim myArray(10)

   myArray(1) = 10
   myArray(2) = "Hello World"
   myArray(3) = 15.34
   myArray(4) = True

   Sub myButton_OnClick
    x = VarType(myArray)
    Alert x
    End Sub
 </SCRIPT>
</HEAD>
<BODY BGCOLOR="white">
 <CENTER>
  <INPUT TYPE="button" NAME="myButton" VALUE="Click Me">
 </CENTER>
</BODY>
</HTML>
```

## Fixed arrays

Most of the time, we know in advance how many values we need to store in an
array. We can therefore dimension it to the appropriate size, or number of
elements, prior to accessing it, by using a `Dim` statement like the following:

```
Dim myArray(5)
```

This line of code creates an array, named *myArray*, with six elements. Why six?
All VBScript arrays start with location 0, so this `Dim` statement creates an array
whose locations range from *myArray(0)* to *myArray(5)*.

Example 3-16 contains a simple example of a fixed array. The script begins by
instructing the VBScript engine to check that all our variables are correctly
declared, then uses the `Dim` statement to dimension *myArray* as an array
containing six elements, with indexes ranging from 0 to 5. The next six lines of
code populate the array with values by explicitly assigning a value to each array
element. This entire process of declaring and populating the array is done outside
of a defined subroutine. This means two things:

- The array is declared, and our values assigned to the array, as the HTML file downloads to the browser.

- *myArray* is available to all subroutines and functions on the page. This is known as scope, and we'll cover this in depth later in this chapter.

*Example 3-16. Using a Fixed Array*

```
<HTML>
 <HEAD>
  <SCRIPT LANGUAGE="vbscript">
    OPTION EXPLICIT
    Dim myArray(5)
    myArray(0) = 12
    myArray(1) = 3
    myArray(2) = 13
    myArray(3) = 64
    myArray(4) = 245
    myArray(5) = 75

    Sub cmdButton1_OnClick
        Dim myValue
        myValue = myArray(CInt(Document.frmForm1.txtText1.Value))
        alert myValue
    End Sub

  </SCRIPT>
 </HEAD>
<BODY BGCOLOR="white">
  <FORM NAME="frmForm1">
    Enter a Number between 0 and 5<BR>
    <INPUT TYPE="text" NAME="txtText1"><BR>
    <INPUT TYPE="button" NAME="cmdButton1" VALUE="Click Me">
  </FORM>
</BODY>
</HTML>
```

When we enter a number into the text box and click the button, the subroutine *cmdButton1_OnClick* is run. This simply displays a message box containing the value of the array element whose index we entered. As we saw earlier, the value in the intrinsic HTML text box, of course, is a string. But we cannot use strings for array indexes; they must be numeric. Therefore, we have to convert the incoming string to an integer. This is done by the line

```
myValue = myArray(CInt(Document.frmForm1.txtText1.Value))
```

This line of code is quite complex, so let's break it down into its constituent parts to see what's going on... as the computer sees it. *Document.frmForm1.-txtText1.Value* is a string containing the number the user has typed in. If the value input by the user is a 5, for example:

```
Document.frmForm1.txtText1.Value = "5"
```

---

### *Populating Arrays: The Array Function* VBS 2.0

If you're used to programming in Visual Basic or Visual Basic for Applications, and you want to populate an array with a series of values, you use the intrinsic *Array* function. The function allows you to quickly assign a range of comma-delimited values to an array. For instance, assigning values to the array in Example 3-16 with the *Array* function would be quite easy:

```
myArray = Array(12,3,13,64,245,75)
```

Unfortunately, though, VBScript Version 1.0 does not support the *Array* function. This means that if you want to assign values to multiple array elements at the same time, you must do it individually for each element, as we have done in Example 3-16. This, of course, makes populating an array with predefined values a very cumbersome process.

Thankfully, the *Array* function has been added to VBScript 2.0, allowing you to save time and space in coding. To use the *Array* function, simply declare a variant variable, then assign the values of the array to the variable using the *Array* function. Any data type (even mixed data types) can be used with the *Array* function, as Example 3-17 shows.

---

Next, the *CInt* function converts this value from a string to an integer:

```
CInt(Document.frmForm1.txtText1.Value) =  5
```

Once we've converted the array index to an integer, we can extract the value stored at that position in *myArray*. In this case, we assign it to a separate variable, *myValue*:

```
myValue = myArray(5)
```

Since 75 is stored in the sixth array element, the value that we are actually assigning to *myArray* is 75, as follows:

```
myValue = 75
```

Being the inquisitive type, you've probably already entered a number greater than 5 or less than 0 just to see what happens, right? You get an error message, "Subscript out of range." The subscript is the index number, and in a real application, we'd have checked that the number entered was within the limits—or bounds—of the array, prior to using the number. We'll see how this is done in the next section.

*Example 3-17. Using the Array Function*

```
<HTML>
<HEAD>
<SCRIPT LANGUAGE="VBScript">
```

*Example 3-17. Using the Array Function (continued)*

```
Dim myArray
myArray = Array("Hello", "World", 2, 1)

Sub cmdShowElement_OnClick
    Alert myArray(0)
    Alert myArray(1)
    Alert myArray(2)
    Alert myArray(3)
End Sub
```

```
</SCRIPT>
</HEAD>
<BODY BGCOLOR="white">
<CENTER>
<H3>Array()</H3>
<INPUT TYPE="button" NAME="cmdShowElement" VALUE="Show Array Elements">
</BODY>
</HTML>
```

Fixed arrays are fine when we know in advance how many values or elements we need. But there are many cases where we do not have prior knowledge of this, and we need a way to expand our array should we have to. We can do this by declaring and using a dynamic array.

### Dynamic arrays

One convenient use of an array is to store input from the user, and to allow users to input as many items of data as they like. Our application therefore has no way of knowing how to dimension the array beforehand. This type of problem calls for a *dynamic array*. Dynamic arrays allow you to expand the number of array elements by using the `ReDim` statement to redimension the array while the program is running.

A dynamic array is declared by leaving out the number of elements, like this:

```
Dim myDynamicArray()
```

When you need to resize the array, use the `ReDim` keyword:

```
ReDim myDynamicArray(10)
```

You can also declare a dynamic array, and specify the initial number of elements at the same time, using `ReDim`:

```
ReDim anyDynamicArray(4)
```

There is no limit to the number of times you can redimension a dynamic array, but obviously, messing around with variables in this way carries an element of risk. As soon as you redimension an array, the data contained within it is lost. Don't panic... if you need to keep the data, use the **Preserve** keyword:

```
ReDim Preserve myDynamicArray(10)
```

In actual fact, **ReDim** creates a new array (hence its emptiness). **Preserve** copies the data from the old array into the new array. Another important point to note is that if you resize an array by contracting it, you lose the data in the deleted array elements.

Example 3-18 shows how to use a dynamic array to save multiple inputs from the user. When the user clicks on the Add to Array button, the contents of the text box are added to *myArray*, an array that is dynamically resized beforehand. When the user clicks on the Show Array Contents button, a dialog box like the one shown in Figure 3-2 displays the data stored to the array.

*Example 3-18. Using Dynamic Arrays*

```
<HTML>
<HEAD>
<TITLE>Dynamic Array Application</TITLE>
<SCRIPT LANGUAGE="vbscript">
   OPTION EXPLICIT                      'require all variables to be declared
   ReDim myArray(0)                     'create a dynamic array with 1 element
   Dim intIndex            'declare variable to track the array index number
   Dim CRTN        'variable for a neat Carriage Return trick in VBScript 1
   CRTN = Chr(10) & Chr(13)                 'assign carriage return to CRTN
   intIndex = 0              'assign the first index number to our counter

   Sub cmdButton1_OnClick

      myArray(intIndex) = Document.frmForm1.txtText1.Value
                                       'Store the user input in the array
      intIndex = intIndex + 1         'increment the array counter by one
      ReDim Preserve myArray(intIndex)   'increase the size of the array
      Document.frmForm1.txtText1.Value = ""    'Empty the text box again
   End Sub

   Sub cmdButton2_OnClick
      Dim x, y, strArrayContents 'declare some variables we're going to need

      'repeat this process as many times as there are array elements
      'note: the last element will always be empty because we've
      'incremented the counter *after* the assignment.
      'try changing the above sub so that we always fill every element
         For x = 0 to intIndex - 1
            'assign a short description and the element no to the variable
            strArrayContents =  strArrayContents & "Element No." & _
               CStr(x) & " = "
            'add to this the contents of the element and our carriage return
            strArrayContents =  strArrayContents & myArray(x) & CRTN
            'go back and do it again for the next value of x
```

*Example 3-18. Using Dynamic Arrays (continued)*

```
        Next
        'when we're done show the result in a message box
        y = MsgBox(strArrayContents,0,"Dynamic Array Application")
    End Sub

  </SCRIPT>
 </HEAD>
<BODY BGCOLOR="white">
  <FORM NAME="frmForm1">
   <INPUT TYPE="text" NAME="txtText1"><BR>
   <INPUT TYPE="button" NAME="cmdButton1" VALUE="Add to array"><P>
   <INPUT TYPE="button" NAME="cmdButton2" VALUE="Show Array Contents">
  </FORM>
</BODY>
</HTML>
```

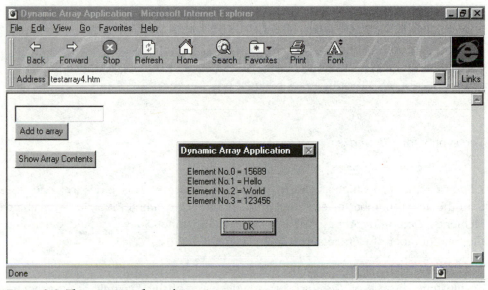

*Figure 3-2. The contents of our dynamic array*

---

**TIP**          Example 3-18 uses a variable, *CRTN*, which is set to `Chr(13) &`
                 `Chr(10)` to emulate a carriage return character. However, VBScript
                 2.0 includes an intrinsic constant, `vbCrLf`, which performs the
                 same function somewhat more gracefully.

---

Because HTML text box controls return string data, you can save any type of data
in your array, but they will automatically be saved as string variants. This means
that you must remember to convert the data saved in arrays before using them in
calculations. This in turn requires that you check to make sure that data is actually

numeric before accepting it or using it. VBScript provides several functions to check data, which will be discussed in depth in Chapter 14.

The above example is fine as it stands, except that, as you can see from the source code, we have to keep track of the size of the array by using the *intIndex* variable. But VBScript allows a much cleaner approach to the problem of finding out how many elements there are in the array.

### Determining array boundaries: UBound and LBound

The functions *UBound* and *LBound* can be used to find the lower index and the upper index, respectively, of an array. However, because VBScript arrays can only start at 0, *LBound* is somewhat redundant. *UBound* can be put to good use, though, to find the current size of a dynamic array.

---

### *VBScript and the Option Base Statement*

In VB and VBA, you can use the `Option Base` statement to define the initial position of an array. The `Option Base` statement, however, is not supported by VBScript. All VBScript arrays begin at position zero.

---

The syntax for *UBound* is:

```
x = UBound(arrayname)
```

*UBound* returns the highest index number of an array. This is always one less than the actual number of elements in the array. For example, if *myArray* has ten elements, *Ubound(myArray)* returns the number nine. So we would determine the total number of elements in an array as follows:

```
myArraySize = UBound(array) + 1
```

To illustrate the use of *UBound*, let's rewrite parts of the dynamic array program in Example 3-18; the results are shown in Example 3-19. Instead of using an integer variable, like *intIndex* in Example 3-18, to continually track the size of the dynamic array, Example 3-19 simply uses the *UBound* function.

*Example 3-19. The UBound Function*

```
<HTML>
 <HEAD>
 <TITLE>Dynamic Array Application No.2</TITLE>
  <SCRIPT LANGUAGE="vbscript">
    OPTION EXPLICIT    'require all variables to be declared
    ReDim myArray(0)   'create a dynamic array with 1 element
    Dim CRTN                'variable for a neat carriage return trick in VBS1
    CRTN = Chr(10) & Chr(13)'assign carriage return to CRTN
```

*Example 3-19. The UBound Function (continued)*

```
Sub cmdButton1_OnClick
    'Store the value enter by the user in the array
    myArray(UBound(myArray)) = Document.frmForm1.txtText1.Value
    'grow the array to be one element greater than its current size
    'Preserve its contents
    ReDim Preserve myArray(UBound(myArray) + 1)
    'Empty the text box for the user
    Document.frmForm1.txtText1.Value = ""
End Sub

Sub cmdButton2_OnClick
    'declare some variables we're going to need
    Dim x, y, strArrayContents
    'repeat this process as many times as there are array elements
    For x = 0 to UBound(myArray) - 1
        'assign a short description and the element no to the variable
        strArrayContents =  strArrayContents & "Element No." & _
                            CStr(x) & " = "
        'add to this the contents of the element and our carriage return
        strArrayContents =  strArrayContents & myArray(x) & CRTN
    'go back and do it again for the next value of x
    Next
    'when we're done show the result in a message box
    y = MsgBox(strArrayContents,0,"Dynamic Array Application #2")
End Sub
</SCRIPT>
 </HEAD>
<BODY BGCOLOR="white">
  <FORM NAME="frmForm1">
   <INPUT TYPE="text" NAME="txtText1"><BR>
   <INPUT TYPE="button" NAME="cmdButton1" VALUE="Add to array"><P>
   <INPUT TYPE="button" NAME="cmdButton2" VALUE="Show Array Contents">
  </FORM>
</BODY>
</HTML>
```

The arrays that we have looked at so far are termed single-dimension (or one-dimensional) arrays. They hold one element of data in each index location, which is fine for most needs. However, there are times when you need to hold a full set of data for each element. These are termed *multidimensional arrays*.

### Multidimensional arrays

To get a sense of when using multidimensional arrays is appropriate, let's look at two situations in which our web page benefits from using arrays. First, the simple case of the single-dimension array. Let's say we're an importer who is putting together a web page that will display to users the country of origin of our company's products when they click a button. We can use a single-dimension array to hold the data, in this case a string containing the country of origin. We have one piece of data for each element, as follows:

| Element No. | Data |
| --- | --- |
| 0 | Product 1 Country of Origin |
| 1 | Product 2 Country of Origin |
| 2 | Product 3 Country of Origin |

Then the marketing department suggests that the page be "improved." Instead of just showing the country of origin of each product, they also want to show its weight and any potential shipping hazard. If we continue to use a single-dimension array, this poses something of a problem, as we can see from the following table:

| Element No. | Data |
| --- | --- |
| 0 | Product 1 Country of Origin |
| 1 | Product 1 Weight |
| 2 | Product 1 Hazards |
| 3 | Product 2 Country of Origin |
| 4 | Product 2 Weight |
| 5 | Product 2 Hazards |
| 6 | Product 3 Country of Origin |
| 7 | Product 3 Weight |
| 8 | Product 3 Hazards |
| etc. | |

As you can see, there is no structure to this data; it's all held sequentially, and as a result can be very difficult to access. The solution is to use a multidimensional array. A multidimensional array allows you to have a separate array of data for each element of your array. Therefore, each element of the array in turn contains an array.

To continue our product importer example, let's say that we have four products, and for each product we want to store three items of data. We would define the multidimensional array as follows:

```
Dim ourProductData(3,2)
```

This is the equivalent of the data table shown below, which consists of four rows and three columns. Each data cell of the table can therefore be viewed as a coordinate, with the first cell (the one containing Product 1's country of origin) starting at 0,0. The row number defines the first value of the coordinate, while the column number defines the second.

|  | Country of Origin | Weight | Hazards |
|---|---|---|---|
| **Product 1** | Element (0,0) |  | Element (0,2) |
| **Product 2** |  |  |  |
| **Product 3** |  |  |  |
| **Product 4** | Element (3,0) |  | Element (3,2) |

---

### *VBScript and User-Defined Structures*

If you're an experienced VB or VBA programmer, you might prefer another so-lution—an array of user-defined structures—to a multidimensional array. How-ever, this solution is not available with VBScript. VBScript does not support the Type... End Type construct, and therefore does not allow you to define a struc-tured data type.

---

*NOTE*  Multidimensional arrays can contain up to 60 dimensions, though it is extremely rare to use more than two or three dimensions.

---

Figures 3-3 and 3-4 illustrate the difference between a one-dimensional array and a multidimensional array—in this case a two-dimensional array. Notice how the two-dimensional array can be thought of as a one-dimensional array (the top row) with each element having its own individual array dropping down from it to form a column.

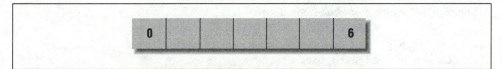

*Figure 3-3. A one-dimensional array*

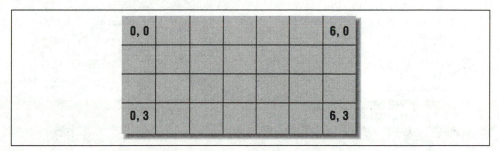

*Figure 3-4. A two-dimensional array*

If in our sample application, which is shown in Example 3-20, we set ourselves a rule—that the country of origin will always be in element 0, the weight in element 1, etc.—then we have a method by which we can quickly access each individual element of data. So if we need to access the weight for Product 3, we use the following line of code.

```
strDataString = strShippingData(2,1) ' row #3 column #2
```

Because we know that the weight will always be in column 2, we can use a constant to improve the readability of the code—something known as self-commenting code. This is an ideal job for a constant, as the following code fragment shows:

```
Dim WEIGHT = 1
strDataString = strShippingData(2, WEIGHT)
```

In this case, the most important part of creating our web page occurs before we actually begin writing our script, when we decide how we want to structure our multidimensional array. Once that is done, implementing the goal for which the web page is created—to display shipping information about a selected product—is fairly straightforward. Since the user clicks any of four buttons to display shipping information about a particular product, a single routine can handle the display of information, as long as it knows which "row" of the multidimensional array contains that product's information. The ONCLICK attribute of each product button's <INPUT> tag defines a single routine, named *Shipping*, as the button's event handler, and passes to it a single parameter, the row containing that product's information in the multidimensional array. The *Shipping* routine then simply retrieves the value of each element in the subarray belonging to the designated row. The result resembles Figure 3-5.

*Example 3-20. Using a Multidimensional Array*

```
<HTML>
 <HEAD>
  <TITLE>Product Shipping Data</TITLE>
   <SCRIPT LANGUAGE="vbscript">

    OPTION EXPLICIT'instruct vbscript to check all variable names
     Dim strShippingData(3,2)              'declare a multidimension array
     Dim COUNTRY, WEIGHT, HAZARDS, CRTN    'declare the constants
     'assign values to the constants
     COUNTRY =0
     WEIGHT=1
     HAZARDS=2
     CRTN=Chr(10) & Chr(13)
     'assign values to the array
     strShippingData(0, COUNTRY)="Finland"
     strShippingData(1, COUNTRY)="Malawi"
```

*Example 3-20. Using a Multidimensional Array (continued)*

```
    strShippingData(2, COUNTRY)="USA"
    strShippingData(3, COUNTRY)="Outer Mongolia"
    strShippingData(0,WEIGHT)="Weight = 34 Kilos"
    strShippingData(1,WEIGHT)="Weight = 17 Kilos"
    strShippingData(2,WEIGHT)="Weight = 10 Kilos"
    strShippingData(3,WEIGHT)="Weight = 15 Kilos"
    strShippingData(0,HAZARDS)="No Hazard"
    strShippingData(1,HAZARDS)="Highly Inflammable"
    strShippingData(2,HAZARDS)="No Hazard"
    strShippingData(3,HAZARDS)="Highly Inflammable"

    'declare a subroutine that can be used by all the buttons
    Sub Shipping(Index)
        'declare variables to be used in this sub
        Dim x, y, strMessage, strCaption
        'we want a line for each data item - use the constants
        For x = COUNTRY TO HAZARDS
            strMessage = strMessage & strShippingData(Index,x)
            strMessage = strMessage & CRTN
        Next
        'construct a caption from the index number
        strCaption = "Shipping Data for Product No." & CStr(Index + 1)
        'finally, show a message box to the user
        y = MsgBox(strMessage,0,strCaption)
    End Sub
  </SCRIPT>
</HEAD>

<BODY BGCOLOR="white">
 <FONT FACE="ARIAL" SIZE=3>
   <B>Product No.1</B><BR>
   Details of the first product go here
   <INPUT TYPE="BUTTON" NAME="cmdShipping" OnClick="Shipping(0)"
                VALUE="Click for Shipping Data"><P>
   <B>Product No.2</B><BR>
   Details of the second product go here
   <INPUT TYPE="BUTTON" NAME="cmdShipping" OnClick="Shipping(1)"
                VALUE="Click for Shipping Data"><P>
   <B>Product No.3</B><BR>
   Details of the third product go here
   <INPUT TYPE="BUTTON" NAME="cmdShipping" OnClick="Shipping(2)"
                VALUE="Click for Shipping Data"><P>
   <B>Product No.4</B><BR>
   Details of the fourth product go here
   <INPUT TYPE="BUTTON" NAME="cmdShipping" OnClick="Shipping(3)"
                VALUE="Click for Shipping Data"><P>
 </FONT>
 </BODY>
</HTML>
```

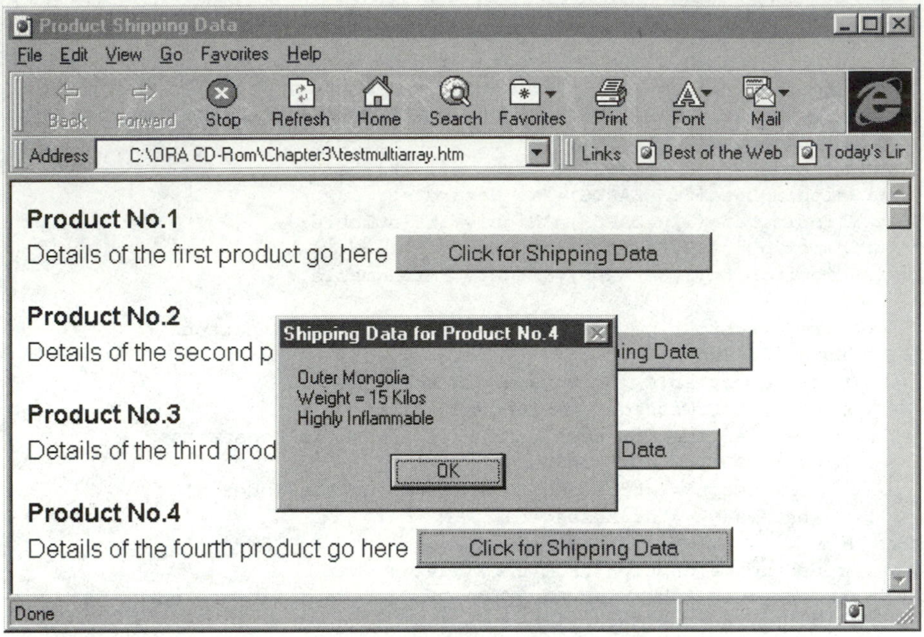

*Figure 3-5. The output of the multidimensional array example application*

So in simple terms, you can use a multidimensional array as a rudimentary database that is located within the client machine's memory. When you access a particular element of a multidimensional array, the value of the first dimension indicates a particular record of your database, while the value of the second dimension designates a particular field belonging to that record.

### Dynamic multidimensional arrays

Earlier you saw how a one-dimensional dynamic array can be resized while your program is executing. Multidimensional arrays can be dynamic too, and the rules for redimensioning them are similar, but since you have more than one dimension to think about, you have to take care how you use and redimension them. The rules for using a dynamic multidimensional array are:

- You can ReDim a multidimensional array to change both the number of dimensions and the size of each dimension. This is illustrated by Example 3-21, where the *myArray* dynamic array is originally defined as a two-dimensional array with 11 elements in the first dimension and 6 in the second when the user clicks the Click One button, but is then redimensioned into a three-dimensional array with 5 elements in the first dimension, 11 in the second, and 3 in the third when the user clicks the Click Two button.

*Example 3-21. Redimensioning a Two-Dimensional Array*

```
<HTML>
<HEAD>
```

*Example 3-21. Redimensioning a Two-Dimensional Array (continued)*

```
<SCRIPT LANGUAGE="vbscript">
Dim myArray(), strMsg

strMsg = "myArray" & vbCrLf

Sub  cmdButtonOne_OnClick

ReDim myArray(10,5)
strMsg = strMsg & "Dimension 1: " & UBound(myArray,1) & " elements " & vbCrLf
strMsg = strMsg & "Dimension 2: " & UBound(MyArray,2) & " elements"
Alert strMsg

End Sub

Sub cmdButtonTwo_OnClick

ReDim myArray(4,10,2)
strMsg = strMsg & "Dimension 1: " & UBound(myArray,1) & " elements " & vbCrLf
strMsg = strMsg & "Dimension 2: " & UBound(MyArray,2) & " elements"
strMsg = strMsg & "Dimension 3: " & UBound(MyArray,3) & " elements"
Alert strMsg

End Sub

</SCRIPT>
</HEAD>
<BODY BGCOLOR="white">
<CENTRE>
<INPUT TYPE="button" NAME="cmdButtonOne" VALUE="Click One">
<P>
<INPUT TYPE="button" NAME="cmdButtonTwo" VALUE="Click Two">
</CENTER>
</BODY>
</HTML>
```

- If you use the **Preserve** keyword, you can only resize the last array dimension, and you can't change the number of dimensions at all. For example:

```
...
ReDim myArray(10,5,2)
...
ReDim Preserve myArray(10,5,4)
...
```

### Using UBound with multidimensional arrays

As you saw earlier, the *UBound* function returns the highest subscript (element number) in an array—that is, its *Upper Boundary*. You can also use *UBound* with a multidimensional array, except that to find the largest element of a multidimensional array, you need to also specify a dimension:

```
largestElement = UBound(arrayname, dimensionNo)
```

To sum up, use static arrays to hold predetermined blocks of data in memory. If you don't know the precise size of an array prior to defining it, use a dynamic array. Finally, if you need to reference more than one data field per data item, use a multidimensional array.

We have now covered the basics of variables and constants, apart from one major issue. You may have noticed in some of the previous examples that some variables and constants were declared at the very beginning of the script, outside of any subroutines, while some were declared within particular subroutines. Precisely where in a program or script you declare a variable or constant determines its scope and its lifetime.

## Scope

A variable's scope determines where within a script you are able to access that particular variable, and whether that variable is *visible* within a particular routine. In a nutshell, variables declared outside of subroutines and functions can be accessed by the whole script, while those declared within a subroutine or function can only be accessed in the procedure in which they've been declared. In addition, VBscript Version 2.0 includes two new keywords, `Public` and `Private`, that control the visibility of variables that are defined outside of individual routines.

### Script-level scope

A variable has *script-level scope* when it can be accessed by all the subroutines and functions contained in a particular script. Variables and constants that have script-level scope also reside in memory for the lifetime of the script. That is to say, as long as the script remains in memory, its script-level variables and constants also remain in memory. To create a variable with script-level scope, you must declare it outside of any subroutine or function. It is common practice to declare script-level variables at the very start of the script, immediately after the `<SCRIPT>` tag. If you have more than one `<SCRIPT>` tag in your HTML page, it doesn't matter which `<SCRIPT>` tag you use. However, declaring script-level variables after the first `<SCRIPT>` tag helps to eliminate possible confusion and makes your script more readable.

---

### *Visual Basic and Script-Level Scope*

If you program in Visual Basic, you'll probably recognize that script-level scope is really the VBScript equivalent of Visual Basic's global variables.

---

Example 3-22 demonstrates the use of script-level variables and constants. When the user clicks on the Click Me button, the number that was entered in the *txtText1* text box is stored to the variable *lngMyVar*. Since it is defined immediately after the first <SCRIPT> tag, it is a script-level variable that is visible to all routines within the web page. This is apparent from the *MyButton_OnClick* event procedure, which assigns a value to *lngMyVar* and then calls the *MySecondProcedure* subroutine. *MySecondProcedure* accesses *lngMyVar* to display its value in the *txtText2* text box, even though *lngMyVar* was not passed as a formal parameter to the procedure. (For a discussion of passing parameters, see Chapter 4.) If *lngMyVar* had not been visible throughout the web page, *MyButton_OnClick* would still have been able to assign a value to *lngMyVar*, but the *MySecondProcedure* routine would not have been able to access that value.

The *MyButton2_OnClick* event procedure, which is fired when the user clicks the Now Click Me button, illustrates the use of a script-level constant. Because MY_CONST is defined and assigned a value immediately after the first <SCRIPT> tag, it is visible to *MyButton2_OnClick*, which adds it to the value that the user entered in the *txtText1* text box, then both assigns the result to *lngMyVar* and displays it in the *txtText2* text box. *MyButton3_OnClick* is similar to *MyButton2_OnClick*, but it is located in the section of code after the second <SCRIPT> tag. Nevertheless, the MY_CONST constant, which is defined in the first <SCRIPT> tag, is visible to it.

*Example 3-22. Script-Level Scope*

```
<HTML>
 <HEAD>
  <SCRIPT LANGUAGE="vbscript">
  OPTION EXPLICIT
   'any variable or constant declared here will be available to
   'all scripts in the document
   Dim lngMyVar
   Dim MY_CONST
   MY_CONST=5

   Sub MyButton_OnClick
    'lngMyVar does not need to be declared here - it's global
    lngMyVar = Document.frmForm1.txtText1.Value
    'lngMyVar is now set to the value of txtText1
    'let's use it in an unrelated procedure just to check that it is global
    Call MySecondProcedure()
   End Sub

   Sub MySecondProcedure()
     'display the value of lngMyVar
     Document.frmForm1.txtText2.Value = lngMyVar
   End Sub
```

*Example 3-22. Script-Level Scope (continued)*

```
   Sub MyButton2_OnClick
     'let's add the value of global constant to the value you entered
     lngMyVar = CLng(Document.frmForm1.txtText1.Value) + MY_CONST
     Document.frmForm1.txtText2.Value = lngMyVar
   End Sub

 </SCRIPT>

</HEAD>

<BODY BGCOLOR="white">
 <CENTER>
  <FORM NAME="frmForm1">
   Enter a number here <INPUT TYPE="text" NAME="txtText1"><P>
   <INPUT TYPE="button" NAME="MyButton" VALUE="Click Me"><P>
   <INPUT TYPE="button" NAME="MyButton2" VALUE="Now Click Me"><P>
   <INPUT TYPE="button" NAME="MyButton3" VALUE="... and Me"><P>
   <INPUT TYPE="text" NAME="txtText2">
  </FORM>
 </CENTER>

 <SCRIPT LANGUAGE="vbscript">

  Sub MyButton3_OnClick
    'this procedure is even within a different SCRIPT tag but the script
    'level or global variables and constants still work
    lngMyVar = CLng(Document.frmForm1.txtText1.Value) + (MY_CONST * 2)
    Document.frmForm1.txtText2.Value = lngMyVar
  End Sub

 </SCRIPT>

 </BODY>
</HTML>
```

### Procedure-level scope

A variable that is declared within an individual procedure (that is, within a subroutine or a function) can only be used within that procedure, and is therefore said to have *procedure-level scope*. As soon as the procedure is complete, references to the variables defined within that procedure are erased from the computer's memory. You can therefore use the same name when defining different variables in different procedures, as in the case of the simple *x* variable commonly used in the `For..Next` loop. Procedure-level variables are ideal for temporary, localized storage of information.

To prove that variables that have been declared (either implicitly by simply using their name, or explicitly using the `Dim` statement) within a procedure do not have scope outside that procedure, take a look at Example 3-23. There are two event handlers for the two buttons on the form. In the first event handler, *cmdButton1_OnClick*, two constants are used to hold the words "Hello" and "World." These are then concatenated and assigned to a local variable, *myLocalVar*, which is then shown in the text box. When you click the second button, the *cmdButton2_OnClick* event handler assigns the value of another local variable, also called *myLocalVar*, to the text box. You can tell that it's a different variable from the first *myLocalVar* because, instead of displaying the string "Hello World," this time the text box is blank, since this *myLocalVar* variable is empty. However, if *myLocalVar* had been declared as a script-level variable, clicking the second button would also show "Hello World" in the text box. So you can see that the two variables, *myLocalVar* and *myLocalVar*, are treated by the program as two completely separate variables, as in fact they are, despite the fact that they have the same name. A variable that is declared within a procedure can only be used within that procedure, the program can only "see" it in that procedure, and once the procedure finishes executing, the variable is destroyed.

*Example 3-23. Procedure-Level Scope*

```
<HTML>
<HEAD>
<TITLE>Procedure Level Scope</TITLE>
<SCRIPT LANGUAGE="vbscript">

Sub cmdButton1_OnClick
    MY_CONST1 = "Hello"
    MY_CONST2 = "World"
    myLocalVar = MY_CONST1 & " " & MY_CONST2
    Document.Form1.Text1.Value = myLocalVar
End Sub

Sub cmdButton2_onClick
    Document.Form1.Text1.Value = myLocalVar
End Sub
</SCRIPT>
</HEAD>
<BODY BGCOLOR="white">
<FORM NAME="Form1">
<CENTER>
<INPUT TYPE="button" NAME="cmdButton1" VALUE="Click Me">
<INPUT TYPE="button" NAME="cmdButton2" VALUE="Click Me">
<P>
<INPUT TYPE="text" NAME="Text1">
<CENTER>
</FORM>
</BODY>
</HTML>
```

## Public scope `VBS 2.0`

A further level of scope has been introduced into Version 2.0 of VBScript with the inclusion of the `Public` declaration keyword. Used outside of a procedure in place of the `Dim` statement, `Public` allows a variable to be seen not only by all procedures in all scripts in the current document, but also by all scripts in all procedures in all currently loaded documents. The `Public` declaration is therefore an important means of transferring data between documents. Its use—along with that of the new `Private` declaration—allows you to expose or protect variables throughout a complete application, and beyond! The use of variables with public scope is illustrated in Examples 3-24 through 3-26.

## *Private* `VBS 2.0`

The `Private` declaration allows you to protect a variable by restricting its scope to the document in which it has been declared. As with the `Public` declaration, the `Private` keyword can only be used outside a procedure; its use within a procedure will generate an error.

Examples 3-24 through 3-26 form a single example that demonstrates the use of public and private variables. The HTML source in Example 3-24 contains a `<FRAMESET>` tag that divides the browser window into two equal columns. The left frame, which is named FrameOne, displays the file *PUBLIC1.HTM* shown in Example 3-25; the right frame, FrameTwo, displays the file *PUBLIC2.HTM* shown in Example 3-26. The document in FrameOne declares two variables: *myPublicVar*, a public variable, and *myPrivateVar*, a private variable. No variables are declared in FrameTwo, which simply references the variables in the left-hand document. When the user clicks on the Show myPublicVar button in FrameOne, its *cmdButton1_OnClick* event procedure increments *myPublicVar* by one and displays its value in a message box. When the user clicks on the Show myPublicVar button in FrameTwo, its *cmdButton1_OnClick* event procedure simply displays its current value. The fact that it is able to do this successfully indicates that *myPublicVar* is visible to all documents, even though it was defined in FrameOne. The two lower command buttons in FrameOne are both labeled Show myPrivateVar, although the first button increments *myPrivateVar* by two before displaying it, while the second simply displays its current value. When the user clicks on the Show *myPrivateVar* button in FrameTwo, on the other hand, an "Object does not support this property or method" error is generated, since the private variable is not visible to the procedures in FrameTwo.

*Example 3-24. Frameset for the Public/Private Variables Example*

```
<HTML>
<FRAMESET COLS=50%,50%>
 <FRAME SRC="public1.htm" NAME="FrameOne">
 <FRAME SRC="public2.htm" NAME="FrameTwo">
</FRAMESET>
</HTML>
```

*Example 3-25. Using Private and Public Declarations*

```
<HTML>
<HEAD>
<SCRIPT LANGUAGE="vbscript">
OPTION EXPLICIT
    Public myPublicVar
    Private myPrivateVar
    Sub cmdButton1_OnClick
        myPublicVar = myPublicVar + 1
        Alert myPublicVar
    End Sub
    Sub cmdButton2_OnClick
        myPrivateVar = myPrivateVar + 2
        Alert myPrivateVar
    End Sub
</SCRIPT>
</HEAD>
<BODY BGCOLOR="white">
<H3>public1</H3>
<INPUT TYPE="button" NAME="cmdButton1" VALUE="Show myPublicVar"><BR>
<INPUT TYPE="button" NAME="cmdButton2" VALUE="Show myPrivateVar"><BR>
<INPUT TYPE="button" NAME="cmdButton3" VALUE="Show myPrivateVar"><BR>
<SCRIPT LANGUAGE="vbscript">
    Sub cmdButton3_OnClick
        Alert myPrivateVar
    End Sub
</SCRIPT>
</BODY>
</HTML>
```

*Example 3-26. Accessing Publicly Declared Variables*

```
<HTML>
<HEAD>
<SCRIPT LANGUAGE="vbscript">
    OPTION EXPLICIT
    Sub cmdButton1_onClick
        Alert Top.FrameOne.myPublicVar
    End Sub
    Sub cmdButton2_onClick
        Alert Top.FrameOne.myPrivateVar
    End Sub
</SCRIPT>
</HEAD>
<BODY BGCOLOR="white">
<H3>public2</H3>
<INPUT TYPE="button" NAME="cmdButton1" VALUE="Show myPublicVar"><BR>
<INPUT TYPE="button" NAME="cmdButton2" VALUE="Show myPrivateVar (causes
error)">
</BODY>
</HTML>
```

In summary, we've seen that a variable is a handle to a memory location that makes it easily recognizable to the human eye. A variable can change its value through the course of its lifetime, while a constant keeps its value. We've examined fixed, dynamic, and multidimensional arrays, and discussed the use of arrays for storing a series of related data items within an easily recognizable package, which allows you to create mini databases in memory. Finally, we introduced scope, which determines the visibility and lifetime of variables and constants. Variables declared outside a procedure can be used in all procedures and last for the life of the script, while variables declared inside a procedure can only be used in that procedure and are resident in memory only while that procedure is actually executing.

The next thing we need to learn about variables is how to manipulate them. We need to be able to perform calculations on the data we have stored in memory, we need to compare one piece of data with another, and so on. The notations we use to instruct the program to perform these manipulations and comparisons are known as *operators*.

# Operators

There are four groups of operators in VBScript: arithmetic, concatenation, comparison, and logical. You'll find some to be instantly recognizable and familiar, while others require a much deeper understanding of mathematics than either the scope of this book or my knowledge of math is able to offer. However, if you have the need to use these types of operators, it is likely that you know the mathematics fundamentals behind them. We will look at each group of operators in turn before discussing the order of precedence VBScript uses when it encounters more than one type of operator within an expression.

## Arithmetic Operators

Arithmetic operators are listed in Table 3-3.

*Table 3-3. Arithmetic Operators*

| Oper-ator | Operation | Description | Example |
|---|---|---|---|
| + | Addition | Used to add numeric expressions. The addition operator can also be used to concatenate (join together) two string variables; however, it's preferable to use the concatenation operator with strings, to eliminate ambiguity. | `result = expression1 + expression2` |

*Table 3-3. Arithmetic Operators (continued)*

| Oper-ator | Operation | Description | Example |
|---|---|---|---|
| – | Subtraction | Used to find the difference between two numeric values or expressions. Also used to denote a negative value. Unlike its addition counterpart, the negative operator cannot be used with string variables. | `result = expression1 – expression2` |
| / | Division | Returns a floating-point number. | `result = expression1 / expression2` |
| * | Multiplication | Used to multiply two numerical values. | `result = expression1 * expression2` |
| \ | Integer Division | Performs division on two numeric expressions and returns an integer result (no remainder or decimal places). | `result = expression1 \ expression2` |
| Mod | Modulo | Performs division on two numeric expressions and returns only the remainder. If either of the two numbers is a floating-point number, it is rounded to an integer value prior to the modulo operation. | `result = expression1 Mod expression2` |
| ^ | Exponentiation | Raises a number to the power of the exponent. | `result = number ^ exponent` |

## Concatenation Operator

There is only one concatenation operator, the ampersand symbol (&). It is used to bind a number of string variables together, creating one string from two or more individual strings. Any nonstring variable or expression is converted to a string prior to concatenation. The syntax to use is: `result = expression1 & expression2`.

Example 3-27 is a sample program that illustrates concatenation. When the user enters text into the top two text boxes and clicks the Click Me button, the *MyButton_OnClick* procedure concatenates the two strings and displays them in the third text box.

*Example 3-27. The Concatenation Operator*

```
<HTML>
 <HEAD>
  <SCRIPT LANGUAGE="vbscript">
```

*Example 3-27. The Concatenation Operator*

```
Sub MyButton_OnClick
   Document.frmMyForm.txtText3.Value _
   = Document.frmMyForm.txtText1.Value & Document.frmMyForm.txtText2.Value
  End Sub
 </SCRIPT>
 </HEAD>

<BODY BGCOLOR="white">
 <FORM NAME="frmMyForm">
   <INPUT TYPE="text" NAME="txtText1"><BR>
   <INPUT TYPE="text" NAME="txtText2"><BR>
   <INPUT TYPE="text" NAME="txtText3"><BR>
   <INPUT TYPE="button" NAME="MyButton" VALUE="Click Me">
 </FORM>
 </BODY>
</HTML>
```

Incidentally, Example 3-27 also demonstrates the use of another type of concatenation operator that you can use in VBScript. Actually, it's not really a concatenation operator; it was included in the VB language to facilitate easily readable code. The code line concatenation "operator" is the underscore, _. As you may recall from our overview of VBScript in "Some Scripting Basics" earlier in this chapter, when you use the underscore at the end of a line of code and precede it with a space, the following line is treated as though it were part of the same line. In other words, the VBScript engine concatenates the two lines of code into one. As you can see from the preceding example, it eliminates lines of code that stretch off into the distance—or exit stage right!

---

*NOTE*        It's a good exercise to modify Example 3-27 by replacing the & operator with the other arithmetic operators, just to see what the results are.

---

## Comparison Operators

There are three main comparison operators: < (less than), > (greater than), and = (equal to). They can be used individually, or any two operators can be combined with each other. The syntax is:

    result = expression1 operator expression2

The result of an expression that uses a comparison operator is True (–1), False (0), or Null. A Null occurs only if either *expression1* or *expression2* itself has a Null value.

Table 3-4 lists the combinations of <, >, and = that produce a True result.

*Table 3-4. Comparison Operations That Evaluate to True*

| Operator | True If |
|----------|---------|
| > | *expression1* greater than and not equal to *expression2* |
| < | *expression1* less than and not equal to *expression2* |
| <> | *expression1* not equal to (less than or greater than) *expression2* |
| >= | *expression1* greater than or equal to *expression2* |
| <= | *expression1* less than or equal to *expression2* |
| = | *expression1* equal to *expression2* |

Comparison operators can be used with both numeric and string variables. However, if one expression is numeric and the other is a string, the numeric expression will always be "less than" the string expression. If both *expression1* and *expression2* are strings, the "greater" string is the one that is the longer. If the strings are of equal length, the comparison is case sensitive. (Lowercase letters are "greater" than their uppercase counterparts.)

---

### Using + as a Concatenation Operator

The mathematical addition operator (+) can also be used for string concatenation. However, its use is not recommended, since it makes code more difficult to read. How easily can you tell, for instance, whether the following assignment statement is supposed to sum the values of two variables or concatenate them?

```
varThree = varOne + varTwo
```

Rewriting this code using the & concatenation operator leaves absolutely no doubt about what the code is expected to do:

```
varThree = varOne & varTwo
```

---

### The Is operator

While not strictly a comparison operator, the `Is` operator determines whether two object reference variables refer to the same object. Thus, it tests, in some sense, for the "equality" of two object references. Its syntax is:

```
result = object1 Is object2
```

If both *object1* and *object2* refer to the same object, the result is True; otherwise, the result is False. We will look at how variables can refer to objects in Chapter 14.

## Logical Operators

Logical operators allow you to evaluate one or more expressions and return a logical value. VBScript supports six logical operators: And, Or, Not, Eqv, Imp, and Xor.

---

### Logical Operators and Bitwise Operators

Each of the logical operators used here can also be used as a bitwise operator. That is, if the argument or arguments supplied to the operator evaluate to logical expressions, the operation returns a logical (True or False) value. On the other hand, if the arguments are numeric values, the operator performs a bitwise evaluation of the two values and returns a numeric result. For instance, 3 And 1 returns 1, because the low-order bit is "on" in both values. However, since most web content providers rarely, if ever, need to use bitwise operators to create web pages, they will not be discussed in detail in this book.

---

### And

The syntax for the **And** operator is

```
result = expression1 And expression2
```

The **And** operator is used to perform logical conjunction; that is to say, it only returns true if both *expression1* and *expression2* evaluate to True. If either expression is False, then the result is False. If either expression is Null, then the result is Null. For example:

```
If x = 5 AND y < 7 Then
```

In this case, the code after the **If** statement will be executed only if the value of *x* is five, and the value of *y* is less than seven.

### Or

The syntax for the **Or** operator is

```
result = expression1 Or expression2
```

The **Or** operator is used to perform logical disjunction; in other words, if either *expression1* or *expression2* evaluates to True, or if both *expression1* and *expression2* evaluate to True, then the result is True. Only if neither expression is True does the `Or` operator return False. If either expression is Null, then the result is also Null. For example:

```
If x = 5 OR y < 7 Then
```

In this case, the code after the `If` statement will be executed if the value of *x* is five or if the value of *y* is less than seven.

### Not

The `Not` operator is used to perform logical negation on a single expression; that is, if the expression is True, the `Not` operator causes it to become False, and if it is False, the operator causes its value to be True. If the expression is Null, though, the result of using the `Not` operator is still a Null. Its syntax is

```
result = Not expression1
```

For example:

```
If Not IsNumeric(x) Then
```

The *IsNumeric* function returns True if the value passed to it is or can be converted to a number; otherwise, it returns False. In this example, because of the `Not` operator, the code following the `If` statement will be executed if the function returns False.

### Eqv

The `Eqv` operator performs logical equivalence; that is, it determines whether the value of two expressions is the same. `Eqv` returns True when both expressions evaluate to True or both expressions evaluate to False, but it returns False if either expression evaluates to True while the other evaluates to False. Its syntax is

```
result = expression1 Eqv expression2
```

### Imp

The `Imp` operator is used to perform logical implication (if *expression1* is True, then *expression2* is also True). Its syntax is

```
result = expression1 Imp expression2
```

Table 3-5 shows the results returned by the `Imp` operator.

*Table 3-5. Results Returned by the Imp Operator*

| Expression1 | Expression2 | Result |
|-------------|-------------|--------|
| True | True | True |
| True | False | False |
| True | Null | Null |

*Table 3-5. Results Returned by the Imp Operator (continued)*

| Expression1 | Expression2 | Result |
|-------------|-------------|--------|
| False | True | True |
| False | False | True |
| False | Null | True |
| Null | True | True |
| Null | False | Null |
| Null | Null | Null |

### Xor

The `Xor` operator is used to perform logical exclusion, and is the converse of `Eqv`. That is, it determines whether two expressions evaluate to different values. Its syntax is

```
result = expression1 Xor expression2
```

When both expressions are either True or False, then the result is False. If only one expression is True, then the result is True. If either expression is Null, the result is also Null.

## Operator Precedence

If you include more than one operator in a single line of code, you need to know the order in which the VBScript engine is going to evaluate them. Otherwise, the results may be completely different than you intend. The rules that define the order in which a language handles operators is known as the *order of precedence*.

If the order of precedence results in operations being evaluated in an order other than the one you intend—and therefore the value that results from these operations is "wrong" from your point of view—you can explicitly override the order of precedence through the use of parentheses. However, the order of precedence still applies to multiple operators within parentheses.

When a single line of code includes operators from more than one category, they are evaluated in the following order:

   Arithmetic operators
   Concatenation operators
   Comparison operators
   Logical operators

Within the arithmetic and logical categories, there is also an order of precedence. However, neither the single concatenation operator nor the comparison operators have an order of precedence. If multiple comparison operators appear in a single line of code, they are simply evaluated from left to right as the VBScript engine encounters them. The orders of precedence of the arithmetic and logical operators are shown in Tables 3-6 and 3-7, respectively. If the same arithmetic or logical operator is used multiple times in a single line of code, the operators are evaluated from left to right.

*Table 3-6. Order of Precedence of Arithmetic Operators*

| | |
|---|---|
| 1 | ^ Exponentiation |
| 2 | * Multiplication and / Division (no order of precedence between the two) |
| 3 | \ Integer Division |
| 4 | Mod Modulo Arithmetic |
| 5 | + Addition and – Subtraction (no order of precedence between the two) |

*Table 3-7. Logical Operators Order of Precedence*

| | |
|---|---|
| 1 | Not |
| 2 | And |
| 3 | Or |
| 4 | Xor |
| 5 | Eqv |
| 6 | Imp |

# Summary

In this chapter, you've seen how to integrate your script with an HTML document, and you have had an in-depth look at the principles of using variables and constants in VBScript. Before moving on, take a moment to recap some of the important points we've covered:

- The `<SCRIPT>` or `<SCRIPT FOR>` tags can be placed anywhere within either the `<HEAD>` or `<BODY>` sections of your HTML document. If you're concerned about your script appearing as plain text in older browsers that don't support the `<SCRIPT>` tag, you should comment out your script by using the HTML comment symbols (`<!--` and `-->`).

- VBScript supports only a single data type, the Variant. The Variant data type in turn has many data subtypes, which are assigned automatically by the VBScript engine. To determine the subtype of a particular variant variable or constant, use the *VarType* function.

- Variables can have their values changed. Constants retain their original value throughout their lifetime.

- The VBScript engine always treats data input into HTML forms as string data. If your application is expecting some other data type, you can use one of the type conversion functions to convert the data into another data subtype.

- There are four types of arrays: fixed one-dimensional, fixed multidimensional, dynamic one-dimensional, and dynamic multidimensional. Arrays can hold any of the variant data subtypes. Use the *UBound* function to return the highest array index. Use the *ReDim* function to create and maintain a dynamic array.

- Variables and constants declared outside a procedure have script-level scope, while variables and constants declared within a procedure can only be used within that procedure.

# 4

# *Program Flow and Structure*

Now that you understand the types and uses of variables in VBScript, you are halfway to being able to program using VBScript. The next topic to master is how to structure scripts and programs and how to handle program flow, or how to create a decision-making path, within your scripts. In this chapter, we'll examine the features that VBScript provides to make decisions within your program and to automatically cause your program to branch in the appropriate direction. In this section, you'll start writing programs and scripts with multiple execution paths, so that simple programs or scripts start to take on the feel of more substantial applications. We'll then look at how to create the basic procedural templates that you use to hold the various subsections of your programs and scripts, in the process contributing to the program's overall efficiency by separating the script into logical and easily managed segments. Finally, we'll look briefly at naming conventions, one of the means used to write self-documenting scripts, to enable other people to quickly understand and follow your work, and, more importantly, to allow you to maintain your script many months after its creation. When you have completed this chapter, you'll have all the basic knowledge needed to venture into the rest of the book, where we delve into the development of real-life examples, in the process showing you how to achieve the goal of dynamic, interactive, and robust web pages.

## Control Statements

*Control statements*, as the name suggests, allow you to control the way the execution sequence of your script is handled by the VBScript engine. Control statements can be divided into two distinct groups:

- Those that control program flow by means of a decision-making process

- Those that control flow by repeating an action a certain number of times, or until a certain condition is met

## Conditional Decision-Making Statements

In creating any application, there are countless times when you want your script to make a decision and to execute different sections of code based on that decision. Not infrequently, you'll even want your program to make another decision based on the result of the first decision. Without a means of writing a decision-making mechanism within a script, it is inconceivable that anything other than the most rudimentary application could ever be produced. Consequently, conditional statements are central to the logical flow and perceived "intelligence" of a properly constructed application. VBScript provides you with several conditional statements:

- If...Then
- If...Else...Then
- If...ElseIf...Then
- Select Case

### If...Then

The most common means of creating a decision-making structure within a script is the `If...Then...End If` control block. It follows a logical sequence that can be read aloud, exactly as you would verbalize the problem. **If** this is true **Then** do something. The `If...Then...End If` control block is constructed as follows:

```
If condition Then
 code to execute if condition is met
End If
```

Let's look at a simple problem. We want the program to show an alert box only if the user enters a number greater than 100. In the HTML page shown in Example 4-1, when the user clicks on the Click Me button, the *cmdMakeADecision_OnClick* procedure stores the value that the user entered into the txtUserNumber text box to the *lngTheNumber* variable. It then uses the `If...Then` statement to determine if it is greater than 100; if it is, the program displays a message box on the user's browser.

*Example 4-1. The If...Then Construct*

```
<HTML>
 <HEAD>
  <SCRIPT LANGUAGE="vbscript">
  <!--
```

*Example 4-1. The If...Then Construct (continued)*

```
Sub cmdMakeADecision_OnClick()
  Dim lngTheNumber                        'Create a variable
  lngTheNumber = CLng(txtUserNumber.Value)    'Copy in the user response
  If lngTheNumber > 100 Then              'Check if its over 100
    Alert "Greater than 100"              'If it is then show an Alert
  End If                                  'Close the If structure
End Sub
-->
</SCRIPT>
</HEAD>

<BODY BGCOLOR="white">
  Enter a number <INPUT TYPE="text" NAME="txtUserNumber">
  <INPUT TYPE="button" NAME="cmdMakeADecision" VALUE="Then Click Me">
</BODY>
</HTML>
```

## If...Then...Else

As you can see, controlling the program by executing a particular section of code only when a given condition is met is very straightforward. But what if you want the program to execute one section of code only if the condition is met, and another section of code only if the condition is not met? Given that the section of code after **End If** will always execute, we need an additional criterion in our logical statement, **If** this is true **Then** do something, otherwise do something **Else**. This is handled by the **If...Then...Else...End If** control block, which is constructed as follows:

```
If condition Then
  code to execute if condition is met
Else
  code to execute only if condition is not met
End If
```

Let's amend our simple example to display another alert box if our original condition is not met; this modified version of our web page is shown in Example 4-2. Now, when our program stores the value that the user enters into the text box to *lngTheNumber* and performs the comparison, it also displays a second message box if the comparison fails—that is, if *lngTheNumber* is less than or equal to 100.

*Example 4-2. The If...Then...Else Construct*

```
<HTML>
 <HEAD>
  <SCRIPT LANGUAGE="vbscript">
   <!--
   Sub cmdMakeADecision_OnClick()
    Dim lngTheNumber
    lngTheNumber = CLng(txtUserNumber.Value)
     If lngTheNumber > 100 Then
```

*Example 4-2. The If...Then...Else Construct (continued)*

```
      Alert "Greater than 100"
    Else
      Alert "Less than or equal to 100"
    End If
  End Sub
  -->
 </SCRIPT>
</HEAD>

<BODY BGCOLOR="white">
  Enter a number <INPUT TYPE="text" NAME="txtUserNumber">
  <INPUT TYPE="button" NAME="cmdMakeADecision" VALUE="Then Click Me">
 </BODY>
</HTML>
```

This works great for conditions where you only need to make a straightforward decision: If *this* Then *that* Else *the other*. But, as we all know, not all real-life decisions are that easy. There are many occasions where you need a third or fourth alternative.

### Nested If statements

VBScript lets you handle multiple decisions in several ways. The first is through the use of nested If statements, which allow a decision to be made based on a previous decision. In a nested If...Then... statement, the inner statement is only activated if the outer condition is met. Here are a couple of examples:

```
If condition Then
    If condition Then
        If condition Then
            If condition Then
                code to execute only if all conditions are true
            End If
        End If
    End If
End If

If condition Then
    If condition Then
        code to execute only if the first and second conditions are met
    Else
        code to execute only if the first condition is met and the
         second condition is not met
    End if ' refers to the second If
Else
    code to execute if first if condition is not met
End if 'refers to first if
```

Let's add this to our example HTML page. In Example 4-3, the program first tests *lngTheNumber* to see if it is greater than 100. If the test fails, the program displays an alert box indicating that its value is 100 or less. If the test succeeds, the program performs an additional test, and displays a message box that indicates whether the value lies between 100 and 199, or whether it is greater than or equal to 200.

*Example 4-3. Using Nested If Statements*

```
<HTML>
 <HEAD>
  <SCRIPT LANGUAGE="vbscript">
  <!--
   Sub cmdMakeADecision_OnClick()
    Dim lngTheNumber
    lngTheNumber = CLng(txtUserNumber.Value)
    If lngTheNumber > 100 Then
       If lngTheNumber < 200 Then
          Alert "Greater than 100 but less than 200"
       Else
          Alert "Greater than or equal to 200"
       End If
    Else
       Alert "Less than or equal to 100"
    End If
   End Sub
  -->
  </SCRIPT>
 </HEAD>

 <BODY BGCOLOR="white">
   Enter a number <INPUT TYPE="text" NAME="txtUserNumber">
   <INPUT TYPE="button" NAME="cmdMakeADecision" VALUE="Then Click Me">
 </BODY>
</HTML>
```

## ElseIf

Let's say we need a conditional test to determine whether or not we should execute code that follows the `Else` statement. One way of doing this is with a nested `If` statement:

```
If condition1 Then
    code to execute if condition1 is met
Else
   If condition2 Then
       code to execute if condition2 is met and condition1 is not met
   End If
End If
```

Another way of doing this involves using the `ElseIf` statement. `ElseIf` performs exactly the same as `If`, but it takes the place of an `Else`.

```
If condition1 Then
 code to execute if condition1 is met
```

```
ElseIf condition2 Then
 code to execute if condition2 is met and condition1 is not met
End If
```

As you can see, the code following the `ElseIf` statement, which would normally execute should the first condition not be met, is itself conditional. Further `Else`s and `ElseIf`s can be placed after `ElseIf`. Note also that an `ElseIf` statement does not need its own corresponding `End If` statement, as Example 4-4 shows.

*Example 4-4. Using If...ElseIf*

```
<HTML>
  <HEAD>
  <SCRIPT LANGUAGE="vbscript">
  <!--
  Sub cmdMakeADecision_OnClick()
   Dim lngTheNumber
   lngTheNumber = CLng(txtUserNumber.Value)
   If lngTheNumber > 100 Then
    Alert "Greater than 100"
   ElseIf lngTheNumber > 50 then
    Alert "Greater than 50 but less than or equal to 100"
   Else
    Alert "Less than or equal to 50"
   End If
  End Sub
  -->
  </SCRIPT>
</HEAD>

<BODY BGCOLOR="white">
  Enter a number <INPUT TYPE="text" NAME="txtUserNumber">
  <INPUT TYPE="button" NAME="cmdMakeADecision" VALUE="Then Click Me">
</BODY>
</HTML>
```

Note that the first comparison in Example 4-4 determines whether or not *lngThe-Number* is greater than 100; if it is, an alert box is displayed. If it is not, the script uses the `ElseIf` statement to perform a second comparison that determines whether or not *lngTheNumber* is greater than 50. If it is, an alert box indicating that the value of *lngNumber* ranges from 51 to 100 is displayed; otherwise, an alert box informs the user that *lngTheNumber* is 50 or less.

### And, Or

As you may have gathered, particularly from looking at the first syntax example in the "Nested If statements" section earlier in this chapter, relying only on the `If...Else...End If` construct to handle complex decisions can result in code that is extremely difficult to read and understand, and that is consequently difficult to debug. Fortunately, as we saw in the last chapter, VBScript provides a rich set of logical operators that allow the formation of complex arguments and that can be used along with variations of the `If...End If` construct to improve the clarity of your code. Let's look at the ways in which these can be used to construct conditional statements that will handle multiple logical conditions.

Using the `And` conditional operator means that two conditions have to be True for the overall statement itself to be True. If either one is False, then the whole statement is False, as the following pseudo-code example shows:

```
If condition1 AND condition2 THEN
    code to execute if both conditions evaluate to true
Else
    code to execute if one or more of the conditions is false
End if
```

Using the `Or` conditional operator means that either of two expressions can be True for the statement itself to be True. Naturally the statement is still True if both are True. So the only situation that leads to the statement being False occurs if both conditions are False.

```
If condition1 OR condition2 THEN
    code to execute if either condition evaluates to true
Else
    code to execute if neither condition evaluates to true
End if
```

Using multiple `And` and `Or` conditional operators within a conditional statement can become a somewhat confusing affair. Use parentheses to split up the statement into understandable sections. However, be careful to place the parentheses in the logical order you require; otherwise, you'll change the logical order, and give a completely different meaning to the statement, as we can see in this example:

```
If (condition1 And condition2) Or (condition3) Then
```

This statement evaluates to True, and the code that follows the `Then` statement is executed, if either of the following conditions is True:

- Both *condition1* and *condition2* are True.

- Only *condition3* is True.

(Of course, if all three conditions are True, the statement also evaluates to True.) Let's change the placement of the parentheses and see how this changes the logic:

```
If condition1 And (condition2 Or condition3) Then
```

Now, *condition1* must be True and either *condtion2* or *condition3* must also be True for the overall condition to evaluate to True. In the first line, only one condition (*condition3*) needed to be met, but now two conditions (1 and either 2 or 3) must be met.

*Understanding True and False statements*

We've seen that a conditional statement depends on being either True or False, and in most cases you can see quite clearly that it's one or the other. However, there are times when you can become unsure whether a statement is going to evaluate to True or not. To get a sense of what True and False mean, let's look at a condition that evaluates to True:

```
x = 9
y  = 1
If x + y = 10 Then
```

This is an easy example to start off, but what about this:

```
x = False
If x = False Then
```

It is important to understand that, in the above example, **x** itself is False, but the statement is True. The value of **x** is False, and the question posed by the conditional statement is whether **x** evaluates to False, as in fact it does. In conditional statements, we are testing to find out whether the *overall* statement is True. Here's another example:

```
x = True
If Not x = False then
```

OK, I'm making this purposely abstruse to try and get the point across. You can see that you can even use what is basically a double negative, and finally another double negative. This could be verbalized as "Is x Not False?" The answer is, "Yes...it's not," so therefore it's True. Let's look at a final example:

```
x = 0
If Not x Then
```

You'll remember that False evaluates to 0, and True evaluates to a nonzero value, or –1. Therefore, the above statement is True.

*Using True and False*

Within an `If...End If` control statement, you can put the built-in literal constants True and False to good use. For example, in the following code fragment, True evaluates to –1:

```
If x = True Then
    code to execute if x is True
Else
    code to execute if x is False
End if
```

## Using an implied True

The preceding code can actually be rewritten without the word True. VBScript will assume an implied True in a simple condition, as follows:

```
If x then
    code to execute if x is any value other than zero
Else
    code to execute if x is zero
End if
```

Because this `If...Else...End If` statement does not explicitly use the constant True in its evaluation, the condition is evaluated somewhat differently than the earlier condition that uses an explicit True. In particular, when True is implied, *x* evaluates to True whenever the value of *x* is nonzero; when True is an explicit condition, *x* evaluates to True whenever the value of *x* is –1.

---

*WARNING*    Note that when using the True keyword explicitly as part of a conditional statement, True will only evaluate to –1. It is easy to fall into
the trap of believing that "True" evaluates to any nonzero value.

---

## Using Not

Under normal circumstances, the `If...Then` statement has to evaluate to True for the code to execute. However, by using **NOT** in the evaluation, you can reverse this so that the code executes only if the condition is False. You will remember from the last chapter that **Not** is used for logical negation. This means that the result of an evaluation is reversed: True is made False, and False is made True:

```
    If Not condition Then
        code to execute if condition is False
    End if
```

`If...Then...End If` is a very important part of any language, and you'll find that you will use it in many different circumstances to control program flow. If this is your first experience with the `If...Then...End If` construct, make sure you understand how it works and how you can use it before proceeding to the rest of the chapter.

## Select Case

In situations where you may have too many **Elses** for your code to be easily understandable and manageable, Visual Basic provides an alternative construct in the **Select Case** statement. **Select Case** statements are constructed as a series of options. The code belonging to only one of the options will execute, depending upon the condition being evaluated. The general form of the `Select Case` construct is:

```
Select Case expression
Case condition1
   code to execute if condition1 is true
Case condition2
   code to execute if condition2 is true
....
End Select
```

---

### *Note for Visual Basic and VBA Programmers*

If you are used to using `Select Case` in VB or VBA, you may be in for a surprise when you come to use it in VBScript. For reasons known only to themselves, Microsoft has left out the main functionality of `Select Case` in VBScript for MSIE3.0. Hopefully, this will be rectified in later versions of MSIE, but for the moment, you must explicitly specify a Case value. This means that statements such as `Case Is > 5` and `Case "a" To "z"`, both of which are legal in VB or VBA, are illegal when you use VBScript. You cannot use the `Is` and `To` keywords within the `Case` statement, which, as you can appreciate, seriously limits the flexibility afforded by `Select Case`.

---

The `Select Case`'s *expression* is evaluated first of all, and the result is compared with a list of `Case` conditions. The code immediately following a matched `Case` condition is executed. The program then resumes execution on the line directly after the `End Select` statement. If none of the `Case` conditions matches the result of the `Select Case` expression, the program resumes execution at the line directly after `End Select`. As you can see, this is analogous to a series of linked `If..Then...Else...End If` statements.

The conditions used next to the list of `Case` statements can be a single argument such as:

```
Case 5
```

or they can be a series of arguments delimited by a comma, like the following:

```
Case 5,10,15
```

The condition in a `Case` statement can be a numeric value, but it can also be a string value like the following:

```
Case "Hello"
```

If you do use the `Select Case` construct to evaluate a string, the comparison is case-sensitive. That is, the string specified in *expression* must match the string specified by one of the conditions exactly, including its case, for a match to occur.

Example 4-5 contains the HTML and VBScript code for a page that uses the `Select Case` construct.

*Example 4-5. The Select Case Construct*

```
<HTML>
 <HEAD>
  <SCRIPT LANGUAGE="vbscript">
  <!--
   Sub cmdMakeADecision_OnClick()
    Dim strSelected, intIndex

    intIndex = selUserSelection.SelectedIndex
    strSelected =  selUserSelection.Options(intIndex).Text

     Select Case strSelected
     Case "This"
       Alert "You have chosen this"
     Case "That"
       Alert "I see you want that, huh?"
     Case "The Other"
        Alert "Do you really want the other?"
     End Select

   End Sub
  -->
  </SCRIPT>
 </HEAD>

<BODY BGCOLOR="white">
  <SELECT NAME="selUserSelection">
   <OPTION>This
   <OPTION>That
   <OPTION>The Other
  </SELECT>
  <INPUT TYPE="button" NAME="cmdMakeADecision" VALUE="Click Me">
 </BODY>
</HTML>
```

You'll notice in Example 4-5 that although three items are defined by the `<OPTION>` tag and therefore appear in the web page's drop-down list box, there are only two `Case` options. This means that, if the user selects the "The Other" option and clicks the Click Me button, nothing happens. In a real web page that used three options, of course, we would simply include an additional `Case` statement to handle a user's selection of "The Other." In some cases, though, you may not know all of the possible values for the individual `Case` statements in advance, or you may be primarily concerned with a limited number of values out of all possible values. In that case, you can include the `Case Else` statement in your `Select Case` structure.

`Case Else` operates in the same way as an `Else` in `If..Then...Else`. If none of the Case conditions can be matched to the `Select Case` expression, then the code immediately following `Case Else` is executed. Again, execution then resumes after `End Select`. It is prudent—and considered good programming practice—to use a `Case Else` to handle any exceptional cases. Example 4-6 is a modified version of the web page from Example 4-5 that uses `Case Else`.

*Example 4-6. Using the Case Else Statement*

```
<HTML>
 <HEAD>
  <SCRIPT LANGUAGE="vbscript">
  <!--
   Sub cmdMakeADecision_OnClick()
    Dim strSelected, intIndex

    intIndex = frmForm1.selUserSelection.SelectedIndex
    strSelected = frmForm1.selUserSelection.Options(intIndex).Text

     Select Case strSelected
     Case "This"
       Alert "You have chosen this"
     Case "That"
       Alert "I see you want that, huh?"
     Case Else
       Alert "So you don't want this or that"
     End Select

   End Sub
  -->
  </SCRIPT>
 </HEAD>

<BODY BGCOLOR="white">
 <FORM NAME="frmForm1">
  <SELECT NAME="selUserSelection">
   <OPTION>This
   <OPTION>That
   <OPTION>The Other
  </SELECT>
  <INPUT TYPE="button" NAME="cmdMakeADecision" VALUE="Click Me">
 </FORM>
 </BODY>
</HTML>
```

To summarize, conditional statements are used to determine which part of the script should execute, allowing your script to perform in various ways depending upon the prevailing circumstances. To handle the decision-making process, you can use `If..Then` for simple and straightforward reasoning, or you can enhance this by using `Else` and `ElseIf` to handle even the most complicated problems with multiple outcomes. As an alternative to `Else` and `ElseIf`, you can also use the `Select Case` statement as a clear and concise method to implement decision making in your code.

Let's now look at the other collection of control statements, known as looping statements, which handle the repetitive execution of code.

## Looping Statements

Looping statements provide the means by which you control the repetitive execution of your code. But why would you want to repeat part of your code? There are an infinite number of cases in which, for purposes of counting and calculating, of generating output, etc., your application needs to execute almost the same procedure over and over again. In some cases, it is possible to write these lines of code inline one after the other, but your code would quickly become so large as to be unmanageable. In other cases, you may not know in advance how many times a particular block of code needs to be repeated, making inline code completely ineffective as a way of repeatedly performing the same operations. VBScript therefore provides looping statements that allow you to write only a few lines of code that can be executed a given number of times, or whose execution can be controlled by some outside value. By modifying and evaluating the values of variables with each repetition, it is possible to build a section of code that, with each iteration, performs as though it were a separate customized section of your program.

VBScript provides four methods of repeatedly executing a segment of code:

- `For...Next` repeats code a given number of times.

- `For Each...Next` repeats code for each of a number of objects (VBScript 2.0 only).

- `Do...Loop` repeats code an indefinite number of times until a condition is True or while a condition is True.

- `While...Wend` repeats code while a condition is True.

### For...Next

The `For...Next` loop executes a given number of times as specified by a loop counter. To use the `For...Next` loop, you must assign a value to a counter variable. This counter is either incremented or decremented automatically with each iteration of the loop. In the `For` statement, you specify the value that is to be assigned to the counter initially and the maximum value the counter will reach for the block of code to be executed. The values of counter variables must be numeric. The `Next` statement delimits the end of the block of code that is to execute repeatedly, and also serves as a kind of flag that indicates that the counter variable is to be modified. The general syntax of the `For...Next` statement is:

```
For counter = initial_counter_value To maximum_counter_value
    ' code to execute on each iteration
Next
```

---

### *Note for Visual Basic and VBA Programmers*

In later editions of Visual Basic, as well as in VBA, the syntax for using `Next` is

```
Next [counter]
```

where *counter* is optional. However, the VBScript engine generates a run-time error ("Expected End of Statement") if you try to use *counter* with `Next`.

---

Example 4-7 illustrates the use of a simple loop using `For...Next`. Before you execute this code, try to work out what will happen.

*Example 4-7. Using a For...Next Loop*

```
<HTML>

  <SCRIPT LANGUAGE="vbscript">
  <!--
    Document.Write  "<BODY BGCOLOR='white'>"

    For x = 1 to 10
      Document.Write "This is line number "
      Document.Write CStr(x)
      Document.Write "<BR>"
    Next
    Document.Write "</BODY>"
  -->
  </SCRIPT>

</HTML>
```

By default, VBScript automatically increments the counter by one each time the loop executes. However, you can specify a different value by using the `Step` keyword. You can even decrement the counter during each iteration of the loop by using a negative step value.

```
For counter = initial_counter_value To maximum_counter_value _
Step increment
  code to execute on each interation
Next
```

Example 4-8 is a modified version of the code in Example 4-7 that uses the `Step` keyword to increment the counter by four for each iteration of the loop, while Example 4-9 uses the `Step` keyword to decrement the counter by four each time that the loop executes:

*Example 4-8. For...Next with a Step Statement*

```
<HTML>

  <SCRIPT LANGUAGE="vbscript">
  <!--
    Document.Write  "<BODY BGCOLOR='white'>"

    For x = 4 to 20 Step 4
      Document.Write "The loop counter is "
      Document.Write CStr(x)
      Document.Write "<BR>"
    Next
    Document.Write "</BODY>"
  -->
  </SCRIPT>

</HTML>
```

*Example 4-9. For...Next with a negative Step statement*

```
<HTML>

  <SCRIPT LANGUAGE="vbscript">
  <!--
    Document.Write  "<BODY BGCOLOR='white'>"

    For x = 20 to 4 Step -4
      Document.Write "The loop counter is "
      Document.Write CStr(x)
      Document.Write "<BR>"
    Next
    Document.Write "</BODY>"
  -->
  </SCRIPT>

</HTML>
```

Although most of our examples have used literal constants to define the starting value, the end value, and the step value of the loop counter, it is also possible to use variables. For example:

```
For x = nStartValue To nEndValue Step nStep
```

By freeing us from having to decide how many times the loop must execute when we write our script, and instead allowing the number of iterations to be determined dynamically when the script is executed, this substantially increases the power and flexibility of the `For...Next` loop.

### For Each...Next `VBS 2.0`

Although the `For Each...Next` construct appears in the documentation for VBScript Version 1, it was not implemented until Version 2. The `For Each...Next` loop allows you to visit all items within a collection, and to execute a block of code on each of those items smoothly and with very little code. The syntax to use is:

```
For Each item In collection
...
Next
```

---

## VB Programmer's Note

When you use the `For Each` statement, you probably use some form of strong typing when you dimension your *item* variable by using the `As` keyword, as in the following code fragment:

```
Dim myControl As Control
For Each myControl In Layout1.Controls
```

However, as you saw in Chapter 3, *Getting Started*, VBScript does not support strong typing, and all VBScript variables are dimensioned as variants. Because of this, the `As` keyword generates a compile-time error. This does make life easy in one sense: you don't have to worry about what type your item variable should be, since it will be automatically cast when the assignment is made in the `For Each` statement.

---

The collection through which you are looping using `For Each...Next` can be a collection of like objects—such as every control on a form—or it can be an array. When the `For Each...` line of the loop has been executed, *item* becomes a reference to a particular item or object within the collection, thus allowing you to access the properties and the methods of the item, using the syntax:

```
item.property
```

Looping through controls or elements of an array is useful when you need to apply the same or similar code to the items, as, for example, when you want to disable all the controls on a form. Or you might simply want to display the ID property (that is, the control name) of every control that has been placed on a layout control, as in the following code fragment:

```
Dim myControl

For Each myControl in Layout1.Controls
    Alert myControl.ID
Next
```

The **For Each...Next** loop will visit all items in the collection, in turn, until the end of the collection is met, at which time execution will continue with the first line following the **Next** statement. If there are no items in the collection, the **For Each...Next** loop is ignored. At any time during the execution of the code with the loop, you can insert any number of **Exit For** statements (discussed in the following section), which will force the loop to halt, and again execution will continue with the first line of code after the **Next** statement.

---

*WARNING*     The **For Each...Next** loop does not work with HTML intrinsic controls in an HTML form. The Elements object—which contains a collection of form controls—is not a collection of the type that VB-Script understands. Therefore, the code you expect to use:

```
For Each myControl in Document.Form1.Elements
```

results in an error. If you want your script to iterate the intrinsic controls on an HTML form, you can use a **For...Next** loop and set the upper limit of the loop counter by reading the value of the Elements.Count property. For details, see Chapter 6, *The Element Object and HTML Intrinsic Controls.*

---

Example 4-10 shows how you can use the **For Each...Next** loop with an array. A script-level array, *myArray*, is populated with values using the *Array* function. When the user clicks on the Click Me button, a **For Each...Next** loop is used to search for an element whose value is 40. A counter variable, *i*, is used to track the number of times the loop has iterated; it starts out with a value of 1 the first time the loop executes. If the value is found (as it should be, since the value of *myArray(2)* is 40), an alert box is displayed that informs the user that the element was found in the third position of the array.

*Example 4-10. Using For Each...Next*

```
<HTML>
<HEAD>
<SCRIPT LANGUAGE="vbscript">
   OPTION EXPLICIT
   Dim myArray
   myArray = Array(10,20,40,60,80)
```

*Example 4-10. Using For Each...Next (continued)*

```
Sub cmdButton1_onClick
    dim myElement
    dim i
    For Each myElement in myArray
        i = i + 1
        If myElement = 40 Then
            Alert "Found It at " & i
            Exit For
        End if
    Next
End Sub
</SCRIPT>
</HEAD>
<BODY BGCOLOR="white">
<H3>For Each...Next</H3>
<INPUT TYPE="button" NAME="cmdButton1" VALUE="Click me">
</BODY>
</HTML>
```

---

*WARNING*    When looping through a collection of controls with `For Each...Next`, it often is essential to know what type of control you are currently referencing. In VB, you use the `TypeOf` statement to do this, as follows:

```
If TypeOf myControl Is textbox then
```

However, contrary to the VBScript documentation, `TypeOf` is not part of VBScript, and its use generates an error. The only way to distinguish one control from another is to use part of the ID (or the control's name), but this means that you must follow a naming convention for the all the controls on your layout. For example, if you consistently start the names of all your text box controls with "txt" (as in `txtName`, `txtZipCode`, etc.), you can determine the object type with a code fragment like the following:

```
If Left(myControl.ID,3) = "txt" Then
```

This code would correctly identify all your text boxes and ignore all other controls. For more information on naming conventions, see the section "VBScript Coding Conventions" later in this chapter.The VBScript 2.0 documentation of the `For Each...Next` construct indicates that the use of the item variable after the `Next` statement is optional. However, this is not true; anything after the `Next` statement will generate an error. Therefore, the `Next` statement must appear on a line of its own.

---

### Exit For

In addition to waiting for the loop to terminate normally, you can also exit a `For...Next` or a `For Each...Next` loop early by testing for a particular condition with `If...Then` and using the `Exit For` statement if the condition is met.

The script resumes execution at the line immediately after the `Next` statement. Any number of `Exit For` statements can be placed anywhere within the `For...Next` loop. The following pseudo-code example illustrates the use of the `Exit For` statement:

```
For counter = initial_counter_value To maximum_counter_value
    code to execute on each iteration
    If condition Then
        Exit For
    End If
    code to execute on each iteration
Next
```

### Do...Loop

In our discussion of the `For...Next` loop, we saw that the use of variables to determine the origin, upper limit, and step value of the loop counter substantially increases the flexibility of the `For...Next` statement, and allows the number of times that the loop is to be repeated to be determined at run-time, rather than when we write the script. Nevertheless, the loop itself always depends on a counter to determine whether or not a block of code is executed. Sometimes, particularly in some situations when we don't know in advance how many times we need to repeat the block of code, it is useful to base the repetition of operations on some condition, rather than on the value of a counter. This is handled by the `Do...Loop` structure.

`Do...Loop` repeats the code that is contained within its boundaries indefinitely—literally! That's almost certainly not what you're looking for, so you need to specify within the code the conditions under which the loop is to stop repeating. You can specify the "halt" condition in several ways:

- By adding the `Until` keyword after `Do`, which instructs the VBScript engine to Do something Until the condition is True. Its syntax is:

```
Do Until condition
    code to execute
Loop
```

  If *condition* is True before your code gets to the `Do...Loop`, the code within the `Do...Loop` is ignored.

- By adding the `While` keyword after `Do`. Using `Do While` repeats the code while a particular condition is True. When the condition becomes False, the loop is automatically exited. The syntax of the `Do While` statement is:

```
Do While condition
 code to execute
Loop
```

  Again, the code within the `Do...Loop` is ignored if *condition* is False when the program arrives at the loop.

However, in some cases, your script may need to execute the loop at least once. You might, for example, evaluate the values held within an array, and terminate the loop if a particular value is found. In that case, you would need to execute the loop at least once. To accomplish this, you can place the `Until` or the `While` keyword along with the condition *after* the `Loop` statement. `Do...Loop Until` always executes the code in the loop at least once, and continues to loop until the condition is True. Likewise, `Do...Loop While` always executes the code at least once, and continues to loop while the condition is True. The syntax of these two statements is as follows:

```
Do
 code to execute
Loop Until condition

Do
 code to execute
Loop While condition
```

You'll also encounter situations in which you intend to execute the loop continually until a condition is true, except in a particular case. This type of exception is handled using the **Exit Do** statement. You can place as many **Exit Do** statements within a Do...Loop structure as you require. As with all exits from a `Do...Loop`, either exceptional or normal, the program continues execution on the line directly following the `Loop` statement. The following code fragment illustrates the use of **Exit Do**:

```
Do Until condition1
   code to execute
   If condition2 Then
      Exit Do
   End if
   more code to execute - only if condition2 is false
Loop
```

Example 4-11 is a sample HTML document that uses the `Do...Loop` control structure. It demonstrates how many times (if any) the code within the loop executes, based on values the user inputs into the Initial Value and End Value text boxes. (In addition, you'll notice that the **Exit Do** statement is automatically executed after the loop executes 500 times!)

*Example 4-11. Using the Do...Loop Construct*

```
<HTML>
 <HEAD>
  <SCRIPT LANGUAGE="vbscript">
  <!--
  OPTION EXPLICIT
   Sub cmdDoWhileLoop_OnClick()
    Dim  intCounter, intStart, intEnd
    'set the tell-tale to zero
```

*Example 4-11. Using the Do...Loop Construct (continued)*

```
    intCounter = 0
    ' convert to integers
    ' NOTE: there is no verification of data type here
    intStart = CInt(txtStartNumber.Value)
    intEnd = CInt(txtEndCondition.Value)
    'reset the telltale counter text box
    txtOutputCounter.Value = CStr(intCounter)
    Do While intStart < intEnd

    'the following code will continue to execute while
    'the first number you entered is less than the
    'second number

    intStart = intStart + 1     'increment start number by one
    intCounter = intCounter + 1'increment the tell tale counter

    'check to make sure the tell-tale counter doesn't go over 500
      If intCounter = 500 Then
        Exit Do    'jump out of the loop
      End If
    Loop
    ' whichever we way got here,
    ' show the value of the tell-tale counter
    txtOutputCounter.Value = CStr(intCounter)
  End Sub

  Sub cmdDoLoopWhile_OnClick()
    Dim  intCounter, intStart, intEnd
    intCounter = 0
    intStart = CInt(txtStartNumber.Value)
    intEnd = CInt(txtEndCondition.Value)
    txtOutputCounter.Value = CStr(intCounter)

    'this code will always execute at least once
    Do
    intStart = intStart + 1
    intCounter = intCounter + 1
      If intCounter = 500 then
        Exit Do
      End If
    'here is where we check the condition
    Loop While intStart < intEnd
    'this counter will always show at least one
    txtOutputCounter.Value = CStr(intCounter)
  End Sub

  -->
 </SCRIPT>
</HEAD>

<BODY BGCOLOR="white">
 <CENTER>
```

*Example 4-11. Using the Do...Loop Construct (continued)*

```
      Enter An Initial Value for your Condition
      <INPUT TYPE="text" NAME="txtStartNumber"><P>
      Enter An End Value for your Condition
      <INPUT TYPE="text" NAME="txtEndCondition"><P>
      <INPUT TYPE="button" NAME="cmdDoWhileLoop" VALUE="Do While">
      <INPUT TYPE="button" NAME="cmdDoLoopWhile" VALUE="Loop While"><P>
      The Loop repeated <INPUT TYPE="text" NAME="txtOutputCounter"> times<P>
      <I>To demonstrate the difference between Do While and Loop While, <BR>
      enter the same value for both start and end.<I>
    </CENTER>
  </BODY>
</HTML>
```

### While...Wend

If you haven't used the `While...Wend` control structure previously, you don't really need to be concerned with it. Microsoft included `While...Wend` for those programmers who had previous experience with the `While` control structure and are therefore more comfortable with it than with `Do...Loop`. However, Microsoft recommends that `Do...Loop` be used because it affords much more flexibility than the older `While..Wend`.

To summarize, you can use decision-making control structures that evaluate program and input variables and then execute parts of your program only under a specific set of circumstances. You can also use looping control structures to repeat sections of code while or until a certain condition is met. Having a good understanding of control structures allows you to build virtually any kind of program under an almost unlimited range of circumstances. The ability to support control structures such as the ones we've discussed here is what really sets scripted HTML documents apart from normal HTML documents, which, as we know, cannot make decisions for themselves. By using control structures, you add some pseudo-intelligence and "life" to your web documents, in the process transforming them into much more than simple documents. Instead, they become programs.

As you have already seen in the previous examples, scripts are made up of one or more procedures. Procedures help to separate the work the program or script has to do into smaller, more easily manageable sections. To refine the VBScript model we've looked at so far, let's now look at how we subdivide our program logically into Functions and Procedures.

## Functions and Procedures

Functions and procedures (or subroutines) are central to modern programming. Dividing our script into subroutines helps us to maintain and write programs by segregating related code into smaller, manageable sections. It also helps us to reduce the number of lines of code we have to write, by allowing us to reuse the same subroutine or function many times in different situations and from different parts of the program. In this section, you will learn about the different types of subroutines, how and why they are used, and how using subroutines helps you to optimize your code.

## Defining Subroutines: The Sub...End Sub Construct

You have already seen the `Sub...End Sub` construct used many times in the previous examples to define a subroutine. Blocks of code defined as subroutines with the `Sub...End Sub` construct can be called in several ways:

- Automatically. Some subroutines provide the means by which an object or control—such as a button—interfaces with the script. For instance, when the user clicks on a button, that button's *OnClick* subroutine is automatically executed, if it exists. For subroutines of this type, the routine's name can only be constructed in one way, as follows:

  ```
  Sub objectname_event
  ```

  For example, *Sub cmdMyButton_OnClick* is a valid name of a subroutine. This tells the VBScript engine that when the object with the name *cmdMyButton* fires an *OnClick* event (which occurs when the user clicks on it with the mouse), the subroutine's code is to be executed. This type of subroutine is known as an *event handler* or an *event procedure*.

- By referring to it by name. A subroutine can be executed at any time by referring to it by name in another part of the script. (For additional details, including the syntax required to call subroutines, see the section "Calling a Subroutine" later in this chapter.) While it is possible to execute event procedures in this way, this method is most commonly used to execute *custom subroutines*. Custom subroutines are constructed to perform particular tasks within a program, and can be assigned virtually any name that you like. They allow you to place code that's commonly used, or that is shared by more than one part of a program, in a single place, so that you don't have to duplicate the same code throughout your application.

Example 4-12 illustrates the use of a custom subroutine to contain code that is common to more than one part of an application. It provides a simple example of some common code that is placed in a custom subroutine. The web page in Example 4-12 contains three command buttons. But rather than handling the user's click of a particular button separately, each button's *OnClick* event procedure simply calls the *ShowAlertBox* routine. Had we not included the *ShowAlertBox* subroutine, which contains code common to all three event

### Subroutine Names

There are several very straightforward rules to remember when giving names to your subroutines:

1. The name can contain any alphabetical or numeric characters and the underscore character.

2. The name cannot start with a numeric character.

3. The name cannot contain any spaces. Use the underscore character to separate words to make them easier to read.

For example,

```
Sub 123MySub()
Sub My Sub Routine()
```

both contain illegal subroutine names. However,

```
Sub MySub123()
Sub MySubRoutine()
```

are legal subroutine names.

handlers in our web page, we would have had to create a script several times longer than the one shown in Example 4-12.

Along with showing how to use a custom subroutine to share code, Example 4-12 also demonstrates how to pass variables from one procedure to another, a topic discussed in greater depth in the section "Passing Variables into a Subroutine" later in this chapter. In particular, the *ShowAlertBox* routine is passed the caption of the button on which the user has clicked, so that it can display it in an alert box.

*Example 4-12. Using a Custom Subroutine to Share Code*

```
<HTML>
 <HEAD>
  <SCRIPT LANGUAGE="vbscript">
  <!--
   Dim LINE_FEED
   LINE_FEED = Chr(13) & Chr(10)

   Sub cmdButton1_OnClick
    Call ShowAlertBox(cmdButton1.Value)
   End Sub

   Sub cmdButton2_OnClick
    ShowAlertBox cmdButton2.Value
   End Sub
```

*Example 4-12. Using a Custom Subroutine to Share Code (continued)*

```
Sub cmdButton3_OnClick
  ShowAlertBox cmdButton3.Value
End Sub

Sub ShowAlertBox(strButtonValue)
  dim strMessage
  strMessage = "This is to let you know" & LINE_FEED
  strMessage = strMessage & "you just pressed the button" & LINE_FEED
  strMessage = strMessage & "marked " & strButtonValue
  Alert strMessage
End Sub

  -->
  </SCRIPT>
</HEAD>

<BODY BGCOLOR="white">
  <CENTER>
   <INPUT TYPE="button" NAME="cmdButton1" VALUE="First Button"><P>
   <INPUT TYPE="button" NAME="cmdButton2" VALUE="Second Button"><P>
   <INPUT TYPE="button" NAME="cmdButton3" VALUE="Third Button"><P>
  </CENTER>
</BODY>
</HTML>
```

## Calling a Subroutine

In Example 4-12, you may have noticed that the *cmdButton1_OnClick* event procedure uses a different syntax to invoke the *ShowAlertBox* routine than the *cmdButton2_OnClick* and *cmdButton3_OnClick* procedures. In the call to *ShowAlertBox* from the *cmdButton2_OnClick* procedure:

```
showAlertBox Top.cmdButton2.Value
```

it is unclear that this is actually a call to a subroutine named *showAlertBox*. Presumably, *showAlertBox* could be a variable. In fact, in order to identify *showAlertBox* as a subroutine, we have to rely on a visual clue: it is followed by another variable on the same line of code. This assumes, of course, that the code is correct, and that we haven't inadvertently omitted an equal sign between two variables.

In contrast, invoking a procedure by using a `Call` statement like the following:

```
Call showAlertBox(Top.cmdButton1.Value)
```

makes the code much more readable, and as a result is considered good programming practice.

The rules for calling procedures are quite simple. If you use the `Call` statement, you must enclose the argument list in parentheses. If you do not use `Call`, you cannot use parentheses unless you're passing a single variable.

## Passing Variables into a Subroutine

The ability to pass variables from one procedure to another is an important part of using custom subroutines. It allows us to write custom "black box" routines that can behave differently depending on where the routine has been called from, and also on the particular data values that the routine receives from the calling program.

The data is passed from a calling routine to a subroutine by an *argument list*. The argument list is delimited with commas and can contain any data subtypes, including objects and arrays. For instance, the *mySubRoutine* procedure shown next expects three arguments: *intDataIn1*, *strDataIn2*, and *lngDataIn3*:

```
Sub AnotherSubRoutine()
    some code....
    Call mySubRoutine (intvar1, strvar2, lngvar3)
    more code which executes after mySubRoutine
End Sub

Sub mySubRoutine(intDataIn1, strDataIn2, lngDataIn3)
    code which uses incoming data
End Sub
```

When *mySubRoutine* is called from *AnotherSubRoutine*, it is passed three variables as arguments: *intvar1*, *strvar2*, and *lngvar3*. So as you can see, the names of variables passed in the calling routine's argument list do not need to match the names in the custom procedure's argument list. However, the number of variables in the two argument lists does need to match, or a run-time error results.

In addition, because VBScript is so flexible in its use of data types, you must take care when building subroutines that use data passed into them. The variables designated in the custom subroutine's argument list are automatically assigned the data types of the calling program's argument list. If a custom subroutine attempts to perform some inappropriate operation on the data passed to it, an error results, as the following code fragment illustrates:

```
Sub AnotherSubRoutine()
    some code....
    intVar1 = "Hello World"
    Call mySubRoutine (intvar1, strvar2, lngvar3)
    more code which executes after mySubRoutine
End Sub
```

```
Sub mySubRoutine(intDataIn1, strDataIn2, lngDataIn3)
    code which uses incoming data
    intResult = intDataIn1 * 10 'this will generate an error
End Sub
```

The custom subroutine *mySubRoutine* assumed that *intDataIn1* would be an integer, but instead the calling program passed it a string variable, *intVar1*. Therefore VBScript automatically cast *intData1* as a string. The subroutine then produced a run-time error when it attempted to perform multiplication on a nonnumeric variable. As you can see, while loosely typed languages like VBScript have many advantages, one of their major drawbacks is the fact that you must be on your guard for rogue data at all times.

## Passing Parameters by Reference and by Value

If you program in VB or VBA, you're probably accustomed to indicating whether parameters are passed to subroutines by value or by reference. You do this in the argument list of the `Sub` statement by preceding the name of the argument with either no keyword or the `ByRef` keyword to pass an argument by reference, or with the `ByVal` keyword to pass the argument by value. VBScript does support the `ByVal` keyword, although it is unnecessary. It does not support the `ByRef` keyword, nor does it allow you to pass values by reference to subroutines. This makes the behavior of VBScript quite different from VBA: whereas VBA by default passes variables to subroutines by reference, VBScript only passes variables to them by value.

## Defining Functions: The Function...End Function Construct

As we've seen, subroutines created by the `Sub...End Sub` construct are used to manipulate data that is passed to them (assuming that the subroutine accepts parameters) or to perform some useful operation. However, subroutines have one major shortcoming: it's not easy to get them to return data, like the results of their manipulations, or information on whether or not they were able to handle data successfully. It is possible to make a subroutine "return" a value by having it update the value of a script-level variable. For instance, we could use the following code fragment to create a subroutine that cubes any value that is passed to it as a parameter:

```
<SCRIPT LANGUAGE="vbscript">
    Dim cube        ' script-level variable

    Sub CubeIt(x)
        cube = x^3
```

```
    End Sub
</SCRIPT>
```

Another routine can then access the result with a code fragment like the following:

```
Dim intVar
intVar = 3
Call CubeIt(intVar)
Alert cube
```

This approach, though, suffers from two limitations. First, it means that the script-level variable must remain in memory for the entire life of our script, even though the variable itself may be used only briefly, if at all. This is a very minor concern, since a shortage of memory is not a problem on most Windows 95 or Windows NT systems. Second, and much more important, it creates a variable that can be accessed and modified from anywhere within our script. This makes it very easy for a routine to accidentally modify the value of a variable that is used elsewhere in the script.

Through its support for functions, VBScript supports a much safer way of retrieving some value from a routine. Functions share many of the same characteristics as subroutines defined with the `Sub...End Sub` construct:

- Through their optional argument list, they can be used to manipulate data that is passed to them.

- Since they can be called from anywhere in a script, they can be used to contain code that is shared by more than one part of the application.

However, unlike subroutines, functions return some value to the calling procedure. This can be either the result of some manipulation that the function performs on the arguments supplied to it (as, for example, when a function is passed a number and returns its cube), or it can be some indicator (like a True or False value) that the function has completed its operations successfully. This makes functions ideal for such uses as storing the code for frequently used calculations and conversions.

Functions are defined by using the `Function...End Function` construct, and by placing the function's code between these two statements. The full form of the `Function...End Function` statements is:

```
Function functionname(argumentlist)
End Function
```

A function's argument list is defined in exactly the same way as a subroutine's: the list of arguments is separated by commas and is enclosed in parentheses.

So how do we have our function return a value to the calling procedure? Within the body of our function, we simply assign the value that we want our function to return to a variable whose name is the same as the name of the function, as illustrated by the following code fragment:

```
Function functionname(argumentlist)
    ...some calculation or manipulation
    functionname = result of calculation or manipulation
End Function
```

This variable is automatically initialized through the use of the `Function` statement. This means that, if you're accustomed to defining your variables before using them, and especially if you've included the `Option Explicit` statement in your script, you should *not* use the `Dim` statement to explicitly initialize the variable for the function's return value.

---

## Defining a Function's Return Value

If you've used VB or VBA to create functions, you probably have used the `As` keyword to define the data type of the value returned by a function, as in the following statement:

```
Function CubeIt( ByVal x As Long) As Long
```

However, since VBScript only supports the variant data type, the `As` keyword is not supported, and you don't have to worry about the data type returned by your custom function. All functions defined by the `Function` statement return data of type variant.

---

To implement our earlier *CubeIt* procedure as a function rather than a subroutine, we dispense with the need to define a global variable to hold the cube of the argument passed to the function, as the following code fragment shows:

```
<SCRIPT LANGUAGE="vbscript">
    Function CubeIt(x)
        CubeIt = x^3
    End Function
</SCRIPT>
```

Once a custom function is correctly defined using the `Function...End Function` statement, it can be called just as if it were an intrinsic function that is built into the VBScript language. Unlike a call to a subroutine, though, this means that the argument list, if one is present, must always be surrounded by parentheses. (If the function accepts no parameters, the opening and closing parentheses are typically still used, although they're not required.) The function call itself can take either of two forms. The most common form involves using the function name and its argument list on the right side of an expression, and assigning its return value to a variable on the left side of the expression. For example, the most common way to call the *CubeIt* function is as follows:

```
y = CubeIt(x)
```

This assigns the value returned by the *CubeIt* function to the variable **x**.

In some cases, though, you may not actually be concerned with a function's return value. This doesn't happen very often; usually, you call a function precisely in order to have it return some value, so ignoring its return value renders the function useless. Nevertheless, if you do want to discard a function's return value, you can use a second method of invoking the function by using the `Call` statement, as follows:

```
Call CubeIt(x)
```

Example 4-13 provides a real-world example—a program that converts inches to either millimeters or meters—that shows how functions are defined and called. Along with two event procedures, it contains a function, *sngMetric*, that has a single argument, **strInches**, which is a string containing the number of inches that the user has input into the form's text box. The function converts this value to a single-precision number, multiplies by 27.3, and, by storing it to the variable *sngMetric*, returns the result. The *cmdButton1_OnClick* and *cmdButton2_OnClick* event handlers call the function as necessary, and pass the appropriate values to it. As you can see, the result returned by the *sngMetric* function is immediately displayed in a message box.

*Example 4-13. Calling a Function and Returning a Result*

```
<HTML>
 <HEAD>
  <SCRIPT LANGUAGE="vbscript">
  <!--
     Sub cmdButton1_OnClick
      Dim strImperial
      strImperial = txtText1.Value
      Alert CStr(sngMetric(strImperial)) & " mm"
     End Sub

     Sub cmdButton2_OnClick
      Dim strImperial
      strImperial = txtText1.Value
      Alert CStr(sngMetric(strImperial)/1000) & " m"
     End Sub

     Function sngMetric(strInches)
      Dim sngInches
      sngInches = CSng(StrInches)
      sngMetric = sngInches * 27.3
     End Function
  -->
```

*Example 4-13. Calling a Function and Returning a Result (continued)*

```
    </SCRIPT>
</HEAD>

<BODY BGCOLOR="white">
    Input Inches: <INPUT TYPE="text" NAME="txtText1">
    <INPUT TYPE="button" NAME="cmdButton1" VALUE="Show Millimeters">
    <INPUT TYPE="button" NAME="cmdButton2" VALUE="Show Meters">
</BODY>
</HTML>
```

## Exiting a Routine with the Exit Statement

Ordinarily, when you call a function or a subroutine, all code between the initial `Function` or `Sub` statement and the concluding `End Function` or `End Sub` statement is executed. In some cases, though, you may not want all of a routine's code to be executed.

For example, imagine a situation in which you only want to execute a subroutine if a particular condition is met. One way of implementing this in your code is to test for the condition before calling the subroutine, as follows:

```
....some code
If condition Then
    Call MySubRoutine()
End if
....more code
```

However, if you call the routine from multiple locations in your code, and you want to apply this test to each call, you'll have to include this control structure at every place in the script in which you call the subroutine. To avoid this redundant code, it's better to call the subroutine regardless of the condition, and to place the test within the subroutine. One way of doing this is as follows:

```
Sub MySubRoutine()
    If condition then
        ......all our subroutine code
    End if
End Sub
```

This is all well and good, and quite legal. However, in any large and complex subroutine, the `End If` statement becomes visually lost, especially if there are several conditions to be met. The preferred alternatives to this are the `Exit Sub` and the `Exit Function` statements, which are used with the `Sub...End Sub` and `Function...End Function` constructs, respectively. Our conditional test at the beginning of a subroutine then appears as follows if we use the `Exit Sub` statement:

```
Sub MySubRoutine()
    If Not condition Then
```

```
        Exit Sub
    End if
    ....all our subroutine code
    End Sub
```

`Exit Sub` and `Exit Function` immediately pass execution of the program back to the calling procedure; the code after the `Exit` statement is never executed. As you can see from the code fragment above, the code is clean and clearly understandable. If the particular condition is not met, the remainder of the subroutine is not executed. Like the `Exit Do` and `Exit For` statements, any number of `Exit Sub` or `Exit Function` statements can be placed anywhere within a procedure, as the following code fragment demonstrates:

```
    Function functionname(argumentlist)

      ...some calculation or manipulation

        If condition1 Then
            functionname = result of calculation or manipulation
            Exit Function
        End If

    ....perhaps some more code

        If condition2 Then
            functionname = result of calculation or manipulation
            Exit Function
        End If

    End Function
```

You've now seen how to structure VBScript programs, how to construct subroutines that can be used by various parts of your program, and how to build functions that perform calculations and other manipulations that pass the result back to the calling part of the program. You now should be familiar with and ready to use the main building blocks of a VBScript program. So let's look at a full client-side application that uses nearly everything you've learned in the last two chapters.

# *The Web Calculator Example Application*

The sample calculator application in Example 4-14, which is shown in Figure 4-1, uses a wide range of VBScript variables, conditional operators, control structures, and constructs. If you're familiar with server-side scripting, imagine, as you go though this example, how you might go about creating this application using server-side scripts; it would be nearly impossible. In this way, this example clearly shows both the power of VBScript and the power of client-side processing.

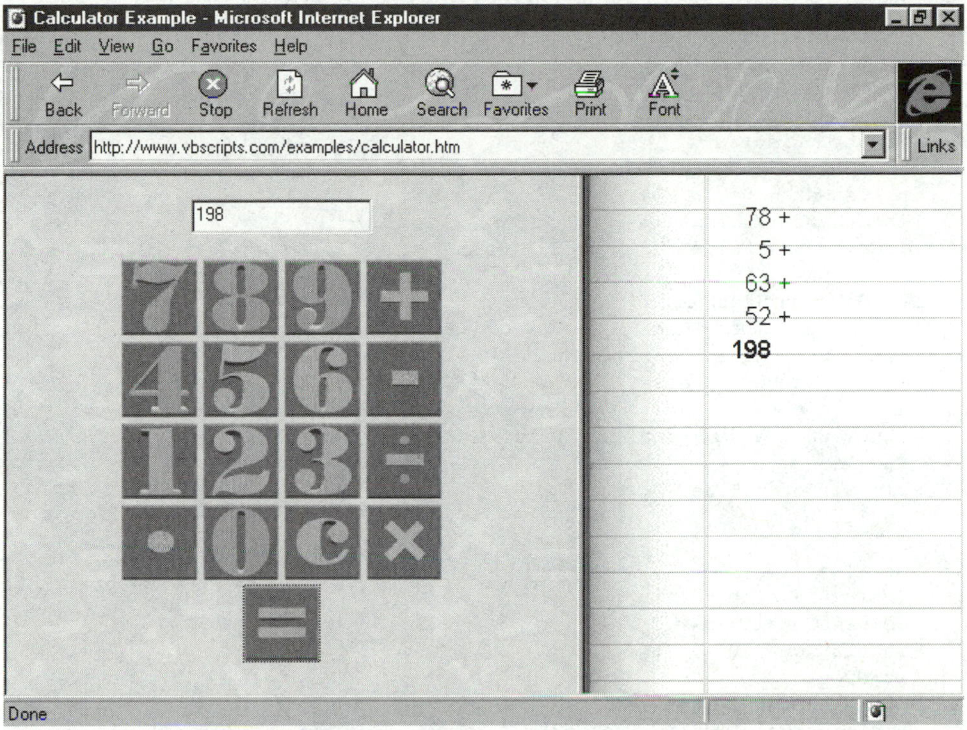

*Figure 4-1. The client-side calculator example*

The ActiveX Layout Control (which is discussed in Chapter 8, *The HTML Layout Control*) has been used to create the interface and align the controls for this example. The complete application consists of the following HTML documents:

- *CALCULATOR.HTM*, which is the frameset document
- *CALC.HTM*, the document displayed in the left frame, which contains the "guts" of the application, *CALCLAYOUT.ALX*
- *ADDLIST.HTM*, the document displayed in the right frame

The source code shown in Example 4-14 is part of *CALCLAYOUT.ALX*; to avoid putting you to sleep, it excludes the statements that define controls, which, as you'll see later, are fairly lengthy in the case of ActiveX controls. (The complete application and source code are included, however, on the accompanying CD-ROM.)

*Example 4-14. VBScript Code from CALCLAYOUT.ALX*

```
<SCRIPT LANGUAGE="vbscript">
  <!--
   OPTION EXPLICIT
   Dim dblLastTotal
```

*Example 4-14. VBScript Code from CALCLAYOUT.ALX (continued)*

```
Dim strPreviousOp
Dim blnNewNumber, blnCalcTot
Dim intListNdx
Dim strCalcList()
Dim strOpList()

intListNdx = 0
blnNewNumber = True
blnCalcTot = False

Sub DoNumber(intNumber)
 If blnNewNumber Then
  txtText1.Value = CStr(intNumber)
  blnNewNumber = False
 Else
  txtText1.Value = txtText1.Value & CStr(intNumber)
 End If
 blnCalcTot = True
End Sub

Sub Clear()
 txtText1.Value = ""
 dblLastTotal = 0
 intListNdx = 0
 strPreviousOp = ""
 blnNewNumber = True
 Redim strCalcList(intListNdx)
 Redim strOpList(intListNdx)
 Call DoAddList(False)
End Sub

Sub DoCalcList()
 intListNdx = intListNdx + 1
 Redim Preserve strCalcList(intListNdx)
 Redim Preserve strOpList(intListNdx)
   strOpList(intListNdx) = strPreviousOp
   strCalcList(intListNdx) = CDbl(txtText1.Value)
   Call DoAddList(False)
End Sub

Sub DoOperator(strOperator)

  If txtText1.Value > "" Then
   If blnCalcTot Then
     Call DoCalcList()
   If intListNdx > 1 then
    Select Case strPreviousOp
    Case "+"
     txtText1.Value = dblLastTotal + CDbl(txtText1.Value)
    Case "-"
     txtText1.Value = dblLastTotal - CDbl(txtText1.Value)
    Case "*"
```

*Example 4-14. VBScript Code from CALCLAYOUT.ALX (continued)*

```vbscript
      txtText1.Value = dblLastTotal * CDbl(txtText1.Value)
    Case "/"
      txtText1.Value = dblLastTotal / CDbl(txtText1.Value)
    End Select
  End If

 End If
    dblLastTotal = CDbl(txtText1.Value)
    strPreviousOp = strOperator
    blnNewNumber = True
 End If

 If txtText1.Value = "" And strOperator = "-" Then
   txtText1.Value = "-"
   blnNewNumber = False
 End If

End Sub

Sub DoEquals()
 Call DoOperator(strPreviousOp)
 blnCalcTot = False
 DoAddlist(True)
End Sub

Sub DoAddlist(blnShowTotal)
Dim x
 Top.ListFrame.Document.Open
  Top.ListFrame.Document.Write "<HTML>"
  Top.ListFrame.Document.Write "<BODY BACKGROUND='notebook.gif'>"
  Top.ListFrame.Document.Write "<FONT FACE='arial' SIZE=3><B>"
  Top.ListFrame.Document.Write "<CENTER><TABLE>"

   For x = 1 to intListNdx
     Top.ListFrame.Document.Write "<TD>" & strOpList(x)
     Top.ListFrame.Document.Write "<TD ALIGN=RIGHT>" & strCalcList(x) _
                                  & "<TR>"
   Next

    If blnShowTotal = True Then
      Top.ListFrame.Document.Write "<TD><TD ALIGN=RIGHT><B>"
      Top.ListFrame.Document.Write  txtText1.Value
      Top.ListFrame.Document.Write "<TR>"
    End If

  Top.ListFrame.Document.Write "</TABLE></B></BODY>"
  Top.ListFrame.Document.Write "</HTML>"
 Top.ListFrame.Document.Close

End Sub

Sub Imageplus_MouseDown(Button, Shift, X, Y)
```

*Example 4-14. VBScript Code from CALCLAYOUT.ALX (continued)*

```
        Call DoOperator("+")
    End Sub

    Sub ImageMinus_MouseDown(Button, Shift, X, Y)
        Call DoOperator("-")
    End Sub

    Sub ImageEquals_MouseDown(Button, Shift, X, Y)
        Call DoEquals()
    End Sub

    Sub ImageDot_MouseDown(Button, Shift, X, Y)
        Call DoNumber(".")
    End Sub

    Sub ImageDivide_MouseDown(Button, Shift, X, Y)
        Call DoOperator("/")
    End Sub

    Sub ImageC_MouseDown(Button, Shift, X, Y)
        Call Clear()
    End Sub

    Sub Image9_MouseDown(Button, Shift, X, Y)
        Call DoNumber(9)
    End Sub

    Sub Image8_MouseDown(Button, Shift, X, Y)
        Call DoNumber(8)
    End Sub

    Sub Image7_MouseDown(Button, Shift, X, Y)
        Call DoNumber(7)
    End Sub

    Sub Image6_MouseDown(Button, Shift, X, Y)
        Call DoNumber(6)
    End Sub

    Sub Image5_MouseDown(Button, Shift, X, Y)
        Call DoNumber(5)
    End Sub

    Sub Image4_MouseDown(Button, Shift, X, Y)
        Call DoNumber(4)
    End Sub

    Sub Image3_MouseDown(Button, Shift, X, Y)
        Call DoNumber(3)
    End Sub

    Sub Image2_MouseDown(Button, Shift, X, Y)
```

*Example 4-14. VBScript Code from CALCLAYOUT.ALX (continued)*

```
        Call DoNumber(2)
    End Sub

    Sub Image1_MouseDown(Button, Shift, X, Y)
        Call DoNumber(1)
    End Sub

    Sub Image0_MouseDown(Button, Shift, X, Y)
        Call DoNumber(0)
    End Sub

    Sub ImageTimes_MouseDown(Button, Shift, X, Y)
        Call DoOperator("*")
    End Sub
-->
</SCRIPT>
```

Let's break this listing down and take you through the main sections to see what we're doing. We'll start where the user will start, by clicking on one of the number buttons:

```
    Sub Image5_MouseDown(Button, Shift, X, Y)
        Call DoNumber(5)
    End Sub
```

Because I wanted a button that was more appealing than the usual gray 3-D button, I've used a .GIF image that's displayed by an ActiveX image control. Unfortunately, the ActiveX Image control doesn't support a *Click* event which would be activated whenever the user clicks on the image. However, the *Mouse-Down* event is actually the first part of the real *Click* event (a *Click* event is simply a *MouseDown* followed by a *MouseUp*), so we can use it to simulate a mouse click. The major difference is that, unlike the *Click* event, *MouseDown*—as its name suggests—is activated as soon as the mouse button is pressed. In normal usage, the difference is rarely noticed. You'll also notice that the value of the button is passed to the **DoNumber** subroutine. This means that we don't need a separate subroutine for each number or button, but that instead we can use a single one for all numbers. Finally, the button's number is passed as a numerical value; it's not passed as a string that's enclosed within quotation marks.

The **DoNumber** subroutine is used to show the current number in the text box above the keypad. The subroutine appears as follows:

```
    Sub DoNumber(intNumber)
        If blnNewNumber Then
            txtText1.Value = CStr(intNumber)
            blnNewNumber = False
        Else
            txtText1.Value = txtText1.Value & CStr(intNumber)
        End If
        blnCalcTot = True
    End Sub
```

Notice the use of `If...Else` to make a decision. If the number entered is a new one (that is, if the previous number has been processed), our program simply has to display the number in the text box above the keypad. However, if this number is one digit of a larger number, then we have to concatenate it to the string currently in the text box. This is accomplished by setting a flag, *blnNewNumber*, a Boolean variable that has script-level scope. When the program starts, this flag is set to True—i.e., any digit that the user selects is interpreted as the start of a new number. Whenever a new number is entered, the *blnNewNumber* flag is toggled (meaning that its value is reversed) to False, so that the next number to be entered is concatenated to this number. Finally, this subroutine sets another script-level flag, *blnCalcTot*, that is used later to indicate that the program can calculate a total.

The user can click on as many numeric buttons as needed to build a number. The first nonnumeric button the user will probably click is one of the arithmetic operator keys, +, –, /, or *. Here again, these buttons are .GIF images stored inside an image control, and I've defined a *MouseDown* event procedure for each of them. This simply calls the `DoOperator` subroutine, passing it a string containing the mathematical operator. The first few lines of the `DoOperator` subroutine are:

```
Sub DoOperator(strOperator)
   If txtText1.Value > "" Then
      If blnCalcTot Then
         Call DoCalcList()
```

The routine first determines whether or not there is a current value entered in the text box; if not, of course, the key press is meaningless. Next, it checks the *blnCalcTot* flag, which indicates whether or not it is OK to perform a calculation. If a value is present and *blnCalcTot* is True, control passes to another subroutine, `DoCalcList`, which appears as follows:

```
Sub DoCalcList()
   intListNdx = intListNdx + 1
   Redim Preserve strCalcList(intListNdx)
   Redim Preserve strOpList(intListNdx)
   strOpList(intListNdx) = strPreviousOp
   strCalcList(intListNdx) = CDbl(txtText1.Value)
   Call DoAddList(False)
End Sub
```

`DoCalcList` uses two script-level arrays. The first, *strCalcList*, contains the numbers entered by the user, while the other, *strOpList*, contains the operators that the user has selected. When the subroutine is invoked, the index counter, *intListNdx*, is incremented by one. Because this is done before any array elements are accessed, this means that the first array element that the routine actually uses is the second (i.e., the element that has an index value of 1). The two arrays are then redimensioned to the new size, and the variable *strPreviousOp* is copied into the *strOpList* array. You may have noticed that up to this point we haven't actually used *strPreviousOp*. That's because *strPreviousOp* is the operator key that the user clicked previously. On the first go round, there isn't a previous operator, so *strPreviousOp* is an empty variable. Next, the routine copies the value of the text box—which represents the number to be used in the calculation—into the *strCalcList* array. Finally, the subroutine calls a further subroutine, DoAddList, passing it a `False` value. DoAddList contains all the code to produce the calculation listing in the right-hand frame. Once control returns from DoAddList, DoCalcList is finished, and program control returns to DoOperator.

So let's go back to examining DoOperator. The next line of code,

```
If intListNdx > 1 then
```

simply checks to make sure that this is the second number in a series. *intListNdx*, as we just saw, is a global variable that keeps track of the array used to print the Calculation listing. If *intListNdx* is 1, we know that this is the first figure in the calculation, and therefore that there is no calculation to perform. If *intListNdx* is greater than one, we are looking at the second or subsequent figure in the calculation. In that case, DoOperator uses the `Select Case` control structure to direct the program to the correct arithmetical operator and to perform the simple calculation:

```
Select Case strPreviousOp
    Case "+"
        txtText1.Value = dblLastTotal + CDbl(txtText1.Value)
    Case "-"
        txtText1.Value = dblLastTotal - CDbl(txtText1.Value)
    Case "*"
        txtText1.Value = dblLastTotal * CDbl(txtText1.Value)
    Case "/"
        txtText1.Value = dblLastTotal / CDbl(txtText1.Value)
    End Select
End If
End If
```

Note that the calculation is performed on the previous total, which is stored in another global variable, *dblLastTotal*.

The next block of code is executed whether or not this is the first number of a series:

```
dblLastTotal = CDbl(txtText1.Value)
strPreviousOp = strOperator
blnNewNumber = True
End If
```

The current total displayed in the text box is stored for use with the next number. The current operator also becomes the previous operator. Finally, now that we have performed the calculation, the next digit to be entered starts a new number, so the *blnNewNumber* flag is set to True.

The last section of `DoOperator` only executes if no number appears in the text box and the user has clicked on the minus button. This places the negative symbol in the text box, since the user obviously is beginning to enter a negative number:

```
If txtText1.Value = "" And strOperator = "-" Then
  txtText1.Value = "-"
  blnNewNumber = False
End If

End Sub
```

When the user clicks the equals symbol, a separate short routine, `DoEquals`, is executed:

```
Sub DoEquals()
    Call DoOperator(strPreviousOp)
    blnCalcTot = False
    DoAddlist(True)
End Sub
```

It calls the `DoOperator` subroutine, sets the *blnCalcTot* flag to False, and calls the `DoAddList` subroutine, this time passing it a True value, which instructs `DoAddList` to print the result of the calculation.

The only other subroutine to look at is `Clear`, which is called when the user clicks the "C" or Clear button:

```
Sub Clear()
    txtText1.Value = ""
    dblLastTotal = 0
    intListNdx = 0
    strPreviousOp = ""
    blnNewNumber = True
    Redim strCalcList(intListNdx)
    Redim strOpList(intListNdx)
    Call DoAddList(False)
End Sub
```

The `Clear` subroutine simply resets and reinitializes all the flags and the two arrays. Finally, it calls the `DoAddList` subroutine so that the right-hand frame is cleared.

In looking at this code listing, you may have noticed that there is a pattern in the way that things like variables and procedures are named. This pattern is deliberate, rather than accidental; the code attempts to follow the Microsoft guidelines for coding conventions as nearly as possible.

# *VBScript Coding Conventions*

Coding conventions are recommended guidelines to follow for creating scripts that are understandable or more easily read. Most of the conventions used in VBScript have come from earlier languages, and many are general conventions used throughout programming, some dating back to the early days of C and beyond.

But why bother with coding conventions? Coding conventions serve one main purpose: consistency. Code that has been written using a consistent notation or a coding convention is easier to read, and the reader will grasp the purpose of the program elements much more quickly and be able to follow the program logic much more easily. The reader could be a colleague who takes over a project that you originally put together, or the reader could be you, trying to decipher your own code. You'd be surprised how quickly you can forget just what a particular function was supposed to do, or why you put a particular variable where you did, and what data type the variable is. You'd be even more surprised by the number of programmers who, when looking at their own code months after writing it, find it to be totally incomprehensible and unreadable. By using a consistent coding convention, you save yourself time and trouble in maybe six months' time, when you must alter or maintain part of your program.

There are three kinds of coding conventions that you can use with VBScript:

- Variable, constant, and procedure naming conventions
- Object and control naming conventions
- Commenting and formatting conventions

Their use is strictly optional; you can determine which conventions you want to follow, as well as the degree to which you wish to adhere to a particular convention.

## *Variable, Constant, and Procedure Naming Conventions*

Variables in VBScript have a naming convention that loosely follows the naming convention developed for Windows programming, known as Hungarian notation (named after the nationality of the Microsoft programmer who came up with the system). All variables start with a lowercase prefix, generally three characters long, that denotes the variable's data subtype. Abbreviations for the data subtypes supported by VBScript are shown in Table 4-1. This is followed by the variable's descriptive name, with the first letter of each word in upper case and the rest in lower case. Multiple words are joined together, and no underscores are used. If you have to use abbreviations, try to use the same abbreviation consistently throughout the program. While variable names can legally contain up to 255 characters, you'll find that variable names become very difficult to read (and even more troublesome to type) after about 30 characters.

*Table 4-1. Abbreviations for VBScript Data Subtypes*

| Data Sub Type | Prefix |
|---------------|--------|
| Boolean       | bln    |
| Byte          | byt    |
| Date (Time)   | dtm    |
| Double        | dbl    |
| Error         | err    |
| Integer       | int    |
| Long          | lng    |
| Object        | obj    |
| Single        | sng    |
| String        | str    |

For example, here are some legal variable names that use Hungarian notation:

```
blnFlag
intCounter
dblUserInput
strMessageBody
```

Function names should also follow the variable naming convention. The function's prefix should reflect the data subtype that is returned by the function. For example:

```
Function dblMetricSize(dblImperialSize)
Function strUpperCaseWord(strLowerCaseWord)
```

As we saw earlier, constants should be uppercase, and have underscores between words; this allows you to easily distinguish constants from variables. It's also useful, though, to be able to visually differentiate HTML code from VBScript constants. To do this, although it's not listed in the Microsoft coding guidelines, I recommend that you use multiple-word names for constants, to set them apart from HTML elements, which are always single words. Here are a couple of sample constant names.

```
MIN_LEFT_MARGIN
DEFAULT_COLOR
```

When naming subroutines, the first word of the name should be a verb such as Do or Create. This helps to create self-commenting code. Subroutine names are always made up of mixed-case words, with the first letter in upper case. For example:

```
Sub CreateInputArray()
Sub DoCalcList()
```

## Object and Control Naming Conventions

Objects and HTML intrinsic controls follow a naming convention similar to that for variables and functions. A three-character lowercase prefix (see Table 4-2) contains the standard abbreviation for the type of control or object, and is followed by a descriptive name in mixed case. Control names should either describe the control's function or indicate the control type along with a series name.

*Table 4-2. Abbreviations for Control and Object Types*

| Object | Prefix |
| --- | --- |
| Check Box | chk |
| Combo Box / Drop Down List | cbo |
| Command Button / Submit | cmd |
| Form | frm |
| Frame | fra |
| Image | img |
| List Box | lst |
| Radio Button | rdo |
| Text Box / Text Area | txt |

Here are some examples of control names:

```
txtText1
txtZipCode
frmOrderForm
cmdSubmitOrder
```

## Commenting and Formatting Conventions

All functions and subroutines should start with a short description of their purpose. This description can include a line or two of what are known as "maintenance headers," which detail who wrote the script and when the script was last modified. For procedures that accept arguments and for functions that accept arguments and return values, you can also give a brief description of the parameters and the return value. For example, the following comments might be included with a *dblConvertToMetric* function:

```
<SCRIPT>
<!--
'***********************************************
'* Purpose: Converts an imperial measurement *
'*          to metric                        *
'* Inputs : dblImperialMeasure: User Input   *
'* Returns: Converted measurement            *
'* Author : Paul Lomax                       *
'* Last Modified: 10/10/96                   *
'***********************************************
 Function dblConvertToMetric(dblImperialMeasure)
 ......
-->
</SCRIPT>
```

Following a consistent method of formatting code also aids the readability of a script. In fact, code should be formatted in some way even in standard HTML pages that do not include any scripts. Code formatting is achieved by indenting lines that relate to each other so that they are in the same vertical path (or column). You will find that this becomes very important when trying to debug large scripts with lots of `If..Then...Else...End If` statements. For example, the following shows how a web page that includes scripting code might be formatted:

```
<HTML>
<HEAD>
<TITLE>
Some Title
</TITLE>

<SCRIPT>
    <!--
    Sub MySampleSub()
       For x = 1 To 10
          If x > 5 Then
                do some code
                do some more code
                even more code
          End If
       Next
    End Sub
    -->
</SCRIPT>

</HEAD>

<BODY BGCOLOR="black">
    Some HTML Stuff here
</BODY>

</HTML>
```

As you can see, all lines of code that relate to each other are indented the same number of spaces (three spaces in this code fragment), which makes it easy to see at a glance where a particular block of code starts and finishes.

# Summary

In this chapter you've seen how to create dynamic scripts using conditional and looping control structures. You have also explored using subroutines and functions to subdivide your scripts into logical procedural elements. Finally, you've read about the conventions that you might use to enhance the readability of the scripts you write. Some of the more salient points in this chapter include the following:

- The `If...Then...End If` structure can be used for simple decision making and branching. `If...Then...Else` also allows for code to be executed when a given condition is not met. Both statements can be nested to handle more complex scenarios.

- Use `ElseIf` to test for a condition before executing the code within an `Else` clause.

- `And` and `Or` can be included in a conditional statement to evaluate multiple expressions.

- The `Select Case` control structure allows a series of options to be evaluated and, depending on the result, a particular portion of code executed.

- The main looping statement, `For...Next`, repeats a loop a given number of times. `Exit For` is used to terminate the loop prematurely.

- In VBScript 2.0 you can use the `For Each...Next` loop to repeat a block of code for every item in a collection of items such as an array.

- `Do While...Loop` iterates while a particular condition remains True. `Do...Loop While` repeats at least once while a particular condition remains True.

- `Do Until...Loop` repeats until a particular condition is True. `Do...Loop Until` executes at least once until a particular condition is True.

- `Exit Do` is used to exit from a `Do...Loop` prematurely.

- The `Sub...End Sub` construct is used for custom routines and event handlers. Execution of the particular routine can be halted and control passed back to the calling routine by using the `Exit Sub` statement.

- A function, defined by the `Function...End Function` construct, is used to manipulate data and return the result to the calling procedure. Execution of a function can be halted and control passed back to the calling routine using `Exit Function`.

- The variable and function naming convention uses a three-letter lowercase prefix to denote the data subtype of the variable or of the value returned by the function.

- The constant naming convention recommends the use of all capitals and underscores between words.

- The formatting convention recommends indentation and the use of comments to improve code readability.

*In this chapter:*
- *Objects and Their Properties, Methods, and Events*
- *The MSIE Scripting Object Model*
- *Summary*

5

# Controlling the Browser

So far, you've learned how to construct programs using the VBScript language. However, if VBScript consisted only of such things as the variables, looping and branching statements, and functions and subroutines that we've discussed in the previous two chapters, it wouldn't be of much use to you as a Web developer interested in creating active content. That's because these language elements, however central they are to VBScript or to any other programming language, do not provide any access or interface to the browser or the browser's environment. But in fact, much of the power of VBScript results not so much from the language when viewed in isolation, as from your ability to use the elements of the language to control the client's web browser and other application objects.

In this chapter, we'll begin our examination of how to use VBScript to control content on the client's computer by focusing on the browser, in this case Microsoft Internet Explorer 3.0. The relationship between VBScript and MSIE—that is, the interface of MSIE that allows it to understand VBScript code and that allows VBScript to access information from MSIE—is defined by two specifications. The ActiveX Scripting Technical Specification defines the OLE interfaces that a scripting engine (like VBScript or JavaScript) needs to implement in order to run successfully on a host (which is typically the browser on the client machine). But while the scripting engine is implemented as an OLE server component, so too is Microsoft Internet Explorer, part of which is an OLE automation server; that is, MSIE uses OLE to expose some of its environment and its functionality to the scripting engine. The precise description of the properties, methods, and events that MSIE makes available to VBScript (or to any scripting engine that complies with the ActiveX Scripting Technical Specification) is defined by the Microsoft Internet Explorer Scripting Object Model.

In other words, through its use of OLE, MSIE exposes some of its objects, properties and methods for other applications—like VBScript—to interact with and manipulate. If you're not familiar with Visual Basic, you may find this somewhat confusing. So before exploring each of the objects exposed through the MSIE Scripting Object Model, we'll begin by examining just what the terms "object," "property," "method," and "event" mean. If you use Visual Basic, or if you're already familiar with these terms, you can skip the first part of this chapter and start with the section "The MSIE Scripting Object Model," where we explore in detail each of the main components of the model, and see how VBScript is used to access the properties, invoke the methods, and handle the events of each object in the model.

## Objects and Their Properties, Methods, and Events

An *object* is simply a software component that has a virtual structure. It is a program or part of a program that encompasses a set of conceptual entities. An object is designed to hold a particular kind of data that defines its behavior, including how it can be acted upon and how it reacts to outside influences. It is often easiest to explain the concept of a software object by imagining it as having a physical form. For example, we can compare a person to a software object. So imagine yourself as an object. You have *properties*, which include such attributes as your height, weight, etc. If someone asks your weight, you will tell them (don't forget, software objects never think twice about answering...and they are never economical with the truth!). You have *methods*, which are the things that you do; for example, one of your methods is walking. Someone could ask you to walk somewhere, give you relevant variables about how to perform this task (i.e., directions), and you could do it successfully. And you have *events*, which are things that happen to you (or external stimuli that you receive). Someone talking to you is an event. You can respond to the event by replying to him or her; this is analogous to an *event handler*.

An object itself can also contain other objects, which have their own properties, events, and methods. To continue our example—still imagining yourself as the object—hair is a contained object (apologies to follically challenged readers) whose properties include color and length. When such "containerized" objects are accessed, they are treated as properties of the main object. Therefore, we might say that "my hair" refers to the *Hair* object belonging to the *Me* object. In programming terms, accessing the containerized object as though it were a property of the main object actually returns a reference to that object. In other words,

```
Me.Hair
```

returns a reference to the Hair object. We'll discuss referencing objects as properties in much greater depth later in the chapter.

Let's look at each of the main parts of an object in detail.

## What Are Properties?

*Properties* are attributes that characterize an object's appearance or state. Different objects have different properties, depending on their purpose. For example, an interface object that is displayed on the screen usually has a Left property that determines the number of pixels from the left side of the screen its left edge should be drawn. In contrast, an object that is never actually displayed (like a Timer control that automatically "fires" at regular intervals) does not need this property. A property is very much like a variable or a constant: each property has a value. Some object properties are directly analogous to variables: their values can be changed by the programmer or by the user while the program is executing. For example, entering text into a text box changes the value of the text box object's Text property. Other object properties are similar to constants: their values sometimes can be set during the design stage when using the ActiveX control pad, but they can never be changed during execution of the program. These are known as *read-only properties*, since, although you cannot set them, your program can still access the values of these properties.

The syntax used to access an object's properties in VBScript is known as *dot notation*. With dot notation, you use the object name followed by a dot followed by the property name. For example:

```
MyObject.Height
txtText1.Text
```

### Getting and setting property values

To retrieve the value of a property for use in your program, use the object and property names on the right side of an assignment statement, as in the following examples:

```
strMyString = txtText1.Text
sngObjectHeight = MyObject.Height
```

The first assignment statement stores the text in a text box control named *txtText1* to a variable named *strMyString*. The second stores the height of the *MyObject* object to a single precision variable named *sngObjectHeight*.

To set the value of a property, use the object/property expression on the left side of an assignment statement, as in the following examples:

```
txtText1.Text = "Hello World"
MyObject.Height = 100
```

The first assignment statement places the string "Hello World" into an ActiveX text box control named *txtText1*, while the second changes *MyObject*'s height to 100.

### Accessing objects as properties

Properties aren't just used to access the settings of an object; properties can also be used in your script to reference one object from the property of another object. For example, the *Window* object has a property named *Parent*. When you access the *Parent* property of a *Window* object, you are in fact telling the program to access another object—in this case, the *Parent* object of the current window (that is, the larger object that contains the window). So the code

```
Window.Parent.Name
```

returns the name of the current window's parent. In the same way, to access the properties of the *History* object for the current window, you use *History* as a property of the current window like this:

```
Window.History.Length
```

Taking this to its logical conclusion, you could therefore access the properties of an associated object. This code fragment returns the value of the *Length* property of the *History* object (that is, the number of items stored to the *History* object) for the current window's parent window:

```
Window.Parent.History.Length
```

Although this is a single statement, let's break it down into individual steps:

1. Starting with the *Window* object, `Window.Parent` allows us to retrieve a reference to the current window's parent.

2. The reference to the *Parent* object then allows us to retrieve a reference to the History object.

3. The reference to the History object allows us to retrieve the value of the *History* object's *Length* property.

In this way, we can say that we're *navigating the object hierarchy* from our current position (the current window) to some object in which we're interested (the *History* object and its *Length* property).

Referring to one object as a property of another object within the browser's object hierarchy is an important concept, as you'll see throughout this chapter. In fact, this part of VBScript has probably caused more confusion than the rest of the language put together, mainly because it is the least understood, and because Microsoft documentation regarding referencing various browser objects is scant, to say the least. To understand how you reference one object from another object, it is vital that you understand the concept of the browser's object hierarchy. (For more details on the hierarchy itself, read the section "The MSIE Scripting Object Model" later in this chapter.) The browser consists of many objects that are contained in a hierarchy, starting with the browser window itself, which may contain a *Frame* object or many *Frame* objects, each of which contains a *Document* object, which may contain a *Form* object, which may contain an intrinsic HTML control like a text box control object.

Now, let's say you need to access the text (which is stored in the *Value* property) that the user has typed into a text box called *text1*. The syntax you use will depend on where the script is being run in relation to the object you are accessing. The way to construct the syntax is to work your way backwards from the property to the main browser window, using the names of objects in between, delimited by dots. So let's look at how this is done, using several slightly different examples of a text box's *Value* property.

First of all, we'll assume that the text box is placed within a form on an HTML document, which is displayed without any frames. The steps from the *Value* property to the main window are:

1. Value (Property)

2. Name of Text Box object

3. Name of Form object

4. Document (object)

5. Main Window

So to return the value, you would reverse this order and translate it into the appropriate syntax:

```
x = Document.FormName.TextBoxName.Value
```

---

**TIP**      Note that, unlike other objects in the hierarchy, the Document does not have a *Name* property that can be set and used to refer to the *Document* object.

---

You could also use the `Top` keyword to denote the Main Window to complete the hierarchy, like this:

```
x = Top.Document.FormName.TextBoxName.Value
```

but unless there are multiple frames present, the main window and therefore the `Top` keyword are implicit and are not necessary.

As you can see, objects become properties of the object that is above them in the object hierarchy. For example *TextBoxName* is a reference to an object, but it can be a property of the *Form* object.

Now let's look at an example in which the form that contains the text box is in a document in a different frame than the document which contains the script. In this case, the steps are:

1. Value (property)

2. Name of Text Box object

3. Name of Form object

4. Document (object)

5. Frame (object)

6. Main Window

So to retrieve the *Value* property, you would use the syntax:

```
x = Top.FrameName.Document.FormName.TextBoxName.Value
```

---

*TIP*            Note that either the frame's name or ordinal number (i.e., Frames(0)) can be used to reference a *Frame* object.

---

Here's a brief summary:

- In all instances, to retrieve a property value, you must use both the property name (in this case, *Value*) and the object name (in this example, *text1*). The rest of the code line will depend upon the objects between the main window and the object.

- If the text box is contained within a form, you must use the name of the form, again delimited with a dot.

- The next object in the hierarchy is the document. The use of the *Document* object is optional when there are no *Frame* objects, but it must be used if the object is within a frame.

- If the document is contained within a *Frame* object, you must use either the frame's name or its ordinal number (see the section, "The Frame Object" later in this chapter for more details).

- The browser window is at the top of the object hierarchy, and the keyword *Top* is used to reference it within the code syntax. Again the *Top* keyword is implicit where there are no frames present. However, you must use the keyword *Top* if you are referencing objects within frames.

Before we move on from this subject, let's look a little more closely at referencing objects and objects' properties within frames. If you are writing code that accesses an object within another frame, you must specify either the frame's name or its ordinal number. It is not always easy to understand which frame is going to be *Frames(0)*, the first frame created, and which is *Frames(1)*, the second frame created—especially in a complex frameset document—so it is safer to use, and easier to debug or understand, code that uses the name of a frame. You can easily name a frame by supplying an HTML **NAME** attribute to its **<FRAME>** tag, like this:

```
<FRAMESET COLS=50%,50%>
    <FRAME NAME="myFirstFrame" SRC="mydoc.html">
    <FRAME NAME="mySecondFrame" SRC="anotherdoc.html">
</FRAMESET>
```

### Accessing objects in nested frames

We've seen that, to access a property of some other object, you must describe a path from the object (that is, the window or the frame) in which your script is running to the object whose property you'd like to access. But when your web page has nested frames—that is, where multiple frames are nested inside of a single frame—you may be having difficulty accessing the properties of one of the nested frames. Let's look at the following **<FRAMESET>** page to see how this might be done:

```
<FRAMESET COLS=50%,50%>
    <FRAME NAME="myFirstFrame" SRC="mydoc.html">
    <FRAMESET NAME="mySecondFrame" ROWS=50%,50%>
        <FRAME NAME="myThirdFrame" SRC="anotherdoc.html">
        <FRAME NAME="myFourthFrame" SRC="yetanotherdoc.html">
    </FRAMESET>
</FRAMESET>
```

This HTML tag divides the browser window into two vertical frames: *myFirstFrame*, which occupies the left half of the window, and *mySecondFrame*, which occupies the right half. Note that *mySecondFrame* is actually a frameset—that is, it's defined by the **<FRAMESET>** tag, and not by the **<FRAME>** tag. The *mySecondFrame* frame is in turn split in half horizontally, and is divided into *myThirdFrame* on the top and *myFourthFrame* on the bottom.

Now, let's say we need to write a script that is stored in *MYDOC.HTML* (which is located in the *myFirstFrame* frame) and must reference a text box in *YETANOTHERDOC.HTML* (which is displayed in the *myFourthFrame* frame). The line of code needed to do this is:

```
Top.myFourthFrame.Document.Form1.Text1.Value = "Hello World"
```

If you've been following the discussion so far, this code may surprise you. Because this is a nested frameset, *myFourthFrame* is actually contained by *mySecondFrame*. Therefore, you would expect to reference *mySecondFrame* first before referencing *myFourthFrame* with a statement like the following:

```
Top.MySecondFrame.MyFourthFrame.Document.Form1.Text1.Value = _
    "Hello World"      'WRONG
```

But the reason that the first statement is correct, and the second incorrect, is that the nested frameset *mySecondFrame* is defined within the overall frameset document in which it is nested, and therefore all the frames are directly contained by the main browser window. To put this another way, because *mySecondFrame* is a frameset (that is, a container whose sole purpose is to hold other frames) rather than a frame (that is, a container whose purpose is to hold documents) it is not treated as a frame within the MSIE object hierarchy.

To illustrate this point further, let's make a slight change to the way that our frames are defined. Here's a **<FRAMESET>** named *TheFrame* that once again divides the screen vertically into two frames: a left frame, named *myFirstFrame*, and a right frame, named *mySecondFrame:*

```
<FRAMESET NAME="TheFrame" COLS=50%,50%>
    <FRAME NAME="myFirstFrame" SRC="myDoc.html">
    <FRAME NAME="mySecondFrame" SRC="yourDoc.html">
</FRAMESET>
```

Note that, unlike the previous example, *mySecondFrame* is defined by the **<FRAME>** tag, rather than the **<FRAMESET>** tag. The *mySecondFrame* frame loads an HTML page named *YOURDOC.HTML*. As the HTML source code for *YOURDOC.HTML* shows, it contains a **<FRAMESET>** tag that in turn divides *mySecondFrame* into two equal frames horizontally:

```
<FRAMESET ROWS=50%,50%>
    <FRAME NAME="myThirdFrame" SRC="anotherdoc.html">
    <FRAME NAME="myFourthFrame" SRC="yetanotherdoc.html">
</FRAMESET>
```

On the top is *myThirdFrame*; on the bottom, *myFourthFrame*.

If you simply inspect the browser windows, these two methods of creating nested frames appear to be identical. However, if you try to reference the text box in *myFourthFrame* from a script in *myFirstFrame*, the code line

```
Top.myFourthFrame.Document.Form1.Text1.Value = "Hello World"
```

now produces an "Object doesn't support this property or method" error. Instead, the line of code needed to reference the text box in *YETANOTHERDOC.HTML* now follows the logical rules applied earlier in the section "Accessing objects as properties."

```
Top.mySecondFrame.myFourthFrame.Document.Form1.Text1.value _
    = "Hello world"
```

You can see from this that a frameset is not treated as a frame by VBScript. Only an object defined with the HTML `<FRAME>` tag and containing a valid document is treated as a valid frame.

---

NOTE        If a document fails to load into a particular frame, or a document is not specified for a frame, the *Frame* object is not created, and any references to that frame will result in a run-time error. A valid document must successfully load into the frame at download time for the frame object to be correctly created.

---

## What Are Events?

Events are slightly more difficult to explain. Events are "incidents" that happen to the object. To put it another way, you could imagine events as outside forces that act upon the object in some way. You can program the object to react in a certain way to an event by adding code to what is known as an *event handler*. To help make this clear, let's take the *Button* object as an example. When the user clicks the *Button* object, the *OnClick* event is triggered. As you've seen in the examples in previous chapters, you can write code in an event handler that causes your program to respond in a certain way when the button is clicked. Typically, the code for an event handler is located in a procedure whose name follows the general format:

```
object_event
```

For example, the event handler:

```
Sub cmdMyButton_OnClick()
    Alert "I've been clicked"
End Sub
```

causes the message to appear whenever *cmdMyButton*'s *OnClick* event occurs. If you do not provide any code for an event handler, the event is ignored by the object.

Again, different objects have different events, and in VBScript, you can only use those events that are predefined for a particular object. You cannot add new events to an object.

## What Are Methods?

Methods are programs that are built into a particular object to perform a particular function. You cannot amend the way the method operates, but in most cases you can pass data to the method in order to customize it for a particular purpose. Methods are therefore things that the object does, as opposed to events, which are things that are done to the object. Methods are invoked using the dot notation we saw earlier:

```
objectname.method
```

For example, one method that you've already seen in our earlier examples was the *Document* object's *Write* method. This method accepts a variable containing the string that's to be displayed in the document, as the following line of code shows:

```
Document.Write "HelloWorld"
```

Now that you understand the basic concept of objects, let's see how all this fits into MSIE by exploring the details of the MSIE Scripting Object Model.

# The MSIE Scripting Object Model

The MSIE Scripting Object Model defines a number of browser objects that can be accessed from a scripting language, along with their associated properties, events, and methods. In our discussion of objects, we noted that commonly an object is a subobject of another "container" object. The MSIE Scripting Object Model defines a hierarchy of eleven objects, as follows:

- **Window object**. This is the top-level object, and consists of the browser window itself.

- **Frame object**. Every window can contain one or more frame objects. Frames can be thought of as windows within a window.

- **History object**. Contains history list data for the current window.

- **Navigator object**. Contains information about the application in the current window.

- **Location object**. Contains information regarding the current URL.

- **Script object**. Contains scripts defined using the `<SCRIPT>` tag in the current window. The *Script* object, though, does not expose any properties, methods, or events, and therefore cannot be directly addressed through your VBScript code.

- **Document object**. Refers to the document in the current window. Each window or frame object can contain only one document.

- **Link object**. An array of hyperlinks in the particular document.

- **Anchor**. An array of anchors in the particular document.

- **Form**. An array of forms in the particular document.

- **Element**. An array of HTML form elements—that is, of HTML intrinsic controls or HTML form objects—in the particular document or form.

If you've spent more than ten minutes using a browser, most of the items in this list are almost certainly familiar to you, although you've probably never thought of them as objects before. You usually interact with these objects by using the browser interface and the mouse, but now you can use a script to programmatically control the browser and its objects.

We've mentioned that the MSIE Scripting Object Model specifies an object and a number of subobjects. The diagram in Figure 5-1 describes the MSIE Active Scripting Object hierarchy.

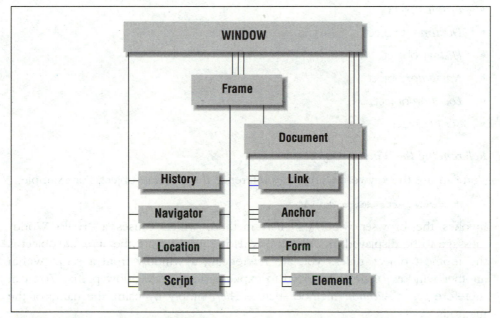

*Figure 5-1. The MSIE Scripting Object model*

As you can see from Figure 5-1, the *Window* object is the ultimate parent of all the objects in the model. The *Window* object always contains the *History, Navigator, Location,* and *Document* objects. These four objects are singular, in that a *Window* object can contain only one of each. The *Window* object can also contain one or more *Script* objects, which exist if you have used the HTML `<SCRIPT>` tag to define a script. The *Window* object also contains one or more *Frame* objects. As you can see from the diagram, the *Frame* object can contain all the same types of objects as the *Window* object. The *Document* object can also contain one or more *Link, Anchor, Form,* or *Element* objects. The *Element* objects can be owned either by a *Form* object or by the *Document* object itself if the *Element* object is placed outside a *Form* object.

Let's now look at each object in detail to find out how to reference the object from within your script. We will also consider the properties, methods, and events that each type of object makes available to your script.

## The Window Object

The *Window* object is the top of the object hierarchy, and when you reference the *Window* object you are actually interacting directly with the Browser window itself. The *Window* object itself contains the following six objects:

- *Frame* object
- *Document* object
- *History* object
- *Navigator* object
- *Location* object
- *Script* object

### Referencing the Window Object

You can use the keyword `Window` to reference the *Window* object. For example,

```
Window.Alert "Hello World"
```

invokes the browser window's *Alert* method, which causes a "Hello World" message to be displayed in a dialog box. However, because the *Window* object is the topmost object, unless you are referencing a window from a script within another window, there is no need to explicitly use the Window prefix. You can therefore call a *Window* method such as *Alert* simply by using the name of the method:

```
Alert "Hello World"
```

An alternative way of referencing the topmost *Window* object is by using the *Top* keyword. The topmost window (which is the window referenced by *Top*) is the window that contains one or more *Frame* objects, each of which is also treated as though it were a window itself. The syntax to access the document in the topmost window is

```
Top.Document
```

Again, if you are only dealing with one window, the *Top* property refers back to the current window anyway, so its use is redundant. *Top* should therefore only be used when you have multiple windows or frames open.

If you have created a frame or a window and assigned it a name, you can access the frame or window's properties and methods by name, as in

```
MyWindow.Document.txtText1.Value = "Hello World"
```

which places the string "Hello World" in the text box named *txtText1* that is displayed by the document in the window named *MyWindow*.

As we've seen, if the main browser window contains one or more frames defined with the HTML <FRAME> tag, these are treated as windows within a window, and you can also access them by their index number. For example, let's say you have created an HTML page containing two frames in the browser window. The window is the *Top* object and will contain the HTML document with the <FRAMESET> definition. The two frames each containing their own HTML documents can be accessed as Frames(0) and Frames(1), as in

```
Top.Frames(1).Document....
```

This is because the *Window* object contains an array of frames; each element of the array is a Frame object. Arrays of objects and controls such as this are often referred to as *collections*. The *Window* object only has one collection, the *Frame* collection.

### Window object properties

The following properties return a *Window* object, and are *read-only*. That is, you can only access the property; you cannot set it.

- **Parent**. Returns the *Window* object of the current window's parent. If the current window is the topmost window in the current object hierarchy, the parent property returns the current *Window* object. In other words, `Window.Parent` returns itself if the window does not have a parent.

- **Self**. Returns the current *Window* object.

- **Top**. Returns the topmost *Window* object. If the current window is the topmost window in the current object hierarchy, it returns the current *Window* object.

Figure 5-2 shows how *Parent*, *Self*, and *Top* are evaluated from a script running in the current window.

The following properties return other objects associated with the *Window* object, and are read-only. As with the properties that return *Window* objects, you can only access these properties; you cannot set them.

- **Frames**. The Frames property returns an array—or, more precisely, a collection object—of frames contained by the current window. Individual *Frame* objects have the same set of properties as a *Window* object; you can retrieve

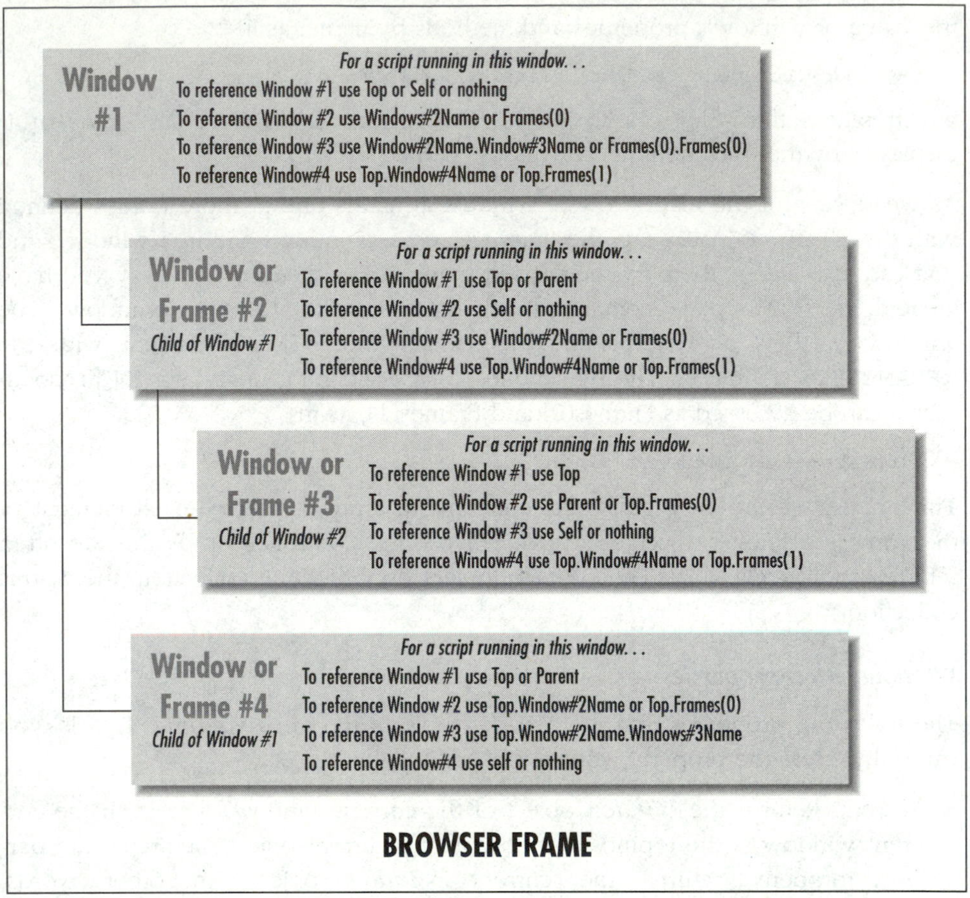

*Figure 5-2. The evaluation of Parent, Self, and Top*

them by accessing a particular frame within the frames collection. Unless you have given the frame a name in the HTML <FRAME> definition, you must refer to a frame by its ordinal position within the frames collection; so, for example:

```
Top.Frames(0).Location.Href
```

You can find out how many frames there are within the current window by using the *Count* property of the *Frames* collection; this is necessary if you need to iterate through the frames. Its syntax is:

```
Top.Frames.Count
```

Remember though that, like all collections, the *Frames* collection starts with *Frame(0)*, but the *Count* property returns the total number of frames. This means that an index whose value is equal to *Count* –1 (and not equal to

*Count*) accesses the last element of the *Frames* collection. So to iterate all the frames in the current window, you would use the code fragment:

```
For i = 0 to Top.Frames.Count - 1
    x = Top.Frames(i).Name
Next
```

The *Count* property of the *Frames* collection returns 0 if there are no frames present in the current window. *Frames* are added to the *Frames* collection in the order in which they are defined in the HTML `<FRAMESET>` document. The first frame defined in the document will be in position 0 of the collection, the second in position 1, and so on.

---

## UBound and the Count Property

You might expect that you can determine the number of *Frame* objects in the *Frames* collection by using the *UBound* function, which returns the upper bound of an array. *UBound*, however, does not work with collections. Instead, the number of items in a collection can be determined by retrieving the value of that collection's *Count* property. This is true of Visual Basic as well: *UBound* does not work with collections, and instead the collection object's *Count* property indicates the number of objects in the collection. With MSIE 3.02 you can also use the collection object's *Length* property; see the sidebar "A Collection's Count Property" in Chapter 6, *The Element Object and HTML Intrinsic Controls*.

---

If you're developing web applications using VBScript 2.0, you can also use the `For...Each` construct to iterate the frames contained in the *Frame* collection. In that case, you can replace the earlier `For...Next` construct with the following code fragment:

```
For Each objFrame in Top.Frames
    x = objFrame.Name
Next
```

See the discussion in "The Frame Object" later in this chapter for a more detailed discussion of referencing frames.

- **Location**. Returns the *Location* object for the current window. Use in conjunction with the properties of the *Location* object.

- **History**. Returns the *History* object for the current window. Use in conjunction with the properties of the *History* object.

- **Navigator**. Returns the *Navigator* object for the current window. Use in conjunction with the properties of the *Navigator* object.

- **Document**. Returns the *Document* object for the current window. Use in conjunction with the properties of the *Document* object.

- **Status**. The *Status* property is used to set and return the text message in the status bar of the browser. For example, in Example 5-1, the message in the browser's status bar changes to "This takes you to any link" whenever the user moves the mouse over the "Any Link" hypertext. To clear the status bar after the user moves the mouse away from the hyperlink, a timeout is set at 4 seconds—see the explanation of the *SetTimeout* and *ClearTimeout* methods later in this section for more details.

*Example 5-1. The Status Property*

```
<HTML>
 <HEAD>
  <SCRIPT LANGUAGE="vbscript">
   Sub AnyLink_MouseMove(s,b,x,y)
       Top.Status = "This takes you to any link"
       hTimeOut = SetTimeout("Top.Status=''",4000)
   End Sub
  </SCRIPT>
 </HEAD>

 <BODY BGCOLOR="white">
   <A HREF="" ID="AnyLink">Any Link</A>
 </BODY>
</HTML>
```

- **DefaultStatus**. The default status property should allow you to set a message that appears in the status bar of the browser when there is no system or predefined message to be displayed. However, the property acts exactly like the *Status* property.

- **Name**. This property allows you to retrieve or to set the name of the specified window. For example, both of the following assignment statements copy the name of the current window into the variable *strWindowName*:

```
strWindowName = Name
strWindowName = Window.Name
```

To access the name of the first frame within the topmost window's frame collection, you would use an assignment statement like the following:

```
strFrameName = Top.Frames(0).Name
```

### Window object methods

- **Alert**. Displays a message box with an alert (exclamation) icon and an OK button. Its syntax is

```
Alert string
```

### Setting the Name Property in a Script

The *Name* property of a window can be set using HTML only by providing a `NAME` attribute to the `<FRAME>` tag or a `TARGET` attribute to the `<A>` tag. That means that the *Name* property of the topmost window, or of any window frame whose name was not defined using the `NAME` attribute, is a null string unless a name was explicitly assigned in a script. Since the only real value of the *Name* property is to identify the window or frame in a script, it's usually not a good idea to *rename* windows or frames, since this might "break" an otherwise working script.

The method takes one argument, which is a string containing the text to be displayed in the message box. For instance, Example 5-2 uses the *Alert* method to display a message box whenever the user clicks on the *cmdShowAlert* button.

It's particularly important that the argument you supply when calling the method be a string. To see the importance of this, take a look at Example 5-3, which includes a check box and two buttons. The check box's *Checked* property is True when the box is checked and False when it is not checked; these are Boolean values. An event handler is attached to each of the buttons; one is incorrect, while the other is not. The faulty one passes the value of the check box's *Checked* property directly to the *Alert* method. But since this value is a Boolean rather than a string, the *Alert* method is unable to interpret it correctly, and always displays "false" in the message box, whether or not the button is checked. In contrast, the Right button always shows the correct value, since the event handler always converts the Boolean variable to a string before passing it to the *Alert* method. Again, this serves to illustrate the drawbacks of a loosely typed language. In other programming languages, the attempt to pass a Boolean value as a string would have generated a run-time error. So remember to be ever vigilant for type mismatches that may go undetected, only showing themselves as unpredictable results.

*Example 5-2. Using the Alert Method*

```
<HTML>
 <HEAD>
  <SCRIPT LANGUAGE="vbscript">
   Sub cmdShowAlert_OnClick
       Alert "This is an Alert"
   End Sub
  </SCRIPT>
 </HEAD>
```

*Example 5-2. Using the Alert Method (continued)*

```
<BODY BGCOLOR="white">
  <INPUT TYPE="button" NAME="cmdShowAlert" VALUE="Show Alert">
</BODY>
</HTML>
```

*Example 5-3. Handling Non-string Values with Alert*

```
<HTML>
 <HEAD>
  <SCRIPT LANGUAGE="vbscript">
   Sub cmdFaultyTest_OnClick
       Alert Document.frmMyForm.chkMyCheck.Checked '****WRONG****
   End Sub

   Sub cmdGoodTest_OnClick
       Alert CStr(Document.frmMyForm.chkMyCheck.Checked)
   End Sub
  </SCRIPT>
 </HEAD>

 <BODY BGCOLOR="white">
  <FORM NAME="frmMyForm">
   Click Me First
   <INPUT TYPE="checkbox" NAME="chkMyCheck"><P>
   <INPUT TYPE="button" NAME="cmdFaultyTest" VALUE="WRONG">
   <INPUT TYPE="button" NAME="cmdGoodTest" VALUE="RIGHT">
 </BODY>
</HTML>
```

- **Confirm**. The *Confirm* method displays a message box containing a message
  and two buttons, *OK* and *Cancel*. If the user clicks OK, the method returns a
  value of True; if the user clicks Cancel, the method returns False. Its syntax is

  ```
  bool = Confirm string
  ```

  The method takes a single argument, which is a string containing the message
  to be displayed. Example 5-4 illustrates the use of the *Confirm* method to confirm user input. When the user clicks on the Confirm button, the *Confirm*
  method is used to display a message box asking whether he or she is sure;
  the user can then confirm the choice by selecting the OK button, and can cancel it by selecting the Cancel button.

  Notice that, in Example 5-4, we've stored the method's return value to a variable, *blnResponse*, which is then evaluated in the `If...Then...Else`
  construct that begins on the following line. In Example 5-5, on the other
  hand, we've eliminated the need for this variable by directly evaluating the
  method's return value in the `If...Then...Else` construct.

*Example 5-4. Using the Confirm Method*

```
<HTML>
 <HEAD>
```

*Example 5-4. Using the Confirm Method (continued)*

```vbscript
<SCRIPT LANGUAGE="vbscript">
  Sub cmdConfirmIt_OnClick
      Dim blnResponse

      blnResponse = Confirm("Are You Sure?")

      If blnResponse = True then
          Alert "You were sure!"
      Else
          Alert "You pressed Cancel."
      End if

  End Sub
  </SCRIPT>
</HEAD>


<BODY BGCOLOR="white">
  <INPUT TYPE="button" NAME="cmdConfirmIt" VALUE="Confirm">
</BODY>
</HTML>
```

*Example 5-5. Directly Handling a Method's Return Value*

```vbscript
<HTML>
 <HEAD>
  <SCRIPT LANGUAGE="vbscript">
   Sub cmdConfirmIt_OnClick

      If Confirm("Are You Sure?") = True then
          Alert "You were sure!"
      Else
          Alert "You pressed Cancel."
      End if

   End Sub
  </SCRIPT>
 </HEAD>


<BODY BGCOLOR="white">
  <INPUT TYPE="button" NAME="cmdConfirmIt" VALUE="Confirm">
</BODY>
</HTML>
```

- **Prompt**. The *Prompt* method solicits input from the user by opening a message box that contains a message and a text box. Its syntax is:

  ```
  string = Prompt(messagestring, defaultinput)
  ```

  where ***messagestring*** is the message that is to appear in the dialog, and ***defaultinput*** is the string that appears in the text box when the dialog first opens. ***string***, the value returned by the method, is the text string input by the user; if the user clicks Cancel, or if the user clicks OK without entering any text, a zero-length string is returned. Example 5-6 illustrates the *Prompt* method; when the user clicks on the User Input button, a dialog opens that prompts the user to enter his or her name.

*Example 5-6. The Prompt Method*

```
<HTML>
 <HEAD>
  <SCRIPT LANGUAGE="vbscript">
   Sub cmdPromptIt_OnClick
       Dim strInput

       strInput = Prompt("Please enter your name","")

       Alert "Hello " & strInput

   End Sub
  </SCRIPT>
 </HEAD>


<BODY BGCOLOR="white">
   <INPUT TYPE="button" NAME="cmdPromptIt" VALUE="User Input">
 </BODY>
</HTML>
```

- **Open**. The *Open* method creates a new browser window and gives you control over its appearance. Its syntax is:

  ```
  x = window.open (url, newwindowname, "optionslist")
  ```

  The *url* parameter is a string containing the relative or absolute path name of the file to open within the new window. *newwindowname* indicates the name of the window that is to display the document indicated by *url*. It performs the same function as the `target` attribute of the `<a>` tag in HTML. If *newwindowname* already exists, the window is reused; that is, the document whose URL is *url* will be displayed in the existing window. If *newwindowname* does not exist, it will be opened.

  *optionslist* is a comma-separated list of configuration options for the new window. All but two options take the form *option=bool*, where *option* is a string literal that indicates the particular option, and *bool* is either "yes," "no," or a variable that evaluates to True or False. The remaining two options, *width* and *height*, take an integer value indicating a number of pixels. The list as a whole must be enclosed in quotation marks. Individual options are shown in Table 5-1. All of *optionslist* must appear on a single line, or a run-time error ("Unterminated string constant") results; the line continuation character, _, cannot appear within *optionslist*.

*Table 5-1. The Optionslist Parameter of the Open Method*

| Option | Description | Default Value |
|---|---|---|
| directories = yes \| no | Not implemented in MSIE 3.0 | |
| height = *integer* | Sets the window height to *integer* pixels | system-defined |
| location = yes \| no | Not implemented in MSIE 3.0 | |
| menubar = yes \| no | Displays or hides the menu bar | no |
| resizable = yes \| no | Not implemented in MSIE 3.0 | |
| scrollbars = yes \| no | Not implemented in MSIE 3.0 | |
| status = yes \|no | Displays or hides the status bar | no |
| toolbar = yes \| no | Displays or hides the toolbar | no |
| width = *integer* | Sets the window width to *integer* pixels | system-defined |

Example 5-7 illustrates the use of the *Open* method. When the user clicks on the Open New Window button, MSIE opens a new browser window that displays the document at *www.vbscripts.com/examples/opened.htm*. The browser window is named *myNewWindow*, is 200 pixels wide by 200 pixels high, and includes a status bar and a menu bar.

*Example 5-7. Using the Window.Open Method*

```
<HTML>
 <HEAD>
  <SCRIPT LANGUAGE="vbscript">
   Sub cmdOpenIt_OnClick
    dim strOptions

    strOptions = "toolbar=No, location=No, directories=Yes, "
    strOptions = strOptions & "status=Yes, menubar=Yes, scrollbars=No, "
    strOptions = strOptions & "resizable=Yes, width=200, height=200"
    Window.Open "http://www.vbscripts.com/examples opened.htm", _
             "myNewWindow", strOptions
   End Sub
  </SCRIPT>
 </HEAD>

<BODY BGCOLOR="white">
  <INPUT TYPE="button" NAME="cmdOpenIt" VALUE="Open New Window">
 </BODY>
</HTML>
```

- **Close**. The *Close* method closes a window. Although the documentation suggests that any window can be closed, actually the method can only be used to close the window containing the code that calls the *Window.Close* method;

it is not possible to close another window. You must therefore provide a button and code within the window to be closed, similar to the following:

```
Sub cmdClose_OnClick
    Window.Close
End Sub
```

- **SetTimeout** and **ClearTimeout**. The *SetTimeout* method sets a timer that can be used to call a procedure after a certain number of milliseconds have elapsed. Its syntax is:

```
ID = [window].setTimeout expression, mSecs
```

where **expression** indicates the function to be called, and **mSecs** is the number of milliseconds after which **expression** should be called. The method returns the ID of the timer object; this can then be used as an argument to the *ClearTimeout* method to switch the timer off. The syntax of the *ClearTimeout* method is:

```
clearTimeout ID
```

---

*NOTE*          Do not confuse this method with the Timer control used in VB. The Timer control repeatedly executes a routine at a specified interval, whereas *SetTimeout* defines a countdown to a one-time call to a particular routine.

---

Example 5-8 illustrates the use of both the *SetTimeout* and *ClearTimeout* methods. As the page loads, a call is made to the S*etTimeOut* method, specifying that the *noclick* subroutine is to be executed after 3,000 milliseconds (3 seconds) have elapsed. If the user clicks the button prior to the end of the time-out period, the call to the time-out procedure, *noclick*, is canceled. Otherwise, the subroutine, which displays an alert box reminding the user to click the button, is executed.

*Example 5-8. The SetTimeOut and ClearTimeOut Methods*

```
<HTML>
<HEAD>
   <SCRIPT LANGUAGE="vbscript">
      OPTION EXPLICIT

      Dim timerID
      timerID = SetTimeout("noclick()", 3000)

      Sub cmdButton_OnClick

          ClearTimeOut timerID
          Alert "The button was clicked!"
      End Sub
```

*Example 5-8. The SetTimeOut and ClearTimeOut Methods (continued)*

```
    Sub noClick()
        Alert "Please click the button!"
    End Sub

  </SCRIPT>
</HEAD>

<BODY BGCOLOR="white">
  <INPUT TYPE="button" NAME="cmdButton" VALUE="Click Me!">
</BODY>
</HTML>
```

---

**WARNING**   Interestingly, the *SetTimeOut* method runs within the JScript engine. Because of this, you must include empty parentheses after the subroutine name, when designating the routine to be called from the *SetTimeout* method. For example:

```
    timerID = SetTimeout("noclick()", 3000)
```

---

The *SetTimeout* method can also be used to call other *Window* object methods directly. For example:

```
timerID = setTimeOut("Alert('This is a message')", 3000)
```

This is ideal for clearing the status bar after you have shown a message in the status bar; otherwise, your message remains in the status bar until another message is shown, creating confusion for the user. For example:

```
timerID = setTimeOut("Status('')",3000)
```

- **Navigate**. Loads the file specified by a URL into the window. Its syntax is:

```
[window].Navigate url
```

where *url* is the URL of the document to be displayed in the browser window.

Ordinarily, using simple HTML, you must always "hardcode" the name of the document that is to be loaded when the user selects a hyperlink. In contrast, by invoking the *Navigate* method, it is possible to dynamically load web pages whose names are not known in advance. By using the *Navigate* method, it's also possible to make an event—like the click of a button—context-sensitive, so that it causes a particular document to be loaded in some cases, while a different document is loaded in other cases.

A rudimentary example, which is impossible to do using a single HTML hyperlink, appears in Example 5-9. Example 5-9 actually consists of two HTML documents: *NAVMAIN.HTM*, which defines the two frames in a browser window, and *NAVIGATE.HTM*, which displays a command button in the left-hand frame and is responsible for loading one of two documents, *NAV1.HTM* or *NAV2.HTM*, in the right-hand frame. You can easily modify this code to load an unlimited number of documents from a single button.

*Example 5-9. The Navigate Method*

```
<HTML>
 <FRAMESET COLS=50%,50%>
  <FRAME NAME="LeftFrame" SRC="navigate.htm">
  <FRAME NAME="RightFrame" SRC="nav1.htm">
 </FRAMESET>
</HTML>
navmain.htm
<HTML>
 <HEAD>
  <SCRIPT LANGUAGE="vbscript">
   Dim intCounter
   intCounter=1

   Sub cmdNav1_OnClick
       intCounter = intCounter + 1
       If intCounter > 2 Then
           intCounter = 1
       End If

       strNewDocName = "Nav" & CStr(intCounter) & ".htm"

       Top.RightFrame.Navigate strNewDocName

   End Sub

  </SCRIPT>
 </HEAD>

 <BODY BGCOLOR="white">
   <INPUT TYPE="button" NAME="cmdNav1" VALUE="Load New Page">
 </BODY>
</HTML>
navigate.htm
```

### Window object events

The *Window* object supports two events, *OnLoad* and *OnUnload*.

*   OnLoad. The *OnLoad* event, as you probably guessed, is triggered when a document is loaded into a frame or window. VBScript provides two methods for defining an event handler for the *OnLoad* event; the first is the "official," documented method, and the second is undocumented. The documented method for defining the *OnLoad* event handler is to indicate the name of a subroutine in the ONLOAD attribute of the HTML document's <BODY> tag. For

## VBScript's OnLoad Event and Visual Basic's Form_Load Event

If you're experienced with Visual Basic, you probably recognize that the *On-Load* event corresponds exactly to the Visual Basic *Form_Load* event, despite the unusual HTML syntax that's used to define a window's *OnLoad* event handler. However, if you prefer, you can instead define a *Window_OnLoad* event procedure that the browser executes whenever the document is loaded in the browser window.

instance, the following <BODY> tag indicates that a subroutine named *Init-Window* should be executed when the page is loaded in the browser window:

```
<BODY Language="vbscript" OnLoad="InitWindow">
```

Note the use of the **LANGUAGE** attribute as well to indicate the scripting language in which the *OnLoad* event handler is written. This is identical to the way in which an *OnLoad* event handler is defined using JavaScript. Example 5-10 illustrates the use of the **ONLOAD** attribute to define a handler for the *OnLoad* event. The **ONLOAD** attribute defines a subroutine, *myOnloadStuff*, that is to execute when the page is loaded into the browser. It causes an alert box to display "Welcome to my page".

*Example 5-10. Using the ONLOAD Attribute to Define an OnLoad Event Handler*

```
<HTML>
 <HEAD>
  <SCRIPT LANGUAGE="vbscript">
   Sub myOnLoadStuff
       Alert "Welcome to my page"
   End Sub
  </SCRIPT>
 </HEAD>

 <BODY BGCOLOR="white" Language="vbscript" OnLoad="myOnloadStuff">
   <CENTER>
    <H1>HELLO</H1>
   </CENTER>
 </BODY>
</HTML>
```

If you're accustomed to storing event handlers in event procedures (that is, in subroutines whose names are formed by separating the name of the object and the event with an underscore, as in *cmdMyButton_OnClick*), this use of the **ONLOAD** attribute may be confusing and difficult to remember. In that case, you may prefer to use a standard event procedure to contain the code for your OnLoad event handler. Although it isn't documented, the VBScript engine automatically executes any code stored to an event procedure named *Window_OnLoad* when a document is loaded into a browser window. Example 5-11 is a rewritten version of the HTML document in Example 5-10 that attaches its initialization code directly to the *Window_OnLoad* event procedure.

*Example 5-11. Defining a Window_OnUnload Event Procedure*

```
<HTML>
<HEAD>
 <SCRIPT LANGUAGE="vbscript">
  Sub Window_OnLoad
      Alert "Welcome to my page"
  End Sub
 </SCRIPT>
</HEAD>

<BODY BGCOLOR="white">
  <CENTER>
   <H1>HELLO</H1>
  </CENTER>
</BODY>
</HTML>
```

There is yet a third way of defining the startup code that is to execute when an HTML document is loaded into a browser window. You can simply create script-level code—code that is placed within the `<SCRIPT>` and `</SCRIPT>` tags, but outside of any procedure. As Example 5-12 shows, this script is also executed as the documented loads.

*Example 5-12. Using Script-Level Code to Emulate an OnLoad Event Handler*

```
<HTML>
 <HEAD>
  <SCRIPT LANGUAGE="vbscript">
   Document.Write "<CENTER><H1>HELLO WORLD</H1>"
  </SCRIPT>
 </HEAD>

<BODY BGCOLOR="white">

 </BODY>
</HTML>
```

- **OnUnload**. The *OnUnload* event is triggered when the document in the current window is unloaded, whether under program control or as a result of user action. The event handler for the *OnUnload* event can be defined in much the same way as the event handler for the *Unload* event. The official, documented method involves using the `ONUNLOAD` attribute of the HTML `<BODY>` tag to define a subroutine that executes when the *OnUnload* event is fired. This is illustrated in Example 5-13. To test it, simply load the document and then open any other web page, or return to your previous web page by clicking the Back button; when you move away from the current page, a dialog is displayed. Although it's not documented, you can also define an *OnUnload* event procedure by including a subroutine named *Window_OnUnload*. The VBScript engine automatically executes this code when the document is unloaded and the *OnUnload* event is fired. Example 5-14 is a rewritten version of Example 5-13 that defines a *Window_OnUnload* event procedure.

*Example 5-13. Using the ONUNLOAD Attribute to Define an OnUnload Event Handler*

```
<HTML>
 <HEAD>
  <SCRIPT LANGUAGE="vbscript">
  Sub DoUnloadStuff()
       Alert "Good Bye Come Again Soon!!"
  End Sub
  </SCRIPT>
 </HEAD>

 <BODY BGCOLOR="white" LANGUAGE="vbscript" OnUnload="DoUnloadStuff">
  <H1>Hello</H1>
 </BODY>
</HTML>
```

*Example 5-14. Defining a Window_OnUnload event procedure*

```
<HTML>
 <HEAD>
  <SCRIPT LANGUAGE="vbscript">
  Sub Window_OnUnload
       Alert "Good Bye, Come Again Soon!!"
  End Sub
  </SCRIPT>
 </HEAD>

 <BODY BGCOLOR="white" >
  <H1>Hello</H1>
 </BODY>
</HTML>
```

## The Frame Object

A *Frame* object is actually a particular kind of *Window* object, so you can use all the same objects, properties, events, and methods that apply to a *Window* object, except that you must replace the object references to the *Window* object with references to the *Frame* object. However, care must be taken when referencing a particular frame from another frame. Much confusion has arisen as to how to reference a particular frame either to write a document within it or to navigate it to another URL.

## VBScript's OnUnload Event and Visual Basic's Form_Unload Event

The VBScript *OnUnload* event corresponds very closely to Visual Basic's *Form_Unload* event. There are, however, two major differences. The first is the rather peculiar syntax (using the ONUNLOAD attribute of the <BODY> tag) to define an *OnUnload* event handler, although you also can also use the undocumented *Window_OnUnload* event procedure to hold your event handler. The second is that, when the Visual Basic *Unload* event is fired, the event procedure is passed an integer variable by reference; this allows the pending unloading of the form to be canceled if its value is changed to zero. In contrast, the browser does not pass any parameters to the *OnUnload* event procedure, and the scheduled unloading of the document cannot be canceled.

Let's first look at a simple frames example. The HTML page in Example 5-15 simply contains a <FRAMESET> tag that specifies two frames that split the window into two equal halves vertically. The two frames are named *LeftFrame* and *RightFrame*, and contain the two HTML documents *FRAMEL.HTM* and *FRAMETMP.HTM*, respectively.

*Example 5-15. A Simple Frames Example*

```
<HTML>
<FRAMESET COLS=50%,50%>
 <FRAME NAME="LeftFrame" SRC="FrameL.htm">
 <FRAME NAME="RightFrame" SRC="FrameTmp.htm">
</FRAMESET>
</HTML>
```

The VBScript code that controls the two frames is held within *FRAMEL.HTM*, the HTML document displayed in the browser's left-hand frame, *LeftFrame*. Its source code is shown in Example 5-16. The right-hand frame initially displays a document, *FRAMETMP.HTM*, which is shown in Example 5-17. However, when the user clicks on the Load New URL button in the left frame, the *OnClick* event procedure in *FRAMEL.HTM* is supposed to load *FRAMER.HTM*, which is shown in Example 5-18.

*Example 5-16. The Source Code for FRAMEL.HTM*

```
<HTML>
 <HEAD>
  <TITLE>Left hand frame</TITLE>
 </HEAD>

<BODY BGCOLOR="white">
  <SCRIPT LANGUAGE="vbscript">
```

*Example 5-16. The Source Code for FRAMEL.HTM (continued)*

```
    Sub cmdLoadURL_OnClick
        RightFrame.Location.Href = "framer.htm"    ' Generates an error
    End Sub
</SCRIPT>

<H1>FRAMEL</H1>
This is the left hand frame.
<FORM>
    <INPUT TYPE=button NAME=cmdLoadURL VALUE="Load New URL">
</FORM>
</BODY>
</HTML>
```

*Example 5-17. The HTML Code for FRAMETMP.HTM*

```
<HTML>
 <HEAD>
  <TITLE>Temporary Document</TITLE>
 </HEAD>

 <BODY BGCOLOR="white">
   <H1>FrameR</H1>
   This is a temporary document in the right hand frame.
 </BODY>
</HTML>
```

*Example 5-18. The HTML Code for FRAMER.HTM*

```
<HTML>
 <HEAD>
  <TITLE>Right hand frame</TITLE>
 </HEAD>

 <BODY BGCOLOR="white">
   <H1>FRAMER</H1>
   This is the new right hand frame.
 </BODY>
</HTML>
```

If you click on the button, though, VBScript generates a run-time error instead of loading the new Web page. The culprit is the VBScript line

```
    RightFrame.Location.Href = "framer.htm"
```

The problem here is that, since the script is executing in *LeftFrame*, which is therefore the current frame, this statement necessarily assumes that *RightFrame* is an object contained within *LeftFrame*. Since this is not the case, VBScript generates an "Object required" error message, because it cannot identify *RightFrame* as a *Frame* object.

To correct this problem, it is necessary to reference *RightFrame* by describing the path from the current frame to the *RightFrame*, the frame on the right-hand side of the browser window. This requires that we move upward one step in our object hierarchy before coming back down to reference *RightFrame*. This can be done with the following statement:

```
Top.RightFrame.Location.Href = "framer.htm"
```

Let's see how this works. Since *LeftFrame* is the current frame, the *Top* property ascends the object hierarchy by returning a reference to the *Window* object that contains *LeftFrame* (as well as all other frames in the current browser instance). *Top.RightFrame* then descends the object hierarchy by identifying the other frame in the current browser instance. Finally, *Location.Href* sets the *Href* property of the *RightFrame Frame* object's *Location* object, which causes the browser to load the document found at that URL.

Since *RightFrame* and *LeftFrame* share the same *Parent* object, it is also possible to ascend and descend the object hierarchy by using the *Parent* property instead of the *Top* property, as in the following statement:

```
Parent.RightFrame.Location.Href = "framer.htm"
```

---

*WARNING*    When referencing an object in another frame, you must start the reference at the "top" of the hierarchy. You cannot, for example, start the reference with *LeftFrame*, move up to the *Top* object, and then move down to *RightFrame*, like this:

```
LeftFrame.Top.RightFrame.Location.HRef = "ThisIsWrong.html"
```

You must start your reference with the topmost *Window* object and work your way down, as follows:

```
Top.RightFrame.Location.Href = "ThisIsCorrect.html"
```

---

This is just a simple web page that uses frames. As you know, frames can be nested within other frames, which heightens the complexity of a web page. In the case of our example, *FRAMER.HTM* might itself contain only the `<FRAMESET>` tag, which in turn splits the right-hand frame into two equal parts horizontally, named *Rupper* and *Rlower*. As a result, the browser would appear as shown in Figure 5-3. To change the document in the *Rlower* frame from a script in the left frame, you can use the statement

```
Top.RightFrame.RLower.Location.Href = "http....."
```

So the *Top* property moves us to the topmost *Window* object. One of the *Frame* objects contained within the browser window is *RightFrame*, and one of the frame objects contained within *RightFrame* is *RLower*. `Location.Href` in turn identifies the *Href* property of *RLower's Location* object. You can now see clearly that the hierarchy of objects must be reflected in the syntax that you use, which is somewhat similar to a `PATH` statement in DOS or UNIX.

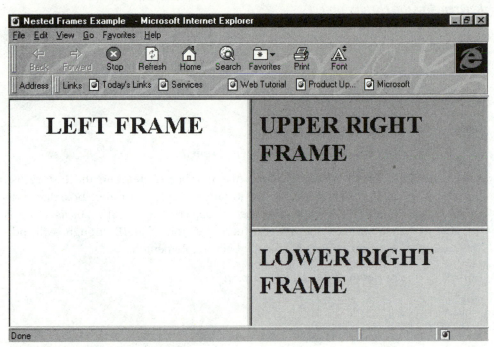

*Figure 5-3. A nested frame document*

## The History Object

WARNING    The *History* object represents the history list of recently opened documents, and, when and if it is actually implemented in a future version of MSIE, it can probably be put to good use by some
imaginative programmer somewhere. However, the existing documentation for the *History* object indicates a major weakness: it lacks
a device (either a property or a value returned by a method) to indicate where within the history list the user currently is. The documentation indicates that, if you're working with a fully implemented
*History* object, you can find out how long the list is, you can move
to the start or the end, you can take steps backward and forward
within the list, and you can even move to a particular indexed item
within the list. But you are unable to find out where in the list you
are starting from. The *History* object is not currently implemented in
MSIE 3.0. The *History* object's *Length* property always returns 0, and
calls to the *History* object's methods generate an error.

*Referencing the History object*

Since the *History* object is an object of the *Window* object, the following references are valid:

```
Window.History....
Top.History....
Top.Frames(1).History....
```

*History object properties*

The History object has only a single property, *Length*:

- **Length**. The *Length* property returns the number of items in the history list. The web page in Example 5-19, for instance, displays an alert box that indicates the number of items in the *History* object. Under MSIE 3.0, its value is always 0. A nonzero value under a future version of MSIE, though, will indicate that the *History* object has finally been implemented.

*Example 5-19. The History Object's Length Property*

```
<HTML>
 <HEAD>
  <SCRIPT LANGUAGE="vbscript">
   Sub cmdShowLength_OnClick
    Alert "Current History Length=" & CStr(History.Length)  & " Items"
   End Sub
  </SCRIPT>
 </HEAD>

<BODY BGCOLOR="white">
 <INPUT TYPE="button" NAME="cmdShowLength" VALUE="History Length">
 </BODY>
</HTML>
```

*History object methods*

The three documented methods of the *History* object allow you to perform relative navigation backward and forward from the current History list item, and to move directly to a particular item in the History list. Unfortunately, though, these methods are not implemented in MSIE 3.0; calls to them produce a syntax error. The methods are:

- **Back**. Moves back in the History list *n* number of entries. It is the programmatic equivalent of the user clicking the Back button of the browser *n* number of times. Its syntax is:

  [*Window*].**Back** *n*

- **Forward**. Moves forward in the History list *n* number of entries. It is the programmatic equivalent of the user clicking the browser's Forward button *n* number of times.

  [*Window*].**Forward** *n*

- **Go**. Moves to the *n*th item in the History list. Unlike other arrays in VBScript, the History array starts at 1. Therefore, the following line moves to the first item in the history list:

```
History.Go 1
```

The following line moves to the last item in the History list:

```
History.Go History.Length
```

There are currently no *History* object events.

## The Navigator Object

An object within the *Window* object, the *Navigator* object presents information about the browser application. The properties and method of the MSIE *Navigator* object correspond exactly to those of Netscape's *Navigator* object, which allows you to determine which browser is displaying your scripted web pages. This information can be useful for the JavaScript programmer, since the same script can run on both browsers, and the values of *Navigator* object properties can be used to determine the browser platform. It's not useful for the VBScript programmer concerned with handling browser differences, though, since currently Navigator does not support VBScript.

The *Navigator* object is an object of the *Window* object, and therefore the following references are all valid:

```
Window.Navigator ....
Top.Navigator ....
Top.Frames(1).Navigator ....
```

As you can see, it's legal to reference the properties of the *Navigator* object for one of a series of frames, even though this serves little purpose. Since the application that is running in one frame must also be the application that is running in the same overall browser window, their values must be the same. For this reason, it's best, and least confusing, to access the Navigator object from the *Top* window object.

The *Navigator* object has the following four properties, all of which are read-only:

- **appCodeName**. Returns the code name of the browser application. MSIE3.0 returns "Mozilla." This is the same value returned by Versions 2.0 and 3.0 of Netscape Navigator.

- **appName**. Returns the application name of the browser. MSIE3.0 returns "Microsoft Internet Explorer." In contrast, Versions 2.0 and 3.0 of Netscape Navigator return "Netscape" as the value of this property.

- **appVersion**. Returns the platform and version number of the browser. MSIE3.0 returns "2.0 (compatible; MSIE 3.0A; Windows 95)".

- **userAgent**. This property returns the user agent string that is sent by the browser to the server in the HTTP request header to identify the browser type. MSIE3.0 returns "Mozilla/2.0 (compatible; MSIE 3.0A; Windows 95)".

Example 5-20 displays the values returned by each of the *Navigator* object's properties.

*Example 5-20. Accessing the Navigator Object's Properties*

```
<HTML>
<HEAD>
<SCRIPT LANGUAGE="vbscript">
  Document.Open
  Document.Write "<BODY BGCOLOR=white>"
  Document.Write "appCodeName: <B>" & Navigator.appCodeName & "</B><BR>"
  Document.Write "appName    : <B>" & Navigator.appName & "</B><BR>"
  Document.Write "appVersion : <B>" & Navigator.appVersion & "</B><BR>"
  Document.Write "userAgent  : <B>" & Navigator.userAgent & "</B><BR>"
  Document.Close
</SCRIPT>
</HEAD>
</HTML>
```

The *Navigator* object has no methods or events.

## The Location Object

The *Location* object is contained within the *Window* object, and is responsible for storing the current URL. If the browser window contains frames, each Frame object also has its own *Location* object for storing that frame's URL. The *Location* object is very useful for programmatically setting and returning the individual components of the URL. Note that modifying any of the individual properties of the *Location* object causes the document represented by the newly formed URL to be loaded.

### Referencing the Location object

Since the *Location* object is an object of the *Window* object, the following references are all valid:

```
Window.Location ....
Top.Location ....
Top.Frames(1).Location ....
```

### Location object properties

The various properties of the *Location* object indicate the complete URL or one of its components. By retrieving the value of any of these properties, you can gather information about the window's current URL. By modifying the value of any property, you can have the browser open a new document. The *Location* object properties are:

- **href**. Returns or sets the complete current URL.

- **protocol**. Returns or sets the current file protocol. For example, if the browser is pointing to the URL *http://www.ora.com/*, the statement:

  `Top.Location.Protocol`

  returns `http:`

- **host**. Returns or sets the host and port of the current URL. For example, if the browser is pointing to the URL *http://www.ora.com:8080/*, the statement:

  `Top.Location.Host`

  returns `www.ora.com:8080`. However, if the URL uses a default port that is not shown as part of the URL, the host property returns only the hostname.

- **hostname**. Returns or sets the hostname of the current URL. For example, if the browser is pointing to the URL *http://www.ora.com/*, the statement:

  `Top.Location.HostName`

  returns *www.ora.com*

- **port**. Returns or sets the port of the current URL. For example, if the browser is pointing to the URL *http://www.ora.com:8080/*, the statement:

  `Top.Location.Port`

  returns `8080`. However, if the URL uses a default port and the port is not shown as part of the URL, a zero-length string is returned.

- **pathname**. Returns or sets the pathname of the current URL—that is, the location on the remote server where a particular document or file is stored. For example with the browser pointing to the URL *http://www.ora.com/new/ new.htm*, the statement:

  `Top.Location.Pathname`

  returns *new/new.htm.*

- **search**. Returns or sets the query string or search string of the current URL, if one is present. The query string or search string is used to transfer data from the browser to the server, using the *GET* method. Many times when you use search engines such as Yahoo! or Lycos, the address line of the browser is completely filled with a seemingly neverending search string like this real URL from a Lycos search: *http://www.lycos.com/cgi-bin/pursuit?first=11&cat- =lycos&query=uk*. When the search string arrives at the server, it is parsed into field and value pairs. For example, if the browser is pointing to the URL *http://www.ora.com/new/new.htm?p=string*, the statement:

  `Top.Location.Search`

  returns `p=string`. Since this is a field name/value pair, *p* is the field and *string* is the value of that field.

- **hash**. The hash portion of the URL is the section that refers to an anchor within a web page. For example, many Frequently Asked Questions (FAQ) pages have anchors defined using the `<A NAME="xyz"></A>` HTML tag, allowing you to jump directly to the topic you wish to read on the current web page by clicking a hyperlink. The URL reflects this by adding the hash character (#) and the anchor name after the HTML filename. Unfortunately, the *hash* property is not currently implemented. In fact, neither the *Location.href* property nor the *Location.hash* property reflects the hash. A URL containing a hash, such as *http://www.ora.com/main.html#new*, is returned as *http://www.ora.com/main.html* by the *href* property, and the *hash* property always returns an empty string.

Example 5-21 contains the source code for a neat little application that demonstrates the *Location* object's properties. As Figure 5-4 shows, it requires that your browser window be divided into two frames, which can be done by opening the following HTML document:

```
<HTML>
<FRAMESET COLS=50%,50%>
 <FRAME NAME="LeftFrame" SRC="location.htm">
 <FRAME NAME="RightFrame" SRC="FrameTmp.htm">
</FRAMESET>
</HTML>
```

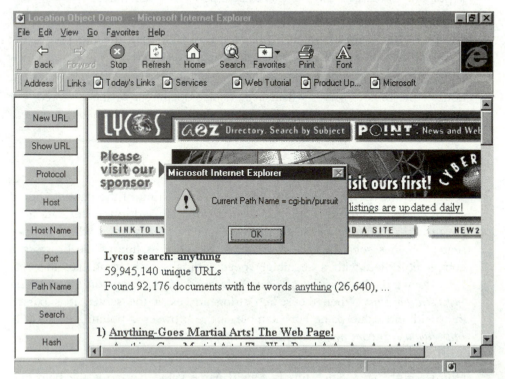

*Figure 5-4. The LOCATION.HTM sample application*

The document displayed by *RightFrame* is unimportant. Once you've gotten your browser to display the two frames, including the sample code from *LOCA-TION.HTM* in *LeftFrame*, you can click on the New URL button in *LeftFrame* to open a new web document in *RightFrame*. When the document is displayed in the right-hand frame, you can click any of the buttons to get information about the current URL. You might also try this out when accessing a search engine, since this allows you to retrieve information from the *Search* property.

*Example 5-21. Examining the Location Object's Properties*

```
<HTML>
 <HEAD>
  <SCRIPT LANGUAGE="vbscript">

   Sub cmdNewURL_OnClick
       Top.RightFrame.Location.href = Prompt("Enter a URL","")
   End Sub

   Sub cmdShowURL_OnClick
       Alert "Current URL = " & Top.RightFrame.Location.href
   End Sub

   Sub cmdProtocol_OnClick
       Alert "Current Protocol = " & Top.RightFrame.Location.Protocol
   End Sub

   Sub cmdHost_OnClick
       Alert "Current Host = " & Top.RightFrame.Location.Host
   End Sub

   Sub cmdHostName_OnClick
       Alert "Current Host Name = " & Top.RightFrame.Location.HostName
   End Sub

   Sub cmdPort_OnClick
       Alert "Current Port = " & Top.RightFrame.Location.Port
   End Sub

   Sub cmdPathName_OnClick
       Alert "Current Path Name = " & Top.RightFrame.Location.PathName
   End Sub

   Sub cmdSearch_OnClick
       Alert "Current Search = " & Top.RightFrame.Location.Search
   End Sub

   Sub cmdHash_OnClick
       Alert "Current Hash = " & Top.RightFrame.Location.Hash
   End Sub

  </SCRIPT>
 </HEAD>
```

*Example 5-21. Examining the Location Object's Properties (continued)*

```
<BODY BGCOLOR="white">
 <CENTER>
  <INPUT TYPE="button" NAME="cmdNewURL" VALUE="New URL"><P>
  <INPUT TYPE="button" NAME="cmdShowURL" VALUE="Show URL"><P>
  <INPUT TYPE="button" NAME="cmdProtocol" VALUE="Protocol"><P>
  <INPUT TYPE="button" NAME="cmdHost" VALUE="Host"><P>
  <INPUT TYPE="button" NAME="cmdHostName" VALUE="Host Name"><P>
  <INPUT TYPE="button" NAME="cmdPort" VALUE="Port"><P>
  <INPUT TYPE="button" NAME="cmdPathname" VALUE="Path Name"><P>
  <INPUT TYPE="button" NAME="cmdSearch" VALUE="Search"><P>
  <INPUT TYPE="button" NAME="cmdHash" VALUE="Hash"><P>
 </CENTER>
 </BODY>
</HTML>
```

The *Location* object currently has no methods or events.

## The Document Object

Each window or frame can contain only one *Document* object. An object contained within the *Window* object, the *Document* object can contain any number of the following:

- *Link* objects

- *Anchor* objects

- *Form* objects

- *Element* objects

The *Document* object supports a number of properties and methods, but it does not support any events.

### Referencing the Document object

The manner in which you reference the *Document* object depends in large measure on whether or not it is the *current document* (i.e., the document in whose frame or window the script resides). If it is the current document, it can be referenced as follows:

```
Window.Document....
Document....
```

You can reference the document in the topmost window as follows (unless the script resides in the same document, in which case you can use either of the above references):

```
Top.Document
```

Finally, you can reference the document in a frame other than the frame in which the script resides, as follows:

```
Top.Frames(i).Document....
```

### Document object properties

The *Document* object supports the following properties:

- **Links**. The *Links* property returns the *Link* object, which is an array of links contained within the *Document* object. It is used in conjunction with the *Link* object properties; see "The Link Object" later in this chapter for a full description of its use.

- **Anchors**. Returns an *Anchor* object, which is an array of anchors defined with the HTML <A> tag within the document. It is used in conjunction with the *Anchor* object properties; see "The Anchor Object" later in this chapter for a full description of its use.

---

# VBScript Color Strings

The following color strings are automatically recognized by VBScript when they are assigned to the *Document.bgColor*, *Document.fgColor*, *Document.LinkColor*, *Document.aLinkColor*, and *Document.vLinkColor* properties:

| | | |
|---|---|---|
| Aqua | Black | Blue |
| Fuchsia | Gray | Green |
| Lime | Maroon | Navy |
| Olive | Purple | Red |
| Silver | Teal | White |
| Yellow | | |

In addition, VBScript 2.0 includes a number of intrinsic color constants; see Appendix C, *VBScript 2.0 Intrinsic Constants*, for details.

---

- **Forms**. Returns a *Form* object, which is an array of forms defined with the HTML <FORM> tag within the document. It is used in conjunction with the *Form* object properties; see "The Form Object" for a full description of its use.

- **LinkColor**. This property can be used to set, as well as to retrieve, the color used to display hyperlinks on an HTML page. Although the documentation indicates that *LinkColor* can only be set as the document is being loaded, in fact it can also be set dynamically after the page has been loaded. The property value can be set as an RGB color value (i.e., 000000) or as a color string (i.e., "white"). Example 5-22 is a sample program that uses the *LinkColor* property to change the color of hyperlinks.

- **aLinkColor**. Gets or sets the active link color—that is, the color of a link while the mouse pointer is held down over a link, but before it is released. This feature, though, is not supported by MSIE 3.0, and the property has been included so that the MSIE object model for scripting remains compatible with the JavaScript *Document* object.

- **vLinkColor**. Gets or sets the color used to display the visited links in a document. Although the documentation indicates that the property's value can only be set at parse time, as the document is being loaded, it can in fact be set at any time. The property value can be set as an RGB color value (i.e., 000000) or as a color string (i.e., "white"). Example 5-22 illustrates the use of the *vLinkColor* property to change the color of visited hyperlinks.

*Example 5-22. Changing the LinkColor and vLinkColor Properties*

```
<HTML>
 <HEAD>
  <SCRIPT LANGUAGE="vbscript">
       Document.LinkColor = "Blue"
       Document.vLinkColor = "Yellow"

   Sub CmdButton1_OnClick
       Document.LinkColor = "Red"
       Document.vLinkColor = "Green"
   End Sub
  </SCRIPT>
 </HEAD>

 <BODY BGCOLOR="white">
  <FONT FACE="arial" SIZE=3>
<CENTER>
<A NAME="test"></A>
<A HREF="linkcolors.htm">This is a link</A><BR>
<A HREF="#test">This is another link</A>
<P>
<INPUT TYPE="button" NAME="cmdButton1" VALUE="Change Link Colors">
</CENTER>
 </BODY>
</HTML>
```

- **bgColor**. This property allows you to read the background color of the document, or to change its color at any time. *bgColor* accepts either RGB color values or color names. Example 5-23 shows how to use the bgColor property to change a document's background color at run-time.

- **fgColor**. This property allows you to change the foreground or text color of the document, or to change its color at any time. *fgColor* accepts either RGB color values or color names. Example 5-23 shows how to use the *fgColor* property to change a document's foreground color at run-time.

*Example 5-23. Changing the Foreground and Background Colors*

```
<HTML>
 <HEAD>
  <SCRIPT LANGUAGE="vbscript">
   Document.bgColor = "White"

   Sub cmdChangeBGColor_OnClick
       intIndex = Document.Colors.Background.SelectedIndex
       strColorChoice = Document.Colors.Background.Options(intIndex).Text
       Document.bgColor = strColorChoice
   End Sub

   Sub cmdChangeFGColor_OnClick
       intIndex = Document.Colors.ForeGround.SelectedIndex
       strColorChoice = Document.Colors.ForeGround.Options(intIndex).Text
       Document.fgColor = strColorChoice
   End Sub
  </SCRIPT>
 </HEAD>

<BODY>
 <CENTER>
  <H2>COLOR CHANGING EXAMPLE</H2>
  <FORM NAME="Colors">
   <SELECT NAME="BackGround">
    <OPTION>White
    <OPTION>Black
    <OPTION>Blue
    <OPTION>Red
    <OPTION>Yellow
    <OPTION>Fuchsia
    <OPTION>Gray
    <OPTION>Lime
    <OPTION>Maroon
    <OPTION>Navy
    <OPTION>Olive
    <OPTION>Purple
    <OPTION>Silver
    <OPTION>Teal
   </SELECT>

   <INPUT TYPE="button" NAME="cmdChangeBGColor" VALUE="Change the
          Background">
   <P>

   <SELECT NAME="ForeGround">
    <OPTION>White
```

*Example 5-23. Changing the Foreground and Background Colors (continued)*

```
    <OPTION>Black
    <OPTION>Blue
    <OPTION>Red
    <OPTION>Yellow
    <OPTION>Aqua
    <OPTION>Fuchsia
    <OPTION>Gray
    <OPTION>Lime
    <OPTION>Maroon
    <OPTION>Navy
    <OPTION>Olive
    <OPTION>Purple
    <OPTION>Silver
    <OPTION>Teal
   </SELECT>
   <INPUT TYPE="button" NAME="cmdChangeFGColor" VALUE="Change the
          Foreground">

   </FORM>
  </CENTER>
 </BODY>
</HTML>
```

# RGB Colors

The RGB color system (the acronym stands for Red, Green, and Blue) is used to produce a given color on screen. To produce a particular color, you specify a value for each of the three primary colors, ranging from 0 (lowest intensity) to 255 (highest intensity). The value for each of the colors must be expressed as a hexadecimal value. For example, the integer value 100 is represented by 64 in hexadecimal. You can use the *Hex* conversion function to convert integer values to hexadecimal values. Once you have a hexadecimal value for each of the three colors, you simply concatenate the values together to form the RGB value string, as the following example shows:

```
red = 100 (hex 64)

blue = 25 (hex 19)

green = 60 (hex 3C)

RGB = "64193C"
```

You can then use this string to set properties such as `Document.LinkColor`:

```
    Document.LinkColor = "64193C"
```

- **location**. This is a *read-only* property that returns the complete URL for the current *Document* object. Its value is identical to that of the *Location* object's *Href* property.

- **lastModified**. Returns a read-only string containing the date the document at the current URL was last modified.The use of the *lastModified* property is illustrated in Example 5-24.

*Example 5-24. Retrieving the Date the Current Document was Last Modified*

```
<HTML>
 <HEAD>
  <SCRIPT LANGUAGE="vbscript">
   Sub cmdLastModified_OnClick
       Alert Document.LastModified
   End Sub
  </SCRIPT>
 </HEAD>

 <BODY BGCOLOR="white">
  <INPUT TYPE="button" NAME="cmdLastModified" VALUE="Last Modified">
 </BODY>
</HTML>
```

- **title**. The *title* property is *read-only* and simply returns a string containing the page title. As Example 5-25 shows, this is the string defined by the HTML `<TITLE>` tag.

*Example 5-25. Retrieving the Document's Title*

```
<HTML>
 <HEAD>
 <TITLE>
 A Page with a Title
 </TITLE>
  <SCRIPT LANGUAGE="vbscript">
   Sub cmdShowTitle_OnClick
       Alert Document.Title
   End Sub
  </SCRIPT>
 </HEAD>

 <BODY BGCOLOR="white">
  <INPUT TYPE="button" NAME="cmdShowTitle" VALUE="Show Title">
 </BODY>
</HTML>
```

- **cookie**. The *cookie* property creates or reads a unique text file for the current page that is stored on the user's computer. It's the only procedure within VBScript that allows interaction with the user's operating and file systems. Cookies are useful for storing small amounts of data, such as the date the user last visited the site or user preferences for viewing the site. Setting a cookie replaces the current content of the cookie text file. Also note that attempting to set the cookie for a document running locally under the `file:` protocol will result in an error. Cookies can only be baked from an `HTTP:` domain.

To set a cookie, use:

```
document.cookie = string
```

To retrieve a cookie, use:

```
string = document.cookie
```

The cookie string must contain at least one user-defined variable name and value pair, and can contain the following attributes, again as `name=value` pairs:

— **domain**. Along with the path, the `domain` is used by the browser to determine if a cookie is associated with a particular HTML document. The host name of the current document is compared with existing cookies to find a match. If a match is found, the client then performs a path match. The domain attribute defaults to the name of the domain creating the cookie.

— **path**. Once the client has matched the domain, it then checks the `path` attribute. The path specified in the `path` attribute only has to match partially to be successful. For example, the `path` attribute "/ora" matches *orafiles/index.html* and */ora/index.html*. The default path is the path of the document that created the cookie.

— **secure**. `secure` is an optional attribute which specifies if a secure connection between the client and server is required to transmit the cookie. The value of this attribute is not relevant to a client-side script, since the cookie is accessed locally and is not transmitted to a server across the Internet.

— **expires**. A cookie cannot be stored indefinitely on a client computer; all cookies must include an expiration date. The `expires` attribute itself is optional. No doubt these last two sentences strike you as contradictory, but in fact they're not. If you write a cookie without an expiration date, the file only exists during the current browser session. As soon as the browser is closed, the cookie vanishes (not even a crumb left!). The `expires` attribute also provides the mechanism for deleting a cookie: simply set the value of `expires` to be before the current date.

There's one slight wrinkle here: `expires` requires a particular date and time format, which is:

```
day, dd-mmm-yy hh:mm:ss GMT
```

Those of you familiar with JavaScript may recognize the format. Unfortunately, VBScript doesn't have a "convert to GMT" function, so you'll have to build the date string yourself, either by hardcoding the date or by converting the date to the required string format and concatenating the "GMT" onto the end.

---

*TIP*     Always remember to delimit the `name=value` pairs in the cookie
        string with a semicolon. For example:

        `myVar1=avalue;myVar2=anothervalue;expires=Friday,`
        `02-Nov-98 10:00:00 GMT`

---

There is a complete sample application using cookies, including a neat function to reformat the date into one that is acceptable for the `Expires` attribute, in Chapter 10, *Date and Time in VBScript*.

- **referrer**. The referrer property is *read-only* and is supposed to return the URL that contained the link that the user selected to reach the current document. If the user enters the current document's URL on the browser's address line and thereby reaches the document without clicking a link, the referrer is supposed to return a null string. However, in MSIE 3.0, the referrer property is broken, and always returns the URL of the current document.

## Document object methods

All the methods of the *Document* object are concerned with writing to or creating documents at run time, or "on-the-fly." This makes them central to creating an interactive web document. Using the *Document* object's methods, you can create a flexible HTML document that may appear differently on screen depending upon any number of circumstances. For example, you can create a document that says "Good Afternoon" or "Good Evening" depending upon the time of day the user downloads the page into the browser. You can also create new and unique HTML documents from the browser without referring back to the server. For example, you can create a page in the browser made up from data the user has input into a form, so that the user can check the data before submitting it to the server. Unfortunately, what you cannot do with MSIE 3.0 is add to a document once it has been displayed within the browser, nor can you change the HTML content of the document other than by employing ActiveX controls. Once the HTML document has been loaded into the browser, its contents are fixed.

The *Document* object supports the following methods:

- **write**. The *write* method appends a given string to the current document when it is loading into the browser. Its syntax is:

`Document.Write ` *string*

The string is written without formatting, so you must include any appropriate HTML tags within it. For instance, the call to the *write* method in the fragment

```
Document.Write "<H1>Hello World</H1><P>"
```

writes a header line to the current document and follows it with a paragraph break.

You may wonder where the *Document.Write* method places the string within the document. Examples 5-26 and 5-27 illustrate two different ways of using the *Document.Write* method. Example 5-26 completely replaces the current document with the phrase "Hello There," and uses no background color or formatting. However, it does demonstrate that the underlying HTML document is unaffected by *Document.Write*: if the user clicks the Refresh button, the original document is again displayed. Example 5-27, on the other hand, places the string at the current position within the HTML text stream. By adding some conditional statements to the above scripts, you could create a different document for almost every visitor, if you so desired.

*Example 5-26. Using Document.Write to Create a New Document*

```
<HTML>
 <HEAD>
  <SCRIPT LANGUAGE="vbscript">
    Sub cmdWriteToDoc_OnClick
        Document.Write "Hello There<P>"
        Document.Close
    End Sub

  </SCRIPT>
 </HEAD>

 <BODY BGCOLOR="white">
  <H2>A Document Write Example</H2><P><CENTER>
   <INPUT TYPE="button" NAME="cmdWriteToDoc" VALUE="Write Now">
 </BODY>
</HTML>
```

*Example 5-27. Using Document.Write to Append Text to a Document*

```
<HTML>
 <BODY BGCOLOR="white">
  <CENTER>
  <H2>A Document Write Example</H2>

  <SCRIPT LANGUAGE="vbscript">
    Document.Write "<H3>Hello There</H3>"
  </SCRIPT>

Some more HTML stuff
```

*Example 5-27. Using Document.Write to Append Text to a Document (continued)*

```
<SCRIPT LANGUAGE="vbscript">
  Document.Write "<P>Another Document.Write Statement"
</SCRIPT>

</BODY>
</HTML>
```

- **writeLn**. The *writeLn* method is basically identical to the *Write* method, except that it appends a carriage return or a newline character to the end of the string written by the method. As you know, HTML ignores newlines unless they appear within `<PRE>` tags. This means that, in the majority of cases, the *Write* and *writeLn* methods behave identically.

- **open**. The *open* method opens a new document object buffer in memory and readies it for writing. Its full syntax is

  ```
  document.open [mimetype]
  ```

  However, *mimetype* is ignored by MSIE 3.0, which assumes that it is always writing text to an HTML document. Typically, the call to the *Document.Open* method is followed by one or more calls to *Document.Write*. In that case, any information currently held within the document is overwritten by *Document.Write*. Without the call to the *Document.Open* method, text written by the *Document.Write* method is simply appended to the existing document if one has already been displayed. Example 5-28 illustrates the use of the *Document.Open* method, and writes the text that the user inputs into a text box in the left frame into the right frame. In order to define the frameset successfully, you must begin by loading an HTML document like the following, which in turn loads *WRITE4.HTM* into the left frame:

  ```
  <HTML>
  <FRAMESET COLS=50%,50%>
   <FRAME NAME="LeftFrame" SRC=" Write4.htm">
   <FRAME NAME="RightFrame" SRC="FrameTmp.htm">
  </FRAMESET>
  </HTML>
  ```

  Since the HTML document in Example 5-28 immediately writes to the right-hand frame when it loads, if the *RightFrame* object is not loaded in the right-hand frame using the `<FRAME SRC>` tag, calls to the *Document* object belonging to *RightFrame* necessarily result in an error. This means that you must also be sure to create the "dummy" file *FRAMETMP.HTM* before trying to load the web pages.

- **Close**. The *Close* method closes the *Document* object stream and writes the resulting document to the browser window. Example 5-28 illustrates the use of the *Document.Close* method.

*Example 5-28. Using the Document Object Methods*

```
<HTML>
<HEAD>
 <SCRIPT LANGUAGE="vbscript">
  Sub DoRightFrame()
      Top.RightFrame.Document.Open
      Top.RightFrame.Document.Write "<BODY BGCOLOR='white'>"
      Top.RightFrame.Document.Write "<H2>Right Frame</H2></BODY></HTML>"
      Top.RightFrame.Document.Close
  End Sub

  Sub cmdWriteItNow_OnClick
      Dim strToWrite
      strToWrite = Document.frmStuffToWrite.txtWriteString.Value

      Top.RightFrame.Document.Open
      Top.RightFrame.Document.Write "<BODY BGCOLOR='white'>"
      Top.RightFrame.Document.Write "<H2>Right Frame</H2>"
      Top.RightFrame.Document.Write "<CENTER><H3>" & strToWrite
      Top.RightFrame.Document.Write "</H3></CENTER></BODY></HTML>"
      Top.RightFrame.Document.Close
  End Sub

 </SCRIPT>
</HEAD>

<BODY BGCOLOR="white" OnLoad="DoRightFrame" LANGUAGE="vbscript">
 <H2>Left Frame</H2>
 <FORM NAME="frmStuffToWrite">
  <INPUT TYPE="text" NAME="txtWriteString">
  <INPUT TYPE="button" NAME="cmdWriteItNow" VALUE="Show Right Frame">
 </FORM>
</BODY>
</HTML>
```

- **Clear**. The *Clear* method is not implemented in MSIE3.x; however, its use does not cause an error.

## The Link Object

The *Link* object is a child of the *Document* object, and represents an array of links in the HTML document. A *link* is any anchor (<A>) tag that includes an HREF attribute. The *Link* object supports a number of properties and events, although it supports no methods.

### Referencing the Link object

The *Link* object is accessed through the *Document* object's *Links* property. The *Links* property returns a *Link* object, which consists of an array of links. Typically, you work with only a single link at a time by indicating which element of the array you wish to access. For example:

```
Window.Document.Links(n)....
Window.Frames(n).Document.Links(n)...
Top.Frames(n).Document.Links(n)...
```

all access the *n* link of the *Link* object, where *n* is an array index number that ranges from 0 to *Total_Number_of_Links* *-1*. *Total_Number_of_Links* can be determined by retrieving the value of the *Link* object's *Length* property. References to the *Links.Length* property are an exception to this typical method of referencing the *Link* object, since they cannot use an array index:

```
Window.Document.Links.Length
```

It is also possible to assign a reference to the *Links* object to a variable, and then to use that variable to access the object's properties, as the following code fragment shows:

```
Set objLink = Document.Links
Alert objLink(0).Href
```

### Link object properties

Of the properties supported by the *Link* object, only one, the *Length* property, applies to the entire object. All of the remaining properties apply to the individual array elements held by the *Link* object. All properties are read-only; they cannot be modified by accessing the *Link* object directly. Notice that, with the exception of *Document.Target*, these properties are also shared by the *Location* object. The *Link* object supports the following properties:

- **Length.** This (so far) is an undocumented property that returns the number of links in a document; if there are no links, it returns 0. Notice that the value of the *Length* property is one greater than the upper bound of the array held within the *Link* object. Unless you know beforehand exactly which *Link* item you wish to reference, it is important to retrieve the value of the *Length* property in order to iterate the Links array.

- **href.** Returns a string containing the complete URL of a link (e.g., *http://www.microsoft.com*).

- **protocol.** Returns a string containing the protocol section of a link URL (i.e., *http*).

- **host.** Returns a string containing the host name and port of a link URL (i.e., *www.vbscripts.com:8080*).

- **hostname**. Returns a string containing the hostname section of a link URL (i.e., *www.vbscripts.com*).

- **port**. Returns a string containing the port number section of a link URL (i.e., 8080).

- **pathname**. Returns the path and file section of a link URL (i.e., */examples/ index.html*).

- **search**. Returns the search sections (or the query string) of a link URL (i.e., *?P=xyz*). The search section of the URL is used to hold the name and value pairs transmitted to the server in a `GET` method.

- **hash**. Returns the hash section of a link URL, or a NULL if the hash portion is absent from the URL. The hash section of a URL refers to the name of an anchor within an HTML document (i.e., *http://www.ora.com/main.html#new*).

- **target**. Returns the name of the target frame or window for the link. This is the same as the value of the `TARGET` attribute of the `<A>` tag, which allows the user to select a hyperlink in one frame that affects the document displayed in another frame.

The application in Example 5-29 makes use of all the *Link* object properties. It requires that an initial HTML file like the following be used to define two frames, and to load *LINKOBJ.HTM*:

```
<HTML>
<FRAMESET COLS=50%,50%>
 <FRAME NAME="LeftFrame" SRC="linkobj.htm">
 <FRAME NAME="RightFrame" SRC="dummy.htm">
</FRAMESET>
</HTML>
```

When the user clicks the New Page button, the *cmdNewURL_OnClick* event procedure executes. This opens a VBScript dialog that prompts the user for a new URL. When the user closes the dialog by clicking the OK button, the browser then loads this page by simply assigning the new URL (which is returned by the *Prompt* method) to the *RightFrame Location* object's *HRef* property. When the user clicks the Link Summary button, a dialog like the one shown in Figure 5-5 appears. It's produced by the *cmdLinkSummary_onClick* event procedure, which begins by examining the *Link* object's *Length* property for the document displayed in *RightFrame*. It then retrieves the value of the *HRef* property for each link in the *Link* object's array. Finally, when the user enters the number of a link in the text box and clicks the Link Details button, the *cmdLinkDetails_OnClick* event procedure executes and opens a dialog like the one shown in Figure 5-6 that displays property information from that link's element in the *Link* object array. Notice that if the user enters a value that exceeds the number of elements in the *Link* object, or fails to enter a value, the procedure adjusts the value accordingly.

*Example 5-29. Retrieving Information from the Link Object*

```
<HTML>
<HEAD>
<SCRIPT LANGUAGE="vbscript">

Dim CRLF
CRLF = chr(13) & chr(10)

Sub cmdNewURL_OnClick
Top.RightFrame.Location.href = Prompt("Enter a URL","")
End Sub

Sub cmdLinkSummary_onClick

Dim intNoOfLinks, x
Dim strLinksMsg, strLinksTitle
intNoOfLinks = Top.RightFrame.Document.Links.Length
strLinksMsg = "There are " & CStr(intNoOfLinks) & _
              " links on this page:" & CRLF & CRLF

For x = 0 to intNoOfLinks - 1
    strLinksMsg = strLinksMsg & CStr(x) & "-" & _
                  Top.RightFrame.Document.Links(x).href & CRLF
Next

strLinksTitle = "Links for " & Top.RightFrame.Document.Title
x = MsgBox(strLinksMsg,0,strLinksTitle)

End Sub

Sub cmdLinkDetails_OnClick

Dim intLinkIndex
Dim docLinkDoc
Dim strLinksTitle,strLinksMsg

Set docLinkDoc = Top.RightFrame.Document
If Len(Trim(Top.LeftFrame.Document.frmLinksNo.txtLink.Value)) > 0 Then
    intLinkIndex = CInt(Top.LeftFrame.Document.frmLinksNo.txtLink.Value)
    if intLinkIndex > docLinkDoc.Links.Length -1 then
        intLinkIndex = docLinkDoc.Links.Length - 1
    End If
else
    intLinkIndex = 0
End If
If docLinkDoc.Links.Length > 0 then
    strLinksMsg = "URL: " & docLinkDoc.Links(intLinkIndex).HRef & CRLF
    strLinksMsg = strLinksMsg & "Protocol: " & _
                  docLinkDoc.Links(intLinkIndex).Protocol & CRLF
    strLinksMsg = strLinksMsg & "Host: " & _
                  docLinkDoc.Links(intLinkIndex).Host & CRLF
    strLinksMsg = strLinksMsg & "HostName: " & _
                  docLinkDoc.Links(intLinkIndex).HostName & CRLF
```

```
    strLinksMsg = strLinksMsg & "Port: " & _
                docLinkDoc.Links(intLinkIndex).Port & CRLF
    strLinksMsg = strLinksMsg & "PathName: " & _
                docLinkDoc.Links(intLinkIndex).PathName & CRLF
    strLinksMsg = strLinksMsg & "Search: " & _
                docLinkDoc.Links(intLinkIndex).Search & CRLF
    strLinksMsg = strLinksMsg & "Hash: " & _
                docLinkDoc.Links(intLinkIndex).Hash & CRLF
    strLinksMsg = strLinksMsg & "Target: " & _
                docLinkDoc.Links(intLinkIndex).Target

    strLinksTitle = "Links Details for " & docLinkDoc.Title & _
                "Link No." & CStr(intLinkIndex)
    x = MsgBox(strLinksMsg,0,strLinksTitle)
End If

End Sub
</SCRIPT>
</HEAD>

<BODY BGCOLOR="white">
   <INPUT TYPE="button" NAME="cmdNewURL" VALUE="New Page"><P>
   <INPUT TYPE="button" NAME="cmdLinkSummary" VALUE="Link Summary"><P>
   <INPUT TYPE="button" NAME="cmdLinkDetails" VALUE="Link Details"><P>
   <FORM NAME="frmLinksNo">
    <INPUT TYPE="text" NAME=txtLink SIZE=10>
   </FORM>
 </BODY>
</HTML>
```

### Link object events

The events supported by the *Link* object are fired when one of a document's links
is affected by some external event. Their event procedures can be used for such
purposes as displaying text in the browser's status bar. The key to using these
events is to give each link a name within the HTML anchor tag defining the link.
For example:

```
<A HREF="http://www.ora.com/" NAME="link1">Goto ORA</A>
```

You can then create an event handler for the *Link* object in the same way that
you would for the intrinsic HTML controls. For example:

```
Sub link1_OnMouseOver
    ...
End Sub
```

The Microsoft documentation for the *Link* object provides examples using the
classic JavaScript-style inline event handlers that are included with the HTML
definition.

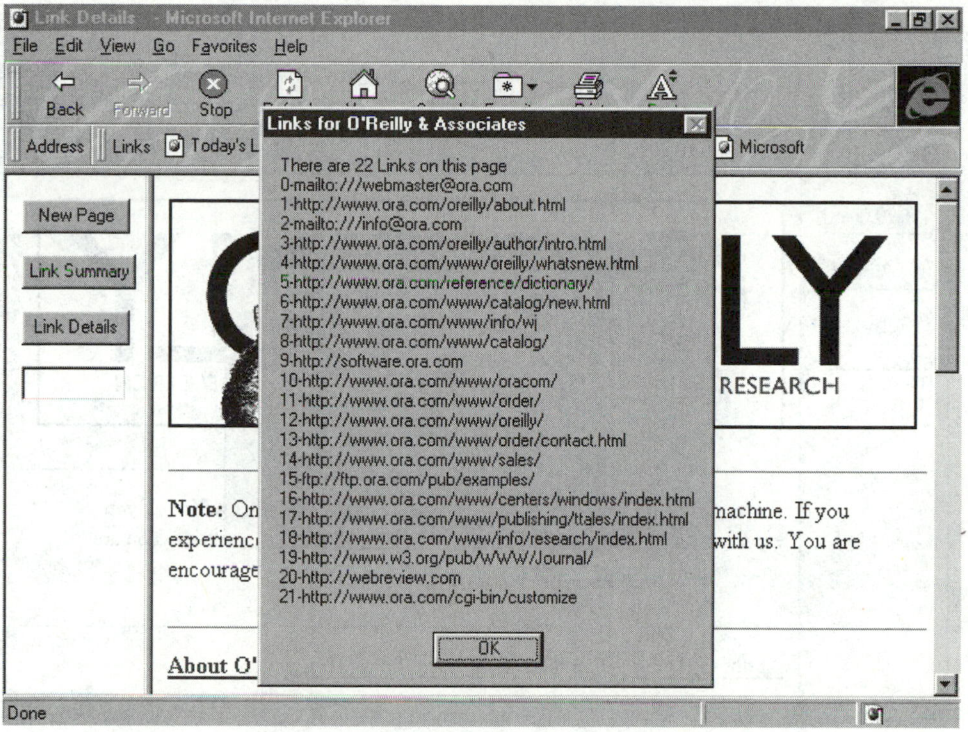

*Figure 5-5. A summary of links on a web page*

For example:

```
<A HREF="http://www.ora.com/" Language='vbscript'
OnMouseOver="status='lets go to ORA'">Goto ORA</A>
```

However, anything more than just a simple one-line command in an inline script becomes very difficult to read, and therefore difficult to maintain.

For this reason, I would recommend sticking to the more VB-oriented method of creating event handlers by assigning a name to the link and creating a separate subroutine.

The events supported by the *Link* object are:

- **mouseMove**. This event is triggered when the mouse pointer passes over a link. The syntax of the *mouseMove* event procedure is

```
Sub linkname_MouseMove(shift, button, x, y)
```

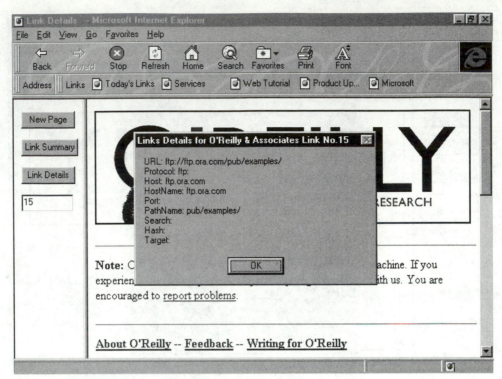

*Figure 5-6. The details of one of the links*

The four parameters that VBScript automatically passes to the event when it is invoked are described in Table 5-2.

*Table 5-2. Parameters Passed to the MouseMove Event Procedure*

| Parameter | Description |
| --- | --- |
| *shift* | Should indicate the state of the shift key; however, in the current version of MSIE (3.x), the *shift* parameter always returns 1. |
| *button* | Should indicate which mouse button (if any) was clicked; however in the current version of MSIE (3.x), the *button* parameter always returns 0. |
| *x* | Horizontal position of the mouse pointer in pixels from the top of the browser window. |
| *y* | Vertical position of the mouse pointer in pixels from the left edge of the browser window. |

- **onMouseOver**. The *OnMouseOver* event is triggered when the mouse pointer passes over a link. The *onMouseOver* event does not accept any parameters, making it a simplified version of the *mouseMove* event. As a result, it is useful in situations in which you only need to know that the mouse is somewhere over the link, but do not need to know the mouse coordinates. There's also an additional difference: unlike *mouseMove*, which is fired whenever the mouse is moved within the area of the link, *onMouseOver* is fired only once, as the mouse moves into the area of the link; it is not fired again until the mouse moves away from the link and then returns.

The syntax for *onMouseOver* is:

```
Sub linkname_OnMouseOver
```

Example 5-30 shows how *onMouseOver* can be used with the *Window* object's *Status* method to provide the user with information about the link. This example also demonstrates the use of the *SetTimeOut* method to clear the status bar.

*Example 5-30. Displaying a Message When the Mouse is Over the Link*

```
<HTML>
 <HEAD>
  <SCRIPT LANGUAGE="vbscript">
   Sub link1_OnMouseOver
       Status = "Click Me Please!"
       timerID = SetTimeOut("Status=''",2000)
   End Sub
  </SCRIPT>
 </HEAD>
 <BODY>
  <A HREF="" NAME="link1">Click Me</A>
 </BODY>
</HTML>
```

- **onClick**. The *onClick* event is triggered when the user clicks on a link. Its syntax is

  ```
  Sub linkname_OnClick
  ```

  Example 5-31 is a web page containing a simple example that uses the *OnClick* event.

*Example 5-31. The Link Object's OnClick Event*

```
<HTML>
 <HEAD>
  <SCRIPT LANGUAGE="vbscript">
       Sub link1_onClick
       Alert "Off you go then...."
   End Sub
  </SCRIPT>
 </HEAD>

 <BODY BGCOLOR="white">
   <A NAME="link1" HREF="http://www.vbscripts.com/">VBScripts.COM</A>
 </BODY>
</HTML>
```

*Link object methods*

Two undocumented methods for the *Link* object appear in the Script Wizard of the ActiveX Control Pad. The first is a *Count* method, which returns the number of links on the document and is identical to the *Link* object's *Length* property. The second is the *Item* method, which is currently not implemented.

## The Anchor Object

The *Anchor* object is a child object of the *Document* object. It represents an array of anchors (which are defined by the HTML `<A>` tag) on the page, as distinct from links (which are defined by an HTML `<A>` tag that includes the `HREF` attribute). The *Anchor* object has only two properties; it currently supports no methods or events.

*Referencing the anchor object*

The *Anchor* object can only be accessed via the `Anchors` array, as in:

```
Document.Anchors(n)...
```

where *n* is a number between 0 and the maximum number of anchors.

*Anchor object properties*

- **name**. The *name* property returns a *read-only* string containing the anchor name. For example,

  ```
  Document.Anchors(3).Name
  ```

  returns the name of the fourth anchor *on* the page. Anchor names are assigned with the `NAME` attribute of the `<A>` tag. Although any anchor can be assigned a name, named anchors are typically used to allow fast jumps within the page. The anchor is declared with `<A NAME="myanchor"></A>`, and the hyperlink to this anchor is defined as `<A HREF="#myanchor">Go to My Anchor</A>`.

- **count**. Although its use with the *Anchor* object is not documented, the standard Visual Basic *count* property can be used with all object arrays to determine the number of elements in the array. *count* is a Visual Basic property that returns the number of items in a collection of a particular object. Fortunately, *count* works with the *Anchor* object to determine the number of anchors in the array, as the following code fragment illustrates:

  ```
  Document.Anchors.Count
  ```

- **length**. Like the *Count* property, *Length* is an undocumented property that returns the number of elements in the *Anchor* object.

Example 5-32 shows how VBScript differentiates between links and anchors. When the user clicks on the Links button, an Alert box indicates that the web page contains two links; this is the case because there are two anchor tags that include the `HREF` attribute. On the other hand, when the user clicks on the Anchor Name button, a dialog box lists the names of four anchors; this is the number of anchor tags on the web page that do not include an `HREF` attribute.

*Example 5-32. Working with the Anchor Object*

```
<HTML>
 <HEAD>
  <SCRIPT LANGUAGE="vbscript">
    Dim CRLF
    CRLF = Chr(13) & Chr(10)

    Sub cmdLinkCount_OnClick
        Alert CStr(Document.Links.Length)
    End Sub

    Sub cmdAnchorName_OnClick
        Dim x, y
        Dim strMsg

        strMsg = "This page contains " & CStr(Document.Anchors.Count) & _
        "Anchors" & vbCRLF

        For x = 0 to Document.Anchors.Count - 1
            strMsg = strMsg & Document.Anchors(x).Name & vbCRLF
        Next

        ' Fix bug with name including null-terminated string
        For x = 1 to Len(strMsg)
            If Mid(strMsg, x, 1) = Chr(0) Then
                strMsg = Left(strMsg, x - 1) & " " & _
                         Right(strMsg, Len(strMsg) - x)
            End If
        Next

        y = MsgBox(strMsg,0,"Anchors")

    End Sub

  </SCRIPT>
</HEAD>


<BODY BGCOLOR="white">
  <A NAME="link1" HREF="http://www.vbscripts.com/">VBScripts.COM</A><P>
  <A NAME="link2" HREF="#anchor4">Goto Anchor 4</A>
  <A NAME="anchor1"></A><BR>
  <A NAME="anchor2"></A><BR>
  <A NAME="anchor3"></A><BR>
  <A NAME="anchor4"></A><BR>
```

*Example 5-32. Working with the Anchor Object (continued)*

```
    <INPUT TYPE="button" NAME="cmdLinkCount" VALUE="Links"><P>
    <INPUT TYPE="button" NAME="cmdAnchorName" VALUE="Anchor Name">
</BODY>
</HTML>
```

---

### The Anchor Name and Chr(0)

If you look closely at the script in Example 5-32, you may notice what appears
to be a rather peculiar `For` loop:

```
    For x = 1 to Len(strMsg)
        If Mid(strMsg, x, 1) = Chr(0) Then
            strMsg = Left(strMsg, x - 1) & " " & _
                      Right(strMsg, Len(strMsg) - x)
        End If
    Next
```

This is because of a bug in the *Anchor* object's *Name* property: whenever you
retrieve the value of the *Name* property, MSIE returns a C string (rather than a
VBScript string) that terminates with a null character, or *Chr*(0). This loop replaces each NULL with a space. If you retrieve the value of the *Name* property
from an *Anchor* object in any of your scripts, it's a good idea to include it. If
Microsoft fixes the bug in a future version of MSIE, this extra loop should have
no effect on your application.

---

## The Form Object

The *Form* object is a child of the *Document* object, and represents an array of
forms in the document. A form may contain one or more *Element* objects. (For a
detailed discussion of the *Element* object, see Chapter 6, *The Element Object and
HTML Intrinsic Controls.*)

### Referencing the Form object

The *Form* object can be referenced either by name or by its ordinal number in the
*Document* object's `Forms` array. So, if you've assigned a form a name by
including the **NAME** attribute in its HTML <FORM> tag, you can reference a form
from a script in the same document as the form, as follows:

```
    Document.frmMyForm....
    Window.Document.frmMyForm....
```

If the form is contained within another document than the script, you can reference it as follows:

```
    Top.Frames(1).Document.frmMyForm...
    Top.MyFrame.Document.frmMyForm...
```

However, if you haven't assigned a name to your form, you can refer to it by its ordinal number—that is, by the order in which the form appears in the document. The first form defined by the <FORM> tag is *Forms(0)*, the second *Forms(1)*, and so on. Once again, if the script is in the same document as the form, you can access the first form on the page as follows:

```
Document.Forms(0)....
Window.Document.Forms(0)....
```

If the browser window is divided into frames, and the form is in a different document than the script, you can reference it as follows:

```
Top.Frames(1).Document.Forms(0)....
Top.MyFrame.Document.Forms(0)....
```

In any case, the reference to the *Document* object always has to precede the reference to the *Form* object, as shown above. The *Window* or *Frame* object reference is optional, depending upon the location of the calling script. The *Window* object reference is always optional, and if the *Form* object is in the same document as the script, you need only start your reference with the *Document* object. However, if you are dealing with frames and the form is in a different document than the script, you must precede the *Document* reference with references to the *Top* and *Frame* objects.

### Form object properties

Form object properties are analogous to the attributes of the HTML form definition. For example, the attributes of the tag

```
<FORM ACTION="http://www.anydomain.com/cgi-bin/mycgi.cgi"
METHOD="POST">
```

directly correspond to the properties of the form's *Form* object.

In your VBScript code, you can either read or set the value of a *Form* object property. The following properties are supported by the *Form* object:

- **action.** The *Form* object's *action* property corresponds to the HTML <FORM> tag's ACTION attribute; that is, the *action* property contains the URL of the application (typically a CGI application or a server-side script) that is to receive and process the form's data. It is possible either to read the value of the property or to assign the property a string that contains the URL of the application that is to process the form's data. For example, the following statement sets the *Form* object's *action* property:

```
Document.frmMyForm.Action = _
                "http://www.anydomain.com/cgi-bin/mycgi.cgi"
```

In contrast, the following statement retrieves the current value of the *Form* object's *action* property:

```
strFormAction = Document.frmMyForm.Action
```

- **encoding**. You can use the *encoding* property either to read or to set the MIME type for encoding the form; it corresponds directly with the HTML `ENC-TYPE` attribute. For example, the statement

```
Document.frmMyForm.encoding= "text/html"
```

  sets the *Form* object's *encoding* property, while

```
strFormEncode = Document.frmMyForm.encoding
```

  retrieves the current value of the *Form* object's *encoding* property.

- **method**. The *method* property corresponds to the `<FORM>` tag's `METHOD` attribute, and defines the method (either `GET` or `POST`) used to send the form's field and data pairs to the server. This is a read-write property. Consequently, the statement

```
Document.frmMyForm.method= "GET"
```

  indicates that the form should be sent to the server by using the `GET` method, while the statement

```
strFormMethod = Document.frmMyForm.method
```

  retrieves the method used to submit the form to the server.

- **target**. The *Form* object's *target* property corresponds to the `<FORM>` tag's `TARGET` attribute, and determines the frame or window that is to be used to display the results of processing the form. The *target* property is also read-write. So the statement

```
Document.frmMyForm.target = "ResultsWindow"
```

  instructs the server to send a window or frame named *ResultsWindow*, while the statement

```
strFormtarget = Document.frmMyForm.target
```

  retrieves the name of the window or frame that is currently configured to receive the form's data.

- **elements**. The *elements* property returns the *element* collection object for the form; the *element* object in turn contains an array of elements. The individual elements in the *element* object array can be intrinsic HTML controls defined using the HTML `<INPUT>` tag, or embedded elements and ActiveX controls defined using the HTML `<OBJECT>` tag. Given the variety of HTML intrinsic controls, Chapter 6 is devoted to the *element* object, and in particular to HTML intrinsic controls.

### Form object methods

The *Form* object supports a single method:

- **submit**. The *submit* method is the programmatic equivalent of the user's clicking a form's Submit button. That is, the *submit* method provides a way to submit a form's data to a server under program control, rather than under user control (which occurs when the user clicks the Submit button). For example, the statement

```
Document.frmMyForm.Submit
```

submits the *frmMyForm* form object's data to a web server.

### Form object events

Finally, the *Form* object supports a single event:

- **onSubmit**. The *onSubmit* event is triggered either when the user clicks a Submit button or when the *Form* object's *submit* method is invoked, but before the form's data is actually sent. This allows the event handler for *onSubmit* to be used to verify the form prior to final submission to the server. It can also be used to halt the submission process altogether. For details, see Chapter 14, *Form Input Validation*.

# Summary

In this chapter, we've examined the objects that Microsoft Internet Explorer makes available to scripts. You've seen how the objects relate to each other in the object hierarchy, and have studied each object in detail, exploring the properties, events, and methods for each. You have also learned what properties, events, and methods are, and how important they are to the event-driven programming model that is at the core of VBScript.

Coverage of one object, the *Element* object, has been deliberately omitted from this chapter, since it involves sufficient detail to deserve its own separate treatment. In Chapter 6 you will find out more about one of the *Element* object's major components, HTML intrinsic controls. The chapter provides detailed discussion of the properties, events, and methods of HTML intrinsic controls, some of which you should already be very familiar with from the many examples you have already seen.

# The Element Object and HTML Intrinsic Controls

In the last chapter, you were introduced to the MSIE Scripting Object Model and took a close look at the objects that the browser makes available to your Visual Basic script. This chapter continues the discussion of the MSIE Scripting Object Model by focusing on the final object in the model, the *Element* object, which consists of the HTML intrinsic controls that are specified by the HTML `<INPUT>` tag, as well as other controls defined by the `<OBJECT>` tag. We'll look at each of the HTML intrinsic controls in detail, exploring their properties, methods, and events.

*Element* objects are, in the main, child objects of the *Form* object. However, it is possible to use the button control outside of a form, in which case the *Element* object can be a child of the *Document* object without being a child of a *Form* object. You must note that when an HTML intrinsic control is used outside a form, you cannot access its properties. For example, if a button control is defined outside of an HTML `<FORM>` tag, the button still appears on the web page when the browser displays it, as you'll see when you use your browser to display the web page in Example 6-1. This proves that an HTML intrinsic object can exist outside of an HTML form. You would expect, of course, that its properties and events should be exposed, and that you should be able to create an event handler for the button, like the *cmdButton1_OnClick* event procedure in Example 6-1. But in fact, the line of code that attempts to access the object's *Value* property fails because the properties of HTML intrinsic controls defined outside of forms are inaccessible to VBScript.

*Example 6-1. An HTML Intrinsic Control Defined Outside of a <FORM> Tag*

```
<HTML>
 <HEAD>
  <SCRIPT LANGUAGE="vbscript">
```

*Example 6-1. An HTML Intrinsic Control Defined Outside of a <FORM> Tag (continued)*

```
   Sub cmdButton1_OnClick
    Alert Document.cmdButton1.Value
   End Sub
 </SCRIPT>
</HEAD>

<BODY BGCOLOR="white">
 <INPUT TYPE="button" NAME="cmdButton1" VALUE="Button One">
</BODY>
</HTML>
```

The code in Example 6-2 does work, though, because the command button is now enclosed within a form and is referenced as a child of the *Form* object.

*Example 6-2. An HTML Intrinsic Control Defined Inside a <FORM> Tag*

```
<HTML>
 <HEAD>
  <SCRIPT LANGUAGE="vbscript">
    Sub cmdButton1_OnClick
     Alert Document.frmMyForm.cmdButton1.Value
    End Sub
  </SCRIPT>
 </HEAD>

 <BODY BGCOLOR="white">
  <FORM NAME="frmMyForm">
   <INPUT TYPE="button" NAME="cmdButton1" VALUE="Button One">
  </FORM>
 </BODY>
</HTML>
```

Individual *Element* objects are usually referred to by name, but you can also refer to them by their ordinal number (beginning at zero) within the *Elements* array. (As you saw in the previous chapter, *Elements*, which is a property of the *Form* object, consists of an array of *Element* objects.) You can use the *Count* property (e.g., `lngValues = Document.frmMyForm.Elements.Count`) to find the number of elements in an *Elements* array. Example 6-3 shows how to access the *Count* property to determine the number of elements in any *Elements* array and how to retrieve the property of a particular Element object.

*Example 6-3. Working with the Element Object*

```
 <HTML>
 <HEAD>
  <SCRIPT LANGUAGE="vbscript">
    Sub cmdButton1_OnClick
     Alert Document.frmMyForm.Elements.Count
     Alert Document.frmMyForm.Elements(1).Value
    End Sub
  </SCRIPT>
```

*Example 6-3. Working with the Element Object (continued)*

```
</HEAD>

<BODY BGCOLOR="white">
<FORM NAME="frmMyForm">
 <INPUT TYPE="button" NAME="cmdButton1" VALUE="Button One">
 <INPUT TYPE="button" NAME="cmdButton2" VALUE="Button Two">
</FORM>
</BODY>
</HTML>
```

---

# *The Accessibility of ActiveX Controls*

Unlike HTML intrinsic controls, which cannot be accessed from VBScript code unless they appear within an HTML form, ActiveX controls are subject to no such restriction. They can be placed anywhere within the body of an HTML document and are fully accessible, as you will see later in this chapter.

---

Referring to elements by their ordinal number is useful when you need to access a series of controls to perform a single operation on some or all of them, like reading or changing a particular property common to them all. This is illustrated in Example 6-4. When the user clicks the On Switch button, each of the page's seven check boxes is turned on. Similarly, when the user clicks the Off Switch button, each check box is turned off. In each case, this is done by an event handler that uses a `For...Next` loop to access each element of the *Elements* array by its ordinal position within the array and to change the value of its *Checked* property.

*Example 6-4. Accessing Element Objects by Their Position in the Elements Array*

```
<HTML>
 <HEAD>
  <SCRIPT LANGUAGE="vbscript">

    Sub cmdButton1_OnClick
    Dim x
     For x = 0 to 6
      Document.frmMyForm.Elements(x).Checked = True
     Next
    End Sub

    Sub cmdButton2_OnClick
    Dim x
     For x = 0 to 6
      Document.frmMyForm.Elements(x).Checked = False
     Next
    End Sub
```

*Example 6-4. Accessing Element Objects by Their Position in the Elements Array (continued)*

```
  </SCRIPT>
  </HEAD>

<BODY BGCOLOR="white">
<FORM NAME="frmMyForm">
<TABLE>
  <TD>Option One<TD><INPUT TYPE="checkbox" NAME="chk1" VALUE="One"><TR>
  <TD>Option Two<TD><INPUT TYPE="checkbox" NAME="chk2" VALUE="Two"><TR>
  <TD>Option Three<TD><INPUT TYPE="checkbox" NAME="chk3" VALUE="Three"><TR>
  <TD>Option Four<TD><INPUT TYPE="checkbox" NAME="chk4" VALUE="Four"><TR>
  <TD>Option Five<TD><INPUT TYPE="checkbox" NAME="chk5" VALUE="Five"><TR>
  <TD>Option Six<TD><INPUT TYPE="checkbox" NAME="chk6" VALUE="Six"><TR>
  <TD>Option Seven<TD><INPUT TYPE="checkbox" NAME="chk7" VALUE="Seven"><TR>
</TABLE>
  <INPUT TYPE="button" NAME="cmdButton1" VALUE="ON Switch">
  <INPUT TYPE="button" NAME="cmdButton2" VALUE="OFF Switch">

  </FORM>
  </BODY>
</HTML>
```

---

## A Collection's Count Property

A number of objects in the MSIE object model are collection objects—that is, they are containers that hold an array of objects. The *Elements* object is an example of such a collection object. In MSIE 3.x, you can determine how many objects are stored in the collection by retrieving the value of its *Count* property. In MSIE 3.02, a *Length* property has been added that also reports the number of objects stored to the collection. From preliminary indications, though, it appears that only the *Length* property will be used to retrieve a count of the objects stored to a collection in future versions of MSIE; the *Count* property will no longer be supported.

---

When you write script-level code—that is, script which is outside an event handler or subroutine—the script executes as the document is loaded into the browser. In this case, you must make sure that any references to intrinsic controls in the script are made *after* the definition of the control. In Example 6-5, for instance, the *Value* property of the *txtText* control is accessed before *txtText* is defined in the HTML code. Because the script engine knows nothing of *txtText* when it encounters the reference to its *Value* property, it displays an "Object doesn't support this property or method" error.

*Example 6-5. Accessing an Undefined HTML Intrinsic Control*

```
<HTML>
<HEAD>
```

*Example 6-5. Accessing an Undefined HTML Intrinsic Control (continued)*

```
<SCRIPT LANGUAGE=VBSCRIPT>
   Document.frmForm1.txtTest.Value = CStr(Now())    ' Error
</SCRIPT>
</HEAD>

<BODY>
  <FORM NAME="frmForm1">
     <INPUT TYPE="text" NAME="txtTest"><P>
   </FORM>
</BODY>
</HTML>
```

The correct way to handle this situation is to enclose the code in a *Window_OnLoad* event as shown in Example 6-6. The *Window_OnLoad* event is not fired until the page is fully created and all the controls used on the page are registered with the scripting engine. In a situation in which you don't want the code to be placed within an event handler—such as a call to the *Document.Write* method—you should move the code below the HTML intrinsic control's definition so that it executes after the control has been defined and registered.

*Example 6-6. The Window_onLoad Event Procedure*

```
<HTML>
<HEAD>
<SCRIPT LANGUAGE=VBSCRIPT>
Sub window_onLoad()
   Document.frmForm1.txtTest.Value = CStr(Now())
End Sub
</SCRIPT>
</HEAD>

<BODY>
  <FORM NAME="frmForm1">
     <INPUT TYPE="text" NAME="txtTest"><P>
   </FORM>
</BODY>
</HTML>
```

One of the main advantages of using the HTML intrinsic controls is that they are predefined within the browser application, and as a result they are present on almost all browsers. This means that using them is both straightforward and fast; you don't need to force the browser to download a new control from the Web, as you often have to do with some ActiveX controls. Furthermore, if you are revising an existing HTML document or adding VBScript code to it, you can very simply and quickly add a certain amount of interactivity to the controls you already have on your current HTML document. However, as you go through this chapter, you'll begin to realize that there are a number of major limitations involved in using HTML intrinsic controls. This is quite understandable, since HTML controls were never designed to be interactive controls on the web page; they were designed to accept the data given to them and simply to pass that data along to the server when requested. Therefore, if your application needs to closely control its controls, you'll do best by using the standard ActiveX controls that we'll discuss in Chapter 7, *Using the ActiveX Control Pad*

---

### For...Each and the Element Object

You might think that, instead of having to retrieve the value of the *Count* property and use it as the upper bound of the *Elements* array, you can simply use the `For Each...Next` construct to iterate each member of the *Elements* collection. But the `For Each...Next loop`, which was introduced into VBScript with Version 2, and which you can use to iterate through a collection of objects or an array, does not work on HTML form controls. So, for instance, if we attempt to replace the *CmdButton1_OnClick* event procedure in Example 6-4 with the following event procedure:

```
Sub cmdButton1_OnClick
  Dim objCheck
  For Each objCheck in Document.frmMyForm.Elements ' Wrong
  objCheck.Checked = True
  Next
End Sub
```

the `For Each` statement generates an "object does not support this property or method" error.

---

## The Element Object

The *Element* object is in fact an array of intrinsic controls. The array is constructed as the HTML page downloads to the browser, and controls are added to the array in the order in which they appear within the HTML code. There are very few situations in which you need to access the *Element* object itself. The vast majority of times, you will be accessing individual controls by their name, as in:

```
Document.Form1.txtMyText.Value = "Hello World"
```

The only time you should need to access the *Element* Object directly is when dealing with the Radio button control, which will be discussed later in this chapter.

### Referencing the Element Object

The *Element* object is a child of the *Form* object, not of the *Document* object, which means that each form has one *Element* object. If there is more than one form in the document, there may be many *Element* objects within the document. To access the *Element* object, you must first refer to the document and then to the form. If your script and the form are in the same frame or window, you can reference the *Element* object as follows:

```
Document.FormName.Elements....
Window.Document.FormName.Elements...
```

If your script and the form are in different frames, you must navigate to the *Element* object from the topmost window:

```
Top.FrameName.Document.FormName.Elements...
Top.Frames(i).Document.FormName.Elements...
```

## Element Object Properties

The *Element* object has a single property, *Length*.

**Length.** The *Length* property returns the number of HTML intrinsic controls in the *Element* collection. Intrinsic controls are numbered from 0, which means that, when you iterate the controls, the ordinal number of the last control will always be `Elements.Length -1`.

---

*TIP*          If you are a VB programmer you can think of the *Element* object as the Controls collection. Although not documented, there is an *Elements.Count* property which operates in the same way as *Elements.Length*: it returns the number of elements—or HTML intrinsic controls in the form.

---

One unfortunate omission from the properties of the HTML intrinsic controls is a *Type* property, which would allow you to iterate the elements of the *Elements* array to pick out controls of a particular type. In the VBA programming language, this is typically handled by the `TypeOf` statement, but VBScript does not support it. There is a way around this, though. If you always use the VBScript Coding Conventions that were presented at the end of Chapter 4, *Program Flow and Structure*, the names of intrinsic controls of the same type will always start with the same first three letters. Our event handlers shown earlier in Example 6-4 could therefore be rewritten to explicitly handle check box controls by identifying them based on their name, as the following code fragment shows:

```
Sub cmdButton1_OnClick
    Dim x
    For x = 0 to Document.frmMyForm.Elements.Length - 1
        If Left(Document.frmMyForm.Elements(x).Name,3) = "chk" Then
            Document.frmMyForm.Elements(x).Checked = True
        End If
```

```
        Next
    End Sub
```

Note that, aside from determining the type of a control based on the first three letters of its name, the code fragment also determines how many times the loop should iterate by retrieving the value of the *Element* object's *Length* property. You might wonder why you'd bother with all this extra coding when you know how many checkboxes there are on the form. But just imagine when, a few months down the line, you add a couple more option buttons or checkboxes to the web page, forget to amend the code, and then scratch your head wondering why they don't all clear. There's also a worse situation: if you add another type of control—say, like a text box—above the checkboxes, the text box control then becomes the object located at *Elements(0)*, and the checkboxes are moved to positions 1 through 7 in the *Elements* array. So you can imagine the problems that even a small change to this form can cause. The code fragment shown above works with any number of checkboxes, from none on up, regardless of their position in the form. This is a good example of clean, flexible, and easily maintainable code.

# HTML Intrinsic Controls

There are ten HTML intrinsic controls, each of which (apart from the SELECT and TEXTAREA controls) is defined by the `TYPE` element of the `<INPUT>` tag. These ten controls are:

- The command button

- The Reset button

- The Submit button

- The checkbox control

- The radio button

- The password control

- The text box control

- The textarea control

- The Select or list box control

- The hidden control

The remainder of this chapter will focus on each of these controls. For each control (or groups of controls), a sample application demonstrates the properties, methods, and events associated with the control. The complete application appears at the beginning of each section and then is broken down throughout the section as we discuss individual features.

*WARNING*      Before examining the properties, events, and methods of the HTML
                intrinsic controls, a word of caution. The MSIE Scripting Object Mod-
                el documentation that is available from Microsoft at the time of this
                writing contains a large reference section detailing the *Element* ob-
                ject's properties, events, and methods.  Do not confuse this with
                what is actually implemented and working in MSIE 3.0. There are
                far more properties, methods, and events detailed in the documenta-
                tion than are actually available. Again, at the time of writing, the fea-
                tures that are covered in this chapter have actually been
                implemented in Internet Explorer; those that are not discussed ei-
                ther do not work or are simply not yet implemented.

## The Command Button, Reset, and Submit Controls

The three command button controls supported by HTML share the same properties, events, and methods, so it's best to view them as a single group.
Consequently, a single sample application, which appears in Example 6-7, illustrates the properties, events, and methods of all three controls.

*Example 6-7. The Submit, Reset, and Command Button Controls*

```
<HTML>
 <HEAD>
  <SCRIPT LANGUAGE="vbscript">
  Sub cmdButton2_OnClick
   Dim CRLF
   Dim strProperties
   CRLF = Chr(13) & Chr(10)
    strProperties = "Button Name: "
    strProperties = strProperties & Document.frmMyForm.cmdButton1.Name _
                    & CRLF
    strProperties = strProperties & "Form Elements: "
    strProperties = strProperties &_
        Document.frmMyForm.cmdButton1.Form.Elements.Count & CRLF
    strProperties = strProperties & "Value: "
    strProperties = strProperties & Document.frmMyForm.cmdButton1.Value
   x = MsgBox(strProperties,0,"Test Button Properties")
  End Sub

  Sub cmdButton3_OnClick
    Document.frmMyForm.cmdButton1.Value = _
              Document.frmMyForm.txtButtonCaption.Value
  End Sub

  Sub cmdButton4_OnClick
    Document.frmMyForm.cmdButton1.Click
  End Sub

  Sub cmdButton1_OnClick
    Alert "The test button has just been clicked"
```

*Example 6-7. The Submit, Reset, and Command Button Controls (continued)*

```
  End Sub

 </SCRIPT>
</HEAD>

<BODY BGCOLOR="white">
 <FORM NAME="frmMyForm">
  <INPUT TYPE="submit" NAME="cmdButton1" Value="Test Button"><P>
  <INPUT TYPE="button" NAME="cmdButton2" Value="Display Test Button
            Properties"><P>
  <INPUT TYPE="text" NAME="txtButtonCaption" Value="">
  <INPUT TYPE="button" NAME="cmdButton3" Value="Change Button Caption"><P>
  <INPUT TYPE="button" NAME="cmdButton4" Value="Click Test Button">
 </FORM>

</BODY>
</HTML>
```

### Command button properties

The button, reset, and submit controls all support the following three properties:

- **Form**. The *Form* property returns the *Form* object that is the parent of the button. Through its ability to retrieve its parent *Form* object, all the *Form* properties become available to the *Button* object. This is illustrated by the following code fragment from Example 6-7, which displays the number of controls in the *Elements* object:

```
strProperties = strProperties & "Form Elements: "
strProperties = strProperties &
Document.frmMyForm.cmdButton1.Form.Elements.Count & CRLF
```

  This is a somewhat contrived example, since the number of controls in a form can be accessed much more efficiently with the following (less cyclical) line of code:

```
strProperties = strProperties & Document.frmMyForm.Elements.Count &
CRLF
```

  Nevertheless, it does illustrate that the full range of properties of a button's parent become accessible through the button's *Form* property.

- **Name**. The *Name* property is read-only, and simply returns the name assigned by the **NAME** attribute of the button's **<INPUT>** tag. If the button was not given a name when it was created, the property returns a zero-length string. The following fragment from Example 6-7 retrieves the name of the cmdButton1 button:

```
strProperties = "Button Name: "
strProperties = strProperties & Document.frmMyForm.cmdButton1.Name &
CRLF
```

## *The Name Property of Element Objects*

Although I have stated that the *Name* property is read-only, it actually can be changed programmatically. "Aha," you say, "a read-only property you can change? That makes sense. Not!" Let me explain. The property itself can be amended from a script. However, any calls to the control's events can only be made to the event handlers attached to the old name. To see how this works, take a look at Example 6-8. This web page contains two command buttons, cmdButton1 and cmdButton2. When you click on cmdButton1, an alert box is displayed informing you that you clicked on cmdButton1. When you click on cmdButton2, the *Name* property of cmdButton1 is changed to cmdButton3. If you then click cmdButton3 (which used to be cmdButton1), the *cmdButton1_ OnClick* event handler is invoked (although this time it reports the new name of *cmdButton3*). The *cmdButton3_OnClick* event handler is ignored.

Therefore, while the *Name* property has been changed at the highest level, the scripting engine has already compiled the code, and without a refresh or re-compilation of the script (which would change the *Name* property back to cmdButton1 anyway), the script will always reference the *cmdButton1_On-Click* event handler when this control is clicked, regardless of the new name that's been programmatically assigned to it. This means that, as far as the scripting engine is concerned, the *Name* property cannot be changed.

There can be little practical use for changing a control's name during execution, aside from possibly providing an alias for a control, as in the following code fragment:

```
If Top.rightFrame.Document.Name = "myDocument.htm" Then
    Document.frmForm1.txtText1.Name = "txtText1"
Else
    Document.frmForm1.txtText1.Name = "txtAnotherName"
End if
```

This would allow two documents, one referring to *txtText1* and the other referring to *txtAnotherName*, to both refer to the same control. But to save yourself many hours of grief trying to debug later code changes, I would strongly recommend that you just think of the *Name* property as read-only.

*Example 6-8. Changing an HTML Intrinsic Control's Name Property*

```
<HTML>
<HEAD>
<SCRIPT LANGUAGE="vbscript">
   Sub cmdButton1_OnClick
       Alert "You just clicked " & Document.frmForm1.cmdButton1.Name
   End Sub
```

*Example 6-8. Changing an HTML Intrinsic Control's Name Property (continued)*

```
Sub cmdButton2_OnClick
    Document.frmForm1.cmdButton1.Name = "cmdButton3"
    Alert "cmdButton1.Name changed to cmdButton3"
End Sub

Sub cmdButton3_onClick
    Alert "This will never be displayed"
End Sub

</SCRIPT>
</HEAD>
<BODY BGCOLOR="white"><CENTER>
<FORM NAME="frmForm1">
<INPUT TYPE="button" NAME="cmdButton1" VALUE="cmdButton1">
<BR>
<INPUT TYPE="button" NAME="cmdButton2" VALUE="cmdButton2">
</FORM>
</BODY>
</HTML>
```

- **Value**. The *Value* property corresponds directly to the VALUE attribute of the HTML <INPUT> tag. The *Value* property contains the caption shown on the face of the button. This caption can be read by your VBScript program as well as set programmatically at run-time. The following code fragment from Example 6-7, for example, retrieves the current caption of the cmdButton1 button:

```
strProperties = strProperties & "Value: "
strProperties = strProperties & Document.frmMyForm.cmdButton1.Value
```

The following procedure from Example 6-7, on the other hand, sets the button's *Value* property to the string that the user has entered into the page's text box.

```
Sub cmdButton3_OnClick
    Document.frmMyForm.cmdButton1.Value =
Document.frmMyForm.txtButtonCaption.Value
End Sub
```

## Command button events

The three command buttons all support a single event:

- **OnClick**. As you've already seen in countless examples, the *OnClick* event is automatically fired when the user clicks on that button. In Example 6-7, for example, when the user clicks the button labeled Test Button, the *cmdButton1_OnClick* event procedure is executed automatically and causes a dialog box to appear. The code for *cmdButton1_OnClick* is as follows:

```
Sub cmdButton1_OnClick
    Alert "The test button has just been clicked"
End Sub
```

## Command Button Methods

The button, reset, and submit controls support a single method:

- **CLICK**. The *Click* method allows you to programmatically click a button. That is, whereas ordinarily a button is clicked by the user, the *Click* method allows your program to generate the button click. The exact meaning of the *Click* method depends on the particular kind of button to which it's applied. When a Submit button's *Click* method is called, the browser automatically submits the form's data to the URL specified by the ACTION attribute of the <FORM> tag. When a Reset button's *Click* method is called, the form's controls are reset to their default states. Interestingly, since invoking a button's *Click* method does not trigger its *OnClick* event, the *Click* event does not cause the *OnClick* event procedure to execute. This means that calling a command button's (i.e., a button whose TYPE attribute is "button") *Click* method has no real effect on the button; it merely gives it the focus and causes it to appear to be clicked. It also means that any preliminary processing done by a Reset or Submit button's *OnClick* event procedure will not occur if the *Click* method is used to submit or to reset the form's data. In Example 6-7, the *Click* method is illustrated in the ***cmdButton4_OnClick*** event procedure, which causes cmdButton1, the form's Submit button, to be clicked under program control:

```
Sub cmdButton4_OnClick
    Document.frmMyForm.cmdButton1.Click
End Sub
```

When the user clicks cmdButton4 (the button whose caption is "Click Test Button"), the button's *OnClick* event handler calls the *Click* method of cmdButton1 ("Test Button"). Since cmdButton1 is a Submit button, Internet Explorer attempts to submit the form's data, which in this case consists of the single text box, to a server. Note, though, that the dialog produced by the call to the *Alert* method in the Submit button's own *OnClick* event procedure never appears, indicating that calling a button's Click method does not trigger an *OnClick* event. This means that, if you want to emulate a user click on a button under program control, you'll have to do it with a code fragment like the following, which invokes the button's *OnClick* event procedure programmatically, before calling its *Click* method:

```
cmdButton1_OnClick
Document.frmMyForm.cmdButton1.Click
```

## The Checkbox Control

The checkbox control is an on/off button, or toggle, that appears as a small square. A check mark appears within the square when the control is on (or true), and it disappears when the control is off (or false). Example 6-9 allows you to view the properties, as well as call the methods and handle the events, of a sample checkbox control.

*Example 6-9. The Checkbox Control*

```
<HTML>
 <HEAD>
  <SCRIPT LANGUAGE="vbscript">
   Sub cmdButton2_OnClick
      Dim CRLF
      Dim strProperties
      CRLF = Chr(13) & Chr(10)
      strProperties = "Checkbox Name: "
      strProperties = strProperties & _
              Document.frmMyForm.chkCheckBox1.Name& CRLF
      strProperties = strProperties & "Form Elements: "
      strProperties = strProperties & _
              Document.frmMyForm.chkCheckBox1.Form.Elements.Count & CRLF
      strProperties = strProperties & "Value: "
      strProperties = strProperties & _
              Document.frmMyForm.chkCheckBox1.Value & CRLF
      strProperties = strProperties & "Checked: "
      strProperties = strProperties & _
              CStr(Document.frmMyForm.chkCheckBox1.Checked)
      x = MsgBox(strProperties,0,"Test CheckBox Properties")
   End Sub

   Sub cmdButton3_OnClick
      Document.frmMyForm.chkCheckBox1.Value = _
              Document.frmMyForm.txtButtonCaption.Value
   End Sub

   Sub cmdButton4_OnClick
      Document.frmMyForm.chkCheckBox1.Click
   End Sub

   Sub chkCheckBox1_OnClick
      Alert "The test check has just been clicked"
   End Sub

   Sub cmdButton5_OnClick
      Document.frmMyForm.chkCheckBox1.Checked = True
   End Sub

   Sub cmdButton6_OnClick
      Document.frmMyForm.chkCheckBox1.Checked = False
   End Sub

  </SCRIPT>
 </HEAD>

<BODY BGCOLOR="white">
 <FORM NAME="frmMyForm">
```

*Example 6-9. The Checkbox Control (continued)*

```
   Test Check<INPUT TYPE="checkbox" NAME="chkCheckBox1" Value="TestCheck">
<P>
   <INPUT TYPE="button" NAME="cmdButton2" Value="Display Test Check
          Properties"><P>
   <INPUT TYPE="text" NAME="txtButtonCaption" Value="">
   <INPUT TYPE="button" NAME="cmdButton3" Value="Change Check Box Value">
<P>
   <INPUT TYPE="button" NAME="cmdButton4" Value="Click Test Check Box"><P>
   <INPUT TYPE="button" NAME="cmdButton5" Value="Set Test Check TRUE"><P>
   <INPUT TYPE="button" NAME="cmdButton6" Value="Set Test Check FALSE">
   </FORM>
  </BODY>
</HTML>
```

---

*TIP*                    The keywords `True` and `False` are built-in or intrinsic constants of
                         VBScript. They evaluate to −1 and 0, respectively.

---

### Checkbox properties

The *checkbox* control supports the same three properties as the command button
controls, along with an additional property. The properties are:

- **Form**. The *Form* property returns the *Form* object that is the parent of the
  checkbox. All the *Form* object's properties can then be accessed from the
  *Checkbox* object. In Example 6-9, the following code fragment retrieves the
  number of controls in the *Element* object by retrieving the *Form* property of
  *chkCheckBox1*:

  ```
  strProperties = strProperties & "Form Elements: "
  strProperties = strProperties &
  Document.frmMyForm.chkCheckBox1.Form.Elements.Count & CRLF
  ```

- **Name**. *Name* is a *read-only* property (but see the earlier sidebar, "The Name
  Property of Element Objects") that returns the name assigned to a checkbox
  control by the **NAME** attribute of the HTML `<INPUT>` tag. If the checkbox was
  not assigned a name by the `<INPUT>` tag, the value of the *Name* property is
  a zero-length string. In Example 6-9, the following code fragment retrieves
  the name of *chkCheckBox1*:

  ```
  strProperties = "Checkbox Name: "
  strProperties = strProperties & Document.frmMyForm.chkCheckBox1.Name _
                  & CRLF
  ```

- **Value**. The *Value* property stores the string assigned by the **VALUE** attribute
  of the HTML `<INPUT>` tag. *Value* is a read/write property: its value can be
  both read and set by a VBScript program. Unlike the *Caption* property of a
  Visual Basic checkbox control, which is roughly equivalent to the *Value* prop-

erty of an HTML intrinsic checkbox control, the *Value* property does not appear on the screen. The following code fragment from Example 6-9 retrieves the *Value* property of *chkCheckBox1*:

```
strProperties = strProperties & "Value:
strProperties = strProperties & Document.frmMyForm.chkCheckBox1.Value
& CRLF
```

- **Checked**. The *Checked* property reflects the state of the control—that is, whether or not it is checked. *Checked* contains a Boolean value that is True if the box is checked, and False if it is not. In addition to reading this property, you can also set its value at run-time; this is the programmatic equivalent of clicking the checkbox. If the value of the *Checked* property is to be used as part of a string, it is safest to convert it to a string by using the *CStr* function before concatenating it to the string. (For a more complete explanation, see the discussion of the *Alert* method in Chapter 5, *Controlling the Browser.*) In Example 6-9, the first code fragment shown below retrieves the current state of the checkbox control, while the second and third fragments check and uncheck the control, respectively:

```
strProperties = strProperties & "Checked: "
strProperties = strProperties &
CStr(Document.frmMyForm.chkCheckBox1.Checked)

Sub cmdButton5_OnClick
   Document.frmMyForm.chkCheckBox1.Checked = True
End Sub

Sub cmdButton6_OnClick
   Document.frmMyForm.chkCheckBox1.Checked = False
End Sub
```

It's also possible to toggle the state of a *checkbox* control by reversing its value. This is accomplished by a statement like the following, which has the same result as invoking the control's *Click* method:

```
Document.frmMyForm.chkCheckBox1.Checked = _
        Not (Document.frmMyForm.chkCheckBox1.Checked)
```

### Checkbox events

The checkbox control supports a single event, *onClick*:

- **onClick**. The *onClick* event is triggered whenever the user clicks on a checkbox. It is not triggered, however, by a call to the checkbox's *Click* method. In Example 6-9, the *chkCheckBox1_OnClick* event procedure causes a dialog to appear whenever the button is clicked:

```
Sub chkCheckBox1_OnClick
   Alert "The test check has just been clicked"
End Sub
```

Note that the most important effect of a user click—reversing the state of the checkbox—is handled automatically by the browser, and therefore should not be handled by the *OnClick* event procedure.

### Checkbox methods

The HTML intrinsic checkbox control supports a single method:

- **click**. The *Click* method allows you to programmatically click a checkbox, which has the effect of giving it the focus and reversing its state (that is, a checked box becomes unchecked, while an unchecked box becomes checked). However, calling a checkbox's *Click* method does not trigger its *OnClick* event. In Example 6-9, for instance, the *cmdButton4_OnClick* event procedure is used to reverse the state of the form's checkbox control by calling its *Click* method:

```
Sub cmdButton4_OnClick
    Document.frmMyForm.chkCheckBox1.Click
End Sub
```

But this does not cause the checkbox's *OnClick* event procedure to execute, since the dialog informing you that you've clicked the checkbox does not appear.

---

*WARNING*    Even worse, in MSIE 3.0, the *Click* method appears to disable the *OnClick* event that ordinarily would be fired by the next *user* click on the checkbox. If you've included an *OnClick* event procedure for a particular checkbox because your application requires something more to occur than simply reversing the state of a checkbox when the user clicks on it, you should use the *Click* method with extreme caution until this bug is corrected.

---

## The Radio Button Control

The radio button (or option button) control is most commonly included as one of a group of radio buttons, only one of which can be chosen. It indicates that the user can make a selection from a group of mutually exclusive alternatives—a "this or that" decision for the user. Where the user can make multiple choices (a "this *and* that" decision), a checkbox control should be used instead. Radio buttons are grouped together by assigning each control within the group the same name. This then informs the browser to only allow one of the group to be "on" or "checked" at any one time. If the user clicks another radio button in the group, the button that is currently "on" is switched "off," and the button that was clicked is switched "on."

Because more than one control has the same name, you cannot reference a radio button control in the same way that you reference any other control, since VBScript must be able to identify to which particular control in the group a particular assignment or subroutine call applies. Therefore, you cannot use a statement like the following:

```
strName = Document.FormName.RadioControl.Value ' Invalid object reference
```

A radio control's properties, events, and methods are accessible only when the radio control is referenced as part of the elements array. This means that, to retrieve the text (or caption) assigned to a particular control, you would have to use a statement like

```
strName = Document.FormName.Elements(IndexNumber).Value
```

## The Element Object and Control Arrays

If you're familiar with Visual Basic, you'll recognize that the *Elements* array is very similar to a Visual Basic control array. In a control array, each control shares the same name with every other control in the array. A particular control is identified by its index number in the array. However, HTML *Element* objects don't actually support the concept of control arrays. You can't, for example, create an array of HTML textboxes on a form, each identified by its own unique index number. The *Elements* array is global to *all* controls of all types on the form. Another important point about the *Elements* array, if you are used to handling collections or control arrays in Visual Basic, is that the *Elements* array is not a true collection in terms that VBScript can understand. As a result, you cannot translate the techniques you use in working with a VB form directly to HTML and the *Element* object. For example, the `For Each...Next` construct does not work with HTML elements.

This is quite logical because the program would have no way of knowing which particular radio control to access if there were several with the same name, whereas using `Elements(indexNumber)` uniquely identifies a control.

It's also important to recognize that there is a major difference between the ways a web server and a VBScript routine handle the control. Above all, this applies to determining which radio button is checked. If you've used radio buttons in your HTML forms before, you know that only the value of the selected radio button (that is, the text string used to describe it in the form) is sent to the server when the form is submitted. Therefore, the server-side script that handles the incoming data only needs to reference the name of the group of radio buttons to find out which value the user chose (e.g., EDUCATION=Some College). However, you don't have this luxury in VBScript. The only way you can discover which Radio button has been selected is to test each one of them in turn until the selected button is found. One way of doing that is shown in the sample program in Example 6-10, and is examined more fully in the discussion of the *Checked* property in the next section, "Radio button properties."

*Example 6-10. The Radio Button Control*

```
<HTML>
 <HEAD>
  <SCRIPT LANGUAGE="vbscript">
   Sub cmdButton2_OnClick
     Dim CRLF
     Dim strProperties
     CRLF = Chr(13) & Chr(10)
     strProperties = "Name: "
     strProperties = strProperties & _
                     Document.frmMyForm.elements(0).Name & CRLF
     strProperties = strProperties & "Form Elements: "
     strProperties = strProperties & _
                  Document.frmMyForm.elements(0).Form.Elements.Count
                     & CRLF
     strProperties = strProperties & "Value: "
     strProperties = strProperties & _
                    Document.frmMyForm.elements(0).Value & CRLF
     strProperties = strProperties & "Checked: "
     strProperties = strProperties & _
                    Document.frmMyForm.elements(0).Checked & CRLF

     x = MsgBox(strProperties,0,"Test Radio Button 1 Properties")
   End Sub

   Sub cmdButton3_OnClick
     Document.frmMyForm.elements(0).Value = _
                    Document.frmMyForm.txtButtonCaption.Value
   End Sub

   Sub cmdButton4_OnClick
     Document.frmMyForm.elements(0).Click
   End Sub

   Sub ClickRadio(intButtonNo)
     Alert "Radio Button No." & CStr(intButtonNo) & _
           " has just been clicked"
   End Sub

   Sub cmdButton5_OnClick
     Document.frmMyForm.elements(0).Checked = True
   End Sub

   Sub cmdButton6_OnClick
     Document.frmMyForm.elements(1).Checked = True
   End Sub
```

*Example 6-10. The Radio Button Control (continued)*

```
Sub cmdButton7_OnClick
    Dim x
    For x = 0 to Document.frmMyForm.Elements.Count-1
        If Left(Document.frmMyForm.Elements(x).Name,3) = "rdo" Then
            If Document.frmMyForm.elements(x).Checked Then
                Alert "Selected Value = " & _
                        Document.frmMyForm.elements(x).Value
                Exit For
            End If
        End If
    Next
End Sub

</SCRIPT>
</HEAD>

<BODY BGCOLOR="white">
<FORM NAME="frmMyForm">
  Test Radio Button 1<INPUT NAME="rdoButton" TYPE="radio" Checked
OnClick="ClickRadio(1)" Language="vbscript" Value="TestRadio"><BR>
  Test Radio Button 2<INPUT NAME="rdoButton" TYPE="radio"
OnClick="ClickRadio(2)" Language="vbscript" Value="NewRadio"><BR>
  <INPUT TYPE="button" NAME="cmdButton2" Value="Display Radio Button 1
Properties"><P>
  <INPUT TYPE="text" NAME="txtButtonValue" Value="">
  <INPUT TYPE="button" NAME="cmdButton3" Value="Change Radio Button 1
Value"><P>
  <INPUT TYPE="button" NAME="cmdButton4" Value="Click Radio Button 1"><P>
  <INPUT TYPE="button" NAME="cmdButton5" Value="Set Radio Button 1 =
TRUE"><P>
  <INPUT TYPE="button" NAME="cmdButton6" Value="Set Radio Button 2 =
TRUE"><P>
  <INPUT TYPE="button" NAME="cmdButton7" Value="Selected Value"><P>

</FORM>
</BODY>
</HTML>
```

### Radio button properties

The radio button control has the same four properties as the checkbox control:

- **Form.** The *Form* property returns the *Form* object that is the parent of the radio button. This makes all of the form's properties accessible from the *Radio Button* object. For example, the following code fragment from Example 6-10 determines how many controls exist on a form by accessing the *Forms* object through the first item in the *Elements* array:

```
strProperties = strProperties & "Form Elements: "
strProperties = strProperties &
Document.frmMyForm.elements(0).Form.Elements.Count & CRLF
```

- **Name**. The *Name* property is *read-only*; it cannot be set under program control (but, again, see the earlier sidebar, "The Name Property of Element Objects"). It returns the name assigned to a radio button by using the NAME attribute of the HTML <INPUT> tag. If the radio button has not been given a name, the value of the *Name* property is a zero-length string. The following code fragment from the *cmdButton2_OnClick* event procedure in Example 6-10 retrieves the name of the first radio button (which is found in the first position of the *Elements* array) on the form:

```
strProperties = "Name: "
strProperties = strProperties & Document.frmMyForm.elements(0).Name & _
            CRLF
```

This is the same value that is returned by the statement

```
strProperties = strProperties & Document.frmMyForm.elements(1).Name & _
            CRLF
```

In other words, to repeat an obvious point, you cannot distinguish among radio buttons in the same group by the value of their *Name* property.

The *OnClick* event procedure shown in Example 6-11 shows how you would use the radio button's *Name* property in conjunction with the *Element* object to determine which radio button has been selected. For this operation to succeed, however, you must use a naming convention for your controls. Example 6-11, for instance, assumes that the names of all radio buttons start with "rdo."

*Example 6-11. Determining Which Radio Button has Been Selected*

```
Sub cmdButton7_OnClick
    Dim x
    For x = 0 to Document.frmMyForm.Elements.Count-1
        If Left(Document.frmMyForm.Elements(x).Name,3) = "rdo" Then
            If Document.frmMyForm.elements(x).Checked Then
                Alert "Selected Value = " & _
                        Document.frmMyForm.elements(x).Value
                Exit For
            End If
        End If
    Next
End Sub
```

- **Value**. The *Value* property corresponds directly to the VALUE attribute of the HTML <INPUT> tag; it indicates the string that the browser sends to the server if that radio button is selected. The *Value* property can be read by a VBScript program, and can also be set programmatically at run time. For example, the following fragment from the *cmdButton2_OnClick* event procedure in Example 6-10 retrieves the value of the first radio button in the *Elements* array:

```
strProperties = strProperties & "Value: "
strProperties = strProperties & Document.frmMyForm.elements(0).Value &
CRLF
```

The *cmdButton3_OnClick* event procedure in Example 6-10, on the other hand, assigns a string input by the user to the radio button's *Value* property:

```
Sub cmdButton3_OnClick
    Document.frmMyForm.elements(0).Value =
Document.frmMyForm.txtButtonValue.Value
End Sub
```

- **Checked**. The *Checked* property is a Boolean value that indicates whether or not a particular radio control is selected or checked. This is a read-write property; you can use VBScript both to retrieve the state of a particular radio button and to check or uncheck it. Its implementation, though, is somewhat different from that of the HTML intrinsic checkbox control, as well as from that of the option button control in Visual Basic—which means that you should be particularly careful about setting the value of a radio button's *Checked* property programmatically. Unlike the checkbox control or the VB option button control, setting a radio button's checked property to False does not "uncheck" it. Instead, the only way to programmatically uncheck a radio button control is to set the value of the *Checked* property of another radio button control in the same group to True. This automatically sets the value of the *Checked* property of all other radio buttons in the group to False.

---

**WARNING**     In fact, in MSIE 3.0, it is easy to check a radio button when you actually mean to uncheck it. Since a radio button can only be unchecked by checking another radio button, VBScript erroneously checks a radio button whenever you attempt to *set* the value of its *Checked* property. For example, if *Elements(1)* represents a check box that is unchecked, the following statement checks it, even though it is explicitly intended to uncheck it:

```
Document.frmForm.Elements(1).Checked = False
```

---

Since retrieving the value of a radio button's *Checked* property has no effect on its state, you can read the value of its *Checked* property just as you would any other control. In Example 6-10, for instance, the following code fragment retrieves the *Checked* property of the first radio button in the *Elements* array:

```
strProperties = strProperties & "Checked: "
strProperties = strProperties & _
                Document.frmMyForm.elements(0).Checked & CRLF
```

Similarly, if the intent of your code is to explicitly turn a radio button on, you can do it using a routine like *cmdButton5_OnClick* from Example 6-10:

```
Sub cmdButton5_OnClick
```

```
      Document.frmMyForm.elements(0).Checked = True
End Sub
```

In most cases, though, you'll want to determine which button in the group has been checked by the user. To do this, you can't access the radio buttons by name, as you can with the server-side result of the form submission, since they all have the same name. Instead, you have to enumerate each radio button control. But because they can only be accessed as individual elements in the *Elements* array, the only way to do this is to enumerate all the controls on the form, to first determine if the control is a radio button, and if it is, to determine whether it is checked. This is illustrated by the *cmdButton7_OnClick* procedure in Example 6-10; if the user clicks on the Selected Value button, the browser executes the following script and displays the *Value* property of the radio button that is checked:

```
Sub cmdButton7_OnClick
   Dim x
   For x = 0 to Document.frmMyForm.Elements.Count-1
       If Left(Document.frmMyForm.Elements(x).Name,3) = "rdo" Then
           If Document.frmMyForm.elements(x).Checked Then
               Alert "Selected Value = " & _
                       Document.frmMyForm.elements(x).Value
               Exit For
           End If
       End If
   Next
End Sub
```

### Radio button events

Like the checkbox control, the radio button control supports a single event, *onClick*:

- **OnClick**. The *OnClick* event is triggered whenever the user clicks on a particular radio button. It does not occur when a radio button's *Click* method is invoked. Ordinarily, when an *OnClick* event is generated, VBScript automatically executes the routine whose name is *ControlName_OnClick*. This won't work, though, because radio button objects cannot be referenced by name. Instead, you have to identify the routine that contains a particular radio button's *OnClick* event handler within the HTML <INPUT> tag, as in the following statements from Example 6-10:

```
Test Radio Button 1<INPUT NAME="rdoButton" TYPE="radio"
   OnClick="ClickRadio(1)" Language="vbscript" Value="TestRadio"><BR>
Test Radio Button 2<INPUT NAME="rdoButton" TYPE="radio"
   OnClick="ClickRadio(2)" Language="vbscript" Value="NewRadio"><BR>
```

You then have to create a subroutine whose name corresponds to the name of your event handler. In Example 6-10, for instance, the *ClickRadio* procedure appears as follows:

```
Sub ClickRadio(intButtonNo)
    Alert "Radio Button No." & CStr(intButtonNo) & _
        " has just been clicked"
End Sub
```

Example 6-10 uses a single event handler for both buttons. We can determine which radio button was clicked by examining the value of *intButtonNo*, the parameter that is passed to the event handler. The *ClickRadio* routine itself simply opens a dialog that indicates which radio button was clicked.

### Radio button methods

The radio button control supports a single method:

- **Click**. The *Click* method allows you to programmatically click a radio button. However, the *Click* method does not set the checked value to True, as physically clicking on the control does. This can cause problems when you assume that because the control is checked it should be True. Therefore, to fully simulate a click action, you must first set the checked property to True, and then invoke the *Click* method. In addition, the Click method does not cause the radio button's *OnClick* event procedure to be invoked. The *Click* method is illustrated in the *cmdButton4_OnClick* event procedure in Example 6-10:

```
Sub cmdButton4_OnClick
    Document.frmMyForm.elements(0).Click
End Sub
```

The routine causes the Test Radio Button 1 button to be checked. However, it does not fire an *OnClick* event that causes the *ClickRadio* subroutine (which is defined as the *OnClick* event handler for both radio buttons) to be executed.

## The Text, Textarea, and Password Controls

The text, textarea, and password controls share a common set of properties, methods, and events, and therefore can be treated together. The text control allows the user to input a single line of text without carriage returns. In contrast, the textarea control, which is defined using the <TEXTAREA></TEXAREA> HTML tags, permits the user to enter large amounts of free-form text in multiple lines, separating individual lines with hard or soft carriage returns, depending upon the attributes set within the <TEXTAREA> HTML tag. Finally, the password control echoes the user's keyboard input as asterisks, thus masking the input. It is important to note that when the *Value* property of a password control is displayed programmatically, VBScript displays the clear unmasked entry, rather than an encoded string.

Example 6-12 contains a sample web page that illustrates the use of these three controls.

*Example 6-12:. The HTML Text Controls*

```
<HTML>
 <HEAD>
  <SCRIPT LANGUAGE="vbscript">
   Sub cmdButton1_OnClick
       Dim CRLF
       Dim strProperties
       CRLF = Chr(13) & Chr(10)
       strProperties = "Name: "
       strProperties = strProperties & _
                     Document.frmMyForm.txtTestText1.Name & CRLF
       strProperties = strProperties & "Form Elements: "
       strProperties = strProperties & _
             Document.frmMyForm.txtTestText1.Form.Elements.Count & CRLF
       strProperties = strProperties & "Value: "
       strProperties = strProperties & Document.frmMyForm.txtTestText1.Value
       x = MsgBox(strProperties,0,"Test Box 1 Properties")
   End Sub

   Sub cmdButton2_OnClick
       Document.frmMyForm.txtTestText1.Focus
   End Sub

   Sub cmdButton3_OnClick
       Document.frmMyForm.txtTestText1.Focus
       Document.frmMyForm.txtTestText1.Select
   End Sub

   Sub txtTestText1_OnChange
       Alert "I've changed"
   End Sub

   Sub txtTestText1_OnBlur
       Document.frmMyForm.txtTestText2.Value = _
             Document.frmMyForm.txtTestText1.Value
   End Sub

   Sub txtTestText1_OnSelect
       Alert "I'm selected"
   End Sub

   Sub txtTestText1_OnFocus
       Alert "I've got the Focus"
   End Sub

  </SCRIPT>

 </HEAD>

<BODY BGCOLOR="white">
```

*Example 6-12:. The HTML Text Controls (continued)*

```
<FORM NAME="frmMyForm">
 Test Text 1<INPUT TYPE="text" NAME="txtTestText1"><BR>
 Test Text 2<INPUT TYPE="text" NAME="txtTestText2"><BR>
 <INPUT TYPE="button" NAME="cmdButton1" Value="Display Text Box 1
         Properties"><P>
 <INPUT TYPE="button" NAME="cmdButton2" Value="Focus to Text Box 2"><P>
 <INPUT TYPE="button" NAME="cmdButton3" Value="Select Text Box 1"><P>
 </FORM>

 </BODY>
</HTML>
```

## Properties of the text, textarea, and password controls

The three intrinsic HTML text box controls support the same three properties as intrinsic HTML buttons:

- **Form**. The *Form* property returns the *Form* object that is the parent of the text box control. This makes all form properties accessible from the text, textarea, or password control. For instance, the following code fragment from Example 6-12 uses the text control's *Form* property to access the *Count* property of the *Elements* object:

```
strProperties = strProperties & "Form Elements: "
strProperties = strProperties &
Document.frmMyForm.txtTestText1.Form.Elements.Count & CRLF
```

- **Name**. *Name* is a *read-only* property (but remember the earlier sidebar, "The Name Property of Element Objects") that returns the name assigned to the control by the **NAME** attribute of the HTML input tag. If the control was not assigned a name, the value of the *Name* property is a zero-length string. The following code fragment from Example 6-12 retrieves the name of the text box control:

```
strProperties = "Name: "
strProperties = strProperties & _
                Document.frmMyForm.txtTestText1.Name & CRLF
```

- **Value**. *Value* is a read-write property that contains the text stored within the text box control. This can be set using the **TEXT** attribute of the HTML **<INPUT>** tag for text and password controls, or by placing text between the **<TEXTAREA>** and **</TEXTAREA>** tags. The following code fragment from Example 6-12 retrieves the current value of the first text box:

```
strProperties = strProperties & "Value: "
strProperties = strProperties & Document.frmMyForm.txtTestText1.Value
```

You can also change the text contained within any of the three text box controls by modifying its *Value* property at run time.

For example, the following procedure from Example 6-12 copies the text in *txtTestText1* to *txtTestText2*:

```
Sub txtTestText1_OnBlur
    Document.frmMyForm.txtTestText2.Value = _
            Document.frmMyForm.txtTestText1.Value
End Sub
```

---

### The Value Property and the Text Property

If you're familiar with Visual Basic, you'll immediately recognize that the *Value* property of the intrinsic HTML text box controls corresponds directly to the *Text* property of the standard Visual Basic text box control. Note, though, that data retrieved from an HTML text box control—and in fact all data retrieved from an HTML form—are string data. So don't forget to explicitly convert the strings returned to the correct variant data subtype before performing calculations, etc. For more information on validating form data, see Chapter 14, *Form Input Validation*.

---

Notice that the behavior of the password control's *Value* property is very similar to that of the Visual Basic text box control's *Text* property if a character has been assigned to the *PasswordChar* property. That is, when your program reads the value of either of these properties, it retrieves the actual text entered by the user, rather than a string containing the character used to conceal that text.

---

*WARNING*     Note that the password control does not support any of the four events supported by the HTML text and textarea controls. This is somewhat surprising, given that the password control is just a simple variation on the standard HTML intrinsic text control. Nevertheless, you should be aware of it so that you don't create an application whose successful operation depends on one of these events, like waiting for the focus to change from the password control before authenticating the user password.

---

### Text box control events

Again, unlike the controls that we've examined so far in this chapter, all of which support only a single *onClick* event, the text and textarea controls support a broader range of events:

- **onBlur**. The *onBlur* event is triggered when focus moves away from the text control, whether as a result of user action or under program control (because of a call to the *Focus* method that causes the focus to move from one control to another).

  In Example 6-12, the *txtTestText1_OnBlur* event procedure is responsible for copying the contents of the first text box to the second, whenever the focus moves away from the first text box:

---

### *OnBlur and LostFocus*

If you're a Visual Basic programmer, you'll recognize that the VBScript *onBlur* event corresponds closely to Visual Basic's *LostFocus* event. You may be wondering, though, why the names of these two similar events differ so much.

It may be argued that the reason for events such as *onBlur* is compatability with JavaScript—there is an *OnBlur* event in the JavaScript *Text* object. But surely there is no reason for VBScript to emulate, nor for it to be compatible with, JavaScript in this manner. In fact, the reason actually has nothing to do with either VBScript or JavaScript. The *OnBlur* event is part of the MSIE object model, and is not part of the VBScript language itself.

The MSIE object model must be compatible with other browsers' object models, and because Microsoft to some extent has to play catch-up as far as the browser object model is concerned, there are several instances of events and methods implemented in the MSIE object model that have obviously not come from a Microsoft parentage. Their similarity to JavaScript actually clouds the real reason behind this apparent change of event names: it's simply that Java-Script was written from scratch, obviously with an HTML browser in mind, so HTML object events such as *OnBlur* became part of the language. It is not possible for Microsoft to change the browser object model to allow the renaming of an event such as *OnBlur* to *LostFocus*.

---

```
Sub txtTestText1_OnBlur
    Document.frmMyForm.txtTestText2.Value = _
            Document.frmMyForm.txtTestText1.Value
End Sub
```

- **onFocus**. Unlike the *onBlur* event, which fires when the focus moves away from a text box control, the *onFocus* event is triggered when the user moves the focus to it. Interestingly, the *onFocus* event is not triggered when the focus moves to a text box under program control (i.e., as a result of the *Focus* method); it is triggered only when the focus moves as a result of user action. The *txtTestText1_OnFocus* event procedure in Example TEXT illustrates the use of the *OnFocus* event by opening a dialog whenever the text box receives the focus:

```
Sub txtTestText1_OnFocus
   Alert "I've got the Focus"
End Sub
```

- **onChange**. The *onChange* event is triggered when the focus moves away from a text control whose *Value* property has changed. It is fired only when the contents of a text control have changed as a result of user action; the *onChange* event is not triggered when the contents of a text control have been changed programmatically, as a result of assigning a new string to the control's *Value* property. In Example 6-12, the *txtTestText1_OnChange* button opens a dialog indicating that the control's text has changed when the user gives the focus to another control:

```
Sub txtTestText1_OnChange
   Alert "I've changed"
End Sub
```

- **onSelect**. Microsoft's documentation on the MSIE Object Scripting Model mentions a fourth event supported by the text and textarea controls, *onSelect*. *onSelect* is supposed to be triggered when a text box control's text is highlighted as a result of a call to its *Select* method. (*onSelect* is not supposed to be fired when the user selects some or all of the text in a text control.) However, *onSelect* is not implemented in MSIE 3.0.

---

### *OnChange and Change*

If you program in Visual Basic, you should be aware of a significant difference between the VBScript *OnChange* event and the Visual Basic *Change* event. The VBScript *OnChange* event is fired only once, when the focus moves away from a text or textarea control whose contents have changed. Its behavior is basically identical to the JavaScript *TextArea.OnChange* event. In contrast, the Visual Basic Change event is fired whenever a change occurs to the contents of a text box on a keystroke-by-keystroke basis. This difference makes the *OnChange* event handler extremely useful for validating user input into a text control.

---

### *Text box control methods*

In contrast to the controls that we've examined previously, all of which supported only the *Click* method, the three HTML intrinsic text box controls support a richer array of methods.

---

### *Focus and SetFocus*

If you program in Visual Basic, you probably recognize that the *Focus* method for text box controls in VBScript corresponds more or less closely to the VB-Script *SetFocus* method. There is, however, an important difference: when the focus moves to a control (or, for that matter, remains with a control) as a result of a call to its *SetFocus* method, in Visual Basic, the control's *GotFocus* event is fired. In contrast, in VBScript, a call to a control's *Focus* method does not trigger its *OnFocus* event.

---

- **Focus**. Moves the focus to the text control if it does not already have the focus, but does not fire its *onFocus* event. (For those who are unfamiliar with Windows programming, the control that has the focus is the control that will receive the user's keyboard input.) For example, when the user clicks on the cmdButton2 button in Example 6-12, its event handler moves the focus to the first text box, *txtTestText1*:

```
Sub cmdButton2_OnClick
    Document.frmMyForm.txtTestText1.Focus
End Sub
```

- **Blur**. According to the documentation, the *Blur* method moves the focus away from the designated control if it has the focus; however, in MSIE 3.x, it appears not to be implemented. But even if it did work, you do not have control over where the focus (if any) is moved to. If you want to move the focus away from a control under program control, the best way is simply to explicitly move the focus to another control.

- **Select**. The *Select* method selects (or highlights) all of the text contained in any of the three text box controls. It assumes that the control referenced in the call to the method already has the focus; if it does not, the call to the method has no effect. (This means that, for example, calling the *Select* method from a command button's *OnClick* event handler without calling the *Focus* method immediately beforehand does not work, since the command button receives the focus when the user clicks on it.) In addition, if the text box does not contain any text, the call to the *Select* method has no effect. In Example 6-12, if the user clicks the Select Text Box 1 button, the *cmdButton3_OnClick* event procedure executes and highlights the text in the first text box control:

```
Sub cmdButton3_OnClick
    Document.frmMyForm.txtTestText1.Focus
    Document.frmMyForm.txtTestText1.Select
End Sub
```

# The Select Control

The Select control is the HTML equivalent of a drop-down list box. Because it's a specialized HTML object, its syntax is unusual in two respects. First, it's one of only two intrinsic HTML controls (the other is the text area control) that are not defined using the `<INPUT>` tag; instead, drop-down list boxes are defined using the `<SELECT>` tag. Second, each drop-down list box contains one or more sub-objects, each of which is defined by the HTML `<OPTION>` tag and has its own set of properties.

---

*WARNING*　　Unlike other HTML controls such as the text objects, the values that appear in the drop-down list box (which are the objects defined by the `<OPTION>` tags) cannot be set at run time, which seriously reduces the interactivity of this interface object. If your application requires either a variable or a dynamic list of options in a list box, you should consider using the ActiveX ComboBox control.

---

The Select control is simple to use, and it is relatively easy to discover which option the user has chosen and what text that option contains. Our sample program, which is shown in Example 6-13, uses a straightforward single selection `<SELECT>`. It is also possible to use a Select control that allows multiple options to be selected simultaneously. (To do this, you add the **MULTIPLE** attribute to the `<SELECT>` tag.) Handling it simply involves the extra step of enumerating each element stored in the *Option* object (which is covered in the discussion of the *Select* property in the next section, "Select control properties") to determine which options were selected.

Example 6-13 allows you to examine the properties of both the `<SELECT>` control and of each of its associated options. Clicking its Show Select Properties button produces a display like the one shown in Figure 6-1, which lists the properties not only of the Select control, but also of its individual selection options.

*Example 6-13. The Select Control*

```
<HTML>
 <HEAD>
  <SCRIPT LANGUAGE="vbscript">
   Sub cmdTest_OnClick
       Dim intLength, intSelected, intCtr
       Dim strProperties
       Dim CRLF
       Dim objOption
       CRLF = Chr(13) & Chr(10)
       Set objSelect = Document.frmMyForm.selTestSelect
       strProperties = "Name: "
       strProperties = strProperties & objSelect.Name & CRLF
```

*Example 6-13. The Select Control (continued)*

```
        strProperties = strProperties & "Length: "
        strProperties = strProperties & objSelect.Length & CRLF
        strProperties = strProperties & "Selected: "
        strProperties = strProperties & objSelect.selectedIndex & CRLF
        strProperties = strProperties & CRLF & "Options:- " & CRLF
        strProperties = strProperties & "Total Number of Options: "
        strProperties = strProperties & objSelect.Options.Length & CRLF
        strProperties = strProperties & "Option No Selected: "
        strProperties = strProperties & objSelect.Options.selectedIndex & _
                    CRLF

        For i = 0 to objSelect.Options.Length - 1
            strProperties = strProperties & "Properties for Option No."
            strProperties = strProperties & i & ", "
            strProperties = strProperties & "Am I Selected: "
            strProperties = strProperties & _
                        objSelect.Options(i).Selected & ", "
            strProperties = strProperties & "defaultSelected: "
            strProperties = strProperties & _
                        objSelect.Options(i).defaultSelected & _
                        ", "
            strProperties = strProperties & "Text: "
            strProperties = strProperties & objSelect.Options(i).Text & CRLF
        Next
        x = MsgBox(strProperties,0,"Test Select Properties")
    End Sub

    Sub selTestSelect_OnChange
        Alert "I've Changed"
    End Sub

    Sub selTestSelect_OnFocus
        Alert "I've got the focus"
    End Sub

  </SCRIPT>
</HEAD>

<BODY BGCOLOR="white">
 <FORM NAME="frmMyForm">
  <SELECT NAME="selTestSelect">
   <OPTION SELECTED>Option No 1
   <OPTION>Option No 2
   <OPTION>Option No 3
   <OPTION>Option No 4
   <OPTION>Option No 5
   <OPTION>Option No 6
  </SELECT>
  <P>
  <INPUT TYPE="button" NAME="cmdTest" VALUE="Show Select Properties"><P>
 </FORM>
</BODY>
</HTML>
```

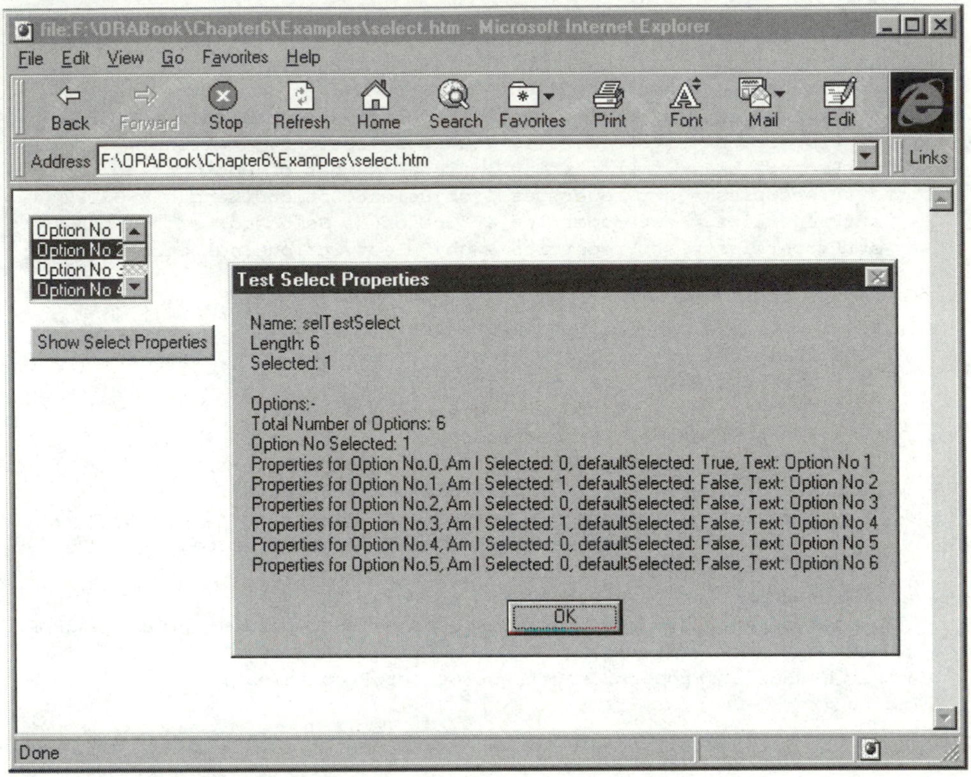

*Figure 6-1. The properties of the HTML Select control and its options*

### Select control properties

Except for two standard properties, *Name* and *Form*, all of the Select control's properties are unique to the control:

- **Form**. The Select control's *Form* property returns reference to the *Form* object, thus allowing the control to access all of the *Form* object's properties.

- **Name**. Like the *Name* property of the other HTML intrinsic controls, the Select control's *Name* property is read-only (but don't forget the earlier sidebar, "The Name Property of Element Objects"); it merely returns the string assigned to the control by the **NAME** attribute of the **<SELECT>** tag. If the control was not assigned a name, the property returns a zero-length string. In Example 6-13, the following statements retrieve the name of the Select control and add it to the string that's to be displayed in an informational dialog.

```
strProperties = "Name: " & CRLF
strProperties = strProperties & _
            Document.frmMyForm.selTestSelect.Name & CRLF
```

- **Length**. The *Length* property returns the number of items displayed in the list box; this corresponds to the number of items defined by the **<OPTION>** tags between the `<SELECT>` and `</SELECT>` tags, and also indicates the number of items contained in the Select control's *Options* array. In using the value of the *Length* property to work with individual list box items, though, remember that the *Options* array (the object returned by the Select control's *Options* property, which is discussed later in this section) is zero-based: the elements in it begin at 0 and end at *length-1*. The following code fragment from Example 6-13 determines the number of listings in the Select control by retrieving the value of its *Length* property:

```
strProperties = strProperties & "Length: "
strProperties = strProperties & _
            Document.frmMyForm.selTestSelect.Length & CRLF
```

- **SelectedIndex**. Returns the index number of the selected option within the *Options* array. (For details on handling a multiple selection list, see the discussion of the *Selected* property later in this section.) The following code fragment from Example 6-13, for instance, retrieves the index of the selected item in the list box to display in a dialog:

```
strProperties = strProperties & "Selected: "
strProperties = strProperties & _
            Document.frmMyForm.selTestSelect.selectedIndex & CRLF
```

- **Options**. The *Options* property returns an *Options* collection. This contains an array of *Option* objects, one for each item in the list box (or one for each item defined by the `<OPTION>` tag for a particular `<SELECT>` tag), and provides a *Length* property that indicates how many *Option* objects are contained in the *Options* collection. Each *Option* object within the *Options* array has its own set of properties, some of which are the same as the properties of the *Select* object, and some of which are different. The properties of the *Options* object, all of which are read-only, are shown in Table 6-1.

### Select control events

The Select control recognizes two events, *onFocus* and *onChange*:

- **onFocus**. The *onFocus* event is triggered when the user moves the input focus from some other control to the list box control. It is also triggered when the list box control regains the focus because its browser window becomes the active window. The following event procedure from Example 6-13 displays a dialog whenever the list box receives the input focus:

```
Sub selTestSelect_OnFocus
    Alert "I've got the focus"
End Sub
```

However, the event does not operate as you may expect. For single-selection list boxes, the *onFocus* event is fired as a result of user actions, in just the way that you would expect, when the user moves the focus to the control from some other control, or when the focus is returned to the list box control after it loses the focus to some other application window. But for multiple-selection list boxes, it is fired only when the focus returns directly to the Select control from another application. Finally, a call to the *Focus* method—which moves the focus to the Select control—never fires the *onFocus* event.

*Table 6-1. Properties of the Select Control's Options Object*

| Property | Applies to | Description |
| --- | --- | --- |
| *defaultSelected* | Each element | *defaultSelected* is a Boolean value that indicates whether a particular *Option* object is the list box's default selection (i.e., the option that was defined using the `SELECTED` attribute of the HTML `<OPTIONS>` tag). If the `SELECTED` attribute was not used to define any member of the list box, the value of the *defaultSelected* property for each member object of the *Options* object is False. In Example 6-13, the following code fragment retrieves the position of the default selection in the *Options* array:<br><br>```Set objOptions = _<br>    Document.frmMyForm.selTestSelect.Options<br>intLength = _<br>Document.frmMyForm.selTestSelect.Length<br>for intCtr = 0 to intLength - 1<br>   if objOptions(intCtr).DefaultSelected =<br>TRUE then<br>       intSelected = intCtr<br>       exit for<br>   end if<br>next``` |
| *length* | Options object | This duplicates the *Select* object's *Length* property. The following fragment from Example 6-13 determines the number of elements in the *Options* array:<br><br>```strProperties = strProperties & "Length: "<br>strProperties = strProperties & _<br>Document.frmMyForm.selTestSe-<br>lect.Options.Length & CRLF``` |
| *selectedIndex* | Options object | The *SelectedIndex* property, which duplicates the *Select* object's *SelectedIndex* property, indicates the index number of the selected option in the *Options* array. Since it is a single variable that is capable of holding a single value, it cannot indicate multiple selections. When more than one option is selected, only the ordinal number of the first selected index is held in this property. For multiple selections, you have to iterate through the options checking the value of the *Selected* property. The following code fragment from Example 6-13 retrieves the index of the selected list box item to display in a dialog:<br><br>```strProperties = strProperties & "Selected: "<br>strProperties = strProperties & _<br>Document.frmMyForm.selTestSe-<br>lect.Options.selectedIndex & CRLF``` |

*Table 6-1. Properties of the Select Control's Options Object (continued)*

| Property | Applies to | Description |
|---|---|---|
| *Selected* | Each element | *Selected* is an integer value that indicates whether a particular option is selected (its value is 1) or not (its value is 0). Examining the value of the *Selected* property for each element of the *Options* array is the only way to determine whether more than one item has been selected in a multiple selection list box. The following code fragment illustrates how to use the *Selected* property to determine whether multiple options have been selected:<br><br>```
set objOption =_
    Document.frmForm.lstPets.Options
for intCtr = 0 to objOption.Length - 1
    if objOption(intCtr).Selected = 1 then
        ' code to handle one of multiple
        selections
    endif
next
```<br>Note that you can treat the value of the *Selected* property as Boolean data only if you don't explicitly compare it to the VBScript True constant. For instance, the code fragment:<br><br>```
Set objListBox = Document.frmMy-
Form.selColors.Options
For intCtr = 0 to objListBox.Length - 1
    If objListBox(intCtr).Selected Then
```<br>can be used to identify whether the items in a Select control have been selected, while the code fragment:<br><br>```
Set objListBox = Document.frmMy-
Form.selColors.Options
For intCtr = 0 to objListBox.Length - 1
    If objListBox(intCtr).Selected = True
Then    ' Wrong
```<br>fails to identify any selected items. |
| *Text* | Each element | The *Text* property contains the string that is defined by the `<OPTIONS>` tag and that appears in the drop-down list box. For example, the following code fragment retrieves the name of the selected item in a single selection list box:<br><br>```
strProperties = strProperties & "Text: "
i = Document.frmMyForm.selTestSe-
lect.Options.selectedIndex
strProperties = strProperties & _
    Document.frmMyForm.selTestSe-
lect.Options(i).Text & CRLF
``` |

- **onChange**. The *onChange* event is fired when the user selects a new item from the list. The following event procedure from Example 6-13 displays a dialog whenever the user selects a different option from the drop-down list box:

```
Sub selTestSelect_OnChange
    Alert "I've Changed"
End Sub
```

## The Select Control's OnFocus Event

In Versions 3.0 and 3.01 of MSIE, the Select Control's *OnFocus* event is always triggered when focus passes from another window to the browser window, if the Select control has focus within the browser window. This can cause more than just a minor irritation. Suppose, for example, your web page has a message box that pops up when the control gets the focus (as in Example 6-13). You then minimize the form when the Select control has the focus. Thereafter, every time that you try to restore the browser window, the *OnFocus* event fires and the message box pops up. However, since the browser does not restore, your web page is stuck in an endless loop. The user's only option is to shut down the browser using the Task Manager.

## Select Control Methods

The Select control supports the following two methods:

- **Focus**. The *Focus* method passes control to the Select control but does not actually cause the control's *OnFocus* event to be fired.

- **blur**. According to the documentation, the *Blur* method moves the focus away from the designated control if it has the focus, and it does just that. However, you do not have control over where the focus (if any) is moved to. If you want to move the focus away from a control under program control, the best way is to explicitly move the focus to another control.

## The removeItem, addItem, and clear Methods

The Microsoft documentation on the *Element* object refers to several methods that do not exist in the MSIE object model: *removeItem*, *addItem* and *clear*. These methods are apparently for use with a nonexistent HTML *Combo* element. The Combo is in fact an ActiveX control. And while the ActiveX combo control is similar to the HTML Select control, you cannot use an ActiveX control's methods with an HTML object.

## The Hidden Control

The Hidden control is used to "store" variables on a form for inclusion in the data sent with the form to the server. Typically, these are data that are read-only and that the application protects by hiding them from the user. Hidden controls are ideal for storing data that you are passing from one page to another, or for concealing data such as usernames, identifiers, etc., that need to be part of the data submitted with a form but that you may not want to show on the HTML page.

Hidden controls are also important when you are using ActiveX controls or the HTML Layout Control to receive input data from the user. In either of these cases, you build your form controls, which look all nice and neat and have some super events and methods for you to code. But at some point you want the data on the form to be passed back to the server. Your problem (assuming that you aren't using Active Server Pages) is that an HTML form—which is the medium that you use to get the data back to the server—doesn't know what an ActiveX control is, and ignores it completely. So what's the solution? Define an HTML form, assigning it a name using the **NAME** attribute, set the *Action* property to the URL of the server script that will process the data, set the **METHOD** attribute to either **POST** or **GET** in the normal way, then define only Hidden controls in the HTML form. The code you place behind your ActiveX "submit" button (which actually submits the data to the server instead of an HTML Submit button) then simply assigns all the values from the ActiveX controls to the appropriate HTML Hidden controls. Your final line of code in the button's *Click* event procedure submits the HTML form by invoking the form's *Submit* method. Example 6-14 shows how this is done.

*Example 6-14. Using Hidden Controls with ActiveX Form Controls*

```
<HTML>
<HEAD>
    <SCRIPT LANGUAGE="VBScript">
<!--
Sub cmdSubmit_Click()
    Document.frmForm1.txtHTMLName.Value = txtName.Value
    Document.frmForm1.txtHTMLEMail.Value = txtEMail.Value
    Call Document.frmForm1.submit()
End Sub
-->
    </SCRIPT>

</HEAD>
<BODY BGCOLOR="white">
<CENTER>
Your Name:
    <OBJECT ID="txtName" WIDTH=181 HEIGHT=24
     CLASSID="CLSID:8BD21D10-EC42-11CE-9E0D-00AA006002F3">
        <PARAM NAME="VariousPropertyBits" VALUE="746604571">
        <PARAM NAME="Size" VALUE="4784;635">
        <PARAM NAME="FontCharSet" VALUE="0">
        <PARAM NAME="FontPitchAndFamily" VALUE="2">
        <PARAM NAME="FontWeight" VALUE="0">
    </OBJECT>
<BR>
Your Email Address:
    <OBJECT ID="txtEMail" WIDTH=159 HEIGHT=24
     CLASSID="CLSID:8BD21D10-EC42-11CE-9E0D-00AA006002F3">
```

*Example 6-14. Using Hidden Controls with ActiveX Form Controls (continued)*

```
        <PARAM NAME="VariousPropertyBits" VALUE="746604571">
        <PARAM NAME="Size" VALUE="4198;635">
        <PARAM NAME="FontCharSet" VALUE="0">
        <PARAM NAME="FontPitchAndFamily" VALUE="2">
        <PARAM NAME="FontWeight" VALUE="0">
    </OBJECT>
<BR>
    <OBJECT ID="cmdSubmit" WIDTH=96 HEIGHT=32
    CLASSID="CLSID:D7053240-CE69-11CD-A777-00DD01143C57">
        <PARAM NAME="Caption" VALUE="Submit">
        <PARAM NAME="Size" VALUE="2540;846">
        <PARAM NAME="FontCharSet" VALUE="0">
        <PARAM NAME="FontPitchAndFamily" VALUE="2">
        <PARAM NAME="ParagraphAlign" VALUE="3">
        <PARAM NAME="FontWeight" VALUE="0">
    </OBJECT>

    <FORM ACTION="http://www.vbscripts.com/test/htmlsubmit.phtml"
        METHOD="POST" NAME="frmForm1">
        <INPUT TYPE=hidden NAME="txtHTMLName">
        <INPUT TYPE=hidden NAME="txtHTMLEMail">
    </FORM>

</BODY>
</HTML>
```

### Hidden control properties

While the Hidden control does not support any events or methods, it does have two properties:

- **Name**. The *Name* property is read-only, and contains the value assigned by the **NAME** attribute of the hidden control's **<INPUT>** tag. The **NAME** attribute is required in order to define a valid hidden control.

- **Value**. The *Value* property contains the value assigned by the **VALUE** attribute of the HTML **<INPUT>** tag. In addition to being able to retrieve the value of the property, your application can also modify its value at run-time, although most commonly the value of a Hidden control is set when creating the HTML page.

## Summary

If you've also read Chapter 5, you've now completed our admittedly hasty overview of the MSIE Object Model. You have now been through every part of the model that is currently implemented in MSIE3.0, so you should have no trouble in recognizing the properties, methods, and events of the various browser objects. Since accessing the browser's object model is critical to most client-side scripts, in subsequent chapters we'll look at other aspects of the VBScript language and how to use it with a script-enabled browser. To summarize the main points:

- The Object Model is a hierarchy of HTML Objects, at the top of which is the *Window* object, which represents the browser window. When referencing objects within the hierarchy, you must start at the top of the model and work your way down. The only exception to this occurs when objects are implicit. However, when referencing objects and controls within other frames, you must start the reference with the *Top* object.

- Since HTML intrinsic controls are part of the browser, they are available to anyone with a script-enabled browser, making them fast and easy to use. In the MSIE object model, they are implemented as elements of the *Element* object array. Since the *Element* object is a child of the *Form* object, the properties, methods, and events of HTML intrinsic controls are accessible only when the controls are placed within an HTML form.

HTML intrinsic controls have a limited range of properties, events, and methods, so you may have to use ActiveX controls to obtain more esoteric functionality.

# 7

In this chapter:
• What Is the ActiveX
  Control Pad?
• Downloading and
  Installation
• Using the ActiveX
  Control Pad
• The ACLIST Utility
• Summary

# Using the ActiveX
# Control Pad

So far, you've seen VBScript used with standard HTML objects, a focus that is particularly important as you attempt to add scripted procedures to current HTML documents. All the examples you've seen have used Notepad or a similar text editor to create the documents. This is appropriate, since the syntax required by HTML to define HTML forms that include intrinsic controls is fairly straightforward and trouble-free.

However useful they are, though, the intrinsic HTML controls have a number of limitations. For one thing, they lack the look and feel of Windows interface components; if you want to create what your users will recognize as a Windows application, they just don't do the trick. For another, the controls are inflexible in a number of ways. We've already seen one instance of this: the HTML Select control does not allow list box items to be added dynamically at run time. But there are countless other instances in which HTML intrinsic controls don't offer the power or the flexibility that you want your application to have. Above all, they comprise a relatively limited range of interface components over which you have comparatively limited control.

As a result, I suspect that, as time goes by, you'll find yourself using ActiveX controls more and more frequently in place of the intrinsic HTML objects. The enormity of the ActiveX control market (ActiveX controls, remember, are used not only in applications developed with VBScript, but in virtually all applications developed with languages like Visual Basic) ensures that a vast array of both general- and special-purpose ActiveX controls is available. And, through their wider range of accessible properties, events, and methods, ActiveX controls offer you a far greater ability to control their behavior.

But aside from the general advantages that ActiveX controls provide, they are readily available on all 32-bit Windows systems. Table 7-1 lists the range of standard ActiveX controls that Microsoft ships with Microsoft Internet Explorer 3.x, which means that you can use controls such as drop-down lists, command buttons, and labels, with relative confidence that visitors to your site who are using MSIE3.0 already have the controls available on their systems and will not have to download them from your site. This removes one of the major drawbacks—the extra time required to download them.

*Table 7-1. Standard Microsoft ActiveX Form Controls*

| Control | Long ID control name | Source File |
| --- | --- | --- |
| CheckBox | Microsoft Forms 2.0 CheckBox | *windows\system\fm20.dll* |
| ComboBox | Microsoft Forms 2.0 ComboBox | *windows\system\fm20.dll* |
| CommandButton | Microsoft Forms 2.0 CommandButton | *windows\system\fm20.dll* |
| Hot Spot | Microsoft ActiveX Hot Spot Control 1.0 | *windows\system\isctrls.ocx* |
| Image | Microsoft ActiveX Image Control 1.0 | *windows\system\isctrls.ocx* |
| Label | Microsoft Forms 2.0 Label | *windows\system\fm20.dll* |
| ListBox | Microsoft Forms 2.0 ListBox | *windows\system\fm20.dll* |
| OptionButton | Microsoft Forms 2.0 OptionButton | *windows\system\fm20.dll* |
| ScrollBar | Microsoft Forms 2.0 ScrollBar | *windows\system\fm20.dll* |
| SpinButton | Microsoft Forms 2.0 SpinButton | *windows\system\fm20.dll* |
| TabStrip | Microsoft Forms 2.0 TabStrip | *windows\system\fm20.dll* |
| TextBox | Microsoft Forms 2.0 TextBox | *windows\system\fm20.dll* |
| ToggleButton | Microsoft Forms 2.0 ToggleButton | *windows\system\fm20.dll* |

### Standard ActiveX Controls

As you can see from the Table 7-1, the majority of standard ActiveX form controls are contained within the file *fm20.dll*, which is installed with MSIE3.0. Due to its size (1,098Kb), it is not designed for transmission across the Internet.

But there is a second major drawback to using ActiveX controls: you have to include them in your application by using the HTML <OBJECT> tag to define the control, and the <PARAM> tag to set the values of its properties. The syntax of the <OBJECT> tag, though, is far more complicated than that of the <FORM> and <INPUT> tags, while at the same time it can be completely unforgiving. If you make an error in defining the object that you'd like included in your application by assigning it an improper CLASSID, the ActiveX control becomes inaccessible and, in most cases, your application fails. Because of this, as the following definition of a command button shows, the definition of an ActiveX control using Notepad can easily become a nightmare:

```
<OBJECT ID="CommandButton1" WIDTH=96 HEIGHT=32
 CLASSID="CLSID:D7053240-CE69-11CD-A777-00DD01143C57">
    <PARAM NAME="Caption" VALUE="Click Me">
    <PARAM NAME="Size" VALUE="2540;846">
    <PARAM NAME="FontCharSet" VALUE="0">
    <PARAM NAME="FontPitchAndFamily" VALUE="2">
    <PARAM NAME="ParagraphAlign" VALUE="3">
    <PARAM NAME="FontWeight" VALUE="0">
</OBJECT>
```

Creating code such as this manually for an HTML document full of ActiveX
controls, debugging it, and trying to get it to work properly is enough to put you
off using ActiveX controls for life! Which is a pity, because as you'll see later in
the chapter, ActiveX controls are the key to producing an interface that not only
looks like a Windows interface, but acts and "feels" like one too...probably
because it *is* a Windows interface.

So how are you going to take advantage of the benefits of ActiveX Controls and
at the same time retain a modicum of sanity? The ActiveX Control Pad is your
answer. The ActiveX Control Pad allows you to very quickly add ActiveX controls
to an HTML page, in the process automatically generating the complex
<OBJECT> and <PARAM> definitions for you. In this chapter, you'll find out how
to obtain and install the ActiveX Control Pad, and how to use it.

# What Is the ActiveX Control Pad?

The ActiveX Control Pad is a tool to help you add ActiveX controls and any associ-
ated script to an HTML page quickly and easily. It isn't a tool to help you *create*
ActiveX Controls; that is still the domain of development tools like Microsoft
Visual C++ and Visual Basic 5.0 and the Visual Basic Control Creation Edition.

The ActiveX Control Pad is comprised of the following four components:

- The HTML editor, a straightforward text editor. This is a rather minimal text
  editor; if you're expecting a fully functional HTML editor that supports the
  point and click addition of HTML tags, you'll be disappointed.

- The Object Editor, which allows you to insert ActiveX Controls and control
  some of their properties. For example, you can select a control like a command button to add to your Web page and use the Object Editor to size it.

- A Properties window, which allows you to view and set the properties of controls that you've added to a Web page in the HTML Layout Control. This Properties window is identical to that in Visual Basic.

- The Script Wizard, which provides a point-and-click interface that allows you
  to add actions to an object's events, and that automatically generates VBScript
  or JavaScript code that can be placed in the HTML file.

## *The <OBJECT> and <PARAM> Tags*

Although it is not essential that you thoroughly understand the <OBJECT> and <PARAM> tags in order to use ActiveX controls, you may find their syntax of interest, since it gives you some insight into how controls and objects interface with HTML documents and the browser.

The <OBJECT> tag tells the browser to load a particular control. It also supplies several pieces of data to the browser, which are then passed to the control on initialization. These are supplied as attributes of the <OBJECT> tag and include:

- **ID**. The name of the control; for example, *IeTimer1*.

- **Width**. The width in pixels of the control. Most controls require this property to be set on initialization, although you may encounter controls whose width and height are fixed and "hardcoded" into the control.

- **Height**. The height of the control in pixels.

- **CLASSID**. The class identifier, or CLSID, is a 128-bit (16-byte) binary value that serves to uniquely identify a particular ActiveX component. (As you can imagine, with a possible 0—255 value for each of 16 place-holders, there are enough unique combinations to allow a brand-new ActiveX control to be created every second of the day, well into the next century!) The actual value must be preceded by the string "CLSID:" For example, an <OBJECT> tag with a **CLASSID** attribute might appear as follows:

```
<OBJECT ID="IeTimer1" WIDTH=39 HEIGHT=39
CLASSID="CLSID:59CCB4A0-727D-11CF-AC36-00AA00A47DD2">
```

- The class identifier is generated by either of two programs, *UUIDGEN* or *GUIDGEN*, both of which are included with the software components used to create ActiveX controls. When the web page is loaded, MSIE uses the class identifier to "look up" the control in the registry, in order to determine if it is already installed on the system.

- **Codebase**. An optional attribute that indicates a source from which the ActiveX control can be downloaded if it cannot be found on the client; see the sidebar "The Codebase Attribute" for details of how to use the **CODEBASE** attribute.

The parameters needed to initialize the properties of an ActiveX control are specified in the <PARAM> tags, with one tag used for each property. The number and variety of <PARAM> tags that appear in an object definition will depend on the individual control, and also on the number of properties whose value you want to set when you place a control in the HTML page—either manually, using the ActiveX Control Pad, or using the HTML Layout Control.

*—Continued—*

Let me expand a little on this point. The designers of the control have created many properties, such as the background color of the control or its font color. They have also specified default values for these properties. As the control is loading, the default values are assigned to the properties. Because the default property values are stored within the control, you need not pass any data to the control when you are using default values. However, if you wish to have a control load with property values other than those set by the control's designer, you need to pass these new values to the control. This is done by specifying both the property name and its value in the `<PARAM>` tag. So a `<PARAM>` tag can be defined as, "A nondefault value that's assigned to a particular property."

For example, let's say you are using a new type of ActiveX command button that has a default caption of "OK." If you leave the caption value as its default, the *Caption* property need not appear in the PARAM list. However, if you change the caption value to "CLICK ME," then a `<PARAM>` tag is needed to assign a nondefault property value as the control initializes. In the case of our example, the `<PARAM>` tag might appear as follows:

```
<PARAM NAME="Caption" Value="CLICK ME">
```

Unlike the `<OBJECT>` tag, `<PARAM>` tags do not have a corresponding close tag. The `<OBJECT>` tag definitions should be closed with `</OBJECT>` after the `<PARAM>` parameters have been defined.

The ActiveX Control Pad can be used in conjunction with the HTML Layout Control, a WYSIWYG tool for placing ActiveX controls on a web page that supports two-dimensional HTML. The HTML Layout Control is covered in the next chapter. First of all, though, you'll need a copy of the ActiveX Control Pad.

## Downloading and Installation

One of the nicest things about the ActiveX Control Pad is that it is available for free from the Microsoft Site Builder Workshop (*http://www.microsoft.com/workshop/*). Simply follow the links for the ActiveX Control Pad, and once you have registered, you can download the Control Pad's self-extracting archive file, *SETUPPAD.EXE*.

Installing the ActiveX Control Pad and its associated HTML Layout Control is simplicity itself. The file that you download is a self-extracting and self-running installation program. All that you have to do is locate the file (*SETUPPAD.EXE*) in your Windows Explorer and double-click the file to extract the required files and launch the installation procedure. Follow the on-screen directions—of which there are very few—and there you go.

### The CODEBASE Attribute

CODEBASE is an attribute of the `<OBJECT>` tag that tells the browser where to find the control for download. The attribute's value is a URL that contains the name of an executable file (i.e., a file with an extension of .OCX, .EXE, or .DLL), a cabinet file (a file with a .CAB extension that contains multiple compressed files), or an .INF file (which details installation instructions and in turn contains the URLs of files needed for the installation). You can use absolute or relative location references for the CODEBASE URL; for example, an absolute reference may be something like *http://www.mydomain.com/ocxfiles/ietimer.- ocx*, while a relative (to the HTML file) reference could be simply the ActiveX filename, if both the HTML file and the ActiveX control reside in the same directory. The following CODEBASE attribute, for example, uses an absolute URL to identify the location from which a control named IeTimer1 can be downloaded:

```
<OBJECT ID="IeTimer1" WIDTH=39 HEIGHT=39
 CLASSID="CLSID:59CCB4A0-727D-11CF-AC36-00AA00A47DD2"
 CODEBASE="http://www.mydomain.com/ietimer.ocx">
    <PARAM NAME="_ExtentX" VALUE="1005">
    <PARAM NAME="_ExtentY" VALUE="1005">
</OBJECT>
```

Note that, when the browser encounters the `<OBJECT>` tag, it first attempts to use the class identifier to determine the precise filename and its location from the Windows registry, in the event that it has already been installed on the local machine. If the file is found, the CODEBASE attribute is ignored and the local file used. Otherwise, the URL provided by the CODEBASE attribute is used to download the file.

Along with allowing you to indicate the name of a file, the CODEBASE attribute can also be used to handle version control. Simply suffix the filename with `#Version=` and the version code, as the following example shows:

```
http://www.vbscripts.com/examples/files/mycontrol.ocx#Version=4.
70. 0. 1085
```

You can obtain the version number of an ActiveX control by locating the file using Window Explorer, right-clicking the filename and selecting Properties from the pop-up menu, then simply selecting the Version tab in the File Properties dialog box.

# Using the ActiveX Control Pad

To demonstrate the various parts of the ActiveX Control Pad and how they work, let's use the Control Pad to create a sample page. To launch the ActiveX Control Pad, click the Start button and select the Programs option. There should be a folder named ActiveX Control Pad that contains an entry named "Microsoft ActiveX Control Pad"; when you select it, it launches the ActiveX Control Pad, as shown in Figure 7-1. As you can see, the ActiveX Control Pad always launches as a text editor, and creates a basic HTML template called *Page1* (a refreshing change from the usual "untitled").

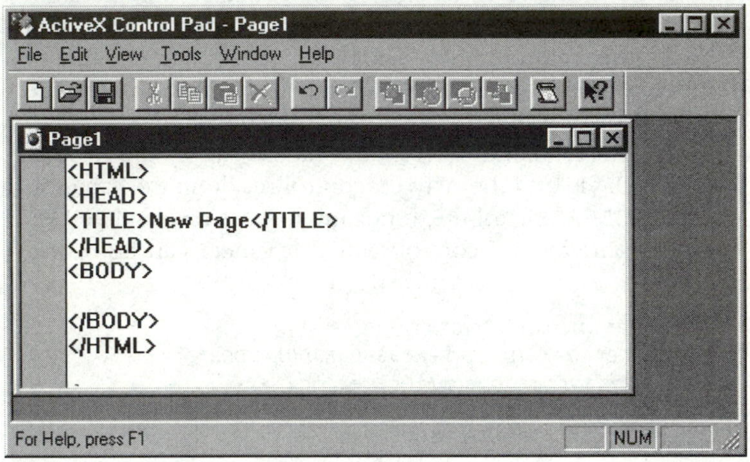

*Figure 7-1. The ActiveX Control Pad*

## The ActiveX Control Pad Menus

The ActiveX Control Pad contains six top-level menus (File, Edit, View, Tools, Window, and Help). As with all Windows applications, the majority of menu items are either self-explanatory or will be instantly familiar to you (like Save or Save As...). So let's focus on the menu items that are unique to the ActiveX Control Pad and are therefore likely to be unfamiliar. These are shown in Table 7-2.

*Table 7-2. ActiveX Control Pad Menu Options*

| Top-Level Menu | Menu Item | Description |
| --- | --- | --- |
| File Menu | New HTML | Opens a new HTML template like the one that is shown when you first open the ActiveX Control Pad. |
| File Menu | New HTML Layout | Opens a new .ALX layout document. For details, see Chapter 8, *The HTML Layout Control.* |
| Edit Menu | Insert ActiveX Control | Displays the Insert ActiveX Control dialog for you to choose the required control whose <OBJECT> tag should be inserted into your page. |

*Table 7-2. ActiveX Control Pad Menu Options (continued)*

| Top-Level Menu | Menu Item | Description |
| --- | --- | --- |
| Edit Menu | Insert HTML Layout | Allows you to open and insert a previously built .ALX Layout Document. For details, see Chapter 8. |
| Tools Menu | Script Wizard | Launches the ActiveX Script Wizard. |
| Tools Menu | Options | Selecting this option produces a submenu with two further options, HTML Layout... and Script... The first option lets you set several defaults for the HTML Layout Control's grid. The second allows you to specify the default language (either VBScript or JavaScript) for the Script Wizard, as well as choose whether the Wizard is launched in code view or list view. |

## The ActiveX Control Pad Toolbar

Like most of Microsoft's recent interfaces, the ActiveX Control Pad features a dockable toolbar. This means you can drag the toolbar from its default position under the menu bar, turn it into a floating toolbar, resize it, and move it around at will. For most applications, though, its default position should suffice.

Moving from left to right in Figure 7-1, the first three groups of buttons on the toolbar—containing nine buttons in all (New, Open, Save, Cut, Copy, Paste, Delete, Undo, and Redo)—are common to most applications and do not require explanation. The fourth group, which consists of four buttons, is used with the HTML Layout Control. These buttons are typically disabled; they're only highlighted when more than one control is placed on an HTML layout page. They are used to move a control back and forth from front to back, and their use is explained in detail in Chapter 8. The last two buttons are the Script Wizard, which launches the ActiveX Script Wizard, and the Help button.

## Using the ActiveX HTML Editor

Although you can use the ActiveX Control Pad's HTML Editor to create a standard HTML document, it's really just the same thing as using Notepad. There are no menus or lists of insertable HTML tags, no dragging and dropping of new controls, no point and click, just straightforward text editing. The ActiveX Control Pad, after all, was never designed as just another HTML authoring tool. The main functions of the Control Pad are to insert ActiveX controls and to create Active Scripting automatically. Of course, if you want to use your favorite HTML editor to create the basic web page, you can do that and then use the File Open menu option to open the HTML file with the ActiveX Control Pad.

If MSIE3.0 is defined as your default browser, and you have installed the ActiveX Control Pad, you can open any HTML file using the ActiveX Control Pad from the Windows Explorer. When you right-click the filename, you'll notice that a new option, Edit with ActiveX Control Pad, appears on the context menu. Selecting this option launches the ActiveX Control Pad and loads the file into the editor's window.

## Inserting an ActiveX Control

Let's take a look at one of the real reasons that you'd want to use the ActiveX Control Pad: inserting an ActiveX Control. The Control Pad generates the code necessary to define the control, and places it in the HTML file wherever your cursor was when you started the process. Therefore, assuming you have the default template open, put your cursor under the <HEAD> tag.

To insert an ActiveX Control, select the Insert ActiveX Control option from the Edit menu. The ActiveX Control Pad opens an Insert ActiveX Control dialog, like the one shown in Figure 7-2, that lists all the insertable controls registered on your system. The exact contents of the dialog's list box depend on which ActiveX or OCX controls you have loaded in the past. At a minimum, you should see the Microsoft Forms 2.0 controls which are part of Windows 95, and you may also see several MSIE 3.0 controls that have been loaded with the final version of MSIE 3.0. If you have Visual Basic or Microsoft Visual C++ installed on your machine, you'll see a plethora of controls, most of them custom controls. These too can be added to your active content documents.

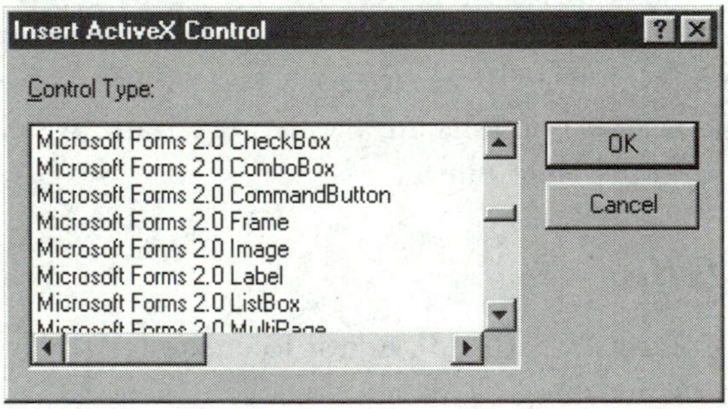

*Figure 7-2. The Insert ActiveX Control dialog*

To add the control to your web page, simply highlight it and click OK. So to begin creating our sample web page with the ActiveX Control Pad, select the Microsoft Forms 2.0 CommandButton control and click OK. This launches the Object Editor shown in Figure 7-3 and the Properties window shown in Figure 7-4.

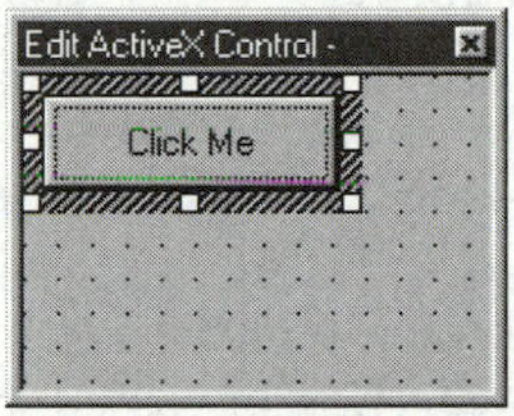

*Figure 7-3. The ActiveX Object Editor*

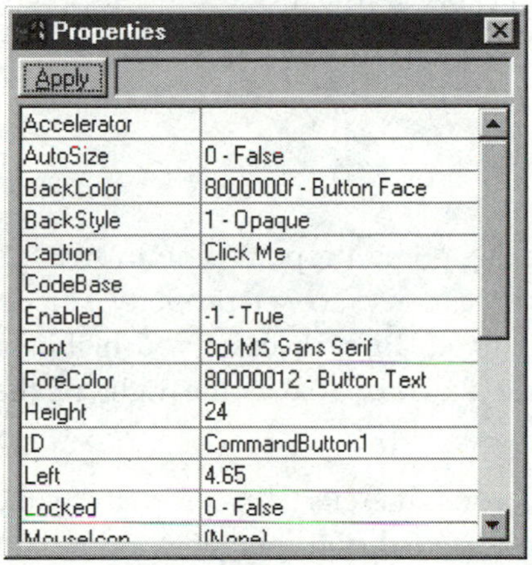

*Figure 7-4. The ActiveX Properties Editor*

## Using the ActiveX Object Editor

Many of the properties of an ActiveX control can be changed from either the Object Editor or the Properties window. The Object Editor is mainly used to control the "visual" properties of an object that affect the way it appears on screen; this includes such properties as height, width, captions, etc. The properties that you can change using the Object Editor are:

- **The object's size**. You can drag with the mouse to change the size of an object. When the cursor is placed over any of the small square blocks along the object's border, it changes into a double arrow. By dragging, you can adjust the object's width, height, or, if you place the cursor over one of the corner blocks, both at once.

- **The button's caption**. To change the caption on the button, click the button in the Object Editor. A wide marquee appears around the button. Now click in the center of the button, and a flashing text cursor bar appears. To enter or change the caption, simply type the required text onto the button. As you type, the *Caption* property in the Properties window is updated to show the new caption.

Although the Object Editor gives the impression that a control can be placed in any location on the screen, the *Left* and *Top* properties are ignored. For example, if you drag the button to the right, the *Left* property in the Properties window changes to reflect the button's new position. However, as soon as you close the Object Editor, the *Left* property is reset to its default value of 4.56. The only way to specify where the object should appear on screen other than directly editing the HTML file is to use the ActiveX HTML Layout Control, which is discussed in Chapter 8.

Most properties of an ActiveX Control can only be set by using the Properties window, which is almost identical in appearance and functionality to the Properties window in Visual Basic.

## Using the Properties Window

The Properties window allows you to set the design-time properties of an ActiveX object. There are several different methods you can use to set property values, depending on the property being edited or changed. In each case, you highlight the property that you'd like to modify and use the text box to the right of the Apply button to set an object's property.

If the property is a variable-length text string, you can select the property name and type the new value in the text box at the top of the Properties window. To set the final version of the text you have entered, click the Apply button to the left of the text box. The *Caption* property of a button is an example of such a text string, as shown in Figure 7-5.

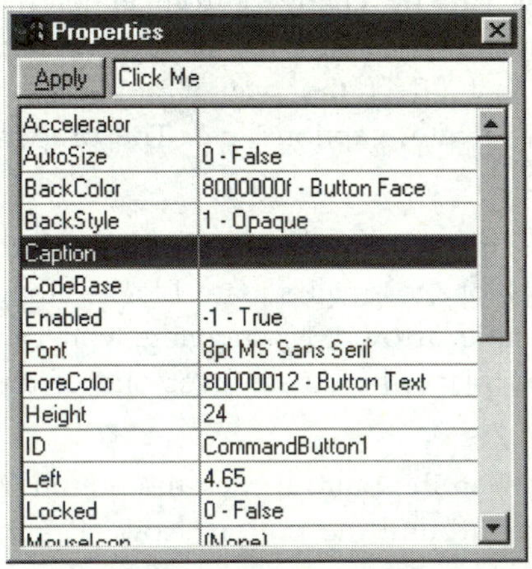

| Properties | ☒ |
|---|---|
| Apply | Click Me |
| Accelerator | |
| AutoSize | 0 - False |
| BackColor | 8000000f - Button Face |
| BackStyle | 1 - Opaque |
| Caption | |
| CodeBase | |
| Enabled | -1 - True |
| Font | 8pt MS Sans Serif |
| ForeColor | 80000012 - Button Text |
| Height | 24 |
| ID | CommandButton1 |
| Left | 4.65 |
| Locked | 0 - False |
| Mouselcon | (None) |

*Figure 7-5. Changing a caption property using the Properties Editor*

The second method of setting a property applies to those properties whose values can vary among a limited number of values. *AutoSize*, which determines whether or not a control is automatically resized to fit its contents, is a good example of this type of property: it is a Boolean value that can either be True or False. To set this property, highlight the property name and then select its value from the drop-down list box to the right of the Apply button, as shown in Figure 7-6. Another way to set this type of property is to double-click the property value. Each double click moves down the list of values by one item.

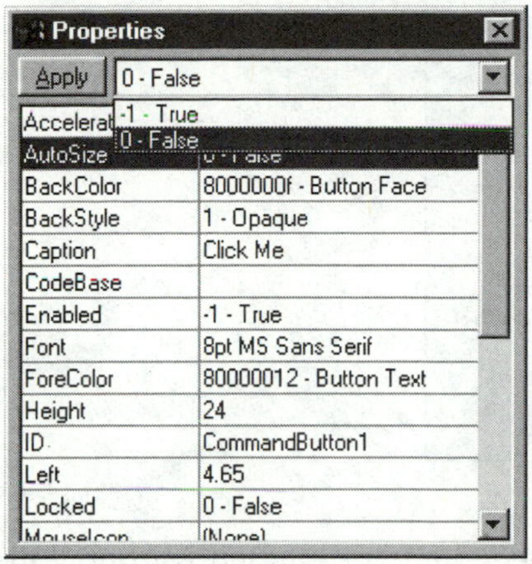

*Figure 7-6. Changing a property with several options*

The final method of setting a property value applies to those properties, like colors and fonts, that can take on an almost unlimited range of values. In these cases, a small button with three dots as the caption appears to the right of the list box at the top of the Property window, as Figure 7-7 illustrates. Clicking this button displays the relevant dialog box, from which you can choose a property value. (To open the dialog, you can also double-click on the property name.) So, if you select the *Font* property and click the button, the Font dialog shown in Figure 7-8 appears, which allows you to change the font face, size, and style.

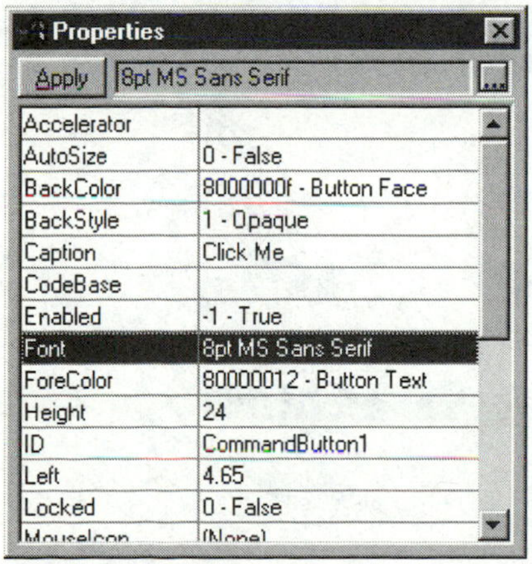

*Figure 7-7. Changing the font property*

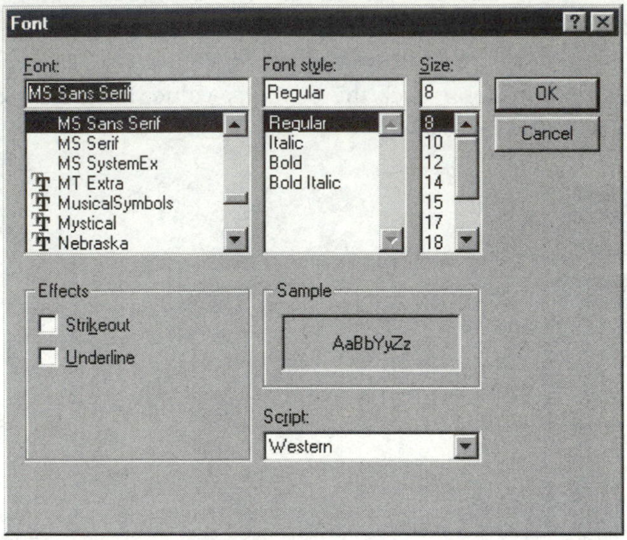

Figure 7-8. The Font dialog box

Once you have set the button's *Caption* property and are satisfied with how the button looks, close the Object Editor. This closes the Properties window as well, and automatically generates the required object definition in your HTML file, as shown in Figure 7-9.

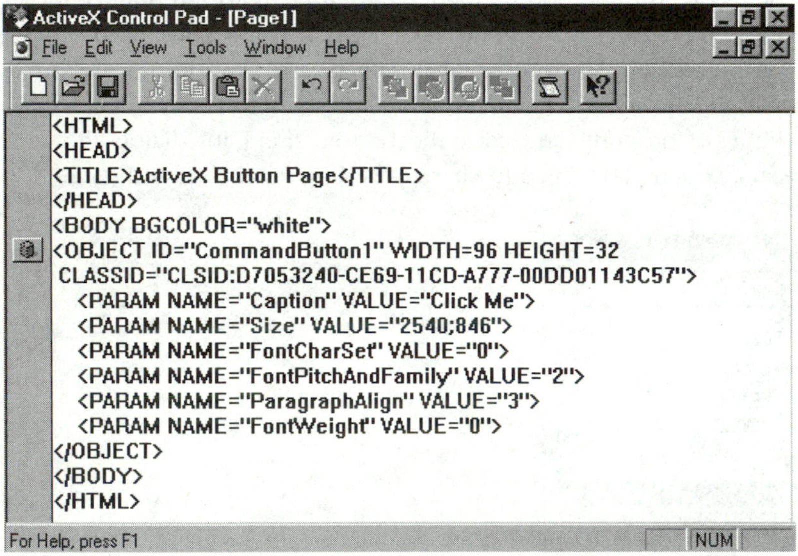

```
<HTML>
<HEAD>
<TITLE>ActiveX Button Page</TITLE>
</HEAD>
<BODY BGCOLOR="white">
<OBJECT ID="CommandButton1" WIDTH=96 HEIGHT=32
 CLASSID="CLSID:D7053240-CE69-11CD-A777-00DD01143C57">
   <PARAM NAME="Caption" VALUE="Click Me">
   <PARAM NAME="Size" VALUE="2540;846">
   <PARAM NAME="FontCharSet" VALUE="0">
   <PARAM NAME="FontPitchAndFamily" VALUE="2">
   <PARAM NAME="ParagraphAlign" VALUE="3">
   <PARAM NAME="FontWeight" VALUE="0">
</OBJECT>
</BODY>
</HTML>
```

Figure 7-9. The command button's <OBJECT> tag

A further addition to the screen is the object icon in the margin to the left of the <OBJECT> tag. Clicking this icon reopens the Object Editor and the Properties window and allows you to change the object's properties. So that's how easy it is to place an ActiveX Control within an HTML document using the ActiveX Control Pad. Now let's look at how easy it is to attach some active scripting to the object.

## Using the ActiveX Script Wizard

I don't want to sound like a Luddite, but there is nothing that you can do with the Script Wizard that you can't accomplish using Notepad! That said, the Script Wizard is very handy for reminding you of the properties, events, and methods available for both HTML intrinsic controls and for ActiveX controls.

The Script Wizard lets you create event handlers for controls that you have already placed onto the HTML page and for the *Window* object. You select the control you want to attach an event handler to, and select the event you wish to code. Then you can either enter the code manually in the event handler code window or you can select other objects, properties, or methods from a hierarchical list to build the code. Once you are satisfied with your event handler, you close the Script Wizard, which places the code into the HTML file.

Despite its convenience, there are a number of drawbacks to using the Script Wizard:

- You cannot use the Script Wizard to write code that is outside a subroutine. You can't, for instance, use the Script Wizard to create the code that defines and populates a global array. Although you can create custom subroutines and functions, all code must be within a procedure.

- You can only use the objects available on the current document. You can't, for example, reference the *Value* property of a text box that resides in a document in another frame; this still requires manual coding.

- The code for the event handler generated by the wizard for HTML intrinsic controls is often written inline in the HTML definition of the control. This makes the HTML file extremely difficult to read, understand, and maintain, as the following example shows:

```
<INPUT LANGUAGE="VBScript" TYPE=text ONCHANGE="call
window.prompt(&quot;Enter the
name&quot;, &quot;Rudy&quot;) window.status = &quot;This is some
code&quot; call
window.alert(&quot;thank-you&quot;)" NAME="txtMyText">
```

Separate script blocks (i.e., <SCRIPT>...</SCRIPT> tags) are created for each ActiveX control, which means that your code is split up throughout the page, one block for each control. Whether or not you find this annoying is a matter of personal preference; you may actually prefer code for a particular control to reside immediately above the control definition.

The only HTML controls that can be scripted by the Script Wizard are those defined using the <INPUT> tag. So coding to handle the <SELECT> and <TEXTAREA> controls must be done by hand.

In these cases, you need to open the raw source code and get down to some good old-fashioned coding.

---

*WARNING*     The Script Wizard is not a debugging or code checking tool! Although the ActiveX Control Pad and the Script Wizard were never advertised as debugging tools, it's easy to fall into the trap of expecting the Wizard to check your code as it translates it to the web page. For example, you could create an event handler that includes an If...Then conditional statement, but forget to type the Then keyword. If you click OK, the code is translated onto the HTML document, only to fail the first time the page loads. In other words, the Script Wizard will transfer whatever garbage you type into the code window directly into the HTML document.

---

The ActiveX Script Wizard can generate code for both VBScript and JavaScript. When first installed, the Script Wizard by default creates VBScript code, but if for some reason you want to change the default scripting language, select Options|Script from the ActiveX Control Pad's Tools menu, then select the required check box. This is also the dialog box that you use to change the default script view from list to code, or vice versa; this is discussed in detail later in this section, as well as in the sidebar "List View or Code View?"

To open the Script Wizard, either select the Script Wizard option from the Tools menu or click the Script Wizard button on the toolbar. The Script Wizard as it first appears is shown in Figure 7-10. As you can see, the Script Wizard window consists of three panes:

- **The Events pane**. The left-hand pane lists all the ActiveX controls, as well as some of the HTML intrinsic objects, that you've added to your page, along with the browser's Window object. By clicking on the plus icon to the left of the control, you can open a list of the events associated with that particular object.

- **The Action pane**. The right-hand pane lists all the ActiveX Controls that you've added to the page, the browser's *Window* object, a Global Variables object, a *Procedures* object, and a *GoToPage* method. This window is used to link methods and properties to object events. Properties are shown with a list icon, methods are shown with an exclamation mark icon, and objects are shown with a cube icon.

- **The Script pane.** The pane running across the bottom of the window is the Script pane. The Script pane shows the event handler or custom procedure that is currently being edited. This pane is split into two sections. A single line at the top of the pane holds the procedure or event handler's prototype, which is the event name and any associated argument lists. The lower section of the pane is where the script's code goes.

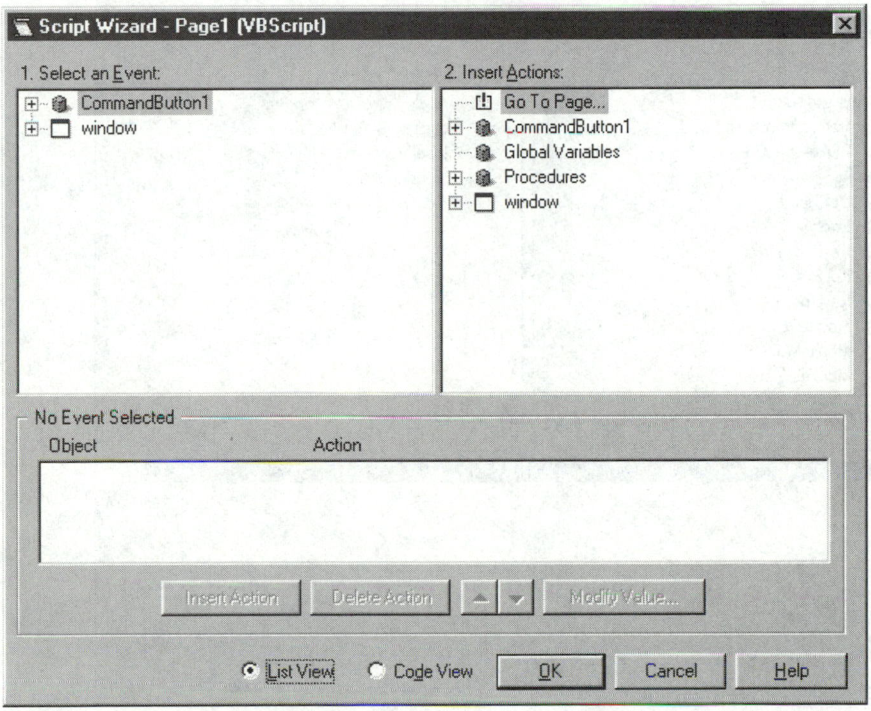

*Figure 7-10. The ActiveX Script Wizard*

To demonstrate how the Script Wizard works, let's continue with the example by doing the following:

1. Click the plus sign to the left of the *CommandButton1* object in the Events pane. A list of its events is displayed.

2. Highlight the *Click* event. (Incidentally, note that event names for ActiveX controls are different from those of HTML intrinsic objects.) By highlighting this event, you are telling the Script Wizard that whatever method or property you wish to invoke will be fired by CommandButton1's *Click* event.

3. Move to the right-hand pane and double-click the top item, Go To Page...
   This opens the Go To Page dialog, in which you can type a URL like *http//
   www.ora.com* and click OK. The Script Wizard then places an entry in the
   Script pane. In List View, the entry appears in plain English, as Figure 7-11
   shows; in Code View, the script window displays the raw true VBScript code
   that will be generated, as seen in Figure 7-12.

4. Now click OK. The Script Wizard automatically generates the required
   VBScript code and adds it to the HTML page, as Figure 7-13 shows.

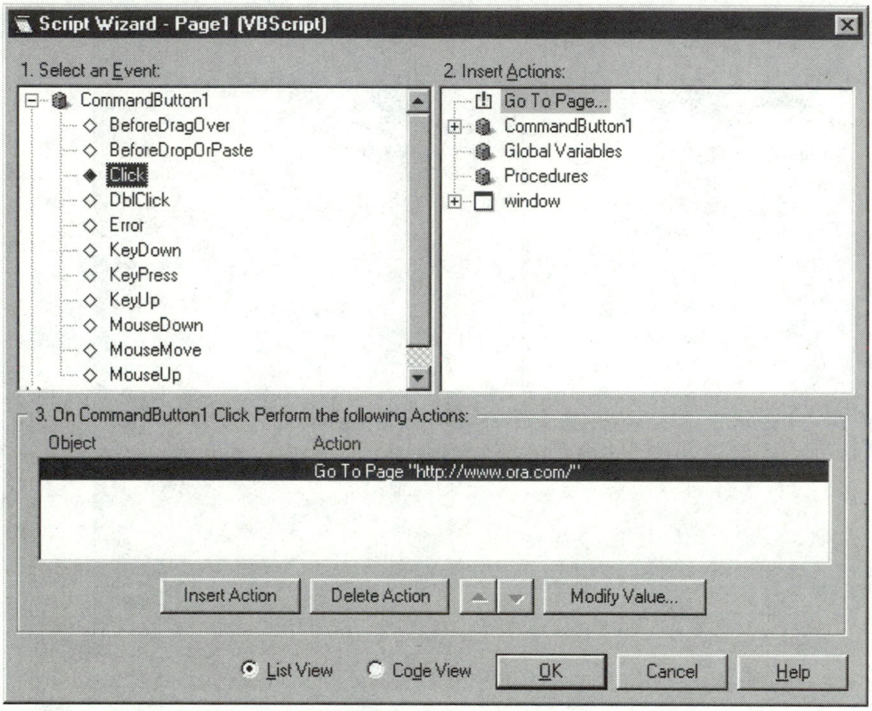

*Figure 7-11. The GoToPage method in List View*

Note that a new icon has appeared in the left-hand margin to denote the presence
of the script. As with the object icon, when you click the script icon, the Script
Wizard is launched and opens the relevant script in the script pane. Save the file
as *BUTTON.HTM*. You can try the file out through the browser when you are
online to view the O'Reilly home page.

## The ACLIST Utility

A useful addition to your scripting toolbox is the Microsoft ActiveX Control Lister,
*ACLIST.EXE*. This is something of a halfway house to the ActiveX Control Pad,

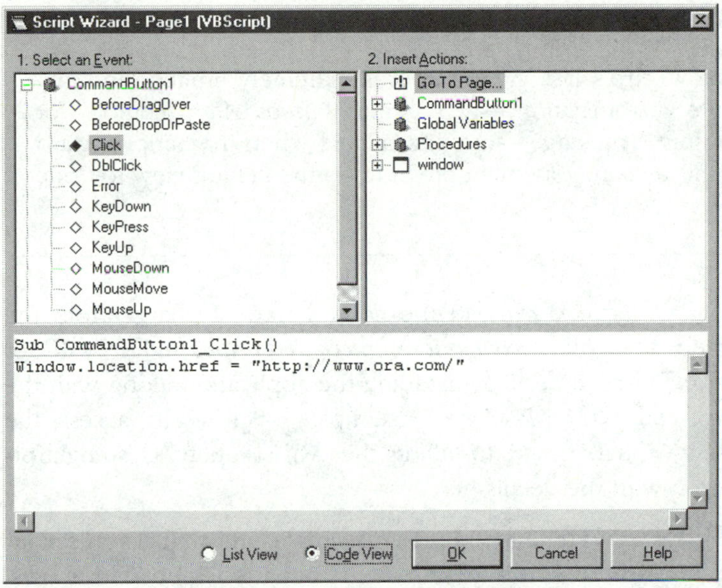

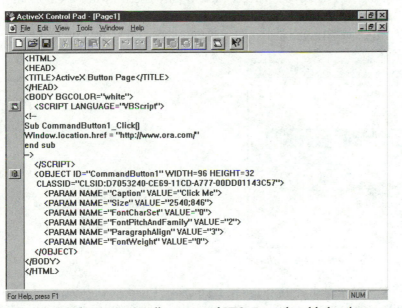

Figure 7-12. The GoToPage method in Code View

```
<HTML>
<HEAD>
<TITLE>ActiveX Button Page</TITLE>
</HEAD>
<BODY BGCOLOR="white">
  <SCRIPT LANGUAGE="VBScript">
<!--
Sub CommandButton1_Click()
Window.location.href = "http://www.ora.com/"
end sub
-->
  </SCRIPT>
  <OBJECT ID="CommandButton1" WIDTH=96 HEIGHT=32
   CLASSID="CLSID:D7053240-CE69-11CD-A777-00DD01143C57">
     <PARAM NAME="Caption" VALUE="Click Me">
     <PARAM NAME="Size" VALUE="2540;846">
     <PARAM NAME="FontCharSet" VALUE="0">
     <PARAM NAME="FontPitchAndFamily" VALUE="2">
     <PARAM NAME="ParagraphAlign" VALUE="3">
     <PARAM NAME="FontWeight" VALUE="0">
  </OBJECT>
</BODY>
</HTML>
```

Figure 7-13. The automatically generated VBScript code added to the page

and is very handy for those occasions when you are using Notepad to create a page, and need to add maybe an odd ActiveX control or two. It allows you to select a control and copy its <OBJECT> tag into your web page.

---

## *List View or Code View?*

Note that the Script Wizard's List View format is extremely limited, and any methods that require customization—such as the *Window.Alert* method (for which you must supply a message)—are unavailable when the Script Wizard is in List View. For this reason, you might prefer to set the default view to Code View.

---

At the time of writing, you can download the control free of charge from the Microsoft VBScript web site, *http://www.microsoft.com/vbscript/*, either with or without the Visual Basic source code. Downloading the application along with the source code provides you with some neat examples of how to access the Windows registry using Visual Basic.* Installing the ACList utility is straightforward, so I'll not bore you with the details here.

The ActiveX Control Lister is a straightforward and simple utility that scans your registry for ActiveX controls and shows them in a list box, as Figure 7-14 shows. You select the control or controls you wish to add to the page, then copy them to the Clipboard by clicking CTRL+C, or right-clicking anywhere in the list box and selecting Copy from the pop-up menu. Next, move to Notepad and insert the <OBJECT> tags either by typing CTRL+V or selecting Paste from the Edit menu.

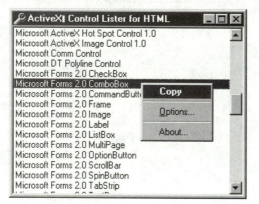

*Figure 7-14. The ActiveX Control Lister utility*

The correct CLSID and default attributes are then pasted into your document and off you go again, without the time and trouble of having to load the ActiveX Control Pad to obtain the control's CLSID.

---

* For more information on the Windows registry, see *Inside The Windows 95 Registry*, by Ron Petrusha, published by O'Reilly & Associates.

# *Summary*

In this chapter, we've documented Microsoft's ActiveX Control Pad and the ActiveX Control Lister, which are tools for incorporating ActiveX controls into your scripts, and we've covered the following points:

- The ActiveX Control Pad, which is available as a free download from Microsoft's web site, is not intended to be an HTML Editor. Instead, it allows you to quickly add inline HTML `<OBJECT>` and `<PARAM>` tags that define ActiveX controls.

- You can use the ActiveX Control Pad to change and edit Properties of the ActiveX controls you have added to your HTML page.

- The Script Wizard can be used to generate VBScript and JavaScript from point and click operations. However, there are drawbacks to using it, and quite a bit of manual coding is still required.

- The Script Wizard is *not* a code checking or debugging tool.

- If you want a quick way of finding ActiveX controls registered on your system, and of pasting their HTML definitions into your source code, use the ACLIST utility.

# 8

In this chapter:
• The Toolbox
• Creating an HTML Layout
• Summary

# The HTML Layout Control

In the last chapter, we looked at the ActiveX Control Pad. One of its components that we didn't cover, though, is the HTML Layout Control, which is also installed automatically when you install either MSIE 3.0 or the full version of the ActiveX Control Pad. If you have experience with visual programming languages such as Visual Basic, you will take to the Layout Control almost instantly; if you haven't, don't worry—it's very easy to use, and the results can be truly astonishing when compared to even the best authored HTML files.

The idea behind the HTML Layout Control is to give you control over the onscreen placement of ActiveX controls, even to the point of overlapping controls, something that is impossible in normal HTML. If you've seen some of the examples of cascading style sheets, or have used them yourself, you'll immediately see the similarity in the source code. The HTML Layout Control brings you what has been termed two-dimensional HTML. This is possible because controls can be placed in exact positions on screen, measured from the top and the left of the web page, and they can be arranged in layers, one on top of the other.

To see its abilities, look at the form in Figure 8-1, which was literally created in a few minutes, using the HTML Layout Control. Imagine, if you can, trying to create this web document using standard HTML code. I think you'd agree that it would be extremely complex because of its use of multiple tables, if not more or less impossible because of the alignment of the list boxes, text boxes, and option buttons. Yet only about 15 minutes' work went into laying the form out and then placing it in the left-hand column of a table. The source for the HTML file that creates this form is shown in Figure 8-2; given the complexity of the web page (at least from the viewpoint of standard HTML), you may find its simplicity surprising.

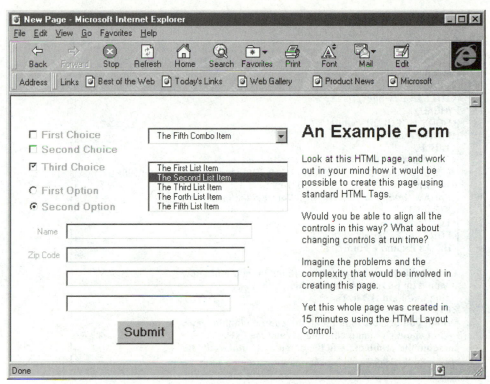

*Figure 8-1. A complex form created in a few minutes with the HTML Layout Control*

As Figure 8-2 shows, the HTML file contains no direct definitions of anything other than the layout file, *FORM.ALX*, that was created by the HTML Layout Control and that is brought into the web document using the `<OBJECT>` tag. The ActiveX Control Pad adds the HTML Layout Control to the HTML file (it is actually the HTML Layout Control that is defined by the `CLASSID="CLSID: 812AE312-8B8E-11CF-93C8-00AA00C08FDF"` attribute), and it is the HTML Layout Control that renders the layout at run time. The HTML layout definition, which is stored in an .ALX file, is therefore treated as a set of variables by the HTML Layout Control. A separate instance of the HTML Layout Control is used for each layout definition on your HTML page. Each HTML Layout Control (or .ALX file) is downloaded to the client along with the web page whenever the server receives a request. However, since the .ALX files are quite small, their impact on a web site's performance is minimal.

Other than writing code that is not contained within a subroutine, you never need to worry about the source code for the layout at all. But if you want to see what it looks like, a short section of it is reproduced in Figure 8-3. If you're familiar with the files used by Visual Basic, the contents of the .ALX file will immediately bring

```
ActiveX Control Pad - [Page2.htm]                        _ □ ×
File  Edit  View  Tools  Window  Help                    _ ₫ ×

<HTML>
<HEAD>
<TITLE>New Page</TITLE>
</HEAD>
<BODY BGCOLOR="white">
<FONT FACE="arial" SIZE=1>
<TABLE>
<TD VALIGN=TOP>
<OBJECT CLASSID="CLSID:812AE312-8B8E-11CF-93C8-00AA00C08FDF"
ID="form_alx" STYLE="LEFT:0;TOP:0">
<PARAM NAME="ALXPATH" REF VALUE="file:form.alx">
</OBJECT>
<TD>
<FONT FACE="arial" SIZE=2>
<H2>An Example Form</H2>

Look at this HTML page, and work out in your mind how
it would be possible to create this page
using standard HTML Tags.
<P>
Would you be able to align all the controls in this way?
What about changing controls at run time? <P>
Imagine the problems and the complexity that would be
involved in creating this page <P>

For Help, press F1                                  NUM
```

*Figure 8-2. HTML source for the document in Figure 8-1*

to mind the Visual Basic .FRM file. In short, the HTML Layout Control achieves the goal we alluded to right at the start of this book: a Windows-style interface for web documents.

The HTML Layout Control is simply a container for other ActiveX controls that sits within the HTML page. It looks, feels, and operates very much like a Visual Basic form. You can place more than one Layout Control on a single web page, and you can create a Layout Control that is used by several web pages, allowing you to reuse code and functionality quickly and easily.

The combination of ActiveX controls and objects (to provide a Windows-style interface that users are familiar with), the HTML Layout Control (to place these controls in the exact screen location where they are needed), and VBScript (to add fast and easy programmability to tie the controls together) will change not only the way that you construct web pages, but also change the type of web pages you construct. For the first time, you can faithfully translate a Windows interface to the web.

The uses of the layout control, like those of any visual programming system, go far beyond creating business forms. Using the wide variety of ActiveX controls

```
form.alx - Notepad
File   Edit   Search   Help

<SCRIPT LANGUAGE="VBScript">
<!--
Sub Layout2_OnLoad()
For x = 0 to 4
 call ListBox1.AddItem(ListData(x),x)
Next

For x = 0 to 5
 call ComboBox1.AddItem(ComboData(x),x)
Next
end sub
-->
</SCRIPT>
<DIV BACKGROUND="#ffffff" ID="Layout2" STYLE="LAYOUT:FIXED;WIDTH:247pt;HEIGHT
    <OBJECT ID="CheckBox1"
      CLASSID="CLSID:8BD21D40-EC42-11CE-9E0D-00AA006002F3" STYLE="TOP:17pt;LEF
         <PARAM NAME="BackColor" VALUE="16777215">
         <PARAM NAME="ForeColor" VALUE="33023">
         <PARAM NAME="DisplayStyle" VALUE="4">
         <PARAM NAME="Size" VALUE="3493;600">
         <PARAM NAME="Caption" VALUE="First Choice">
         <PARAM NAME="FontCharSet" VALUE="0">
         <PARAM NAME="FontPitchAndFamily" VALUE="2">
         <PARAM NAME="FontWeight" VALUE="0">
    </OBJECT>
    <OBJECT ID="CheckBox2"
      CLASSID="CLSID:8BD21D40-EC42-11CE-9E0D-00AA006002F3" STYLE="TOP:32pt;LEF
         <PARAM NAME="BackColor" VALUE="16777215">
```

*Figure 8-3. The .ALX file used to produce the form example*

already available on the Web, or even by using a humble label control, you can create some really ... dare I say it ... cool (argghh I've said it) web pages. The example you're going to see, to introduce you to the HTML Layout control, will show you the very beginnings of what's possible. The rest, again, is up to your imagination and creativity.

To start the HTML Layout Control and create a new HTML Layout file, you must have the ActiveX Control Pad running. Then select the New HTML Layout option from the File menu. This creates a new HTML Layout window and opens the layout control's toolbox.

# The Toolbox

When the toolbox first opens, it has two property sheets and looks something like Figure 8-4. The top sheet, labeled "Standard," contains the ActiveX Controls that will always work, assuming that the user has MSIE 3.0 and Windows 95 or Windows NT. As you move your mouse across an icon on the toolbox, the icon becomes a clickable button, making it easier to select it. The toolbox is a resizable, floating toolbox than you can position anywhere on the screen.

*Figure 8-4. The HTML Layout Control toolbox*

## Adding New Controls to the Toolbox

The HTML Layout Control's toolbox is flexible, and allows you to add new controls as they become available. You can find a wealth of new controls on the Microsoft Internet Workshop site (*http://www.microsoft.com/workshop*). As you go through Microsoft's ActiveX Gallery, which contains listings and descriptions of available controls, the controls are automatically downloaded and registered on your machine, making them available for you to use in your web pages. See Chapter 9, *An HTML Layout Common Menu Object*, for details on how to make new controls available to users of your web site.

When you're adding new controls to the HTML Layout Control Toolbox, don't add them to the Standard property sheet, which is already populated with some standard ActiveX controls; instead, add them to the second and subsequent property sheets. To add a control to the toolbox do the following:

1. Click the property sheet on which you'd like the control's icon to appear. This should bring it to the foreground.

2. Right-click on the body of the property sheet (rather than on its tab) to open its context menu, and select the Additional Controls... menu options. This opens the Additional Controls dialog shown in Figure 8-5. If you're familiar with Visual Basic, you'll note immediately that it bears a striking resemblance to Visual Basic's Custom Controls dialog, which allows you to insert objects and controls in the Visual Basic toolbox.

3. Make sure that the Controls box is checked, and that the Selected Items Only box is not checked. (Otherwise, the dialog won't display any controls, or it will only list those controls whose icons are already displayed in the toolbox.)

4. Select the control or controls you'd like to add to the property sheet by checking their boxes in the Available Controls list box. Note that, whenever you highlight a new object, its path and filename are displayed at the bottom of the Additional Controls dialog box.

5. Click the OK button to add the new control's (or controls') icon to the toolbox.

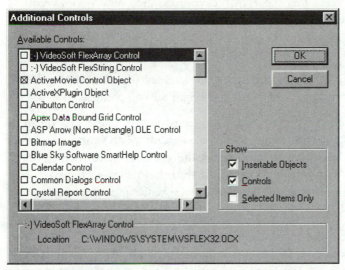

*Figure 8-5. The Additional Controls dialog*

Besides being able to add frequently used controls to the toolbox, you can also delete unwanted controls and customize the appearance of existing ones. To delete a control, right-click on the control's toolbox button, then select the Delete *<controlname>* option from the context menu. When you do this, make sure that you've selected the control that you actually want to delete; once you select the Delete menu option, the control is removed from the property sheet without any additional confirmation prompts. To customize the appearance of a control in the toolbox, right-click on the control's toolbox button, then select the Customize *<controlname>* option from the context menu. You can modify the following aspects of the control's appearance in the toolbox:

- The control's tool tip text. This is the text that is displayed when the mouse cursor pauses for a brief period when it is over the control.

- The control's icon. The HTML layout control allows you to edit the control's existing icon or to assign it a new icon by selecting any bitmap (files with .BMP and .DIB extensions) or icon (.ICO) files on your system.

## Renaming and Adding Toolbox Sheets

If you start to fill up the toolbox pages, you can adopt either of two solutions. First, you can resize the toolbox so that each page displays more icons. Second, you may want to organize your controls so that groups of controls appear on their own property sheets. This can be easily achieved by adding new toolbox property sheets and, if necessary, by renaming your existing ones.

To rename a property sheet, right-click on the tab strip (rather than on the body of the property sheet itself) of the sheet you'd like to rename, and select Rename from the context menu. Note that the HTML Layout Control only permits you to rename the property sheet on which you've clicked.

To add a new property sheet, right-click on any tab strip (rather than on the body of any property sheet), then select the New Page option from the context menu. The HTML Layout Control adds a new page at the back of the existing pages and names it New Page. You can then rename it and begin adding controls to it.

The context menu also allows you to delete existing toolbox pages. To delete a page, right-click on the tab strip (rather than on the body of the property sheet) of the sheet that you'd like to delete, then select the context menu's Delete Page option. Be sure, though, that you've clicked on the tab belonging to the page you want to delete, since the program will delete the page without additional warning or a confirmation dialog box.

You can also change the order in which pages appear in the toolbox. To do this, right-click on the tab belonging to any page, then select the Move option from the context menu. This opens the Page Order dialog box, which allows you to rearrange all of the toolbox's pages.

A final neat feature of the toolbox that's ideal for development teams is the ability to import and export toolbox pages. These options are available by clicking on any page's tab and selecting either the Import Page or Export Page option from the context menu.

# Creating an HTML Layout

When the layout control first opens, it presents you with an empty layout window. To show you how to use the HTML Layout Control to add ActiveX objects to your web page, we'll begin by discussing the layout window itself before covering how to work with controls themselves.

## Setting the Layout Properties

You can think of the layout window as simply a background object that can contain other objects and controls. The layout window itself has several properties that can be set at design time. These are:

- **BackColor**. The window's background color. As with all ActiveX controls, this can be either selected from the list of Windows system colors or from the Color Dialog box.

- **Height**. The window's height, expressed in pixels.

- **Width**. The window's width, expressed in pixels.

- **ID**. This is the name that is used to refer to the *Layout* object that you create when you save the file. It can be different from the actual file name. For Visual Basic programmers, the layout window's ID property corresponds to a form's *Name* property.

To access the layout window's properties, either right-click anywhere in the layout window and select the Properties option from the context menu, or, when no other objects or controls are selected in the layout window, select the Properties option from the View menu.

The height and width of the layout window as you see it onscreen is the size that it will appear when added to your HTML page. To adjust its size, either modify the Height and Width properties in the Properties window, or drag the frame of the layout window.

---

*WARNING*    The ActiveX Control Pad supports a multidocument interface. This means that if you have both a layout window and an HTML text editor open in the ActiveX Control Pad, you can move between one and the other at will. However, if your HTML text editor is maximized and you move to the layout window, the layout will be automatically maximized too, and if you save it in this way, it will be saved as a maximized layout.

---

## Adding a Control to the Layout

To add a control to the Layout window, simply select the control you wish to add from the toolbox. The selected control now appears as a depressed button. Then you can use one of two methods to place the control in the Layout window:

- Click in the general area of the Layout window where you want the control to appear. The control will be placed on the layout at the point that you clicked, and will be its default size.

- Click and hold the mouse down. If the control is sizable, this allows you to drag the borders of the control so that you can size it to your satisfaction.

To add the controls used in the sample application in this chapter, select the label control in the toolbox and add a label to the layout. Next, select the label control icon from the toolbox again and add a second label to the layout. Once this is done, add two command buttons to the layout. The result is shown in Figure 8-6.

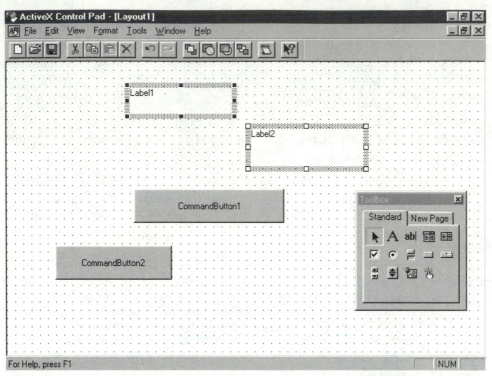

*Figure 8-6. The Layout window with two labels and two command buttons added*

## Moving and Resizing Controls

Moving a control is extremely easy: simply select the control by clicking on it, then drag it and drop it at the precise location where you want it placed. Resizing a control is also easy:

1. Select the control by clicking on it.

2. Position the mouse cursor over any of the eight small squares that appear in the control's border, depending on the direction of the location where you want them. The two center horizontal squares allow you to size the control vertically. The two center vertical squares allow you to size the control horizontally. The four corner squares allow you size the control both horizontally and vertically.

3. When the cursor changes to a double arrow, drag the border or borders of the control until you've sized it as you want.

You can also move multiple controls simultaneously so that their positions relative to each other remain the same. To do this, click and depress the mouse button at a position in the Layout window that does not have a control. Then drag so that the marquee that is formed by the mouse movement includes all the controls you wish to move. When you release the mouse button, all controls surrounded by the marquee will be selected. (You can also select more than one control by clicking on one control to select it, and then depressing the Ctrl key while you click on each additional control.) Once you've selected the controls, you can move all of the controls by dragging just one control.

The layout control has a helpful feature for aligning controls called a *grid*. The grid is the matrix of black dots on the layout window that appears at design-time only; again, this is instantly recognizable if you have experience with Visual Basic. You can change the grid settings by selecting Options|HTML Layout from the Tools menu. This allows you to change the size of the grid cells: the smaller the figure, the more compact the grid, and the more precise control you have over placing your controls. Another option is *Snap to Grid*, which speeds up the placement of controls. When Snap to Grid is set, a control automatically aligns to the nearest grid coordinate, even if you place it several pixels away. A final option is *Show Grid*, which determines whether or not the grid is displayed in the Layout window.

To see how this works, try resizing and repositioning the labels that you just placed on the layout page. Their actual size is not important here; the idea is for you just to get a feel of using the Layout Control.

## Using the Property Editor

To change the property values of a control found in the Layout window, you must first select the control. Then you can either select the Properties option from the View menu or right-click on the control and select the Properties option from the context menu. (If the Properties window is already open, you can simply select the control whose properties you'd like to examine.) The Property window used by the HTML Layout Control is the same as that used in the ActiveX Control Pad, which was discussed in the last chapter.

To experiment with using the Properties window to modify the properties of a control, change the size of the font used for the two labels to 48 point, by modifying the *Font* property of each control, and change the foreground color of one label to red and the other to blue. (Foreground color is controlled by the *Fore-Color* property.) Then change the *Caption* property to "This is a label" for *Label1* and to "Another label" for *Label2*. Next, drag *Label2* so that it slightly overlaps *Label2*, and set the *BackStyle* property of both labels to Transparent. Similarly, you can change the *Caption*, *ForeColor*, and *BackColor* properties of the command buttons. Just play around and experiment with the different effects you can create—free of the restrictions of HTML controls! Your Layout window should resemble Figure 8-7.

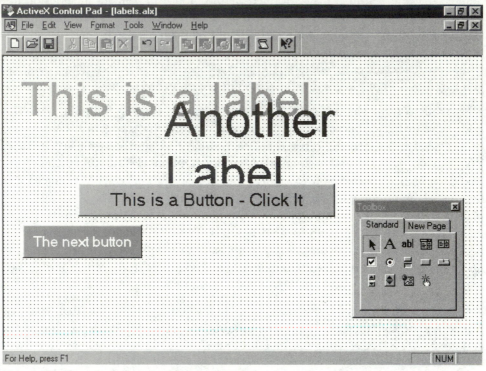

*Figure 8-7. The sample layout with its properties set*

## Working with Layers

One of the advantages of the HTML Layout Control is that ActiveX controls can be layered—that is, one can sit on top of another. This means you can add a control, then add another control that overlaps the first. Within the layout control's design-time environment, you can also change which control is at the front and which is at the back (and which are in between, if you are using more than two controls) by using the four layer buttons on the tool bar. These allow you to:

- Bring the selected control to the front

- Move the selected control forward one layer

- Move the selected control back one layer

- Send the selected control to the back

## Using the Script Wizard

The Script Wizard, which we discussed in the previous chapter, *Using the ActiveX Control Pad*, is also available when you're using the HTML Layout Control. You can start the Script Wizard in any of the following three ways:

- Right-click anywhere in the Layout window, then select the Script Wizard option from the context menu.

- Click the Script Wizard button on the toolbar.

- Select the Script Wizard option from the Tools menu.

One major difference when you use the Script Wizard from the Layout Control is the unavailability of most of the subobjects, methods, and properties of the *Window* object. If the Script Wizard is opened from the ActiveX Control Pad, the *Window* object is available in both the Event and Actions panes, and the Actions pane displays a long list of properties and methods for the *Window* object. But as Figure 8-8 shows, the *Window* object is unavailable in the Event pane, and only the *Window* object's *Location* object is available in the Actions pane, if the Script Wizard is opened from the HTML Layout Control. This doesn't prevent you from using Windows methods, setting Windows properties, or accessing objects contained within the *Window* object; it just means that you have to code these manually.

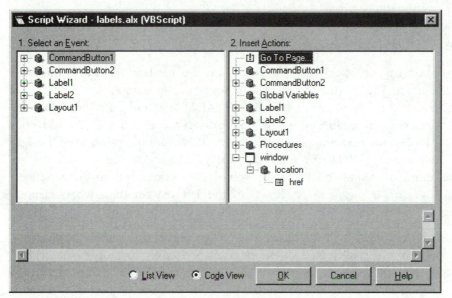

*Figure 8-8. The Script Wizard as it appears from the Layout Control*

To attach some code to our sample layout, click the plus sign to the left of CommandButton1 in the Events pane, and select the *Click* event. With the Script Wizard in its code view, type the following code into the script window:

```
Label1.Caption = "I've been changed"
```

Next, click the plus sign to the left of CommandButton2 in the Events pane and select the *MouseDown* event. Then type the following code into the script window:

```
For x = 48 to 20 step -2
    Label1.Font.Size = x
Next
```

Finally, select the *MouseUp* event for CommandButton2, and enter the code:

```
For x = 20 to 48 step 2
    Label1.Font.Size = x
Next
```

As you can see, when CommandButton2 is pressed, the font size of *Label1* is reduced from 48 points to 20 points in steps of 2 points. When the button is released, the label returns to its original state. Once you've added the code, click OK, and the Script Wizard will transfer the code you've written into the .ALX file. This source code, though, isn't available in your HTML document. Instead, the Script Wizard adds it to the layout source document, so you can't actually see it without opening the source.

## Saving Your Layout and Adding It to the HTML File

To save your Layout, click the Save button on the toolbar or choose the Save option from the File menu. In the case of our sample layout, save the file as *LABELS.ALX*. (Note that all layout files use the .ALX file extension.) Then close the Layout window by selecting the Close option from the File menu. To add your layout to the HTML document, select the Insert HTML Layout option from the Edit Menu, then select *LABELS.ALX* from the dialog. This adds the `<OBJECT>` tag that's required to define the layout to your HTML document. As with ActiveX controls and scripts, an icon is shown in the left margin that, when clicked, launches the HTML Layout Control, which in turn opens the layout file.

There's one final detail to take care of before we finish this sample application. The layout that we just created does not reach the edge and top of our HTML document. This is because, as with HTML tables, the HTML document has a default top and left margin. So change the background color of the HTML page to white by adding the `BGCOLOR="white"` attribute to the `<BODY>` tag. You can also try to get around this using the `LEFTMARGIN=0` and `TOPMARGIN=0` attributes of the body tag, although you'll never succeed in getting a Layout control to sit flush against the edge of the document. The source code for your finished HTML page should look like Figure 8-9. Finally, save the HTML file as *LABELS1.HTM*.

Now that you've saved your work, try using your browser to view it. When you click the This is a Button – Click It button, the first label's caption should change, as shown in Figure 8-10. And when you click the next button, the text of the first

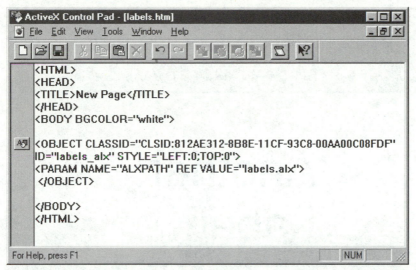

*Figure 8-9. The HTML code for LABELS.HTM*

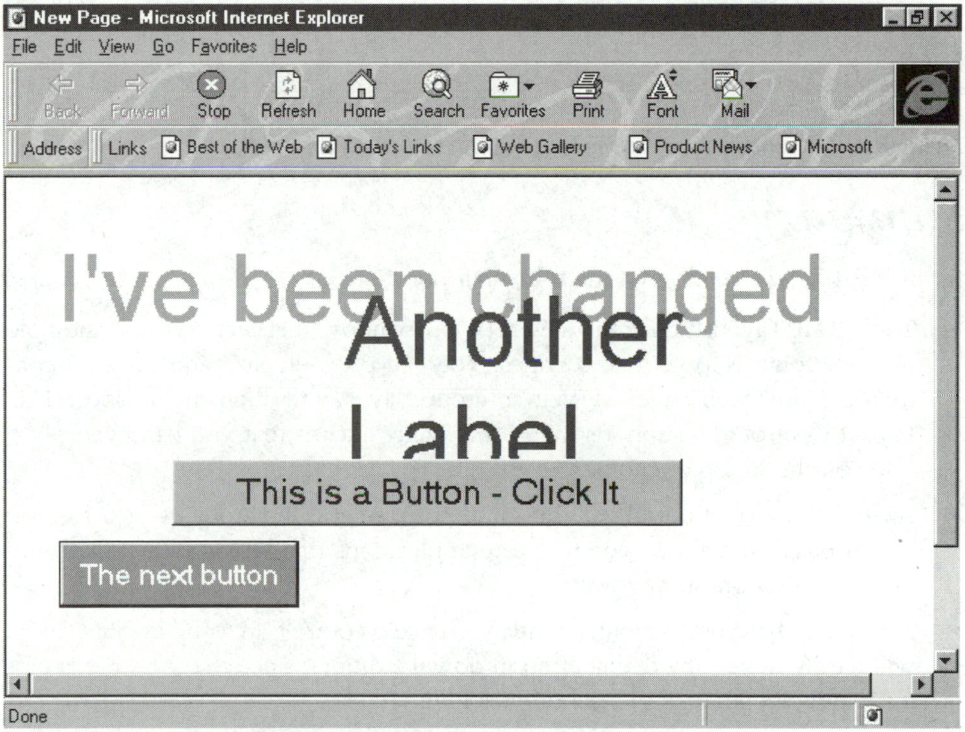

*Figure 8-10. The Labels example when the user clicks CommandButton1*

label should first be reduced in size, as shown in Figure 8-11, and then return to its normal size.

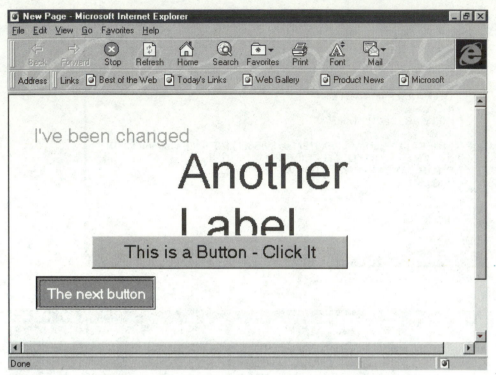

*Figure 8-11. The Labels example when the user presses CommandButton2*

## Summary

In this chapter, we've covered the following points:

- The HTML Layout Control is a WYSIWYG window that lets you add multiple ActiveX controls to your web pages. You can precisely size and position controls on your web page, as well as group, layer, and align them. The HTML Layout Control also supports 2D HTML, which means that you can even place one control on top of another.

- An HTML Layout Control has the same purpose and functionality as a form in Visual Basic, and allows you to create applications that look and feel like Windows applications in a browser.

- Assuming that you use only standard ActiveX controls in your layouts, users will hardly notice any degradation in download time, since the .ALX file is typically only a couple of thousand bytes long.

- The HTML Layout Control defines your layout to HTML by using the <OBJECT> tag in your HTML file, and it saves your layout in a separate file with an .ALX extension. The HTML Layout Control reads the file and renders the layout at run time.

- You can make changes to the ALX file without altering anything on the HTML document, making maintenance quick and easy, especially if the same .ALX file is used over many HTML documents.

- You can add multiple HTML Layouts to a single web page, or a single layout to many pages, or even multiple layouts to multiple pages.

# 9

*In this chapter:*
- *Creating the Menu Bar*
- *Adding the Menu Layout to an HTML Document*
- *Summary*

# An HTML Layout Common Menu Object

Chapter 8 introduced you to the HTML Layout Control and showed how you can quickly and easily lay out a web page containing ActiveX controls. In this chapter, you'll discover how the HTML Layout Control can help you create the type of powerful web applications that have until now been the sole domain of Windows visual development environments. The application you'll create is a three-page web site, all of whose pages use a common horizontal menu bar. The menu is created using the HTML Layout Control and is added to the HTML page like any other ActiveX object.

This chapter will also discuss:

- How to use VBScript to interface an HTML page with the HTML layout object as though the latter were part of the current page

- How to bring the functionality and feel of web documents closer to those of Windows applications, by using such features as keyboard accelerators

- How to copy properties from one control to another and set properties of multiple controls at the same time

- Considerations in adding downloadable ActiveX controls to your web page

Most important, though, this chapter illustrates how you might use the HTML Layout Control to build reusable software components within your web site. One of the main goals of Windows programmers over recent years has been, and still is, the creation *reusable code*—blocks of code that, once written, can be snapped together and used in a variety similar situations. Not only does code reuse make economic sense for the person paying for the software to be written, it also makes both logical and logistical sense for the person writing the code. Why should you rewrite code over and over again to do very similar tasks?

Take a menu bar in a web application. Each menu on each page of the site has a similar—if not identical—number of buttons, and the buttons have the same captions and the same destination URLs. You wouldn't want to create the same menu over and over again with only slight modifications for the particular page on which it is shown, for example, to disable the button pointing to the current page, or maybe to change the color of the current page's menu button to give an added visual clue as to the current page. Ideally, you would create the menu once, and add code that could automatically customize the menu bar for the current page.

## Creating the Menu Bar

So let's start our example by creating the menu bar. This requires that you do the following:

1. Open the ActiveX Control Pad and select the New HTML Layout option from the File menu.

2. Add three command buttons to the Layout window. Don't worry at this stage about where you place them or their size. Your Layout window might appear as shown in Figure 9-1.

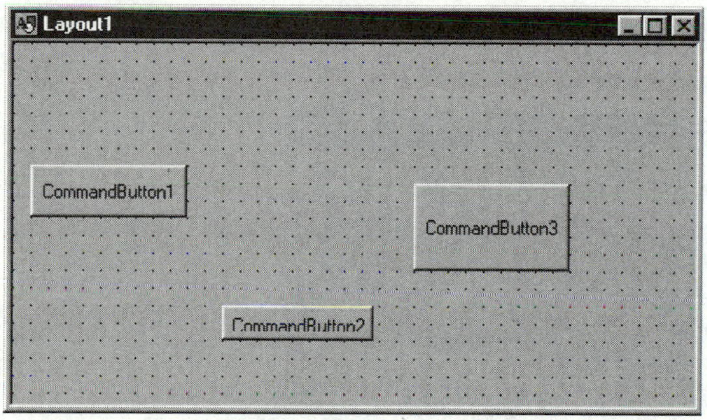

*Figure 9-1. The three menu bar buttons placed in the Layout window*

3. Select CommandButton1, open the Properties window, and set the value of its *Height* property to 26, and its *Width* property to 107. Then close the Properties window.

4. Select all three command button controls so that CommandButton1 is the dominant control (see TIP). This is a preliminary step to copying the values of CommandButton1's *Height* and *Width* properties to the other two buttons.

## *The Dominant Control and Copying Control Properties*

The HTML Layout Control allows you to use some of the options available on the Format menu to pass certain properties to other controls from what is known as a *dominant control*. When you select multiple controls (as in CommandButton1, CommandButton2, and CommandButton3 in Figure 9-1), the dominant control is the one whose handles are formed by white-filled rectangles; the handles of the other controls are formed by black-filled rectangles. The dominant control is always the control that is included in the selection last if the controls are selected using the Ctrl key. It's the control that's closest to the starting corner of the selection marquee, if the controls are selected according to their location in the Layout window. If the wrong control is designated the dominant control, you can correct this by holding down the Ctrl key and clicking twice on the control that you want to be dominant, once to deselect it and once to select it again, thereby making it the most recently selected (and therefore the dominant) control.

5. Select the Make Same Size option from the Format menu, then select the Both option from its submenu. All the buttons should now be the same size as the dominant control, CommandButton1. Your Layout window should resemble Figure 9-2.

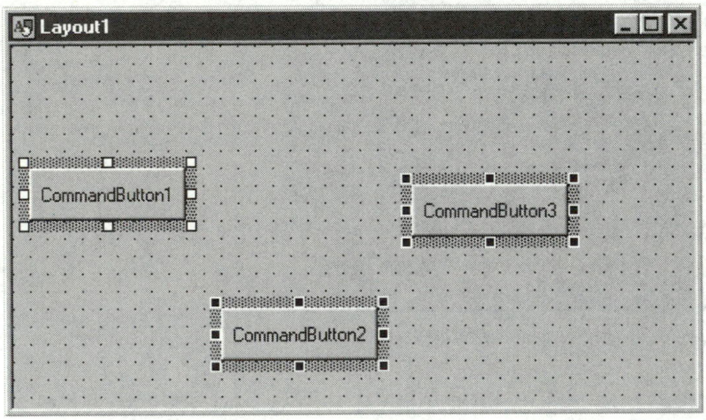

*Figure 9-2. The buttons resized to the height and width of CommandButton1*

6. With all three buttons still selected, select the Align option from the Format menu, then select the Tops option from its submenu. This copies the value of the dominant control's *Top* property to the two other selected controls.

7. Again with all three buttons selected, select the Horizontal Spacing option from the Format menu, then choose the Make Equal option from its submenu to equally space the buttons. Now that you've finished aligning and spacing the controls, your Layout window should resemble Figure 9-3.

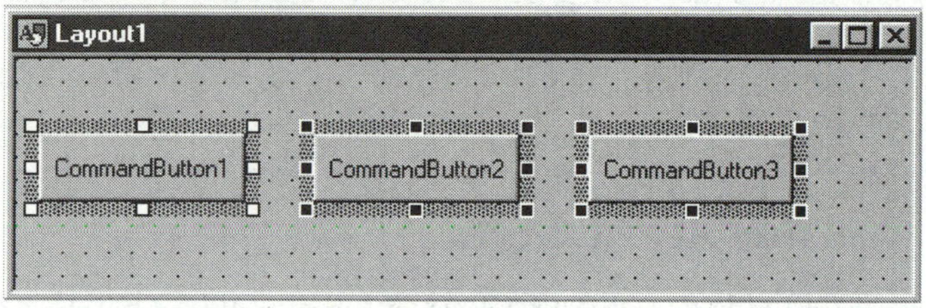

*Figure 9-3. All the buttons aligned and spaced*

Now that we've finished laying out our menu, we need to set some of the controls' properties to integrate them with the web pages that we'll build, and to make them more accessible to users. This requires that you do the following:

1. Change the *BackColor*, *ForeColor,* and *FontSize* properties of the three controls. The values that you use for each property are completely up to you, although they should be the same for each button.

---

## Changing the Properties of Several Controls at Once

In addition to copying properties from one control to other selected controls, you can also use the HTML Layout Control to set properties for a group of controls at the same time. First, you select all of the controls whose properties you'd like to change. Next, open the Properties window by clicking the right mouse button on one of the selected controls and selecting the Properties option from the context menu. When multiple controls are selected, the Properties window shows actual values for those properties whose value is the same for all selected controls, and displays the string "(Mixed)" for those properties whose values differ among the selected controls. If the selection includes different types of controls, the Properties window only displays those properties that are common to each control in the collection. This leaves you free to change any property value, including those of the mixed properties, and have the new values apply to each control that you've selected.

---

2. Close the Properties window and, while you still have all the controls selected, move them up toward the top of the layout by dragging any one of them. They will all move in unison. Of course, the same thing could have been achieved by resetting their *Top* property.

3. Reopen the Properties window and separately set the values of the *Caption* and *Accelerator* properties for each of the three controls. Change CommandButton1's *Caption* property to "Home Page" and its *Accelerator* property to "o." (When you finish, note that the button's caption appears as "H<u>o</u>me Page." Then change the *Caption* properties of CommandButton2 and CommandButton3 to "Links Page" and "What's New," and change their *Accelerator* properties to "k" and "N," respectively.

---

### *Using Accelerators*

Accelerators are keyboard shortcuts, and are indicated by the underlined letters in a caption. A user can quickly access a button or a menu item without the mouse by using the Alt key plus the underscored character. For example, Alt+F is the common windows accelerator to open the File menu, as though the user had clicked on the word File. The standard ActiveX controls that have a *Caption* property (the CommandButton, Label, OptionButton, and CheckBox controls) also have an *Accelerator* property. You set this property by entering a single letter that appears in the caption. (Obviously, it's pointless defining a letter that does not appear in the caption as an accelerator key, like "a" for the caption "Button.") Accelerators are also case-sensitive, so to set the *Accelerator* property for the caption "Window" you would use "W"; if you use "w," the last letter will be the accelerator. One other note of caution: the following accelerators, which are used by MSIE 3.0 and override any accelerator that you set, should not be used in your applications: a, E, F, G, H, and V. Neither should the Netscape accelerators B, O, D, and W be used.

---

4. Reduce the height of the Layout window so that it's just deeper than the buttons.

5. Finally, change the value of the Layout window's *BackColor* property to white. The Layout window should now resemble Figure 9-4.

*Figure 9-4. The final main menu layout*

The basic layout is now complete. Next, we want to write the script that calls the correct page when a button is clicked. To define the behavior of a click on each button, do the following:

1. Launch the Script Wizard.

2. Select the *Click* event for CommandButton1 in the Event pane, and double-click "Go To Page" in the Actions pane. The text `Window.location.href = ""` is automatically added to the script window.

3. Enter "`home.htm`" between the empty quotation marks.

4. Repeat steps 2 and 3 for ComandButton2 and CommandButton3, using "links.htm" and "new.htm," respectively.

5. Click OK to close the Script Wizard.

6. Save the layout as *MAINMENU.ALX*.

## Adding the Menu Layout to an HTML Document

The next step involves integrating our menu layout into our HTML documents. This can be done as follows:

1. Using the *Page1* template that's open in the ActiveX Control Pad, substitute "Home Page" for "New Page" in the `<TITLE>` tag, and add the `BGCOLOR="white"` attribute to the `<BODY>` tag.

2. Add a `<CENTER>` tag under the `<BODY>` tag to center the text that follows.

3. Insert a new blank line immediately below the `<CENTER>` tag, and select the Insert HTML Layout option from the Edit menu. When the file dialog appears, select your layout file, *MAINMENU.ALX*. The ActiveX Control Pad adds the object definition for your layout to the HTML document, which should now resemble Figure 9-5.

Now you can add some code to customize the menu bar as it is loaded into the HTML page. You'll remember that one of the ideas for customizing this menu is that the button that refers to the current page be disabled. This prevents the user clicking and reloading the same page—not that it would do any harm, it's just a total waste of time! This means, for instance, that when the home page is showing, only the Links Page and the What's New buttons can be clicked.

The simplest place to write the code to customize the menu bar is within the HTML document itself. The reason for this is that the document knows where it is, but the menu bar is unaware of which HTML page is loading it. Think of it from the menu bar's point of view: is it the home page that is loading the menu bar, or the Links page? It simply doesn't know. You can write a short piece of code in the HTML document, however, that references the menu bar and disables a particular button.

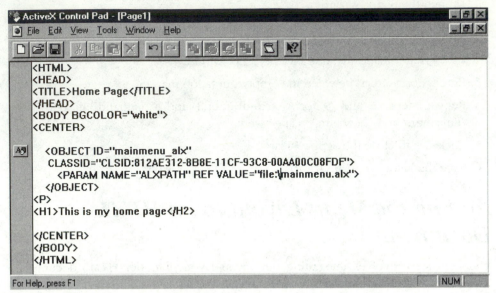

*Figure 9-5. The main menu object definition*

To add this customization, launch the Script Wizard and click the plus sign to the left of the *mainmenu_alx* object in the Events window. Unfortunately, as you can see, the only object you have available is the overall *Layout*; you cannot access the controls within the layout. But since you now know how to code in VBScript, manually coding the script is no problem. The event you need is the *Layout's* one and only event, "OnLoad," which means that this script will execute as the layout loads. Click *OnLoad* and, with the Script window in Code view, enter the following line:

```
mainmenu_alx.CommandButton1.Enabled=False
```

This means that every time the main menu layout loads in this particular page, CommandButton1 will be disabled.

To finish up this page, Click OK and add an `<H1>` tag with a heading that reads something like "This is the Home Page" under the `</OBJECT>` tag. Finally, save the HTML source for this page, which should look like Figure 9-6, as *HOME.HTM*.

To save yourself a lot of extra work, you can create the other two pages from this one by using the Save As menu option. First, create the Links page by making the following changes to the HTML source code:

1. Change the code for the *mainmenu_alx_OnLoad* event procedure to read

   ```
   mainmenu_alx.CommandButton2.Enabled=False
   ```

2. Change the page title and heading to reflect the fact that this is the Links page.

3. Select the Save As option from the File menu, and name the file *LINKS.HTM*.

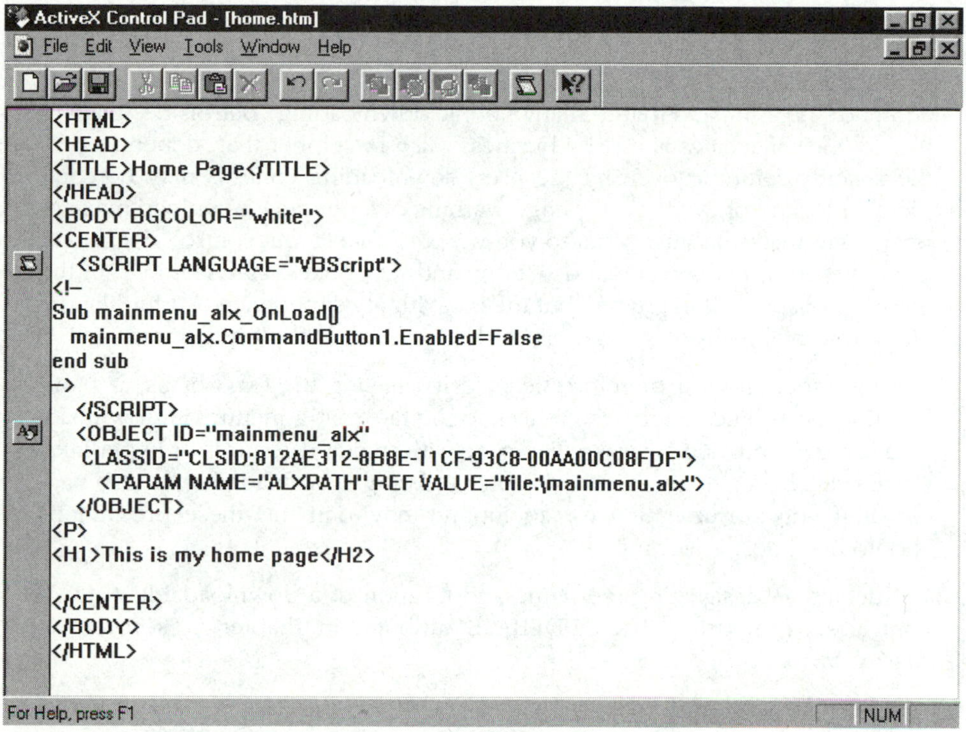

```
ActiveX Control Pad - [home.htm]
File   Edit   View   Tools   Window   Help

<HTML>
<HEAD>
<TITLE>Home Page</TITLE>
</HEAD>
<BODY BGCOLOR="white">
<CENTER>
  <SCRIPT LANGUAGE="VBScript">
<!--
Sub mainmenu_alx_OnLoad()
  mainmenu_alx.CommandButton1.Enabled=False
end sub
-->
  </SCRIPT>
  <OBJECT ID="mainmenu_alx"
   CLASSID="CLSID:812AE312-8B8E-11CF-93C8-00AA00C08FDF">
     <PARAM NAME="ALXPATH" REF VALUE="file:\mainmenu.alx">
  </OBJECT>
<P>
<H1>This is my home page</H2>

</CENTER>
</BODY>
</HTML>

For Help, press F1                                          NUM
```

*Figure 9-6. HOME.HTM in the text editor*

Finally, create the What's New page by making the following changes to the existing HTML source code:

1. Change the code for the *mainmenu_alx_OnLoad* event procedure to read

    ```
    mainmenu_alx.CommandButton3.Enabled=False
    ```

2. Change the page title and heading to reflect the fact that this is the What's New page.

3. Select the Save As option from the File menu, and name the file *NEW.HTM*.

You are now ready to try out your new common menu bar, so either launch your browser and open *HOME.HTM*, or, if MSIE is your default browser, select *HOME.HTM* from the Documents option on the Start menu. The home page of the finished application is shown in Figure 9-7. (Don't forget to try out the accelerator keys.) This example clearly demonstrates that a single .ALX layout file can be shared among multiple HTML files, and that the individual HTML documents can interact with the layout individually via a script.

## *Active Control Security*

If you are designing a page using ActiveX controls which is targeted at a public audience, bear in mind that to many people downloading controls designed to run on their machines is a risky business. Also remember that, depending on the security setting chosen by the user, downloading controls may be completely blocked or, worse, a message warning of a pending download may appear. I say worse because what to you was a simple layout control, containing a couple of harmless command buttons and text boxes, can seem (from the warnings displayed) to anyone but the most highly experienced surfer like the virus from hell ready to wipe their hard drive clean at the first opportunity!

Careful attention must therefore be paid to allaying the fears of users. Your HTML page should include references to the fact that a menu will download. You can even provide an alternative page with standard controls or hyperlinks. Once users become accustomed to controls being downloaded with web pages (or if you are designing for an Intranet environment) these precautions should be almost irrelevant.

For details on designating the name and location of a downloadable ActiveX control, see the sidebar "The CODEBASE Attribute," in Chapter 7, *Using the Ac-tiveX Control Pad.*

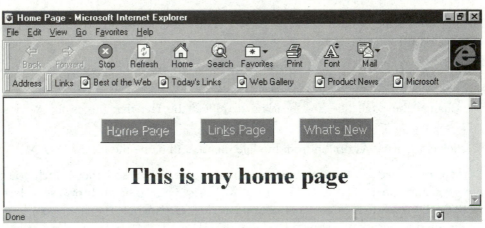

*Figure 9-7. The Main Menu Layout in the home page*

*WARNING*   When you add an HTML layout control to an HTML page in the ActiveX Control Pad, the `ALXPATH` parameter is set to the fully qualified path of the .ALX file on your local drive. For example,

```
file://c:\mydirectory\mylayout.alx
```

If you plan to use the layout file from a web server, you'll need to manually alter the `ALXPATH` parameter in the `<OBJECT>` definition for the layout in the HTML file. The `ALXPATH` parameter will work with relative paths, just like the `<A HREF>` tag, which means that if the HTML page and the .ALX file reside in the same directory on the server, you need to specify only the name of the file. For example:

```
<PARAM NAME="ALXPATH" REF VALUE="mainmenu.alx">
```

If you fail to change the path parameter, the page will work perfectly on your machine, and your machine alone, as it will find and use your local copy of the .ALX file. Unfortunately, anyone else loading the page will be faced with a pretty bleak looking HTML document!

# *Summary*

An HTML layout can be treated as if it were a complete new object or control, available to all of your web pages. This reusability of Windows objects and controls is in keeping with modern concepts of object-oriented programming, and promises to save you a good deal of time and trouble. In this chapter, I've shown you how to use the HTML Layout Control to create a single reusable menu bar that can be incorporated into multiple web page applications. Now that you know how to create one reusable component, you can doubtless think of other components that you can create to enhance and add interactivity to your web pages.

# 10

# Date and Time in VBScript

Using variables based on the date and time on the client's machine is probably the easiest way to "personalize" a web page when it's displayed by the browser. It gives the user the feeling that a particular page is unique to her or him, or that a dialogue is more personal than when the user sees a page that is identical to the one everyone will see. VBScript provides a rich set of functions to return and manipulate the date and time on the client machine, and in this way to personalize the web pages displayed on the client. But VBScript's date and time functions can be used for much more than simply displaying the date and/or time onscreen. A date can be treated like any mathematical quantity for use in calculations or to determine the day of the week that a particular date falls on. In this chapter, we'll see how VBScript can be used both to personalize the user's viewing experience and to perform numeric calculations. We'll also look at some of the issues and problems involved in manipulating date and time data on the web.

The source of date and time information doesn't necessarily have to be the client's machine. The correct time is available, for instance, from the U.S. Naval Observatory (*http://tycho.usno.navy.mil/howclock.html*), but this involves an additional set of network transfers. The date and time on the server can also be determined and transmitted to the client's browser, although it requires the additional steps of determining where the client is located and establishing the precise time difference between the server and the client. This is a tremendous waste of resources when the correct time is literally inches away from the browser.

A problem though, is that date and time formats differ from country to country. For instance, it was difficult for me to remember, as a British citizen who was starting to work with Americans in the Saudi oil industry, that 6/4/95 meant the 4th of June, and not the 6th of April. This is a fairly easy problem, though. In Scandinavia, 95.6.4 is a valid date format. Aside from the order of digits, there are enormous variations in the date delimiter: some countries use dashes, some use slashes, and some use dots. You can specify the valid date format for your computer using the Control Panel's Regional Settings applet in Windows 95 and Windows NT. All time and date functions that execute on the machine use this format, which thus permits a date to be validated easily on the client machine. But what happens when an unusual date format from a client machine reaches the web server, which by its very nature has to handle input and requests form every corner of the globe? Later in the chapter, you'll see how to use VBScript to rearrange or reformat the date data to match your own requirements at the client, prior to sending the date to the server, thereby ensuring that useable date formats reach your CGI or other server-side processes.

This chapter is divided into seven sections:

- "Checking the Validity of a Date" shows you how to determine if your program can treat data entered by the user as a valid date.

- "Returning the Client Machine's Date and Time" shows you how to use a range of simple functions to display the date and the time in a web page on the browser.

- "Splitting Up the Time" shows how to dissect the time into its constituent parts (hours, minutes, and seconds).

- "Splitting Up the Date" discusses dissecting the date variable into its constituent parts (the year, month, day, and day of the week).

- "Calculating with Dates and Times" covers mathematical operations with dates and times.

- "Reformatting Date Expressions" discusses rearranging the date on the client machine before submitting it to the server.

- "A Cookie Example" shows how to reformat the date and time for the *Cookies Expires* variable, as well as how to write and read cookie files.

- "A Countdown Example" features an example web page that displays the number of days to a particular date.

## Checking the Validity of a Date

How do you check if "12 June 1961" is a real date? And if it is, are "6-12-61," "6/ 12," "12 Jun," and "Jun 12 1961" real dates too? You know that they are all valid because your brain has been taught to recognize certain numerical and character elements that, when combined in a wide variety of ways, constitute a date. To the computer, though, input such as this is just a series of characters, nothing more.

To ensure that the user enters a valid date, you could spend the next several months writing a data validation script. But when you use the script to validate form input on the Web, users from Sweden will complain that they can't use your form because the dates they entered, such as 61.12.6, were rejected as invalid! So back to the drawing board.

A much simpler (and painless) solution is to use the VBScript *IsDate* function. Its syntax is

```
bool = IsDate(stringargument)
```

*IsDate* accepts any string argument, and returns True if the string is a valid date and False if it is not.

The validation of a date is localized; that is, a date input using a date format that's valid in one country can be invalid in another. The *IsDate* function determines the correct format from the Control Panel's Regional Settings applet and compares the input string value to the range of valid formats used by Windows on the client machine. This means that your script will operate in all countries independently of their local date/time format. You should always use *IsDate* before performing calculations and formatting functions on dates, to eliminate the run-time errors that occur when you try to manipulate a nondate string as though it were a date. Example 10-1, for instance, uses the *IsDate* function to validate the date entered by a user into an HTML form.

*IsDate* can also be used to validate times, although it is much less flexible. It recognizes only two valid time separators, ":" and ".".

*Example 10-1. The IsDate Function*

```
<HTML>
<HEAD>
<TITLE>IsDate()</TITLE>
 <SCRIPT LANGUAGE="vbscript">
 <!--
  Sub cmdButton1_OnClick
      If IsDate(Document.frmForm1.txtDateVal.Value) Then
          Alert "Valid Date"
      Else
          Alert "NOT a Valid Date"
      End If
  End Sub
 -->
 </SCRIPT>
</HEAD>
 <BODY BGCOLOR="white">
  <CENTER>
  <H3>Using IsDate() to Validate a Date</H3>
   <FORM NAME="frmForm1">
    <INPUT TYPE="text" NAME="txtDateVal">
    <INPUT TYPE="button" NAME="cmdButton1" VALUE="Check Date">
   </FORM>
```

*Example 10-1. The IsDate Function (continued)*

```
  </CENTER>
 </BODY>
</HTML>
```

# *Returning the Client Machine's Date and Time*

---

## *Windows Short Dates and Long Dates*

Windows Short and Long dates refer to the built-in date formats of the Windows system. The exact format depends on your Regional Settings. However, the following is the American date settings format:

- **Short Date**: *m/d/yy*, where *m* is the month, *d* is the day, and *yy* is the year. Months and days do not have leading zeroes, and the century is not used in the year.

- **Long Date**: *dddd, MMMM dd, yyyy*, where *dddd* is the day, spelled out, *MMMM* is the month, spelled out, *dd* is the day (including a leading zero where necessary), and *yyyy* is the year, including the century.

---

VBScript includes a number of functions that allow you to access the date or the time on the client machine:

- **Now**. The VBScript *Now* function returns a variant type 7 variable that contains both the date and time on the client machine. Example 10-2 illustrates the use of the *Now* function. As Figure 10-1 shows, it returns the date and time in the Short Date format defined in the Control Panel's Regional Settings applet. Its syntax is:

  *vartype7* = Now()

- **Date**. The VBScript *Date* function returns a variant type 7 variable containing the date on the client machine in the Short Date format defined in the Control Panel's Regional Settings applet. Its syntax is:

  *vartype7* = Date()

- **Time**. The *Time* function returns a variant type 7 variable containing the time on the client machine in the 12-hour clock format (i.e., with A.M. and P.M.) defined as the 12-hour clock format in the Control Panel's Regional Settings applet. Its syntax is:

  *vartype7* = Time()

*Example 10-2. Retrieving the Date and Time with Now*

```
<HTML>
<HEAD>
<TITLE>Now(), Date() & Time()</TITLE>
 <SCRIPT LANGUAGE="vbscript">
 <!--
  Sub cmdButton1_OnClick
      Alert Now()
  End Sub
  Sub cmdButton2_OnClick
      Alert Date()
  End Sub
  Sub cmdButton3_OnClick
      Alert Time()
  End Sub
 -->
 </SCRIPT>
</HEAD>
 <BODY BGCOLOR="white">
 <FONT FACE="arial" SIZE=2>
  <CENTER>
   <FORM NAME="frmForm1">
    <B>Using Now() to Return the Current Date and Time</B><BR>
    <INPUT TYPE="button" NAME="cmdButton1" VALUE="Show Date and Time"><P>
    <B>Using Date() to Return the Current Date</B><BR>
    <INPUT TYPE="button" NAME="cmdButton2" VALUE="Show Date"><P>
    <B>Using Time() to Return the Current Time</B><BR>
    <INPUT TYPE="button" NAME="cmdButton3" VALUE="Show Time">
   </FORM>
  </CENTER>
 </BODY>
</HTML>
```

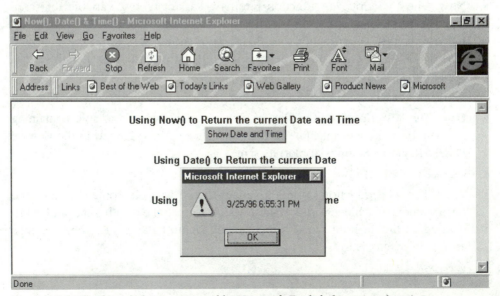

*Figure 10-1. The date and time returned by Now with English (American) settings*

# *Splitting Up the Time*

VBScript includes three functions that you can use to dissect any string value representing the time into its component parts. Each function returns an integer variant subtype. The functions, each of which is used in Example 10-3, are:

- **Hour**. The VBScript *Hour* function has the following syntax:

  ```
  intVar = Hour(dateexpression)
  ```

  It returns an integer variant subtype whose value can range from 0 to 23, representing the hour of the day for *dateexpression*. This means that, regardless of the computer's regional settings, *Hour* always returns a value using the 24-hour clock format, as Figure 10-2 shows. *dateexpression*, the argument passed into the *Hour* function, must be a valid date, date/time, or time value. The *Hour* function allows you to localize the greeting on your welcome page, as the following code snippet shows:

  ```
  Dim h
  h = Hour(Now)
  If h < 12 Then
      Document.Write 'Good Morning'
  ElseIf h > 12 and h < 19 Then
      Document.Write 'Good Afternoon'
  Else
      Document Write 'Good Evening'
  End If
  ```

- **Minute**. The syntax of the VBScript *Minute* function is:

  ```
  intVar = Minute(dateexpression)
  ```

  The function returns a variant integer data subtype whose value ranges from 0 to 59, representing the minutes of the hour in *dateexpression*. The argument *dateexpression* must be a valid date/time or time value.

- **Second**. The syntax of the *Second* function is:

  ```
  intVar = Second(dateexpression)
  ```

  The function returns a variant integer data subtype whose value ranges from 0 to 59, representing the seconds in *dateexpression*. For the function to execute successfully, *dateexpression* must be a valid date/time or time value.

*Example 10-3. VBScript Functions to Split up the Time*

```
<HTML>
<HEAD>
<TITLE>Hours, Minutes and Seconds</TITLE>
 <SCRIPT LANGUAGE="vbscript">
 <!--
  Sub cmdButton1_OnClick
      Alert Hour(Now())
  End Sub
```

*Example 10-3. VBScript Functions to Split up the Time (continued)*

```
  Sub cmdButton2_OnClick
      Alert Minute(Now())
  End Sub
  Sub cmdButton3_OnClick
      Alert Second(Now())
  End Sub
 -->
 </SCRIPT>
</HEAD>
<BODY BGCOLOR="white">
<FONT FACE="arial" SIZE=2>
 <CENTER>
  <FORM NAME="frmForm1">
   <B>Using Hour() to Return the Current Hour</B><BR>
   <INPUT TYPE="button" NAME="cmdButton1" VALUE="Show Hour"><P>
   <B>Using Minute() to Return the Current Minute</B><BR>
   <INPUT TYPE="button" NAME="cmdButton2" VALUE="Show Minute"><P>
   <B>Using Second() to Return the Current Seconds</B><BR>
   <INPUT TYPE="button" NAME="cmdButton3" VALUE="Show Seconds">
  </FORM>
 </CENTER>
</BODY>
</HTML>
```

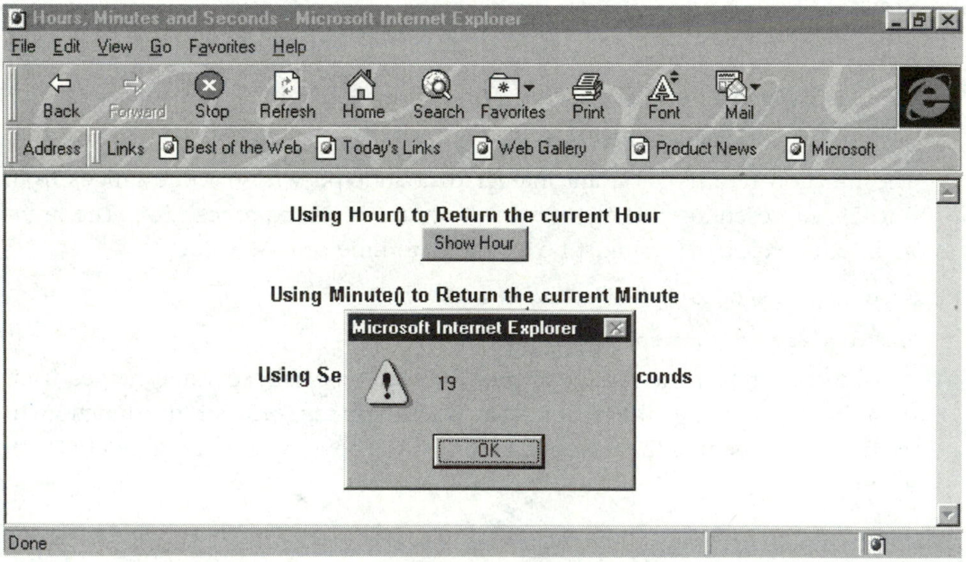

*Figure 10-2. The Hour function*

# Splitting Up the Date

VBScript also provides a number of functions that allow you to extract a component part of the date from a date variable, or to determine the day of the week on which a particular date fell.

# Year, Month, and Day

Just as the *Hour*, *Minute*, and *Second* functions separate the time into its component parts, the *Year*, *Month*, and *Day* functions are used to access the individual components of the system date. They are extremely useful when you need to reformat a date, since they permit you to isolate the individual parts of the date and rearrange them as necessary. For an example of this, see "Reformatting Date Expressions" later in this chapter.

The three VBScript functions that permit you to split up the date, each of which is used in Example 10-4, are:

- **Year**. The *Year* function has the following syntax:

  ```
  intVar = Year(dateexpression)
  ```

  *Year* returns a variant integer data subtype value with a value between 100 and 9999, which represents the year of *dateexpression*. Regardless of the computer's date settings, *Year* always returns a three-digit (for years from 100 to 999) or four-digit (for all years from 1000 on) value. *dateexpression*, the argument passed to the *Year* function, must be a valid date value.

- **Month**. The syntax of the *Month* function is:

  ```
  intVar = Month(dateexpression)
  ```

  *intVar* is an integer variant data subtype whose value can range from 1 to 12, representing the month of *dateexpression*. *dateexpression* must be a valid date value.

- **Day**. The syntax of the *Day* function is:

  ```
  intVar = Day(dateexpression)
  ```

  *Day* returns an integer variant data subtype that can take on a value ranging from 1 to 31, representing the day of the month of *dateexpression*. *dateexpression*, the argument passed to the *Day* function, must be a valid date/time or time value.

*Example 10-4. VBScript Functions to Split up the Date*

```
<HTML>
<HEAD>
<TITLE>Year, Month and Day</TITLE>
 <SCRIPT LANGUAGE="vbscript">
 <!--
  Sub cmdButton1_OnClick
      Alert Year(Now())
  End Sub
  Sub cmdButton2_OnClick
      Alert Month(Now())
  End Sub
  Sub cmdButton3_OnClick
```

*Example 10-4. VBScript Functions to Split up the Date (continued)*

```
      Alert Day(Now())
  End Sub
  -->
</SCRIPT>
</HEAD>
<BODY BGCOLOR="white">
<FONT FACE="arial" SIZE=2>
  <CENTER>
    <FORM NAME="frmForm1">
      <B>Using Year() to Return the Current Year</B><BR>
      <INPUT TYPE="button" NAME="cmdButton1" VALUE="Show Year"><P>
      <B>Using Month() to Return the Current Month</B><BR>
      <INPUT TYPE="button" NAME="cmdButton2" VALUE="Show Month"><P>
      <B>Using Day() to Return the Current Day</B><BR>
      <INPUT TYPE="button" NAME="cmdButton3" VALUE="Show Day">
    </FORM>
  </CENTER>
</BODY>
</HTML>
```

## Determining the Day of the Week

Besides splitting up the date into its component parts, you sometimes need to know the day of the week on which a particular date falls. For example, will June 12, 1999, be either a Saturday or a Sunday? You probably don't know, and I certainly don't! For most of us, the only way to find out is to look at a calendar. Thankfully, VBScript, which lacks a calendar, has a built-in function that returns the day of the week. It doesn't return the actual name of the day as a string (like Sunday, Monday, etc.); instead, it returns a number representing the day of the week. The function can take either of two forms:

```
intVar = Weekday(dateexpression)
intVar = Weekday(dateexpression, firstday)
```

The first variation of the function returns *intVar*, an integer variant subtype whose value ranges from 1 (for Sunday, the first day of the week) to 7 (for Saturday, the last day of the week).

In the second variation of the function, you can specify a different starting day of the week in *firstday*. The function then returns the day of the week relative to the first day of the week. For instance, if you set the value of *firstday* to 2, indicating that Monday is the first day of the week, and attempt to determine the day of the week on which October 1, 1996, falls, the function returns a 2. That's because October 1, 1996, is a Tuesday, the second day of a week whose first day is Monday. If you use VBScript version 2.0, you can use a constant shown in Table 10-2 in place of an integer for *firstday*.

Example 10-5 illustrates the use of the *Weekday* function. The program makes use of a simple array to store the names of the seven days of the week, starting with Sunday at ordinal position 1. When the button is clicked, the *Weekday* function returns a number for the day of the week, which is used to access the array and display the name of the day.

*Example 10-5. The Weekday Function*

```
<TITLE>Day of the week</TITLE>
 <SCRIPT LANGUAGE="vbscript">
 <!--
  Dim days(7)
  days(1) = "Sunday"
  days(2) = "Monday"
  days(3) = "Tuesday"
  days(4) = "Wednesday"
  days(5) = "Thursday"
  days(6) = "Friday"
  days(7) = "Saturday"

  Sub cmdButton1_OnClick
      Alert days(Weekday(Now()))
  End Sub
 -->
 </SCRIPT>
</HEAD>
<BODY BGCOLOR="white">
<FONT FACE="arial" SIZE=2>
  <CENTER>
    <FORM NAME="frmForm1">
      <B>Using Weekday() to Return the Current Day of the Week</B><BR>
      <INPUT TYPE="button" NAME="cmdButton1" VALUE="Show Day">
    </FORM>
  </CENTER>
 </BODY>
</HTML>
```

## DatePart  `VBS 2.0`

The *DatePart* function introduced in VBScript 2.0 is a single function encapsulating the individual *Year, Month, Day, Hour, Minute,* and *Second* functions. Its syntax is:

**DatePart**(*interval, date*[, *firstdayofweek*[, *firstweekofyear*]])

The arguments for *DatePart* are as follows:

- **interval**. A string argument that tells *DatePart* which part of the date you wish to return. Valid values for `interval` are shown in Table 10-1. `Interval` must be either a variable or a literal string enclosed in quotation marks.

- **date**. A valid date expression whose component part you wish to retrieve.

*Table 10-1. Interval Strings for Use with DatePart, DateAdd, and DateDiff*

| String | Part of the Date To Return (Interval) | Return Value | Note |
|---|---|---|---|
| yyyy | Year | Integer representing year | |
| Q | Quarter | 1–4 | |
| M | Month | 1–12 | |
| Y | Day of year | 1–366 | Day of year and Day operate identically in the *DateAdd* and *DateDiff* functions |
| d | Day | 1–31 | |
| w | Weekday | 1–7 | Value relative to the first day of the week as specified by *firstdayofweek* |
| ww | Week of year | 1–52 | Weekday and Week of year operate identically in the *DateDiff* function |
| h | Hour | 0–24 | |
| n | Minute | 0–59 | Incorrectly stated as "m" in the VBScript documentation. |
| s | Second | 0–59 | |

- **firstdayofweek** (optional). Determines the first day of the week for function calls whose *interval* value is "w" or "ww." At first glance, this argument may seem somewhat odd. However, for business applications and for dealing with countries whose week starts on a Friday or Saturday, it is invaluable. Its value can be either an integer from 1 to 7 or one of the constants shown in Table 10-2. If not specified, its default value is 1 (for Sunday).

*Table 10-2. Day of the Week Constants (VBScript 2.0 only)*

| Constant | Value | Meaning |
|---|---|---|
| vbUseSystem | 0 | Use National Language Support (NLS) API setting |
| vbSunday | 1 | Sunday (default) |
| vbMonday | 2 | Monday |
| vbTuesday | 3 | Tuesday |
| vbWednesday | 4 | Wednesday |
| vbThursday | 5 | Thursday |
| vbFriday | 6 | Friday |
| vbSaturday | 7 | Saturday |

- **firstweekofyear** (optional). You use this with an *interval* of "ww" when a commercial rule specifies what constitutes the first week of the calendar year.

Its value can be either one of the integers or one of the constants shown in Table 10-3. Unfortunately, it does not allow you to specify a week number, which would probably have been of more use to businesses, by allowing a week number relative to the start of a financial year to be returned.

*Table 10-3. First Week of the Year Constants*

| Constant | Value | Description |
|----------|-------|-------------|
| vbUseSystem | 0 | Use National Language Support (NLS) API setting |
| vbFirstJan1 | 1 | The week in which January 1 occurs (default) |
| VbFirstFourDays | 2 | Week with a minimum of four days in new year |
| VbFirstFullWeek | 3 | The first full week of the new year |

Example 10-6 not only demonstrates the use of the *DatePart* function, but also allows you to examine the different values returned by the function by defining the values passed to it as parameters.

*Example 10-6. Using the DatePart Function*

```
<HTML>
<HEAD>
    <SCRIPT LANGUAGE="vbscript">
OPTION EXPLICIT

   Dim vDateOption
   Dim vDOWOption 'First Day of Week
   Dim vWOYOption 'First Week of Year
   vDOWOption = vbSunday
   vWOYOption = vbFirstJan1

   Sub cmdButton1_onClick

       If Not isDate(frmForm1.txtStartDate.Value) Then
          Alert "Start date is Invalid"
          Exit Sub
       End If

       frmForm1.txtText1.Value = DatePart(vDateOption, _
                            frmForm1.txtStartDate.Value, _
                            vDOWOption, _
                            vWOYOption)
   End Sub
    </SCRIPT>
</HEAD>
<BODY BGCOLOR="white">

<FONT FACE="arial" SIZE=2>

<CENTER> <H3>DatePart</H3>

<FORM NAME="frmForm1">
```

*Example 10-6. Using the DatePart Function (continued)*

```
<TABLE>
  <TR
    <TD><FONT SIZE=2>Start Date </TD>
    <TD><INPUT TYPE="text" NAME="txtStartDate"></TD>
  </TR>

  <TR>
    <TD><INPUT LANGUAGE="vbscript" TYPE=radio VALUE="yyyy"
ONCLICK="vDateOption = &quot;yyyy&quot;" NAME="rdoOption"></TD>
    <TD><FONT SIZE=2>Year</TD>
    <TD><INPUT LANGUAGE="vbscript" TYPE=radio VALUE="q"
ONCLICK="vDateOption = &quot;q&quot;" NAME="rdoOption"></TD>
    <TD><FONT SIZE=2>Quarter</TD>
  </TR>

  <TR>
    <TD><INPUT LANGUAGE="vbscript" TYPE=radio VALUE="m"
ONCLICK="vDateOption = &quot;m&quot;" NAME="rdoOption"></TD>
    <TD><FONT SIZE=2>Month</TD>
    <TD><INPUT LANGUAGE="vbscript" TYPE=radio VALUE="y"
ONCLICK="vDateOption = &quot;y&quot;" NAME="rdoOption"></TD>
    <TD><FONT SIZE=2>Day of year</TD>
  </TR>

  <TR>
    <TD><INPUT LANGUAGE="vbscript" TYPE=radio VALUE="d"
ONCLICK="vDateOption = &quot;d&quot;" NAME="rdoOption"></TD>
    <TD><FONT SIZE=2>Day</TD>
    <TD><INPUT LANGUAGE="vbscript" TYPE=radio VALUE="w"
ONCLICK="vDateOption = &quot;w&quot;" NAME="rdoOption"></TD>
    <TD><FONT SIZE=2>Weekday</TD>
  </TR>

  <TR>
    <TD><INPUT LANGUAGE="vbscript" TYPE=radio VALUE="ww"
ONCLICK="vDateOption = &quot;ww&quot;" NAME="rdoOption"></TD>
    <TD><FONT SIZE=2>Week of year</TD>
    <TD><INPUT LANGUAGE="vbscript" TYPE=radio VALUE="h"
ONCLICK="vDateOption = &quot;h&quot;" NAME="rdoOption"></TD>
    <TD><FONT SIZE=2>Hour</TD>
  </TR>

  <TR>
    <TD><INPUT LANGUAGE="vbscript" TYPE=radio VALUE="n"
ONCLICK="vDateOption = &quot;n&quot;" NAME="rdoOption"></TD>
    <TD><FONT SIZE=2>Minute</TD>
    <TD><INPUT LANGUAGE="vbscript" TYPE=radio VALUE="s"
ONCLICK="vDateOption = &quot;s&quot;" NAME="rdoOption"></TD>
    <TD><FONT SIZE=2>Second</TD>
  </TR>
</TABLE>
<BR><BR>
```

*Example 10-6. Using the DatePart Function (continued)*

```
<TABLE>
<TH>First Day of the Week</TH>
  <TR>
    <TD><INPUT LANGUAGE="vbscript" TYPE=radio
ONCLICK="vDOWOption = vbUseSystem" NAME="rdoDOWOption"></TD>
    <TD><FONT SIZE=2>Use National Language Support (NLS) API setting</TD>
  </TR>
  <TR>
    <TD><INPUT LANGUAGE="vbscript" TYPE=radio
ONCLICK="vDOWOption = vbSunday" NAME="rdoDOWOption"></TD>
    <TD><FONT SIZE=2>Sunday</TD>
  </TR>
  <TR>
    <TD><INPUT LANGUAGE="vbscript" TYPE=radio
ONCLICK="vDOWOption = vbMonday" NAME="rdoDOWOption"></TD>
    <TD><FONT SIZE=2>Monday</TD>
  </TR>
  <TR>
    <TD><INPUT LANGUAGE="vbscript" TYPE=radio
ONCLICK="vDOWOption = vbTuesday" NAME="rdoDOWOption"></TD>
    <TD><FONT SIZE=2>Tuesday</TD>
  </TR>
  <TR>
    <TD><INPUT LANGUAGE="vbscript" TYPE=radio
ONCLICK="vDOWOption = vbWednesday" NAME="rdoDOWOption"></TD>
    <TD><FONT SIZE=2>Wednesday</TD>
  </TR>
  <TR>
    <TD><INPUT LANGUAGE="vbscript" TYPE=radio
ONCLICK="vDOWOption = vbThursday" NAME="rdoDOWOption"></TD>
    <TD><FONT SIZE=2>Thursday</TD>
  </TR>
  <TR>
    <TD><INPUT LANGUAGE="vbscript" TYPE=radio
ONCLICK="vDOWOption = vbFriday" NAME="rdoDOWOption"></TD>
    <TD><FONT SIZE=2>Friday</TD>
  </TR>
  <TR>
    <TD><INPUT LANGUAGE="vbscript" TYPE=radio
ONCLICK="vDOWOption = vbSaturday" NAME="rdoDOWOption"></TD>
    <TD><FONT SIZE=2>Saturday</TD>
  </TR>
</TABLE>

<BR><BR>

<TABLE>
<TH>First Week of the Year</TH>
  <TR>
    <TD><INPUT LANGUAGE="vbscript" TYPE=radio
ONCLICK="vWOYOption = vbUseSystem" NAME="rdoWOYOption"></TD>
```

*Example 10-6. Using the DatePart Function (continued)*

```
    <TD><FONT SIZE=2>Use National Language Support (NLS) API setting</TD>
  </TR>
  <TR>
    <TD><INPUT LANGUAGE="vbscript" TYPE=radio
ONCLICK="vWOYOption = vbFirstJan1" NAME="rdoWOYOption"></TD>
    <TD><FONT SIZE=2>Week containing Jan 1st (default)</TD>
  </TR>
  <TR>
  <TR>
    <TD><INPUT LANGUAGE="vbscript" TYPE=radio
ONCLICK="vWOYOption = vbFirstFourDays" NAME="rdoWOYOption"></TD>
    <TD><FONT SIZE=2>Week with min. four days in new year</TD>
  </TR>
  <TR>
    <TD><INPUT LANGUAGE="vbscript" TYPE=radio
ONCLICK="vWOYOption = vbFirstFullWeek" NAME="rdoWOYOption"></TD>
    <TD><FONT SIZE=2>First full week of the new year</TD>
  </TR>
</TABLE>
<BR>
        <INPUT TYPE=button VALUE="Click me" NAME="cmdButton1">
  
        <INPUT TYPE=text NAME="txtText1">
    </FORM>
</BODY>
</HTML>
```

# Calculations with Dates and Times

Until a decimal calendar becomes popular, we're stuck with an awkward system of days, months, and years, which makes it difficult to perform date calculations easily. Most of us actually are forced to use a calendar (or our fingers) to add up days. But if your web page is VBScript-enabled, you can use built-in VBScript functions to perform date calculations.

If some or all of the date or time values on which you want to perform calculations are entered into an HTML form by the user, however, you may recall from the discussion of form data in Chapter 3, *Getting Started*, that they are strings, and that it is therefore impossible to perform arithmetic operations on them. Consequently, before manipulating a date or time value, a necessary preliminary step is to convert it from a variant string to a variant date or time value.

## Converting Strings to Dates or Times

As we saw in "Checking the Validity of a Date," earlier in this chapter, the *IsDate* function can be used to determine whether an item of data can be converted into a variant of the date or time subtype. If the data are capable of conversion, either of the following two functions can actually be used to convert them:

- **DateValue**. The syntax of the *DateValue* function is:

  *varType7* = DateValue(*stringexpression*)

  It returns a date variant (variant type 7) containing the date represented by **stringexpression**. The date value is formatted according to the Short Date setting defined by the Regional Settings applet in Control Panel. *DateValue* can successfully recognize a **stringexpression** in any of the date formats recognized by *IsDate*. *DateValue* does not return time values in a date/time string; they are simply dropped. However, if **stringexpression** includes a valid date value but an invalid time value, a run-time error results. Example 10-7 demonstrates the use of the *DateValue* function to convert data input by the user into a date variant subtype.

*Example 10-7. Using the DateValue Function*

```
<HTML>
<HEAD>
<TITLE>DateValue()</TITLE>
<SCRIPT LANGUAGE="vbscript">
<!--
Sub cmdButton1_OnClick
Dim dv

 If Not IsDate(Document.frmForm1.inputdate.Value) Then
     Alert "Not A Valid Date"
     Exit Sub
 End If

 dv = DateValue(Document.frmForm1.inputdate.Value)

 Alert dv

End Sub
-->
</SCRIPT>
</HEAD>
<BODY BGCOLOR="white">
<FORM NAME="frmForm1">
<CENTER>
Enter a Date <INPUT TYPE="text" NAME="inputdate"><BR>
<INPUT TYPE="button" NAME="cmdButton1" VALUE="Date Value">
</FORM>
</CENTER>
</BODY>
</HTML>
```

- **TimeValue**. The syntax of the *TimeValue* function is:

  *varType7* = TimeValue(*stringexpression*)

  *TimeValue* is identical in operation to *DateValue*. If **stringexpression** is a valid date, it converts it to a variant type 7 date/time value. This means that, if you want to manipulate time data input by the user into a form, and perform calculations on them, you should first test the data using the *IsDate* function and, if they are valid time data, use *TimeValue* to convert them from a string to a variant time subtype. Example 10-8 demonstrates the use of the *Time-Value* function to convert data input by the user into a date/time variant subtype.

*Example 10-8. Using the TimeValue Function*

```
<HTML>
<HEAD>
<TITLE>TimeValue()</TITLE>
<SCRIPT LANGUAGE="vbscript">
<!--
Sub cmdButton1_OnClick
Dim dv

  If Not IsDate(Document.frmForm1.inputtime.Value) Then
      Alert "Not A Valid Time"
      Exit Sub
  End If

  tv = TimeValue(Document.frmForm1.inputtime.Value)

  Alert tv

End Sub
-->
</SCRIPT>
</HEAD>
<BODY BGCOLOR="white">
<FORM NAME="frmForm1">
<CENTER>
Enter a Time <INPUT TYPE="text" NAME="inputtime"><P>
<INPUT TYPE="button" NAME="cmdButton1" VALUE="Time Value">
</FORM>
</CENTER>
</BODY>
</HTML>
```

## Performing Calculations with Dates or Times

Except for those of us with pretty odd brains, we've all struggled and grappled with the mind-bending calculations needed to add or subtract a certain number of days to or from a particular date. For example, add 132 days to October 10, 1973. Easy, huh? Apart from everything else, was 1974 a leap year? Or try this: how many days, months, quarters, hours, minutes, and seconds are there between September 20, 1996, and June 3, 1954? This illustrates, as if any illustration were necessary, just how difficult our calendar is to deal with in mathematical terms. Nevertheless, we are called upon, time and again, to perform such calculations, especially in commercial applications. Fortunately, as you would expect, VBScript comes armed with several functions that save your gray matter from going pop! The set of functions that we'll examine is used for performing date and time calculations as well as for assembling a date from integers that represent individual date and time components.

### DateAdd `VBS 2.0`

The *DateAdd* function lets you add or subtract a number of time intervals to or from a given date or time, and returns the resulting date or time. So, for example, you can find out what the date and time were 30,786 minutes ago, or what date it will be in 23 quarters. The syntax for *DateAdd* is:

```
DateAdd(interval, number, date)
```

The arguments passed to the *DateAdd* function are:

- **interval**. A string argument that indicates what unit of time *number* represents. Valid values were shown earlier in Table 10-1. *interval* must be either a variable or a literal string enclosed in quotation marks.

- **number**. The number of intervals to add or subtract from the date. To subtract, *number* should be negative. For those of you into ancient history, however, you should be aware that the VBScript engine does not recognize dates before the year 100 A.D., and they will generate an error.

- **date**. An expression that evaluates to a valid date in terms of the client computer's regional settings. It represents the starting date for the calculation.

Example 10-9 shows how you can use the *DateAdd* function, and also allows you to experiment with using different *interval* values.

*Example 10-9. Using DateAdd to Perform Calculations on the Current Date and Time*

```
<HTML>
<HEAD>
    <SCRIPT LANGUAGE="vbscript">
    OPTION EXPLICIT

    dim vDateOption

    Sub cmdButton1_onClick
        frmForm1.txtText1.Value = dateAdd(vDateOption, _
                frmForm1.txtDiffValue.Value, Now())
    End Sub
    </SCRIPT>
</HEAD>
<BODY BGCOLOR="white">
<FONT FACE="arial" SIZE=2>
<CENTER>
<H3>DateAdd</H3>
```

*Example 10-9. Using DateAdd to Perform Calculations on the Current Date and Time*

```
    <FORM NAME="frmForm1">
Enter a value to add (or use a negative value to subtract)<BR>
from today's date.<BR>
<INPUT TYPE="text" NAME="txtDiffValue"><BR><BR>
Then select a date/time unit to perform the calculation on<BR>
<TABLE>
  <TR>
    <TD><INPUT LANGUAGE="vbscript" TYPE=radio VALUE="yyyy"
ONCLICK="vDateOption = &quot;yyyy&quot;" NAME="rdoOption"></TD>
    <TD><FONT SIZE=2>Year</TD>
    <TD><INPUT LANGUAGE="vbscript" TYPE=radio VALUE="q"
ONCLICK="vDateOption = &quot;q&quot;" NAME="rdoOption"></TD>
    <TD><FONT SIZE=2>Quarter</TD>
  </TR>

  <TR>
    <TD><INPUT LANGUAGE="vbscript" TYPE=radio VALUE="m"
ONCLICK="vDateOption = &quot;m&quot;" NAME="rdoOption"></TD>
    <TD><FONT SIZE=2>Month</TD>
    <TD><INPUT LANGUAGE="vbscript" TYPE=radio VALUE="y"
ONCLICK="vDateOption = &quot;y&quot;" NAME="rdoOption"></TD>
    <TD><FONT SIZE=2>Day of year</TD>
  </TR>

  <TR>
    <TD><INPUT LANGUAGE="vbscript" TYPE=radio VALUE="d"
ONCLICK="vDateOption = &quot;d&quot;" NAME="rdoOption"></TD>
    <TD><FONT SIZE=2>Day</TD>
    <TD><INPUT LANGUAGE="vbscript" TYPE=radio VALUE="w"
ONCLICK="vDateOption = &quot;w&quot;" NAME="rdoOption"></TD>
    <TD><FONT SIZE=2>Weekday</TD>
  </TR>

  <TR>
    <TD><INPUT LANGUAGE="vbscript" TYPE=radio VALUE="ww"
ONCLICK="vDateOption = &quot;ww&quot;" NAME="rdoOption"></TD>
    <TD><FONT SIZE=2>Week of year</TD>
    <TD><INPUT LANGUAGE="vbscript" TYPE=radio VALUE="h"
ONCLICK="vDateOption = &quot;h&quot;" NAME="rdoOption"></TD>
    <TD><FONT SIZE=2>Hour</TD>
  </TR>

  <TR>
    <TD><INPUT LANGUAGE="vbscript" TYPE=radio VALUE="n"
ONCLICK="vDateOption = &quot;n&quot;" NAME="rdoOption"></TD>
    <TD><FONT SIZE=2>Minute</TD>
    <TD><INPUT LANGUAGE="vbscript" TYPE=radio VALUE="s"
ONCLICK="vDateOption = &quot;s&quot;" NAME="rdoOption"></TD>
    <TD><FONT SIZE=2>Second</TD>
  </TR>

</TABLE>
```

*Example 10-9. Using DateAdd to Perform Calculations on the Current Date and Time*

```
<INPUT TYPE=button VALUE="Click me" NAME="cmdButton1">
<BR><BR>
Result.... <INPUT TYPE=text NAME="txtText1">
<BR><BR><BR>
<B>Note: The MS Documentation for the VBScript DateAdd() function<BR>
 incorrectly shows minute as "m" - it should be "n".
</BODY>
</HTML>
    </FORM>
</BODY>
```

### DateDiff `VBS 2.0`

So now that you can add or subtract a number of time intervals to or from a given date, how do you attack the problem from the other perspective: how many time intervals are there between two dates? For example, how many days, or hours, or minutes have passed since the current user last visited your web page? (If you combine this function with the Cookie example later in this chapter you can easily find the answer to this question.)

The *DateDiff* function simply returns the number of time intervals (you specify what the intervals are) between two dates. Here's the syntax:

```
DateDiff(interval, date1, date2 [,firstdayofweek[, firstweekofyear]])
```

For an explanation of the two optional arguments, *firstdayofweek* and *firstweekofyear*, refer to the *DatePart* function earlier in this chapter. The required arguments are:

- **interval.** The unit of time in which the difference between dates should be calculated. For a list of the valid string values for *interval*, see Table 10-1. Note that, when using *DateDiff*, Day and Day of year return the same result, as do Week and Week of year.

- **date1 and date2.** The two date/time values whose difference the function is to compute. If *date2* chronologically precedes (is older than) *date1*, the result will be negative. For example:

```
DateDiff("d", 10/10/97, 10/10/96)  ' returns -365
DateDiff("d", 10/10/96, 10/10/97)  ' returns 365
```

Example 10-10 illustrates the operation of the *DateDiff* function and again lets you experiment by using different arguments.

*Example 10-10. Using the DateDiff Function*

```
<HTML>
<HEAD>
    <SCRIPT LANGUAGE="vbscript">
    OPTION EXPLICIT
```

*Example 10-10. Using the DateDiff Function (continued)*

```
Dim vDateOption
Dim vDOWOption 'First Day of Week
Dim vWOYOption 'First Week of Year
vDOWOption = vbSunday
vWOYOption = vbFirstJan1

Sub cmdButton1_onClick

    If Not isDate(frmForm1.txtStartDate.Value) Then
        Alert "Start date is Invalid"
        Exit Sub
    End If

    If Not isDate(frmForm1.txtEndDate.Value) Then
        Alert "End date is Invalid"
        Exit Sub
    End If

    frmForm1.txtText1.Value = DateDiff(vDateOption, _
                             frmForm1.txtStartDate.Value, _
                             frmForm1.txtEndDate.Value, _
                             vDOWOption, _
                             vWOYOption)

End Sub

    </SCRIPT>
</HEAD>
<BODY BGCOLOR="white">

<FONT FACE="arial" SIZE=2>

<CENTER> <H3>DateDiff</H3>
<FORM NAME="frmForm1">
<TABLE>
  <TR>
    <TD><FONT SIZE=2>Start Date </TD>
    <TD><INPUT TYPE="text" NAME="txtStartDate"></TD>
    <TD><FONT SIZE=2>End Date</TD>
    <TD><INPUT TYPE="text" NAME="txtEndDate"></TD>
  </TR>

  <TR>
    <TD><INPUT LANGUAGE="vbscript" TYPE=radio VALUE="yyyy"
ONCLICK="vDateOption = &quot;yyyy&quot;" NAME="rdoOption"></TD>
    <TD><FONT SIZE=2>Year</TD>
    <TD><INPUT LANGUAGE="vbscript" TYPE=radio VALUE="q"
ONCLICK="vDateOption = &quot;q&quot;" NAME="rdoOption"></TD>
    <TD><FONT SIZE=2>Quarter</TD>
  </TR>
```

*Example 10-10. Using the DateDiff Function (continued)*

```
   <TR>
      <TD><INPUT LANGUAGE="vbscript" TYPE=radio VALUE="m"
ONCLICK="vDateOption = &quot;m&quot;" NAME="rdoOption"></TD>
      <TD><FONT SIZE=2>Month</TD>
      <TD><INPUT LANGUAGE="vbscript" TYPE=radio VALUE="y"
ONCLICK="vDateOption = &quot;y&quot;" NAME="rdoOption"></TD>
      <TD><FONT SIZE=2>Day of year</TD>
   </TR>

   <TR>
      <TD><INPUT LANGUAGE="vbscript" TYPE=radio VALUE="d"
ONCLICK="vDateOption = &quot;d&quot;" NAME="rdoOption"></TD>
      <TD><FONT SIZE=2>Day</TD>
      <TD><INPUT LANGUAGE="vbscript" TYPE=radio VALUE="w"
ONCLICK="vDateOption = &quot;w&quot;" NAME="rdoOption"></TD>
      <TD><FONT SIZE=2>Weekday</TD>
   </TR>

   <TR>
      <TD><INPUT LANGUAGE="vbscript" TYPE=radio VALUE="ww"
ONCLICK="vDateOption = &quot;ww&quot;" NAME="rdoOption"></TD>
      <TD><FONT SIZE=2>Week of year</TD>
      <TD><INPUT LANGUAGE="vbscript" TYPE=radio VALUE="h"
ONCLICK="vDateOption = &quot;h&quot;" NAME="rdoOption"></TD>
      <TD><FONT SIZE=2>Hour</TD>
   </TR>

   <TR>
      <TD><INPUT LANGUAGE="vbscript" TYPE=radio VALUE="n"
ONCLICK="vDateOption = &quot;n&quot;" NAME="rdoOption"></TD>
      <TD><FONT SIZE=2>Minute</TD>
      <TD><INPUT LANGUAGE="vbscript" TYPE=radio VALUE="s"
ONCLICK="vDateOption = &quot;s&quot;" NAME="rdoOption"></TD>
      <TD><FONT SIZE=2>Second</TD>
   </TR>
</TABLE>

<BR><BR>

<TABLE>
<TH>First Day of the Week</TH>
   <TR>
      <TD><INPUT LANGUAGE="vbscript" TYPE=radio
ONCLICK="vDOWOption = vbUseSystem" NAME="rdoDOWOption"></TD>
      <TD><FONT SIZE=2>Use National Language Support (NLS) API setting</TD>
   </TR>
   <TR>
      <TD><INPUT LANGUAGE="vbscript" TYPE=radio
ONCLICK="vDOWOption = vbSunday" NAME="rdoDOWOption"></TD>
      <TD><FONT SIZE=2>Sunday</TD>
   </TR>
   <TR>
      <TD><INPUT LANGUAGE="vbscript" TYPE=radio
```

*Example 10-10. Using the DateDiff Function (continued)*

```
ONCLICK="vDOWOption = vbMonday" NAME="rdoDOWOption"></TD>
    <TD><FONT SIZE=2>Monday</TD>
  </TR>
  <TR>
    <TD><INPUT LANGUAGE="vbscript" TYPE=radio
ONCLICK="vDOWOption = vbTuesday" NAME="rdoDOWOption"></TD>
    <TD><FONT SIZE=2>Tuesday</TD>
  </TR>
  <TR>
    <TD><INPUT LANGUAGE="vbscript" TYPE=radio
ONCLICK="vDOWOption = vbWednesday" NAME="rdoDOWOption"></TD>
    <TD><FONT SIZE=2>Wednesday</TD>
  </TR>
  <TR>
    <TD><INPUT LANGUAGE="vbscript" TYPE=radio
ONCLICK="vDOWOption = vbThursday" NAME="rdoDOWOption"></TD>
    <TD><FONT SIZE=2>Thursday</TD>
  </TR>
  <TR>
    <TD><INPUT LANGUAGE="vbscript" TYPE=radio
ONCLICK="vDOWOption = vbFriday" NAME="rdoDOWOption"></TD>
    <TD><FONT SIZE=2>Friday</TD>
  </TR>
  <TR>
    <TD><INPUT LANGUAGE="vbscript" TYPE=radio
ONCLICK="vDOWOption = vbSaturday" NAME="rdoDOWOption"></TD>
    <TD><FONT SIZE=2>Saturday</TD>
  </TR>
</TABLE>

<BR><BR>

<TABLE>
<TH>First Week of the Year</TH>
  <TR>
    <TD><INPUT LANGUAGE="vbscript" TYPE=radio
ONCLICK="vWOYOption = vbUseSystem" NAME="rdoWOYOption"></TD>
    <TD><FONT SIZE=2>Use National Language Support (NLS) API setting</TD>
  </TR>
  <TR>
    <TD><INPUT LANGUAGE="vbscript" TYPE=radio
ONCLICK="vWOYOption = vbFirstJan1" NAME="rdoWOYOption"></TD>
    <TD><FONT SIZE=2>Week containing Jan 1st (default)</TD>
  </TR>
  <TR>
  <TR>
    <TD><INPUT LANGUAGE="vbscript" TYPE=radio
ONCLICK="vWOYOption = vbFirstFourDays" NAME="rdoWOYOption"></TD>
    <TD><FONT SIZE=2>Week with min. four days in new year</TD>
  </TR>
  <TR>
    <TD><INPUT LANGUAGE="vbscript" TYPE=radio
```

*Example 10-10. Using the DateDiff Function (continued)*

```
ONCLICK="vWOYOption = vbFirstFullWeek" NAME="rdoWOYOption"></TD>
    <TD><FONT SIZE=2>First full week of the new year</TD>
  </TR>
</TABLE>
<BR>
        <INPUT TYPE=button VALUE="Click me" NAME="cmdButton1">
  
        <INPUT TYPE=text NAME="txtText1">
</BODY>
</HTML>
    </FORM>
</BODY>
```

## DateSerial

The *DateSerial* function returns a variant 7 data subtype (a date) from the three date components (year, month, and day). For the function to succeed, all three components must be present, and all must be numeric values. The value returned by the function takes the Short Date format defined by the Regional Settings applet in the Control Panel of the client machine. The syntax of *DateSerial* is:

```
varType7 = DateSerial(year, month, day)
```

Each of the arguments supplied to the function supports a range of values that are recognized as valid. These are:

- **year**: 100 to 9999. *DateSerial* assumes that years apply to the current century for values from 0 to 99.

- **month**: 1 to 12.

- **day**: 1 to 31. The precise upper limit depends on the month.

If the value of a particular element exceeds its normal limits, *DateSerial* adjusts the date accordingly. For example, if you tried *DateSerial(96,2,31)*—February 31, 1996—*DateSerial* would return March 2, 1996.

Example 10-11 illustrates the use of the *DateSerial* function. Simply enter a figure for the three constituents of the date (day, month, and year), and click the button to allow the program to convert these figures into a valid date.

*Example 10-11. The DateSerial Function*

```
<HTML>
<HEAD>
<TITLE>DateSerial()</TITLE>
<SCRIPT LANGUAGE="vbscript">
<!--
Sub cmdButton1_OnClick
```

*Example 10-11. The DateSerial Function (continued)*

```
d = Document.frmForm1.dayinput.Value
m = Document.frmForm1.monthinput.Value
y = Document.frmForm1.yearinput.Value

Alert DateSerial(y, m, d)

End Sub
-->
</SCRIPT>
</HEAD>
<BODY BGCOLOR="white">
<FORM NAME="frmForm1">
<CENTER>
Enter a Day <INPUT TYPE="text" NAME="dayinput"><P>
Enter a Month <INPUT TYPE="text" NAME="monthinput"><P>
Enter a Year <INPUT TYPE="text" NAME="yearinput"><P>
<INPUT TYPE="button" NAME="cmdButton1" VALUE="Show Date">
</FORM>
</CENTER>
</BODY>
</HTML>
```

The fact that *DateSerial* automatically adjusts the date it returns to correct individual date components whose values exceed the valid ranges suggests that *DateSerial* can be used to perform date calculations as well as to piece together a date from its components. And in fact, the arguments passed to the function can be expressions as well as explicit numbers, which does allow you to perform date arithmetic when calling the function. For example, the following code fragment adds 100 months to the current date:

```
d = Day(Now())
m = Month(Now())
y = Year(Now())
DateSerial(y, m + 100, d)
```

The code fragment begins by splitting a valid date into its constituent parts using the *Day*, *Month*, and *Year* functions. When 100—which of course exceeds the upper range of the month argument—is added to the current month, *DateSerial* automatically calculates the correct date and reforms the date using the Short Date format.

Example 10-12 illustrates the use of the *DateSerial* function to perform date calculations by adding a certain number of days to a given date. Enter the start date and the number of days to add, then click the button to see the result.

*Example 10-12. Using DateSerial to Add Days to a Date*

```
<HTML>
<HEAD>
<TITLE>Calculating Dates</TITLE>
<SCRIPT LANGUAGE="vbscript">
```

*Example 10-12. Using DateSerial to Add Days to a Date (continued)*

```
<!--
Sub cmdButton1_OnClick

  If Not IsDate(Document.frmForm1.inputdate.Value) Then
      Alert "Not A Valid Date"
      Exit Sub
  End If

  y = Document.frmForm1.days.Value
  x = DateValue(Document.frmForm1.inputdate.Value)

  Alert DateSerial(Year(x), Month(x), Day(x) + y)

End Sub
-->
</SCRIPT>
</HEAD>
<BODY BGCOLOR="white">
 <CENTER>
  <FORM NAME="frmForm1">
    Enter a Date <INPUT TYPE="text" NAME="inputdate"><BR>
    Enter No of Days to Add <INPUT TYPE="text" NAME="days" SIZE=10><BR>
    <INPUT TYPE="button" NAME="cmdButton1" VALUE="CALCULATE">
  </FORM>
 </CENTER>
</BODY>
</HTML>
```

### TimeSerial

Like *DateSerial*, the *TimeSerial* function pieces together a valid time value from its component parts. It returns a variant type 7 (the date subtype) from the three time components (hours, minutes, and seconds), all of which must be numeric values. The general syntax of the *TimeSerial* function is:

```
varType7 = TimeSerial(hour, minute, second)
```

Each argument can be represented by a numeric expression as well as by an explicit numeric value. The arguments supplied to the function support values in the following ranges:

- **hour**: 0 to 23

- **minute**: 0 to 59

- **second**: 0 to 59

As you've probably guessed by now, *TimeSerial* operates in exactly the same fashion as *DateSerial*. This means that, if the value of a particular argument exceeds its normal limits, *TimeSerial( )* adjusts the time accordingly. Note, however, that if *hour* exceeds 24, the day variable is incremented. When you are dealing purely with time variables, and have not specified a date, the day is taken as 0, but if you spill the hours into the next "day," the day variable becomes 1. Day 1 in VBScript terms is January 31, 1899, so your result may appear somewhat screwy.

Example 10-13 provides a simple "time" calculator that returns a time value based on the values you supply for hours, minutes, and seconds. You can use it to test VBScript's handling of individual time components that exceed their valid ranges.

*Example 10-13. The TimeSerial Function*

```
<HTML>
<HEAD>
<TITLE>TimeSerial()</TITLE>
<SCRIPT LANGUAGE="vbscript">
<!--
  Sub cmdButton1_OnClick

     s = Document.frmForm1.secondinput.Value
     m = Document.frmForm1.minuteinput.Value
     h = Document.frmForm1.hourinput.Value

     Alert TimeSerial(h, m, s)

  End Sub
-->
</SCRIPT>
</HEAD>
<BODY BGCOLOR="white">
<FORM NAME="frmForm1">
<CENTER>
Enter a Second <INPUT TYPE="text" NAME="secondinput"><P>
Enter a Minute <INPUT TYPE="text" NAME="minuteinput"><P>
Enter an Hour <INPUT TYPE="text" NAME="hourinput"><P>
<INPUT TYPE="button" NAME="cmdButton1" VALUE="Show Time">
</FORM>
</CENTER>
</BODY>
</HTML>
```

### Timer

The *Timer* function is not documented for either VBScript or VBScript 2. However, it returns the number of seconds elapsed since midnight, to an accuracy of 6 decimal places. Not very useful, you may think. However, the most popular use of the *Timer* function is as a method of accurately timing some portion of your script. For example, when optimizing your code, you may want to know if method A is quicker than method B for achieving a particular result. To do this, simply call and store the *Timer* value immediately prior to performing the task, then as soon as the task is completed, call the *Timer* function again and subtract the starting figure to end up with an accurate elapsed time.

Example 10-14 uses a mathematical function called The Sieve of Eratosthenes (he's the guy who accurately calculated the circumference of the earth in about 300 B.C.), a favorite benchmark when testing the capabilities of software and computer languages. Basically, it returns all the prime numbers up to a given number. The example shows how to use the *Timer* function, and it will give you some idea of the speed at which VBScript runs. By modifying the program to work with other languages, like Visual Basic, you can get some sense of how much slower VBScript is.

*Example 10-14. Using Timer to Test the Speed of VBScript*

```
<HTML>
<HEAD>
<TITLE>Timer</TITLE>
<SCRIPT LANGUAGE="vbscript">

   Sub cmdCommand1_OnClick
       Dim t
       Dim sSeive

       t = Timer

       sSeive = doSeive(frmForm1.txtMaxNumber.Value)
       Alert sSeive & " - processed in " & (Timer-t) & " seconds"
   End Sub

   Function doSeive(iMax)
       ReDim iNumbers(iMax)
       Dim i, j
       Dim sReturn

       For i = 2 to iMax
           For j = 2 to iMax
               If cInt((i * j)) > CInt(iMax) Then
                   Exit For
               Else
                   iNumbers(cInt(i * j)) = 1
               End if
           Next
       Next

       For i = 1 to iMax
           If iNumbers(i) <> 1 Then
               If sReturn = " " Then
                   sReturn = i
               Else
                   sReturn = sReturn & "," & i
               End if
       Next
```

*Example 10-14. Using Timer to Test the Speed of VBScript (continued)*

```
        DoSeive = sReturn
    End Function

</SCRIPT>

</HEAD>
<BODY BGCOLOR="white">
<CENTER>
<H3>The Sieve of Eratosthenes</H3>
<BR>
<FORM NAME="frmForm1">
Find Prime Numbers up to <INPUT TYPE="text" NAME="txtMaxNumber">
  
<INPUT TYPE="button" NAME="cmdCommand1" VALUE="Run">
</FORM>
</CENTER>
</BODY>
</HTML>
```

# Reformatting Date Expressions

Earlier, we used the *IsDate* function to check at the client whether or not a date entered into an HTML form was valid. The ability to establish that a date is valid is important, since you can then use the *Day, Month, Year,* and other date and time functions for further processing. But there is one problem with *IsDate*: it establishes that the date is valid only in accordance with the date formatting rules that are in effect on the client computer.

What happens, however, when the date is not only being used on the client computer, but is also being sent to the server? The client may, for instance, transmit the date to the server, where you plan to add it to your database. You can imagine the havoc that dates formatted in many different ways can cause, when entered into your database. In cases such as these, you can reformat the date before submitting it to the server. To ensure that the date is valid on your server, you use the *Day, Month,* and *Year* functions to break a localized date into its constituent components, and then concatenate them, along with the required date separator characters, into the format that is used on the server. Once you've done this, however, the resulting date may no longer be considered valid on the client machine.

Example 10-15 shows how to verify that a date input into an HTML form is valid, split it up into day, month, and year, and reassemble it in the Month, Year, Day format using a "–" character as the separator. In the real world, you would store this as a string variable, which would be passed to the server with the rest of the data. A procedure such as this one assures you that, first of all, you're going to receive a valid date, and second, that the date will be formatted in the style you require.

*Example 10-15. Reformatting a Local Date*

```
<HTML>
<HEAD>
<TITLE>Reformating the Date</TITLE>
<SCRIPT LANGUAGE="vbscript">
<!--
Sub cmdButton1_OnClick
  If Not IsDate(Document.frmForm1.inputdate.Value) Then
     Alert "Not A Valid Date"
     Exit Sub
  End If

  dv = DateValue(Document.frmForm1.inputdate.Value)
  Alert  Month(dv) & "-" & Year(dv) & "-" & Day(dv)

End Sub

-->
</SCRIPT>
</HEAD>
 <BODY BGCOLOR="white">
  <CENTER>
   <FORM NAME="frmForm1">
    Enter a valid date
    <INPUT TYPE="text" NAME="inputdate"><P>
    <INPUT TYPE="button" NAME="cmdButton1" VALUE="Reformat">
   </FORM>
  </CENTER>
 </BODY>
</HTML>
```

## *FormatDateTime* `VBS 2.0`

To save space in the original version of VBScript, Microsoft engineers left out the VB and VBA *Format* function. In an attempt to add some "lite" formatting functionality, VBScript 2.0 has several targeted formatting functions, one of which is *FormatDateTime*. This function allows you to format a date/time expression using one of five predefined formats, based on the computer's localized settings. However, unless you are certain that the client machine will have a regional setting compatible with that of the server, you should be careful of using this function to format dates and times. Bearing this in mind, you'd probably be smart to stick to manually formatting dates and times using the known intervals of month, day, and year in situations where you are unsure of the regional settings of the client.

The syntax of *FormatDateTime* is:

```
FormatDateTime(date[,format])
```

The new intrinsic constants to use for the format argument are listed in Table 10-4.

*Table 10-4. The format argument of the FormatDateTime Function*

| Constant | Value | Description |
|---|---|---|
| vbGeneralDate | 0 | Displays a date and/or time. If there is a date part, displays it as a short date. If there is a time part, displays it as a long time. If present, both parts are displayed. |
| VbLongDate | 1 | Uses the long date format specified in the client computer's regional settings. |
| VbShortDate | 2 | Uses the short date format specified in the client computer's regional settings. |
| VbLongTime | 3 | Uses the time format specified in the computer's regional settings. |
| VbShortTime | 4 | Uses a 24-hour format (hh:mm). |

# A Cookie Example

Example 10-16 shows how to read and write a cookie. (For more details on the *Document.Cookie* property, see "The Document Object" in Chapter 5, *Controlling the Browser.*) You can use the cookie to store all kinds of data that can help enhance your interaction with a user, which should in turn improve the experience the user gains from visiting your web site.

Date and time manipulation is important when using cookies, not only because a popular use of cookies is to store the date when a user last visited the site, but more importantly because an integral part of the cookie definition is the expiration date of the cookie, which must be set in order to store a cookie for longer than the current browser session. Example 10-16 therefore shows how to use the *DateAdd*, *DatePart*, and *IsDate* functions.

The example also introduces some new VBScript 2.0 string manipulation functions: *Split*, a mini-parsing tool, and *Replace*, to replace a substring within a string. For more details on string manipulation functions, see Chapter 14, *Form Input Validation*, and Appendix B, *VBScript Version 2.*

---

NOTE          You must run the web page in Example 10-16 from a web server domain in order to see the results. In case it isn't possible for you to do this, I've placed the page at the following URL for you to try out: *http://www.vbscripts.com/test/cookies.htm.*

---

> ## *Converting to GMT: MakeLegalCookieDate*
>
> To be stored on a user's hard drive for longer than the current browser session, a cookie must have an expiration date set. The `Expires` parameter, however, must be formatted in a particular way in order to be accepted. The required format is:
>
> ```
> day, dd-mmm-yy hh:mm:ss GMT
> ```
>
> Unfortunately, VBScript does not include a built-in function to convert a date to this format. But you can use the *MakeLegalCookieDate* function, which is included in Example 10-16, to convert a VBScript date to a date that's correctly formatted for the cookie's `Expires` parameter.

*Example 10-16. Reading and Writing a Cookie*

```
<HTML>
<HEAD>
  <TITLE>Learning VBScript Cookie Example</TITLE>
  <SCRIPT LANGUAGE="vbscript">
  OPTION EXPLICIT
  Sub window_onLoad()
      Call DoCookiesList()
  End Sub

  Sub DoCookiesList()
      'Get a list of the cookie variable names and display them
      'in the combo box.
      Dim sCookie
      Dim vaCookies
      Dim sCookieVar
      Dim i

      'read the cookie string
      sCookie = Document.Cookie

      'split the cookie string up into name=value pairs
      'the Split() function creates an array
      vaCookies = Split(sCookie, ";")

      'iterate through the array splitting up the Name=Value pairs
      'and add the variable names to the combobox list
      frmCookies.cboCookieVar.Clear
      For i = 0 to UBound(vaCookies)
          sCookieVar = Left(vaCookies(i), _
                            inStr(1, vaCookies(i), "=")-1)
          frmCookies.cboCookieVar.AddItem Trim(sCookieVar)
      Next

  End Sub

  Sub cmdAmendCookieValue_OnClick
```

*Example 10-16. Reading and Writing a Cookie (continued)*

```
    Dim sCookieVar
    Dim sOldVal
    Dim sOldPair
    Dim sNewPair
    Dim sCookie

    If frmCookies.cboCookieVar.ListIndex = -1 Then
        Alert "Please select a cookie variable"
        Exit Sub
    Else
        '
        'build a string of the old name=value pair
        sCookieVar = _
frmCookies.cboCookieVar.List(frmCookies.cboCookieVar.ListIndex)
        sOldVal = GetCookieValue(frmCookies.cboCookieVar.ListIndex)
        sOldPair = sCookieVar & "=" & sOldVal

        'build a new name=value pair for this cookie variable
        sNewPair = sCookieVar & "=" & _
                   Trim(frmCookies.txtAmendCookieValue.Value)
        sCookie = Document.Cookie

        'replace the old pair with the new pair
        sCookie = Replace(sCookie, sOldPair, sNewPair) _
                  & ";expires=" & _
                  MakeLegalCookieDate(dateadd("d",7,Now()))

        Document.Cookie = sCookie
        Alert "New Cookie Value Saved"
    End If

End Sub

Sub cmdRemoveCookie_OnClick
    'The way to delete a cookie is to set an expiration
    'date prior to today.
    Dim vExpire
    Dim sCookieExpire
    Dim sCookie

    'read the current cookie string
    sCookie = Document.Cookie

    'expiration will be yesterday
    vExpire = DateAdd("d", -1, Now())

    'now create the new legal expiration string
    sCookieExpire = ";expires=" & MakeLegalCookieDate(vExpire)

    'rewrite the cookie with the new expiration date
    sCookie = sCookie & sCookieExpire
    Document.Cookie = sCookie
End Sub
```

*Example 10-16. Reading and Writing a Cookie (continued)*

```
Sub cmdAmendCookieExpires_OnClick
    Dim vExpire
    Dim sCookieExpire
    Dim sCookie

    'read the current cookie string
    'sCookie = Document.Cookie

    'check new expiration date
    If Not isDate(frmCookies.txtNewCookieExpires.Value) Then
        Alert "Invalid Expiration Date"
        Exit Sub
    Else
        vExpire = frmCookies.txtNewCookieExpires.Value
    End If

    'now create the new legal expiration string
    sCookieExpire = ";expires=" & MakeLegalCookieDate(vExpire)

    'rewrite the cookie with the new expiration date
    sCookie = sCookie & sCookieExpire
    Document.Cookie = sCookie

End Sub

Sub cmdShowCookie_OnClick
    If frmCookies.cboCookieVar.ListIndex = -1 Then
        Exit Sub
    Else
        Alert GetCookieValue(frmCookies.cboCookieVar.ListIndex)
    End If
End Sub

Sub cmdAddCookie_OnClick
    Dim sCookie

    sCookie = Document.Cookie
    sCookie = sCookie & ";" & Trim(frmCookies.txtNewCookieVar.Value) _
                & "=" _
                & Trim(frmCookies.txtNewCookieValue.Value) & ";" _
                & "expires=" & _
                MakeLegalCookieDate(dateadd("d",7,Now()))

    Document.Cookie = sCookie
    Call DoCookiesList()
End Sub

Function GetCookieValue(iCookieIndex)
    Dim vaCookies
    Dim sCookiePair

    vaCookies = Split(Document.Cookie, ";")
    sCookiePair = vaCookies(iCookieIndex)
```

*Example 10-16. Reading and Writing a Cookie (continued)*

```
        GetCookieValue = Mid(sCookiePair, (InStr(1, sCookiePair, "=") +1))

End Function

Function MakeLegalCookieDate(vDate)

    'purpose: To convert the date into a format that is legal
    '          to use for the Expires attribute in a cookie file
    ' author: Paul Lomax copyright O'Reilly & Associates 1997
    '   note: Requires the use of VBScript 2.0

    Dim sDays
    Dim sDay
    Dim sMonths
    Dim sMonth

    On Error Resume Next
    MakeLegalCookieDate = ""

    If Not IsDate(vDate) Then
        Alert "Not a valid date"
        Exit Function
    End If

    sDays = Array("Sunday", "Monday", "Tuesday", _
                "Wednesday", "Thursday", "Friday", "Saturday")
    sMonths = Array("Jan", "Feb", "Mar", "Apr", "May", "Jun", _
                "Jul", "Aug", "Sept", "Oct", "Nov", "Dec")

    sDay = sDays(Weekday(vDate, vbSunday)-1)
    sMonth = sMonths(DatePart("m", vDate)-1)

    If Err.Number > 0 Then
        Alert Err.Number & " " & Err.Description
        Exit Function
    End If

    MakeLegalCookieDate = sDay & ", " _
                            & DoubleDigit(DatePart("d",vDate)) & "-" _
                            & sMonth & "-" _
                            & DatePart("yyyy",vDate) & " " _
                            & DoubleDigit(DatePart("h",vDate)) & ":" _
                            & DoubleDigit(DatePart("n",vDate)) & ":" _
                            & DoubleDigit(DatePart("s",vDate)) & " " _
                            & "GMT"

End Function


Function DoubleDigit(sMaybeSingle)

  If Len(sMaybeSingle) = 1 then
     DoubleDigit = "0" & sMaybeSingle
```

*Example 10-16. Reading and Writing a Cookie (continued)*

```
    Else
        DoubleDigit = sMaybeSingle
    End If

  End Function
    </SCRIPT>
</HEAD>
<BODY BGCOLOR="white">
<CENTER><FONT FACE="arial" SIZE=2><B>
<H3>This example will only operate from a web domain</H3>
<BR>
<H4>This example requires VBScript 2</H4>
<BR>
    <FORM NAME="frmCookies">
This is a list of the Variables for the current Cookie

<OBJECT ID="cboCookieVar" WIDTH=171 HEIGHT=24
 CLASSID="CLSID:8BD21D30-EC42-11CE-9E0D-00AA006002F3">
    <PARAM NAME="VariousPropertyBits" VALUE="746604571">
    <PARAM NAME="DisplayStyle" VALUE="3">
    <PARAM NAME="Size" VALUE="4493;635">
    <PARAM NAME="MatchEntry" VALUE="1">
    <PARAM NAME="ShowDropButtonWhen" VALUE="2">
    <PARAM NAME="FontCharSet" VALUE="0">
    <PARAM NAME="FontPitchAndFamily" VALUE="2">
    <PARAM NAME="FontWeight" VALUE="0">
</OBJECT>

<BR>
  Select a cookie and click the button to display the value
  of the selected cookie.
        <INPUT TYPE=button VALUE="Show Cookie Value" NAME="cmdShowCookie">
<BR>

<HR>

  Select a cookie variable from the list above and enter a new value
  to store against it, then click the button.<BR>
  New Value
        <INPUT TYPE=text NAME="txtAmendCookieValue">
  
        <INPUT TYPE=button VALUE="Amend Cookie Value"
NAME="cmdAmendCookieValue">
<BR>

<HR>

  Enter a new Cookie Variable Name, then enter a value for it, and click
the
  "Add Cookie Variable" Button <BR>
  Name
        <INPUT TYPE=text NAME="txtNewCookieVar">
  
  Value
```

*Example 10-16. Reading and Writing a Cookie (continued)*

```
        <INPUT TYPE=text NAME="txtNewCookieValue">
  
        <INPUT TYPE=button VALUE="Add Cookie Variable" NAME="cmdAddCookie">
<BR>

<HR>

    To change the Expiration date of the current cookie, enter a new
    date and click "Change Cookie Expiration"<BR>
     <FONT SIZE=1>
      n.b. Setting a date prior to now will delete the cookie
     </FONT><BR>
    New Expiration Date
        <INPUT TYPE=text NAME="txtNewCookieExpires">
  
        <INPUT TYPE=button VALUE="Change Cookie Expiration"
NAME="cmdAmendCookieExpires">
<BR>

<HR>

    To remove the cookie attached to this document, click this button.
        <INPUT TYPE=button VALUE="Remove Cookie" NAME="cmdRemoveCookie">
     </FORM>
</BODY>
</HTML>
```

# A Countdown Example

The program in Example 10-17 illustrates the use of a number of the date functions discussed in this chapter, as well as the placement of VBScript code in the HTML text stream. The program creates a variable headline that indicates the number of days remaining in the current year, as Figure 10-3 shows. The headline is created by a mixture of text and VBScript code as the HTML page loads into the browser; notice that the scripts contained within the <SCRIPT> tags contain no procedure or function definitions.

One possible difficulty is that we don't want to "hardcode" a year ending date (like 12/31/97) in our VBScript code, since this means that our application either becomes outdated after the end of the year, or that we have to remember to modify it annually. Instead of specifying a precise year, the program simply converts the string "12/31" into a date. When no year is specified, *DateValue* extracts the year from the computer's system date. That allows this web page to operate successfully for about another 8000 years.

The number of days to the end of the current year is then easily calculated by subtracting the current date and time from the end of the year.

*Figure 10-3. Countdown to a new year*

*Example 10-17. A Sample Date Program*

```
<HTML>
<HEAD>
<TITLE>Countdown to New Year</TITLE>
</HEAD>

 <BODY BGCOLOR="white">
  <CENTER>
   <IMG SRC="oldtime.jpg"><P>
   <H2>There are only

     <SCRIPT LANGUAGE="vbscript">
         x = DateValue("12/31")
         y = Now()
         z = int(x - y)

         Document.Write z
     </SCRIPT>

     days of

     <SCRIPT LANGUAGE="vbscript">
         Document.Write Year(Now())
     </SCRIPT>

     left
   </H2>
  </CENTER>
```

*Example 10-17. A Sample Date Program (continued)*

```
</BODY>
</HTML>
```

# Summary

Here's a quick summary of the time and date functions that you have seen in this chapter:

- You can use the *IsDate* function to verify that a string expression represents a valid date.

- A variety of functions can be used to return the current date, time, or one of its components, based on the system clock on the user's machine. These include *Now* (which returns both the date and the time), *Date*, *Time*, *Year*, *Month*, *Day*, *Weekday*, *Hour*, *Minute*, and *Second*.

- *DatePart* can be used to return a specific part of the given date, for example the day or month.

- *DateAdd* can be used to add or subtract a particular number of time intervals to or from a given date.

- *DateDiff* returns the number of time intervals between two dates.

- The *DateValue* and *TimeValue* functions can be used to convert a valid string value to a variant date and a time, respectively.

- The *DateSerial* and *TimeSerial* functions can be used to construct a date or a time value from its individual date or time components.

---

### Millennium-Ready?

Hopefully I'll have this book finished in time for the new millennium! But how ready will your VBScript web pages be? VBScript, like VB and VBA, is millennium-proof for a good few years at least. Here's how:

When VBScript sees a two-digit year, it assumes that all values equal to or greater than 30 are in the twentieth century (i.e., 30 = 1930, 97 = 1997), and that all values less than 30 are in the twenty-first century (i.e., 29 = 2029, 5 = 2005). Of course, if you don't want sleepless nights rewriting scripts in the year 2029, I'd suggest that you insist on a four-digit year, which will make your scripts work perfectly for about the next 8000 years!

---

# 11

# *Describing Your Hyperlinks*

One of the real strengths of the Web is its support for hyperlinks, which allow a user to navigate from the current document to another, related document by simply clicking on a block of text. Interestingly, this is also one of the weaknesses of the Web. Users typically spend a good deal of time (in the process sometimes becoming very disoriented) following links that turn out to be uninteresting or irrelevant. And probably the most common use of the Back button is to back out of a series of uninteresting links and return to some original starting point.

One of the reasons for this frustration is that, in an ordinary web page, the hyperlink itself provides most of the available information about a link, and that information is often inadequate for allowing the user to decide whether to follow the link or not. For instance, when you move your mouse over a hyperlink in a Microsoft Internet Explorer window, the mouse cursor changes from an arrow to a pointing hand, and the status bar changes to read "Shortcut to" with some variation of the URL of the linked document.

In this chapter, we'll explore several techniques for adding some additional interactivity to your HTML documents by using VBScript to display more detailed descriptions of the documents to which hyperlinks lead.

## *Link Descriptions Using HTML Intrinsic Objects*

One of the methods of "activating" your hyperlinks involves using only HTML intrinsic controls. You add an HTML text box control to your form whose purpose is to display a message about the document that will be displayed when the user clicks a hyperlink. The text box displays a message about a particular hyperlink as the user moves the mouse cursor over that hyperlink.

But how can you determine whether the mouse is positioned over a hyperlink? As you may recall from the discussion of the MSIE object model in Chapter 6, *The Element Object and HTML Intrinsic Controls*, Internet Explorer uses the *Link* object to keep track of all information relating to a document's hyperlinks. The *Link* object supports two events that are triggered by the mouse moving over a particular hyperlink: *MouseMove* and *OnMouseOver*. Both can be used to track mouse movement so that you can add extended information about hyperlinks to your application.

## The MouseMove Event

The *MouseMove* event is triggered whenever the mouse pointer passes over a particular *named* hyperlink. If, for instance, a document includes the hyperlink

```
<A HREF="http://www.ora.com" NAME="OraLink">
```

its event handler can be defined in either of two ways:

- By using the HTML <SCRIPT FOR> tag. For example,

```
<SCRIPT LANGUAGE="vbscript" FOR="OraLink" EVENT="MouseMove(shift,
button, x, y)">
    alert "Mouse over OraLink at coordinates " & x & ", " & y
</SCRIPT>
```

  defines the *MouseMove* event handler when the mouse passes over *OraLink*. This is the method that is discussed in Microsoft's documentation of the MSIE object model.

- By creating an event procedure for the link's *MouseMove* event. For example,

```
Sub OraLink_MouseMove(shift, button, x, y)
    alert "Mouse over OraLink at coordinates " & x & ", " & y
End Sub
```

  Note that the event handler applies to a particular link rather than to the Links collection object as a whole.

As you can see, regardless of which method is used to define the event handler, four parameters are passed to the *MouseMove* event handler:

- **shift**. Indicates the state of the Shift key at the time the *MouseMove* event was triggered. In MSIE 3.0, its value is always 1.

- **button**. Indicates which mouse button (if any) was clicked or held at the time the *MouseMove* event was triggered. In MSIE 3.0, its value is always 0.

- **x**. The horizontal position of the mouse (that is, the position along the X axis) in pixels when the *MouseMove* event was triggered. The X axis starts at the left hand side of the screen, position 0.

- **y.** The vertical position of the mouse (that is, the position along the Y axis) in pixels when the *MouseMove* event was triggered. The Y axis starts at the top of the screen, position 0.

However, since we're only concerned with whether the mouse is over our hyperlink or not, we don't need to make use of any of these variables. In Chapter 12, *Image Maps Made Easy*, you'll see the x and y coordinates used in an image map example, since we need to know the precise coordinates of the mouse to determine which portion of the image map the user selected.

## The OnMouseOver Event

Like *MouseMove*, the *OnMouseOver* event is triggered when the mouse passes over a hyperlink. It differs from *MouseMove* in two ways. First, it can be used to define an event handler both to named and unnamed links. Second, the event handler does not have any parameters; VBScript does not pass any arguments to it when the event is triggered. The *OnMouseOver* event handler can be defined in the same two ways as the *MouseMove* event handler, as well as in one additional way:

```
<A LANGUAGE="vbscript" NAME="Link1" OnMouseOver="call showLink(0)"
HREF="">
About Khalifa Desert Holidays</A><BR>
```

Here, the *OnMouseOver* event handler is defined along with the link itself. When the *OnMouseOver* event is triggered, VBScript calls a custom procedure and passes it a number that identifies the link that called the procedure. For example:

```
Sub ShowLink(LinkNo)
    Alert "Mouse over link " & LinkNo + 1
End Sub
```

## Creating the Link Description Example

In our sample web page, we'll create six hyperlinks with the `<A>` tag. So that you can see how to use the two mouse movement events to add additional text to describe a hyperlink, we'll create a *MouseMove* event handler for three of the links and an *OnMouseOver* event handler for the three remaining links. The page uses an HTML intrinsic text box control, named *Text1*, to hold the text that describes the currently selected hyperlink. The event handler simply retrieves a string that describes its link from a string array, and places it in the text box.

To add the extended descriptions of hyperlinks to a web page, follow these steps:

1. Build a single-dimension public string array to hold the text describing each link. Using an array allows us to separate the text from the code (we don't have to "hardcode" the descriptions into our program), making it easier to

maintain the web page. Since our web page has six hyperlinks, we want to define a string array with six elements as follows:

```
Dim DescribeLink(5)
DescribeLink(0) = "Find out all about us"
DescribeLink(1) = "So good you'll want to stay for life"
DescribeLink(2) = "The under 17's stay longer for free"
DescribeLink(3) = "Our new Hotel now open in Communicado"
DescribeLink(4) = "Frequently Asked Questions about Desert Holidays"
DescribeLink(5) = "All the latest news and gossip"
```

2. Construct the custom procedure and event handlers for the two types of mouse movement events. For this example, we'll use the following custom procedure to display an extended description of links *Link1*, *Link2*, and *Link3*:

```
Sub ShowLink(LinkNo)
   text1.value = DescribeLink(CInt(LinkNo))
End Sub
```

Each of the remaining three links has its own *MouseMove* event procedure, as follows:

```
Sub Link4_MouseMove(s,b,x,y)
   text1.value = DescribeLink(3)
End Sub
```

```
Sub Link5_MouseMove(s,b,x,y)
   text1.value = DescribeLink(4)
End Sub
```

```
Sub Link6_MouseMove(s,b,x,y)
   text1.value = DescribeLink(5)
End Sub
```

3. Modify the `<A>` tags that define links *Link1*, *Link2*, and *Link3* by defining the *OnMouseOver* event:

```
<A LANGUAGE="vbscript" NAME="Link1" OnMouseOver="call showLink(0)"
HREF="">
Rates and Tariffs</A><BR>
```

```
<A LANGUAGE="vbscript" NAME="Link2" OnMouseOver="call showLink(1)"
HREF="">
Rates and Tariffs</A><BR>
```

```
<A LANGUAGE="vbscript" NAME="Link3" OnMouseOver="call showLink(2)"
HREF="">
Rates and Tariffs</A><BR>
```

As you can see, the first three links all call the same *ShowLink* custom procedure, which is simply passed a number indicating which link is responsible for invoking the procedure. We can do this because the *OnMouseOver* event lets you define an event handler in the anchor (`<A>`) tag. This allows you not only to designate a custom procedure as an event handler, but also to indicate what parameters should be passed to the procedure. The result is more compact, "tidier" code.

Links *Link4, Link5,* and *Link6* all have their own event handler. Of course, we would prefer to have a single event handler for all three links, but the way in which the *MouseMove* event procedure is defined does not make this possible. It would be very convenient, for example, to group a set of links together, develop a common event handler for them, and use each link's index number in the Links object collection to distinguish it from other links. In that case, the *MouseMove* event procedure would be much clearer and simpler:

```
Sub Link(I)_MouseMove(s,b,x,y)' WRONG:  not supported by VBScript
    text1.value = DescribeLink(I)
End Sub
```

Unfortunately, however, VBScript does not support this syntax, and does not pass a link's index number in any form when firing the *MouseMove* event. So we have no alternative but to write separate explicit event handlers instead. Each event handler uses the number of its link to retrieve the text from the public string array and display it in an HTML text box above the links.

The complete source code for the first example is shown in Example 11-1; Figure 11-1 shows the result when the mouse pointer passes over Link2.

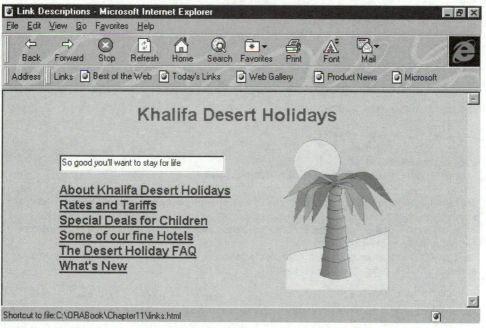

*Figure 11-1. The link description shown in an HTML Text Box*

*Example 11-1. Using an HTML Intrinsic Text Box to Describe Links*

```
<HTML>
<HEAD><TITLE>Link Descriptions</TITLE>
<SCRIPT language="vbscript">
```

*Example 11-1. Using an HTML Intrinsic Text Box to Describe Links (continued)*

```
Dim DescribeLink(5)
DescribeLink(0) = "Find out all about us"
DescribeLink(1) = "So good you'll want to stay for life"
DescribeLink(2) = "The under 17's stay longer for free"
DescribeLink(3) = "Our new Hotel now open in Communicado"
DescribeLink(4) = "Frequently Asked Questions about Desert Holidays"
DescribeLink(5) = "All the latest news and gossip"

Sub ShowLink(LinkNo)
    text1.value = DescribeLink(CInt(LinkNo))
End Sub

Sub Link4_MouseMove(s,b,x,y)
    text1.value = DescribeLink(3)
End Sub

Sub Link5_MouseMove(s,b,x,y)
    text1.value = DescribeLink(4)
End Sub

Sub Link6_MouseMove(s,b,x,y)
    text1.value = DescribeLink(5)
End Sub

</SCRIPT>
</HEAD>

<BODY BGCOLOR="#80FFFF" TEXT="#FF0000">

<P>
<FONT FACE="arial" SIZE=2>
<CENTER>
<H2>Khalifa Desert Holidays</H2>
<TABLE WIDTH=80%>
<TD ALIGN=LEFT>
<INPUT TYPE="text" NAME="text1" SIZE=40><P>
<B>
<A LANGUAGE="vbscript" NAME="Link1" OnMouseOver="call showLink(0)" HREF="">
About Khalifa Desert Holidays</A><BR>
<A LANGUAGE="vbscript" NAME="Link2" OnMouseOver="call showLink(1)" HREF="">
Rates and Tariffs</A><BR>
<A LANGUAGE="vbscript" NAME="Link3" OnMouseOver="call showLink(2)" HREF="">
Special Deals for Children</A><BR>

<A NAME="Link4" HREF="" VALUE=3>Some of Our Fine Hotels</A><BR>
<A NAME="Link5" HREF="" VALUE=4>The Desert Holiday FAQ</A><BR>
<A NAME="Link6" HREF="">What's New</A><BR>
<TD ALIGN=CENTER>
<IMG SRC="desert.gif">
<TR>
</TABLE>

</BODY>
</HTML>
```

# Link Descriptions Using the Status Bar

Now that we've added an extended description of each link, it's very easy to modify the HTML page in Example 11-1 to display each link's descriptive text in the status bar at the bottom of the browser as well. We can do this quite simply by adding the following single line of code to the *ShowLink* custom procedure:

```
Status = DescribeLink(CInt(LinkNo))
```

In addition, we have to modify each of the three *MouseMove* event handlers as follows:

```
Sub Link4_MouseMove(s,b,x,y)
    text1.value = DescribeLink(3)
    Status = DescribeLink(3)
End Sub

Sub Link5_MouseMove(s,b,x,y)
    text1.value = DescribeLink(4)
    Status = DescribeLink(4)
End Sub

Sub Link6_MouseMove(s,b,x,y)
    text1.value = DescribeLink(5)
    Status = DescribeLink(5)
End Sub
```

As you may recall from the discussion of the MSIE object model in Chapter 5, *Controlling the Browser, Status* is a property of the *Window* object. Assigning the value of a string array element to the *Status* property causes the browser to display the string in the status bar.

If you try out this modification, however, you'll quickly notice a problem: once some text is displayed in the status bar, it remains there until another *Status* method is called to replace it. As a result, the browser's status bar may describe a link that the mouse has left long ago, so that any indication of which link the text refers to has been lost. I certainly find this confusing, and I'm sure users do as well.

If you recall the methods supported by the *Window* object, a solution seems readily at hand. The *Window* object supports a *setTimeout* method that activates a *Timer* object to automatically perform some action (like calling a function) after a specified number of milliseconds has elapsed. So we could use the *setTimeout* method to clear the status bar after a specified length of time (let's say approximately 4 seconds) by assigning a null (or empty) string to the *Window* object's status property. This requires that we add the following line of code to each of the four event handlers:

```
tID = setTimeout("Status=''",4000)
```

Of course, you can also add a line of similar code to clear the text box as well, like this:

```
tID = setTimeout("text1.value=''",4000)
```

The complete code for the amended example is shown in Example 11-2. Figure 11-2 shows the result when the mouse pointer passes over Link2.

*Example 11-2. Displaying Link Information in the Status Bar*

```
<HTML>
<HEAD><TITLE>Link Descriptions</TITLE>
<SCRIPT language="vbscript">
  Dim DescribeLink(5)
    DescribeLink(0) = "Find out all about us"
    DescribeLink(1) = "So good you'll want to stay for life"
    DescribeLink(2) = "The under 17's stay longer for free"
    DescribeLink(3) = "Our new Hotel now open in Communicado"
    DescribeLink(4) = "Frequently Asked Questions about Desert Holidays"
    DescribeLink(5) = "All the latest news and gossip"

  Sub ShowLink(LinkNo)
      text1.value = DescribeLink(CInt(LinkNo))
      Status = DescribeLink(CInt(LinkNo))
      tID = setTimeout("Status=''",4000)
      tID = setTimeout("text1.value=''",4000)
  End Sub

  Sub Link4_MouseMove(s,b,x,y)
      text1.value = DescribeLink(3)
      Status = DescribeLink(3)
      tID = setTimeout("Status=''",4000)
      tID = setTimeout("text1.value=''",4000)
  End Sub

  Sub Link5_MouseMove(s,b,x,y)
      text1.value = DescribeLink(4)
      Status = DescribeLink(4)
      tID = setTimeout("Status=''",4000)
      tID = setTimeout("text1.value=''",4000)
  End Sub

  Sub Link6_MouseMove(s,b,x,y)
      text1.value = DescribeLink(5)
      Status = DescribeLink(5)
      tID = setTimeout("Status=''",4000)
      tID = setTimeout("text1.value=''",4000)
  End Sub

</SCRIPT>
</HEAD>

<BODY BGCOLOR="#80FFFF" TEXT="#FF0000">
```

*Example 11-2. Displaying Link Information in the Status Bar (continued)*

```
<P>
<FONT FACE="arial" SIZE=2>
<CENTER>
<H2>Khalifa Desert Holidays</H2>
<TABLE WIDTH=80%>
<TD ALIGN=LEFT>
<INPUT TYPE="text" NAME="text2" SIZE=40><P>
<B>
<A LANGUAGE="vbscript" NAME="Link1" OnMouseOver="call showLink(0)" HREF="">
About Khalifa Desert Holidays</A><BR>
<A LANGUAGE="vbscript" NAME="Link2" OnMouseOver="call showLink(1)" HREF="">
Rates and Tariffs</A><BR>
<A LANGUAGE="vbscript" NAME="Link3" OnMouseOver="call showLink(2)" HREF="">
Special Deals for Children</A><BR>
<A NAME="Link4" HREF="" VALUE=3>Some of our fine Hotels</A><BR>
<A NAME="Link5" HREF="" VALUE=4>The Desert Holiday FAQ</A><BR>
<A NAME="Link6" HREF="">What's New</A><BR>
<TD ALIGN=CENTER>
<IMG SRC="desert.gif">
<TR>
</TABLE>

</BODY>
</HTML>
```

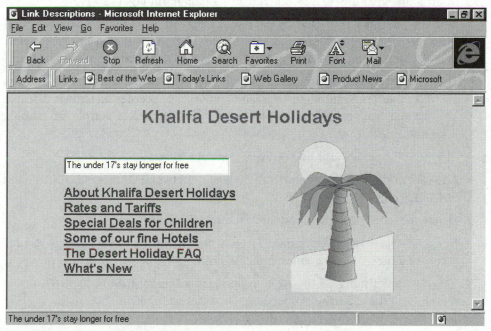

*Figure 11-2. The link description shown in both the text box and the status bar*

# *Link Descriptions Using an ActiveX Label Control*

Although we've succeeded in better describing our links, there are still some problems with the way we've done that in Examples 11-1 and 11-2. First of all, the HTML intrinsic text box control that we've used in examples is not a read-only control; we cannot easily prevent the user from entering text into the text box. Second, the text box itself is rather too conspicuous. The reason is that we have no real control over it: the browser, rather than our script, controls such settings as the font size and attributes and the text box's background color.

In this section, we'll continue working with our Khalifa Desert Holidays page by replacing the HTML text box control with an ActiveX label control. This makes our web page far more aesthetically pleasing. The ActiveX label control gives a much cleaner, more professional look to the page, and allows you the flexibility to change such attributes as the font size, the background color, etc.

To modify the web page shown in Example 11-2, do the following:

1. Using the ActiveX Control Pad, open the HTML document shown in Example 11-2

2. Insert a line after the `</H2>` tag and add a paragraph tag (`<P>`).

3. Insert a line after the `<P>` tag and select the Insert ActiveX Control option from the Edit menu. When the Insert ActiveX Control dialog appears, select the Microsoft Forms 2.0 Label control in the Object Type drop-down list box.

4. The ActiveX Control Pad next opens the Edit ActiveX Control window as well as the Properties window. Set the label control's properties as shown in Table 11-1. When you press the Apply button, the ActiveX Control Pad should resemble Figure 11-3.

5. Close the Properties and Edit ActiveX Control windows.

6. Add an additional paragraph tag (`<P>`) between the `</OBJECT>` and `<TABLE>` tags.

7. Delete the `<INPUT>` tag that defines the HTML intrinsic text box control.

8. In each *MouseMove* event procedure, change the string "Text1.Value" to read "Label1.Caption". Do the same in the *ShowLink* procedure.

9. Tidy up the clearing of the caption and status bar by having the *setTimeOut* method call the *ClearDesc* procedure. Now the *setTimeOut* code reads:

```
tID = SetTimeout("ClearDesc()", 4000)
```

10. Add the `ClearDesc` subroutine, the code for which is as follows:

```
Sub ClearDesc()
    Status = ""
    Label1.Caption = ""
End Sub
```

*Table 11-1. Nondefault Properties of the ActiveX Label Control*

| Property | Value | Comments |
|----------|-------|----------|
| Font | 12pt MS Sans Serif, Bold, Italic | |
| BackColor | 00ffff80 – Unknown | To match the document's background color |
| ForeColor | 000080ff – Unknown | |
| Width | 329 | |
| TextAlign | 2 – Center | |

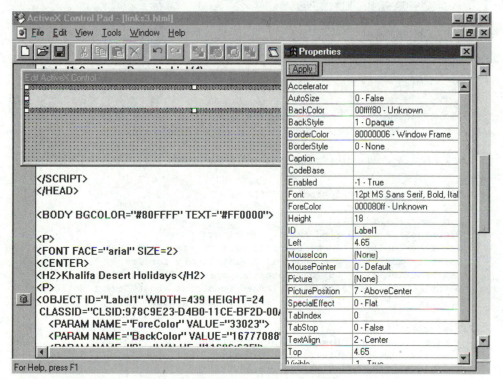

*Figure 11-3. Inserting the ActiveX Label control*

The complete source code for this example is shown in Example 11-3. Figure 11-4 shows the browser window when the mouse pointer passes over *Link5*.

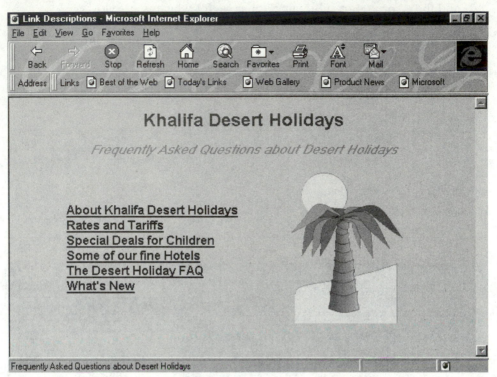

*Figure 11-4. The link description displayed in an ActiveX Label control*

*Example 11-3. Describing Links with the ActiveX Label Control*

```
<HTML>
<HEAD><TITLE>Link Descriptions</TITLE>
<SCRIPT language="vbscript">
    Dim DescribeLink(5)
    DescribeLink(0) = "Find out all about us"
    DescribeLink(1) = "So good you'll want to stay for life"
    DescribeLink(2) = "The under 17's stay longer for free"
    DescribeLink(3) = "Our new Hotel now open in Communicado"
    DescribeLink(4) = "Frequently Asked Questions about Desert Holidays"
    DescribeLink(5) = "All the latest news and gossip"

  Sub ShowLink(LinkNo)
      Label1.Caption = DescribeLink(CInt(LinkNo))
      Status = DescribeLink(CInt(LinkNo))
      tID = setTimeout("ClearDesc()",4000)
  End Sub

  Sub Link4_MouseMove(s,b,x,y)
      Label1.Caption = DescribeLink(3)
      Status = DescribeLink(3)
      tID = setTimeout("ClearDesc()",4000)
  End Sub
```

*(continued)*

hyperlinks more descrip-
ther they really want to

*seOver* events to capture

nich is used to display a

d to activate the built-in
number of seconds have
n that was written when
ed.

escriptive text, and other
rent types of controls—
ifferent and imaginative

event, this time taking
so that we can create a

```
showLink(0)" HREF="">

showLink(1)" HREF="">

showLink(2)" HREF="">

ls</A><BR>
2</A><BR>
```

*Example 11-3. Describing Links with the ActiveX Label Control*

```
</BODY>
</HTML>
```

# *Summary*

In this chapter, we've explored techniques for making
tive, thereby allowing our users to better decide wh
follow a particular link. We've done this as follows:

- By using the Link object's *MouseMove* and *OnMou*
  mouse movement across a particular link.

- By setting the *Window* object's *Status* property, w
  message in the status bar.

- By calling the *Window* object's *SetTimeOut* metho
  *Timer* object, which calls a routine after a particular
  elapsed. This allows us to clear the textual descriptic
  the *MouseMove* and *OnMouseOver* events were trigger

Using the *MouseMove* event, you can dynamically add d
information helpful to the user, to a whole host of diffe
both HTML intrinsic controls and ActiveX controls—in c
ways.

In the next chapter, we'll continue to use the *MouseMov*
advantage of the coordinate values passed to the event,
client-side image map from a .GIF image.

# 12

# *Image Maps Made Easy*

Image maps offer a neat way to present a graphical menu of pages within a web site. However, traditionally, the use of image maps has involved two problems:

- File size. By their very nature, the graphics files used as image maps tend to be quite large.

- The programming required to create a clickable image map. Typically, image maps are controlled from the web server, and require a server-side script in order to operate.

This chapter will show you how to create a straightforward image map and an image navigation bar, and how to use VBScript to determine which section of the image the mouse is over, and which section of the image the user has clicked. We'll begin by creating the image map itself and exploring the coordinate system used with image maps.

## *The Screen Coordinate Scheme*

As you know, the video display is made up of pixels, and any given pixel can be identified by its coordinates on the screen. This coordinate system uses the top left-hand corner of the screen as its starting point; the topmost and leftmost pixel is located at coordinate 0, 0. The pixels are arranged in a matrix going across the screen on the X axis from left to right, and down the screen on the Y axis from top to bottom (see Figure 12-1). The number of pixels on each axis depends on the individual computer's display resolution. One system, for example, might have a video display that is 640 pixels wide (along the X axis) and 480 pixels high (along the Y axis), while another might be set at 1024 pixels along the X axis and 768 pixels down the Y axis. The precise settings are a matter of the capabilities of the display adapter and the system's monitor, as well as of personal preference and the usage to which the computer is put.

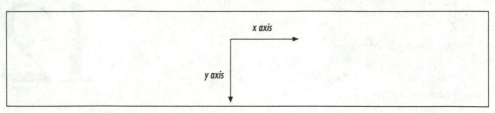

*Figure 12-1:. The video display's X and Y axes*

In Chapter 11, *Describing Your Hyperlinks*, we saw that, when the *MouseMove* event is fired, VBScript passes four arguments to the *MouseMove* event handler, two of which are the X and Y coordinates of the mouse pointer when the event was triggered. This allows us to determine the exact position of the mouse pointer on the screen. But the coordinate system used by the *MouseMove* event has a different starting point than the general screen coordinate system. Whereas the latter begins from the top left corner of the screen, the X and Y coordinates returned by the *MouseMove* event are relative to the top left corner of the image, rather than of the screen as a whole. This makes working with client-side image maps much simpler, since you don't have to concern yourself with where on the screen the image itself has been placed. Instead, you can simply work with the image in isolation.

## Defining a Clickable Image Map

The starting point for creating a clickable image map, of course, is to find an image that will form the image map. Once your final image is available, you calculate where the clickable areas of the image map will be, by dividing the image into rectangles. (The only disadvantage to using VBScript with image maps is that you cannot specify a clickable area other than a rectangle or a square.)

Each clickable area of the image is defined by two coordinates, which describe the rectangle mathematically (see Figure 12-2):

- The top left pixel of the image's clickable area, which is denoted as *x1, y1*.

- The bottom right pixel of the image's clickable area, which is denoted as *x2, y2*.

Again, both *x1* and *x2* represent the number of pixels from the left-hand edge of the image (i.e., along the X axis), while *y1* and *y2* are the number of pixels from the top of the image (i.e., along the Y axis). Most graphics packages have an option that displays the coordinates of the pixel at which the mouse cursor is pointing, so you can use this feature to note the boundaries that you want to denote as clickable areas on the image. Once you've completed this rather tedious task, you'll end up with a table of coordinates that describes the image's clickable rectangular coordinates. We'll use the image shown in Figure 12-3 as our example in this chapter; its table of coordinates is shown in Table 12-1. Remember that these coordinates represent the position of pixels relative to the upper left-hand corner of the image, not of the screen.

*Table 12-1. The Coordinate Table for the Example Image Map (shown in Figure 12-3)*

| Area | x1 | y1 | x2 | y2 |
|------|-----|-----|-----|-----|
| 1 | 0 | 0 | 140 | 130 |
| 2 | 220 | 60 | 350 | 173 |
| 3 | 0 | 130 | 214 | 277 |
| 4 | 250 | 185 | 357 | 277 |
| 5 | 360 | 50 | 500 | 277 |

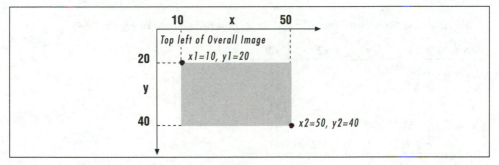

*Figure 12-2:. Working out the image's coordinates*

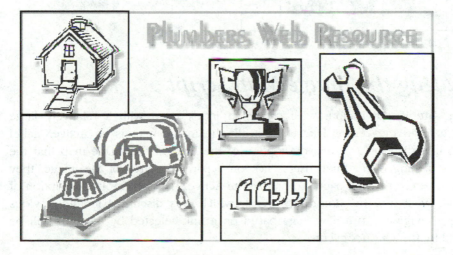

*Figure 12-3. The main image map boundaries*

The image shown in Figure 12-3 is suitable for the Plumbers Web Resource home page, which allows the user to navigate to any of the web site's five major sections. However, users also appreciate the ability to move freely from one section to the beginning of another section. The best way of implementing this is to create a navigation bar image map. As Figure 12-4 shows, this consists of an icon bar or a toolbar containing only the clickable images from our larger image map. Once we've created the image, of course, we have to determine the coordinates of each button, as shown in Table 12-2. Note that the uniform nature of the navigation bar is reflected in the coordinate matrix. Along the X axis, the start of the clickable area of each image is one pixel greater than the end of the clickable area of the previous image. Area 1, for instance, extends from pixels 0 to 36, while Area 2 extends from pixels 37 to 91. Along the Y axis, the clickable area of each button begins at the top of the image (pixel 0) and extends to the bottom of the image (pixel 41).

*Table 12-2. The Coordinate Table for the Navigation Bar (shown in Figure 12-4)*

| Area | x1 | y1 | x2 | y2 |
|------|-----|----|-----|----|
| 1 | 0 | 0 | 36 | 41 |
| 2 | 37 | 0 | 91 | 41 |
| 3 | 92 | 0 | 132 | 41 |
| 4 | 133 | 0 | 187 | 41 |
| 5 | 188 | 0 | 222 | 41 |

*Figure 12-4. The image map navigation bar boundaries*

# Creating the Image Map Script

As our sample application, we'll create an index page with a relatively large image map in the center. Directly beneath the image map is an ActiveX label control that displays a textual description of the link on the image map that the cursor is resting over. When users click on a particular area of the image, they will be taken to the link page. To handle the ActiveX label control's description of the link, we'll use the *MouseMove* event, which was discussed in the previous chapter. Navigating to a new page based on a link selected by the user will be handled by the *OnClick* event.

The first step in creating our web page is to define the image that provides the image map in our HTML source code. For this, we use the <IMG> tag within an <A>, or anchor, tag, as follows:

```
<A ID="link1" HREF="">
<IMG SRC="plumber.gif" BORDER=0>
</A><BR>
```

Note that the hyperlink has been assigned a name by using the ID attribute, and that the HREF attribute, which defines the URL that the client is to request from a server if the link is selected, is an empty string. This has two implications. First, if the user clicks on the hyperlink but outside of one of the defined clickable areas, the page reloads. This is because the HREF references relative URLs, and an empty URL relative to the current document is the current document itself. This behavior isn't a design feature, it's simply a side effect of having to specify an HREF attribute to create a hyperlink. But since both the page and the image are stored in the browser's cache, the process of reloading the current page should be almost instantaneous. Second, when the user clicks on a predefined area of the image, we can override the HREF element (which is now inactive) with an *OnClick* event procedure.

Having placed the image in our web page, let's next see how to handle the *MouseMove* event. Remember, our goal here is to describe a link as the mouse passes over it. When the *MouseMove* event is triggered, VBScript passes it four parameters, only two of which—X and Y—are of interest to us. We can use their values to determine if the mouse is within a clickable area of the image, as the following *MouseMove* event procedure shows:

```
Sub link1_MouseMove(s,b,x,y)
    lastX = x
    lastY = y
    If (OverIcon(x, y,   0,  0, 140, 130)=true) Then
        DisplayLink "Back to Home Page"
    ElseIf (OverIcon(x, y, 220,  60, 350, 173)=true) Then
        DisplayLink "Join in this years Plumber of the Year Awards"
    ElseIf (OverIcon(x, y,   0, 130, 214, 277)=true) Then
        DisplayLink "Discounted Plumbing Supplies"
    ElseIf (OverIcon(x, y, 250, 185, 357, 277)=true) Then
        DisplayLink "Join in our International Plumbers Forum"
    ElseIf (OverIcon(x, y, 360,  50, 500, 277)=true) Then
        DisplayLink "Links to Tool Manufacturers and Suppliers"
    Else
        DisplayLink ""
    End If
End Sub
```

This procedure begins by assigning the values *X* and *Y* to two global variables, *lastX* and *lastY*; this allows the program to use them later in the *OnClick* event. Note that the *OnClick* event itself does not give us access to the mouse postion in terms of X and Y coordinates, so we have to use the global *lastX* and *lastY* variables. Next, a series of `If...ElseIf` conditional statements determines whether the coordinates are within a designated area. (Notice that 0,0 and 140,130, for instance, correspond to the coordinates of Area 1 in Table 12-1.) To do this, the event procedure calls a custom function, *OverIcon*, and passes it the X and Y mouse coordinates and the description of the rectangle, X1,Y1,X2,Y2:

```
Function OverIcon(x, y, rx1, ry1, rx2, ry2)
    OverIcon =  x>=rx1 AND x<=rx2 AND y>=ry1 AND y<=ry2
End Function
```

If the mouse coordinates X and Y fall within the boundaries of the rectangle, the function returns True; if they don't, the function returns False. A return value of True then forces the *DisplayLink* custom procedure, which displays the text passed to it as a parameter in both the ActiveX label control and the status bar at the bottom of the browser:

```
Sub DisplayLink(text)
    Label1.Caption = text
    Status = text
    tID = SetTimeout("ClearLink()", 4000)
End Sub
```

Notice that a timeout has been set at four seconds. This means that, when four seconds have elapsed, the *ClearLink* subroutine will be called to remove the text from both the caption and the status bar. Its source code is as follows:

```
Sub ClearLink()
    Label1.Caption = ""
    Status = ""
End Sub
```

To complete our web page, we need to add the code for the *Link* object's *OnClick* event. This is very similar to the code for the *MouseMove* event, except that, if the mouse is within a designated area of the map, a new page will be loaded. Remember that the *OnClick* event passes no coordinates from the mouse, so we've saved the last position of the mouse (immediately prior to the click taking place) in the *lastX* and *lastY* variables. We can now determine which part of the image the user has clicked upon. The code for the *OnClick* event procedure is as follows:

```
Sub link1_OnClick()
  If OverIcon(lastX, lastY,  0, 0, 140, 130) Then
      location.href = "plumber.html"
  ElseIf OverIcon(lastX, lastY,  220, 60, 350, 173) then
      location.href = "plumb1.html"
  ElseIf OverIcon(lastX, lastY, 0, 130, 214, 277) then
      location.href = "plumb2.html"
  ElseIf OverIcon(lastX, lastY,  250, 185, 357, 277) then
      location.href = "plumb3.html"
```

*ttinued)*

50, 500, 277) then

rmines whether the mouse pointer was
, indicating that the mouse was over a
*HRef* property of the browser's *Location*
he page that the browser is currently
e, causing the browser to load that page.
d variables are used in place of X and Y,
ve us access to the mouse's coordinates.

s script is shown in Example 12-1, while the
Figure 12-5.

bers Web Resource Index Page

TLE>

```
40, 130)=true) Then
me Page"
, 60, 350, 173)=true) Then
his years Plumber of the Year Awards"
130, 214, 277)=true) Then
ed Plumbing Supplies"
50, 185, 357, 277)=true) Then
our International Plumbers Forum"
360, 50, 500, 277)=true) Then
o Tool Manufacturers and Suppliers"
```

very
el to
are
hese

```
tY,   0, 0, 140, 130) Then
plumber.html"
, lastY,   220, 60, 350, 173) then
plumb1.html"
, lastY, 0, 130, 214, 277) then
"plumb2.html"
X, lastY,   250, 185, 357, 277) then
"plumb3.html"
tX, lastY,   360, 50, 500, 277) then
= "plumb4.html"
```

*Example 12-1. HTML Source for the Plumbers Web Resource Index Page (co*

```
 End If
End Sub


Function OverIcon(x, y, rx1, ry1, rx2, ry2)
    OverIcon =  x>=rx1 AND x<=rx2 AND y>=ry1 AND y<=ry2
End Function

Sub DisplayLink(text)
    Label1.Caption = text
    Status = text
    tID = SetTimeout("ClearLink()", 4000)
End Sub

Sub ClearLink()
    Label1.Caption = ""
    Status = ""
End Sub

</SCRIPT>

<BODY BGCOLOR="white">
<CENTER>
<A ID="link1" HREF="">
<IMG SRC="plumber.gif" BORDER=0>
</A><BR>

<OBJECT ID="Label1" WIDTH=484 HEIGHT=24
 CLASSID="CLSID:978C9E23-D4B0-11CE-BF2D-00AA003F40D0">
    <PARAM NAME="ForeColor" VALUE="16711680">
    <PARAM NAME="BackColor" VALUE="16777215">
    <PARAM NAME="VariousPropertyBits" VALUE="27">
    <PARAM NAME="Size" VALUE="12801;630">
    <PARAM NAME="FontEffects" VALUE="1073741827">
    <PARAM NAME="FontHeight" VALUE="240">
    <PARAM NAME="FontCharSet" VALUE="0">
    <PARAM NAME="FontPitchAndFamily" VALUE="2">
    <PARAM NAME="ParagraphAlign" VALUE="3">
    <PARAM NAME="FontWeight" VALUE="700">
</OBJECT>
</CENTER>
</BODY>
</HTML>
```

The code for the pages within the web site that contain the navigation bar is
similar to the code shown in Example 12-1. However, it does not use a lab
describe the hyperlink, and it uses a different system of coordinates, which
based on the navigation bar and are shown earlier in Table 12-2. One of t
pages is shown in Figure 12-6, while its code is show in Example 12-2.

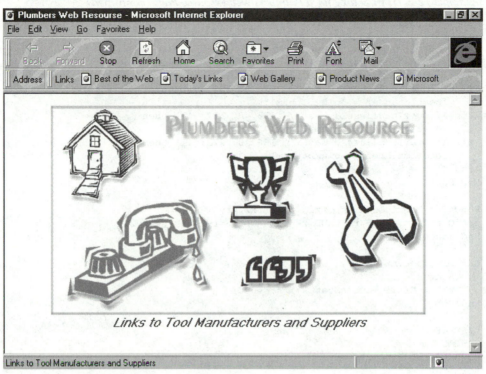

*Figure 12-5. The Plumbers Web Resource index page*

*Example 12-2. HTML Source for a Plumbers Web Resource Page*

```
<HTML>
<HEAD>
<TITLE>Plumbers Awards</TITLE>
<SCRIPT LANGUAGE="vbscript">
Dim lastX, lastY

Sub menu_MouseMove(s,b,x,y)
  lastX = x
  lastY = y
  If (OverIcon(x, y,   0, 0, 36, 41)=true) Then
      DisplayLink "Back to Home Page"
  ElseIf (OverIcon(x, y, 37, 0, 91, 41)=true) Then
      DisplayLink "Discounted Plumbing Supplies"
  ElseIf (OverIcon(x, y,  92, 0, 132, 41)=true) Then
      DisplayLink "Join in this year's Plumber of the Year Awards"
  ElseIf (OverIcon(x, y,  133, 0, 187, 41)=true) Then
      DisplayLink "Join in our International Plumbers Forum"
  ElseIf (OverIcon(x, y,  188, 0, 222, 41)=true) Then
      DisplayLink "Links to Tool Manufacturers and Suppliers"
  Else
      DisplayLink ""
  End If
End Sub
```

*Example 12-2. HTML Source for a Plumbers Web Resource Page (continued)*

```
Sub menu_OnClick()
 If OverIcon(lastX, lastY,  0, 0, 36, 41) Then
     location.href = "plumber.html"
 ElseIf OverIcon(lastX, lastY, 37, 0, 91, 41) then
     location.href = "plumb2.html"
 ElseIf OverIcon(lastX, lastY, 92, 0, 132, 41) then
     location.href = "plumb1.html"
 ElseIf OverIcon(lastX, lastY, 133, 0, 187, 41) then
     location.href = "plumb3.html"
 ElseIf OverIcon(lastX, lastY, 188, 0, 222, 41) then
     location.href = "plumb4.html"
 End If
End Sub

Function OverIcon(x, y, rx1, ry1, rx2, ry2)
     OverIcon =  x>=rx1 AND x<=rx2 AND y>=ry1 AND y<=ry2
End Function

Sub DisplayLink(text)
     Status = text
     tID = SetTimeout("Status=''", 4000)
End Sub

</SCRIPT>
</HEAD>
<BODY BGCOLOR="white">
<CENTER>
<A ID="menu" HREF="">
<IMG SRC="menubar.gif" BORDER=0>
</A>
<P>
<h2>Plumber of the Year Awards</H2>
</BODY>
</HTML>
```

*Figure 12-6. One of the web site pages with the image map navigation bar*

# *Summary*

Using client-side image maps is much quicker and easier than using their server-side counterparts. In this chapter, we've seen how you can go about implementing client-side image maps. The following points are worth keeping in mind when developing your own image maps:

- Whether you're using client-side or server-side maps, you still have to go through the tedium of describing the areas mathematically as a set of rectangular coordinates. This, incidentally, points to the only drawback of using VBScript to handle image maps: without some sophisticated algorithms, you can only use a rectangular clickable area.

- Remember that the coordinates you use in the script are relative to the top corner of the image, and not the top corner of the screen or the top corner of the browser window.

- You create a client-side image map by embedding the `<IMG>` tag inside of the `<A>` tag, just as you do to define a "normal" graphical link. However, you also assign the hyperlink a name using the anchor tag's `ID` attribute, and you provide an empty string as the value of its `HREF` attribute, which prevents the browser from loading a new page when the user clicks anywhere on the image.

- You use the *Link* object's *MouseMove* event to determine which portion of the image the mouse pointer is over. When the *MouseMove* event is fired, the VBScript engine passes it the mouse's coordinates relative to the top left corner of the image.

- You use the *Link* object's *OnClick* event to activate the link on which the user has clicked. However, since mouse coordinates are not passed to the *OnClick* event procedure, you must store the mouse coordinates passed to the *Mouse-Move* event procedure to two global variables, in order to make them available to the *OnClick* event procedure. Otherwise, you won't be able to determine where within your image map the user clicked.

# 13

## Building Dynamic HTML Pages

The ability to create dynamic HTML documents—that is, to build web pages "on the fly"—on the browser without having to refer back to the server is the pinnacle of interactivity on the Web today. Almost by definition, there's nothing more "active" than a web page that can itself spawn other web pages from within the client environment. Once you can create a dynamic page or a set of dynamic pages from a single client-side script, you have equipped the user with a truly interactive medium in which to work.

Prior to client-side scripting, the only way to vary the content of an HTML page was to write a server-side script (either a CGI script or application, or a server-side include) that used a predetermined set of variables and data to create an HTML document on the fly and dispatch it to the browser to display. Now, you can download a single file that contains a client-side script such as VBScript to the browser. As the script is executed at the browser, it creates the final HTML display. These two methods of producing dynamic HTML pages are illustrated in Figure 13-1.

A simple example illustrates the difference between these two methods of creating a dynamic web page. Say you want to display the date and time on your web page. To do this using a server-side include, you would write a script that takes the date/time variable from the server and builds the resultant value into the HTML file, as this Active Server Pages script shows:

```
<HTML>
<HEAD>
<TITLE>Show the time and date</TITLE>
</HEAD>
<BODY BGCOLOR="white">
<% Response.Write Now() %>
</BODY>
</HTML>
```

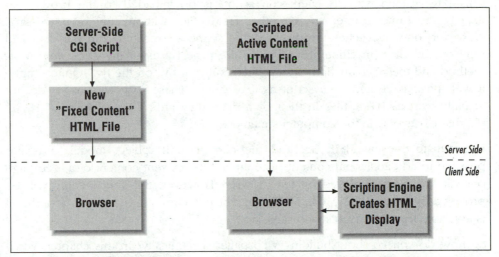

*Figure 13-1. The difference between server-generated and browser-generated pages*

Although this page is built dynamically by the server, its contents are fixed once the server transmits it to a client. Furthermore, the date and time are likely to be different on the server and the client (that is, the client and the server are likely to be located in different time zones), in which case the time reported in the web page will be incorrect. To address this latter problem, it is possible to create a database of time zones and time offsets based on domain suffixes, but this is extremely complex, inefficient, and by no means accurate. The VBScript code for achieving the same (or a better) result is:

```
<HTML>
<HEAD>
<TITLE>Show the time and date</TITLE>
</HEAD>
<BODY BGCOLOR="white">
<SCRIPT LANGUAGE="vbscript">
 Document.Write Now()
</SCRIPT>
</BODY>
</HTML>
```

## Frames and Dynamic Web Pages

You don't always have to rely on a script to create a dynamic web page for the browser as a whole. Instead, you can use a script that's included within a document displayed in one frame to create a totally new page that's displayed in another frame.

This page, along with its client-side script, is downloaded to the browser in exactly the same manner as any other HTML file, without any preprocessing. However, once it reaches the browser, the script is executed, and the date and time on the client machine are added to the page by using the *Document.Write* method and the *Now* function. This is what is meant by "on the fly." Quite simply, a web page is created by a script as it executes. These new web pages do not actually exist as HTML files in their own right; they are a kind of "virtual" HTML file that exists only in the computer's memory.

Unfortunately, using MSIE 3.x and the current MSIE object model, it is not possible to add additional content or to amend the current content of a web page once it has been displayed by the browser. However, this functionality will be provided by Dynamic HTML in MSIE 4.0, which is currently being beta tested and is available from Microsoft's web site.

So how do you go about building web pages dynamically? In this chapter, you'll see how to use the *Document* object's *Open*, *Write*, and *Close* methods to:

- Create complete dynamic pages that are downloaded to the browser
- Add content to documents dynamically
- Build new pages from a script that already resides on the browser

## Document Object Methods

Let's begin with a review of the *Document* object's methods that are used to create dynamic web pages. (For a detailed discussion, see "The Document Object," in Chapter 5, *Controlling the Browser*.)

### Document.Open

Use *Document.Open* for creating new HTML documents from within a script. *Document.Open* clears the document's memory buffer and prepares it to accept text from the *Document.Write* method. Do not use *Document.Open* to write individual fragments of text (such as individual variables) within a larger web page; this causes your script to overwrite any text already written either in the static portion of your HTML document or by earlier portions of your script.

### Document.Write

Use *Document.Write* to pass HTML tags and variable values into the document's memory buffer. All values must be passed as strings within quotation marks.

## Document.WriteLn

Basically, the *WriteLn* method is the same as *Document.Write*, except that it automatically adds an extra linefeed character at the end of the text string that it writes. Since normal HTML ignores line breaks, though, this is only significant when writing text formatted with the HTML <PRE> tag.

## Document.Close

Like *Document.Open*, *Document.Close* is only used with new HTML pages. It sends the contents of the document's memory buffer to the HTML display.

---

*NOTE*     Be careful not to overwrite your current document accidentally. If one of your procedures calls the *Document.Write* method to act on the current window or frame, the display will be overwritten by the new document, as Example 13-1 demonstrates. Figure 13-2 displays the web page that results when the user clicks on the "Click Me" button in the original web page defined by the HTML file in Example 13-1. Note that the underlying HTML file is left unchanged, as you can see if you view the HTML document's source by selecting the Source option from the MSIE View menu. As Figure 13-3 shows, this continues to correspond to the original HTML document shown in Example 13-1.

---

*Example 13-1. Overwriting an Existing Web Page*

```
<HTML>
<HEAD>
<TITLE>Oops</TITLE>
<SCRIPT LANGUAGE="vbscript">
 Sub CmdButton1_OnClick
  Document.Write "<H2>Where's it all gone?</H2>"
 End Sub
</SCRIPT>
<BODY BGCOLOR="white">
<CENTER>
<INPUT TYPE="button" NAME="CmdButton1" VALUE="Click Me">
</BODY>
</HTML>
```

# Building a Document on Download

There are two main methods you can use to create partially or completely dynamic pages on download to the browser. The first method is to use <SCRIPT> tags without subroutines, so that the code within the <SCRIPT> tags is executed by the browser as soon as it is read, which causes the dynamic

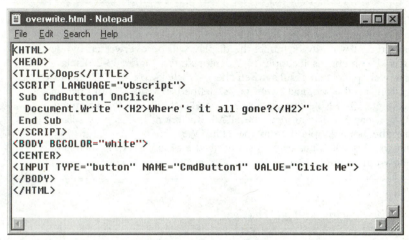

*Figure 13-2. Overwriting an existing web page*

```
<HTML>
<HEAD>
<TITLE>Oops</TITLE>
<SCRIPT LANGUAGE="vbscript">
 Sub CmdButton1_OnClick
   Document.Write "<H2>Where's it all gone?</H2>"
 End Sub
</SCRIPT>
<BODY BGCOLOR="white">
<CENTER>
<INPUT TYPE="button" NAME="CmdButton1" VALUE="Click Me">
</BODY>
</HTML>
```

*Figure 13-3. HTML source for the web page in Figure 13-2*

---

### *Dynamic Documents and the Microsoft Script Debugger*

If you use the *Document.Open*, *Document.Write*, and *Document.Close* methods to create a document on the fly, the underlying document remains the same, as you have seen in Figure 13-3. However, if you view the source using the Script Debugger (see Chapter 15, *Error Handling and Debugging*), you will see the source code for the newly created dynamic document, rather than the underlying document. Be careful not to save this source while in the debugger, or the underlying document will be overwritten by the dynamic document and will therefore be lost.

content to be added to the display immediately, when the document is down-loaded. Example 13-2 uses this approach to mix static HTML text and dynamic content created by VBScript within a single web page. As Figure 13-4 shows, the dynamic HTML is inserted into the existing HTML text stream at the point that the browser encounters the <SCRIPT> tags and the calls to the *Document.Write* method.

*Example 13-2. Using <SCRIPT> to Insert Dynamic Content into the HTML Text Stream*

```
<HTML>
<HEAD>
<TITLE>On the Fly 1</TITLE>
</HEAD>
<BODY BGCOLOR="white">
<FONT FACE="arial" SIZE=2>
<CENTER>
<H2>On the Fly</H2>
<P>
<SCRIPT LANGUAGE="vbscript">
    Document.Write "<H3>Scripted Line 1</H3>"
</SCRIPT>
<P>
<H3>Fixed Line 1</H3>
<SCRIPT LANGUAGE="vbscript">
    Document.Write "<H3>Scripted Line 2</H3>"
</SCRIPT>
</CENTER>
</BODY>
</HTML>
```

The second method to create a page dynamically when it is downloaded to the browser involves calling a scripted procedure, and is illustrated in Example 13-3. <SCRIPT> tags still need to be inserted within the HTML stream in the places where you need the scripted lines to be displayed. However, these tags are simply used to call a single procedure that in turn is responsible for calling the *Document.Write* method, which inserts text dynamically into the web page. As you can see from Figure 13-5, the resulting page displayed by the browser is iden-tical to the web page built by the HTML source in Example 13-2.

*Example 13-3. Calling Procedures to Insert Dynamic Content into the HTML Text Stream*

```
<HTML>
<HEAD>
<TITLE>On the Fly 2</TITLE>
<SCRIPT LANGUAGE="vbscript">
Sub DoScriptedLine(i)
 Document.Write "<H3>Scripted Line " & i & "</H3>"
End Sub
</SCRIPT>
</HEAD>
```

*Example 13-3. Calling Procedures to Insert Dynamic Content into the HTML Text Stream*

```
<BODY BGCOLOR="white">
<FONT FACE="arial" SIZE=2>
<CENTER>
<H2>On the Fly</H2>
<P>

<SCRIPT LANGUAGE="vbscript">
 Call DoScriptedLine(1)
</SCRIPT>

<P>
<H3>Fixed Line 1</H3>

<SCRIPT LANGUAGE="vbscript">
 Call DoScriptedLine(2)
</SCRIPT>

</CENTER>
</BODY>
</HTML>
```

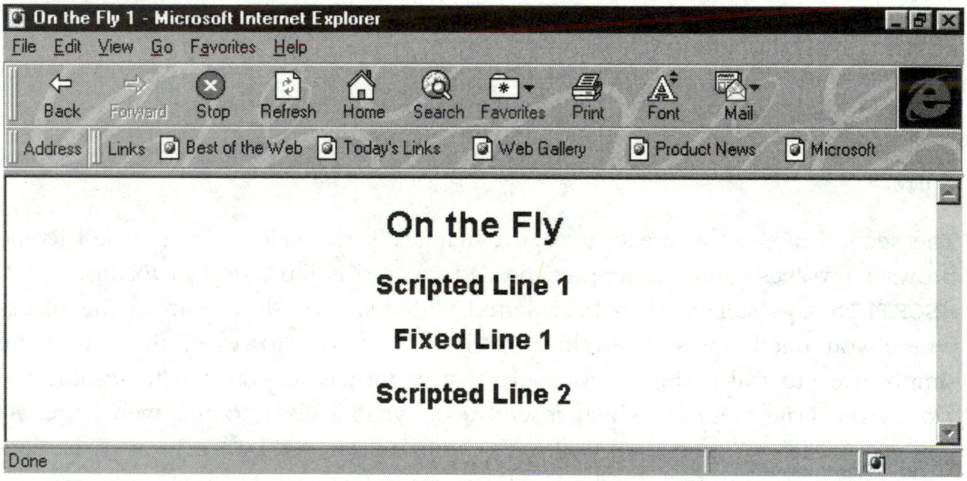

*Figure 13-4. Web page built with scripts and HTML*

You can utilize the complete range of VBScript functions to create variable pages at the browser. The HTML source code in Example 13-4, for instance, uses the built-in *Weekday* function to create a different page every day of the week; one possible page that the HTML source, along with its accompanying script, builds is shown in Figure 13-6. The program contains a number of predefined arrays:

- *days*, to hold the names of the days of the week

- *backs*, to hold the background colors of the browser window

- *forec*, to hold the foreground (text) colors of the browser window

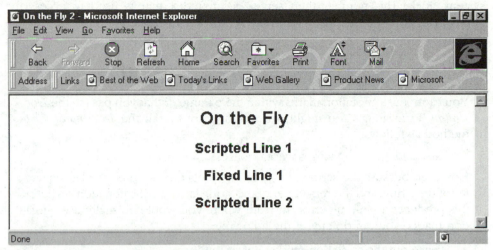

*Figure 13-5. An HTML page created on the fly*

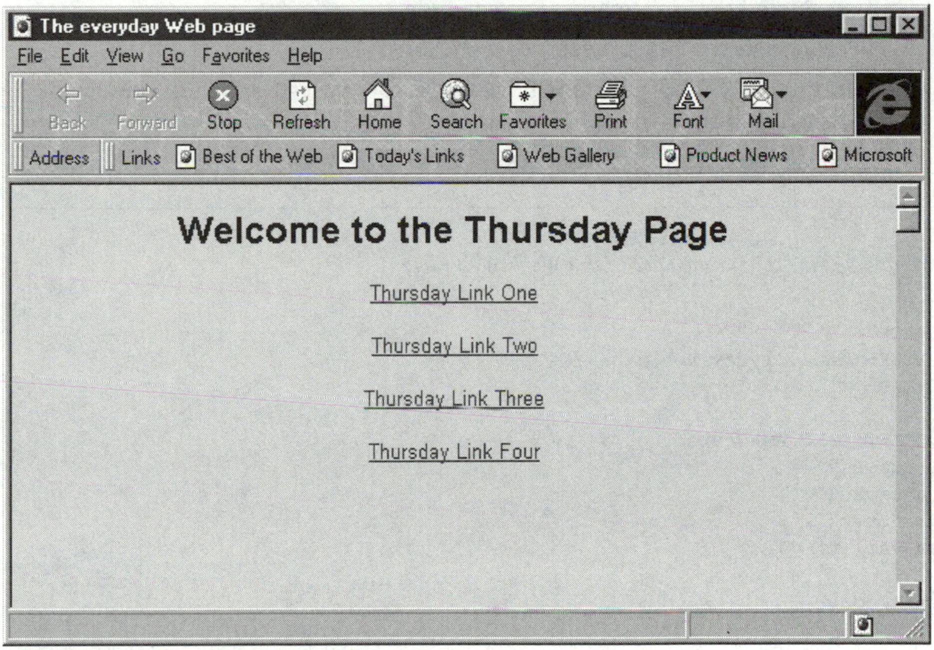

*Figure 13-6. A different page every day of the week*

- *varlinks*, a two-dimensional array that contains the links for each day. The first dimension represents the day of the week, while the second dimension contains one of four links for that day.

As the page is downloaded to the browser, an ordinal number representing the day of the week is obtained by retrieving the date from the client machine's system clock. This number then serves as an index that is used to access the appropriate array elements and build the HTML tags to create the page.

---

## Document.Write and Quotation Marks

You cannot use quotation marks within the parameter that you pass to the *Document.Write* string. You might, for instance, try to call the *Document.Write* method as follows:

```
Document.Write "<BODY BGCOLOR="white">" ' ERROR
```

However, because the scripting engine interprets the "=" to be the last character of the string, and the remainder of the string lacks a concatenation operator, this produces a run-time error. Instead, where you would normally use quotation marks, you can do any of the following:

- Leave out the quotation marks. For example,

```
Document.Write "<BODY BGCOLOR=white>"
```

- Use single quotation marks. For example,

```
Document.Write "<BODY BGCOLOR='white'>"
```

- Substitute *Chr(34)*—the ASCII value of the quotation mark character— for each quotation mark. For example,

```
Document.Write "<BODY BGCOLOR=" & Chr(34) & white & Chr(34) & ">"
```

---

*Example 13-4. A Dynamic Day of the Week Web Page*

```
<HTML>
<HEAD>
<TITLE>The everyday Web page</TITLE>
</HEAD>

<SCRIPT LANGUAGE="vbscript">
Dim days(7)
Dim backs(7)
dim forec(7)
dim varlinks(7,4)

dim iToday

days(1) = "Sunday"
days(2) = "Monday"
days(3) = "Tuesday"
days(4) = "Wednesday"
days(5) = "Thursday"
days(6) = "Friday"
days(7) = "Saturday"
backs(1) = "white"
backs(2) = "aqua"
backs(3) = "green"
```

*Example 13-4. A Dynamic Day of the Week Web Page (continued)*

```
backs(4) = "orange"
backs(5) = "red"
backs(6) = "teal"
backs(7) = "yellow"
forec(1) = "aqua"
forec(2) = "green"
forec(3) = "yellow"
forec(4) = "teal"
forec(5) = "white"
forec(6) = "red"
forec(7) = "orange"
varlinks(1,1) = "<A HREF=a.html>Sunday Link One</A><P>"
varlinks(1,2) = "<A HREF=a.html>Sunday Link Two</A><P>"
varlinks(1,3) = "<A HREF=a.html>Sunday Link Three</A><P>"
varlinks(1,4) = "<A HREF=a.html>Sunday Link Four</A><P>"
varlinks(2,1) = "<A HREF=a.html>Monday Link One</A><P>"
varlinks(2,2) = "<A HREF=a.html>Monday Link Two</A><P>"
varlinks(2,3) = "<A HREF=a.html>Monday Link Three</A><P>"
varlinks(2,4) = "<A HREF=a.html>Monday Link Four</A><P>"
varlinks(3,1) = "<A HREF=a.html>Tuesday Link One</A><P>"
varlinks(3,2) = "<A HREF=a.html>Tuesday Link Two</A><P>"
varlinks(3,3) = "<A HREF=a.html>Tuesday Link Three</A><P>"
varlinks(3,4) = "<A HREF=a.html>Tuesday Link Four</A><P>"
varlinks(4,1) = "<A HREF=a.html>Wednesday Link One</A><P>"
varlinks(4,2) = "<A HREF=a.html>Wednesday Link Two</A><P>"
varlinks(4,3) = "<A HREF=a.html>Wednesday Link Three</A><P>"
varlinks(4,4) = "<A HREF=a.html>Wednesday Link Four</A><P>"
varlinks(5,1) = "<A HREF=a.html>Thursday Link One</A><P>"
varlinks(5,2) = "<A HREF=a.html>Thursday Link Two</A><P>"
varlinks(5,3) = "<A HREF=a.html>Thursday Link Three</A><P>"
varlinks(5,4) = "<A HREF=a.html>Thursday Link Four</A><P>"
varlinks(6,1) = "<A HREF=a.html>Friday Link One</A><P>"
varlinks(6,2) = "<A HREF=a.html>Friday Link Two</A><P>"
varlinks(6,3) = "<A HREF=a.html>Friday Link Three</A><P>"
varlinks(6,4) = "<A HREF=a.html>Friday Link Four</A><P>"
varlinks(7,1) = "<A HREF=a.html>Saturday Link One</A><P>"
varlinks(7,2) = "<A HREF=a.html>Saturday Link Two</A><P>"
varlinks(7,3) = "<A HREF=a.html>Saturday Link Three</A><P>"
varlinks(7,4) = "<A HREF=a.html>Saturday Link Four</A><P>"

iToday = Weekday(Now())

Document.Write "<BODY BGCOLOR=" & backs(iToday) & ">"
Document.Write "<FONT FACE=arial SIZE=2 COLOR=" & forec(iToday) & ">"
Document.Write "<CENTER><H2>Welcome to the "
Document.Write days(iToday)
Document.Write " Page</H2><P>"
For i = 1 to 4
 Document.Write varlinks(iToday,i)
next
Document.Write "</CENTER></BODY>"

</SCRIPT>
</HTML>
```

# *Adding Variables to a Web Page at Download Time*

Another important use for *Document.Write* is to add variable values into the content of a web page as it downloads into the browser. When adding separate variables, do not use *Document.Open* or *Document.Close*, since these overwrite any text that the browser has already interpreted. Instead, simply include a <SCRIPT> section that either writes the variable HTML text directly into the HTML text stream, or calls a scripted procedure that writes to the document.

Example 13-5, for instance, creates a web page that includes a document footer containing the current time and date, the type of browser being used, and the date the document was last modified. Each of these elements was simply inserted into the HTML text stream when the document was displayed, by calling the *Document.Write* method along with the relevant VBScript function or MSIE object method. Figure 13-7 shows what the page looks like through the browser.

*Example 13-5. Adding a Footer to a Web Page*

```
<HTML>
<HEAD>
<TITLE>Document Footer</TITLE>
</HEAD>
<BODY BGCOLOR="white">
<FONT FACE="arial" SIZE=2>
<CENTER>
<H2>A Document Footer Example</H2>
</CENTER>
<P>
<BLOCKQUOTE>
<B>
This example demonstrates how you can add a variable footer
to your web pages displaying the current date and time, the
type of browser, and the date and time the document
was last modified. This short code snippet can be
quickly and easily added to any web page.
</BLOCKQUOTE>

<HR>
<CENTER>
<FONT SIZE=1>
<SCRIPT LANGUAGE="vbscript">
    Document.Write Now() & "<BR>"
    Document.Write Navigator.userAgent & "<BR>"
    Document.Write "Last Modified: " & Document.LastModified
</SCRIPT>
</FONT>
</CENTER>
</B>

</BODY>
</HTML>
```

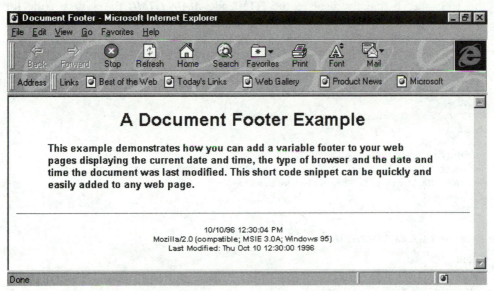

*Figure 13-7. Web page with a dynamic footer*

The variables you use to build the page using the *Document.Write* method do not have to be part of the HTML of the page itself; as with all your client-side scripts created with VBScript, you can pass variables around from document to document. The following example demonstrates how to import values from a different document when creating a web page. This application allows the user to choose or to modify the color scheme for a web site at any time, by selecting the foreground and background colors from drop-down <SELECT> lists. As the new page loads, the selected color values are obtained from the form document and included in the new document's <BODY> tag. A neat extension to this application would be to store the user-defined foreground and background colors in a cookie file (see Chapter 10, *Date and Time in VBScript*). This frees an application from having to continuously display the form, and makes the values available every time the user visits the site. You could then have a separate page containing the color selection form, which the user visits to change the color scheme when required.

This sample application consists of four HTML files. The first, *USERDEF.HTML*, which is shown in Example 13-6, contains a <FRAMESET> tag that divides the browser window into two frames. It is the top frame, named *config*, that allows the user to dynamically alter the web site's foreground and background colors at any time. It continually displays *CONFIG.HTML*, the color configuration form document, which is shown in Example 13-7. The bottom frame is named *main*, and although it initially displays the simple welcome message shown in Figure 13-8, it is the frame that is responsible for displaying pages as the user navigates through the web site. It initially displays the HTML file *MAIN.HTML,* the source code for which is shown in Example 13-8. The Internet Explorer window when these HTML pages are first loaded is shown in Figure 13-8.

*Example 13-6. USERDEF.HTML*

```
<HTML>
<HEAD>
<TITLE>User Defined Colors</TITLE>
</HEAD>

<FRAMESET ROWS=15%,85%>
 <FRAME NAME="config" SRC="config.html" SCROLLING=No NORESIZE>
 <FRAME NAME="main" SRC="welcome.html">
</FRAMESET>
</HTML>
```

*Example 13-7. CONFIG.HTML*

```
<HTML>
<HEAD>
 <SCRIPT LANGUAGE="vbscript">
  Sub ok_OnClick
      If Right(top.main.location.href, 12) = "welcome.html" then
          top.main.location.href = "main.html"
      Else
          top.main.location.href = ""
      End If
  End Sub
 </SCRIPT>
<BODY BGCOLOR="white">
<FONT FACE="arial" SIZE=2>
<CENTER>
<FORM NAME="colors">
 Background Color
  
 <SELECT NAME="bgcol">
 <OPTION SELECTED>White
 <OPTION>Blue
 <OPTION>Green
 <OPTION>Black
 <OPTION>Yellow
 <OPTION>Red
 <OPTION>Orange
 <OPTION>Cyan
 </SELECT>

  
  

 Fore Color
  

 <SELECT NAME="fcol">
```

*Example 13-7. CONFIG.HTML (continued)*

```
<OPTION>White
<OPTION>Blue
<OPTION>Green
<OPTION SELECTED>Black
<OPTION>Yellow
<OPTION>Red
<OPTION>Orange
<OPTION>Cyan
</SELECT>

 
 
<INPUT TYPE="button" NAME="ok" VALUE="OK">
</FORM>
</CENTER>
</BODY>
</HTML>
```

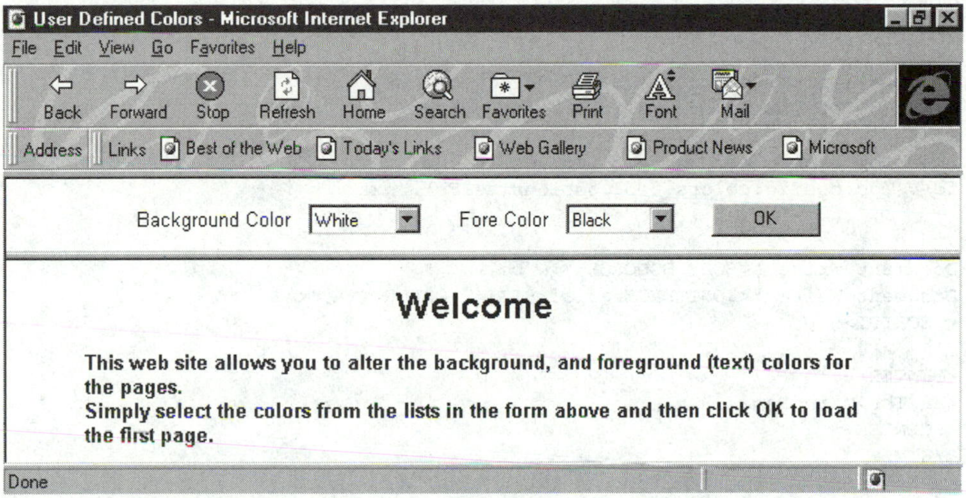

*Figure 13-8. Selecting a site's background and font colors*

When *MAIN.HTML*, whose source code is shown in Example 13-8, loads, it first obtains the index of the selected item from both the *fcol* and *bgcol* HTML drop-down lists in *CONFIG.HTML*. Note that, to do this, it simply navigates through the MSIE object model hierarchy. It first references the topmost window, followed by the Main frame and the *colors* form object. It then retrieves the value of the *SelectedIndex* property from the form object's *bgcol* and *fcol* HTML intrinsic controls. It then uses this index value to retrieve the text of the selected item from the Element object's `options` array. This string—which is a color name—is then added to the `<BODY>` tag, thereby creating a document whose color scheme has been chosen by the user.

If you want, you can easily make further enhancements to this application by adding Link and Visited Link Colors and even Font Size to the form. You may also want to add a validation routine to make sure that the user has not selected the same foreground and background color—which would make the text unreadable! Also note that any document within the web site that supported user-selected colors would have to have the same basic line of script to produce its <BODY> tag.

*Example 13-8. MAIN.HTML*

```
<HTML>
<HEAD>
<TITLE>The Main Web page</TITLE>
</HEAD>

<SCRIPT LANGUAGE="vbscript">
dim selBc
dim selFc
dim bc
dim fc

selBc = Top.config.colors.bgcol.SelectedIndex
selFc = Top.config.colors.fcol.SelectedIndex

bc = Top.config.colors.bgcol.options(selBc).text
fc = Top.config.colors.fcol.options(selFc).text


Document.Write "<BODY BGCOLOR=" & bc & ">"
Document.Write "<FONT FACE=arial SIZE=2 COLOR=" & fc & ">"
</SCRIPT>

<CENTER>
<H2>The Main Page</H2>
</CENTER>
</HTML>
```

# Creating a New Web Page from a Script

So far in this chapter, we've looked at pages created from variables as they download to the browser. Let's now look at how you can create a complete new web page from a script in another document. This example uses a simple order form in a frame to solicit input from the user. When the user clicks the Order Now button, a summary of his or her order is built into a new document and displayed in the right-hand frame. The confirmation document also includes a button for users to confirm their orders and programmatically submit their orders to the server. (For demonstration purposes, the submission coding has been replaced by an Alert box.)

In the old days of server-side scripting, the user would have had to submit the form to the server and wait for the confirmation page to be constructed and sent back to the browser. Once the browser received and displayed it, the user could then submit a confirmation. Now, all the calculations involved in creating the confirmation document, as well as the creation of the confirmation document itself, are done immediately by the browser.

This example also demonstrates how to call a script from a second document that has been created by the first document. Using the <SCRIPT> tag within a *Document.Write* string causes a run-time error, which means that the confirmation document, which our application builds on the fly, cannot contain any scripts. Therefore, any scripts that we want to associate with the new document must be placed in another document and simply called from the new document.

The code for the <FRAMESET>, which divides the browser window vertically into two equal halves, is shown in Example 13-9. Notice that it makes use of Internet Explorer's borderless frames (defined by setting the **FRAMEBORDER** and **FRAMESPACING** attributes of the <FRAMESET> tag to zero) to create the impression of a single document, as Figure 13-9 shows. The right-hand frame initially displays a blank HTML document; the file *BLANK.HTML* simply contains the <HTML> and <BODY> tags, and no other text.

*Example 13-9. Frame Definitions for the Order Application*

```
<HTML>
<HEAD>
<TITLE>Web Order Form</TITLE>
</HEAD>

<FRAMESET COLS=50%,50% frameborder=0 framespacing=0>
 <FRAME NAME="order" SRC="order.html" MARGINWIDTH=0 MARGINHEIGHT=0
SCROLLING=No NORESIZE>
 <FRAME NAME="ConfirmIt" SRC="blank.html" MARGINWIDTH=0 MARGINHEIGHT=0
SCROLLING=No NORESIZE>
</FRAMESET>
</HTML>
```

The source for the left-hand frame, which does all the work for this application, is shown in Example 13-10. As *ORDER.HTML* loads into the browser, *Prices*, an array of prices for the products on sale, is created, and *Shipping*, a global variable containing the shipping and handling charge, is defined and set equal to 10.

The rest of the document at this stage is a standard HTML form, as shown in Figure 13-9.

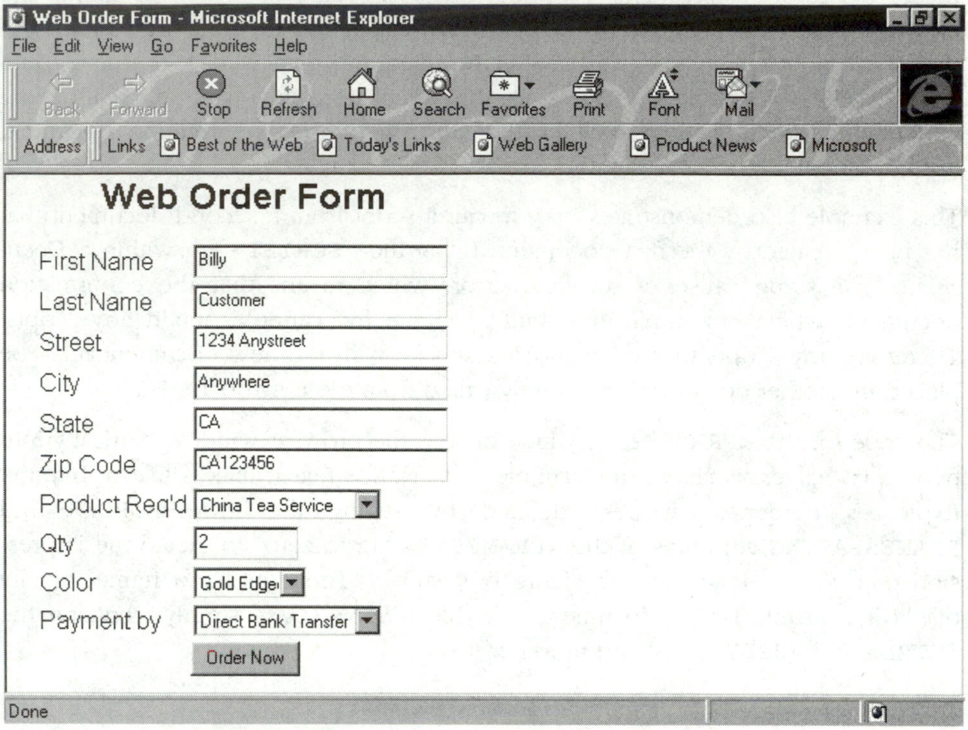

*Figure 13-9. The order form before clicking the Order Now button*

*Example 13-10. ORDER.HTML*

```
<HTML>
<HEAD>
 <SCRIPT LANGUAGE="vbscript">
  Dim Prices(3)
  Dim Shipping
  Prices(0) = 90.00
  Prices(1) = 15.50
  Prices(2) = 12.00
  Prices(3) = 6.00
  Shipping = 10.00

  Sub placeOrder_OnClick
    dim prod
    dim colr
    dim pay
    dim subtot
    prod = Document.order.product.SelectedIndex
    colr = Document.order.color.SelectedIndex
    pay = Document.order.payment.SelectedIndex
    subtot = Prices(prod) * CInt(Document.order.qty.value)
```

*Example 13-10. ORDER.HTML (continued)*

```
Top.ConfirmIt.Document.Open
Top.ConfirmIt.Document.Write "<HTML><HEAD>"

Top.ConfirmIt.Document.Write "</HEAD>"
Top.ConfirmIt.Document.Write "<BODY BGCOLOR=white>"
Top.ConfirmIt.Document.Write "<FONT FACE=arial SIZE=2><B><BR><BR>"
Top.ConfirmIt.Document.Write "Hi " & Document.order.fname.value & _
                             ",<BR>"
Top.ConfirmIt.Document.Write "Thank you for your order for "
Top.ConfirmIt.Document.Write Document.order.qty.value  & " "
Top.ConfirmIt.Document.Write Document.order.color.options(colr).text _
                             & " "
Top.ConfirmIt.Document.Write Document.order.product.options(prod).text
If Document.order.qty.value > 1 Then
 Top.ConfirmIt.Document.Write "s, "
Else
 Top.ConfirmIt.Document.Write ", "
End If

Top.ConfirmIt.Document.Write "which you wish to purchase via "
Top.ConfirmIt.Document.Write Document.order.payment.options(pay).text _
                             & ".<BR>"
Top.ConfirmIt.Document.Write "<P><CENTER>Billing Summary<P>"
Top.ConfirmIt.Document.Write _
     "<TABLE BORDER=1><TR><TD>Qty</TD><TD>Description</TD>"
Top.ConfirmIt.Document.Write "<TD>@ea</TD><TD>Line Val</TD></TR>"
Top.ConfirmIt.Document.Write "<TR><TD>" & Document.order.qty.value & _
                             "</TD>"
Top.ConfirmIt.Document.Write "<TD>" & _
     Document.order.product.options(prod).text & "</TD>"
Top.ConfirmIt.Document.Write "<TD>$" & Prices(prod) & "</TD>"
Top.ConfirmIt.Document.Write "<TD>$" & subtot & "</TD></TR>"
Top.ConfirmIt.Document.Write "<TR><TD></TD><TD>Shipping & Handling</TD>"
Top.ConfirmIt.Document.Write "<TD></TD><TD>$" & Shipping & "</TD></TR>"
Top.ConfirmIt.Document.Write "<TR><TD></TD><TD>TOTAL</TD>"
Top.ConfirmIt.Document.Write _
               "<TD></TD><TD><B>$" & subTot + Shipping & "</TD></TR>"
Top.ConfirmIt.Document.Write _
               "</TABLE><P> To confirm your order, please click OK"

Top.ConfirmIt.Document.Write _
               "<P><INPUT TYPE=button NAME=confirmed VALUE=OK "
Top.ConfirmIt.Document.Write "LANGUAGE=vbscript OnClick=" & Chr(34) _
               & "Call Top.Order.Confirmed()" & Chr(34) & ">"
Top.ConfirmIt.Document.Write "</BODY></HTML>"
Top.ConfirmIt.Document.Close

End Sub

Sub Confirmed()
 Alert "Submitting Order Now"
End Sub
```

*Example 13-10. ORDER.HTML (continued)*

```
 </SCRIPT>
<BODY BGCOLOR="white">
<FONT FACE="arial" SIZE=2>
<CENTER>
<H2>Web Order Form</H2>
<FORM NAME="order">
<TABLE>
<TR>
<TD>First Name</TD>
<TD><INPUT TYPE="text" NAME="fname" SIZE=30></TD>
</TR>
<TR>
<TD>Last Name</TD>
<TD><INPUT TYPE="text" NAME="lname" SIZE=30></TD>
</TR>
<TR>
<TD>Street</TD>
<TD><INPUT TYPE="text" NAME="street" SIZE=30></TD>
</TR>
<TR>
<TD>City</TD>
<TD><INPUT TYPE="text" NAME="city" SIZE=30></TD>
</TR>
<TR>
<TD>State</TD>
<TD><INPUT TYPE="text" NAME="state" SIZE=30></TD>
</TR>
<TR>
<TD>Zip Code</TD>
<TD><INPUT TYPE="text" NAME="zip" SIZE=30></TD>
</TR>
<TR>
<TD>Product Req'd</TD>
<TD>
 <SELECT NAME="product">
 <OPTION>China Tea Service
 <OPTION>14 Inch Dinner Plate
 <OPTION>Cup
 <OPTION>Saucer
 </SELECT>
</TD>
</TR>
<TR>
<TD>Qty</TD>
<TD><INPUT TYPE="text" NAME="qty" SIZE=10></TD>
</TR>
<TR>
<TD>Color</TD>
<TD>
 <SELECT NAME="color">
 <OPTION>White
```

*Example 13-10. ORDER.HTML (continued)*

```
 <OPTION>Blue
 <OPTION>Green
 <OPTION>Black
 <OPTION>Yellow
 <OPTION>Red
 <OPTION>Floral
 <OPTION>Gold Edged
 </SELECT>
</TD>
</TR>
<TR>
<TD>Payment by</TD>
<TD>
 <SELECT NAME="payment">
 <OPTION>Credit Card
 <OPTION>Cash
 <OPTION>Direct Bank Transfer
 </SELECT>
</TD>
</TR>

</TABLE>

 <INPUT TYPE="button" NAME="placeOrder" VALUE="Order Now">
</FORM>
</CENTER>
</BODY>
</HTML>
```

When the user fills out the form and clicks the placeOrder button, *placeOrder_ OnClick*, the event handler for placeOrder, is executed. It starts by determining which items are selected in the product, color, and payment drop-down lists, and then calculates the subtotal. The rest of the event handler opens the document buffer for the right-hand frame and writes the new document, using the values selected by the user. Closing the document has the effect of emptying the buffer onto the screen, as shown in Figure 13-10.

Notice the <INPUT> tag that defines the confirmed button. It uses the LANGUAGE and OnClick attributes to define a custom procedure, *Confirmed*, that is to handle the button's *OnClick* event. As the definition of the event handler shows, however, *Confirmed* is located in the order (or the left-hand) frame. So when the user clicks the Confirmed button in the right-hand frame, the *Confirmed* custom procedure in the left-hand frame is called. In our sample application, this simply displays a dialog box; in the real world, this would submit the order to a web server.

The new document that we've created and displayed in the right-hand frame is a virtual document—that is, it is present in memory only. You can prove this to yourself by right-clicking anywhere in the right frame except on the OK button, and

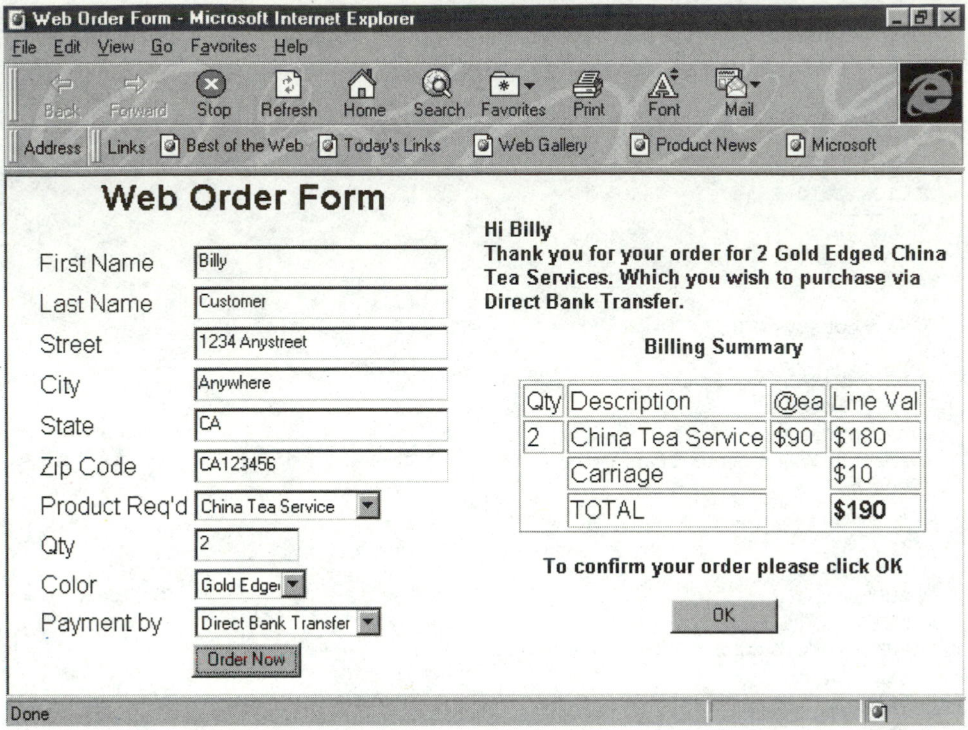

*Figure 13-10. An HTML frame created on the fly*

selecting the View Source option from the context menu. All that Internet Explorer displays as the HTML source for the frame is the original source for *BLANK.HTML*. This is a major disadvantage when you are trying to debug a complex application that uses *Document.Write* to create on-the-fly web pages, since you can never view the physical HTML code that your script is creating. The only workaround to this is to output the string that is giving you problems to an Alert box.

# Summary

In this chapter, you've seen how to create documents dynamically using the *Document.Write* method. You have seen how HTML documents can be created from scripts, using variables and literal strings. Documents can be created either partially or completely by VBScript embedded either in the document itself or in another document altogether. Above all *Document.Write* gives you the flexibility to create new documents "on the fly" as circumstances dictate, without the expense—in terms of time and bandwidth—of referring back to the server. The implications for web development from just this one series of methods—*Document.Open*, *Write*, and *Close*—is enormous. For example, although it is somewhat impractical, you could now theoretically build a complete and infinitely variable web site from a single VBScripted HTML document.

To summarize these three methods of the Document object:

- Use *Document.Write* to place text on the HTML page in the browser.

- *Document.Write* is temporary, in that is does not overwrite the underlying document.

- Use *Document.Open* to open the document memory buffer and create a fresh HTML page, but be careful not to call this method on a page you want to keep within the browser.

- Use *Document.Close* to write the contents of the document memory buffer to the browser.

# 14

## Form Input Validation

Data validation, or form input validation, is an important part of client-side scripting. The idea of any data validation is to reduce or eliminate the amount of invalid or unusable data that is sent to the server for processing, whether that means simply displaying the data back on the client browser or storing it in a database on the server. The usual method for validating data involves writing a CGI script that performs checks on the data transferred to the server when a form's Submit button is clicked. If the CGI application finds that a data item is invalid, a new page, informing the user of the problem, is then sent from the server back to the client—a complex and wasteful process.

It is far better to inform the user of any problems with the data they've entered prior to submitting it to the server. And this is where client-side scripting comes in. As you have already seen, client-side scripting with VBScript allows you to perform at the browser most of the functions that you would usually perform at the server, and a few more besides.

Most of the validation of data entered into an HTML form involves at least some string manipulation. For example, is the string the correct length? Does it contain the required characters? In addition to validating the data, you can also use VBScript to manipulate and modify the data to fit your requirements for further processing. You might, for example, require that all string data be uppercase, and convert it from lower- to uppercase if it is not.

With this in mind, this chapter shows you how to use the built-in string manipulation and data checking functions of VBScript, and demonstrates how these can be used to perform data validation before submitting the data, in the process saving time and bandwidth and producing a much more professional looking application. The chapter begins by showing you how to create object references to simplify the amount of coding required when working with form data. Then it examines a number of functions commonly used for data validation, and provides some examples of data validation routines within client-side VBScript.

# Working with Object References

One of the basic problems of writing validation routines in VBScript is that they are code-intensive; that is, a good deal of coding is required to navigate the object hierarchy in order to properly reference a form or an HTML intrinsic control on a form. Take, for instance, a script that has to obtain values from two text boxes in a frame, add them together, then display the result in a third text box in the frame. Without using the `Set` statement, which we'll discuss shortly, the code might look like this:

```
Parent.Frames(1).Document.Form1.Text3.Value = _
     CLng(Parent.Frames(1).Document.Form1.Text1.Value) + _
     CLng(Parent.Frames(1).Document.Form1.Text2.Value)
Something of a mouthful!
```

It's possible to simplify this, and to reduce the amount of coding that you have to do, by creating an object reference to an HTML form, an HTML intrinsic control, or any other object. To do this, you use the `Set` statement to initialize a variable to which you assign an object reference. Its syntax is:

```
Set variable = object
```

where *variable* is the name of the variable to hold the object reference, and *object* is a valid control or object available within the Microsoft Internet Explorer object model. Note that using the `Set` statement doesn't create a *copy* of the object; instead, it creates a *reference* to a single object.

To illustrate, we can retrieve the contents of an HTML intrinsic text box control with the following line of code:

```
strX = Document.Form1.Text1.Value
```

However, we can do the same thing by creating a variable, *frm*, that contains a reference to the HTML form, and then using it to access the text box control, as the following code fragment does:

```
Set frm = Document.Form1
strX = frm.Text1.Value
```

So why bother? Replacing a long reference to a control or some other object with a single variable can reduce the size and complexity of a script, making the script easier to read, understand, and maintain. For example, we can simplify our earlier example, in which we added values from two text boxes and stored the result in a third text box, as follows:

```
Set frm1 = Parent.Frames(1).Document.Form1
frm1.Text3.Value = CLng(frm1.Text1.Value) + CLng(frm1.Text2.Value)
```

## *Object References and Performance*

To test the performance improvement that results from replacing lengthy object references with object variables, I created a form with 20 text boxes (it has to be a large number to obtain meaningful measurements). I then wrote the code, which repeated a somewhat lengthy reference 19 times in order to add the values of the 19 text boxes and display the result in the twentieth text box. I then used the *Timer* function (which, although it is undocumented in both VBScript 1.0 and 2.0, returns the number of milliseconds elapsed since midnight) before the addition began and after it was completed; the difference between the two values returned by *Timer* is the number of seconds required to perform the addition. Because prevailing system conditions will marginally affect the result, I then called the addition 100 times and divided my result by 100 to achieve a uniform average, which was 0.075 seconds.

I then repeated the test, this time replacing the object reference with a single object variable. With an object variable instead of a lengthy object reference, this time each loop was executed in an average of 0.034 seconds. While the basic numbers appear insignificant, the fact that using the `Set` command and a single object reference can cut the time required for an operation in half is very significant.

There is also another benefit to replacing a long reference to a control with a single object variable: performance. Each of the dots that separate the objects in a reference, and which reflect the navigation from one object to another object in the object hierarchy, represents a function call somewhere deep inside the scripting engine. Each of these "dots," in other words, takes time to resolve as the scripting engine works its way to the object, property, or method being accessed. In contrast, using an object variable means that navigation to the eventual control or property is performed only once during execution of the `Set` statement; thereafter, through the object variable, it can be accessed directly.

It's important to understand that using the `Set` statement to assign an object to a variable does not create a new copy of that object. Instead, it creates a reference to the object, or associates the variable with the object. Only a single instance of the object continues to exist, however. This can be seen in the code fragment defining the *frm* variable; *frm* is simply a reference to `Document.Form1`, so if you then change the value of the text box using the statement

```
frm.Text1.Value = "string"
```

the value of *strX,* after the line of code

```
strX = Document.Form1.Text1.Value
```

executes, will be "string." Because the `Set` statement only creates a reference to an object, any change to the variable will be automatically reflected in the object. The converse is also true: any change to the object will be automatically reflected in the variable or variables that refer to it.

Although we'll use the `Set` statement throughout this chapter, Example 14-1 contains the source code for a simple web page that demonstrates the `Set` statement. When the user enters text into a text box in the HTML form and clicks on the Click Me button, the button's *OnClick* event procedure creates the variable *frm*, which contains an object reference to the HTML form `Document1.Form1`. The form's text box is then accessed from this *frm* object reference, and the value of its *Value* property is displayed in an alert box.

*Example 14-1. Using the Set Statement*

```
<HTML>
<HEAD>
<TITLE>Form Input Validation - Set</TITLE>
 <SCRIPT LANGUAGE="vbscript">
   Sub Command1_OnClick
       Dim frm
       Set frm = Document.Form1
       Alert frm.TextBox1.Value
   End Sub
 </SCRIPT>
</HEAD>
   <BODY BGCOLOR="white">
<CENTER>
<FORM NAME="form1">
 <INPUT TYPE="text" NAME="TextBox1">
 <INPUT TYPE="button" NAME="Command1" VALUE="Click Me">
</FORM>
</CENTER>
</BODY>
</HTML>
```

It's worthwhile to explicitly emphasize that the `Set` statement has nothing to do with data validation *directly*. Instead, since data validation involves using many references to the same form or to objects on a form, you will find that object references defined by the `Set` statement save you time and coding. Let's look now at the main constituents of data validation.

# Data Validation Functions

Typically, when you need to validate data entered into an HTML form, you'll find that you almost invariably use the same basic set of VBScript functions in your code. The bulk of them are string manipulation functions. We'll briefly survey each of these before we examine exactly when in your script you want to validate data entered by the user.

## *Determining a String's Size: Len*

Perhaps the most common operation performed in data validation is counting the number of characters that are contained in a text box. Frequently, you want to do this to make sure that the user has entered the correct number of characters (like a 10-digit social security number, or a 5-digit zip code). Probably even more frequently, you want to make sure that the user has entered something into a text box, and that the number of characters stored to it exceeds zero.

In such cases, you can use the *Len* function, which returns the length of a string or the number of bytes required to represent that string. The string length reported by the *Len* function includes any leading or trailing spaces. Its syntax is:

    Len(*string*)

where *string* is any valid variable, expression, or property. For example,

    x = Len("Hello World")

returns 11.

Example 14-2 illustrates the use of the *Len* function. When the user enters a string into a text box and clicks the form's Click Me button, the form's *OnClick* event procedure uses the *Len* function to display the string's length in an alert box.

*Example 14-2. The Len Function*

```
<HTML>
<HEAD>
<TITLE>Form Input Validation - Len</TITLE>
<SCRIPT LANGUAGE="vbscript">
 Sub Command1_OnClick
     Dim frm
     Set frm = Document.Form1
     Alert Len(frm.TextBox1.Value)
 End Sub
</SCRIPT>
</HEAD>
<BODY BGCOLOR="white">
<CENTER>
<FORM NAME="form1">
 <INPUT TYPE="text" NAME="TextBox1">
 <INPUT TYPE="button" NAME="Command1" VALUE="Click Me">
</FORM>
</CENTER>
</BODY>
</HTML>
```

# Converting a String to Lower Case: LCase

Particularly if you want to compare a string to another string, or to a string constant, you usually have to make sure that the strings have the same case. One of the ways of doing this is to change a string to lower case by using the *LCase* function. Its syntax is:

```
LCase(string)
```

The function converts any alphabetical characters within a given string to lower case and returns the result. Any numeric characters or symbols within the string are ignored. For example:

```
x = LCase("1A2B3C*d")
```

returns:

```
1a2b3c*d
```

There are two major uses for the *LCase* function when performing data validation:

- To impose a uniform format on string data. For instance, a particular field within your database might require lower case data. One option is to specify that data should be entered in lower case on the HTML page containing the form. You must then hope that the user reads and follows these directions. A far better option is to accept the data entered by the user and then convert them to lower case before submitting them to the server. This guarantees that, regardless of the form of the data entered by the user, data in the correct format will be written to the database.

- To format a string input by the user before comparing it with another string, string literal, or string constant. Since string comparisons are case-sensitive ("mystring," for example, does not equal "MyString"), you frequently want to make sure that differences in case do not affect the result of a string comparison. But since you don't have any way of knowing whether the user will enter the data in upper, lower, or a mixed case, you have to convert the user's string, and possibly both strings, to the same case before performing the comparison, as the following code fragment illustrates:

```
strCompare = "MyString"
If LCase(strCompare) = LCase( Document.Form1.Text1.Value) Then
```

Example 14-3 illustrates the use of the *LCase* function in a web page. When the user clicks the Click Me button, the button's *OnClick* event procedure converts the contents of the text box to lower case and displays it in an alert dialog.

*Example 14-3. Converting a String to Lower Case*

```
<HTML>
<HEAD>
```

*Example 14-3. Converting a String to Lower Case (continued)*

```
<TITLE>Form Input Validation - LCase</TITLE>
<SCRIPT LANGUAGE="vbscript">
 Sub Command1_OnClick
     Dim frm
     Set frm = Document.Form1
     Alert LCase(frm.TextBox1.Value)
 End Sub
</SCRIPT>
</HEAD>
<BODY BGCOLOR="white">
<CENTER>
<FORM NAME="form1">
 <INPUT TYPE="text" NAME="TextBox1">
 <INPUT TYPE="button" NAME="Command1" VALUE="Click Me">
</FORM>
</CENTER>
</BODY>
</HTML>
```

## Converting a String to Upper Case: UCase

Just as *LCase* converts a string of alphabetical characters to lower case, the *UCase* function converts them to upper case. Non alphabetic characters (like numbers and special symbols) are ignored.

The syntax of *UCase* is:

```
UCase(string)
```

where **string** is a string variable or string expression to be converted to upper case. *UCase* is used for the same reasons as *LCase*, and is shown in Example 14-4. When the user clicks the Click Me button, the button's *OnClick* event procedure converts the contents of the text box to upper case and displays it in an alert dialog.

*Example 14-4. Converting a String to Upper Case*

```
<HTML>
<HEAD>
<TITLE>Form Input Validation - UCase</TITLE>
<SCRIPT LANGUAGE="vbscript">
 Sub Command1_OnClick
     Dim frm
     Set frm = Document.Form1
     Alert UCase(frm.TextBox1.Value)
 End Sub
</SCRIPT>
</HEAD>
<BODY BGCOLOR="white">
<CENTER>
<FORM NAME="form1">
```

*Example 14-4. Converting a String to Upper Case (continued)*

```
<INPUT TYPE="text" NAME="TextBox1">
<INPUT TYPE="button" NAME="Command1" VALUE="Click Me">
</FORM>
</CENTER>
</BODY>
</HTML>
```

## Extracting a String's Leftmost Characters: Left

The *Left* function allows you to return a given number of characters starting with the leftmost character. Its syntax is:

```
Left(string, length)
```

where **string** is the string variable or string expression, and **length** is the number of characters to extract. If **length** exceeds the length of the string, the complete string is returned; a run-time error is not generated. For example,

```
x = Left("MyString",2)
```

returns "My".

Example 14-5 allows the user to enter a string and to designate the number of leading characters to extract from it. When the user clicks the Click Me button, its *OnClick* event procedure displays an alert box that contains the extracted string. For example, if the user enters "VBScript" into the top text box and 2 into the bottom one, the alert box displays the string "VB." Notice that the script included with the web page includes a validation routine; it uses the *IsNumeric* function to determine whether or not the string entered by the user into the second text box is a valid number. If not, it displays a message informing the user that only numeric data are acceptable.

*Example 14-5. Extracting the Leading Characters of a String*

```
<HTML>
<HEAD>
<TITLE>Form Input Validation - Left</TITLE>
<SCRIPT LANGUAGE="vbscript">
 Sub Command1_OnClick
     Dim noChar
     Dim chars
     Dim frm

     Set frm = Document.Form1
     If Not IsNumeric(frm.TextBox2.Value) Then
         Alert "Number of Characters must be numeric"
         Exit Sub
     Else
         noChar = frm.TextBox2.Value
         chars = Left(frm.TextBox1.Value,noChar)
```

*Example 14-5. Extracting the Leading Characters of a String (continued)*

```
        Alert chars
      End If
 End Sub
</SCRIPT>
</HEAD>
<BODY BGCOLOR="white">
<CENTER>
<FORM NAME="form1">
 Enter a String  
 <INPUT TYPE="text" NAME="TextBox1"> <BR>
 Enter Number of Characters  
 <INPUT TYPE="text" NAME="TextBox2"> <BR>
 <INPUT TYPE="button" NAME="Command1" VALUE="Click Me">
</FORM>
</CENTER>
</BODY>
</HTML>
```

## Extracting a String's Rightmost Characters: Right

The *Right* function allows you to return a given number of characters from a
string beginning with the rightmost character. Its syntax is:

```
Right(string, length)
```

where ***string*** is a string variable or expression, and ***length*** is the number of
characters to extract from the string. If the number of characters specified is more
than the length of the string, the complete string is returned; a run-time error is
not generated. For example,

```
x = Right("MyString",2)
```

returns "ng".

Along with the *Left* function, the *Right* function is used to dissect the string when
its basic format or makeup is known in advance. In other words, if you require an
input to follow a given pattern, you can use these two functions to verify that this
pattern or format has been used. For example, if your web page requires that the
user enters the name of a text file with a .TXT extension into a text box, you can
check that the input is a valid filename with the statement:

```
If UCase(Right(Document.Form1.Text1.Value, 4)) = ".TXT" Then
```

Example 14-6 contains the source code for a web page that allows the user to
enter a string and to designate the number of trailing characters to extract from it.
When the user clicks the Click Me button, its *OnClick* event procedure displays
an alert box that contains the extracted string. For example, if the user enters
"VBScript" into the top text box and 5 into the bottom one, the alert box displays
the string "Script". Notice that, as in Example 14-5, the script attached to this web
page includes a validation routine that checks whether or not the user has
entered a number into the bottom text box.

*Example 14-6. Extracting the Rightmost Characters of a String*

```
<HTML>
<HEAD>
<TITLE>Form Input Validation - Right</TITLE>
<SCRIPT LANGUAGE="vbscript">
 Sub Command1_OnClick
     Dim noChar
     Dim chars
     Dim frm

     Set frm = Document.Form1
     If Not IsNumeric(frm.TextBox2.Value) Then
         Alert "Number of Characters must be numeric"
         Exit Sub
     ElseIf frmTextBox2 < 1 Then
         Alert "Number of Characters must be greater than 0"
         Exit Sub
     Else
         noChar = frm.TextBox2.Value
         chars = Right(frm.TextBox1.Value,noChar)
         Alert chars
     End If
End Sub
</SCRIPT>
</HEAD>
<BODY BGCOLOR="white">
<CENTER>
<FORM NAME="form1">
 Enter a String  
 <INPUT TYPE="text" NAME="TextBox1"> <BR>
 Enter Number of Characters  
 <INPUT TYPE="text" NAME="TextBox2"> <BR>
 <INPUT TYPE="button" NAME="Command1" VALUE="Click Me">
</FORM>
</CENTER>
</BODY>
</HTML>
```

## Extracting Any Substring from a String: Mid

*Mid* is one of the most important functions for string manipulation. It extracts a substring of a given length from a source string. Its syntax is:

```
Mid(string, start[, length])
```

where:

- *string* is the original string from which a substring is to be extracted.

- *start* is the character position in *string* at which the substring starts. The first character of a string is always in the first ordinal position. If *start* is less than one, a run-time error results.

- *length* is an optional parameter that specifies the number of characters to extract. If it is absent, the remainder of the string from the starting point is returned.

For example,

```
x = Mid("Hello World", 7, 2)
```

returns "Wo." If *length* is absent,

```
x = Mid("Hello World", 7)
```

returns "World."

When used in conjunction with the *InStr* function (which is discussed later in this section, and allows you to identify the position in a string at which a substring begins), *Mid* allows you to dissect strings in an infinite number of ways. Complete strings can be parsed and whole sentences chopped up into individual words.

Example 14-7 illustrates the *Mid* function. An HTML form prompts the user to enter a string, a starting position, and a number of characters. When the user clicks the Click Me button, an alert box displays the substring that is extracted based on the user's specifications.

*Example 14-7. Extracting a Substring from a String*

```
<HTML>
<HEAD>
<TITLE>Form Input Validation - Mid</TITLE>
<SCRIPT LANGUAGE="vbscript">
 Sub Command1_OnClick
     Dim noChar
     Dim StartChar
     Dim chars
     Dim frm

     Set frm = Document.Form1
     If Not IsNumeric(frm.TextBox2.Value) OR _
        Not IsNumeric(frm.TextBox3.Value) Then
          Alert "Number of Characters must be numeric"
          Exit Sub
     Else
          noChar = frm.TextBox2.Value
          StartChar = frm.TextBox3.Value
          chars = Mid(frm.TextBox1.Value, StartChar, noChar)
          Alert chars
     End If
 End Sub
</SCRIPT>
</HEAD>
<BODY BGCOLOR="white">
<CENTER>
<FORM NAME="form1">
```

*Example 14-7. Extracting a Substring from a String (continued)*

```
Enter a String  
<INPUT TYPE="text" NAME="TextBox1"> <BR>
Return Number of Characters  
<INPUT TYPE="text" NAME="TextBox2"> <BR>
Starting at Character Number  
<INPUT TYPE="text" NAME="TextBox3"> <BR>
<INPUT TYPE="button" NAME="Command1" VALUE="Click Me">
</FORM>
</CENTER>
</BODY>
</HTML>
```

# Replacing Part of a String: Replace  VBS 2.0

In Visual Basic, you can use the *Mid* function on the left side of an argument to replace a part of a string, but this is not possible in VBScript. VBScript 2.0, however, provides a new function called *Replace* that allows you to specify a substring to be replaced. Its syntax is:

> **Replace**(*string*, *stringToReplace*, *replacementString* [, *start*[, *count*[, *compare*]]])

where:

- *string* is the complete string containing the substring to be replaced.

- *stringToReplace* is the substring that will be sought by the function.

- *start* is the point in *string* at which the search for *stringToReplace* commences. If omitted, the search begins at the start of the string.

- *count* is the number of instances of *stringToReplace* that are to be replaced. If omitted, all instances of the substring after the *start* character are replaced. Care must therefore be exercised when replacing short strings that may form parts of unrelated words.

- *compare* is the type of comparison method used by VBScript. The possible values for this argument are shown in Table 14-1.

*Table 14-1. Values of the Compare Argument to the Replace Function*

| VBScript Constant | Numeric Value | Meaning |
|---|---|---|
| VbBinaryCompare | 0 | Perform a binary comparison |
| VbTextCompare | 1 | Perform a textual comparison |

The return value from *Replace* depends on the parameters you specify in the argument list, as Table 14-2 shows.

*Table 14-2. Values Returned by the Replace Function*

| If | Return Value |
|---|---|
| *string* = "" | Zero-length string ("") |
| *string* is Null | An error |
| *StringToReplace* = "" | Copy of *string* |
| *replacementString* = "" | Copy of *string* with all instances of *stringToReplace* removed |
| *start* > Len(*string*) | Zero-length string ("") |
| *count* = 0 | Copy of *string* |

You must also be aware that if you have specified *start* to be greater than 1, the returned string will start at that character, and not at the first character of the original string, as you might expect. For example, given the statements:

```
sOld = "This is a string to check the Replace function"
sNew = Replace(sOld, "check", "test", 5, 1)
```

*sNew* will contain the value:

```
"is a string to test the Replace function"
```

Example 14-8 illustrates how to use the *Replace* function. It also shows that you have to take care not to overwrite words that contain the substring you are replacing. Because we don't specify a value for *count* in Example 14-8, the call to the *Replace* function replaces every occurrence of "you" in the original string with "we." But in its second occurrence, "you" is part of the word "your," which consequently is modified to become "wer."

*Example 14-8. Replacing a Substring Within a String*

```
<TITLE>Replace()</TITLE>
<SCRIPT LANGUAGE="vbscript">
   Dim sString
   Dim sNewString
   sString = "You have to be careful when you do this " _
      & "or you could ruin your string"

   sNewString = Replace(sString, "you", "we")

</SCRIPT>
</HEAD>
<BODY BGCOLOR="white">
<FONT FACE="arial">
<CENTER>
<H3>Replace()</H3>
<SCRIPT LANGUAGE="vbscript">
   Document.Write sString & "<BR><BR>"
   Document.Write sNewString
</SCRIPT>
</BODY>
</HTML>
```

## *Finding the Starting Position of a Substring: InStr*

The *InStr* function returns the starting position of one string within another. Its syntax is:

```
InStr([start, ]sourcestring, soughtstring)
```

where:

- *start* is an optional parameter that designates the starting point of the search. If it is omitted, the search begins from the first character in *sourcestring*.

- *sourcestring* is the complete string in which you want to find the starting position of a substring.

- *soughtstring* is the substring that you are looking for, and whose starting position you want to identify. If *soughtstring* is not found, *InStr* returns 0.

For example,

```
x = InStr(5, "Hello World", "l")
```

returns 10, while:

```
x = InStr("Hello World", "l")
```

which does not specify a *start* value, returns 3.

Use *InStr* to find substrings when the pattern or format of the data entered by the user is unknown. For example, to verify that an email address entered by the user does not contain the @ character somewhere in the string, you could use the statement:

```
If InStr(Document.Form1.Text1.Value,"@') = 0 Then
```

Frequently, the *InStr* function determines the value of the *start* parameter in the *Mid* function. For example, to extract the domain of an email address, you could use the assignment:

```
strDomain = Mid(Document.Form1.Text1.Value, _
            InStr(Document.Form1.Text1.Value, "@") + 1)
```

which identifies the position of the "@" character within the email address, adds one to it, and extracts the entire string from that point to the end of the string assigned to `Form1.Text1.Value`.

Example 14-9 illustrates the *InStr* function. The user enters the string into the top text box, the substring to locate into the middle text box, and the starting position at which to begin searching the string into the bottom text box. When the user clicks the Click Me button, an alert box displays the character position at which the substring begins. If the substring is not found inside of the string, the alert box displays a dialog informing the user that the search string was not found.

*Example 14-9. Finding the Starting Position of a Substring*

```
<HTML>
<HEAD>
<TITLE>Form Input Validation - InStr</TITLE>
<SCRIPT LANGUAGE="vbscript">
Sub Command1_OnClick
Dim noChar
Dim StartChar
Dim Chars
Dim frm

Set frm = Document.Form1
If Not IsNumeric(frm.TextBox3.Value) Then
  Alert "Number of Characters must be numeric"
  Exit Sub
Else
  noChar = frm.TextBox2.Value
  StartChar = frm.TextBox3.Value
  chars = InStr(StartChar, frm.TextBox1.Value, frm.TextBox2.Value)
  If chars = 0 Then
    Alert "Search String Not Found"
  Else
    Alert "String found at Character " & chars
    End If
End If

End Sub
</SCRIPT>
</HEAD>
<BODY BGCOLOR="white">
<CENTER>
<FORM NAME="form1">
 Enter a Source String  
 <INPUT TYPE="text" NAME="TextBox1"> <BR>
 Enter a Search String  
 <INPUT TYPE="text" NAME="TextBox2"> <BR>
 Starting at Character Number  
 <INPUT TYPE="text" NAME="TextBox3"> <BR>
 <INPUT TYPE="button" NAME="Command1" VALUE="Click Me">
</FORM>
</CENTER>
</BODY>
</HTML>
```

# Searching from the End of a String: *InStrRev* VBS 2.0

*InStr* searches a string from left to right; *InStrRev* searches a string from right to left. The syntax for *InStrRev* is:

```
InStrRev(sourcestring, soughtstring[, start])
```

where:

- *start* is an optional parameter that designates the starting point of the search. If it is omitted, the search begins from the last character in *source-string*.

- *sourcestring* is the complete string in which you want to find the starting position of a substring.

- *soughtstring* is the substring that you are looking for, and whose starting position you want to identify. If *soughtstring* is not found, *InStr* returns 0.

If *soughtstring* is found within *sourcestring*, the value returned by *InStrRev* is the position of *sourcestring* from the start of the string.

Example 14-10 uses both *InStr* and *InStrRev* to highlight the different results produced by each. Using a *sourcestring* of "I like the functionality that *InStrRev* gives", *InStr* finds the first occurrence of "th" at character 8, while *InStrRev* finds the first occurrence of "th" at character 26.

*Example 14-10. Comparing Instr and InstrRev*

```
<HTML>
<HEAD>
    <SCRIPT LANGUAGE="vbscript">
        Dim myString
        Dim sSearch
        myString = "I like the functionality that InsStrRev gives"
        sSearch = "th"

        Sub cmdButton1_OnClick
            frmForm1.txtResult.Value = InStr(myString, sSearch)
        End Sub

        Sub cmdButton2_OnClick
            frmForm1.txtResult.Value = InStrRev(myString, sSearch)
        End Sub
    </SCRIPT>
</HEAD>
<BODY BGCOLOR="white">
<FONT FACE="arial">
<CENTER>
<H3>InStrRev()</H3>
<BR><BR>
Find the string <B>"th"</B> in the phrase "I like <B>th</B>e
functionality <B>th</B>at InSrtRev gives"<BR><BR>

    <FORM NAME="frmForm1">
        <INPUT TYPE=button VALUE="Use InStr" NAME="cmdButton1">
          
        <INPUT TYPE=button VALUE="Use InStrRev" NAME="cmdButton2"><BR>
        <INPUT TYPE="text" NAME="txtResult">
    </FORM>
</BODY>
</HTML>
```

## Converting Between Characters and Their Binary Value: *Asc* and *Chr*

Two other useful functions for checking data or manipulating strings are *Asc* and *Chr.*

Since computers can work only with binary numbers, every character is assigned an integer value between 0 and 255 that represents the value of that character in memory. The *Asc* function returns the ANSI code number that represents a particular character. Its syntax is:

```
Asc(string)
```

If the string you pass to **Asc** has more than one character, the function returns the ANSI code only of the first character.

You can use **Asc** to determine the ANSI code for a particular character. For example,

```
x = Asc("a")
```

returns 97. The most common application for the *Asc* function, though, is to confirm that a particular character lies within a range of characters.

The *Chr* function is the direct reverse of *Asc*: it converts an ANSI code value between 0 and 255 into that value's string representation. Its syntax is:

```
Chr(number)
```

For example,

```
x = Chr(97)
```

returns "a."

If *number* is less than 0 or greater than 255, the *Chr* function generates a run-time error.

These two functions are useful in data validation and string manipulation because they allow you to create algorithms using numeric constants that operate on string values. The simple fact is that scripts can be much more easily written to cope with a range of situations when numbers are used than when strings are used. Let's say you want to ensure that the first character of a particular field is within a range of letters, but that the range of letters is itself determined by an additional variable. This type of situation is common when an invoice number contains alphabetical characters. For example, the location of a branch office might determine the first character of an invoice number, where Manchester branch uses A–D and the London branch uses E–F. By comparing the strings to a numeric value, you can use the same comparison for both branches, as the following code fragment shows:

```
    Dim sBranch
    Dim iInvPrefix

    If sBranch = "Manchester" Then
        iInvPrefix = 0
    Else
        iInvPrefix = 5
    End if

    If Asc(Left(myString, 1)) >= (65 + iInvPrefix) and _
        Asc(Left(myString,1)) <= (68 + iInvPrefix) Then
```

Another use might be to selectively change the case of certain characters. To change a lowercase character to uppercase, simply subtract 32 from its *Asc* code; to change uppercase to lowercase, add 32 to its *Asc* code.

Example 14-11 shows a fairly typical use of the *Asc* function for data validation. When the user types a word in the form's text box and clicks the Click Me button, an alert box indicates whether the string's first character is uppercase, lowercase, or nonalphabetical. It does this by using the *Asc* function to determine whether that character's code value lies between 65 (the value of "A") and 90 (the value of "Z"), on the one hand, or between 97 (the value of "a") and 122 (the value of "z"), on the other. Note that the procedure also performs some data validation by making sure that the "word" entered by the user is not actually a number.

*Example 14-11. Determining the Case of a Character*

```
<HTML>
<HEAD>
<TITLE>Form Input Validation - Asc</TITLE>
<SCRIPT LANGUAGE="vbscript">
Sub Command1_OnClick
    Dim frm
    Set frm = Document.Form1

    If IsNumeric(frm.TextBox1.Value) Then
        Alert "Please enter a word"
        Exit Sub
    End If

    If Asc(frm.TextBox1.Value) >= 65 AND Asc(frm.TextBox1.Value) <= 90 Then
        Alert "The first character is UPPERCASE"
    ElseIf Asc(frm.TextBox1.Value) >= 97 AND _
            Asc(frm.TextBox1.Value) <= 122 Then
        Alert "The first character is lowercase"
    Else
        Alert "The first character isn't alphabetical"
    End If

End Sub
</SCRIPT>
</HEAD>
```

*Example 14-11. Determining the Case of a Character (continued)*

```
<BODY BGCOLOR="white">
<CENTER>
<FORM NAME="form1">
 Enter a word  <INPUT TYPE="text" NAME="TextBox1">
 <INPUT TYPE="button" NAME="Command1" VALUE="Click Me">
</FORM>
</CENTER>
</BODY>
</HTML>
```

## Can a String Be Converted to a Number? IsNumeric

The *IsNumeric* function determines whether a variable or expression passed to the function either is numeric or can be converted to a number. Its syntax is:

```
IsNumeric(expression)
```

where **expression** is any legal expression, variable, or constant. The function returns True (−1) if **expression** is numeric or can be converted into a number, and False (0) if it cannot. For example,

```
IsNumeric("ten")
```

returns False, while

```
IsNumeric("10")
```

returns True, since the string expression "10" can be converted to a number.

As you may remember, all data input into HTML text box controls are stored as variant strings, which requires that you convert numeric strings to numeric variants before using them within numeric expressions. But as the statement

```
x = CInt("ten")
```

shows, the attempt to do this generates a run-time error if the expression cannot successfully be converted to a number. Consequently, the main use of *IsNumeric* for data validation is to ensure that the data entered by a user can be converted into a numeric quantity for use in a numeric expression.

Example 14-12 uses the *IsNumeric* function to determine whether the data input by the user into a text box are a valid numeric expression.

*Example 14-12. Determining if an Entry is Numeric*

```
<HTML>
<HEAD>
<TITLE>Form Input Validation - IsNumeric</TITLE>
<SCRIPT LANGUAGE="vbscript">
Sub Command1_OnClick
Dim frm
    Set frm = Document.Form1
```

*Example 14-12. Determining if an Entry is Numeric (continued)*

```
    If Not IsNumeric(frm.TextBox1.Value) Then
        Alert "This is NOT a numeric entry"
    Else
        Alert "This IS a numeric entry"
    End If
End Sub
</SCRIPT>
</HEAD>
<BODY BGCOLOR="white">
<CENTER>
<FORM NAME="form1">
 <INPUT TYPE="text" NAME="TextBox1">
 <INPUT TYPE="button" NAME="Command1" VALUE="Click Me">
</FORM>
</CENTER>
</BODY>
</HTML>
```

## Can a String Be Converted to a Date?  IsDate

The *IsDate* function is covered at length in "Checking the Validity of a Date" in Chapter 10, *Date and Time in VBScript*.

# Formatting Data  VBS 2.0

Due to considerations of size, the *Format* function which was so useful in Visual Basic was left out of the original version of VBScript. After much wailing and gnashing of teeth from the users of VBScript, Microsoft has included several scaled-down functions in VBScript 2.0 that can be used to format data. These are:

- *FormatDateTime*
- *FormatCurrency*
- *FormatNumber*
- *FormatPercent*

The nice thing about the Visual Basic *Format* function is its almost unlimited flexibility: you specify, in an easy-to-construct string, just how you want the resulting string to look. However, this obviously requires high overhead in terms of the language engine. The new specific formatting functions, although they undoubtedly have their uses, do not afford such flexibility. The reason for this is that much of the formatting used in the functions is based on the Windows system's international settings. If only users from the same locale will be submitting data to you, and you know for a fact that their international settings will be the same as yours, you won't have a problem with these functions. If, however, you want to receive data from all over the world, then these formatting functions can only be safely used on the server. Here, then, is a brief description of the formatting functions.

## *FormatDateTime* VBS 2.0

The *FormatDateTime* function uses named constants to format a date or time value based on the computer's regional settings. A complete explanation can be found in Chapter 10.

## *FormatCurrency, FormatNumber, and FormatPercent* VBS 2.0

The *FormatCurrency*, *FormatNumber,* and *FormatPercent* functions are almost identical. They all take identical arguments, the only difference being that *Format-Currency* returns a formatted number beginning with the currency symbol specified in the computer's regional settings, *FormatNumber* returns just the formatted number itself, and *FormatPercent* returns the formatted number followed by a percentage sign (%). The syntax of these three functions is:

```
FormatCurrency(string[,DecimalPlaces ][,
IncLeadingZero[,UseParenthesis[,GroupDigits]]]])
FormatNumber(string[,DecimalPlaces ][,
IncLeadingZero[,UseParenthesis[,GroupDigits]]]])
FormatPercent(string[,DecimalPlaces ][,
IncLeadingZero[,UseParenthesis[,GroupDigits]]]])
```

Where:

- *string* is a required argument that represents the string to be formatted.

- *DecimalPlaces* is an optional argument that indicates how many decimal places the formatted string should contain after the decimal point. If *Decimal-Places* is not specified, the value in the computer's regional settings is used.

- *IncLeadingZero* is an optional tristate constant that indicates if the formatted string is to have a 0 before numbers between 0 and 1 or 0 and −1.

- *UseParenthesis* an optional tristate constant used to specify whether parentheses should be placed around negative numbers.

- *GroupDigits* is an optional tristate constant that determines whether or not digits in the returned string should be grouped using the delimiter specified in the computer's regional settings. For example, on English language systems, the value 1000000 is returned as 1,000,000 if *GroupDigits* is not False.

---

### Tristate Constants

The tristate constants, which are new to VBScript Version 2.0, are similar to the Boolean constants True and False, except that, as their name suggests and as Table 14-3 shows, there are three values rather than two. However, at the time of this writing, the tristate constants do not work. Therefore, when specifying a function argument that requires a tristate constant, use the numeric value instead.

---

The files *FORMATCURRENCY.HTM*, *FORMATPERCENT.HTM*, and *FORMAT-NUMBER.HTM* on the CD-ROM accompanying *Learning VBScript* allow you to choose the various options and see the differing results.

*Table 14-3. The VBScript Tristate Constants*

| Constant | Value | Meaning |
| --- | --- | --- |
| TristateTrue | −1 | True |
| TristateFalse | 0 | False |
| TristateDefault | −2 | Use the computer's regional settings |

# The Timing of Data Validation

When should you validate data? The obvious answer to this question is "before you use it," and the next best is "before the data is submitted to the server." But should you validate the data as it is entered, or when the user moves away from the input field, or when he or she clicks the Submit button? In this section, we'll examine the advantages and disadvantages of each approach. Your decision about when you will validate data has an impact on how easy or difficult a form is to use, and on how successful you'll be at catching rogue data.

## Moving Away from the Input Field

The first method we'll try out is validating the data as the user moves the focus away from an input field. When using HTML intrinsic controls, this is done by including your data validation code in the *onBlur* event procedure.

If the data validation routine finds incorrect or invalid data, you can, of course, display an Alert box informing the user of his or her misdeeds and hope that they'll correct it. But just showing a message is not going to be sufficient for some users. And if you validate data when the user moves away from the input field, you do not have an opportunity to validate that data again until the focus returns to the field. In other words, the user can accidentally or deliberately circumvent your data validation routine, and pass bad data to your application or to the server, by simply ignoring the warning message.

There is, of course, a solution that prevents the user from ignoring warnings about bad data: you can force the cursor to move back to the invalid data field by using the Focus method. Every time that the user tries to get away from a field containing bad data, he or she is pulled back to it as though attached by a length of elastic.

Although this technique is effective, it can conceal a rather nasty "gotcha" that your users may encounter if you have more than one field in a form that uses this method, as Example 14-13 illustrates. This form contains three text boxes, two of which are validated in their *onBlur* event procedure. One requires numeric input, while the other requires a date value. If the user enters bad data into the numeric field, then tries to move to the date field, he or she is pulled back to the numeric field. This, of course, is what you want. But the attempt to move back to the numeric field means that the script is attempting to move away from the form's other field, the date field, which triggers its data validation routine. But since a blank entry is not a valid date, the focus is pulled back to the date field. This triggers the numeric field's data validation routine, which pulls the focus back to the numeric field. So, alternately, the user is pulled back to the date field, then back to the number field, looping between the two for infinity. Eventually, users who tire of this situation and are well-versed in Windows basics will press *CTRL+ALT+DEL* and terminate the Internet Explorer task. (You can only speculate about what users who do not know how to end a task are going to do.) As you may have guessed, this is not the most elegant method for preventing the user from entering bad data.

If you are validating only one field on a form, this glitch does not occur. So you can safely validate data when the user moves away from the input field. But even so, this method uses the "stay here until you get it right" approach to data validation, which is not very polite. The problem is that it completely locks a user into a field with badly formatted data. But the user may not have the information at hand to know what the correctly formatted data are, and your validation method does not allow him or her to find out.

*Example 14-13. Validating Multiple Fields in OnBlur Event Procedures*

```
<HTML>
<HEAD>
<TITLE>Validate on leaving field</TITLE>
<SCRIPT LANGUAGE="vbscript">
'***********************************
'****          WARNING          ****
'**** THIS SCRIPT CAN CREATE AN ****
'****        INFINITE LOOP      ****
'***********************************
```

*Example 14-13. Validating Multiple Fields in OnBlur Event Procedures (continued)*

```
Dim frm1

  Sub Window_OnLoad
     Set frm1 = Document.Form1
  End Sub

  Sub text1_OnBlur
     If Not IsNumeric(frm1.text1.value) Then
         Alert "Entry must be numeric"
         frm1.text1.focus
     End If
  End Sub

  Sub text2_OnBlur
     If Not IsDate(frm1.text2.value) Then
         Alert "Entry must be a date"
         frm1.text2.focus
     End If
  End Sub
</SCRIPT>
</HEAD>
<BODY BGCOLOR="white">
<CENTER>

<FONT COLOR="red">
<H2>WARNING!! THIS SCRIPT CAN CREATE AN INFINITE LOOP</H2>
</FONT>

<FORM NAME="Form1">
Enter a number  
<INPUT TYPE="text" NAME="text1"><P>
Enter a date  
<INPUT TYPE="text" NAME="text2"><P>
Enter your name  
<INPUT TYPE="text" NAME="text3"><P>
<INPUT TYPE="button" NAME="cmdButton1" VALUE="Submit">
</FORM>
</CENTER>
</BODY>
</HTML>
```

# *During Input*

Let's look at a gentler way to check data. The HTML text box, text area, and select objects have an *OnChange* event that can be used for data validation. This event is fired as the user leaves a field *if the data have changed since the user entered the field*. If the data are the same, the event is not fired.

Validating data during input using the *OnChange* event is illustrated in Example 14-14. The HTML form requires that the user enter a numeric value into the first text box and a date into the second. If you experiment with it a bit, you'll find

---

## VB Programmers Note

The HTML *OnChange* event differs from the ActiveX control's *Change* event, which fires with every keystroke.

---

that it offers a method of validating data that is far superior to using the *OnBlur* event, while at the same time it leaves open a major escape hatch.

Because the user has to change the value of a control before its validation routine is invoked, the infinite loop scenario illustrated in Example 14-13 (in which one field contained invalid data and the second failed its validation test because it remained blank) is impossible.

If the *OnChange* event detects invalid data, you can display a warning message and call the control's *Focus* method to send the user back to the field. However, once the user has returned to a field that contains invalid data, he or she can leave it without making any additional changes. Since unchanged data do not trigger the *OnChange* event, the user will not be brought back to the field, even though its data are invalid. So ultimately, this method fails to prevent the user from ignoring any warning messages. If users want to leave bad data in an input field, they can; they will be warned once and only once.

*Example 14-14. Data Validation Using OnChange*

```
<HTML>
<HEAD>
<TITLE>Validate during input</TITLE>
<SCRIPT LANGUAGE="vbscript">
 Dim frm1

 Sub Window_OnLoad
     Set frm1 = Document.Form1
 End Sub

 Sub text1_OnChange
     If Not IsNumeric(frm1.text1.value) Then
         Alert "Entry must be numeric"
         frm1.text1.focus
     End If
 End Sub

 Sub text2_OnChange
     If Not IsDate(frm1.text2.value) Then
         Alert "Entry must be a date"
         frm1.text2.focus
     End If
 End Sub
</SCRIPT>
```

*Example 14-14. Data Validation Using OnChange (continued)*

```
</HEAD>
<BODY BGCOLOR="white">
<CENTER>
<FORM NAME="Form1">
Enter a number  
<INPUT TYPE="text" NAME="text1"><P>
Enter a date  
<INPUT TYPE="text" NAME="text2"><P>
Enter your name  
<INPUT TYPE="text" NAME="text3"><P>
<INPUT TYPE="button" NAME="cmdButton1" VALUE="Submit">
</FORM>
</CENTER>
</BODY>
</HTML>
```

# When Submitting Data

Typically, the object of data validation is to prevent badly formatted data from ever reaching the server. This means that data submission should rely on the data's having been successfully validated. The sure way to do this is to build data validation into the form's *OnSubmit* event, which is designed specifically to do just this.

Your *OnSubmit* event handler can call whatever functions are necessary to validate the data. If the data are validated successfully and you wish to submit the form data to the server, the *OnSubmit* event must return a value of True. If the form data are invalid, and you wish to stop them from being submitted, the *OnSubmit* event must return a value of False.

The last paragraph has probably confused you, as it did me the first time I found out about it. We're talking about an event handler returning a value. This means that the implementation of the *OnSubmit* is somewhat odd. Because it is an event handler that returns a value, it has to be implemented as a function, as follows:

```
Function form1_OnSubmit
```

You return True and False values like this, for a form named *form1*:

```
form1_OnSubmit = True
form1_OnSubmit = False
```

Once you get the hang of it, it's quite straightforward; it just looks weird at first!

Example 14-15 illustrates the use of the *OnSubmit* event to validate data. The form consists of three fields: a numeric field, a date field, and a string field. The validation routine examines only the first two. If the user has entered nonnumeric data in the first field or an invalid date value in the second field, an alert box indicating the invalid data is displayed. Otherwise, the data are submitted to the server, in this case a fictitious server at *www.yourdomain.com*.

*Example 14-15. Validating Data in the OnSubmit Event Procedure*

```
<HTML>
<HEAD>
<TITLE>Validate OnSubmit</TITLE>
<SCRIPT LANGUAGE="vbscript">
  Dim frm1

  Sub Window_OnLoad
      Set frm1 = Document.Form1
  End Sub

  Function IsFieldNumeric(field)
      If Not IsNumeric(field.value) Then
          Alert "Entry must be numeric - Submit Cancelled"
          field.focus
          IsFieldNumeric = False
      Else
          IsFieldNumeric = True
      End If
  End Function

  Function IsFieldaDate(field)
      If Not IsDate(field.value) Then
          Alert "Entry must be a date - Submit Cancelled"
          field.focus
          IsFieldaDate = False
      Else
          IsFieldaDate = True
      End If
  End Function

  Function Form1_OnSubmit
      Set ChkField = frm1.text1
      If Not IsFieldNumeric(ChkField) Then
          Form1_OnSubmit = False
          Exit Function
      End If

      Set ChkField = frm1.text2
      If Not IsFieldaDate(ChkField) Then
          Form1_OnSubmit = False
          Exit Function
      End If

      Form1_OnSubmit = True

  End Function

</SCRIPT>
</HEAD>
<BODY BGCOLOR="white">
<CENTER>
```

*Example 14-15. Validating Data in the OnSubmit Event Procedure (continued)*

```
<FORM NAME="Form1" ACTION="http://www.yourdomain.com/yourscript.etc"
METHOD="POST">
Enter a number  
<INPUT TYPE="text" NAME="text1"><P>
Enter a date  
<INPUT TYPE="text" NAME="text2"><P>
Enter your name  
<INPUT TYPE="text" NAME="text3"><P>
<INPUT TYPE="submit" VALUE="Submit">
</FORM>
</CENTER>
</BODY>
</HTML>
```

There's another way to validate data before submitting it to the server. This method uses a button control instead of a Submit button. The button's *OnClick* event procedure calls the relevant functions to perform the data validation, and only if all the functions indicate that the data are valid is the form's Submit method called. Example 14-16 is a variation on Example 14-15 that's been reworked to use the Submit method.

*Example 14-16. Data Validation Using a Custom Button*

```
<HTML>
<HEAD>
<TITLE>Validate prior to submission [2]</TITLE>
<SCRIPT LANGUAGE="vbscript">
  Dim frm1

  Sub Window_OnLoad
      Set frm1 = Document.Form1
  End Sub

  Function IsFieldNumeric(field)
      If Not IsNumeric(field.value) Then
          Alert "Entry must be numeric"
          field.focus
          IsFieldNumeric = False
      Else
          IsFieldNumeric = True
      End If
  End Function

  Function IsFieldaDate(field)
      If Not IsDate(field.value) Then
          Alert "Entry must be a date"
          field.focus
          IsFieldaDate = False
      Else
          IsFieldaDate = True
      End If
  End Function
```

*Example 14-16. Data Validation Using a Custom Button (continued)*

```
Sub cmdButton1_OnClick
    Set ChkField = frm1.text1
    If Not IsFieldNumeric(ChkField) Then
        Exit Sub
    End If

    Set ChkField = frm1.text2
    If Not IsFieldaDate(ChkField) Then
        Exit Sub
    End If

    frm1.submit

End Sub

</SCRIPT>
</HEAD>
<BODY BGCOLOR="white">
<CENTER>
<FORM NAME="Form1" ACTION="http://www.yourdomain.com/yourscript.etc"
METHOD="POST">
Enter a number  
<INPUT TYPE="text" NAME="text1"><P>
Enter a date  
<INPUT TYPE="text" NAME="text2"><P>
Enter your name  
<INPUT TYPE="text" NAME="text3"><P>
<INPUT TYPE="button" NAME="cmdButton1" VALUE="Submit">
</FORM>
</CENTER>
</BODY>
</HTML>
```

## Combining Validation Methods

So far in this chapter, we've presented methods for data validation as either/or options: you can choose to validate data as the user inputs data, or as the user moves away from the form, or when the user submits data to the web server. In fact, however, these methods are not mutually exclusive (unless, of course, your web page falls prey to the endless loop described earlier).

Example 14-17 shows how to combine these methods of validating data. The form consists of one numeric and one date field. As the user moves away from either control, its *OnChange* event procedure is triggered, which examines the control's value and, if it is invalid, displays a warning message. As we've seen, though, the user can choose to ignore these warnings. So when the user clicks the Submit button, the data validation routines are called once more. This combination gives users a chance to make changes to data before clicking the Submit button, and ensures that only valid data reach the server.

*Example 14-17. Combining Data Validation Methods*

```
<HTML>
<HEAD>
<TITLE>Validate during input and prior to submission</TITLE>
<SCRIPT LANGUAGE="vbscript">
  Dim frm1

  Sub Window_OnLoad
      Set frm1 = Document.Form1
  End Sub

  Function IsFieldNumeric(field)
      If Not IsNumeric(field.value) Then
          Alert "Entry must be numeric"
          field.focus
          IsFieldNumeric = False
      Else
          IsFieldNumeric = True
      End If
  End Function

  Function IsFieldaDate(field)
      If Not IsDate(field.value) Then
          Alert "Entry must be a date"
          field.focus
          IsFieldaDate = False
      Else
          IsFieldaDate = True
      End If
  End Function

  Sub text1_OnChange
      Set ChkField = frm1.text1
      x = IsFieldNumeric(ChkField)
  End Sub

  Sub text2_OnChange
      Set ChkField = frm1.text2
      x = IsFieldaDate(ChkField)
  End Sub

  Sub cmdButton1_OnClick
      Set ChkField = frm1.text1
      If Not IsFieldNumeric(ChkField) Then
          Exit Sub
      End If

      Set ChkField = frm1.text2
      If Not IsFieldaDate(ChkField) Then
          Exit Sub
      End If

      frm1.submit
  End Sub
```

*Example 14-17. Combining Data Validation Methods (continued)*

```
</SCRIPT>
</HEAD>
<BODY BGCOLOR="white">
<CENTER>
<FORM NAME="Form1" ACTION="http://www.yourdomain.com/yourscript.etc"
METHOD="POST">
Enter a number  
<INPUT TYPE="text" NAME="text1"><P>
Enter a date  
<INPUT TYPE="text" NAME="text2"><P>
Enter your name  
<INPUT TYPE="text" NAME="text3"><P>
<INPUT TYPE="button" NAME="cmdButton1" VALUE="Submit">
</FORM>
</CENTER>
</BODY>
</HTML>
```

# Summary

Time spent designing data validation routines is time well spent. However sophisticated our systems become, the old maxim "garbage in...garbage out" still holds true. The more you can reduce incorrectly formatted data, or—ideally—eliminate it altogether, the better a web application is. To ensure that data submitted to the server are valid, the following methods have been covered:

- Defining an object variable that refers to an HTML form object or an HTML control provides a convenient way both to reduce coding for data validation and to make code more efficient and more readable.

- VBScript provides a number of functions—most of them designed for string manipulation—that are commonly used for data validation. These include *Len, LCase, UCase, Left, Right, Mid, InStr, Asc, Chr, IsNumeric*, and *IsDate*.

- You can validate data as the user moves the focus away from the field, but, if used for more than one field on a form, this method risks creating an endless loop.

- You can validate data as the user changes data in the field, by providing code for an *OnChange* event procedure, but this method allows the user to disregard warning messages.

- The best single technique for validating data is to define a form's *OnSubmit* event procedure.

- While most event procedures are in fact *procedures* (pardon the redundancy), the *OnSubmit* event procedure is unusual in that it is a function. It returns True if an HTML form is to be submitted to a server, and False if it is not.

- You can use more than one technique for validating data in your web pages. The most effective combination is to define *OnChange* event procedures along with an *OnSubmit* event procedure.

# 15

## Error Handling and Debugging

Let me guess—you've been working on an example in an earlier chapter and you jumped to here, right? If you've reached here without having an error message when you tried to run one of your scripts for the first time, then...well, I don't believe it! Errors, bugs, and therefore debugging, are part of life for a programmer. As the saying goes, if you haven't made any mistakes, then you aren't trying hard enough.

Dealing with errors actually involves two very different processes: error handling and debugging. *Error handling* is a combination of coding and methodology that allows your program to anticipate user and other errors. It allows you to create a robust program. Error handling does not involve weeding out bugs and glitches in your source code, although some of the error handling techniques we'll cover in this chapter can be used to great advantage at the debugging stage. In general, error handling should be part of your overall program plan, so that when you have an error-free web page and program running on a user's browser, nothing is going to bring it to a screeching halt. With some sturdy error handling in place, your program should be able to run despite all the misuse that your users can—and certainly will—throw at it.

The following code fragment illustrates some simple error handling:

```
n = 10
x = Document.Form1.Text1.Value
If x = 0 Or Not IsNumeric(x) Then
  Alert "x is an invalid entry"
  End Sub
Else
  y = n / x
  Alert y
End If
```

The error handling in this example is the best kind—it stops an error before it can occur. Suppose you hadn't used the conditional IF...ELSE statement and had allowed any value to be assigned to *x*. Sooner or later, some user will fail to enter a value or will enter a zero. Possibly in both cases, and certainly in the latter case, this generates the "cannot divide by zero" run-time error. So error handling, as this code fragment illustrates, is as much about careful data validation as it is about handling actual errors.

The following code fragment is a "real" error handler that we'll examine later in this chapter, so don't worry about the syntax at this stage. Like the previous code fragment, it aims at handling the "cannot divide by zero" run-time error when and if it occurs:

```
Sub cmdButton1.OnClick
On Error Resume Next
n = 10
x = Document.Form1.Text1.Value
y = n / x
If Err.Number <> 0 Then
   MsgBox "Oops! " & Err.Description
End If
Alert y
End Sub
```

As both of these examples show, the code itself is error-free and doesn't contain any bugs, but without either the data validation code or the error handling code, this program will be brought to its knees the first time a user enters a zero in the text box. *Error handling* therefore is a way to prevent a potentially disastrous error from halting program execution. With error handling, if an error does occur, your program can inform the user in a much more user-friendly manner, and you can still retain control over the program.

*Debugging*, on the other hand, involves finding errors and removing them from your program. There are many types of errors that you can unwittingly build into your scripts, and finding them provides hours of fun for all the family. Errors can result from:

- Including language features or syntax that the scripting engine does not support within the script.

- Failing to correctly implement the intent of the program or some particular algorithm. This occurs when, although code is syntactically correct and does not generate any errors, it produces behavior or results other than those you intended.

- Including components (like ActiveX controls) that themselves contain bugs. In this case, the problem lies with a particular control, rather than with your script, which "glues" the controls together.

The single most important thing you need when debugging is patience: you have to think the problem through in a structured, logical fashion in order to determine why you are witnessing a particular behavior. The one thing that you do have on your side is that programs will never do anything of their own free will (although they sometimes seem to). Let's begin by looking more closely at this structured, logical approach to debugging your scripts.

# Debugging

You've designed your solution and written the code. You start to load it into the browser with high hopes and excitement, only to be faced with a big ugly gray box telling you that the VBScript engine doesn't like what you've done. So where do you start? Well, I find that another cup of coffee helps, but most of the time the error's still there when I rerun the script.

When confronted with a problem, you first need to know the type of error you're looking for. Bugs come in two main flavors:

- **Syntax errors**. You may have spelled something incorrectly or made some other typographical or syntactical error. When this happens, usually the program won't run at all.

- **Logical errors**. Although syntactically correct, your program either doesn't function as you expect, or it generates an error message.

Bugs appear at different times, too:

- **At compile time**. If a compile-time error is encountered, an error message appears as the page is loading. This usually is the result of a syntax error.

- **At run time**. The page loads OK, but the program runs with unexpected results, or fails when executing a particular function or subroutine. This can be the result either of a syntax error that goes undetected at compile time or of a logical error.

Let's look at each type of bug individually. We'll begin by looking at syntax errors, first at compile time and then at run time, before looking at logical errors.

## Syntax Errors at Compile Time

Syntax errors at compile time are usually the easiest to trace and rectify. When the browser loads an HTML page that contains script, it calls the scripting engine to compile the code. If the VBScript engine encounters a syntax error, it cannot compile the program and instead displays an error message.

For instance, an attempt to run the script shown in Example 15-1 produces the error message shown in Figure 15-1. At first glance, it appears that the VBScript engine has done an outstanding job of detecting the error. But when you look at line 7—the line that the error message identifies as containing the error—you see that it simply contains the `End Sub` statement.

*Example 15-1. Script with a Syntax Error*

```
<HTML>
<HEAD>
<TITLE>Syntax Error</TITLE>
<SCRIPT LANGUAGE="vbscript">
Sub cmdButton1_OnClick
  Alert LCase("Hello World")
End Sub
</SCRIPT>
</HEAD>
<BODY BGCOLOR="white">
<INPUT TYPE="button" NAME="cmdButton1" VALUE="OK">
</BODY>
</HTML>
```

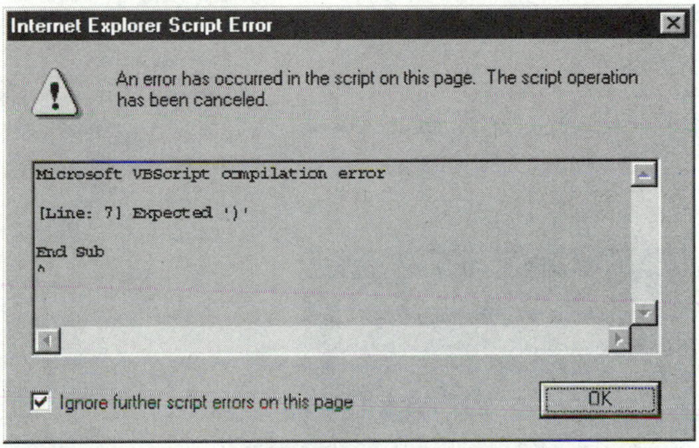

*Figure 15-1. Error message generated by Example 15-1*

This illustrates just one of the problems you face with VBScript syntax errors: the line number identified in the error message is not always the one that has caused the error. The error was generated in this case as the compiler reached the "E" in **End** because it was trying to find the closing parenthesis from the previous line. In this particular example, it only takes a moment to find the offending line and rectify the problem using line 7 as a guide, but error messages from much larger scripts can often point to line numbers far from where the actual syntax error is located.

Language engines, and compilers such as the VBScript engine, must be lean and fast to reduce the overhead involved in creating a run-time executable file in as short a time as possible. The extra bulk that would have to be added to the engine to display a completely accurate message with a correct line number is usually not worth the trouble.

## Syntax Errors at Run Time

Very often, a syntax error in VBScript only appears at run time. Although the VBScript engine can successfully compile the code, it cannot actually execute it. Example 15-2 provides a sample web page that generates a run-time error, which is shown in Figure 15-2.

*Example 15-2. HTML Page that Generates a Run-Time Error*

```
<HTML>
<HEAD>
<TITLE>Syntax Error</TITLE>
<SCRIPT LANGUAGE="vbscript">
Sub cmdButton1_OnClick
 Alet LCase("Hello World")
End Sub
</SCRIPT>
</HEAD>
<BODY BGCOLOR="white">
<INPUT TYPE="button" NAME="cmdButton1" VALUE="OK">
</BODY>
</HTML>
```

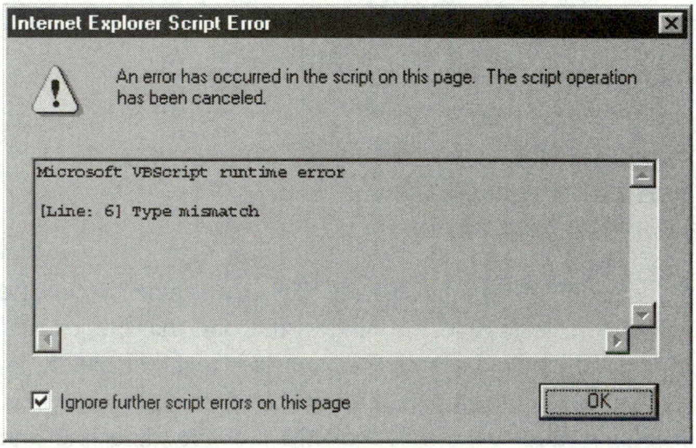

**Internet Explorer Script Error**

⚠ An error has occurred in the script on this page.  The script operation has been canceled.

Microsoft VBScript runtime error

[Line: 6] Type mismatch

☑ Ignore further script errors on this page            OK

*Figure 15-2. Error message generated by Example 15-2*

In this example, even though the *Alet* (misspelling of *Alert*) function does not exist, the line of code appears to the compiler to identify a valid function, since it contains the correct syntax for a function call: **functioname** is followed by **argu-**

*ment list*. The VBScript engine can therefore compile the code into a run-time program, and only when the engine tries to pass *argumentlist* to the nonexistent function *Alet* is an error generated.

## Logical Errors

*Logical errors* occur when your code is syntactically correct—that is to say, the code itself is legal—but the logic you have used for the task at hand is flawed in some way. There are two categories of logical errors: first, there are logical errors that simply produce the wrong program results; then there are the more serious ones, which generate an error message that brings the program to a halt.

### Logical errors that affect program results

This type of logical error can be quite hard to track down because your program will execute from start to finish without falling over, only to produce an incorrect result. There are an infinite number of reasons why this kind of problem can occur, but the cause can be as simple as adding two numbers together when you meant to subtract them. Because this is syntactically correct (how does the scripting engine know that you wanted "−" instead of "+"?), the script executes perfectly.

### Logical errors that generate error messages

The fact that an error message is generated helps you to pinpoint where an error has occurred. However, there are times where the syntax of the code that generates the error is not the problem. Look at this code (the line numbers have been added to make explanation easier):

```
<HTML>
<HEAD><TITLE>Logical Error</TITLE>
<SCRIPT LANGUAGE="vbscript">

1:   Sub cmdButton1_OnClick
2:       Dim myNum
3:       Dim sPhrase

4:       sPhrase = "This is some error"
5:       myNum = GetaNumber(Int(Document.frmForm1.txtText1.Value))
6:       If Instr(myNum, sPhrase, "is") > 0 Then
7:           Alert "Found it!"
8:       End If
9:   End Sub

10:  Function GetaNumber(iNum)
11:      iNum = iNum - 1
12:      GetaNumber = iNum
13:  End Function
```

```
</SCRIPT>
</HEAD>
<BODY BGCOLOR="white">
<FORM NAME="frmForm1">
<INPUT TYPE="hidden" NAME="txtText1" VALUE=0>
<INPUT TYPE="button" NAME="cmdButton1" VALUE="Click Me">
<FORM>
</BODY>
</HTML>
```

When you run this example in the browser, the code compiles correctly. It's only when you click the button that you find that an error halts execution on line 6, with the message "Invalid Procedure Call." But when you check the syntax for *InStr*, you find that it is correct.

The problem with this script is that the initial value of the hidden text field *txtText1* is 0. So when the *GetaNumber* function reduces it by 1, *myNum* is then −1, which is not allowed by the *InStr* function. It could be said that this type of logical error produces a syntax error because the syntax:

```
InStr(-1, "This is some error", "is")
```

is illegal.

In general, syntax errors manifest themselves while the page is loading into the browser, because the scripting engine is compiling the code in the page and comes across some code that it cannot compile. Logical errors, on the other hand, allow the page to be compiled, but raise their ugly head when the script is executing. However, some logical errors may appear to be generated during compile time—that is, as the page is downloading—although this is usually because the code is located outside of a subroutine, and so is run immediately once the program has been compiled. So these are actually run-time errors.

The script in Example 15-3, for instance, generates the error message shown in Figure 15-3. Since the error seems to occur as the page is loading, you might conclude that the script had generated a compile-time error. However, you can see from the error message that the error has occurred at run time, which means that the program has been compiled successfully. In fact, if you click OK, the page loads and the code for the command button runs perfectly.

*Example 15-3. A Logical Array Index Error*

```
<HTML>
<HEAD>
<TITLE>Logical Error</TITLE>
<SCRIPT LANGUAGE="vbscript">
Dim myArray(2)
For x = 0 to 3
 myArray(x) = x
Next

Sub cmdButton1_OnClick
```

*Example 15-3. A Logical Array Index Error (continued)*

```
 Alert "Hello World"
End Sub
</SCRIPT>

</HEAD>
<BODY BGCOLOR="white">
<CENTER>
<H2>A Logical Error</H2>
<P>
<INPUT TYPE="button" NAME="cmdButton1" VALUE="OK">
</CENTER>
</BODY>
</HTML>
```

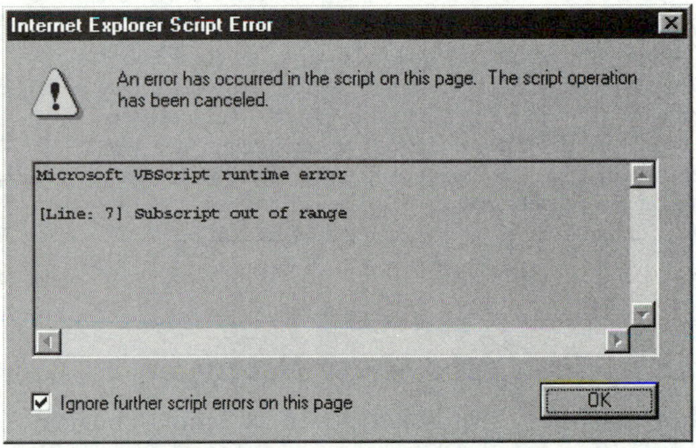

Internet Explorer Script Error

An error has occurred in the script on this page. The script operation has been canceled.

Microsoft VBScript runtime error

[Line: 7] Subscript out of range

☑ Ignore further script errors on this page          OK

*Figure 15-3. Error message generated by Example 15-3*

When you read through the code, you'll find that all the syntax is correct. The only problem is that you've specified a subscript larger than the defined size of the array. In Example 15-3, the error is fairly easy to spot:

```
For x = 0 to 3
```

But it may be slightly harder to track down if you are using a variable to define the upper limit of the loop, as in

```
For x = 0 to upperlimit
```

In this case you would have to try to determine what the value of *upperlimit* is. *upperlimit* may be the result of a calculation somewhere else in the program, or may even have been passed as a parameter into the subroutine, as in the following code fragment:

```
Sub filltheArray(upperlimit)
For x = 0 to upperlimit
  MyArray(x) = x *10
Next
```

This need to determine the value of variables in order to diagnose and eliminate logical errors is where code tracing during program execution comes in.

## The Microsoft Script Debugger

The Script Debugger has been designed to allow you to debug your scripts while they are running in the browser. You can trace the execution of your script and determine the value of variables during execution. The Script Debugger is freely downloadable from the Microsoft web site. (For details, see the Microsoft Script Debugger home page at *http://www.microsoft.com/workshop/prog/scriptIE/*) It arrives in a single self-extracting, self-installing archive file, so that you can be up and running with the debugger in minutes.

---

*NOTE*          At the time of writing, the Script Debugger also installs beta versions of VBScript Version 3 and JScript Version 3, which are required by the Script Debugger.  The only change to the VBScript language engine over Version 2.0 is its support for run-time debugging. The Version 3 files are installed into a separate directory to allow for easy deinstallation of the Script Debugger.

---

> ## The Unavailability of the Script Debugger
>
> Shortly before this book went to press, Microsoft removed the Script Debugger, which had been available for free download, from its web site and classified it as an unsupported piece of software. If you're one of the tens of thousands of VBScript programmers who download the Microsoft Script Debugger prior to its removal from Microsoft's web site, or if you've recently downloaded the Script Debugger from one of the handful of Internet sites from which it is reportedly still available, you'll want to read this section on debugging with the Script Debugger. If you don't have and can't find the Script Debugger, on the other hand, you can skip this section and instead read "Using Alert as a Breakpoint to Trace Execution," which examines a very simple technique that serves as an alternative to a professional debugging tool.

### Launching the Script Debugger

The Script Debugger is not a standalone application, in the sense that you can launch it on its own. Instead, the Script Debugger runs in the context of the browser. When you are running MSIE, there are two ways to access the debugger:

- By selecting the Source option from the View menu. This launches the debugger and displays the current page's source code. Note that if you don't have the debugger installed, Notepad is launched instead.

- Automatically, when a script fails for any reason. This launches the debugger and displays the source code for the current page at the point where the script failed.

Figure 15-4 shows the Script Debugger in action.

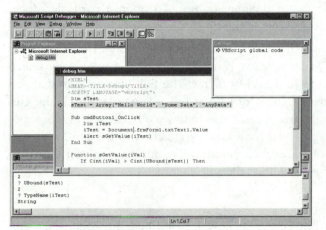

*Figure 15-4. The Microsoft Script Debugger*

### The Script Debugger interface

When you launch the Script Debugger, as Figure 15-4 shows, you're faced with a number of different windows, each with its own special function. These windows are:

- **The Script window**, which contains the code for the current HTML page just as if you'd selected the View Source option to launch Notepad. It is from the Script window that you control how the debugger steps through program execution, and that you watch the execution of the script. The script in this window is read-only.

- **The Edit window**, which displays a read-write version of the current HTML page. The Edit window is not loaded when you first launch the Script Debugger. To edit a script, place your cursor in the Script window at the point you wish to begin editing, and press either *Enter* or some other key. A pop-up message appears to remind you that the script in the Script window is read-only, and asks you if you'd like to open the file for editing. Selecting Yes opens the Edit window.

---

*WARNING*    Editing a script during execution is not recommended, although it is possible. The side effect is that the original script never completes its execution, which means that MSIE is hung in mid-air waiting for the script to complete.

---

- **The Project Explorer** window, which displays a graphical view of the page or pages currently loaded in the browser. I say "pages" because the Script Debugger can handle scripts in different frames. To open a particular document, simply double-click its name in the Project Explorer window.

- **The Call Stack** window, which displays the current hierarchy of calls made by the program. If the Call Stack window is hidden, you can display it by selecting the Call Stack option from the View menu. The Call Stack window allows you to trace the path that program execution has followed to reach the current routine (and, implicitly, that it must also follow to "back out" of these routines). For example, let's say you have a script attached to the OnClick event of a button called cmdButton1, which in turn calls a function named *sMyFunction*. When *sMyfunction* is executing, the call stack will be:

```
cmdButton1_OnClick
sMyFunction
```

This allows you to see how program flow has reached the routine it's currently in. It is all too easy when you have a breakpoint set in a particular function to lose track of how the script reached the function. A quick glance at the Call Stack window will tell you.

- **The Immediate window**. For my money, this is the most important part of the debugger. If you have experience in Visual Basic, you can now breathe a sigh of relief! The Immediate window allows you to interrogate the scripting engine and find the value of variables, expressions, and built-in functions. If the Immediate window is not visible, you can open it by selecting the Immediate Window option from the View menu. To use the Immediate window, type a question mark (?) followed by the name of the variable or value you wish to see, then press *Enter*. For example:

```
? sMyString
"Hello World"
```

### Tracing execution with the Script Debugger

The goal of tracing program execution is to discover, in a logical sequence, how your program is operating. If your program runs, but generates an error message—or produces results that are inconsistent with what you expected—it is obviously not operating according to plan. You therefore need to follow the flow of your program as it executes, and test the value of key variables at various stages and build up an overall "picture" of what is really happening inside of your program.

This should enable you to discover where and why your program is being derailed.

To trace the execution of your script, you need a way to "break into" the script while it is running, and then step through each line of code to determine what execution path is being followed, or perhaps where the script is failing. The Script Debugger gives you two ways to halt execution and pass control over to the debugging environment:

- **Break at Next Statement**. The simplest option is to select the Break at Next Statement from the Script Debugger's Debug menu or from the MSIE Edit menu. Then run your script in the normal way in the browser. As soon as the first line of scripting code is encountered by the browser, execution is suspended, and you have control over the script in the Debugger. However, the part of the script you want to concentrate upon may be many lines of code further on from the first, in which case you will waste time stepping through to the portion that interests you.

- **Set Breakpoint**. Most of the time you will have a good idea where your code is either failing or not producing the desired results. In this case, you can set a breakpoint by placing your cursor on the line of code at which you wish to halt execution, and then either pressing F9 or selecting Set Breakpoint from the Script Editor's Debug menu. A line that has a breakpoint set is highlighted in red. Run your script from the browser. When the code containing the breakpoint is reached, execution is suspended, and you have control over the script in the debugger.

When the code has been suspended, it must be executed manually from the debugger. There are three methods you can use for stepping through a script one line at time. For each method, you can either select an option from the debugger's Debug menu or press a keyboard combination. The options are:

- **Step Into (F8)**. Executes the next line of code. Using Step Into, you can follow every line of execution, even if the next line to be executed is within another subroutine or function.

- **Step Over (Shift-F8)**. Executes the next line of code only within the current subroutine or function. If a call is made to another subroutine or function, the procedure executes in the background before control is passed back to you in the current subroutine.

- **Step Out (Ctrl-Shift-F8)**. This is only required if you have chosen Step Into and your script has called a function or subroutine. In some cases, you may realize that this is a lengthy procedure that has no consequence to your debugging. In this case, you can select Step Out to automatically execute the rest of the function, and break again when control returns to the original subroutine or function.

---

*NOTE*          At the time of writing, the Microsoft Script Debugger Version 1 was
                not able to debug scripts held within Layout Control (.ALX) files.

---

### *Determining the value of a variable, expression, or function at run time*

One of the main functions of the Immediate window is to allow you to check the
value of a particular variable while the script is running. The most frustrating part
about debugging a script prior to the release of the Script Debugger was that you
could only see the results of your script after it had run (or failed). Most debugging requires you to get inside the script and have a wander around while it's in
the middle of execution.

In the absence of a debugger, many programmers and content providers inserted
calls to the *Alert* method or the *MsgBox* function to serve as breakpoints in
various places in a script. The dialog would then display the values of particular
variables or expressions selected by the programmer. Although this can still be
the most efficient method of debugging when you have a very good idea of
what's going wrong with your code, it becomes very cumbersome to continually
move the calls to *Alert* or *MsgBox,* and to change the information the dialogs
display, when you don't really have a good idea of where or why your script is
failing.

---

*NOTE*          Using the Immediate window to display the value of any variable is
                easy.   Simply type a question mark (?) followed by the variable
                name, then press Enter. The Script Debugger will then evaluate the
                variable and display its value in the Immediate window.   Note,
                though, that if your script requires variable declaration because
                you've included the `OPTION EXPLICIT` statement, you must have
                declared the variable and it must be in scope for the debugger to
                successfully retrieve its value;   otherwise, an error dialog is dis-
                played. The debugger cannot evaluate the result of user-defined
                functions;   it can only evaluate intrinsic functions (that is, functions
                that are a built-in part of the scripting language).

---

But you aren't limited to using the Immediate window to view the values of variables; you can also use it to inspect the values of expressions or of VBScript
intrinsic functions. To see how this works, and also to get some experience using
the Script Debugger, try out the web page in Example 15-4. Basically, the user
should be able to enter a number and, if it is actually between zero and two, be
shown the element of the array at that ordinal position. Somewhere in this code is
a sneaky little bug that is causing problems. The script always tells the user that

the number entered into the text box is too large, which indicates that it is greater than the upper boundary of the array. But this isn't the case: the user can enter the numbers 0 or 2 and still be told that the number is too large.

*Example 15-4. A Badly Behaved Web Page*

```
<HTML>
<HEAD><TITLE>Testing the Script Debugger</TITLE></HEAD>
<BODY>
<SCRIPT LANGUAGE="VBSCRIPT">

Dim sTest
sTest = Array("Hello World", "Some Data", "AnyData")

Sub cmdButton1_OnClick
    Dim iTest
    iTest = Document.frmForm1.txtText1.Value
    Alert sGetValue(iTest)
End Sub

Function sGetValue(iVal)
    If iVal > UBound(sTest) Then
        sGetValue = "Number too big"
    Elseif iVal < 0 Then
        sGetValue = "Number too small"
    Else
        sGetValue = sTest(iVal)
    End If
End Function

</SCRIPT>

<FORM NAME=frmForm1>
    Input a Number (0-2): <INPUT TYPE=text NAME=txtText1> <P>
    <INPUT TYPE=button NAME=cmdButton1 VALUE="OK">
</FORM>

</BODY>
</HTML>
```

To debug the script in Example 15-4, you can place a breakpoint on the first line of the *sGetValue* function, since this is probably where the problem lies. Then run the script and enter the number 2 into the text box *txtText1*. When execution is suspended, you can investigate the values of the program's variables. As you can see, the call to the *sGetValue* function has a single argument, *iTest*, which is passed to the function as the *iVal* parameter. So our first step is to determine the value of *iVal* at run time by entering the following into the Immediate window:

```
? iVal
```

Press *Enter*, and the debugger displays the result:

2

Next, find out what the script thinks the upper boundary of the array is, by entering the following in the Immediate window and pressing *Enter*.

```
? UBound(sTest)
```

Note that here you're not simply asking for the value of a variable; you're actually asking the debugger to evaluate the *UBound* function on the *sTest* array and return the result, which is...

```
2
```

So *iVal* is not greater than *UBound(sTest)*. Next, go back to the Script window and press F8 to follow the flow of program control. Execution is suspended on the following line, where the string "Number too big" is assigned to the variable *sGetValue*. That indicates that the scripting engine has evaluated the expression incorrectly and has decided that *iVal* is greater than *UBound(sTest)*. So go back to the Immediate window, and this time try to evaluate the complete expression:

```
? iVal > UBound(sTest)
```

Something interesting happens here: an error message ("Error executing immediate statement") is shown, informing you that the expression cannot be evaluated. Since each half of the expression could be evaluated separately in the Immediate window, but the expression as a whole can't be evaluated, it seems likely that our problem may center in the data types used in the comparison. So try the following:

```
? TypeName(UBound(sTest))
```

Here, you're asking the debugger to evaluate the *UBound* function on the *sTest* array, and, by calling the *TypeName* function, to indicate the data type of the value returned by the *UBound* function. The result is:

```
Long
```

Now find out what data type *iVal* is:

```
? TypeName(iVal)
```

The debugger returns

```
Variant
```

This actually doesn't tell you a great deal, since all VBScript data is variant. But *iVal* is the name within the *sGetValue* function of the *iTest* variable in the button's *OnClick* event procedure. And *iTest* in turn represents the value retrieved from the text box. So go back a step. What type of data is coming in from the text box?

```
? TypeName( iTest)
String
```

Aha! The Script Debugger shows that, in reality, you're performing the following comparison:

```
If "2" > 2 Then
```

which of course is nonsense! Try this in the debugger:

```
? CLng(iVal) > UBound(sTest)
```

And success! The Immediate window shows...

```
False
```

You can see from this debugging exercise that the Immediate window is a powerful tool allowing you to perform function calls, evaluate complete expressions, and try out different ways of writing your code.

### Changing variable values at run time

Another use for the Immediate window is to assign a new value to a variable. In the section "Logical errors that generate error messages," earlier in this chapter, you saw an example in which the value for the variable used to specify the starting position of an *InStr* search was erroneously set to −1, which generated a run-time error. If you were to step through this program, you could check the value of *myNum*:

```
? myNum
−1
```

Then you could assign a legal value in the Immediate window, like this:

```
myNum = 1
```

Simple! In this way, you can continue stepping through program execution.

## Using Alert as a Breakpoint to Trace Execution

In integrated development environments (IDEs) like Visual Basic, you have the luxury of built-in debugging and tracing. You can create a breakpoint, then execute the code one line at a time, checking variables along the way to discover where your bug emanates. However, unless you've managed to download a copy of the Script Debugger from Microsoft's web site before it was withdrawn or to find it on some third-party ftp or web site, there is no built-in method of tracing the execution of an HTML document or a script within an HTML document. So how are you going to find out what the value of a variable is, where execution is taking place, and where your VBScript code is going wrong?

The goal of tracing program execution is to discover, in a logical sequence, how your program is operating. If your program runs, but generates an error message— or produces results that are inconsistent with what you expected—it is obviously not operating according to plan. You therefore need to follow the flow of your

## *How the Visual Basic Debugger and the Script Debugger Differ*

If you have experience with Visual Basic, the debugging concepts covered in this section will be familiar to you. However, there are a few features that aren't available to you in the Script Debugger:

- **No "on the fly" editing**. Because the Script window is read-only, you cannot edit the code during execution, as you can most of the time with VB. Using the Script Debugger, it is possible to open an Edit window while the script is running, and to change the script. However, the original script, as far as MSIE is concerned, is still running, and until it finishes, MSIE is locked up.

- **No instant watch (SHIFT+F9)**. The VB debugger's instant watch facility, which allows you to highlight a variable in your code, press SHIFT+F9, and see the value of the variable, is not available in the Script Debugger.

- **Cannot set watches**. The concept of watches does not exist in the Script Debugger.

- **Cannot set the next statement**. Using the VB Debugger, you can place the cursor on a line of code and, by clicking CTRL+F9, have program execution resume at that line. This is particularly useful to backtrack or to re-execute a section of code. Unfortunately, this feature is not available in the Script Debugger.

program as it executes, and at various stages to test the value of key variables and to build up an overall "picture" of what is really happening inside of your program. This should enable you to discover where and why your program is being derailed.

In the absence of an IDE that allows you to trace program execution, you'll have to devise your own method for following the flow of your program. In this section, we'll look at a technique for doing this, which very simply involves using the *Alert* statement as a breakpoint. The method of defining breakpoints that allow you to trace program execution, examine the values of variables and expressions, and diagnose problems within your code is both quick and easy to use—probably the easiest and quickest debugging technique to use. It simply involves placing one or more Alert boxes in the code so that you can track where a problem occurs and collect diagnostic information about it (like the value of a variable). For example:

```
Alert "I've gotten to #1"
......
Alert "I've gotten to #2"
etc..
```

If you have a lengthy code section that you are trying to debug and don't know which line of code contains the error, start with just one *Alert* message about half way through the code. If the Alert message box appears, you know that the first half of the code is OK. Then move the message further down the script until the error occurs. You then know that the error has occurred at some point just before your *Alert* statement. For instance, the script in Example 15-5 ordinarily produces the error dialog shown in Figure 15-5; however, four *Alert* dialogs have been added to help identify the line number on which the error occurred. (If you use multiple *Alert* messages, don't forget to number them; a series of "I'm here" messages are not of much use!)

*Example 15-5. Script with Calls to the Alert Method*

```
<HTML>
<HEAD>
<TITLE>Finding an Error</TITLE>
<SCRIPT LANGUAGE="vbscript">
Function substr(x, i, y, z)
Alert "at #2"
        v = y - (z * I)
Alert "at #3"
        substr = Mid(x, v, z)
End Function

Sub cmdButton1_OnClick
    Dim i, y, z, v
    y = 50
    z = 5
    i = 11
Alert "at #1"
    v = substr("Hello World", i, y, z)
Alert "at #4"
    Alert v
End Sub
</SCRIPT>
</HEAD>
<BODY BGCOLOR="white">
<CENTER>
<H2>Finding an Error</H2>
<P>
<INPUT TYPE="button" NAME="cmdButton1" VALUE="OK">
</CENTER>
</BODY>
</HTML>
```

The *Alert* message boxes indicate that the error occurs in the line

```
    substr = Mid(x, v, z)
```

When you check the syntax, you will find it is correct: $x$ should be a string, which it is; and $v$ and $z$ must be numeric, which they are.

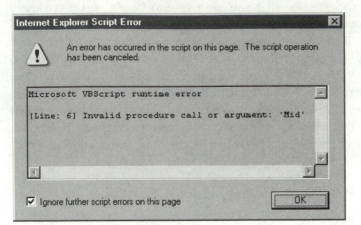

*Figure 15-5. The error produced by Example 15-5*

---

### *Debugging Is Best Done Using Notepad*

Run the HTML document through the browser. Then, if you have a problem, select View | Source. This loads Notepad, which in turn displays your HTML source code. You can then use Notepad to modify the file and to save your changes, and you can simply click the Refresh button to have the browser reload the new version of the HTML page so that you can try it again. This saves you a lot of time in trying to move back and forth between your HTML editor and the browser.

---

Of course, in this case, the line on which the error occurred was obvious. As I mentioned earlier, in small scripts like the one in Example 15-5, the line number of the error is fairly reliable. But things get a lot more confusing when you have calls to many different functions and procedures; you frequently don't understand exactly by what path your program reached a particular function or procedure.

So now we've successfully identified the line on which the error occurs, and we know the path that the script has followed to reach that line. But we still don't know precisely what the error is. To determine this, we need to know what values these variables contain. We can once again use the *Alert* box to find out what the values of certain variables are as the program is executing. So our next step in debugging the script in Example 15-5 is to remove the *Alert* statements numbered #1 through #4, and to insert the following line immediately before the call to the *Mid* function:

```
Alert "v=" & v & " z=" & z
```

When you reload the file and click on the OK button, the *Alert* box, which is shown in Figure 15-6, points to the problem: the value of the variable *v* is –5, which is an illegal value for the starting character position in a *Mid* function call.

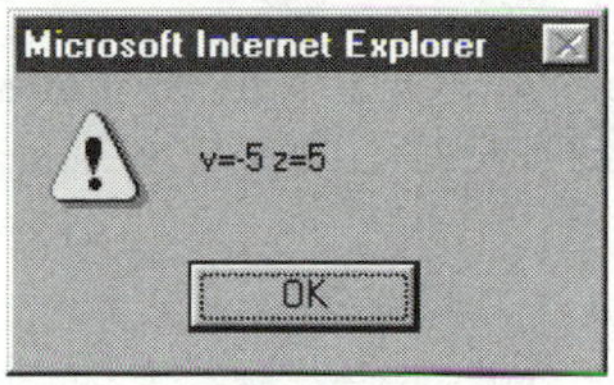

*Figure 15-6. Determining the value of program variables*

Once again, Example 15-5 contains an admittedly simple error, and one that is very easy to detect even without the aid of *Alert* statements, much less other, more sophisticated debugging tools. Nevertheless, it does illustrate how easy it is to use *Alert* statements for a variety of practical debugging operations:

- To determine the line on which an error has occurred. Typically, though, MSIE provides this information in its error dialog, so you rarely need to determine which line produced the error.

- To determine how program flow has reached the line at which the error occurred. Particularly if your script calls a number of functions or subroutines or executes one or more conditional or branching statements before reaching the line with the error, your script will probably fail in some cases while it succeeds in others. In that case, you'll want to follow the path that your program takes to reach the offending line.

- To determine the values of variables and expressions in your program. Almost invariably, debugging involves examining the values of program variables to locate the logical error that has derailed your script.

# Error Handling

Error handling does not involve finding errors in your scripts. Instead, you use error handling techniques to allow your program to continue executing even though a potentially fatal error has occurred. Ordinarily, all run-time errors that are generated by the VBScript engine are fatal, since execution of the current script is halted when the error occurs. Error handling allows you to inform the user of the problem and either to halt execution of the program or, if it is prudent, to continue executing the program.

## The ON ERROR RESUME NEXT Statement

There are two main elements to error handling in VBScript. The first is the ON ERROR statement, which informs the VBScript engine of your intention to handle

errors yourself, rather than to allow the VBScript engine to display a typically unin-
formative error message and halt the program. You do this by inserting a
statement like the following at the start of a procedure:

```
On Error Resume Next
```

This tells the VBScript engine that, should an error occur, you want it to continue
executing the program, starting with the line of code that directly follows the line
in which the error occurred. For example, in the procedure

```
1:Sub cmdButton1_OnClick
2:On Error Resume Next
3:x = 10
4:y = 0
5:z = x / y
6:Alert z
7:End Sub
```

a "Cannot divide by Zero" error is generated on line 5. But because you've placed
the ON ERROR statement in line 2, program execution continues with line 6. The
problem with this is that, when an error is generated, the user is unaware of it;
the only indication that an error has occurred is the blank Alert box (from line 6)
that's displayed for the user.

---

*NOTE*          A particular ON ERROR statement is valid until another ON ERROR
statement in the line of execution is encountered. This means that if
Function A contains an ON ERROR statement, and Function A calls
Function B, but Function B does not contain an ON ERROR statement, the error handling from Function A is still valid. Therefore, if
an error occurs in Function B, it is the ON ERROR statement in Function A that handles the error. When Function A completes execution, the ON ERROR statement it contains is also destroyed.

---

This is where the second element of VBScript's error handling comes in. VBScript
includes an error object, named *Err*, which, when used in conjunction with **On
Error Resume Next**, adds much more functionality to error handling, allowing
you to build robust programs and relatively sophisticated error handling routines.

## The Err Object

The *Err* object is part of the VBScript language and contains information about
the last error to occur. By checking the properties of the *Err* object after a particular piece of code has executed, you can determine if an error has occurred and,
if so, which one. You can then decide what to do about the error; you can, for
instance, continue execution regardless of the error, or you can halt execution of
the program. The main point here is that error handling using ON ERROR and the

*Err* object puts you in control of errors, rather than allowing an error to take control of the program (and bring it to a grinding halt). To see how the *Err* object works, and how you can use it within an error handling regime within your program, let's begin by taking a look at its properties and methods.

### Err object properties

Like all object and control properties, the properties of the *Err* object can be accessed by using the name of the object, *Err*, the dot (or period) delimiter, and the property name. The *Err* object supports the following properties:

- **Number**. The *Number* property is an integer value that contains an error code value between 0 and 65535, representing the last error. If the value of `Err.Number` is 0, no error has occurred. The line of code like the following, then, can be used to determine if an error has occurred:

  ```
  If Err.Number <> 0 Then
  ```

  Although the properties of the *Err* object provide information on the last error to occur in a script, they do not do so permanently. All the *Err* object properties, including the *Number* property, are set either to zero or to zero-length strings after an `End Sub`, `End Function`, `Exit Sub`, or `Exit Function` statement. In addition, however, you can explicitly reset `Err.Number` to zero after an error. Example 15-6 illustrates the importance of resetting the Err object after an error occurs. (The line numbers in the example's code are for easy reference only.)

*Example 15-6. Failing to Reset the Err Object*

```
<HTML>
<HEAD>
<TITLE>Using the Err Object</TITLE>
<SCRIPT LANGUAGE="vbscript">

1:Sub cmdButton1_OnClick
2:Dim x, y ,z
3:On Error Resume Next
4:x = 10
5:y = 0
6:z = x / y
7:If Err.Number <> 0 Then
8:   Alert "There's been an error #1"
9:Else
10:  Alert z
11:End IF
12:
13:z = x * y
14:If Err.Number <> 0 Then
15:   Alert "There's been an error #2"
16:Else
17:   Alert z
```

*Example 15-6. Failing to Reset the Err Object (continued)*

```
18:End If
19:End Sub

</SCRIPT>
</HEAD>
<BODY BGCOLOR="white">
<CENTER>
<H2>Using the Err Object</H2>
<P>
<INPUT TYPE="button" NAME="cmdButton1" VALUE="OK">
</CENTER>
</BODY>
</HTML>
```

The division by zero on line 6 of the script in Example 15-6 generates an error. Therefore, the conditional statement on line 7 evaluates to True, and an Alert box is displayed. Program flow then continues at line 13. Line 13 is a perfectly valid assignment statement that always executes without error, but the *Err.Number* property still contains the error number from the previous error in line 6. As a result, the conditional statement on line 14 evaluates to True, and a second Alert box is displayed. Despite the two error messages, though, there's only been a single error in the script.

The *Err* object can be reset by using the *Clear* method (which is discussed in the "Err object methods" section, later in this chapter) or by setting the *Err.Number* property to 0, as the following assignment statement shows:

```
Err.Number = 0
```

- **Description**. The *Description* property contains a string that describes the last error that occurred. You can use the *Description* property to build your own message box alerting the user to an error, as Example 15-7 shows. Figure 15-7 shows an Alert box that uses the *Description* property to display error information.

*Example 15-7. Using the Description Property to Display Error Information*

```
<HTML>
<HEAD>
<TITLE>Using the Err Object</TITLE>
<SCRIPT LANGUAGE="vbscript">

Sub cmdButton1_OnClick
Dim x, y ,z
On Error Resume Next
x = 10
y = 0
z = x / y
If Err.Number <> 0 Then
    Alert "Error number " & Err.Number & ", " & Err.Description & _
          ", has occurred"
    Err.Number = 0
```

*Example 15-7. Using the Description Property to Display Error Information (continued)*

```
Else
    Alert z
End IF

z = x * y
If Err.Number <> 0 Then
    Alert "Error No:" & Err.Number & " - " & Err.Description & _
          " has occurred"
    Err.Number = 0
Else
    Alert z
End If

End Sub

</SCRIPT>
</HEAD>
<BODY BGCOLOR="white">
<CENTER>
<H2>Using the Err Object</H2>
<P>
<INPUT TYPE="button" NAME="cmdButton1" VALUE="OK">
</CENTER>
</BODY>
</HTML>
```

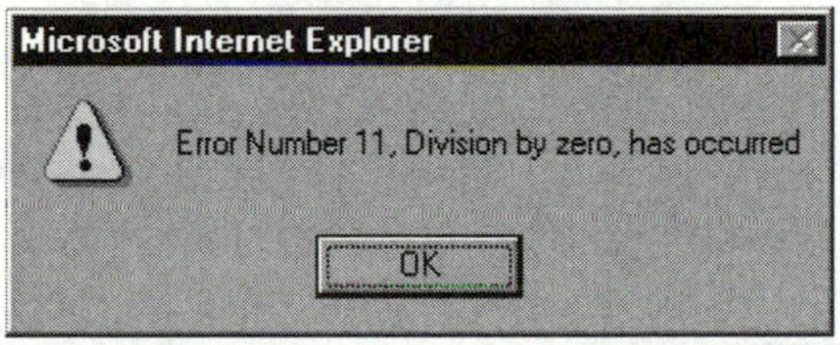

*Figure 15-7. An error message using the Description property*

- **Source**. The *Source* property contains a string expression that indicates the class name of the object or application that generated the error. You can use the *Source* property to provide users with additional information about an error, in particular about where an error occurred. Example 15-8, for instance, makes use of the *Source* property when handling a division by zero error. As Figure 15-8 shows, it indicates that the error was a VBScript run-time error—not a particularly useful item of information. However, the primary use of the *Source* property is to signal an error that is generated by some other object, like an OLE automation server (like Microsoft Excel or Microsoft Word) or an ActiveX control.

*Example 15-8. Using Err.Source to Provide Error Information*

```
<HTML>
<HEAD>
<TITLE>Using the Err Object</TITLE>
<SCRIPT LANGUAGE="vbscript">

Sub cmdButton1_OnClick

Dim x, y ,z
On Error Resume Next
x = 10
y = 0
z = x / y
If Err.Number <> 0 Then
   Alert "Error No:" & Err.Number & " - " & Err.Description & " has
occurred in " & Err.Source
   Err.Number = 0
Else
   Alert z
End If

End Sub

</SCRIPT>
</HEAD>
<BODY BGCOLOR="white">
<CENTER>
<H2>Using the Err Object</H2>
<P>
<INPUT TYPE="button" NAME="cmdButton1" VALUE="OK">
</CENTER>
</BODY>
</HTML>
```

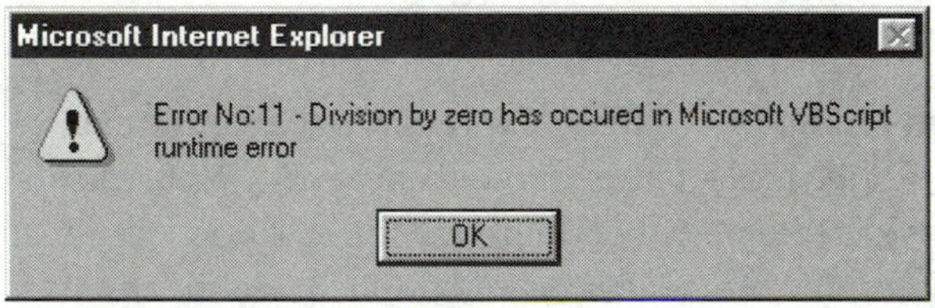

*Figure 15-8. An error message using the Err.Source property*

### Err object methods

The two methods of the *Err* object allow you to raise or clear an error, in the process simultaneously changing the values of one or more *Err* object properties. The two methods are:

• **Raise**. The *Err.Raise* method allows you to generate a run-time error. Its syntax is

```
Err.Raise(ErrorNumber)
```

where ***ErrorNumber*** is the numeric code for the error you'd like to generate.[*] At first glance, generating an error within your script may seem like a very odd thing to want to do! However, there are times, particularly when you are creating large, complex scripts, that you need to test the effect a particular error will have on your script. The easiest way to do this is to generate the error by using the *Err.Raise* method and providing the error code to the ***ErrorNumber*** parameter, then to sit back and note (1) how your error handling routine copes with the error, (2) what the consequences of the error are, and (3) what side effects the error has, if any. The web page in Example 15-9, for instance, allows the user to enter a number into a text box, which is passed as the error code value to the *Err.Raise* method. If the value of the error code is nonzero, an Alert box opens that displays the error code and its corresponding description. Figure 15-9, for instance, displays the Alert box that is displayed when the user enters a value of 13 into the text box.

*Example 15-9. Calling the Err.Raise Method*

```
<HTML>
<HEAD>
<TITLE>Using the Err Object</TITLE>
<SCRIPT LANGUAGE="vbscript">

Sub cmdButton1_OnClick
On Error Resume Next
errN = Document.frm1.errcode.value
Err.Raise(errN)

If Err.Number <> 0 Then
 Alert "Error No:" & Err.Number & " - " & Err.Description
 Err.Number = 0
End If

End Sub

</SCRIPT>
</HEAD>
<BODY BGCOLOR="white">
<CENTER>
<H2>Generating an Error</H2>
<P>
<FORM NAME="frm1">
Enter an Error Code  
```

---

[*] A more complete version of the syntax of the *Raise* method is:

```
Err.Raise(number, source, description)
```

where ***source*** is the name of the object or application that generates the error, and ***description*** is a string describing the error. The latter parameter is particularly useful when handling an application-defined error. This topic—and therefore the complete syntax of the *Raise* method—is beyond the scope of this chapter.

*Example 15-9. Calling the Err.Raise Method (continued)*

```
<INPUT TYPE="text" NAME="errcode">
<INPUT TYPE="button" NAME="cmdButton1" VALUE="Generate Error">
</CENTER>
</BODY>
</HTML>
```

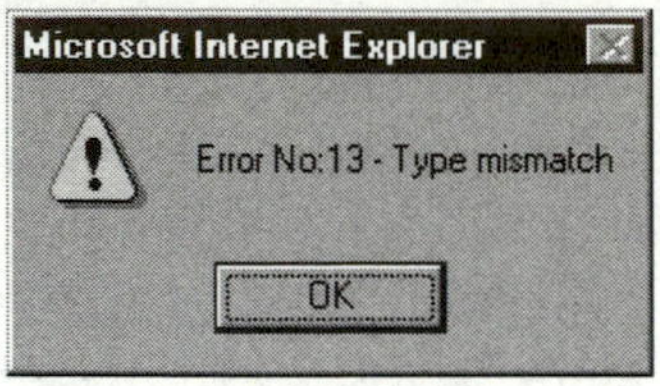

*Figure 15-9. Generating a Type mismatch error at run time*

At present there is no definitive list of VBScript run-time error codes available from Microsoft. Table 15-1, however, lists a few of the most common run-time errors.

*Table 15-1. Some Common VBScript Error Codes*

| Error number | Description |
|---|---|
| 5 | Invalid procedure call |
| 6 | Overflow |
| 7 | Out of memory |
| 9 | Subscript out of range |
| 11 | Division by zero |
| 13 | Type mismatch |

---

NOTE      An Error Code Generator (*ERRCODES1.HTML*), which allows you to generate a complete list of current VBScript error codes and their descriptions, can be found on the CD-ROM accompanying *Learning VBScript*.

---

- **Clear**. The *Clear* method clears the information that the *Err* object is storing about the previous error; it takes no parameters. It sets the value of `Err.Number` to 0 and sets the value of the Err object's *Source* and *Description* properties to a null string. Calling `Err.Clear` is similar to assigning a value of 0 to `Err.Number`, except that this does not clear the values of the Source and Description properties that were assigned by the previous error. Because of this, calling the *Err.Clear* method is preferable to assigning a value of 0 to the *Err* object's *Number* property.

## *Creating an Error Handler with Err Object and On Error*

Using the `On Error Resume Next` statement, as described earlier, forces your program to continue executing, no matter which error has occurred. This does have some benefits, since your program will not suddenly crash without warning. But it also means that you may be blissfully unaware of problems and side effects that occur later in the course of the program. For example, if you calculated a value that is posted to the server, you may be unaware that the value is Null because of an error that had occurred in the program. The Null value will probably then cause all sorts of mischief when you come to analyze and further process the data on the server.

You therefore must decide which errors your program can be allowed to ride though and which are serious enough to halt program execution. Example 15-10 shows how to construct an error handler that uses a conditional statement to decide whether or not to halt program execution. If the error handler decides to halt execution, it displays a message like the one shown in Figure 15-10.

*Example 15-10. A Conditional Error Handler*

```
<HTML>
<HEAD>
<TITLE>Using the Err Object</TITLE>
<SCRIPT LANGUAGE="vbscript">

Function DoErrMsg()

 Dim Msg, MsgBoxType
 Dim CRLF
 CRLF = Chr(13) & Chr(10)
 Msg = "A serious error - "
 Msg = Msg & Err.Description & CRLF
 Msg = Msg & "has occurred in "
 Msg = Msg & Err.Source & CRLF

 If Err.Number = 11 Then
    Msg = Msg & "Halting Execution"
    MsgBoxType = 16
    DoErrMsg = "Fatal"
 Else
    Msg = Msg & "Continuing Execution"
    MsgBoxType = 48
    DoErrMsg = "OK"
 End If

 MsgBox Msg, 48, "My Script Error"
 Err.Clear

End Function
```

*Example 15-10. A Conditional Error Handler (continued)*

```
Sub cmdButton1_OnClick
Dim x, y ,z
On Error Resume Next
x = 10
y = 0
z = x / y
If Err.Number <> 0 Then
   If DoErrMsg() = "Fatal" Then
      Exit Sub
   End IF
End If

Alert z

End Sub

</SCRIPT>
</HEAD>
<BODY BGCOLOR="white">
<CENTER>
<H2>An Error Handler</H2>
<P>
<INPUT TYPE="button" NAME="cmdButton1" VALUE="OK">
</CENTER>
</BODY>
</HTML>
```

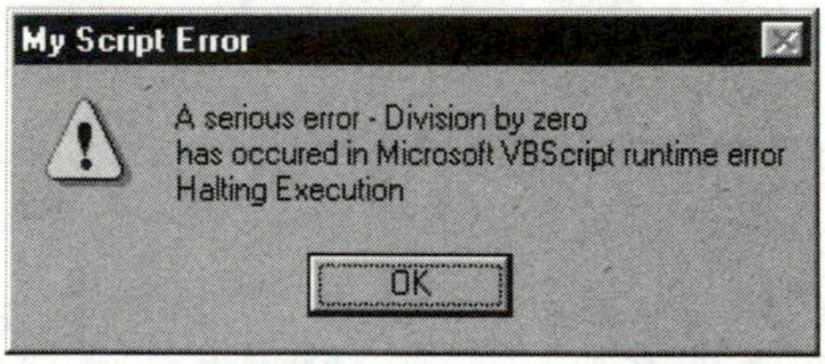

*Figure 15-10. A message generated by the error handler*

Example 15-10 uses an error handling function, *DoErrMsg*, that you can easily add to any script. Note that both the *cmdButton1_OnClick* event procedure and the *DoErrMsg* function reference the *Err* object. They are able to do this because the *Err* object is part of the language and therefore has global scope. So, even though the error occurred in the *cmdButton1* event handler, you can access the properties and methods of the *Err* object from the *DoErrMsg* function without having to explicitly pass the object or its values to the function.

If an error occurs—as determined by the value of **Err.Number**—a call is made to the *DoErrMsg* function. The function constructs the first part of the error message from the *Description* property of the *Err* object. The function then checks to see if the error that has occurred is considered fatal. If so, the function finishes building the error message by adding the warning that execution is being halted, and the function terminates by returning the string "Fatal." If the error is not fatal, the function adds the string "Continuing Execution" to complete the warning and returns "OK." The error message is then displayed to the user, and, finally and most importantly, the current error is cleared from the *Err* object using the *Clear* method. *DoErrMsg* then returns control to the calling procedure.

When execution is passed back to the calling line within the event handler, a check is made to see if the function has deemed this to be a fatal error. If so, the subroutine is exited; if not, execution continues as normal.

Error handling plays a major role in creating a robust application—one that won't fall over at the first sign of trouble, and one that can march smartly through all that users will throw at it. But, as they say, prevention is better than cure, which in this case translates to "Stop errors before they occur." In the next section, we'll take a look at how you go about designing your scripted web pages so that you are able to anticipate errors before they occur.

# Building Robust Applications

A robust application is not an easy thing to achieve, and the work involved in creating an application that can stand up to the rigors of the web magnifies exponentially as the size of the script grows. You have to consider all sorts of possibilities, and the only way you can do this is to break your code down into small manageable sections. For each section you need to decide:

- What are the internal influences on this particular part of the script? In other words, are there any other scripted functions and procedures that influence the variables and values? Are values passed to this section from another part of the script, and are values passed from this script to another function or procedure? How have you controlled the values coming from other areas?

- What are the external influences? Which values have been entered by the user? (This may also include values that have been passed into the current section from another part of the script.)

- If an error does occur within a particular section of your script, how will it affect the lines of code that follow the error? To really test this thoroughly, you must resort to creating deliberate errors using the *Err.Raise* method described earlier in this chapter.

- How are you going to handle errors that occur in a particular section? Again, the error handling techniques described previously will help you.

As you have seen in this chapter, many of the errors that occur at run time are generated by variable data entered by the user. The reason I mention this is that, once you've debugged your code and gotten your script to work nicely, it's not going to fail unless something changes; usually the only thing that can change is input from the outside world. Thankfully, programs don't wear out with use!

As you saw in Chapter 14, *Form Input Validation*, there are many ways in which you can control the data entered by a user. It's just not sufficient to display the message "Please enter a number here" and assume that every user will comply. Your script may even be executed by a user who *intends* to comply, but who assumes that, instead of the number 10, he can enter the string "Ten." After all, that's a number, isn't it? So, before using any data entered by the user, check that the data are in the format that your script requires. This means using functions like *IsNumeric, IsDate*, etc.

---

NOTE          For a full description of form verification techniques, see Chapter 14.

---

For example, you can anticipate and therefore prevent a sizable number of errors by writing code like the following:

```
If Not IsNumeric(input.value) Then
   Alert "I said NUMERIC!"
   Exit Sub
Else
   x = x + input.value
End If
```

In summary, a robust application is one that minimizes the risk of an error occurring and, in the exceptional cases in which one does occur, handles the error with ease, informing the user of the actions being taken, and then continues to execute its way out of trouble.

## Common Problem Areas, and How to Avoid Them

There is much to be said for the old maxim, "The best way to learn is by making mistakes." (If it were completely true, I should have a brain the size of a planet by now!) But in seriousness, once you have made a mistake, found out what you did wrong, and rectified the error, you will—in general—have a much better understanding of the concepts involved and of what is needed to build a successful application. But to save you from having to experience this painful process of trial and error in its entirety, I'd like to share with you some of the most common errors that I, and other programmers I've worked with, have made over more years than I care to remember. These types of errors are actually not unique to VBScript, nor in fact to VB, but apply to programming in general. In approximate order of frequency, they are:

- Straight in at No. 1 in the charts this week are syntax errors generated by typing errors. This is a tough one; typing errors—the misspelled function call or variable name—are always going to creep into code somewhere. They can be difficult to detect particularly because they are typing errors; we tend to train our eyes to see what *should* be there, rather than what is there. When the effect of the typing error is subtle, it becomes even more difficult to detect. For instance, in writing this book, I had spelled `LANGUAGE` as `LANGAUGE` in coding the `<SCRIPT>` tag. The result was that MSIE immediately began reporting JavaScript syntax errors. This isn't surprising, given that, in the absence of a valid `LANGUAGE` attribute, MSIE used its default scripting language, JavaScript. But when confronted with this situation, it takes a while to recognize the obvious—that the `LANGUAGE` attribute for some reason is improperly defined; instead, it seems that Internet Explorer and VBScript are somehow mysteriously "broken." The only real way to reduce the time spent scratching your head is to build code in small executable stages, testing them through the browser as you go. Another good tip is to use individual small sample scripts if you are using a function or set of functions for the first time and aren't sure how they'll work. That allows you to concentrate on just the new functions, rather than on all the rest of the script as well. Another very effective technique to reduce troublesome misspelling of variables is to include the `OPTION EXPLICIT` directive under the first `<SCRIPT>` tag. This way, any undefined variables—which includes misspelled variables—are caught at compile time.

- Running a close second are type mismatches by everyone's favorite data type, the variants. (Type mismatches occur when the VBScript engine is expecting one type of data—like a string—but is actually passed another type of data—like an integer.) Actually, type mismatch errors are fairly uncommon in VBScript, since the variant data type itself takes care of most data typing and of converting data from one subtype to another. That tends, though, to make type mismatch errors all the more frustrating. The best way to reduce or eliminate type mismatch errors is to adhere as closely as possible to a uniform set of VBScript coding conventions. (For a review of coding conventions and their significance, see Chapter 4, *Program Flow and Structure*.) For instance, when you know that a variable is going to hold a string, use a variable name like *strMyVar* to indicate its subtype, etc. Code becomes easier to use if you can tell instantly that some operation (like `strMyString = intMyInt * dteMyDate`) doesn't make sense, but you're none the wiser if your line of code reads `a = b * c`.

- In the third position is an error that occurs frequently when using arrays: *Subscript Out Of Range*. This error and I have been great friends for many years! It actually doesn't take much to eliminate this error for good. All you have to do is check the variable value you're about to use to access the array element against the value of the *UBound* function, which (as Chapter 3, *Getting Started*, showed) lets you know exactly what the maximum subscript of an array is.

- Approximately the fourth most common error is division by zero. If you try to divide any number by zero, you'll kill your script stone dead. While it's very easy to generate a division by zero error in a script, it's also not at all difficult to prevent it from happening. A division by zero error is easy to diagnose: whenever a variable has a value of zero, it's likely to cause a problem. So all your script has to do is check its value and, if it turns out to be zero, not perform the division. There's no rocket science here! Simply use an `If x = 0 Then` conditional statement, where *x* is the variable representing the divisor.

## Summary

However carefully you put your scripts together, errors are going to creep in, whether they result from a typing error on your part, from invalid data entered by users, or from a logical error in your program's design. The first rule of handling errors is to try to prevent errors from occurring in the first place. If they do happen, have some error handling code in place that will allow your program to continue executing and to keep you in control of the program. When you're developing an application, use the Script Debugger to trace execution and to display variable values. Use the *Err* object to obtain and display information about an error, and use its *Raise* method to generate errors so that you can test your application's ability to ride out the storm.

Here's a quick summary of the concepts you've seen in this chapter:

- Use the Script Debugger by setting breakpoints at various points along the script, to discover where your script is falling over. Also use the Script Debugger to display the values of variables that you suspect may be other than what you had intended.

- Use the `On Error Resume Next` statement to force execution to continue on the line that follows an error. Otherwise, VBScript will simply terminate your script when it encounters an error.

- Use the *Err* object's *Number* property to detect an error, and use its *Description* property to display information about the error. Use the *Raise* method to create an error, and the *Clear* method to reset the *Err* object.

- Think about how your script will be used, and attempt to write code in a way that will prevent errors from occurring. Since most errors result from invalid data input by users, above all check the validity of input data before using them.

# 16

# *The VBScript Shopping Cart*

If you've followed this book from start to finish, you should have a good grounding in all aspects of using VBScript and ActiveX controls to create state-of-the-art active content for your web pages. In this chapter, you'll see everything you've learned so far brought together into one application. The VBScript Shopping Cart is a fully functional client-side script that you can modify and use both as a learning aid and as a working shopping cart application on your web site.

As the Web becomes more and more commercial, companies are starting to exploit the vast potential of the Internet as a direct sales medium. Shopping cart applications are therefore becoming very popular, and the high price of a good shopping cart application reflects this growing market.

So what is a shopping cart application? Well, imagine yourself walking into a virtual shop on the Web. You can browse through the aisles of goods (represented by web pages) and select the goods that you want to buy. In a real store, you might put these goods into your shopping cart. In the virtual shop, you add the product references and their quantities to a database. When you get to the real check-out counter, you are told how much the total purchase price is, and you hand over the money. But there is a big problem with virtual shops. Let's say that you download the index page for a shop on the Web. You then navigate to the first product description page. You like one of the products, so you enter the quantity you want to order in the text box provided and press the Submit button. The server software has to store this information in some way so that, if you add another product to your order from another page, that new item will be added to the correct order. Some method is therefore required to link several seemingly unrelated submissions of data at the server. For instance, some shopping cart software utilizes a cookie file on your hard drive to store order information as you browse the store. Then, when you reach the virtual check-out counter, the cookie file is read back into the final order page. Other shopping cart applications assign you a unique number as you enter the site. This number, which follows you as you browse the site, is then used to read and write to a database on the server as you order goods.

In this chapter, we'll develop a shopping cart application for a fictitious company that sells flowers and plants via the Web. The application that we'll develop is unique in that all the product pages for the whole virtual shop are held as an array of variables within a single script file. Once you've downloaded the index page, only the graphics for each product are requested from the server; until you submit your final order to the server, everything else is done locally. Even the order information that's entered into the client is stored to the script's array variables. In fact, except that the graphics for various products in the virtual shop are needed from the server, the application could be operated off-line once the index page was downloaded!

Before we look at the VBScript shopping cart application, it may help you to appreciate how much easier things are with client-side scripting if we examine how shopping carts applications are implemented normally:

- **Server-Side Database Shopping Carts**. When you enter the web site for the first time, you are automatically assigned a user number. This number stays with you as you navigate from page to page through the site. If you add an item to your shopping cart, a form is submitted to the server, which in turn adds a new record to the shopping cart database. The record will most likely consist of your unique ID, the product code, and the quantity. A message is then sent back to the browser informing you that the item was successfully added to your shopping cart. This continues until you reach a point where you wish to complete the purchase and hand over the money. At this stage, the database will be queried, and all current records for your ID will be returned to the browser in the form of an order. You then enter your payment details and submit the order form.

- **Cookie Shopping Carts**. The other popular method of implementing a shopping cart is to use a cookie. In the cookie shopping cart, data is written to a cookie on the client machine. The cookie file will contain a delimited string of product codes and quantities; since the cookie file is unique to the user, a unique ID is not required at this stage. However, it is still a server-side script that performs the data manipulation and handles instructions from the browser.

What both methods have in common is their use of bandwidth to send data back and forth across the Internet, and the time involved in those transmissions. The application you are about to see eliminates almost all data transmissions across the Web until the user is ready to place an order, making it a more flexible, faster application.

# The Design of the User Interface

The VBScript Shopping Cart is contained within a single document or browser window, which is divided into three frames by the HTML <FRAMESET> tag. The window is divided vertically into two columns, while the left column is subdivided horizontally into two rows. As Figure 16-2 shows, the top row of the left-hand frame is reserved for the catalog index, while the bottom frame contains the main program which builds all the pages that are shown in the top left-hand frame and the right-hand frame. The right-hand frame is used to display the product pages (see Figure 16-3), a summary of the order (see Figure 16-4), and the input form for the user's details (see Figure 16-5). Note that, although the browser window is divided into separate frames, MSIE's hidden frame extensions to HTML cause the frameset to appear as a single page.

Figure 16-1 shows the shopping cart as it looks when it downloads to the browser. To enter the virtual shop, the user clicks the View Catalog button and is presented with a list of products, each of which has its own View Details button. Clicking one of these causes a graphic and a full description of the product to load in the right-hand frame. In the bottom of the product frame is a box in which the user can enter the quantity that he or she would like to order. Once the quantity is entered, the user clicks the Add to Order button on the right of the Quantity text box.

To view the current order, the user clicks the View Order button, which displays a summary of the order in the right-hand frame. The user can then remove an item from the order by clicking the button beside the line item to be removed. To submit the order to the server, the user clicks the Finish Order button and completes the order information requested by the form, which is again displayed in the right-hand frame. The user then clicks the Submit button at the bottom of the form.

Apart from the initial documents which are displayed in the top left- and right-hand frames, all other frames are rendered programmatically by using the *Document.Write* method. Furthermore, all scripted routines are run from the web page *CARTMAIN.HTML*, which is located in the bottom left-hand frame. The buttons that appear at certain times in the top left- and right-hand frames actually call subroutines that are located in the bottom left-hand frame.

# The Shopping Cart Code

The script for the shopping cart application has been broken down into its main functions as follows:

- Declaring and assigning values to variables
- Displaying the catalog index

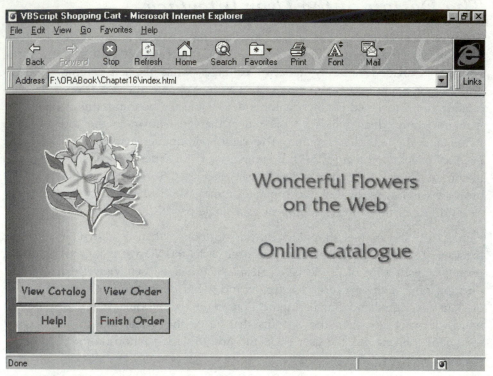

*Figure 16-1. The shopping cart application when it first loads*

- Displaying the product details page

- Adding an item to the order

- Displaying the current order

- Removing an item from the order

- Requesting that the customer provide additional details about the order, and submitting the order to the server

- The format currency function

- The `<FRAMESET>` document

We'll examine each of these functions in turn. Before you actually begin delving into the workings of the script, though, it's a good idea for you to try running the shopping cart example that's included on the accompanying CD-ROM (*CHAPTER16/INDEX.HTM*), to help you understand the shopping cart script. Note that, although the complete shopping cart application consists of a number of HTML files, there is just a single listing for the shopping cart application as a whole in the chapter index for the CD-ROM accompanying *Learning VBScript*.

---

## Variables, Arrays, and Constants

If you're a little bit hazy on how variables are declared, what arrays are, or why you might want to initialize variables, you might want to review Chapter 3, *Getting Started*.

---

## Declaring and Assigning Values to Variables

In the first part of our shopping cart application, we must set out our stall, programmatically speaking. That is, we must tell the language engine what our requirements are in terms of the memory space needed to run our program. We do this by declaring global variables and constants, and assigning them initial values in a single block of code, which is shown in Example 16-1.

### Dimensioning the arrays

Our fictitious virtual shop, Wonderful Flowers on the Web, is offering five products for sale electronically: azaleas, chrysanthemums, irises, daisies, and poinsettias. To hold information about these five products, lines 1 through 9 dimension nine parallel arrays; their function in our shopping cart application is shown in Table 16-1. For ease of programming, we won't use the first array element (the element at position zero); each array is dimensioned with an upper bound of 5, so that it has a total of six elements. (In VB, we could just include an OPTION BASE statement so that our arrays are 1-based instead of 0-based, but OPTION BASE isn't supported by VBScript, so instead we'll just leave the element at position 0 empty.) All arrays are one-dimensional except for the *Options* array, which is two-dimensional and holds the options available for each product. Its first dimension contains one element for each product, while its second dimension has enough elements to hold the maximum number of options offered by any single product.

*Table 16-1. Parallel Product Arrays Used in the Shopping Cart Application*

| Array name | Function in application |
| --- | --- |
| Products | Contains the name of the product |
| CatNos | Holds the product's catalog number |
| Description | Contains text providing an extended description of the product |
| Price | Provides the product's price |
| Per | Provides the unit of the product on which the price is charged |
| OptionHeading | Contains text that names the product's options (e.g., colors) |

*Table 16-1. Parallel Product Arrays Used in the Shopping Cart Application (continued)*

| Array name | Function in application |
|---|---|
| NofOptions | Indicates how many options are available for that product. It indicates the last nonblank element in the second dimension of the *Options* array. |
| Options | Two-dimensional array of product options |
| Graphic | Name of the file containing a graphic image of the product |

Lines 11 to 13 declare three dynamic arrays that are used to store the order details. Dynamic arrays are useful when you're not certain in advance how many items the user will wish to order. Otherwise, you have to dimension arrays that are large enough to hold the maximum possible number of items that the user can order. This is an enormous waste of system resources. And if you underestimate that maximum number, your script will crash when a user attempts to order too many items.

*Example 16-1. The variable initialization block*

```
 1:Dim Products(5)
 2:Dim CatNos(5)
 3:Dim Description(5)
 4:Dim Price(5)
 5:Dim Per(5)
 6:Dim OptionHeading(5)
 7:Dim NoOfOptions(5)
 8:Dim Options(5,3)
 9:Dim Graphic(5)
10:
11:Dim ordProdNo()
12:Dim ordQty()
13:Dim ordOption()
14:Dim CurrentOrderLine
15:Dim CurrentOption
16:
17:Dim DQ
18:Const TD1 = "<TD><FONT SIZE=1>"
19:Const TD1B = "<TD><FONT SIZE=1><B>"
20:Const TD2 = "<TD><FONT SIZE=2>"
21:DQ = Chr(34)
22:
23:Products(1) = "Azalea"
24:CatNos(1) = "A-ZH3-007"
25:Description(1) = _
"A year-round favorite, direct from our greenhouses to your door."
26:Price(1) = 5.64
27:Per(1) = "Plant"
28:OptionHeading(1) = "Bloom Color"
29:NoOfOptions(1) = 2
30:Options(1,1) = "Yellow"
31:Options(1,2) = "White"
32:Graphic(1) = "Azalea.gif"
```

*Example 16-1. The variable initialization block (continued)*

```
33:CurrentOption = ""
34:CurrentOrderLine=0
```

---

NOTE    The line numbers in the code examples in this chapter are for ease of explanation only; they do not appear in the final code. In addition, all comments have been removed from the code examples.

To avoid the possibility of failing to modify the number of array elements when adding or removing products (and to reduce the coding needed to change the number of products), you could instead declare a **MAXPRODUCTS** constant and assign it a value of (in this case) 5. You could then use this constant in each of the array declarations. That way, when the number of products changes, you only need to change a single value. The beginning of this block of code might then appear as follows:

```
Const MAXPRODUCTS = 5
Dim Products(MAXPRODUCTS)
Dim CatNos(MAXPRODUCTS)
```

and so on.

---

### Declaring global variables and constants

Lines 14 and 15 declare two global variables. The first of these, *CurrentOrderLine*, keeps track of the current line item in the order—which in this application is the same as the highest array element number in the OrdProdNo, OrdQty, and *OrdOption* arrays. The second, *CurrentOption*, indicates which option the user chose last. Lines 17 through 20 declare several constants that are used in various parts of the script. As you'll see in the next section, the main use of constants is to replace frequently used literal values with easy-to-remember and easy-to-use tokens.

Line 21 defines a constant that represents the quotation mark character. We can use it in calling the *Document.Write* method, where a literal quotation mark is not possible. Finally, lines 18 through 20 assign some often used HTML strings to constants. This helps to cut down on coding, and makes the code easier to read. Note that the global constant DQ cannot be declared using the Const statement, since its value is *Chr*(34), and only literal values can be assigned to true constants.

***Populating the product detail arrays.*** sUsing arrays in an application is very much like creating a simple database in memory. If the products offered by your virtual shop are not going to change very much from week to week, you can "hardcode" these values into the HTML page, as we are doing in this sample application. If, however, you wish to have the flexibility of changing your products or their attributes frequently, you can create a server-side script that retrieves product information from a server database and builds this section of the HTML as the page is requested from the client.

Lines 26 through 35 place information on one of the products, azaleas, into the arrays holding product information. All five products are very similar, so I won't bore you by presenting all the code or discussing each one here; you can see the complete script at the end of the chapter. Several points about the flexibility that this type of client-side scripting offers you are worth noting here, however.

Because of the use of the *Per* array, you can define a different unit of issue (per) for each product. In this application, prices are per plant.

You can enter a different Option Heading for each item. In this snippet, the options available are Bloom Colors. Other items, though, give the user the option of ordering different sizes of plants.

You can define a variable number of options. For instance, in this code snippet, there are two options: azaleas with yellow bloom colors and azaleas with white ones. This application limits the total number of options to three. To have more than three options, you simply need to amend the *Options* array declaration on line 8.

As you can see, there is nothing that restricts this shopping cart to a florist's shop. It could just as easily be any other type of virtual shop selling any other kind of product or products.

---

*NOTE*        This application is designed to operate through VBScript Version 2.0 and uses several of the language's built-in constants throughout the application. However, if you intend to use this with VBScript Version 1.0, you will need to define your own constants using the following values:

| VBScript 2 Constant | Value |
| --- | --- |
| vbCrLf | Chr(10) & Chr(13) |
| vbYes | 6 |
| vbNo | 7 |
| vbCancel | 2 |
| vbQuestion + vbYesNoCancel | 35 |

---

*Assigning values to the global variables.* Lines 33 and 34 initialize two global variables, *CurrentOption* and *CurrentOrderLine*. Although VBScript does not force you to assign values to variables before using them, it is good programming practice, since it allows other developers you may be working with to see immediately how you intend to use these variables. In the case of *CurrentOrderLine* it is necessary, as you will see later; the value of 0 is used as a test in several places to see if any items have been placed on order by the user.

## Displaying the Catalog Index

When the user clicks the "View Catalog" button the *DoIndex_Click* event handler is called. (The View Catalog button is an ActiveX command button control whose object ID—or name within our web page—is *DoIndex*.) This event handler, which is shown in Example 16-2, creates a new document in the Cart frame (the top left-hand frame) containing a list of product names. Next to each product name is a button that the user can click to view the product details. Figure 16-2 shows the products catalog index page.

---

### Loops, Browser Objects, Object References, and ActiveX Controls

While you're reading this and the next section, you may find that you need to refresh your memory about some of the details discussed here. The *Document.Write* method, which is used to build a browser frame or document on the fly from within a script, is discussed in Chapter 13, *Building Dynamic HTML Pages*. The use of the SET statement to define an object reference is covered in Chapter 14, *Form Input Validation*. The use of browser objects—like each of the View Details buttons—is treated in Chapter 5, *Controlling the Browser*. Finally, the use of the FOR...NEXT loop, which the script uses to include each product in the catalog index, is discussed in Chapter 4, *Program Flow and Structure*.

---

Lines 2 and 3 of the event handler define *i* and *cartndx* as local variables—that is, they exist only while this event handler is executing. Line 5 assigns a reference to the *Document* object in the Cart frame to *cartndx*; this means that the document can now be referenced simply by using the *cartndx* variable. Line 7 opens the document buffer in order to write to it. Lines 8 through 11 write the initial part of the HTML document. Lines 12 through 22 form a flexible loop that executes once for each product that the application is to handle. Line 14 writes the product name, and lines 15 though 20 write the HTML code for the product's View Details button. Although this button definition is split into several lines to make the code easier to read, the HTML `<INPUT>` tag that you are creating to define the button for azaleas programmatically is as follows:

```
<INPUT TYPE=button LANGUAGE="vbscript"
ONCLICK="Parent.Cart2.ShowPage(1)"
    VALUE="View Details">
```

As you can see, the HTML button definition contains several elements within double quotation marks and a variable value (shown above as 1) that is passed to the *ShowPage* subroutine. But the VBScript engine cannot successfully parse a line of code if double quotation marks are used as literals within a call to the *Document.Write* method. Consider the following line of code:

```
Document.Write "ONCLICK="Parent.Cart2.ShowPage(1)""
```

Since the second quotation mark is interpreted by the VBScript engine as marking the end of a string, only the string "ONCLICK=" is being passed to the *Write* method. In order to pass a string that contains quotation marks, you must use their ASCII character code—34—to indicate their placement within the string. So for the VBScript engine to correctly interpret our previous example, we would have to rewrite it as follows:

```
Document.Write "ONCLICK=" & Chr(34) & "Parent.Cart2.ShowPage(1)" &
Chr(34)
```

But since we've defined the constant DQ as *Chr(34)*, we can further simplify this line of code:

```
Document.Write "ONCLICK=" & DQ & "Parent.Cart2.ShowPage(1)" & DQ
```

Lines 17 and 18 illustrate how to call subroutines within another frame. `Cart2` is the name of the frame that contains this script, and `ShowPage` is the name of the subroutine to be called.

Lines 23 and 24 finish off the HTML document and close the buffer, which causes the HTML document shown in Figure 16-2 to be written to the browser.

*Example 16-2. The DoIndex_Click Event Handler*

```
 1:Sub DoIndex_Click
 2:Dim i
 3:Dim cartndx
 4:
 5:Set cartndx = Parent.Cart.Document
 6:
 7:cartndx.Open
 8:cartndx.Write "<HTML><BODY BACKGROUND=" & DQ & "cartbak.gif" & DQ
 9:cartndx.Write "><FONT FACE=" & DQ & "arial" & DQ & "SIZE=2" & ">"
10:cartndx.Write "<CENTER><H3>Catalog Index</H3><P><B>"
11:cartndx.Write "<TABLE>"
12:For i = 1 to UBound(Products)
13:    cartndx.Write "<TD ALIGN=LEFT><FONT SIZE=2><B>"
14:    cartndx.Write Products(i) & "</TD><TD ALIGN=RIGHT>"
15:    cartndx.Write "<INPUT TYPE=button LANGUAGE="
16:    cartndx.Write DQ & "vbscript"  & DQ
17:    cartndx.Write " ONCLICK=" & DQ & "Parent.Cart2.ShowPage("
18:    cartndx.Write i
19:    cartndx.Write ")" & DQ & " VALUE=" & DQ & "View Details"
20:    cartndx.Write DQ & "><BR>"
```

*Example 16-2. The DoIndex_Click Event Handler (continued)*

```
21:    cartndx.Write "</TD></TR>"
22:Next
23:cartndx.Write "</TABLE></CENTER></BODY></HTML>"
24:cartndx.Close
25:End Sub
```

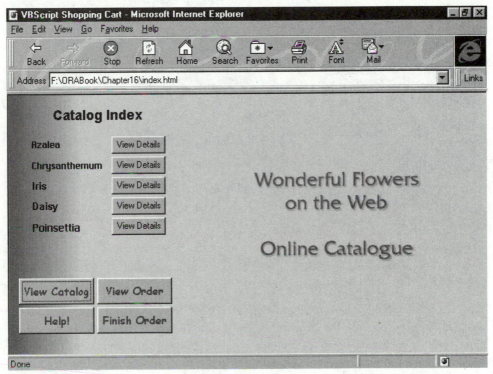

*Figure 16-2. The product's Catalog Index*

## Displaying the Product Details Page

When the user clicks one of the View Details buttons, a page is created in the right-hand frame that describes the product and its available options. Figure 16-3, for instance, shows the page that's created when the user requests details on azaleas. Also shown are the cost per unit of issue, a text box in which to enter the required quantity, and a button to add the item to the order.

The *ShowPage* custom procedure, which is shown in Example 16-3, is responsible for creating the product details page. When the procedure is called, it is passed a single parameter, `ProductNumber`, which represents the index of the product selected by the user from the *Products* array.

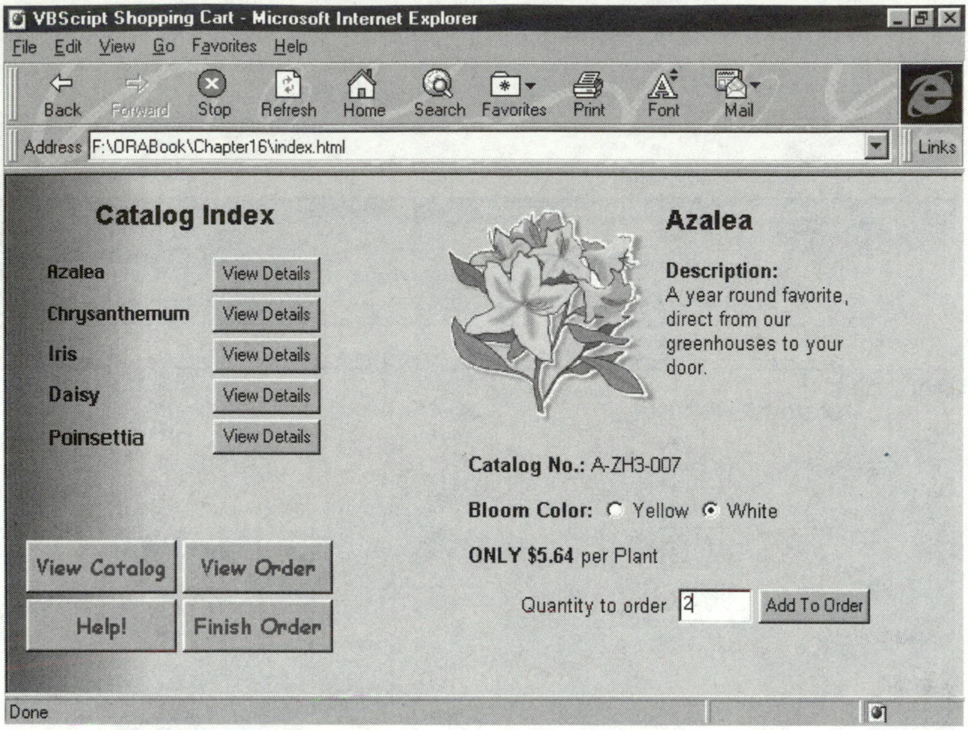

*Figure 16-3. The azalea details page*

Line 2 of the *ShowPage* subroutine defines *TheGoods* as a local variable. Line 4 assigns a reference to the document in the right-hand (Goods) frame to the *TheGoods* variable. Line 6 opens the Goods frame's document buffer before writing text to it. Lines 7 to 10 create the beginning of the HTML source that's written to the frame. Line 8 adds the HTML code to define the graphic for the product selected by the user; the name of the graphics file is extracted from the *Graphic* array. Lines 12 and 13 define the HTML code to display a heading consisting of the product's name; this is extracted from the *Products* array. Lines 14 and 15 are responsible for writing the product's description, while line 19 displays the catalog number.

After displaying the option heading in line 21, the loop in lines 23 to 36 executes as many times as there are options available for this product. The loop is responsible for creating the option buttons that allow the user to choose a particular option. The loop is also responsible for defining the subroutine that's called when the user clicks an option button. (This short subroutine, *DoOption*, simply changes the *CurrentOption* global variable.) One of the lines of HTML code generated by the loop might appear as follows:

```
<INPUT TYPE=radio LANGUAGE="vbscript"
OnClick="Parent.Cart2.DoOption("white")" CHECKED>
```

Note that lines 29 to 33 conditionally add the **CHECKED** attribute to the HTML `<INPUT>` tag only for the first option button, thereby checking it by default. Lines 34 and 35 add the name of the option and a nonbreaking space after the option button.

Once the options have been added to the page, the price of the item is added in lines 38 and 39. The price is formatted using the *FormatNumber* function so that it always displays two digits after the decimal place.

---

*TIP*          VBScript Version 2.0 includes a built-in *FormatCurrency* function to format currency values. However, because the function uses the regional settings from the computer, the currency symbol from the user's locale will be prepended to the number. Therefore, a user viewing this page in the UK, for instance, will see £100.00 instead of $100.00.

---

Lines 40 and 41 define the text box in which the user can enter the quantity he or she wants to order. Lines 42 through 45 define the Add To Order button and also define its event handler, a custom procedure named *DoOrder* that adds the current product to the user's order. The HTML source for one such order button might appear as follows:

```
<INPUT TYPE=BUTTON LANGUAGE="vbscript"
ONCLICK="Parent.Cart2.DoOrder(1)"
        VALUE="Add To Order">
```

Lines 46 to 48 complete the HTML document and close the document buffer, which writes the page into the frame. Line 49 sets the *CurrentOption* global variable to its default value of 1.

A benefit of creating pages in this manner is that only one routine creates product pages, and only one "page" is actually ever defined. Should you wish to change the look or the style of the page, you only need to modify this part of the script, and all your product "pages" will reflect the change.

*Example 16-3. The ShowPage Procedure*

```
1:Sub ShowPage(ProductNumber)
2:Dim TheGoods
3:
4:Set TheGoods = Parent.goods.Document
5:
6:TheGoods.Open
7:TheGoods.Write "<HTML><BODY BGCOLOR=" & DQ & "#FFCCCC" & DQ & ">"
8:TheGoods.Write "<FONT FACE=arial SIZE=2><CENTER>"
```

*Example 16-3. The ShowPage Procedure (continued)*

```
 9:
10:TheGoods.Write "<TABLE WIDTH=90%>"
11:TheGoods.Write "<TR><TD><IMG SRC=" & Graphic(ProductNumber) & "></TD>"
12:TheGoods.Write "<TD VALIGN=TOP ALIGN=LEFT><FONT SIZE=2>"
13:TheGoods.Write "<H3>" & Products(ProductNumber) & "</H3>"
14:TheGoods.Write "<B>Description:</B><BR>"
15:TheGoods.Write Description(ProductNumber)
16:TheGoods.Write "</TD></TR></TABLE>"
17:
18:TheGoods.Write "<BLOCKQUOTE></CENTER>"
19:TheGoods.Write "<B>Catalog No.:</B> " & CatNos(ProductNumber) & "<P>"
20:TheGoods.Write "<FORM NAME=addtoOrder>"
21:TheGoods.Write "<B>" & OptionHeading(ProductNumber) & ": </B>"
22:
23:For opt = 1 to NoOfOptions(ProductNumber)
24:   TheGoods.Write "<INPUT TYPE=radio LANGUAGE="
25:   TheGoods.Write DQ & "vbscript" & DQ
26:   TheGoods.Write " OnClick=" & DQ & "Parent.Cart2.DoOption("
27:   TheGoods.Write "&quot;" & Options(ProductNumber,opt)
28:   TheGoods.Write "&quot;" & ")" & DQ
29:   If opt = 1 Then
30:      TheGoods.Write " CHECKED>"
31:   Else
32:      TheGoods.Write ">"
33:   End If
34:   TheGoods.Write Options(ProductNumber,opt)
35:   TheGoods.Write " "
36:Next
37:
38:TheGoods.Write "<P><B>ONLY $" & FormatNumber(Price(ProductNumber), 2)
39:TheGoods.Write "</B> per " & Per(ProductNumber) & "<P>"
40:TheGoods.Write "<CENTER>Quantity to order  <INPUT TYPE=text"
41:TheGoods.Write " NAME=qty SIZE=6>"
42:TheGoods.Write "<INPUT TYPE=BUTTON LANGUAGE=" & DQ & "vbscript" & DQ
43:TheGoods.Write " ONCLICK=" & DQ & "Parent.Cart2.DoOrder("
44:TheGoods.Write ProductNumber
45:TheGoods.Write ")" & DQ & " VALUE=" & DQ & "Add To Order" & DQ & ">"
46:TheGoods.Write "</FORM>"
47:TheGoods.Write "</CENTER></BODY></HTML>"
48:TheGoods.Close
49:CurrentOption = Options(ProductNumber,1)
50:End Sub
```

# Handling the Customer's Order

Although an important major goal of any shopping cart application is to provide an attractive catalog that the user can browse, it also has an even more important business objective: it serves as a medium for selling the products produced or distributed by the business. In this section, we'll look at the code that allows the user to add an item to his or her order, to view the order in its current state, and to delete an item from the order.

---

### Dynamic Arrays, Data Validation, and Browser Objects

If you'd like to review the REDIM statement and its use in redimensioning arrays dynamically, see Chapter 3. Browser objects and the *Alert* method, which displays a message dialog, are covered in Chapter 5. To review the SET statement, as well as the *MsgBox* and *IsNumeric* functions, and more generally to refresh your memory about techniques for data validation, see Chapter 14. For the *Status* property and the *SetTimeOut* method, which are used to inform the user that an item has been successfully added to the order, see Chapter 11, *Describing Your Hyperlinks*. Finally, if you're unsure how to use VBScript and the *Document.Write* method to generate HTML pages on the fly, see Chapter 13.

---

## Adding an Item to the Order

Along with ordering an item, the user has to indicate which variant of a particular item he or she wants to order, by selecting a product option. Let's take a look at how this product option is handled before we actually examine how the user goes about placing an order for a product.

You may remember from "Displaying the Product Details Page" that, as the product page loads into the right-hand frame, that product's default option is assigned to the *CurrentOption* global variable. If the user clicks one of the option buttons, its event handler calls the *DoOption* procedure, passing it the option name. As you can see, the *DoOption* procedure, which is shown in Example 16-4, is very simple: it assigns the name of the option that the user has clicked to the *CurrentOption* global variable. This way of determining which option has been clicked is preferable to the alternative, which is to check all option buttons for a *Checked* property of True.

*Example 16-4. The DoOption Procedure*

```
1:Sub DoOption(TheOption)
2:    CurrentOption = TheOption
3:End Sub
```

When the user decides to order an item, he or she enters the quantity in the Quantity to order text box and clicks the Add To Order button. The button's event handler calls the *DoOrder* custom procedure shown in Example 16-5. Lines 2 to 4 declare local variables. Line 6 assigns a reference to the form on the product details page to one of the local variables, *OrderForm*. Lines 8 through 11 verify that the data entered into the Quantity to order text box are a number; if not, a warning message is shown, and the procedure ends. Line 13 converts the number to a variant of subtype Double and checks to make sure it is neither zero nor negative; if it is, a message is displayed and the procedure ends. Lines 20 through 22 check the order array for the current product and option combination, since only one line item of the order can contain a particular product and option combination. If the item is already on order, the user is prompted—in line 30—to indicate whether he or she wants to replace the quantity already on order with the number he or she has just entered in the text box. The user can click the Yes button to modify the order, and can cancel the transaction by clicking No or Cancel. If the user clicks Yes, line 32 replaces the order quantity stored in the *ordQty* array with the new order quantity, and the procedure exits in line 34.

If the data validation routines do not detect a possible error, the procedure continues to execute at line 39, where the *CurrentOrderLine* global variable is incremented. Lines 40 to 42 dynamically increase the size of the order arrays to the new value of *CurrentOrderLine*, and lines 44 to 46 assign the order data to the order arrays. Lines 48 to 50 then show a message in the status bar for 3 seconds, to let the user know that the new item has been added to the order.

*Example 16-5. The DoOrder Procedure*

```
1:Sub DoOrder(ProductNo)
2:Dim msg, stat
3:Dim response, t
4:Dim OrderForm
5:
6:Set OrderForm = Parent.goods.Document.addtoOrder
7:
8:If Not IsNumeric(OrderForm.qty.value) Then
9:   Alert "Quantity must be a number"
10:   Exit Sub
11:End If
12:
13:If CDbl(OrderForm.qty.value) <= 0 Then
14:   msg = "Quantity cannot be 0 or less" & vbCrLf
15:   msg = msg & "To remove a line item go to View Order"
16:   Alert msg
17:   Exit Sub
18:End If
19:
20:If CurrentOrderLine > 0 Then
21:   For i = 1 to CurrentOrderLine
22:      If ordProdNo(i) = ProductNo And ordOption(i) = CurrentOption Then
23:         msg = "You already have "
24:         msg = msg & ordQty(i)
25:         msg = msg & " of this item on order " & vbCrLf
26:         msg = msg & "Do you want to replace the current order"
27:         msg = msg & " qty of " & ordQty(i) & vbCrLf
28:         msg = msg & "with this new qty of "
29:         msg = msg & OrderForm.qty.value & "?"
```

*Example 16-5. The DoOrder Procedure (continued)*

```
30:          response = MsgBox(msg, vbQuestion + vbYesNoCancel,"Shopping
Cart")
31:          If response = VBYES Then
32:             ordQty(i) = OrderForm.qty.value
33:          End If
34:          Exit Sub
35:       End If
36:    Next
37:End If
38:
39:CurrentOrderLine = CurrentOrderLine + 1
40:ReDim Preserve ordProdNo(CurrentOrderLine)
41:ReDim Preserve ordQty(CurrentOrderLine)
42:ReDim Preserve ordOption(CurrentOrderLine)
43:
44:ordProdNo(CurrentOrderLine) = ProductNo
45:ordQty(CurrentOrderLine) = OrderForm.qty.value
46:ordOption(CurrentOrderLine) = CurrentOption
47:
48:stat = OrderForm.qty.value & " " & CurrentOption & " "
49:stat = stat & Products(ProductNo) & " added to current order"
50:Parent.Status = stat
51:t = Parent.SetTimeout("Parent.Status=''",3000)
52:End Sub
```

## Displaying the Current Order

To view the status of the current order (or "to take a peek into the shopping basket"), the user clicks the View Order button. The browser window then resembles Figure 16-4, as the right-hand frame changes to display a summary of the goods the user has placed into the shopping basket, including the name, quantity, price per unit of issue, and dollar amount of each item ordered. At the end of each line item is a button that allows the user to remove that line from the order. The code responsible for displaying the current order, the *ShowOrder_Click* event procedure, appears in Example 16-6.

Notice that the event procedure is named *ShowOrder_Click*, rather than *ShowOrder_OnClick*. That's because the View Order button, like the other four main menu buttons, is an ActiveX control. Therefore, a click generates a *Click* event instead of the *OnClick* event that's generated by clicking an HTML button.

Lines 2 and 3 of the *ShowOrder_Click* event procedure declare local variables. Lines 5 to 9 check whether there are any items in the order. If not, a message is displayed, the opening image is reloaded into the frame, and the procedure terminates. If there are items in the order, line 11 assigns a reference to the document in the right-hand frame to a local variable named *TheGoods*, and line 12 initializes the *OrderTotal* variable.

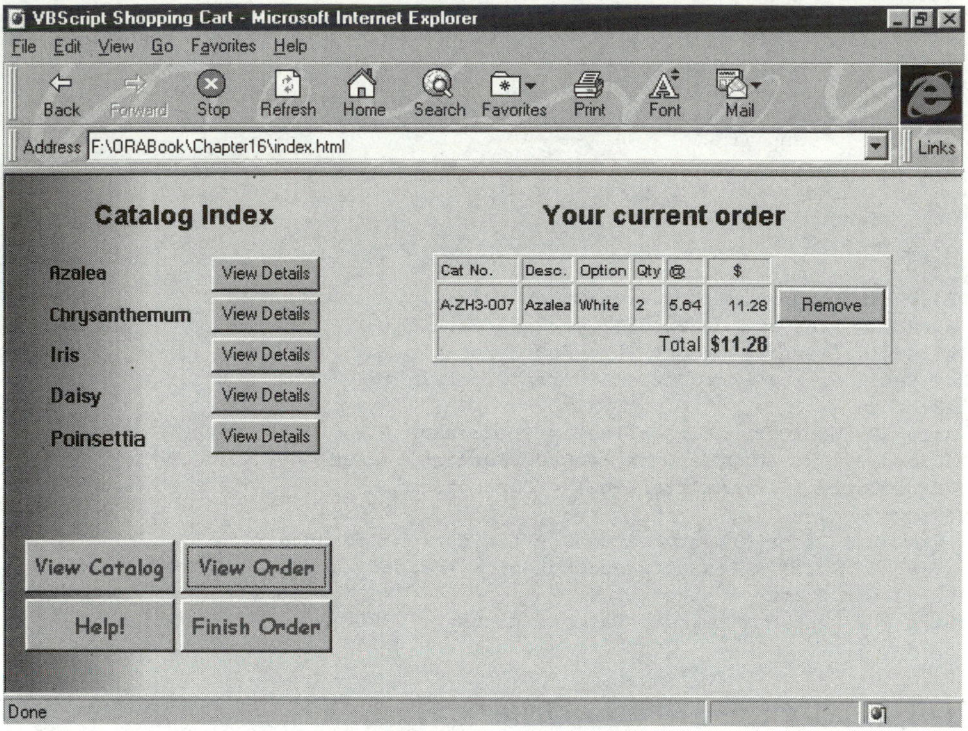

*Figure 16-4. Displaying the contents of the shopping cart*

Line 14 opens the document buffer by using the object reference. Lines 15 to 25 set up the header row of the table used to summarize the order. Line 27 initializes a loop that repeats as many times as there are line items in the order. Lines 28 to 36 display the information for each line item. Lines 37 to 41 create the HTML code for the button that can be clicked to remove a line item. One of the lines of the HTML source that is created by these lines of code, for instance, is the following:

```
<INPUT TYPE=button VALUE=Remove LANGUAGE="vbscript"
       ONCLICK="Parent.Cart2.RemoveOrderLine(1)">
```

Lines 44 to 48 write the HTML code for the order total at the foot of the order summary. Finally, line 49 closes the document buffer.

*Example 16-6. The ShowOrder_Click Event Procedure*

```
1:Sub ShowOrder_Click
2:Dim OrderTotal
3:Dim TheGoods
4:
5:If CurrentOrderLine = 0 Then
6:    Alert "No Goods On Order"
7:    Parent.goods.Location.hRef = "cartgoods.html"
8:    Exit Sub
```

*Example 16-6. The ShowOrder_Click Event Procedure (continued)*

```
 9:End If
10:
11:Set TheGoods = Parent.goods.Document
12:OrderTotal = 0
13:
14:TheGoods.Open
15:TheGoods.Write "<HTML><BODY BGCOLOR=" & DQ & "#FFCCCC" & DQ & ">"
16:TheGoods.Write "<FONT FACE=arial><CENTER>"
17:TheGoods.Write "<H3>Your current order</H3>"
18:TheGoods.Write "<TABLE WIDTH=90% BORDER=1><TR>"
19:TheGoods.Write TD1B & "Cat No.</TD>"
20:TheGoods.Write TD1B & "Desc.</TD>"
21:TheGoods.Write TD1B & "Option</TD>"
22:TheGoods.Write TD1B & "Qty</TD>"
23:TheGoods.Write TD1B & "@</TD>"
24:TheGoods.Write "<TD ALIGN=CENTER><FONT SIZE=1><B>"
25:TheGoods.Write "$</TD></TR>"
26:
27:For i = 1 to CurrentOrderLine
28:    TheGoods.Write "<TR>" & TD1 & CatNos(ordProdNo(i)) & "</TD>"
29:    TheGoods.Write TD1 & Products(ordProdNo(i)) & "</TD>"
30:    TheGoods.Write TD1 & OrdOption(i) & "</TD>"
31:    TheGoods.Write TD1 & ordQty(i) & "</TD>"
32:    TheGoods.Write TD1 & FormatNumber(Price(ordProdNo(i)), 2)
33:    TheGoods.Write "</TD><TD ALIGN=RIGHT><FONT SIZE=1>"
34:    LineTotal = ordQty(i) * Price(ordProdNo(i))
35:    OrderTotal = OrderTotal + LineTotal
36:    TheGoods.Write FormatNumber(LineTotal, 2) & "</TD>"
37:    TheGoods.Write "<TD><INPUT TYPE=button VALUE=Remove"
38:    TheGoods.Write " LANGUAGE=" & DQ & "vbscript" & DQ
39:    TheGoods.Write " ONCLICK=" & DQ & "Parent.Cart2.RemoveOrderLine("
40:    TheGoods.Write i
41:    TheGoods.Write ")" & DQ & "></TD></TR>"
42:Next
43:
44:TheGoods.Write "<TR><TD COLSPAN=5 ALIGN=RIGHT><FONT SIZE=2>"
45:        TheGoods.Write "Total</TD><TD ALIGN=RIGHT><FONT SIZE=2><B>"
46:        TheGoods.Write "$" & FormatNumber(OrderTotal, 2)
47:        TheGoods.Write "</TD><TR>"
48:        TheGoods.Write "</TABLE></CENTER></BODY></HTML>"
49:    TheGoods.Close
50:End Sub
```

## Removing an Item from the Order

If the user clicks one of the "Remove" buttons on the order summary, the *Remove-OrderLine* procedure, which is shown in Example 16-7, is called, and the number of the line to be removed is passed to the procedure. Line 2 declares a local variable.

Line 4 determines whether the line to be removed is *not* the last line of the order. If it is not, the line items that follow the deleted item must be moved up one position, a process handled by the loop from line 5 to line 9. (If it is the last line, the loop is skipped, and execution continues at line 12.) Line 5 initializes the loop, which begins by processing the line immediately after the deleted line and ends with the last line of the order. Lines 6 to 8 assign the line's item data to the preceding line item.

In line 12, the *CurrentOrderLine* variable, which indicates the total number of items in the order, is reduced by one. Lines 13 to 15 reduce the size of the order arrays by 1, to match the new value of *CurrentOrderLine*. Finally, line 16 refreshes the order summary on screen by calling the *ShowOrder_Click* event procedure.

*Example 16-7. The RemoveOrderLine procedure*

```
 1:Sub RemoveOrderLine(ByVal LineNumber)
 2:Dim i
 3:
 4:If LineNumber < CurrentOrderLine Then
 5:    For i = LineNumber + 1 To CurrentOrderLine
 6:        ordProdNo(i-1) = ordProdNo(i)
 7:        ordQty(i-1) = ordQty(i)
 8:        ordOption(i-1) = ordOption(i)
 9:    Next
10:End If
11:
12:CurrentOrderLine = CurrentOrderLine - 1
13:ReDim Preserve ordProdNo(CurrentOrderLine)
14:ReDim Preserve ordQty(CurrentOrderLine)
15:ReDim Preserve ordOption(CurrentOrderLine)
16:Call ShowOrder_Click()
17:End Sub
```

# Submitting the Order to the Server

By browsing the catalog and order items, the user has only indicated what should be ordered, but not where it should be sent or how it will be paid for. This means that, once the user is satisfied with his or her selection of goods, these details should be added to the order, which should then be sent to the server. Two separate procedures are used to handle this aspect of the shopping cart. First of all, an input form is created. When the user clicks the Submit button, the details are transferred from the form to hidden fields in the main script document, and a message box is shown to the user for confirmation. Once that confirmation is received, the data is submitted to the server.

## Dynamic Web Pages, Data Validation, and Error Handling

If you don't fully understand the code in this section, you might want to review the *Document.Write* method, which is used by a script to build web pages on the fly, in Chapter 13. Data validation, including the *UCase* and *MsgBox* functions, is covered in Chapter 14. Finally, the `On Error Resue Next` statement, as well as approaches to error handling, are treated in Chapter 15, *Error Handling and Debugging*.

## The Customer Details Form

When the user clicks the Finish Order button (which is an ActiveX control named *CompleteOrder*), its *Click* event handler, which is shown in Example 16-8, is executed. Lines 3 to 6 make sure that the order contains line items, and that therefore an order is in progress. Line 8 assigns a reference to the document in the right-hand (goods) frame to a local variable, *TheGoods*. Line 10 opens the document buffer to accept output from the *Write* method. Lines 11 to 37 create an HTML table for improved formatting, an HTML form, and its form objects. Lines 38 to 40 define the Submit button by generating the following HTML source code:

```
<INPUT LANGUAGE="vbscript" TYPE=button
ONCLICK="Parent.Cart2.SubmitOrder()" VALUE=Submit>
```

Finally, lines 41 and 42 complete the HTML document and close the document buffer, writing the form document to the right-hand frame, as in Figure 16-5.

*Example 16-8. The CompleteOrder_Click Event Procedure*

```
 1:Sub CompleteOrder_Click
 2:
 3:If CurrentOrderLine = 0 Then
 4:   Alert "No Goods On Order"
 5:   Exit Sub
 6:End If
 7:
 8:Set TheGoods = Parent.goods.Document
 9:
10:TheGoods.Open
11:TheGoods.Write "<HTML><BODY BGCOLOR=" & DQ & "#FFCCCC" & DQ & ">"
12:TheGoods.Write "<FONT FACE=arial SIZE=2><CENTER>"
13:TheGoods.Write "<H3>Order Form</H3>"
14:TheGoods.Write "Please complete all fields then press Submit"
15:TheGoods.Write "<CENTER><P><FORM NAME=orderdetails><TABLE>"
16:TheGoods.Write "<TR>" & TD2 & "Name</TD>"
17:TheGoods.Write "<TD><INPUT TYPE=text NAME=name SIZE=40></TD></TR>"
18:TheGoods.Write "<TR>" & TD2 & "Street</TD>"
19:TheGoods.Write "<TD><INPUT TYPE=text NAME=street SIZE=30></TD></TR>"
20:TheGoods.Write "<TR>" & TD2 & "City</TD>"
21:TheGoods.Write "<TD><INPUT TYPE=text NAME=city></TD></TR>"
```

*Example 16-8. The CompleteOrder_Click Event Procedure (continued)*

```
22:TheGoods.Write "<TR>" & TD2 & "State</TD>"
23:TheGoods.Write "<TD><INPUT TYPE=text NAME=state></TD></TR>"
24:TheGoods.Write "<TR>" & TD2 & "Zip</TD>"
25:TheGoods.Write "<TD><INPUT TYPE=text NAME=zip></TD></TR>"
26:TheGoods.Write "<TR>" & TD2 & "Telephone</TD>"
27:TheGoods.Write "<TD><INPUT TYPE=text NAME=telephone></TD></TR>"
28:TheGoods.Write "<TR>" & TD2 & "Credit Card Type</TD>"
29:TheGoods.Write "<TD><SELECT NAME=crcard>"
30:TheGoods.Write "<OPTION>American Express"
31:TheGoods.Write "<OPTION>MasterCard"
32:TheGoods.Write "<OPTION>Visa</SELECT></TD></TR>"
33:TheGoods.Write "<TR>" & TD2 & "Card Number</TD>"
34:TheGoods.Write "<TD><INPUT TYPE=text NAME=cardnumber SIZE=30></TD></TR>"
35:TheGoods.Write "<TR>" & TD2 & "Expiration Date</TD>"
36:TheGoods.Write "<TD><INPUT TYPE=text NAME=expirydate SIZE=10></TD></TR>"
37:TheGoods.Write "</TABLE></FORM>"
38:TheGoods.Write "<INPUT LANGUAGE=" & DQ & "vbscript" & DQ
39:TheGoods.Write " TYPE=button ONCLICK=" & DQ &
"Parent.Cart2.SubmitOrder()"
40:TheGoods.Write DQ & " VALUE=Submit>"
41:TheGoods.Write "</BODY></HTML>"
42:TheGoods.Close
43:End Sub
```

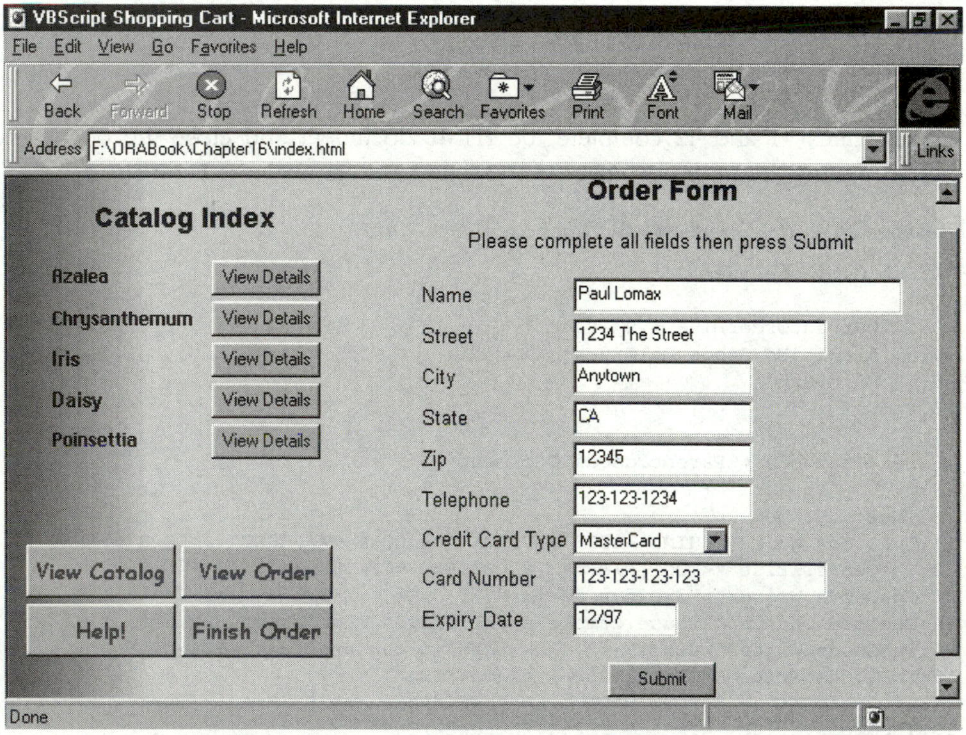

*Figure 16-5. The customer details form*

# *Submitting the Order to the Server*

When the user clicks the Submit button (which is actually a normal HTML button, and not an HTML Submit button), its event handler calls the *SubmitOrder* procedure, which is shown in Example 16-9.

Line 2 of the procedure instructs the scripting engine that, if an error occurs, it should continue executing the procedure at the line following the error. This error handling statement is necessary because the procedure later references the name and value properties of every object within the form in the right-hand frame. Some intrinsic HTML objects that are used in the form don't have a *Value* property, however, which means that references to them generate a run-time error. The ON ERROR statement ensures that error handling goes unseen by the user, and allows program execution to occur without interruption.

Line 9 assigns a reference to the form in the right-hand frame to a local variable, *TheDetails*, and line 10 assigns a reference to the form held within the main script document *CARTMAIN.HTML* to a local variable, *TheOrder*. Lines 14 to 21 check that the user has entered data into each text box in the input form; if a text box is empty, an error message is generated, and the procedure terminates.

Lines 23 to 40 create a message box like the one shown in Figure 16-6 that contains all the user and order details and asks the user to confirm that the order can be submitted to the server. Lines 40 to 44 handle the response from the user. If the user clicks the Yes button, execution continues at line 46; otherwise, a message is displayed and the procedure terminates.

Lines 46 to 54 assign the values entered in the form by the user to the hidden form in the main script document.

Lines 55 to 57 create a single text string for each of the three arrays, *ordProdNo*, *ordQty*, and *ordOption*, using the VBScript 2.0 function *Join*. When the string arrives at the server, it will be dissected by a server-side VBScript application using the *Split* function, which is the converse of *Join*. The strings produced by the *Join* function calls are immediately assigned to the relevant hidden HTML text controls.

Finally, line 58 (which has been disabled in this example) submits the data to the server.

*Example 16-9. The SubmitOrder Procedure*

```
1:Sub SubmitOrder()
2:On Error Resume Next
3:
4:If CurrentOrderLine = 0 Then
5:   Alert "No Goods On Order"
```

*Example 16-9. The SubmitOrder Procedure (continued)*

```
 6:    Exit Sub
 7:End If
 8:
 9:Set TheDetails = Parent.goods.Document.orderdetails
10:Set TheOrder = Document.finalorder
11:
12:selndx = TheDetails.crcard.selectedindex
13:
14:For i = 0 to TheDetails.Elements.length - 1
15:    If TheDetails.Elements(i).Name <> "crcard" Then
16:        If TheDetails.Elements(i).Value  = "" Then
17:            Reject(TheDetails.Elements(i).Name)
18:            Exit Sub
19:        End If
20:    End if
21:Next
22:
23:msg = "Ready to Submit the Following Order" & vbCrLf
24:For i = 0 to TheDetails.Elements.length - 1
25:    If TheDetails.Elements(i).Name <> "crcard" Then
26:        msg = msg & UCase(TheDetails.Elements(i).Name) & ": "
27:        msg = msg & TheDetails.Elements(i).Value & vbCrLf
28:    End If
29:Next
30:msg = msg & "Credit Card Type: "
31:msg = msg & TheDetails.crcard.options(selndx).text
32:msg = msg & vbCrLf & String(20,"=") & vbCrLf & vbCrLf
33:For i = 1 to CurrentOrderLine
34:    msg = msg & Products(ordProdNo(i)) & " "
35:    msg = msg & OrdOption(i) & " x "
36:    msg = msg & ordQty(i) & vbCrLf
37:Next
38:msg = msg & vbCrLf & "Do you wish to continue?"
39:
40:response = MsgBox(msg, 67, "Confirm Submission of Order")
41:If response = VBNO Or response = VBCANCEL Then
42:    Alert "Submission Cancelled"
43:    Exit Sub
44:End If
45:
46:TheOrder.name.Value = TheDetails.name.Value
47:TheOrder.street.Value = TheDetails.street.Value
48:TheOrder.city.Value = TheDetails.city.Value
49:TheOrder.state.Value = TheDetails.state.Value
50:TheOrder.zip.Value = TheDetails.zip.Value
51:TheOrder.telno.Value = TheDetails.telephone.Value
52:TheOrder.cctype.Value = TheDetails.crcard.options(selndx).text
53:TheOrder.ccno.Value = TheDetails.cardnumber.value
54:TheOrder.ccexp.Value = TheDetails.expirydate.value
55:TheOrder.ProdData.Value = Join(ordProdNo, "|")
56:TheOrder.QtyData.Value = Join(ordQty, "|")
57:TheOrder.OptionData.Value = Join(ordOption, "|")
```

*Example 16-9. The SubmitOrder Procedure (continued)*

```
58:'TheOrder.Submit
59:End Sub
```

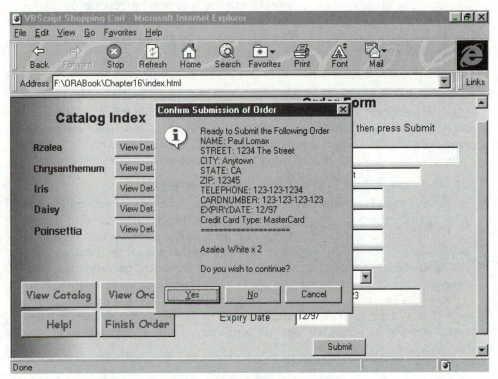

*Figure 16-6. Confirming customer and order details*

If the form validation in the *SubmitOrder* procedure finds an empty field, the *Reject* procedure shown in Example 16-10 is called, and the name of the field containing invalid data is passed to it.

*Example 16-10. The Reject Procedure*

```
1:Sub Reject(ByVal FieldName)
2:Dim msg
3:    msg = "Sorry, we cannot accept this order " & vbCrLf
4:    msg = msg & "without details entered in the " & vbCrLf
5:    msg = msg & UCase(FieldName) & " field" & vbCrLf & vbCrLf
6:    msg = msg & "Please rectify and resubmit"
7:    MsgBox msg, 48, "Error"
8:End Sub
```

---

## The Join and Split Functions

Version 2.0 of VBScript includes two functions, *Join* and *Split*, that are ideal for formatting a string of data to be submitted to a server for processing, or for handling a string of data retrieved from a server or from a cookie. *Join* combines data from a variety of substrings (or variables) into a single string, and allows you to specify a delimiter for each item. Its syntax is:

```
Join(list[, delimiter]
```

where *list* is an array containing the data to be joined, and *delimiter* is an optional argument indicating the character to serve as a delimiter. If *delimiter* is not provided, the space character (" ") is used instead. The function returns a single string containing all the substrings indicated by *list*. *Split* allows you to store a single delimited string to the elements of an array. Its syntax is:

```
Split(expression[, delimiter[, count[, compare]]])
```

where *expression* is the string containing the concatenated substrings, *delimiter* is an optional argument that indicates the character used to delimit each substring, *count* is an optional argument that determines the number of substrings to extract from *expression*, and *compare* is an optional constant (its value can be either **vbBinaryCompare** or **vbTextCompare**) that indicates the type of comparison to be used in evaluating *expression*. If *delimiter* is not provided, it defaults to the space (" ") character; if *compare* is not provided, it defaults to **vbTextCompare**. The function returns a one-dimensional string array containing the substring extracted from *expression*.

---

# Source Code for Shopping Cart Example

In discussing the shopping cart example, I've broken down the application into discrete functions and subroutines (and numbered each line of code) to give you a sense of how the application works. What follows is the complete source code for the shopping cart application, without line numbers and including comments.

## INDEX.HTML: The Frameset Document

```
<HTML>
<HEAD>
<TITLE>VBScript Shopping Cart</TITLE>
</HEAD>
<FRAMESET COLS="40%,60%" FRAMEBORDER=0 FRAMESPACING=0>
 <FRAMESET ROWS="65%,35%" FRAMEBORDER=0 FRAMESPACING=0>
  <FRAME NAME="cart" SRC="prodndx.html" RESIZE=NO>
  <FRAME NAME="cart2" SRC="cartmain.html" RESIZE=NO>
 </FRAMESET>
 <FRAME NAME="goods" SRC="cartgoods.html">
</FRAMESET>
</HTML>
```

## *The Main Menu and the Application Script: CARTMAIN.HTML*

Here's the complete source for the main script document, *CARTMAIN.HTML*. This HTML document is responsible for displaying the main menu (which consists of four ActiveX command button controls) in the lower left frame, and contains all of the application's script.

```
<HTML>
<HEAD>
<SCRIPT LANGUAGE="vbscript">
'
'Declare Arrays to hold details of products
'
Dim Products(5)
Dim CatNos(5)
Dim Description(5)
Dim Price(5)
Dim Per(5)
Dim OptionHeading(5)
Dim NoOfOptions(5)
Dim Options(5,3)
Dim Graphic(5)


'
'Declare the arrays and global variables for the current order
'
Dim ordProdNo()
Dim ordQty()
Dim ordOption()
Dim CurrentOrderLine
Dim CurrentOption


'
'Declare global constants
'
Dim   DQ
Const TD1 = "<TD><FONT SIZE=1>"
Const TD1B = "<TD><FONT SIZE=1><B>"
Const TD2 = "<TD><FONT SIZE=2>"


'
'Initialize current order global variables
'
CurrentOption = ""
CurrentOrderLine=0


'
'Assign values to global constants
'
DQ = Chr(34)
'
'Assign values to the product details arrays
```

```
Products(1) = "Azalea"
CatNos(1) = "A-ZH3-007"
Description(1) = _
"A year-round favorite, direct from our greenhouses to your door."
Price(1) = 5.64
Per(1) = "Plant"
OptionHeading(1) = "Bloom Color"
NoOfOptions(1) = 2
Options(1,1) = "Yellow"
Options(1,2) = "White"
Graphic(1) = "Azalea.gif"

Products(2) = "Chrysanthemum"
CatNos(2) = "A-CF5-198"
Description(2) = _
"A year-round favorite, direct from our greenhouses to your door."
Price(2) = 2.59
Per(2) = "Stem"
OptionHeading(2) = "Stem Size"
NoOfOptions(2) = 3
Options(2,1) = "10in"
Options(2,2) = "14in"
Options(2,3) = "18in"
Graphic(2) = "chrys.gif"

Products(3) = "Iris"
CatNos(3) = "G-JK6-127"
Description(3) = _
"A year-round favorite, direct from our greenhouses to your door."
Price(3) = 9.99
Per(3) = "Box of 10"
OptionHeading(3) = "Bloom Color"
NoOfOptions(3) = 2
Options(3,1) = "Blue"
Options(3,2) = "Red"
Graphic(3) = "iris.gif"

Products(4) = "Daisy"
CatNos(4) = "D-ZH5-087"
Description(4) = _
"A year-round favorite, direct from our greenhouses to your door."
Price(4) = 2.20
Per(4) = "Bunch"
OptionHeading(4) = "Variety"
NoOfOptions(4) = 3
Options(4,1) = "Giant"
Options(4,2) = "Normal"
Options(4,3) = "Dwarf"
Graphic(4) = "daisy.gif"

Products(5) = "Poinsettia"
CatNos(5) = "L-LP3-123"
Description(5) = _
```

```
"A year-round favorite, direct from our greenhouses to your door."
Price(5) = 15.99
Per(5) = "Plant"
OptionHeading(5) = "Bloom Color"
NoOfOptions(5) = 2
Options(5,1) = "Red"
Options(5,2) = "White"
Graphic(5) = "poin.gif"


'========================================================================
'
'This is the event handler for the Show Catalog button
'It creates the catalog index into the top left frame
'
Sub DoIndex_Click
'declare local variables
Dim i
Dim cartndx

    'assign a reference to the document in the top left frame
    'to a local variable
    Set cartndx = Parent.Cart.Document

    'create the document
    cartndx.Open
        cartndx.Write "<HTML><BODY BACKGROUND=" & DQ & "cartbak.gif" & DQ
        cartndx.Write "><FONT FACE=" & DQ & "arial" & DQ & "SIZE=2" & ">"
        cartndx.Write "<CENTER><H3>Catalog Index</H3><P><B>"
        cartndx.Write "<TABLE>"
            For i = 1 to UBound(Products)
                cartndx.Write "<TD ALIGN=LEFT><FONT SIZE=2><B>"
                cartndx.Write Products(i) & "</TD><TD ALIGN=RIGHT>"
                cartndx.Write "<INPUT TYPE=button LANGUAGE="
                cartndx.Write DQ & "vbscript"  & DQ
                cartndx.Write " ONCLICK=" & DQ & "Parent.Cart2.ShowPage("
                cartndx.Write i
                cartndx.Write ")" & DQ & " VALUE=" & DQ & "View Details"
                cartndx.Write DQ & "><BR>"
                cartndx.Write "</TD></TR>"
            Next
        cartndx.Write "</TABLE></CENTER></BODY></HTML>"
    cartndx.Close
End Sub


'========================================================================
'
'This subroutine assigns the number of the option that has
'just been clicked, to the CurrentOption global variable
'
Sub DoOption(TheOption)
    CurrentOption = TheOption
End Sub


'========================================================================
```

```
'
'This subroutine is called by the Add To Order button on the
'product details page. It adds a new line to the current
'order
'
Sub DoOrder(ProductNo)
'declare local variables
Dim msg, stat
Dim response, t
Dim OrderForm

'assign the form object in the right frame to a variable
Set OrderForm = Parent.goods.Document.addtoOrder

'check that a number has been entered
If Not IsNumeric(OrderForm.qty.value) Then
    Alert "Quantity must be a number"
    Exit Sub
    End If

'check that the number is positive
If CDbl(OrderForm.qty.value) <= 0 Then
    msg = "Quantity cannot be 0 or less" & vbCrLf
    msg = msg & "To remove a line item go to View Order"
    Alert msg
    Exit Sub
End If

'only one line item for the same product and option combination
'can be accepted, if the combination already exists in the order
'check that the user wants to replace the current qty
If CurrentOrderLine > 0 Then
    For i = 1 to CurrentOrderLine
        If ordProdNo(i) = ProductNo And ordOption(i) = CurrentOption Then
            msg = "You already have "
            msg = msg & ordQty(i)
            msg = msg & " of this item on order " & vbCrLf
            msg = msg & "Do you want to replace the current order"
            msg = msg & " qty of " & ordQty(i) & vbCrLf
            msg = msg & "with this new qty of "
            msg = msg & OrderForm.qty.value & "?"
            response = MsgBox(msg,vbQuestion + vbYesNoCancel, _
                        "Shopping Cart")
                If response = VBYES Then
                    ordQty(i) = OrderForm.qty.value
                End If
                Exit Sub
        End If
    Next
End If


'increase the order arrays by 1
CurrentOrderLine = CurrentOrderLine + 1
```

```
ReDim Preserve ordProdNo(CurrentOrderLine)
ReDim Preserve ordQty(CurrentOrderLine)
ReDim Preserve ordOption(CurrentOrderLine)

'assign the order values to the array
ordProdNo(CurrentOrderLine) = ProductNo
ordQty(CurrentOrderLine) = OrderForm.qty.value
ordOption(CurrentOrderLine) = CurrentOption

'show a message in the status bar
stat = OrderForm.qty.value & " " & CurrentOption & " "
stat = stat & Products(ProductNo) & " added to current order"
Parent.Status = stat
t = Parent.SetTimeout("Parent.Status=''",3000)
End Sub

'=======================================================================
'
'This subroutine is called by the View Details button next to
'the product name in the Catalog Index. It creates a page for
'the product in the right-hand frame
'
Sub ShowPage(ProductNumber)
'declare local variables
Dim TheGoods

'assign the document in the right frame to a local variable
Set TheGoods = Parent.goods.Document

TheGoods.Open
    TheGoods.Write "<HTML><BODY BGCOLOR=" & DQ & "#FFCCCC" & DQ & ">"
    TheGoods.Write "<FONT FACE=arial SIZE=2><CENTER>"

    TheGoods.Write "<TABLE WIDTH=90%>"
  TheGoods.Write "<TR><TD><IMG SRC=" & Graphic(ProductNumber) & "></TD>"
    TheGoods.Write "<TD VALIGN=TOP ALIGN=LEFT><FONT SIZE=2>"
    TheGoods.Write "<H3>" & Products(ProductNumber) & "</H3>"
    TheGoods.Write "<B>Description:</B><BR>"
    TheGoods.Write Description(ProductNumber)
    TheGoods.Write "</TD></TR></TABLE>"

    TheGoods.Write "<BLOCKQUOTE></CENTER>"
    TheGoods.Write "<B>Catalog No.:</B> " & CatNos(ProductNumber) & "<P>"
    TheGoods.Write "<FORM NAME=addtoOrder>"
    TheGoods.Write "<INPUT TYPE=hidden NAME=productno "
    TheGoods.Write "VALUE=" & ProductNumber & ">"
    TheGoods.Write "<B>" & OptionHeading(ProductNumber) & ": </B>"

        For opt = 1 to NoOfOptions(ProductNumber)
            TheGoods.Write "<INPUT TYPE=radio LANGUAGE="
            TheGoods.Write DQ & "vbscript" & DQ
            TheGoods.Write " OnClick=" & DQ & "Parent.Cart2.DoOption("
            TheGoods.Write "&quot;" & Options(ProductNumber,opt)
            TheGoods.Write "&quot;" & ")" & DQ
```

```
                    If opt = 1 Then
                        TheGoods.Write " CHECKED>"
                    Else
                        TheGoods.Write ">"
                    End If
                TheGoods.Write Options(ProductNumber,opt)
                TheGoods.Write " "
            Next


    TheGoods.Write "<P><B>ONLY $" & FormatNumber(Price(ProductNumber), 2)
    TheGoods.Write "</B> per " & Per(ProductNumber) & "<P>"
    TheGoods.Write "<CENTER>Quantity to order  <INPUT TYPE=text"
    TheGoods.Write " NAME=qty SIZE=6>"
    TheGoods.Write "<INPUT TYPE=BUTTON LANGUAGE=" & DQ & "vbscript" & DQ
    TheGoods.Write " ONCLICK=" & DQ & "Parent.Cart2.DoOrder("
    TheGoods.Write ProductNumber
    TheGoods.Write ")" & DQ & " VALUE=" & DQ & "Add To Order" & DQ & ">"
    TheGoods.Write "</FORM>"
    TheGoods.Write "</CENTER></BODY></HTML>"
TheGoods.Close
CurrentOption = Options(ProductNumber,1)
End Sub


'=================================================
'
'The following event handler is attached to the View Current
'Order button. It creates a detailed list of the current order
'in the right-hand frame
'
Sub ShowOrder_Click
Dim OrderTotal
Dim TheGoods

If CurrentOrderLine = 0 Then
    Alert "No Goods On Order"
    Parent.goods.Location.hRef = "cartgoods.html"
    Exit Sub
End If

Set TheGoods = Parent.goods.Document
OrderTotal = 0

TheGoods.Open
TheGoods.Write "<HTML><BODY BGCOLOR=" & DQ & "#FFCCCC" & DQ & ">"
TheGoods.Write "<FONT FACE=arial><CENTER>"
TheGoods.Write "<H3>Your current order</H3>"
TheGoods.Write "<TABLE WIDTH=90% BORDER=1><TR>"
TheGoods.Write TD1B & "Cat No.</TD>"
TheGoods.Write TD1B & "Desc.</TD>"
TheGoods.Write TD1B & "Option</TD>"
TheGoods.Write TD1B & "Qty</TD>"
TheGoods.Write TD1B & "@</TD>"
TheGoods.Write "<TD ALIGN=CENTER><FONT SIZE=1><B>"
TheGoods.Write "$</TD></TR>"
```

```
    For i = 1 to CurrentOrderLine
        TheGoods.Write "<TR>" & TD1 & CatNos(ordProdNo(i)) & "</TD>"
        TheGoods.Write TD1 & Products(ordProdNo(i)) & "</TD>"
        TheGoods.Write TD1 & OrdOption(i) & "</TD>"
        TheGoods.Write TD1 & ordQty(i) & "</TD>"
        TheGoods.Write TD1 & FormatNumber(Price(ordProdNo(i)), 2)
        TheGoods.Write "</TD><TD ALIGN=RIGHT><FONT SIZE=1>"
            LineTotal = ordQty(i) * Price(ordProdNo(i))
            OrderTotal = OrderTotal + LineTotal
        TheGoods.Write FormatNumber(LineTotal, 2) & "</TD>"
        TheGoods.Write "<TD><INPUT TYPE=button VALUE=Remove"
        TheGoods.Write " LANGUAGE=" & DQ & "vbscript" & DQ
        TheGoods.Write " ONCLICK=" & DQ & "Parent.Cart2.RemoveOrderLine("
        TheGoods.Write i
        TheGoods.Write ")" & DQ & "></TD></TR>"
    Next

TheGoods.Write "<TR><TD COLSPAN=5 ALIGN=RIGHT><FONT SIZE=2>"
TheGoods.Write "Total</TD><TD ALIGN=RIGHT><FONT SIZE=2><B>"
TheGoods.Write "$" & FormatNumber(OrderTotal, 2)
TheGoods.Write "</TD><TR>"
TheGoods.Write "</TABLE></CENTER></BODY></HTML>"
TheGoods.Close
End Sub


'==========================================================
'
'This event handler is attached to the Finish Order button.
'It builds an input form in the right-hand frame for the user
'to enter their personal details
'
Sub CompleteOrder_Click

    If CurrentOrderLine = 0 Then
        Alert "No Goods On Order"
        Exit Sub
    End If

    Set TheGoods = Parent.goods.Document

    TheGoods.Open
        TheGoods.Write "<HTML><BODY BGCOLOR=" & DQ & "#FFCCCC" & DQ & ">"
        TheGoods.Write "<FONT FACE=arial SIZE=2><CENTER>"
        TheGoods.Write "<H3>Order Form</H3>"
        TheGoods.Write "Please complete all fields then press Submit"
        TheGoods.Write "<CENTER><P><FORM NAME=orderdetails><TABLE>"
        TheGoods.Write "<TR>" & TD2 & "Name</TD>"
        TheGoods.Write "<TD><INPUT TYPE=text NAME=name SIZE=40></TD></TR>"
        TheGoods.Write "<TR>" & TD2 & "Street</TD>"
        TheGoods.Write _
                "<TD><INPUT TYPE=text NAME=street SIZE=30></TD></TR>"
        TheGoods.Write "<TR>" & TD2 & "City</TD>"
        TheGoods.Write "<TD><INPUT TYPE=text NAME=city></TD></TR>"
```

```
          TheGoods.Write "<TR>" & TD2 & "State</TD>"
          TheGoods.Write "<TD><INPUT TYPE=text NAME=state></TD></TR>"
          TheGoods.Write "<TR>" & TD2 & "Zip</TD>"
          TheGoods.Write "<TD><INPUT TYPE=text NAME=zip></TD></TR>"
          TheGoods.Write "<TR>" & TD2 & "Telephone</TD>"
          TheGoods.Write "<TD><INPUT TYPE=text NAME=telephone></TD></TR>"
          TheGoods.Write "<TR>" & TD2 & "Credit Card Type</TD>"
          TheGoods.Write "<TD><SELECT NAME=crcard>"
          TheGoods.Write "<OPTION>American Express"
          TheGoods.Write "<OPTION>MasterCard"
          TheGoods.Write "<OPTION>Visa</SELECT></TD></TR>"
          TheGoods.Write "<TR>" & TD2 & "Card Number</TD>"
          TheGoods.Write _
                  "<TD><INPUT TYPE=text NAME=cardnumber SIZE=30></TD></TR>"
          TheGoods.Write "<TR>" & TD2 & "Expiration Date</TD>"
          TheGoods.Write _
                  "<TD><INPUT TYPE=text NAME=expirydate SIZE=10></TD></TR>"
          TheGoods.Write "</TABLE></FORM>"
          TheGoods.Write "<INPUT LANGUAGE=" & DQ & "vbscript" & DQ
          TheGoods.Write " TYPE=button ONCLICK=" & DQ & _
          "Parent.Cart2.SubmitOrder()"
          TheGoods.Write DQ & " VALUE=Submit>"
          TheGoods.Write "</BODY></HTML>"
TheGoods.Close
End Sub


'==============================================================================
'
'This subroutine is used by the validation routine in the
'input form, to display an error message to the user.
'
Sub Reject(ByVal FieldName)
Dim msg
    msg = "Sorry, we cannot accept this order " & vbCrLf
    msg = msg & "without details entered in the " & vbCrLf
    msg = msg & UCase(FieldName) & " field" & vbCrLf & vbCrLf
    msg = msg & "Please rectify and resubmit"
    MsgBox msg, 48, "Error"
End Sub


'==============================================================================
'
'This subroutine is called by the Remove button on the
'order summary. It removes the particular line from the
'current order.
'
Sub RemoveOrderLine(ByVal LineNumber)
Dim i

    If LineNumber < CurrentOrderLine Then
        For i = LineNumber + 1 To CurrentOrderLine
            ordProdNo(i-1) = ordProdNo(i)
            ordQty(i-1) = ordQty(i)
            ordOption(i-1) = ordOption(i)
```

```
            Next
        End If

        CurrentOrderLine = CurrentOrderLine - 1
        ReDim Preserve ordProdNo(CurrentOrderLine)
        ReDim Preserve ordQty(CurrentOrderLine)
        ReDim Preserve ordOption(CurrentOrderLine)
        Call ShowOrder_Click()
End Sub

'================================================================
'
'This subroutine is called by the Submit button on the user details
'input form. It checks that the user has entered all the fields and
'then submits the data to the server.
'
Sub SubmitOrder()
On Error Resume Next

    If CurrentOrderLine = 0 Then
        Alert "No Goods On Order"
        Exit Sub
    End If

    Set TheDetails = Parent.goods.Document.orderdetails
    Set TheOrder = Document.finalorder

    selndx = TheDetails.crcard.selectedindex

    For i = 0 to TheDetails.Elements.length - 1
        If TheDetails.Elements(i).Name <> "crcard" Then
            If TheDetails.Elements(i).Value = "" Then
                Reject(TheDetails.Elements(i).Name)
                Exit Sub
            End If
        End if
    Next

    msg = "Ready to Submit the Following Order" & vbCrLf
    For i = 0 to TheDetails.Elements.length - 1
        If TheDetails.Elements(i).Name <> "crcard" Then
            msg = msg & UCase(TheDetails.Elements(i).Name) & ": "
            msg = msg & TheDetails.Elements(i).Value & vbCrLf
        End If
    Next
    msg = msg & "Credit Card Type: "
    msg = msg & TheDetails.crcard.options(selndx).text
    msg = msg & vbCrLf & String(20,"=") & vbCrLf & vbCrLf
    For i = 1 to CurrentOrderLine
        msg = msg & Products(ordProdNo(i)) & " "
        msg = msg & OrdOption(i) & " x "
        msg = msg & ordQty(i) & vbCrLf
    Next
    msg = msg & vbCrLf & "Do you wish to continue?"
```

```
        response = MsgBox(msg, 67, "Confirm Submission of Order")
            If response = VBNO Or response = VBCANCEL Then
                Alert "Submission Canceled"
                Exit Sub
            End If


        TheOrder.name.Value = TheDetails.name.Value
        TheOrder.street.Value = TheDetails.street.Value
        TheOrder.city.Value = TheDetails.city.Value
        TheOrder.state.Value = TheDetails.state.Value
        TheOrder.zip.Value = TheDetails.zip.Value
        TheOrder.telno.Value = TheDetails.telephone.Value
        TheOrder.cctype.Value = TheDetails.crcard.options(selndx).text
        TheOrder.ccno.Value = TheDetails.cardnumber.value
        TheOrder.ccexp.Value = TheDetails.expirydate.value
        TheOrder.ProdData.Value = Join(ordProdNo, "|")
        TheOrder.QtyData.Value = Join(ordQty, "|")
        TheOrder.OptionData.Value = Join(ordOption, "|")
     'TheOrder.Submit
End Sub


'===================================================================
    '
'The following event handler is attached to the Help button
'and displays a page in the right-hand frame
    '
Sub DoHelp_Click
    Parent.goods.Location.hRef = "help.html"
End Sub


</SCRIPT>
</HEAD>
<BODY BACKGROUND="cartbak.gif">

<TABLE>
<TR><TD>
<OBJECT ID="DoIndex" WIDTH=100 HEIGHT=35
 CLASSID="CLSID:D7053240-CE69-11CD-A777-00DD01143C57">
    <PARAM NAME="ForeColor" VALUE="8388736">
    <PARAM NAME="Caption" VALUE="View Catalog">
    <PARAM NAME="Size" VALUE="3034;894">
    <PARAM NAME="FontName" VALUE="Comic Sans MS">
    <PARAM NAME="FontEffects" VALUE="1073741825">
    <PARAM NAME="FontHeight" VALUE="200">
    <PARAM NAME="FontCharSet" VALUE="0">
    <PARAM NAME="FontPitchAndFamily" VALUE="2">
    <PARAM NAME="ParagraphAlign" VALUE="3">
    <PARAM NAME="FontWeight" VALUE="700">
</OBJECT>
</TD><TD>
<OBJECT ID="ShowOrder" WIDTH=100 HEIGHT=35
 CLASSID="CLSID:D7053240-CE69-11CD-A777-00DD01143C57">
    <PARAM NAME="ForeColor" VALUE="8388736">
```

```
            <PARAM NAME="Caption" VALUE="View Order">
            <PARAM NAME="Size" VALUE="3034;894">
            <PARAM NAME="FontName" VALUE="Comic Sans MS">
            <PARAM NAME="FontEffects" VALUE="1073741825">
            <PARAM NAME="FontHeight" VALUE="200">
            <PARAM NAME="FontCharSet" VALUE="0">
            <PARAM NAME="FontPitchAndFamily" VALUE="2">
            <PARAM NAME="ParagraphAlign" VALUE="3">
            <PARAM NAME="FontWeight" VALUE="700">
    </OBJECT>
    </TD></TR>
    <TR><TD>
    <OBJECT ID="DoHelp" WIDTH=100 HEIGHT=35
     CLASSID="CLSID:D7053240-CE69-11CD-A777-00DD01143C57">
            <PARAM NAME="ForeColor" VALUE="8388736">
            <PARAM NAME="Caption" VALUE="Help!">
            <PARAM NAME="Size" VALUE="3034;894">
            <PARAM NAME="FontName" VALUE="Comic Sans MS">
            <PARAM NAME="FontEffects" VALUE="1073741825">
            <PARAM NAME="FontHeight" VALUE="200">
            <PARAM NAME="FontCharSet" VALUE="0">
            <PARAM NAME="FontPitchAndFamily" VALUE="2">
            <PARAM NAME="ParagraphAlign" VALUE="3">
            <PARAM NAME="FontWeight" VALUE="700">
    </OBJECT>
    </TD><TD>
    <OBJECT ID="CompleteOrder" WIDTH=100 HEIGHT=35
     CLASSID="CLSID:D7053240-CE69-11CD-A777-00DD01143C57">
            <PARAM NAME="ForeColor" VALUE="8388736">
            <PARAM NAME="Caption" VALUE="Finish Order">
            <PARAM NAME="Size" VALUE="3034;894">
            <PARAM NAME="FontName" VALUE="Comic Sans MS">
            <PARAM NAME="FontEffects" VALUE="1073741825">
            <PARAM NAME="FontHeight" VALUE="200">
            <PARAM NAME="FontCharSet" VALUE="0">
            <PARAM NAME="FontPitchAndFamily" VALUE="2">
            <PARAM NAME="ParagraphAlign" VALUE="3">
            <PARAM NAME="FontWeight" VALUE="700">
    </OBJECT>
    </TD></TR>
    </TABLE>
    <FORM NAME="finalorder">
    <INPUT TYPE="hidden" NAME="name">
    <INPUT TYPE="hidden" NAME="street">
    <INPUT TYPE="hidden" NAME="city">
    <INPUT TYPE="hidden" NAME="state">
    <INPUT TYPE="hidden" NAME="zip">
    <INPUT TYPE="hidden" NAME="telno">
    <INPUT TYPE="hidden" NAME="cctype">
    <INPUT TYPE="hidden" NAME="ccno">
    <INPUT TYPE="hidden" NAME="ccexp">
    <INPUT TYPE="hidden" NAME="ProdData">
    <INPUT TYPE="hidden" NAME="QtyData">
    <INPUT TYPE="hidden" NAME="OptionData">
```

```
</FORM>
</CENTER>
</BODY>
</HTML>
```

# 17

# *Handling Other Browsers*

This chapter should really be titled *Handling the Other Browser*. Certainly at the time of writing, only two browsers dominate the market: Netscape Navigator and Microsoft Internet Explorer. Many of the online services (like America Online) have struck deals with Microsoft to supply the MSIE 3.0 browser to their subscribers, which means that you do not have to worry about whether or not an AOL subscriber can see your page. Only time will tell who will eventually win "the browser wars," but one thing is certain: the MSIE browser will certainly account for a growing number of web surfers as time progresses, particularly once it becomes an integral part of the Windows operating system. However, as in the Mac/PC wars, there will still be a large enough band of ardent Netscape supporters who flatly refuse to have anything Microsoft on their machines.

At the moment, only MSIE 3.x supports ActiveX and Active Scripting, which includes VBScript. However, because of the success of ActiveX and VBScript, it seems increasingly likely that future releases of Netscape Navigator will include native support for ActiveX and Active Scripting. But for a while at least, that still leaves a very large installed base of browsers that cannot handle the cool new active content pages you have developed using VBScript. This chapter discusses your options for supporting other browsers and arms you with enough facts to allow you to make decisions about whether and how you are going to provide support for other browsers within your active content web site.

First, you'll find out how to determine which browser is calling your web page. Then, you'll learn about the various methods that are available for handling browsers that are not Microsoft Internet Explorer. But since browsers other than MSIE and Netscape Navigator now account for such a small section of the market, it is probably not really worth the time and trouble to handle other browsers. Consequently, you'll only see a brief discussion of handling these older browsers.

*TIP*            A good way of keeping up to date with the latest market penetra-
                 tion of each browser type is to make a regular visit to Browser-
                 Watch at *http://browserwatch.iworld.com/*.  The site contains up-to-
                 the-minute statistics on the state of the browser market, as well as a
                 comprehensive list of ActiveX controls.

# Determining the Browser

The key to creating a web site that either acts like a chameleon and changes to
accommodate many different types of browsers, or acts like a filter and only
allows access to ActiveX and VBScript to enabled browsers, is determining the
type of browser that's calling the page. As you will see, there are explicit methods
to check the browser type in both server-side and client-side scripts, and later on
you will see an implicit browser check. Regardless of the method that you use,
until you know what type of browser is being used, you cannot take any action.
Obviously, you could ignore the fact that there are others browsers in use that
cannot handle ActiveX and VBScript, and also ignore the fact that a sizable propor-
tion of your active page content will not appear at all on many users' browsers.
For a web site on the WWW, this is a rather blunt and inconsiderate approach;
however, if you're designing pages for a corporate intranet where you know that
only MSIE browsers are used, handling other browsers is not an issue to start with.

So how do you determine what type of browser is requesting your page? When
the user instructs the browser to download a resource from a web server, the
browser transmits a number of *request headers* to the server. These are named
values that are intended to provide the server with any information that might be
needed about the browser's request. One of these is the `User-Agent` request
header, whose value is a string passed by the browser software itself identifying
its type. For example, MSIE3.0 sends the following `User-Agent` value to the
server:

```
Mozilla/2.0 (compatible; MSIE 3.0A; Windows 95)
```

Netscape Navigator 3.0's User-Agent value is as follows:

```
Mozilla/3.0 (Win95; I)
```

You can either make use of this information when the request reaches the server,
by executing a server-side CGI script or Active Server Pages script, or you can
wait for the page to be downloaded to the browser and retrieve the browser type
directly from the browser by using a client-side script.

# Determining the User's Browser from the Server Side

Determining the browser and then handling pages for different browsers can be done very effectively at the server by using the `HTTP_USER_AGENT` variable defined by the CGI interface.*

The following code fragment, for instance, is written using PHP/FI server-side scripting, which I use on most of my web sites to handle various types of browsers:

```
<? if (Reg_Match(".*Mozilla/2",$HTTP_USER_AGENT));
        $browse="nn2";
        if (Reg_Match(".*MSIE 3.",$HTTP_USER_AGENT));
            $browse="ie3";
        endif;
    else;
        if (Reg_Match(".*Mozilla/3",$HTTP_USER_AGENT));
            $browse="nn3";
        else;
            $browse="nf";
        endif;
    endif>
```

This code is written inline at the top of the web page, and the value of the *$browse* variable is then used to include or leave out various page elements. Similar scripts can be written in any of the server-side scripting languages that support the CGI interface. Pages that are specifically enhanced for the particular browser that is calling the web page can therefore be created at the server. This entire process is transparent to the user; users are never aware that a page has been specially created for them, and all they ever see is a page that looks great (hopefully) on their browser—even if they are using the character-based Lynx browser!

CGI provides one interface that allows you to determine the name of the browser. A second is Win-CGI, a variation of the standard CGI interface that was developed expressly for Windows web servers. Although Win-CGI applications can be created in a wide range of languages, like C, C++, Perl, and Delphi, the most commonly used programming language is probably Visual Basic.

If you're not using Visual Basic, you can determine the name of the browser by retrieving the value of the `User Agent` entry in the `[CGI]` section of the temporary initialization file created by the server to handle the request. If you are using Visual Basic along with the C6I32.BAS code module to add support for win-C6I, you can simply retrieve the value of the `CGI_UserAgent` variable. Our earlier

---

* For a discussion of programming using the Common Gateway Interface (CGI), see *CGI Programming on the World Wide Web*, by Shishir Gundavaram, published by O'Reilly & Associates.

code fragment rewritten in Visual Basic to take advantage of the Win-CGI interface would then appear as follows:

```
Dim strBrowser As String
If Instr(1, CGI_UserAgent, "Mozilla/2") > 0 Then
    If Instr(1,CGI_UserAgent, "MSIE 3.") Then
        strBrowser = "ie3"
    Else
        strBrowser = "nn2"
    End If
Else
    If Instr(1, CGI_UserAgent, "Mozilla/3") > 0 Then
        strBrowser = "nn3"
    Else
        strBrowser = "nf"
    End If
End If
```

Finally, if you're using Microsoft Internet Information Server, you can use Active Server Pages and server-side VBScript to determine the browser. Here's the preceding code snippet ported to an Active Server Pages script:

```
<%@ LANGUAGE="VBSCRIPT" %>

<HTML>
<HEAD>
<TITLE>Document Title</TITLE>
</HEAD>
<BODY BGCOLOR="white">
<CENTER><FONT FACE="arial">
<H3>Which Browser?</H3>
<P>
<%
   Dim sUAgent
   Dim strBrowser

   sUAgent = Request.ServerVariables("HTTP_USER_AGENT")

   If Instr(1, sUAgent, "Mozilla/2") > 0 Then
      If Instr(1,sUAgent, "MSIE 3.") Then
         strBrowser = "ie3"
      Else
         strBrowser = "nn2"
      End If
   Else
      If Instr(1, sUAgent, "Mozilla/3") > 0 Then
         strBrowser = "nn3"
      Else
         strBrowser = "nf"
      End If
   End If
%>

</BODY>
</HTML>
```

An advantage of handling the browser type at the server is that you can cater to browsers that have no script interpretation capabilities. However, at the time of this writing, only about 10 percent of all browsers cannot handle either JavaScript or VBScript, and with every passing day, this percentage is becoming smaller. So it's now possible to think seriously about handling the browser type at the client.

## Determining the User's Browser from the Client Side

In addition to being available at the server for use in a CGI script, the user agent variable can also be obtained from within a client-side script. The object models of both MSIE and Netscape Navigator include a *Navigator* object, which has a *userAgent* property that contains the user agent variable. For example, the following code fragment prints the user agent string on an HTML page:

```
<SCRIPT LANGUAGE="vbscript">
document.write Navigator.userAgent
</SCRIPT>
```

There is one problem with this script, though: if the browser is Netscape Navigator, it cannot handle VBScript, which means that your script will never run. If you use VBScript to determine the client's browser type, you can only determine whether the browser is Microsoft Internet Explorer 3.0 or greater, which tends to defeat the object of the exercise somewhat. So to be sure that you can determine the type of a script-capable browser on the client, you must write your browser-checking script in JavaScript, so that it can run successfully on both Netscape's and Microsoft's browsers.

Because JavaScript was the first client-side scripting language, Microsoft made JavaScript (or JScript, as the Microsoft implementation is called) the default language of MSIE. A script written in JavaScript runs on both Netscape Navigator 2.x onwards and MSIE 3.x onwards.

MSIE 3.x is technically classed as a Mozilla 2.0-compatible browser, and the first part of the user agent value returned by MSIE 3.x is identical to that of Netscape Navigator 2.x, as you can see in the following example. (The first string is returned by MSIE, while the second is returned by Netscape Navigator.)

```
Mozilla/2.0 (compatible; MSIE 3.0A; Windows 95)
Mozilla/2.0 (Win95; I)
```

Since the strings are similar, you must therefore check the **User-Agent** value for an occurrence of "MSIE 3" to differentiate between the two classes of browsers. As Figures 17-1 and 17-2 show, the JavaScript snippet shown in Example 17-1 allows you to do this in both Netscape Navigator and MSIE 3.x. Note that we are actually checking to make sure that the version of MSIE running our script is *greater than* MSIE 2.0; this allows us to designate a baseline version, so that our script can (hopefully) run under future versions of MSIE without modification.

*Example 17-1. Using JavaScript to Determine the Browser Type*

```
<HTML>
<HEAD>
<TITLE>Checking for Internet Explorer</TITLE>
</HEAD>
<BODY BGCOLOR="white">
<CENTER><H2>
<SCRIPT LANGUAGE="javascript">
var uagent;
uagent = navigator.userAgent;
if (uagent.substring(25,29)=="MSIE" && uagent.charAt(30) > 2)
   document.write("This is Internet Explorer 3+");
else
   document.write("This isn't Internet Explorer");
</SCRIPT>
</H2>
</BODY>
```

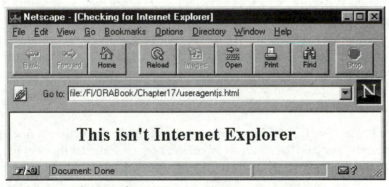

*Figure 17-1. Checking for "MSIE 3." in Netscape Navigator*

*Figure 17-2. Checking for "MSIE 3." in MSIE3.0*

# Handling the Browser

So now that you know what type of browser is requesting your page, what are you going to do with that information? You have three options:

- Blocking other browsers, in which case your site caters to MSIE users exclusively and, because you haven't developed content that can be displayed by other browsers, you refuse their requests for web pages.

- Automatic redirection to VBScript/ActiveX pages.

- Active and nonactive content web pages.

We'll examine each of these in turn.

## Blocking Other Browsers

If, for whatever reason, you intend to support only MSIE with active content, and you are not too bothered about losing a certain number of visitors, there is always the "Go away and get MSIE before you come back" approach. This is illustrated by the code in Example 17-2. You can see the results of this simple code in Figure 17-3, which shows what happens when the routine executes on Netscape Navigator, and in Figure 17-4, which displays the simple page produced on MSIE. Of course, in the real world, you'd be slightly more polite to your Netscape users than I've been in this example. But as you can see, only users of Internet Explorer 3.x will have access to the rest of the web site.

*Example 17-2. Blocking Non-MSIE Browsers*

```
<HTML>
<HEAD>
<TITLE>MS Internet Explorer site only</TITLE>
</HEAD>
<BODY BGCOLOR="white">
<CENTER>
<SCRIPT LANGUAGE="javascript">

var uagent;
uagent = navigator.userAgent;
if (uagent.substring(25,29)=="MSIE"&&uagent.char4+(30)72)
    {
    document.write("<H2><A HREF=activexpages.html>"); 'PAGE NOT PRESENT.
    document.write("Welcome..please come in");
    document.write("</A></H2>");
    }
else
    {
    document.write("<H2>This site can only be viewed<BR>");
    document.write(" with Microsoft Internet Explorer</H2>");
    document.write("<FONT SIZE=1><b>Go get it and come back<br>");
```

*Example 17-2. Blocking Non-MSIE Browsers (continued)*

```
    document.write("<a href=http://www.microsoft.com/ie/ie.htm>");
    document.write("<img src=http://www.microsoft.com/ie")
    document.write("images/ie_animated.gif ");
    document.write("width=88 height=31 border=0");
    document.write(" alt= &quot;Microsoft Internet Explorer&quot;");
    document.write(" vspace=7></a>");
    document.write("<br>Click here to start.</b><br></font>");
    }

</SCRIPT>
</BODY>
```

*Figure 17-3. Blocking access to Netscape Navigator*

*Figure 17-4. Allowing access to MSIE*

This works fine on Netscape Navigator and MSIE 3.x, but what about the people who still use pre-active content browsers? Since this entire web page is created on the fly by the *Document.Write* method, which requires a script-aware browser, they will see absolutely nothing. Furthermore, you may not want to simply block certain users from your site. Fortunately, there is a way to allow non-MSIE users to see the your web page at the same time that you completely segregate Internet Explorer users from everyone else, allowing them to see your active content in all its glory.

## Automatic Redirection to Active Content Pages

There are several ways that you can automatically redirect a user to another page. You can include some VBScript initialization code like the following, which you know will be ignored by Netscape Navigator and therefore only run within MSIE3.0:

```
<HTML>
<HEAD>
<SCRIPT LANGUAGE="vbscript">
    Location.hRef = myactivepages.html
</SCRIPT>
etc...
```

At first glance this may appear to be an ideal solution, until an MSIE user tries to use the Back button from *MYACTIVEPAGES.HTML* and finds that it doesn't work. The reason this doesn't work is that every time the Back button is pressed to return to the original page containing the redirection script, the script immediately transports the user forward again to the page from which he or she is trying to escape, leaving the user forever stuck within *MYACTIVEPAGES.HTML*!

Another, slightly less drastic, approach is to use the script to write a `<META>` refresh tag. The `<META HTTP-EQUIV>` tag can replicate the user's clicking the Refresh button. It can take a new URL as one of its parameters, along with the time delay before the new URL is activated. The following code fragment shows how you can create an HTML `<META>` tag using VBScript:

```
<HTML>
<HEAD>
<SCRIPT LANGUAGE="vbscript">
    Document.Write "<META HTTP-EQUIV="
    Document.Write Chr(34) & refresh & Chr(34)
    Document.Write " CONTENT=" & Chr(34) & _
    "5; url= myactivepages.html" & chr(34) & ">"
</SCRIPT>
etc...
```

This script relies on a technique called *client pull*. If the user has MSIE, the `<META>` tag will be written to the HTML page, and at the end of 5 seconds the browser will automatically request the pages containing Active Content. If, however, the user's browser doesn't support VBScript, the `<META>` tag never appears in the HTML page, and therefore the browser remains within the current page. With this method at least you can alter the time delay to give the user time to move back out of the site or page, but it is still not seamless, which is what you should be trying to achieve, both from an aesthetic and from a user interface design point of view.

So far, we've used the explicit method of determining the browser type—that is, we've used a script to see which browser is being used. There is, however, one implicit method of determining the browser type that takes advantage of a unique feature of MSIE, and that provides an excellent method for implicitly segregating browser types. Internet Explorer supports a special `<IFRAME>` tag which is used to show floating frames. The tag is ignored by Netscape Navigator, so you can use its `SRC` attribute to provide the URL of your active or scripted page to be loaded only on Internet Explorer. In Example 17-3, for instance, the `SRC` attribute of the `<IFRAME>` tag defines the active content page as *MSIEONLY.HTML*, whose source code is shown in Example 17-4. Because MSIE is the only browser that supports the `<IFRAME>` tag, this page can only be loaded into MSIE; Figure 17-5 shows it displayed within the "invisible" floating frame defined by the HTML source in Example 17-3. Other browsers that don't support the `<IFRAME>` tag simply ignore it and the entire web page that it defines. This means that, within the same page, you can use a `<NOFRAMES>` tag to handle older browsers, and place the content to be displayed on the non-frame-aware browser between the `<NOFRAMES>` and `</NOFRAMES>` tags. Figure 17-6 shows how the web page in Example 17-3 appears when displayed by an older browser, CompuServe Mosaic, that does not support frames.

*Example 17-3. Using the <IFRAMES> and <NOFRAMES> Tags*

```
<HTML>
<HEAD>
<TITLE>Handling All Browsers</TITLE>
</HEAD>
<BODY BGCOLOR=#FFFFFF TOPMARGIN=0 LEFTMARGIN=0>
<IFRAME FRAMEBORDER=0 WIDTH=100% Height=100% SRC="msieonly.html">
</IFRAME>
<NOFRAMES>
 <CENTER>
 <H2>This site can only be viewed<BR>
 with Microsoft Internet Explorer</H2>
 <BR>
 <b>Go get it and come back<br>
 <a href="http://www.microsoft.com/ie/ie.htm">
 <img src="http://www.microsoft.com/ie/images/ie_animated.gif" width="88"
height="31" border="0" alt="Microsoft Internet Explorer" vspace="7"></a>
 <br>Click here to start.</b><br>
 </BODY>
</NOFRAMES>
</HTML>
```

*Example 17-4. HTML Source for MSIEONLY.HTML*

```
<HTML>
<HEAD>
<TITLE>MSIE Only Page</TITLE>
</HEAD>
<BODY BGCOLOR="white">
<CENTER>
<H2>
<SCRIPT LANGUAGE="vbscript">
 Document.Write "Welcome MSIE User!"
</SCRIPT>
</BODY>
```

*Figure 17-5. MSIE displaying MSIEONLY.HTML in the floating frame defined by NONMSIE.HTML*

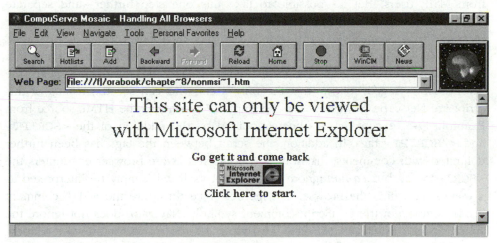

*Figure 17-6. Content defined by the <NOFRAMES> tag on an antique CompuServe Mosaic*

But what about Netscape Navigator, which, after all, supports frames? One of the neat things about this approach is that Netscape Navigator, although it is frame-enabled, ignores the <NOFRAMES> tag in this case because, as far as it is concerned, there hasn't been a frame set defined by the <FRAMESET> tag. As a

result, it treats all the content between the <NOFRAMES> and </NOFRAMES> tags
as normal HTML. Figure 17-7, for example, shows the web page in Example 17-3
displayed by Netscape Navigator.

*Figure 17-7. Netscape Navigator handling the <NOFRAMES> tag*

So by taking advantage of the <IFRAME> tag, you can separate non-MSIE users
from MSIE users. But it's possible to take this one step further—and separate
Netscape Navigator users from other non-MSIE users—by displaying a unique
message to Netscape users. The code within the <NOFRAMES> tags is only read
by browsers other than MSIE. Of these, only Netscape Navigator 2.x onwards can
understand the <SCRIPT> tag. So if you place some JavaScript within the
<NOFRAMES> tag, it follows that the only users who can see the results of this
script are Netscape Navigator users. Example 17-5 contains the HTML source from
Example 17-3, except that it's been modified by the addition of the <SCRIPT>
and </SCRIPT> tags. In addition, the script between the tags has been further
delimited with comments; that way, if a non-script-aware browser encounters the
<SCRIPT> tag but *cannot* ignore it, the script itself will simply be interpreted as
a comment, which the browser can ignore. Since these are the HMTL comment
symbols, and not the JavaScript comment symbols, Navigator does not ignore the
script; instead, Navigator executes the script, and the Navigator browser window
resembles Figure 17-8.

*Example 17-5. Using the <IFRAME> and <SCRIPT> Tags to Differentiate Browsers*

```
<HTML>
<HEAD>
<TITLE>Handling All Browsers</TITLE>
```

*Example 17-5. Using the <IFRAME> and <SCRIPT> Tags to Differentiate Browsers (continued)*

```
</HEAD>
<BODY BGCOLOR=#FFFFFF TOPMARGIN=0 LEFTMARGIN=0>
<IFRAME FRAMEBORDER=0 WIDTH=100% Height=100% SRC="msieonly.html">
</IFRAME>
<NOFRAMES>
 <CENTER>
    <SCRIPT LANGUAGE="javascript">
    <!--
            document.write("<H2>Welcome Netscape Navigator User</H2>");
    //-->
    </SCRIPT>

 <H2>This site can only be viewed<BR>
 with Microsoft Internet Explorer</H2>
 <BR>
 <b>Go get it and come back<br>
 <a href="http://www.microsoft.com/ie/ie.htm">
 <img src="http://www.microsoft.com/ie/images/ie_animated.gif" width="88"
height="31" border="0" alt="Microsoft Internet Explorer" vspace="7"></a>
 <br>Click here to start.</b><br>
 </BODY>
</NOFRAMES>
</HTML>
```

*Figure 17-8. Netscape Navigator displaying a web page built by the script in Example 17-5*

---

TIP      For details on client-side scripting with JavaScript, see *JavaScript: The Definitive Guide*, by David Flanagan, published by O'Reilly & Associates.

## Providing Active and Nonactive Content Web Pages

In the previous section, we allowed all MSIE users to view our active content, and chose to show a message that effectively blocked all users of other browsers from our site. A much better option, though, is to include a hyperlink to nonactive pages within your web site. Or, better still, you can write the web page so that it can be accessed seamlessly by all three types of users. Example 17-6 illustrates how this might be done by creating an HTML form that can be displayed on all three types of browsers.

The HTML source in Example 17-6 uses the `<IFRAME>` tag (as it did in our earlier sample HTML page shown in Example 17-3) to define a completely separate active content page containing a form that is loaded into a floating frame in Internet Explorer, as shown in Figure 17-9. The floating frame, as you can see, is invisible to the user; the user only sees a page loaded into a floating frame that appears to be the standard browser window. Even the address drop-down combo box indicates that *UNIFORM.HTML*, which contains the `<IFRAME>` tag, is the web page displayed in the browser window. The source code for this page, which is defined by the `<IFRAME>` tag's `SRC` attribute, is shown in Example 17-7. In it, all the regular HTML form elements have been replaced with their corresponding ActiveX controls, and a simple VBScript event handler has been added to CommandButton1 to display a Thank You message. To complete the replication of an HTML form, the Submit method is called by the button's event handler.

Other browsers, of course, will ignore the `<IFRAME>` tag.

*Example 17-6. HTML Source for UNIFORM.HTML*

```
<HTML>
<HEAD>
<TITLE>Handling All Browsers</TITLE>
</HEAD>
<BODY BGCOLOR=#FFFFFF TOPMARGIN=0 LEFTMARGIN=0>
<IFRAME FRAMEBORDER=0 WIDTH=100% Height=100% SRC="msieform.html">
</IFRAME>
<NOFRAMES>
  <CENTER>
  <H4>Please complete the following form and press Submit</H4>
  </CENTER>
  <FORM ACTION="" METHOD="POST">
    <BR><PRE>
    Your Name:        <INPUT TYPE=text SIZE=30 NAME="name">
    <BR>
    Postal Address:   <INPUT TYPE=text SIZE=30 NAME="addr">
    <BR>
    EMail Address:    <INPUT TYPE=text SIZE=30 NAME="email">
    <BR>
                      <INPUT LANGUAGE="JavaScript" TYPE=submit
    VALUE="Submit" ONCLICK="window.alert(&quot;Thank You&quot;)">
```

*Example 17-6. HTML Source for UNIFORM.HTML (continued)*

```
    </FORM>
    </PRE>
</NOFRAMES>
</BODY>
</HTML>
```

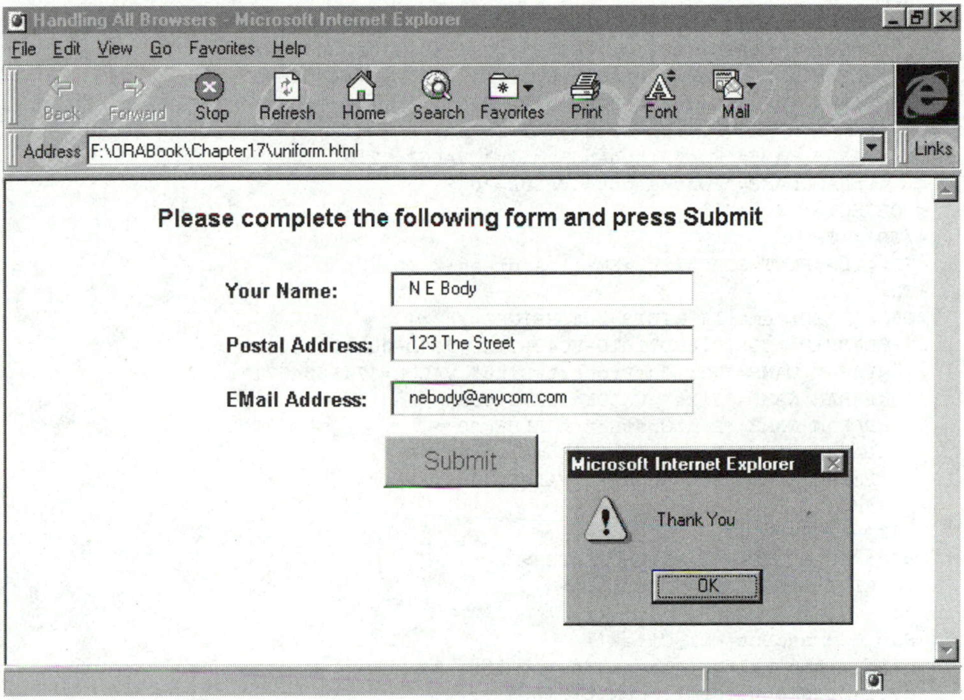

*Figure 17-9. MSIE displaying a form within a floating frame*

*Example 17-7. Source code for a form displayed within a floating frame*

```
<HTML>
<HEAD>
<TITLE>Handling All Browsers</TITLE>
</HEAD>
<BODY BGCOLOR="white">
<FONT FACE="arial">
<CENTER>
<H4>Please complete the following form and press Submit</H4>
<FORM NAME="form1" ACTION="" METHOD="POST">
  <TABLE CELLSPACING=10>
  <TR><TD><FONT SIZE=2><B>Your Name:</TD>
  <TD>
  <OBJECT ID="name" WIDTH=204 HEIGHT=24
    CLASSID="CLSID:8BD21D10-EC42-11CE-9E0D-00AA006002F3">
    <PARAM NAME="VariousPropertyBits" VALUE="746604571">
    <PARAM NAME="Size" VALUE="5392;635">
```

*Example 17-7. Source code for a form displayed within a floating frame (continued)*

```
      <PARAM NAME="FontCharSet" VALUE="0">
      <PARAM NAME="FontPitchAndFamily" VALUE="2">
      <PARAM NAME="FontWeight" VALUE="0">
  </OBJECT>
  </TD></TR>
  <TR><TD><FONT SIZE=2><B>Postal Address:</TD>
  <TD>
  <OBJECT ID="addr" WIDTH=204 HEIGHT=24
      CLASSID="CLSID:8BD21D10-EC42-11CE-9E0D-00AA006002F3">
      <PARAM NAME="VariousPropertyBits" VALUE="746604571">
      <PARAM NAME="Size" VALUE="5392;635">
      <PARAM NAME="FontCharSet" VALUE="0">
      <PARAM NAME="FontPitchAndFamily" VALUE="2">
      <PARAM NAME="FontWeight" VALUE="0">
  </OBJECT>
  </TD></TR>
  <TR><TD><FONT SIZE=2><B>EMail Address:</TD>
  <TD>
  <OBJECT ID="email" WIDTH=204 HEIGHT=24
      CLASSID="CLSID:8BD21D10-EC42-11CE-9E0D-00AA006002F3">
      <PARAM NAME="VariousPropertyBits" VALUE="746604571">
      <PARAM NAME="Size" VALUE="5392;635">
      <PARAM NAME="FontCharSet" VALUE="0">
      <PARAM NAME="FontPitchAndFamily" VALUE="2">
      <PARAM NAME="FontWeight" VALUE="0">
  </OBJECT>
  </TD></TR>
  <TR><TD COLSPAN=2 ALIGN=CENTER>
  <SCRIPT LANGUAGE="VBScript">
  <!--
  Sub CommandButton1_Click()
  call window.alert("Thank You")
  call Document.form1.submit()
  end sub
  -->
  </SCRIPT>
  <OBJECT ID="CommandButton1" WIDTH=104 HEIGHT=35
      CLASSID="CLSID:D7053240-CE69-11CD-A777-00DD01143C57">
      <PARAM NAME="ForeColor" VALUE="255">
      <PARAM NAME="Caption" VALUE="Submit">
      <PARAM NAME="Size" VALUE="2746;926">
      <PARAM NAME="FontName" VALUE="Arial">
      <PARAM NAME="FontHeight" VALUE="240">
      <PARAM NAME="FontCharSet" VALUE="0">
      <PARAM NAME="FontPitchAndFamily" VALUE="2">
      <PARAM NAME="ParagraphAlign" VALUE="3">
      <PARAM NAME="FontWeight" VALUE="0">
  </OBJECT>
  </TD></TR>
  </TABLE>
</FORM>
</CENTER>
</BODY>
</HTML>
```

In Example 17-6, the `<NOFRAMES>` tag is then used to enclose a nonactive version of the same page. The code after the `<NOFRAMES>` tag defines a standard HTML form that will be displayed on older browsers, like CompuServe Mosaic in Figure 17-10, that don't support frames. The form's Submit button also has a Java-Script event handler, which browsers that don't support scripting will ignore, since they won't recognize the `LANGUAGE` or `ONCLICK` attributes. In general, it's important that the HTML code that follows the `<NOFRAME>` tag be extremely simple. For instance, to align the form, we might put the labels for each text box in one column, and the text boxes in another, by using the `<TABLE>` tag. But this technique risks defeating the purpose of the `<NOFRAMES>` tag, since most non-script-, non-frame-enabled browsers were in use before the `<TABLE>` tag was released.

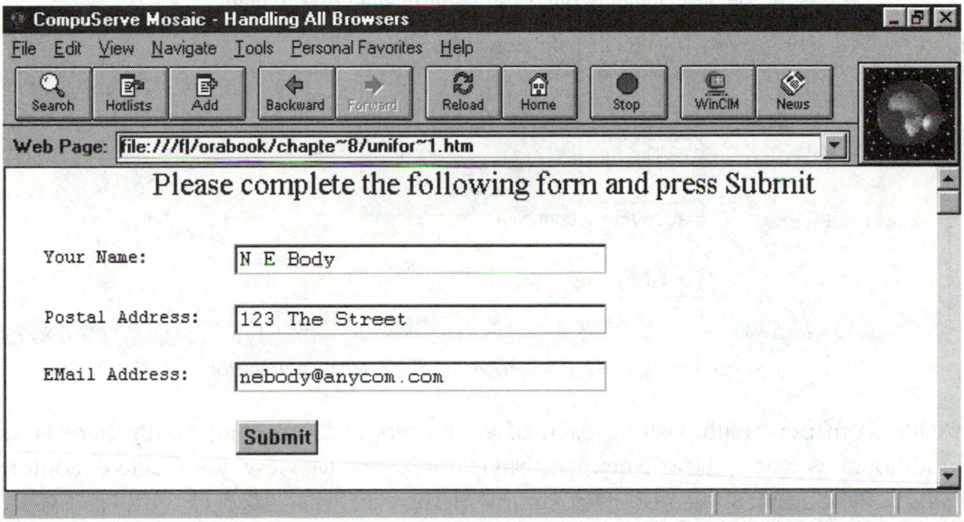

*Figure 17-10. CompuServe Mosaic displaying the HTML source defined by <NOFRAMES>*

As we've mentioned, the JavaScript event handler attached to the Submit button in Example 17-6, while it will be ignored by Mosaic and other non-script-enabled browsers, will execute only on Netscape Navigator. This causes an Alert dialog to be displayed when the user clicks the Submit button, as shown in Figure 17-11.

It's worth noting that our decision to implement a web page that can be displayed both by non-frame-enabled browsers and by Netscape Navigator limits the content that we can have Navigator display, as do peculiarities in the implementation of frames in both Navigator and MSIE. Ordinarily, we might want to take advantage of Navigator's support for frames in displaying the Netscape version of the page. But only pre-frames HTML code can be placed inside of the `<NOFRAMES>` tag. Another option might be to define the Navigator tag after the `<IFRAME>` tag, but before the `<NOFRAMES>` tag. This, however, isn't possible because of the way in which floating frames are implemented in MSIE, and the way the <FRAMESET> tag is supported in Navigator. To give the impression of a complete page using a floating frame, MSIE requires a <BODY> tag whose `Top` and `Left Margin` attributes set to 0; however, Navigator ignores all frameset definitions after the body tag.

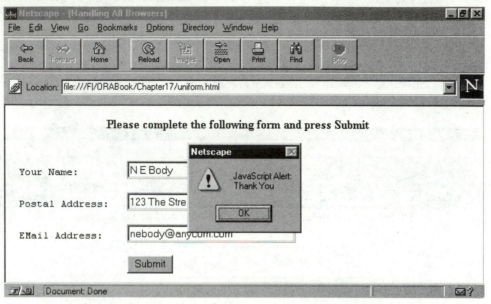

*Figure 17-11. The script in Example 17-6 running in Netscape Navigator*

Aside from personally visiting each of your users and installing MSIE, there is an additional way to allow Netscape Navigator users to view your active content pages, although it's less popular than the method just discussed.

## Netscape Plug-Ins

Netscape Navigator uses a technology comparable to ActiveX that allows software components written by third parties to interface with the browser. It therefore follows that if you wrote a software component that, on the one hand, plugs into Netscape Navigator, and, on the other hand, allows interaction with ActiveX controls, you would have the software version of the travel adapter plug: a virtual conduit between ActiveX and Netscape Navigator.

One company has done just that. NCompass Laboratories has launched a Netscape Navigator plug-in named ScriptActive. It allows Netscape Navigator users to view pages that have been written for MSIE 3.x... sort of! The idea is sound, and I have found it to operate satisfactorily. However, the logistics of using the plug-in soon take the shine off the product:

- As a Netscape user, you register with the company, and download an evaluation version. But here's the rub: the file is a whacking 3.6Mb. I just cannot imagine Netscape Navigator users rushing to download a three megabyte file in the hope that developers like us are also going to download a three megabyte file and convert all our MSIE pages for them to view in Netscape Navigator!

- Apparently NCompass is going to, was going to, or does charge a fee for ScriptActive, but I couldn't get any information about this from their web site (*http://www.ncompasslabs.com/*) on the days I visited, nor have they responded to my many emails asking for more detail to be included here.

- As a designer writing pages enhanced for MSIE 3.x, you would initially think that it's great that Netscape Navigator users who have the ScriptActive plug-in can immediately benefit from ActiveX and VBScript. Wrong! You have to create new files that the plug-in can understand (although NCompass does supply you with an automatic conversion wizard).

- Some of the functionality of ActiveX controls is missing from ScriptActive, or at least it was at the time of writing. If you want to check the current implementation, I suggest that you visit the NCompass Labs web site, *http://www.ncompasslabs.com.*

Obtaining and installing ScriptActive is straightforward, so I won't go into it here. What I do want to discuss are the conversions needed to allow ScriptActive to interface with your MSIE-enhanced pages.

### Converting pages to use the Scriptactive Plug-in

When you install ScriptActive, it creates a program group that includes a Conversion Tool icon. When you launch the Conversion Tool, it appears as shown in Figure 17-12.

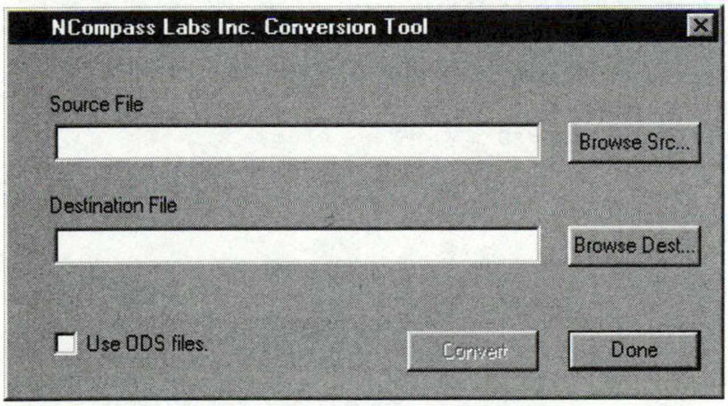

*Figure 17-12. The NCompass Conversion Tool*

Let's look at an example document that uses several ActiveX controls and a short VBScript to see how ActiveScript handles the conversion and how the results appear within Netscape Navigator. Example 17-8 lists the original HTML file created using the ActiveX Control Pad specifically for MSIE 3.x. As you can see from the HTML source, the web page consists of a label, a text box, and a command button. The command button's *Click* event procedure simply displays the string input into the text box within a message box. Figure 17-13 displays the web page that results when Example 17-8 is run by Internet Explorer; as you can see, it contains no surprises.

*Example 17-8. A Simple Web Page Using ActiveX Controls and VBScript*

```
<HTML>
<HEAD>
<TITLE>ScriptActive Test Page</TITLE>
</HEAD>
<BODY BGCOLOR="white">
<FONT FACE="arial"><B>
<CENTER>
<H3>This is a test of the ScriptActive Plug-In</H3>
Enter a phrase and click "Show Me!"
<BR><BR>
    <OBJECT ID="Label1" WIDTH=124 HEIGHT=24
 CLASSID="CLSID:978C9E23-D4B0-11CE-BF2D-00AA003F40D0">
    <PARAM NAME="ForeColor" VALUE="16711680">
    <PARAM NAME="BackColor" VALUE="16777215">
    <PARAM NAME="Caption" VALUE="Your Phrase...">
    <PARAM NAME="Size" VALUE="3281;635">
    <PARAM NAME="FontEffects" VALUE="1073741825">
    <PARAM NAME="FontHeight" VALUE="240">
    <PARAM NAME="FontCharSet" VALUE="0">
    <PARAM NAME="FontPitchAndFamily" VALUE="2">
    <PARAM NAME="FontWeight" VALUE="700">
</OBJECT>
    <OBJECT ID="TextBox1" WIDTH=195 HEIGHT=24
     CLASSID="CLSID:8BD21D10-EC42-11CE-9E0D-00AA006002F3">
        <PARAM NAME="VariousPropertyBits" VALUE="746604571">
        <PARAM NAME="Size" VALUE="5128;635">
        <PARAM NAME="FontCharSet" VALUE="0">
        <PARAM NAME="FontPitchAndFamily" VALUE="2">
        <PARAM NAME="FontWeight" VALUE="0">
    </OBJECT>
<BR><BR>
    <SCRIPT LANGUAGE="VBScript">
<!--
Sub CommandButton1_Click()
 MsgBox TextBox1.Text, 0, "ScriptActive Test"
end sub
-->
    </SCRIPT>
    <OBJECT ID="CommandButton1" WIDTH=96 HEIGHT=32
     CLASSID="CLSID:D7053240-CE69-11CD-A777-00DD01143C57">
```

*Example 17-8. A Simple Web Page Using ActiveX Controls and VBScript (continued)*

```
            <PARAM NAME="ForeColor" VALUE="255">
            <PARAM NAME="Caption" VALUE="Show Me!">
            <PARAM NAME="Size" VALUE="2540;846">
            <PARAM NAME="FontName" VALUE="Comic Sans MS">
            <PARAM NAME="FontEffects" VALUE="1073741827">
            <PARAM NAME="FontHeight" VALUE="240">
            <PARAM NAME="FontCharSet" VALUE="0">
            <PARAM NAME="FontPitchAndFamily" VALUE="2">
            <PARAM NAME="ParagraphAlign" VALUE="3">
            <PARAM NAME="FontWeight" VALUE="700">
        </OBJECT>
    </CENTER>
</BODY>
</HTML>
```

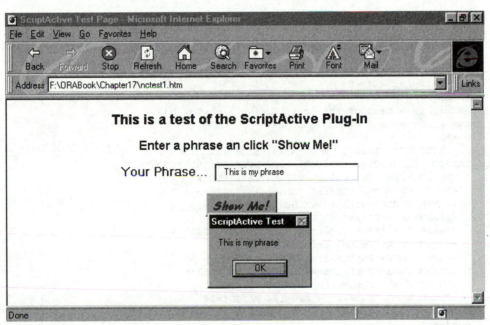

*Figure 17-13. MSIE displaying the web page from Example 17-8*

To allow this page to be displayed on Netscape Navigator, the next step is to use the NCompass Conversion Tool to turn it into a file that can be understood by the NCompass ScriptActive plug-in. When the Conversion Tool runs, it generates two files:

- A converted version of your HTML file. Example 17-9, for instance, shows the converted HTML source for the web page shown in Example 17-8. Since the converted HTML file can be somewhat confusing, it's best, when you generate it, to specify a different filename in the Conversion Tool's Destination File

dialog. Therefore, the Conversion Tool will not overwrite your original file.
This means that you can continue to maintain the original file and convert it
each time you modify it, so that you never have to work directly with the converted HTML file.

- A second file with an .AXS extension. The Conversion Tool generates this file
  in the same directory as it writes the converted HTML file. If you move the
  converted file, you must make sure that ScriptActive can always find its corresponding .AXS file in the same directory. The .AXS file that the Conversion
  Tool generates when it generates the converted HTML page in Example 17-9
  is shown in Example 17-10; as you can see, it contains the script from the
  original web page.

*Example 17-9. The Converted Version of Example 17-8*

```
<HTML>
<HEAD>
<TITLE>ScriptActive Test Page</TITLE>
</HEAD>
<BODY BGCOLOR="white">
<FONT FACE="arial"><B>
<CENTER>
<H3>This is a test of the ScriptActive Plug-In</H3>
Enter a phrase and click "Show Me!"
<BR><BR>
    <OBJECT ID="Label1" WIDTH=124 HEIGHT=24
 CLASSID="CLSID:978C9E23-D4B0-11CE-BF2D-00AA003F40D0">
    <PARAM NAME="ForeColor" VALUE="16711680">
    <PARAM NAME="BackColor" VALUE="16777215">
    <PARAM NAME="Caption" VALUE="Your Phrase...">
    <PARAM NAME="Size" VALUE="3281;635">
    <PARAM NAME="FontEffects" VALUE="1073741825">
    <PARAM NAME="FontHeight" VALUE="240">
    <PARAM NAME="FontCharSet" VALUE="0">
    <PARAM NAME="FontPitchAndFamily" VALUE="2">
    <PARAM NAME="FontWeight" VALUE="700">
    <EMBED NAME="Label1" WIDTH=124 HEIGHT=24
 CLASSID="CLSID:978C9E23-D4B0-11CE-BF2D-00AA003F40D0" TYPE="application/
oleobject"
    PARAM_ForeColor="16711680"
    PARAM_BackColor="16777215"
    PARAM_Caption="Your Phrase..."
    PARAM_Size="3281;635"
    PARAM_FontEffects="1073741825"
    PARAM_FontHeight="240"
    PARAM_FontCharSet="0"
    PARAM_FontPitchAndFamily="2"
    PARAM_FontWeight="700"
></OBJECT>
    <OBJECT ID="TextBox1" WIDTH=195 HEIGHT=24
     CLASSID="CLSID:8BD21D10-EC42-11CE-9E0D-00AA006002F3">
        <PARAM NAME="VariousPropertyBits" VALUE="746604571">
```

*Example 17-9. The Converted Version of Example 17-8 (continued)*

```
        <PARAM NAME="Size" VALUE="5128;635">
        <PARAM NAME="FontCharSet" VALUE="0">
        <PARAM NAME="FontPitchAndFamily" VALUE="2">
        <PARAM NAME="FontWeight" VALUE="0">
        <EMBED NAME="TextBox1" WIDTH=195 HEIGHT=24
    CLASSID="CLSID:8BD21D10-EC42-11CE-9E0D-00AA006002F3"
TYPE="application/oleobject"
        PARAM_VariousPropertyBits="746604571"
        PARAM_Size="5128;635"
        PARAM_FontCharSet="0"
        PARAM_FontPitchAndFamily="2"
        PARAM_FontWeight="0"
    ></OBJECT>
<BR><BR>
    <SCRIPT LANGUAGE="VBScript">
<!--
Sub CommandButton1_Click()
 MsgBox TextBox1.Text, 0, "ScriptActive Test"
end sub
-->
    </SCRIPT>
    <OBJECT ID="CommandButton1" WIDTH=96 HEIGHT=32
     CLASSID="CLSID:D7053240-CE69-11CD-A777-00DD01143C57">
        <PARAM NAME="ForeColor" VALUE="255">
        <PARAM NAME="Caption" VALUE="Show Me!">
        <PARAM NAME="Size" VALUE="2540;846">
        <PARAM NAME="FontName" VALUE="Comic Sans MS">
        <PARAM NAME="FontEffects" VALUE="1073741827">
        <PARAM NAME="FontHeight" VALUE="240">
        <PARAM NAME="FontCharSet" VALUE="0">
        <PARAM NAME="FontPitchAndFamily" VALUE="2">
        <PARAM NAME="ParagraphAlign" VALUE="3">
        <PARAM NAME="FontWeight" VALUE="700">
        <EMBED NAME="CommandButton1" WIDTH=96 HEIGHT=32
    CLASSID="CLSID:D7053240-CE69-11CD-A777-00DD01143C57"
TYPE="application/oleobject"
        PARAM_ForeColor="255"
        PARAM_Caption="Show Me!"
        PARAM_Size="2540;846"
        PARAM_FontName="Comic Sans MS"
        PARAM_FontEffects="1073741827"
        PARAM_FontHeight="240"
        PARAM_FontCharSet="0"
        PARAM_FontPitchAndFamily="2"
        PARAM_ParagraphAlign="3"
        PARAM_FontWeight="700"
    >

    <EMBED SRC="nctest2.AXS" WIDTH=1 HEIGHT=1 LANGUAGE="VBScript">

    </OBJECT>
</CENTER>
</BODY>
</HTML>
```

*Example 17-10. An .AXS File*

```
Sub CommandButton1_Click()
   MsgBox TextBox1.Text, 0, "ScriptActive Test"
End Sub
```

Figure 17-14, which displays the HTML source in Example 17-9 running in Netscape Navigator (complete with the ScriptActive plug-in) shows the results after this rather painless conversion. As you can see, the ActiveX controls are there, as is the VBScript, although it's running from a second file. The only difference in the behavior of the ActiveX controls in the converted HTML page is that the cursor does not appear within the text box control, so, until you start typing, you never know if the text box has the focus, or where the cursor is within the text box.

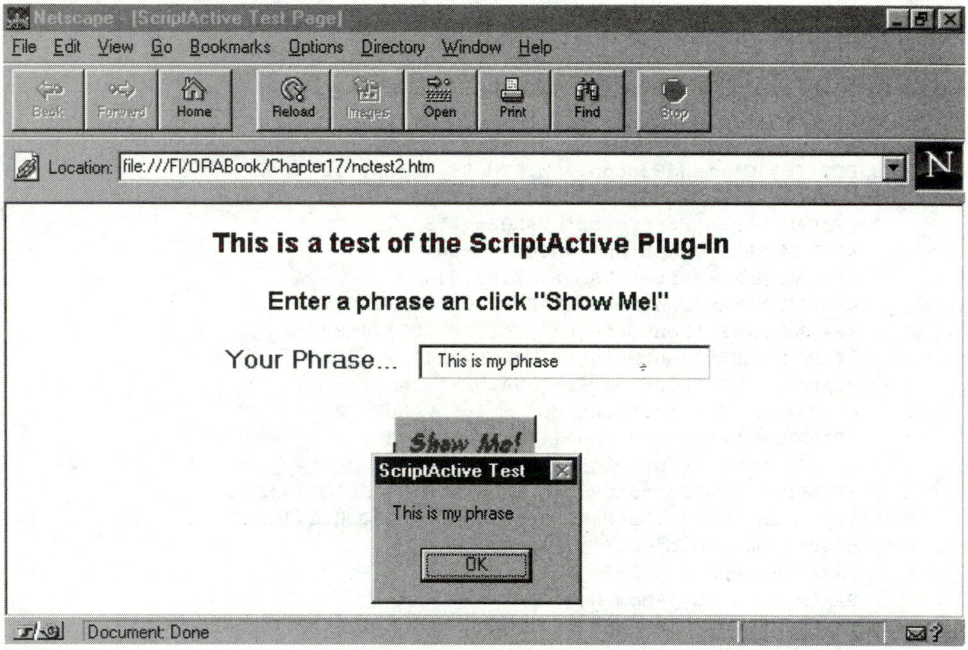

*Figure 17-14. The converted ActiveX and VBScript page running in Netscape Navigator*

In case you're wondering, the converted HTML files (in the case of our example, *NCTEST2.HTM*) run perfectly well within MSIE. The idea, of course, is that you need only a single file to provide content to users with Internet Explorer or with Netscape Navigator and the ScriptActive plug-in. As I've suggested, though, you may want to continue to provide two versions of the web page, the first developed expressly for MSIE and the second converted by the Conversion Tool for Netscape Navigator.

Earlier in the chapter, you saw how to use JavaScript to write a message just to Netscape users. You could extend this idea by including a hyperlink to the NCompass Laboratories web site, thereby giving Netscape users the option of downloading the plug-in (if you are prepared to put converted pages online) or downloading MSIE 3.x.

# *Summary*

Let's recap your options in handling multiple browsers, and list the advantages and disadvantages of each. Ultimately, your decision about which method will suit you best will depend upon your individual set of circumstances, so I make no attempt here to recommend a course of action.

To handle multiple browsers, you can do any of the following:

- Determine the browser type by using the `HTTP_USER_AGENT` variable within a server-side CGI script, by using the `User Agent` value entry or the *CGI_UserAgent* variable in a Win-CGI application, or by retrieving the `HTTP_USER_AGENT` value from the IIS *Request* object's *ServerVariables* collection. You can then construct pages at the server to suit the particular browser that you encounter.

  — ADVANTAGE: Seamless to the user.

  — DISADVANTAGE: Can require that you develop relatively complex server-side scripts and various versions of each page.

- Determine the browser type by using the *Navigator.userAgent* property within a client-side script.

  — ADVANTAGES:

    1. Pages can be created as they arrive at the browser.

    2. Seamless to the user.

    3. Can be used either to block non-MSIE browser types, or to create non-active pages on the fly.

  — DISADVANTAGES:

    1. Ignores non-script-enabled browsers.

    2. Requires that you use JavaScript to include Netscape users.

- Recommend that users take advantage of the ScriptActive plug-in from Ncompass Laboratories.

  — ADVANTAGE: One page fits all (except for older, non-script-enabled browsers).

— DISADVANTAGES:

1. Ignores non-script-enabled browsers.

2. Users have to download and install a very large file.

3. Developers have to create a specially converted HTML file.

4. Some ActiveX functionality is not implemented.

- Use `<IFRAME>` tags to display active content pages in MSIE.

  — ADVANTAGES:

  1. Seamless to all users.

  2. Allows you to support all browser users.

  — DISADVANTAGE: Only basic HTML code can be included within the `<NOFRAMES>` tags.

# VBScript 1.0 Language Quick Reference

This appendix details all the functions, statements, and other keywords available within the VBScript language Version 1.0, listed by category. The categories are:

- Array Handling
- Assignment
- Comment
- Constants and Literals
- Conversions
- Dates and Times
- Declarations
- Error Handling
- Input and Output
- Mathematical Functions
- Operators
- Options
- Program Flow
- String Handling
- Variants

For each entry, I've indicated the type of the language construct and its syntax. There is also a brief description of the keyword, along with an example. Note that most examples are not syntactically correct; many have been broken across multiple lines without using the VBScript line continuation character. Where necessary, individual keywords may appear in more than one category.

# Array Handling

| Keyword | Type | Syntax | Example | Purpose |
|---|---|---|---|---|
| Dim | Statement | Dim *array*([*subscripts*]) | Dim MyArray(10) | Declares an array |
| Erase | Statement | Erase *array* | Erase MyArray | Clears the contents of an array |
| IsArray | Function | IsArray(*var*) | If IsArray(myArray) Then | Returns True if *var* is an array, False if it isn't |
| LBound | Function | LBound(*arrayname*) | lowElement = LBound(myArray) | In VBScript always returns 0 |
| Preserve | Statement | Redim Preserve *array*(*subscripts*) | Redim Preserve myArray(intNewSize) | Copies a dynamic array to a resized dynamic array |
| ReDim | Statement | ReDim *array*() or ReDim *array*([*subscripts*]) | ReDim myArray() | Declares or redimensions a dynamic array (see **Preserve**) |
| UBound | Function | UBound(*arrayname*) | intMax = Ubound(myArray) | Returns the largest subscript of an array |

# Assignment

| Keyword | Type | Syntax | Example | Purpose |
|---|---|---|---|---|
| = | Operator | *variable* = *value* | x = 10 | Assigns a value to a variable or property |
| Set | Statement | Set *variable* = *object* | Set myForm = Parent.Frames(1). Document.Form1 | Assigns an object reference to a variable |

# Comment

| Keyword | Type | Syntax | Example | Purpose |
|---|---|---|---|---|
| ' | Statement | ' *comment_text* | ' This text is a comment | Declares all text following the ' symbol as a comment to be ignored by the language engine |
| Rem | Statement | Rem *comment_text* | Rem This text is a comment | Declares the line starting with Rem as a comment to be ignored by the language engine |

# Constants and Literals

| Keyword | Type | Syntax | Example | Purpose |
|---------|------|--------|---------|---------|
| Empty | Literal | *variable* = Empty | x = Empty | Represents a special uninitialized value |
| False | Constant | *variable* = False | If x = False Then | A Boolean value representing 0 |
| Nothing | Literal | Set *variable* = Nothing | Set myForm = Nothing | Disassociates an object reference from a variable; use in conjunction with `Set` |
| Null | Literal | *variable* = Null | If x = Null Then | Represents no valid data |
| True | Constant | *variable* = True | x = True | Boolean value representing −1 |

# Conversions

| Keyword | Type | Syntax | Example | Purpose |
|---------|------|--------|---------|---------|
| Abs | Function | Abs(*number*) | x = Abs(y) | Returns the unsigned (absolute) value of a number |
| Asc | Function | Asc(*string*) | intMyChar = Asc("T") | Returns the ANSI/ASCII code of a character |
| CBool | Function | CBool(*expression*) | If CBool(x) = True Then | Returns a Boolean variant value from any valid expression |
| CByte | Function | CByte(*expression*) | x = CByte(myVar) | Returns a Byte variant value from any valid expression |
| CDate | Function | CDate(*expression*) | If CDate(myVar) < Now Then | Returns a Date variant value from any valid expression |
| CDbl | Function | CDbl(*expression*) | myDbl = CDbl(myVar) | Returns a double precision variant value from any valid expression |
| Chr | Function | Chr(*number*) | CRLF = Chr(13) & Chr(10) | Returns the character corresponding to the ANSI or ASCII code |
| CInt | Function | CInt(*expression*) | For x = CInt(myVar) to CInt(yourVar) | Returns an Integer variant value from any valid expression |
| CLng | Function | CLng(*expression*) | x = CLng(myForm.txt Numb.Value) | Returns a long integer variant value from any valid expression |
| CSng | Function | CSng(*expression*) | If CSng(myForm.txt Numb.Value) < _ sngMyNum Then | Returns a single precision variant value from any valid expression |
| CStr | Function | CStr(*expression*) | Alert CStr(anyVar) | Returns a string variant value from any valid expression |

| Keyword | Type | Syntax | Example | Purpose |
|---|---|---|---|---|
| DateSerial | Function | DateSerial (*year, month, day*) | newDate = Date-Serial(myYear, myMonth + 10, myDay) | Returns a date subtype variant from valid year, month, and day values |
| DateValue | Function | DateValue(*expression*) | myDate = DateValue(my-Form.Text1. Value) | Returns a date variant from any valid date expression |
| Fix | Function | Fix(*number*) | intResult = Fix((x + y) * (a / 7)) | Returns an integer variant that contains the integer portion of *number*, if *number* is negative, the value returned is rounded up (i.e., −1.5 returns −1). |
| Hex | Function | Hex(*number*) | myHex = Hex(my Number) | Returns a string variant representing the hexadecimal value of a number |
| Int | Function | Int(*number*) | intResult = Int((x + y) * (a / 7)) | Returns an integer variant that contains the integer portion of a *number*; if *number* is negative, the value returned is rounded down (i.e., −1.5 returns −2). |
| Oct | Function | Oct(*number*) | myOct = Oct(my Number) | Returns a string variant representing the octal value of a number |
| Sgn | Function | Sgn(*number*) | If Sgn(my Number) = −1 Then | Returns an integer subtype variant representing the sign of a number. |
| TimeSerial | Function | Time-Serial(*hour, minute, second*) | myTime = TimeSerial (myHour, myMin, mySec + newSec) | Returns a date variant from valid hour, minute, and second values |
| TimeValue | Function | TimeValue (*expression*) | myTime = Time-Value(Docu-ment.Form1.Text 4.Value) | Returns a date variant value from any valid time expression |

*Values Returned by the Sgn Function*

| Value of number | Return value |
|---|---|
| > 0 | 1 |
| = 0 | 0 |
| < 0 | −1 |

# Dates and Times

| Keyword | Type | Syntax | Example | Purpose |
|---|---|---|---|---|
| Date | Function | Date() | Document.Write Date() | Returns the current system date |

| Keyword | Type | Syntax | Example | Purpose |
|---------|------|--------|---------|---------|
| DateSerial | Function | DateSerial (*year,month,day*) | newDate = Date-Serial(myYear, myMonth + 10, myDay) | Returns a date subtype variant from valid year, month, and day values |
| DateValue | Function | DateValue(*expression*) | myDate = DateValue(myForm. Text1.Value) | Returns a date subtype variant value from any valid date expression |
| Day | Function | Day(*dateexpression*) | myDay = Day(Now()) | Returns an integer subtype variant representing the day (1–31) from a valid date expression |
| Hour | Function | Hour(*timeexpression*) | myHour = Hour(Now()) | Returns an integer subtype variant representing the hour (0–23) from a valid time expression |
| Minute | Function | Minute(*timeexpression*) | myMin = Minute(myTime) | Returns an integer subtype variant representing the minute (0–60) from a valid time expression |
| Month | Function | Month(*dateexpression*) | myMonth = Month(Now()) | Returns an integer subtype variant representing the month (1–12) from a valid date expression |
| Now | Function | Now() | Document.Write Now() | Returns the current date and time of the system |
| Second | Function | Second(*timeexpression*) | Document.Form1. Text1.Value = Second(Now()) | Returns an integer subtype variant representing the second (0–60) from a valid time expression |
| Time | Function | Time() | Label1.Caption = Time() | Returns the current system time |
| Timer | Function | Timer() | lngSecs = Timer() | Returns the number of seconds that have elapsed between midnight and the current time |
| TimeSerial | Function | TimeSerial (*hour,minute, second*) | myTime = TimeSerial (myHour, myMin, mySec + newSec) | Returns a date sub type variant from valid hour, minute, and second values |
| TimeValue | Function | TimeValue(*expression*) | myTime = Time-Value(Document. Form1.Text4.Value) | Returns a date subtype variant value from any valid time expression |

| Keyword | Type | Syntax | Example | Purpose |
|---------|------|--------|---------|---------|
| Weekday | Function | Weekday(*dateexpression*) | Document.Write strDaysArray (Weekday (Now())) | Returns an integer subtype variant between 1 and 7 representing the day of the week—starting at Sunday—from a date expression |
| Year | Function | Year(*dateexpression*) | currYear = Year(Now()) | Returns an integer subtype variant representing the year from a valid date expression |

## Declarations

| Keyword | Type | Syntax | Example | Purpose |
|---------|------|--------|---------|---------|
| Dim | Statement | Dim *variablename* | Dim x | Declares a variable |
| End | Statement | End Sub<br>End Function | Sub mySub()<br>...<br>End Sub | Declares the end of a Sub procedure or function |
| Exit | Statement | Exit Do \| For \| Function \| Sub | If x = 10 Then<br>  myFunction = 20<br>  Exit Function<br>End If | Used with Do, For, Function, or Sub to prematurely exit the routine |
| Function | Statement | Function funcname(*arglist*)<br>  Exit Function<br>End Function | Function myFunction (x, y, z) | Declares a function and the argument list passed into the function. Declares the end of a function. Also used with Exit to prematurely end a function. |
| Sub | Statement | Sub *subname*([*arglist*])<br>  Exit Sub<br>End Sub | Sub mySub()<br>...<br>End Sub | Declares a custom procedure or event handler and the argument list, if any. Declares the end of a custom procedure or event handler. Also used with Exit to prematurely end a custom procedure or event handler. |

# Error Handling

| Keyword | Type | Syntax | Example | Purpose |
|---|---|---|---|---|
| Clear | Method | Err.Clear | If strResponse = "OK" Then Err.Clear | Resets the *Err.Number* property to 0 |
| Description | Property | Err.Description | strMsg = strMsg & Err.Description | String describing the last error, as specified in the *Err.Number* property |
| Err | Object | Err.*property* \| *method* | strMsg = strMsg & Err.Description | An object containing information about the last error |
| On Error | Statement | On Error | Sub mySub()<br>    On Error Resume Next | Used in conjunction with **Resume Next** to continue execution with the line directly following the line in which the error occurred |
| Raise | Method | Err.Raise(*error-number*) | Err.Raise(9) | Simulate the occurrence of the error specified by *error-number* |
| Number | Property | Err.Number | If Err.Number > 0 Then | The error code for the last error, or 0 if no error has occurred |
| Source | Property | Err.Source | strMsg = strMsg & Err.Source | Returns the name of the object or application that raised the error |

# Input and Output

| Keyword | Type | Syntax | Example | Purpose |
|---|---|---|---|---|
| InputBox | Function | InputBox(*caption*[, *title*][, *value*][, *x*][, *y*]) | response = InputBox("Please enter a value", "My Application", "") | Displays a dialog box to allow user input |
| MsgBox | Function | MsgBox(*prompt*[, *msgtype*][, *title*]) | response = MsgBox("The value you entered is incorrect", 48, "My Application") | Displays a dialog box. Values for *msgtype* are shown in the next table. |

*Values of the msgtype Parameter to the MsgBox Function*

| msgtype | Message Box Types |
|---------|-------------------|
| 0 | Display OK button only |
| 1 | Display OK and Cancel buttons |
| 2 | Display Abort, Retry, and Ignore buttons |
| 3 | Display Yes, No, and Cancel buttons |
| 4 | Display Yes and No buttons |
| 5 | Display Retry and Cancel buttons |
| 16 | Display critical message icon |
| 32 | Display warning query icon |
| 48 | Display warning message icon |
| 64 | Display information message icon |
| 0 | First button is default |
| 256 | Second button is default |
| 512 | Third button is default |
| 768 | Fourth button is default |
| 0 | Application modal. The user must respond to the message box before continuing work in the current application. |
| 4096 | System modal. All applications are suspended until the user responds to the message box. |

# Mathematical Functions

| Keyword | Type | Syntax | Example | Purpose |
|---------|------|--------|---------|---------|
| Atn | Function | Atn(*number*) | x = Atn(myNumber) | Returns the arctangent of a number |
| Cos | Function | Cos(*number*) | x = Cos(myNumber) | Returns the cosine of an angle |
| Exp | Function | Exp(*number*) | x = Exp(myNumber) | Returns a number raised to a power |
| Log | Function | Log(*number*) | x = Log(myNumber) | Returns the logarithm of a number |
| Randomize | Statement | RANDOMIZE | | Primes the internal random number generator |
| Rnd | Function | Rnd | Int((intHighNo − intLowNo + 1) * Rnd + intLowNo) | Returns a random number |
| Sin | Function | Sin(*number*) | x = Sin(myNumber) | Returns the sine of an angle |
| Sqr | Function | Sqr(*number*) | If Sqr(myNumber) > 2 Then | Returns the square root of a number |
| Tan | Function | Tan(*number*) | x = Tan(myNumber) | Returns the tangent of an angle |

# Operators

| Keyword | Type | Syntax | Example | Purpose |
|---------|------|--------|---------|---------|
| + | Operator | *result = expr1 + expr2* | txtTextBox1.Value = myNumber + − 10 + intAnother | Adds two numerical expressions |
| And | Operator | If *expr1* And *expr2* Then | If x = 10 And y − 2 = myVar Then | Logical conjunction operator |
| / | Operator | *result = expr1 / expr2* | x = myVar / 2 | Division operator |
| = | Operator | If *expr1* = *expr2* Then | If myVar = yourVar Then | Equality operator |
| Eqv | Operator | If *expr1* Eqv *expr2* Then | If x Eqv y Then | Logical equivalence operator |
| ^ | Operator | *result = expr1 ^ expr2* | x = myVar ^ 10 | Exponentiation operator |
| > | Operator | If *expr1* > *expr2* Then | If x > 10 Then | Greater than comparison |
| >= | Operator | If *expr1* >= *expr2* Then | If x >= 10 Then | Greater than or equal to comparison |
| Imp | Operator | If *expr1* Imp *expr2* Then | If myVar Imp yourVar Then | Logical implication |
| <> | Operator | If *expr1* <> *expr2* Then | If x <> 10 Then | Inequality comparison |
| \ | Operator | *result = expr1 \ expr2* | intMyVar = MyNumber \ yourNumber | Integer division operator |
| < | Operator | If *expr1* < *expr2* Then | If myVar < yourVar Then | Less than comparison |
| <= | Operator | If *expr1* <= *expr2* Then | If x <= 10 Then | Less than or equal to comparison |
| Mod | Operator | *result = expr1* Mod *expr2* | If myVar Mod 10 > 0 Then | Modulus arithmetic, returns only the remainder of a division of two numbers |
| * | Operator | *result = expr1 * expr2* | x = myNumber * _ Document.Form1.Text1.Value | Multiplication |
| - | Operator | *result = expr1 − expr2* | Document.Form1.Text2.Text = Document.Form1.Text1.Text − 20 | Subtraction |
| Or | Operator | If *expr1* Or *expr2* Then | If x = 10 Or y > 50 Then | Logical disjunction |

| Keyword | Type | Syntax | Example | Purpose |
|---------|------|--------|---------|---------|
| & | Operator | *result = string & string* | strMsg = "The error number was: " – & Str (Err.Number) | Concatenates two string values |
| Xor | Operator | *expression* Xor *expression* | If (myVar = 10) Xor (yourVar = 20) Then | Logical exclusion. The result of the evaluation is shown in the next table |

*Truth Table for the Xor Operator*

| If expression1 is | And expression2 is | The result is |
|-------------------|--------------------|--------------| 
| True | True | False |
| True | False | True |
| False | True | True |
| False | False | False |

# Options

| Keyword | Type | Syntax | Purpose |
|---------|------|--------|---------|
| Option Explicit | Statement | Option Explicit | Requires variable declaration |

# Program Flow

| Keyword | Type | Syntax | Example | Purpose |
|---------|------|--------|---------|---------|
| Call | Statement | Call *subroutinename* [()] | Call cmdbutton_ OnClick() | Passes execution to a subroutine or event handler |
| Do Loop Until | Statement | Do ... Loop Until *condition* | Do     x = x + 1 Loop until x >= 10 | Executes code at least once and repeats it until a condition is True |
| Do Loop While | Statement | Do ... Loop While *condition* | Do     x = x + 1 Loop while x < 10 | Executes code at least once and repeats it while a condition is True |
| Do Until Loop | Statement | Do Until *condition* ... Loop | Do Until x >= 10     x = x + 1 Loop | Repeats code until a condition is true |
| Do While Loop | Statement | Do While *condition* ... Loop | Do While x < 10     x = x + 1 Loop | Repeats code while a condition is true |
| For...Next | Statement | For *counter = lower* To *upper* [*step*] ... Next | For i = 1 To 10 ... Next | Repeats a block of code until the counter reaches a given number |

| Keyword | Type | Syntax | Example | Purpose |
|---------|------|--------|---------|---------|
| If...Then<br>Else<br>End If | Statement | If *condition* Then<br>  ... (code to execute<br>  if condition is true)<br>Else<br>  ... (code to execute<br>  if condition is false)<br>End If | If x = 10 Then<br>  Alert "x is 10"<br>Else<br>  Alert "x is not 10"<br>End If | Conditional execution of code |
| Select Case | Statement | Select Case *testexpr*<br>Case *expression*<br>  ...<br>Case *expression*<br>  ...<br>Case Else<br>End Select | Select Case x<br>Case 10<br>  Alert "x is 10"<br>Case 20<br>  Alert "x is 20"<br>End Select | Selective execution of code. Where *testexpr* must match *expression* |
| While...<br>Wend | Statement | While expression<br>  ...<br>Wend | While x < 10<br>  x = x + 1<br>Wend | Execution of code block while a condition is true |

# String Handling

| Keyword | Type | Syntax | Example | Purpose |
|---------|------|--------|---------|---------|
| InStr | Function | *result* = InStr(*start*, _<br>*searched*, *sought*) | If InStr(1, Document.Form1.Text1.Value, "@") Then | Returns the starting point of one string within another string, or 0 if the substring is not found |
| LCase | Function | *result* = LCase(*string*) | strDomain = LCase(Document.Form1.Text2.Value) | Converts a string to lower case |
| Left | Function | *result* = Left(*string*, *n*) | strPart = Left(Document.Form1.Text1.Value, 5) | Returns the *n* left-most characters of a string |
| Len | Function | *result* = Len(*string*) | intLen = Len(Document.Form1.Text1.Text) | Returns the length of a string |
| LTrim | Function | *result* = LTrim(*string*) | strEmail = LTrim(TextBox1.Text) | Removes all leading spaces from a string |
| Mid | Function | *result* = Mid(*string*, _<br>*start*, *n*) | strMyVar = Mid(TextBox1.Text, 4, 6) | Returns a string of length *n*, starting at position *start* |
| Right | Function | *result* = Right(*string*, *n*) | strMyVar = Right(TextBox1.Text, 4) | Returns the rightmost *n* characters |
| RTrim | Function | *result* = RTrim(*string*) | If RTrim(myString) = "Hello" Then | Removes all trailing spaces from a string |
| Space | Function | *result* = Space(*n*) | strNew = strOld & Space(5) & strOther | Returns a string consisting of *n* spaces |

| Keyword | Type | Syntax | Example | Purpose |
|---------|------|--------|---------|---------|
| StrComp | Function | *result* = StrComp(*strng1*, _ *strng2*, [*comptype*]) | If StrComp(myString, yourString) = 1 Then | Returns an integer variant representing the result of a comparison of two strings.  comptype can take any of the values shown in the next table.  The function's return value is shown in the following table. |
| String | Function | *result* = String(*n*, *character*) | strBreak = String(80, "-") | Returns a string consisting of n number of *character* |
| Trim | Function | *result* = Trim(*string*) | If Trim(strResponse) = strMyString Then | Removes both leading and trailing spaces |
| UCase | Function | *result* = UCase(*string*) | strMyString = UCase(document. form1.text1.value) | Returns a string of uppercase characters |

*Values of the comptype Parameter of the StrComp Function*

| comptype value | Comparison Method |
|----------------|-------------------|
| 0 (default) | Binary (case sensitive) |
| 1 | Text |

*Values Returned by the StrComp Function*

| Result | Return Value |
|--------|--------------|
| *strng1* < *strng2* | -1 |
| *strng1* = *strng2* | 0 |
| *strng1* > *strng2* | 1 |

# Variants

| Keyword | Type | Syntax | Example | Purpose |
|---------|------|--------|---------|---------|
| IsArray | Function | *result* = IsArray(*expr*) | If IsArray(myVar) Then | Returns True (−1) if *expr* is an array and False (0) if not |
| IsDate | Function | *result* = IsDate(*expr*) | If IsDate(document. form1.text2.value) Then | Returns True (−1) if *expr* is a valid date and False (0) if not |
| IsEmpty | Function | *result* = IsEmpty(*expr*) | If IsEmpty(myVar) Then | Returns True (−1) if *expr* equates to an Empty sub type and False (0) if not |
| IsNull | Function | *result* = IsNull(*expr*) | If Not IsNull(myVar) Then | Returns True (−1) if *expr* equates to an Null sub type and False (0) if not |

| Keyword | Type | Syntax | Example | Purpose |
|---|---|---|---|---|
| IsNumeric | Function | *result* = IsNumeric(*expr*) | If IsNumeric(document.form1.text2.value) Then | Returns True (−1) if *expr* is a valid numeric expression and False (0) if not |
| VarType | Function | result = VarType(expr) | myVType = VarType(document.form1.text2.value) | Returns an integer representing the data subtype of a variant |

# B

## VBScript Version 2

VBScript 2 is a significant release that includes both feature enhancements as well as new areas of functionality. The changes introduced in Version 2 span all areas of the languages, making mundane and complex programming tasks easier, as well as adding a series of new functions that do not even appear in Visual Basic yet. Whereas VBScript Version 1 was developed primarily for use as a client-side scripting language, VBScript Version 2 is a general-purpose language for scripting on both the client and the server. Consequently, some of the features incorporated into VBScript Version 2 are only for use when writing Active Server scripts for IIS; these server-side features (like the *GetObject* function, for instance) are not discussed in this appendix.

At the time of writing, MSIE is still being supplied with VBScript Version 1; VBScript Version 2 is an extra download from the Microsoft VBScript web site (*http://www.microsoft.com/vbscript*). The Version 2 self-extracting executable file actually contains both VBScript Version 2 and JScript (the Microsoft implementation of JavaScript) Version 2. In addition, at the time of writing, a third version of VBScript—VBScript Version 3—has appeared, although only in public beta. The major difference between it and Version 2 is that Version 3 handles support for script debugging, and is installed automatically as part of the Script Debugger from Microsoft.

The fact that Microsoft has invested time and money in creating a second and much improved version of VBScript bodes well for the future of the language. It also shows that they have listened to the marketplace by including much of the functionality asked for by developers through the VBScript mailing list and newsgroups.

This chapter is devoted to the new features in VBScript that can be used on the client. Several of these (such as the functions that allow a script to determine which scripting engine it is running under) are useful primarily if executed on the client, while others (like the new variable declarations) are general enhancements that can be used both on the client and on the server. A few features new to VBScript are intended to be executed primarily or exclusively on the server, in server-side scripts; they are not covered in this appendix.

# Script Engine Identification

Whenever a new version of a language is released, the question of compatibility arises. In the case of VBScript, none of the functions already implemented within Version 1 have changed under Version 2, so your Version 1 script will still operate with the Version 2 scripting engine. However, because there is a large installed base of Version 1 scripting engines (which may well continue to exist for quite some time), you need a method that allows your script to determine if the new features in Version 2 can be safely used in the client's browser. Version 2 therefore includes several functions that return details about the current scripting engine. These functions ensure that, as the language develops, you can create scripts that operate with all flavors of VBScript, while clients equipped with the latest scripting engines can take advantage of the new features.

It may have already occurred to you that there's a problem here: if the functions that return details about the scripting engine have only been implemented in Version 2, then they're useless as a means of determining the version of the scripting engine, since they'll necessarily produce a syntax error when run under Version 1. But in fact, when these scripting engine function calls are used in VBScript 1, the function names are treated as uninitialized variable names by the VBScript 1 scripting engine, so the functions will therefore "return" zero-length or empty strings. The function calls, however, will generate errors when run under Version 1 if the `OPTION EXPLICIT` directive has been used.

The following four scripting engine functions, none of which takes any parameters, have been added to VBScript Version 2:

- **ScriptEngine**. Returns the name of the current scripting engine. VBScript Version 2 onwards will return "VBScript." This function is really only relevant to someone programming in JavaScript, as the Microsoft implementation of the JavaScript engine returns JScript as opposed to JavaScript.

- **ScriptEngineMajorVersion**. If you've installed the Script Debugger, the *ScriptEngineMajorVersion* function currently will return 3; otherwise, it will return 2 for Version 2.

- **ScriptEngineMinorVersion**. Currently returns 0. Microsoft appears to be releasing VBScript in major new versions only (Version 1, Version 2, Version 3).

Should Microsoft at some point release a Version 3.5, for example, the *ScriptEngineMinorVersion* function would return 5.

- **ScriptEngineBuildVersion.** It is unlikely that individual builds of the scripting engine will add more functionality. However, this information can be very useful in cases where a serious bug is known to exist in a particular build. If you can return the build number of the client's scripting engine, you can then work around the bug.

Example B-1 below shows how to return the Script Engine identity values.

*Example B-1. The Scripting Engine Functions*

```
<HTML>
<HEAD>
<SCRIPT LANGUAGE="VBScript">
   Dim CRLF
   CRLF = Chr(13) & Chr(10)

   Sub cmdShowEngine_OnClick
      Dim sMsg
      sMsg = "Script Engine: " & ScriptEngine() & CRLF _
           & "Major Version      : " & ScriptEngineMajorVersion() & CRLF _
           & "Minor Version: " & ScriptEngineMinorVersion() & CRLF _
           & "Build          : " & ScriptEngineBuildVersion()
      MsgBox sMsg
   End Sub
</SCRIPT>
</HEAD>
<BODY BGCOLOR="white">
<INPUT TYPE="button" NAME="cmdShowEngine"
</BODY>
</HTML>
```

# *Variable Declarations*

VBScript Version 2 makes working with constants and variables easier by adding language elements that allow you to more precisely define the scope of a variable, explicitly define constants, and determine the subtype of individual variables. These new language features are:

- **Private.** The `Private` declaration statement allows you to declare a variable whose scope is restricted to the script in which it is declared. Its general syntax is:

    `Private variablename`

    where *variablename* is a single variable or a comma-delimited list of variable names. See Chapter 3, *Getting Started*, for a more detailed explanation of the `Private` statement.

- **Public**. The `Public` declaration statement allows you to declare a variable that is available to the script in which it is declared, to other scripts within the same document, and even to other documents within the browser. Its syntax is:

  ```
  Public variablename
  ```

  where *variablename* is a single variable or a comma-delimited list of variable names. See Chapter 3 for a more detailed explanation of the `Public` statement.

- **Const**. The `Const` declaration statement allows you to create true constants that cannot have their value changed during their lifetime. Once the name of the constant is declared, you can use it in place of the value it represents, to make your code more understandable and self-documenting. Trying to change a constant's value will generate a run-time error. The syntax of the `Const` statement is:

  ```
  Const constname = literalvalue
  ```

  *literalvalue* must be the actual string or numeric value that you want to assign to the constant; the `Const` statement does not allow you to assign the value of a variable or the value returned by a function to a constant.

  Example B-2 shows how to use the `Const` statement—and how *not* to use it!

*Example B-2. Using and Misusing a Constant*

```
<HTML>
<HEAD>
<TITLE>Constant Example</TITLE>
<SCRIPT LANGUAGE="vbscript">

    Const MYCONST = 5

    Sub CmdButton1_OnClick
        Alert MYCONST
        '*** the following line generates an error ***
        MYCONST = 7
    End Sub

</SCRIPT>
</HEAD>
<BODY BGCOLOR="white">
<INPUT TYPE="button" NAME="cmdButton1" VALUE="Constant">
</BODY>
</HTML>
```

- **TypeName**. The *TypeName* function is similar to the *VarType* function, except that, whereas the *VarType* function returns a number representing the data subtype of the variable passed to the function, *TypeName* returns a string containing the actual name of the data subtype. For instance, if you pass an inte-

ger variable to *VarType*, it returns 2, whereas *TypeName* returns "Integer."
Example B-3 illustrates the use of the *TypeName* function.

*Example B-3. The TypeName Function*

```
<HTML>
<HEAD>
<SCRIPT LANGUAGE="vbscript">
    Sub cmdButton1_OnClick
        Dim x

        If IsDate(frmForm1.txtText1.Value) Then
            x = CDate(frmForm1.txtText1.Value)
        ElseIf IsNumeric(frmForm1.txtText1.Value) Then
            x = CDbl(frmForm1.txtText1.Value)
        ElseIf frmForm1.txtText1.Value > "" Then
            x = Trim(frmForm1.txtText1.Value)
        End If

        Alert TypeName(x)

    End Sub
</SCRIPT>
</HEAD>
<BODY BGCOLOR="white">
<FONT FACE="arial">
<CENTER>
<H3>TypeName()</H3>
<BR><BR>
<FORM NAME="frmForm1">
<INPUT TYPE="text" NAME="txtText1"><BR><BR>
<INPUT TYPE="button" NAME="cmdButton1" VALUE="What Type?">
</FORM>
</CENTER>
</BODY>
</HTML>
```

- **Data Type Intrinsic Constants.** In VBScript Version 1, you had to remember which integer value corresponded to which data subtype whenever you interpreted the return value of the *VarType* function. In VBScript Version 2, on the other hand, you can use the constants shown in Table B-1 to represent the integers that *VarType* uses to represent data subtypes.

*Table B-1. Intrinsic Constants for Use With the VarType Function*

| Constant | Value | Description |
|----------|-------|-------------|
| vbEmpty | 0 | Empty (uninitialized) |
| vbNull | 1 | Null (no valid data) |
| vbInteger | 2 | Integer |
| vbLong | 3 | Long integer |
| vbSingle | 4 | Single-precision floating-point number |

*Table B-1. Intrinsic Constants for Use With the VarType Function (continued)*

| Constant | Value | Description |
|----------|-------|-------------|
| vbDouble | 5 | Double-precision floating-point number |
| vbCurrency | 6 | Currency |
| vbDate | 7 | Date |
| vbString | 8 | String |
| vbObject | 9 | Automation object |
| vbError | 10 | Error |
| vbBoolean | 11 | Boolean |
| vbVariant | 12 | Variant (used only with arrays of Variants) |
| vbDataObject | 13 | Data-access object |
| vbByte | 17 | Byte |
| vbArray | 8192 | Array |

- **Array()**. In VBScript 1, filling an array involves assigning individual values on an element-by-element basis. Where array values are known in advance, the *Array* function makes it much easier to define the values of individual elements, since it can be used to create a variant array of values that are passed to it in a comma-delimited list. For example, the statement:

```
myArray = Array(2,3,5,7,12)
```

returns an array consisting of five elements, `myArray`(0)—whose value is 2—through `myArray`(4)—whose value is 12. See Chapter 3 for further details on the *Array* function.

# Data Conversion: The Currency Subtype

Since Version 2 of VBScript adds support for a new data type, the currency subtype, it necessarily requires some means of converting numeric and string data to currency data. The function that does this is *CCur*; its general syntax is:

```
CCur(expression)
```

where **expression** is any numeric or string expression that is able to be converted to a currency value.

# The Dictionary Object

The *Dictionary* object, while not strictly an array, is in many ways very similar to an array; in fact, it is based loosely on the Perl associative array. It contains data that are held in elements like an array, but in a *Dictionary* object these elements are called Items. Accessing the value of these dictionary items is performed by using unique keys, rather than by using the element index numbers with which you access elements in an array. In this way the *Dictionary* object is also very similar to the now ubiquitous *Visual Basic Collection* object.

This makes the *Dictionary* object ideal when you need to access data that are associated with a particular unique named value. If you only need to access your data sequentially, though, an array is a better option.

A good example of a situation in which the *Dictionary* object is preferable to an array is a list of product IDs and product descriptions. Given the product description, your web page is required to return the product ID. To implement this in VBScript using arrays, you would have to use two arrays, one containing the product IDs, and the other containing the product descriptions. (VBScript, remember, doesn't support user-defined data types, which would allow you to define an array that included both items of information in a single array element.) To find a given product's description, your script searches the product ID array sequentially until a match is found, then uses the same index number to retrieve the product description from the product description array. Here's how that code snippet may look:

```
ReturnValue = ""
For x = 0 to UBound(ProductID)
    If ProductID(x) = SearchValue Then
        ReturnValue = ProductDescription(x)
        Exit For
    End If
Next
If ReturnValue = "" Then
    Alert "Product ID cannot be found"
End If
```

Now look how much easier and neater the coding is to implement the same thing using a *Dictionary* object. And there's an added bonus: you can immediately inform the user if the product ID does not exist, as you can see from the following code fragment:

```
If ProdDict.Exists(SearchValue) Then
    ReturnValue = ProdDict.Item(SearchValue)
Else
    Alert "Product ID cannot be found"
End If
```

The first step in using a *Dictionary* object is to create it, for which a special function, *CreateObject*, is available. (The *Dictionary* object is the only object that will allow you to call *CreateObject* on the client side.) To create a *Dictionary* object, you must first declare a variable that will become an object variable of type Dictionary. You then assign a reference to an instance of the *Dictionary* object using the **Set** command, like this:

```
Dim myDict
Set myDict = CreateObject("Scripting.Dictionary")
```

---

## Note for VB Programmers

Because VBScript does not yet support the "As" type definition, and therefore you can only dimension variables as variants, you cannot use early binding in VBScript.

---

You can now use the *myDict* variable as a *Dictionary* object to call *Dictionary* object methods, and set and return *Dictionary* object properties.

## Dictionary Object Properties

The *Dictionary* object includes the following four properties:

- **CompareMode.** Sets or returns the mode used to compare the keys in a *Dictionary* object. The *CompareMode* setting is used by *StrComp*, the string comparison function. *CompareMode* can only be set on a dictionary that does not contain any data. Acceptable values for *CompareMode* are 0 (Binary), 1 (Text), and 2 (Database). Values greater than 2 can be used to refer to comparisons using specific locale IDs (LCIDs). You need to explicitly set the *CompareMode* property only if you do not wish to use the default binary comparison mode.

- **Count.** A read-only property that returns the number of key/item pairs in a *Dictionary* object. The following code fragment shows how you can use the *Count* property.

```
Dim vArray
vArray = DictObj.Items
For i = 0 to DictObj.Count -1
    Document.Write vArray(i)
Next
```

- **Item.** Sets or returns the data item to be linked to a specified key in a *Dictionary* object. If you try to set an item to a nonexistent key, the key is added to the dictionary and the item is linked to it, a sort of implicit "add." However, the dictionary exhibits rather strange behavior when you try to return the item linked to a nonexistent key, since it adds the key to the *Dictionary* object along with a blank item.

    The syntax for setting an item is:

    ```
    dictionaryobject.Item(key) = item
    ```

    The syntax for returning an item is:

    ```
    value = dictionaryobject.Item(key)
    ```

where the parameters are as follows:

`dictionaryobject`

> A reference to a *Dictionary* object

`key`

> A unique string key for this *Dictionary* object

`Item`

> The data associated with `key`

- **key**. Returns the key or replaces an existing key with a new one. As with the *Item* property, if a key that you are attempting to change does not exist, the new key is added to the dictionary and is linked to a blank item.

The syntax for setting a new key is:

`dictionaryobject.Key(key) = newkey`

---

WARNING   **Nonexistent Keys**. Because of the strange (but by-design) behavior of the key in the *Dictionary* object, in which a search for a nonexistent key results in the key being added to the *Dictionary* object without an error or warning, you should check for the existence of a key prior to setting either the *Item* or the *Key* properties, by using the *Exists* method shown in the following section.

---

## Dictionary Object Methods

The *Dictionary* object supports seven methods, which allow you to perform such operations as adding a key, retrieving the value that corresponds to a key, or deleting a key. The methods are:

- **Add**. Adds a key and its associated item to the specified *Dictionary* object. If the key is not unique, an error will be generated. Its syntax is:

  `dictionaryobject.Add key, item`

- **Exists**. Returns True if the specified key exists in the *Dictionary* object, and False if it does not. Its syntax is:

  `dictionaryobject.Exists(key)`

- **Items**. Returns a 0-based array containing all the items in the specified *Dictionary* object. The data items can then be accessed like an array in the normal way, as the following code snippet shows:

```
Dim vArray
vArray = DictObj.Items
For i = 0 to DictObj.Count -1
    Document.Write vArray(i)
Next
```

- **Keys**. Returns a 0-based array containing only the keys in the specified *Dictionary* object. The keys can then be accessed like an array in the normal way, as the following code snippet shows:

```
Dim vArray
vArray = DictObj.Keys
For i = 0 to DictObj.Count -1
    Document.Write vArray(i)
Next
```

- **Remove**. Removes both the specified key and its associated data (i.e., item) from the dictionary. Its syntax is:

```
dictionaryobject.Remove(key)
```

- **RemoveAll**. Clears out the dictionary. In other words, it removes all keys and their associated data from the dictionary. Its syntax is:

```
dictionaryobject.RemoveAll
```

Example B-4 illustrates most of the available properties and methods of the *Dictionary* object, and allows you to see how the object is created and used.

*Example B-4. Properties and Methods of the Dictionary Object*

```
<HTML>
<HEAD>
<SCRIPT LANGUAGE="vbscript">
    Dim dicTestDict
    Dim frm

    Sub Window_OnLoad
        Set dicTestDict = CreateObject("Scripting.Dictionary")
        Set frm = Document.frmForm1
    End Sub

    Sub cmdAddNew_OnClick
        If dicTestDict.Exists(frm.txtNewKey.Value) Then
            Alert "This key already exists"
        Else
            dicTestDict.Add frm.txtNewKey.Value, frm.txtNewItem.Value
            Alert "Key and item added successfully"
        End If
    End Sub

    Sub cmdChangeItem_OnClick
        If Not dicTestDict.Exists(frm.txtKeyChangeItem.Value) Then
            Alert "This key does not exist"
        Else
            dicTestDict.Item(frm.txtKeyChangeItem.Value) = _
                        frm.txtChangeItem.Value
            Alert "Item successfully changed"
        End If
    End Sub
```

*Example B-4. Properties and Methods of the Dictionary Object (continued)*

```
    Sub cmdFindItem_OnClick
        If Not dicTestDict.Exists(frm.txtFindKey.Value) Then
            Alert "This key does not exist"
        Else
            Alert dicTestDict.Item(frm.txtFindKey.Value)
        End If
    End Sub

Sub cmdShowKeys_OnClick
    Dim msg
    Dim i
    Dim keyArray

    keyArray = dicTestDict.Keys

    For i = 0 to dicTestDict.Count - 1
        msg = msg & keyArray(i) & vbCrLf
    Next

    Msgbox msg, 0, "All current Keys"

    End Sub

    Sub cmdShowItems_OnClick
        Dim msg
        Dim i
        Dim itemArray

        itemArray = dicTestDict.Items

        For i = 0 to dicTestDict.Count - 1
            msg = msg & itemArray(i) & vbCrLf
        Next

        Msgbox msg, 0, "All current Items"

    End Sub

    Sub cmdRemoveItem_OnClick
        If Not dicTestDict.Exists(frm.txtRemoveKey.Value) Then
            Alert "This key does not exist"
        Else
            dicTestDict.Remove(frm.txtRemoveKey.Value)
            Alert "Item & Key successfully removed"
        End If
    End Sub

</SCRIPT>
</HEAD>
<BODY BGCOLOR="white">
<FONT FACE="arial"><FONT SIZE=3>
<CENTER>
```

*Example B-4. Properties and Methods of the Dictionary Object (continued)*

```
<H3>Using the Dictionary Object</H3>
</CENTER>
<P>
<FORM NAME="frmForm1">
<HR>
 <B>Add a new Item</B><BR>
  Enter the new Key
  <INPUT TYPE="text" NAME="txtNewKey">  
  Enter the new Item
  <INPUT TYPE="text" NAME="txtNewItem">  
  <INPUT TYPE="button" NAME="cmdAddNew" VALUE="Add New Key / Item">
<BR>
<HR>
 <B>Change an Item</B><BR>
  Enter the Key
  <INPUT TYPE="text" NAME="txtKeyChangeItem">  
  Enter the new Item
  <INPUT TYPE="text" NAME="txtChangeItem">  
  <INPUT TYPE="button" NAME="cmdChangeItem" VALUE="Change Item">
<BR>
<HR>
 <B>Find an Item</B><BR>
  Enter the Key
  <INPUT TYPE="text" NAME="txtFindKey">  
  <INPUT TYPE="button" NAME="cmdFindItem" VALUE="Find Item">
<BR>
<HR>
 <B>Show All Keys</B>  
  <INPUT TYPE="button" NAME="cmdShowKeys" VALUE="Show all Keys">
<BR>
<HR>
 <B>Show All Items</B>  
  <INPUT TYPE="button" NAME="cmdShowItems" VALUE="Show all Items">
<BR>
<HR>
 <B>Remove an Item</B><BR>
  Enter the Key
  <INPUT TYPE="text" NAME="txtRemoveKey">  
  <INPUT TYPE="button" NAME="cmdRemoveItem" VALUE="Remove Item">
<BR>
<HR>

</TABLE>
</FORM>
</CENTER>
</BODY>
</HTML>
```

# *Program Flow: For Each...Next*

A major addition to the VBScript language is the inclusion of the `For Each...Next` loop, which has proven so popular and valuable in Visual Basic 4.0. This special type of loop iterates through collections of objects, or an array, and returns the current object or array element in an object variable. This allows the same code to be applied to each item of an array or collection. Its general syntax is:

```
For Each itemvariablename in collectionvariablename
...
Next
```

For example:

```
Dim myElement
For Each myElement in MyArray
    Document.Write myElement
Next
```

For more detailed information, see Chapter 4, *Program Flow and Structure.*

# *Dates and Times*

Its date and time functions are probably the area in which VBScript Version 2 is most improved over Version 1. VBScript Version 2 features six new date and time functions:

- **DateAdd**. Lets you add or subtract a given number of time intervals from a specified date or time. For more information, see Chapter 10, *Date and Time in VBScript.*

- **DateDiff**. Returns the number of specified time intervals between two dates or times. For more information, see Chapter 10.

- **DatePart**. Returns a given date or time interval from a specified date or time. For more information, see Chapter 10.

- **Weekday**. Returns the ordinal number of the day of the week from a specified date expression. See Chapter 10 for more information

- **WeekdayName**. *WeekdayName* accepts a number between 1 and 7 and returns the real name of the day, starting with 1 as Sunday. Example B-5 illustrates the use of the *WeekdayName* function.

*Example B-5. The WeekdayName Function*

```
<HTML>
<HEAD><TITLE>WEEKDAYNAME</TITLE>
</HEAD>
```

*Example B-5. The WeekdayName Function (continued)*

```
<BODY BGCOLOR="White">
<CENTER>
<H2>
<SCRIPT LANGUAGE="vbscript">
  Document.Write WeekDayName(DatePart("w",Now()))
</SCRIPT>
</H2>
</BODY>
</HTML>
```

- **MonthName**. *MonthName* accepts a number between 1 and 12, and returns the name of the given month. It is illustrated in Example B-6.

*Example B-6. The MonthName Function*

```
<HTML>
<HEAD><TITLE>MONTHNAME</TITLE>
</HEAD>
<BODY BGCOLOR="White">
<CENTER>
<H2>
<SCRIPT LANGUAGE="vbscript">
  Document.Write MonthName(DatePart("m",Now()))
</SCRIPT>
</H2>
</BODY>
</HTML>
```

# *Formatting*

When VBScript was initially released, VB programmers who were beginning to write scripts using VBScript complained bitterly about the failure to include the VB *Format* function in VBScript. Interestingly, it's still absent from VBScript. Instead, Microsoft has added four general-purpose functions, as well as the *Round* function:

- **FormatDateTime**. Allows you to format a date or time expression based on the regional settings of the client computer. See Chapter 10 for more information.

- **FormatCurrency**, **FormatNumber**, **FormatPercent**. These three numerical formatting functions are discussed in depth in Chapter 14, *Form Input Validation*.

- **Round**. Rounds a given number to a specified number of decimal places. Its syntax is:

```
Round(expression[, numdecimalplaces])
```

where ***expression*** is the number to be rounded, and ***numdecimalplaces*** is the number of decimal places to which it is to be rounded. Example B-7 allows you to experiment with how *Round* treats precision; you enter the number to round and the precision you require (up to 16 decimal places).

*Example B-7. The Round Function*

```
<HTML>
<HEAD>
<SCRIPT LANGUAGE="vbscript">
Sub cmdButton_OnClick
    'the round function will round to a
    'maximum of 16 decimal places
    'starts by rounding the nth decimal
    'place specified.

    frmForm1.txtRounded.Value = Round(frmForm1.txtmyNumber.Value, _
                    frmForm1.txtDecPlaces.Value)
End sub
</SCRIPT>
</HEAD>
<BODY BGCOLOR="white">
<FONT FACE="arial">
<CENTER>
<H3>Round()</H3>
<BR><BR>
<FORM NAME="frmForm1">
Enter a number
<INPUT TYPE="text" NAME="txtMyNumber"><BR>
Enter the number of decimal places
<INPUT TYPE="text" NAME="txtDecPlaces"><BR>
<INPUT TYPE="button" NAME="cmdButton" Value="Round Now!">
<BR><BR>
<INPUT TYPE="text" NAME="txtRounded"><BR>
</FORM>
</BODY>
</HTML>
```

# String Manipulation

Although VBScript Version 1 included the standard set of string manipulation functions, VBScript Version 2 includes a number of string handling functions that reflect the needs of client/server applications in general and web applications in particular. The new functions are:

- **Filter**. Produces an array of matching values from an array of source values that either match or do not match a given filter. In other words, individual elements are copied from a source array to a target array if they either match or do not match a filter string. Its syntax is:

  `result = **Filter**(SourceArray, FilterString[, Switch[, Compare]])`

  where the parameters are as follows:

*result*
> An array of the elements filtered from *SourceArray*

*SourceArray*
> An array containing values you wish to filter

*FilterString*
> The string of characters you wish to find within the source array

*Switch*
> A Boolean (True or False) value. If **True**, *Filter* includes all matching values in *result*; if **False**, *Filter* excludes all matching values (or, to put it another way, includes all nonmatching values).

*Compare*
> An optional constant (possible values are **vbBinaryCompare** or **vbTextCompare**) that indicates the type of string comparison to use.

Example B-8 allows you to see the result of allowing or disallowing a *FilterString* from a *Filter* function call.

*Example B-8. Including or Excluding Elements Based on a Filter String*

```
<HTML>
<HEAD>
<SCRIPT LANGUAGE="vbscript">
  Dim blnInclude

  Sub cmdButton_OnClick

      myArray = array("this", "that", "the other", "something")
      myFilter = filter(myArray, "thi", blnInclude)
      sMsg = ""
      For i = 0 to uBound(myFilter)
          sMsg = sMsg & myFilter(i) & vbCrLf
      Next

      MsgBox sMsg, 0, "Filter"

  End Sub
</SCRIPT>
</HEAD>
<BODY BGCOLOR="white">
<FONT FACE="arial">
<CENTER>
<H3>Filter()</H3>
Stored words = "this", "that", "the other" & "something"<BR>
Check this option to INCLUDE words containing "thi"
    <INPUT LANGUAGE="VBScript" TYPE=radio ONCLICK="blnInclude = True"
NAME="optInclude"><BR>
Check this option to EXCLUDE words containing "thi"
    <INPUT LANGUAGE="VBScript" TYPE=radio ONCLICK="blnInclude = False"
NAME="optInclude">
```

*Example B-8. Including or Excluding Elements Based on a Filter String (continued)*

```
<BR><BR>
    <FORM NAME="frmForm1">
        <INPUT TYPE=button VALUE="Filter Now!" NAME="cmdButton">
    </FORM>
</BODY>
</HTML>
```

- **InStrRev**. Determines the starting position of a substring within a string by searching from the end of the string to its beginning. Its syntax is:

```
InstrRev(sourcestring, soughtstring[, start[, compare]])
```

where the parameters are as follows:

*sourcestring*
>    The string to be searched

*soughtstring*
>    The substring to be found within *sourcestring*

*start*
>    The starting position of the search

*compare*
>    The method used to compare *soughtstring* with *sourcestring*; its value can be either **vbBinaryCompare** or **vbTextCompare**.

See Chapter 14 for more details.

- **Join**. Concatenates an array of values into a delimited string using a specified delimiter. Its syntax is:

```
result = Join(sourcearray, delimiter)
```

where the parameters are as follows:

*result*
>    The concatenated string

*sourcearray*
>    Array whose elements are to be concatenated

*delimiter*
>    Character used to delimit the individual values in the string. If none is specified, the space character is used as a delimiter.

Example B-9 illustrates the *Join* function.

*Example B-9. The Join Function*

```
<HTML>
<HEAD>
    <SCRIPT LANGUAGE="vbscript">
        Dim sMyArray()
```

*Example B-9. The Join Function (continued)*

```
        Dim blnInit
        blnInit = True
        ReDim sMyArray(0)

        Sub cmdButton1_OnClick
            If Not blnInit Then
                Redim Preserve sMyArray(UBound(sMyArray)+1)
            Else
                blnInit = False
            End If
            sMyArray(UBound(sMyArray)) = frmForm1.txtText1.Value
            frmForm1.txtText1.Value = ""
        End Sub

        Sub cmdButton2_OnClick
            Alert Join(sMyArray, ",")
        End Sub

    </SCRIPT>
</HEAD>
<BODY BGCOLOR="white">
<FONT FACE="arial">
<CENTER>
<H3>Join()</H3>
<BR><BR>
<FORM NAME="frmForm1">
    Enter a word and click "Save Word".  Do this several
    times and then click "Show Joined Words".<BR>
    <INPUT TYPE="text" NAME="txtText1"><BR>
    <INPUT TYPE="button" NAME="cmdButton1" VALUE="Save Word"><BR><BR>
    <INPUT TYPE="button" NAME="cmdButton2" VALUE="Show Joined Words">
</FORM>
</BODY>
</HTML>
```

- **Replace**. Replaces a number of substrings within a string with another sub-string. *Replace* is discussed in detail in Chapter 14.

- **Split**. The converse function to *Join*, it parses a single string containing delimited values into an array. Its syntax is:

  ```
  Split (expression[, delimiter[, count[, compare]]])
  ```

  where the parameters are as follows:

*expression*

A string to be broken up into multiple strings

*delimiter*

The character used to delimit the substrings in *expression*

*count*

An optional value indicating the number of strings to be returned. If *count* is omitted or its value is −1, all strings are returned.

*compare*

The method of comparison. Possible values are `vbBinaryCompare` or `vbTextCompare`.

The use of the *Split* function is illustrated in Example B-10.

*Example B-10. The Split Function*

```
<HTML>
<HEAD>
<SCRIPT LANGUAGE="vbscript">
    Dim sString
    Dim sMyArray
    sString = "One,Two,Three,Four,Five"
</SCRIPT>
</HEAD>
<BODY BGCOLOR="white">
<FONT FACE="arial">
<CENTER>
<H3>Split()</H3>
<BR><BR>
<SCRIPT LANGUAGE="vbscript">
    Dim i
    myArray = Split(sString, ",")
    For i = 0 to UBound(myArray)
        Document.Write myArray(i) & "<BR>"
    Next
</SCRIPT>
</CENTER>
</BODY>
</HTML>
```

- **StrReverse**. Returns a string that is the reverse of the string passed to it. Its syntax is:

  `StrReverse(str_expression)`

  where ***str_expression*** is the string whose characters are to be reversed. For example, if the string "and" is passed to it as an argument, *StrReverse* returns the string "dna".

# C

# VBScript 2.0 Intrinsic Constants

This appendix details the new VBScript 2.0 intrinsic (built-in) constants.

## Color Constants

| Constant | Value |
|----------|-------|
| vbBlack | &h00 |
| vbRed | &hFF |
| vbGreen | &hFF00 |
| vbYellow | &hFFFF |
| vbBlue | &hFF0000 |
| vbMagenta | &hFF00FF |
| vbCyan | &hFFFF00 |
| vbWhite | &hFFFFFF |

## Comparison Constants

| Constant | Value | Description |
|----------|-------|-------------|
| vbBinaryCompare | 0 | A binary comparison |
| vbTextCompare | 1 | A textual comparison |
| vbDatabaseCompare | 2 | Comparison method defined by the database in which the comparison is made |

# Date and Time Constants

## Day of the Week

| Constant | Value | Description |
|---|---|---|
| vbSunday | 1 | Sunday |
| vbMonday | 2 | Monday |
| vbTuesday | 3 | Tuesday |
| vbWednesday | 4 | Wednesday |
| vbThursday | 5 | Thursday |
| vbFriday | 6 | Friday |
| vbSaturday | 7 | Saturday |
| vbUseSystemDayOfWeek | 0 | Use the day of the week specified in the system settings for the first day of the week |

## First Week of the Year

| Constant | Value | Description |
|---|---|---|
| vbFirstJan1 | 1 | Use the week in which January 1 occurs (default). |
| vbFirstFourDays | 2 | Use the first week that has at least four days in the new year. |
| vbFirstFullWeek | 3 | Use the first full week of the year. |

## Date Formats

| Constant | Value | Display a date/time using |
|---|---|---|
| vbGeneralDate | 0 | For real numbers, display a date and time. If there is no fractional part, display only a date. If there is no integer part, display time only. Date and time display is determined by the computer's system settings. |
| vbLongDate | 1 | The long date format specified in the computer's regional settings. |
| vbShortDate | 2 | The short date format specified in the computer's regional settings. |
| vbLongTime | 3 | The long time format specified in the computer's regional settings. |
| vbShortTime | 4 | The short time format specified in the computer's regional settings. |

# MsgBox Constants

## MsgBox Button Constants

| Constant | Value | Buttons to display |
|---|---|---|
| vbOKOnly | 0 | OK button only |
| vbOKCancel | 1 | OK and Cancel buttons |
| vbAbortRetryIgnore | 2 | Abort, Retry, and Ignore buttons |
| vbYesNoCancel | 3 | Yes, No, and Cancel buttons |
| vbYesNo | 4 | Yes and No buttons |
| vbRetryCancel | 5 | Retry and Cancel buttons |

## MsgBox Icon Constants

| Constant | Value | Icon to display |
|---|---|---|
| vbCritical | 16 | Critical message |
| vbQuestion | 32 | Warning query |
| vbExclamation | 48 | Warning message |
| vbInformation | 64 | Information message |

## MsgBox Default Button on Load

| Constant | Value | Default Button |
|---|---|---|
| vbDefaultButton1 | 0 | First button |
| vbDefaultButton2 | 256 | Second button |
| vbDefaultButton3 | 512 | Third button |

## MsgBox Modality Constants

| Constant | Value | Description |
|---|---|---|
| vbApplicationModal | 0 | Application modal. The user must respond to the message box before continuing work in the application. |
| vbSystemModal | 4096 | System modal. All applications are suspended until the user responds to the message box. |

Message boxes with differing functionality can be achieved by **AND**ing different constants together. For example, the following line of code can be used to create a message box that contains Yes and No buttons, a question icon, and the No button as the default button (i.e., it has focus):

```
iResponse = MsgBox("Are you sure", vbYesNo + vbQuestion +
vbDefaultButton2, "Query")
```

## MsgBox Return Value Constants

| Constant | Value | Button clicked |
|----------|-------|----------------|
| vbOK     | 1     | OK button      |
| vbCancel | 2     | Cancel button  |
| vbAbort  | 3     | Abort button   |
| vbRetry  | 4     | Retry button   |
| vbIgnore | 5     | Ignore button  |
| vbYes    | 6     | Yes button     |
| vbNo     | 7     | No button      |

# String Constants

| Constant | Value | Description |
|----------|-------|-------------|
| vbCr | *Chr*(13) | Carriage return |
| vbCrLf | *Chr*(13) & *Chr*(10) | Carriage return/linefeed combination |
| vbLf | *Chr*(10) | Linefeed |
| vbNewLine | *Chr*(13) & *Chr*(10) or *Chr*(10) | Platform-specific newline character; whatever is appropriate for the platform |
| vbNullChar | *Chr*(0) | Character having the value 0; corresponds to a C language NULL |
| vbNullString | String having value 0 | A null string; corresponds to a C language pointer to a NULL |
| vbTab | *Chr*(9) | Horizontal tab |

# Tristate Constants

| Constant | Value | Description |
|----------|-------|-------------|
| TristateTrue | −1 | True |
| TristateFalse | 0 | False |
| TristateUseDefault | −2 | Use default setting |

# VarType Constants

| Constant | Value | Variant subtype |
|---|---|---|
| vbBoolean | 11 | Boolean |
| vbByte | 17 | Byte |
| vbCurrency | 6 | Currency |
| vbDataObject | 13 | Data access object |
| vbDate | 7 | Date |
| vbDecimal | 14 | Decimal |
| vbDouble | 5 | Double |
| vbEmpty | 0 | Uninitialized (default) |
| vbError | 10 | Error |
| vbInteger | 2 | Integer |
| vbLong | .3 | Long |
| vbNull | 1 | Contains no valid data |
| vbObject | 9 | Object |
| vbSingle | 4 | Single |
| vbString | 8 | String |
| vbVariant | 12 | Variant (used only for arrays of variants) |
| vbArray | 8192 | Array |

# D

## ActiveX Controls
## Quick Reference

This appendix summarizes the properties, events, and methods for each of the standard ActiveX Controls—that is, the controls that are included either with Windows 95 or with the full installation of both MSIE 3.0 and the ActiveX Control Pad.* Do not confuse these ActiveX controls with the intrinsic HTML controls, details of which you can find in Chapter 6, *The Element Object and HTML Intrinsic Controls.*

### The Checkbox Control

The full name of the Checkbox control is the Microsoft Forms 2.0 CheckBox; it's one of the controls included in *FM20.DLL*, the Microsoft Forms 2.0 Object Library. Its properties, events, and methods are listed in Table D-1.

*Table D-1. Properties, Events, and Methods of the Checkbox Control*

**Properties**

| | | | |
|---|---|---|---|
| Accelerator | Alignment | AutoSize | BackColor |
| BackStyle | Caption | CodeBase | Enabled |
| Font | ForeColor | GroupName | Height |
| ID | Left | Locked | MouseIcon |
| MousePointer | Picture | PicturePosition | SpecialEffect |
| TabIndex | TabStop | Top | TripleState |
| Value | Visible | Width | WordWrap |

---

* A complete description of each property, method, and event, along with complete examples, can be found in the forthcoming book *VBScript in a Nutshell*, written by Paul Lomax and published by O'Reilly & Associates.

*Table D-1. Properties, Events, and Methods of the Checkbox Control (continued)*

**Events**

| AfterUpdate | BeforeDragOver | BeforeDropOrPaste | BeforeUpdate |
|---|---|---|---|
| Change | Click | DblClick | Enter |
| Error | Exit | KeyDown | KeyPress |
| KeyUp | MouseDown | MouseMove | MouseUp |

**Methods**

| SetFocus | Zorder | | |
|---|---|---|---|

# ComboBox Control

Like the Checkbox control, the Microsoft Forms 2.0 ComboBox is one of the controls included in *FM20.DLL*, the Microsoft Forms 2.0 Object Library. Its properties, events, and methods are listed in Table D-2.

*Table D-2. Properties, Events, and Methods of the ComboBox Control*

**Properties**

| AutoSize | AutoTab | AutoWordSelect | BackColor |
|---|---|---|---|
| BackStyle | BorderColor | BorderStyle | BoundColumn |
| CodeBase | Column | ColumnCount | ColumnHeads |
| ColumnWidths | DragBehavior | DropButtonStyle | Enabled |
| EnterFieldBehavior | Font | ForeColor | Height |
| HideSelection | ID | IMEMode | IntegralHeight |
| Left | List | ListCount | ListIndex |
| ListRows | ListStyle | ListWidth | Locked |
| MatchEntry | MatchRequired | MaxLength | MouseIcon |
| MousePointer | SelectionMargin | SelLength | SelStart |
| SelText | ShowDownButtonWhen | SpecialEffect | Style |
| TabIndex | TabStop | Text | TextAlign |
| TextColumn | Top | Value | Visible |
| Width | | | |

**Events**

| AfterUpdate | BeforeDragOver | BeforeDropOrPaste | BeforeUpdate |
|---|---|---|---|
| Change | Click | DblClick | DropButtonClick |
| Enter | Error | Exit | KeyDown |
| KeyPress | KeyUp | MouseDown | MouseMove |
| MouseUp | | | |

*Table D-2. Properties, Events, and Methods of the ComboBox Control (continued)*

**Methods**

| | | | |
|---|---|---|---|
| AddItem | Clear | Copy | Cut |
| DropDown | Paste | RemoveItem | SetFocus |
| ZOrder | | | |

## CommandButton Control

The CommandButton control is also included in *FM20.DLL*, the Microsoft Forms 2.0 Object Library. Its properties, events, and methods are listed in Table D-3.

*Table D-3. Properties, Events, and Methods of the CommandButton Control*

**Properties**

| | | | |
|---|---|---|---|
| Accelerator | AutoSize | BackColor | BackStyle |
| Caption | CodeBase | Enabled | Font |
| ForeColor | Height | ID | Left |
| Locked | MouseIcon | MousePointer | Picture |
| PicturePosition | TabIndex | TabStop | Top |
| Value | Visible | Width | WordWrap |

**Events**

| | | | |
|---|---|---|---|
| AfterUpdate | BeforeDragOver | BeforeDropOrPaste | BeforeUpdate |
| Click | DblClick | Enter | Error |
| Exit | KeyDown | KeyPress | KeyUp |
| MouseDown | MouseMove | MouseUp | |

**Methods**

| | | | |
|---|---|---|---|
| SetFocus | ZOrder | | |

## HotSpot Control

The Microsoft ActiveX HotSpot Control, one of the controls included in *ISCTRLS.OCX*, is an invisible run-time control that can be used in implementing image maps. Its properties, events, and methods are shown in Table D-4.

*Table D-4. Properties, Events, and Methods of the HotSpot Control*

**Properties**

| | | | |
|---|---|---|---|
| CodeBase | Enabled | Height | ID |
| Left | MouseIcon | MousePointer | TabIndex |
| TabStop | Top | Visible | Width |

*Table D-4. Properties, Events, and Methods of the HotSpot Control (continued)*

| Events | | | |
|---|---|---|---|
| Click | DblClick | Enter | Exit |
| MouseDown | MouseEnter | MouseExit | MouseMove |
| MouseUp | | | |
| **Methods** | | | |
| Move | ZOrder | | |

# Image Control

The Image control, which is also one of the components included in the Microsoft Forms 2.0 Object Library, is a container that can be used to display Windows bitmaps (.BMP) and metafiles (.WMF), along with .GIF and .JPEG files. The control's properties, events, and methods are listed in Table D-5.

*Table D-5. Properties, Events, and Methods of the Image Control*

| Properties | | | |
|---|---|---|---|
| AutoSize | BackColor | BackStyle | BorderColor |
| BorderStyle | CodeBase | Enabled | Height |
| ID | Left | PictureAlignment | PicturePath |
| PictureSizeMode | PictureTiling | SpecialEffect | Top |
| Visible | Width | | |
| **Events** | | | |
| BeforeDragOver | BeforeDropOrPaste | Enter | Exit |
| MouseDown | MouseMove | MouseUp | |
| **Methods** | | | |
| Move | ZOrder | | |

# Label Control

The properties, methods, and events of the Label control, which is one of the components of the Microsoft Forms 2.0 Object Library, are shown in Table D-6.

*Table D-6. Properties, Events, and Methods of the Label Control*

| Properties | | | |
|---|---|---|---|
| Accelerator | AutoSize | BackColor | BackStyle |
| BorderColor | BorderStyle | Caption | CodeBase |
| Enabled | Font | ForeColor | Height |
| ID | Left | MouseIcon | MousePointer |

*Table D-6. Properties, Events, and Methods of the Label Control (continued)*

| | | | |
|---|---|---|---|
| Picture | PicturePosition | SpecialEffect | TabIndex |
| TextAlign | Top | Visible | Width |
| WordWrap | | | |

**Events**

| | | | |
|---|---|---|---|
| AfterUpdate | BeforeDragOver | BeforeDropOrPaste | BeforeUpdate |
| Click | DblClick | Enter | Error |
| Exit | MouseDown | MouseMove | MouseUp |

**Methods**

| | | | |
|---|---|---|---|
| ZOrder | | | |

# ListBox Control

Another control within the Microsoft Forms 2.0 Object Library is the ListBox control, whose properties, events, and methods are shown in Table D-7.

*Table D-7. Properties, Events, and Methods of the ListBox Control*

**Properties**

| | | | |
|---|---|---|---|
| BackColor | BorderColor | BorderStyle | BoundColumn |
| CodeBase | Column | ColumnCount | ColumnHeads |
| ColumnWidths | Enabled | Font | ForeColor |
| Height | ID | IMEMode | IntegralHeight |
| Left | List | ListIndex | ListStyle |
| Locked | MatchEntry | MouseIcon | MousePointer |
| Selected | SpecialEffect | TabIndex | TabStop |
| Text | TextColumn | Top | Value |
| Visible | Width | | |

**Events**

| | | | |
|---|---|---|---|
| AfterUpdate | BeforeDragOver | BeforeDropOrPaste | BeforeUpdate |
| Change | Click | DblClick | Enter |
| Error | Exit | KeyDown | KeyPress |
| KeyUp | MouseDown | MouseMove | MouseUp |

**Methods**

| | | | |
|---|---|---|---|
| AddItem | Clear | RemoveItem | SetFocus |
| ZOrder | | | |

# OptionButton

This is also a component within the Microsoft Forms 2.0 Object Library. The OptionButton control's properties are listed in Table D-8.

*Table D-8. Properties, methods, and events of the OptionButton Control*

**Properties**

| | | | |
|---|---|---|---|
| Accelerator | Alignment | AutoSize | BackColor |
| BackStyle | Caption | CodeBase | Enabled |
| Font | ForeColor | GroupName | Height |
| ID | Left | Locked | MouseIcon |
| MousePointer | Picture | PicturePosition | SpecialEffect |
| TabIndex | TabStop | Top | TripleState |
| Value | Visible | Width | WordWrap |

**Events**

| | | | |
|---|---|---|---|
| AfterUpdate | BeforeDragOver | BeforeDropOrPaste | BeforeUpdate |
| Change | Click | DblClick | Enter |
| Error | Exit | KeyDown | KeyPress |
| KeyUp | MouseDown | MouseMove | MouseUp |

**Methods**

| | |
|---|---|
| SetFocus | Zorder |

# ScrollBar Control

The ScrollBar control typically is used to provide the user with an additional method of interacting with some standard interface object. A ScrollBar control might be used with a TextBox control, for example, so that the user can not only enter a value into the text box, but also can select that value by adjusting the position of the scroll bar. The ScrollBar control's properties, methods, and events are shown in Table D-9.

*Table D-9. Properties, Events, and Methods of the ScrollBar Control*

**Properties**

| | | | |
|---|---|---|---|
| BackColor | CodeBase | Delay | Enabled |
| ForeColor | Height | ID | LargeChange |
| Left | Max | Min | MouseIcon |
| MousePointer | Orientation | ProportionalThumb | SmallChange |
| TabIndex | TabStop | Top | Value |
| Visible | Width | | |

*Table D-9. Properties, Events, and Methods of the ScrollBar Control  (continued)*

**Events**

| AfterUpdate | BeforeDragOver | BeforeDropOrPaste | BeforeUpdate |
|---|---|---|---|
| Change | Enter | Error | Exit |
| KeyDown | KeyPress | KeyUp | Scroll |

**Methods**

| Move | SetFocus | Zorder | |
|---|---|---|---|

## SpinButton Control

Like the ScrollBar control, the SpinButton control is used to provide an additional means of modifying a control that displays a graduated numeric value. Like most of the other controls that we've discussed in this appendix, it is one of the components of the Microsoft Forms 2.0 Object Library. Its properties, events, and methods are listed in Table D-10.

*Table D-10. Properties, Events, and Methods of the SpinButton Control*

**Properties**

| BackColor | CodeBase | Delay | Enabled |
|---|---|---|---|
| ForeColor | Height | ID | Left |
| Max | Min | MouseIcon | MousePointer |
| Orientation | SmallChange | TabIndex | TabStop |
| Top | Value | Visible | Width |

**Events**

| AfterUpdate | BeforeDragOver | BeforeDropOrPaste | BeforeUpdate |
|---|---|---|---|
| Change | Enter | Error | Exit |
| KeyDown | KeyPress | KeyUp | SpinDown |
| SpinUp | | | |

**Methods**

| SetFocus | Zorder | | |
|---|---|---|---|

## TabStrip Control

One of the more popular controls to emerge recently, the TabStrip control contains one or more tabs (also known as property sheets), which allow user-selectable options to be presented in an organized way. The TabStrip control is also one of the components of the Microsoft Forms 2.0 Object Library; its properties, events, and methods are shown in Table D-11.

*Table D-11. Properties, Events, and Methods of the TabStrip Control*

**Properties**

| | | | |
|---|---|---|---|
| Accelerator | BackColor | Caption | CodeBase |
| Enabled | Font | ForeColor | Height |
| ID | Left | MouseIcon | MousePointer |
| MultiRow | SelectedItem | Style | TabFixedHeight |
| TabFixedWidth | TabIndex | TabOrientation | TabStop |
| Top | Value | Visible | Width |

**Events**

| | | | |
|---|---|---|---|
| BeforeDragOver | BeforeDropOrPaste | Change | Click |
| DblClick | Enter | Error | Exit |
| KeyDown | KeyPress | KeyUp | MouseDown |
| MouseMove | MouseUp | | |

**Methods**

| | |
|---|---|
| SetFocus | Zorder |

# TextBox Control

The TextBox control is also a component of the Microsoft Forms 2.0 Object Library. Its properties, events, and methods are listed in Table D-12.

*Table D-12. Properties, Events, and Methods of the TextBox Control*

**Properties**

| | | | |
|---|---|---|---|
| AutoSize | AutoTab | AutoWordSelect | BackColor |
| BackStyle | BorderColor | BorderStyle | CodeBase |
| CurLine | DragBehavior | Enabled | EnterFieldBehavior |
| EnterKeyBehavior | Font | ForeColor | Height |
| HideSelection | ID | IMEMode | IntegralHeight |
| Left | LineCount | Locked | MaxLength |
| MouseIcon | MousePointer | MultiLine | PasswordChar |
| ScrollBars | SelectionMargin | SelLength | SelStart |
| SelText | SpecialEffect | TabIndex | TabKeyBehavior |
| TabStop | Text | TextAlign | Top |
| Value | Visible | Width | WordWrap |

**Events**

| | | | |
|---|---|---|---|
| AfterUpdate | BeforeDragOver | BeforeDropOrPaste | BeforeUpdate |
| Change | DblClick | Enter | Error |
| Exit | KeyDown | KeyPress | KeyUp |
| MouseDown | MouseMove | MouseUp | |

*Table D-12. Properties, Events, and Methods of the TextBox Control (continued)*

**Methods**

| | | | |
|---|---|---|---|
| Copy | Cut | Paste | SetFocus |
| ZOrder | | | |

## ToggleButton Control

The ToggleButton control is a push button that, when it is clicked, remains depressed to indicate that it is in an "on" state. When clicked again, it appears normal, indicating that it's in the "off" state. The properties, methods, and events of the ToggleButton control, which is also one of the controls within the Microsoft Forms 2.0 Object Library, are shown in Table D-13.

*Table D-13. Properties, Events, and Methods of the ToggleButton Control*

**Properties**

| | | | |
|---|---|---|---|
| Accelerator | Alignment | AutoSize | BackColor |
| BackStyle | Caption | CodeBase | Enabled |
| Font | ForeColor | Height | ID |
| Left | Locked | MouseIcon | MousePointer |
| Picture | PictureProperty | SpecialEffect | TabIndex |
| TabStop | Top | TripleState | Value |
| Visible | Width | WordWrap | |

**Events**

| | | | |
|---|---|---|---|
| AfterUpdate | BeforeDragOver | BeforeDropOrPaste | BeforeUpdate |
| Change | Click | DblClick | Enter |
| Error | Exit | KeyDown | KeyPress |
| KeyUp | MouseDown | MouseMove | MouseUp |

**Methods**

| | |
|---|---|
| SetFocus | Zorder |

# E

# *Active Server Pages*

Active Server Pages (ASP) allows you to create complex, fully-featured, and dynamic web applications by adding Active Scripting to an HTML type document to be executed at the server, so that only the resulting HTML code will be sent to the browser. Here are some examples of the types of applications you can create with ASP:

- Process incoming data from HTML Forms

- Create back-end data processing for shopping carts and other commercial applications

- Link to Access, or the powerful SQL Server (NT4 only) database

- Dynamically optimize your web pages for any of the popular browsers

- Create web-based applications that maintain back office databases

- Migrate three-tier VB client/server applications to a web interface quickly and easily, reusing current OLE Remote Automation objects

Support for ASP is included with Personal Web Server (PWS) for Windows '95 and Internet Information Server (IIS) for Windows NT.

## *How Does ASP Work?*

In short, ASP is server-side scripting. You create ASP applications by adding scripting to the page that will be executed at the server. You then give the HTML document file an .ASP extension because only documents with the special .ASP extension are parsed by the Active Server; otherwise, the server simply transmits ("serves") a static document without parsing it.

Very much as client-side applications can be created by any scripting language, as long as it supports the appropriate COM interfaces, Active Server Pages can be created by any scripting language. But in client-side scripting, JavaScript is the default scripting language, and you have to explicitly indicate that VBScript is being used if you want your scripts to run, whereas VBScript is the default ASP scripting language.

When a request is received at the server for an ASP document, the .ASP file is passed to the ASP server, which adds in any files that you've specified should be included, compiles the server-side scripts, and creates the relevant objects. The scripts are then executed, and the resulting HTML is fed into the output buffer in line with the standard HTML and text, and transmitted to the browser in the normal way. To emphasize this once again, the *result* of a server-side script is HTML, which is inserted into the HTML output stream.

To make this clear, let's take a look at an ASP document—that is, at the "input" to an Active server—and at the document that is produced for it to transmit to the client. Example E-1 contains the sample ASP document. Note that it includes calls to the *FormatDateTime* and *Now* functions, presumably to insert date and time information into the document. It also includes two calls to a custom function, *DoSampleScript*, whose purpose is to select a country of the day and include a link to a web page for that country.

*Example E-1. An Active Server Page*

```
<HTML>
<HEAD>
<META NAME="GENERATOR" Content="Microsoft Visual InterDev 1.0">
<META HTTP-EQUIV="Content-Type" content="text/html; charset=iso-8859-1">
<TITLE>Document Title</TITLE>
<SCRIPT LANGUAGE="vbscript" RUNAT="server">
    Function DoSampleScript
        Dim vArray
        vArray = Array("England", "USA", "France", _
                    "Germany", "Canada", "Italy", _
                    "Brazil")
        DoSampleScript = vArray(DatePart("w",Now()))
    End Function
</SCRIPT>
</HEAD>
<BODY BGCOLOR="white"><FONT FACE="arial">
<CENTER>
<H2>Welcome to my ASP Web</H2>
Today is
<%= FormatDateTime(Now(), vbLongDate) %>
<P>
Today is <A HREF="<%= lCase(DoSampleScript)%>.htm">
<%= DoSampleScript %></A> Day
</BODY>
</HTML>
```

Example E-2, on the other hand, shows how the document in Example E-1 might appear when it's transmitted to a client by an Active server. There is a striking difference between them: whereas the web page in Example E-1 contains scripts, the page transmitted by the server in Example E-2 does not. That's because the scripts have executed on the server, and the language engine has inserted HTML and text into the server's output stream.

*Example E-2. HTML Document Produced by the Active Server Page in Example E-1*

```
<HTML>
<HEAD>
<META NAME="GENERATOR" Content="Microsoft Visual InterDev 1.0">
<META HTTP-EQUIV="Content-Type" content="text/html; charset=iso-8859-1">
<TITLE>Document Title</TITLE>

</HEAD>
<BODY BGCOLOR="white"><FONT FACE="arial">
<CENTER>
<H2>Welcome to my ASP Web</H2>
Today is
Friday, July 18, 1997
<P>
Today is <A HREF="brazil.htm">
Brazil</A> Day
</BODY>
</HTML>
```

Because ASP generates HTML, which it then sends to the browser, you don't need to worry about whether or not the browser can support Active Scripting. (Of course, if your HTML output includes client-side scripts defined with the <SCRIPT> tag, you still have to worry about older browsers not recognizing the tag; and if you choose to output VBScript code in your client-side scripts, then you also need to be aware of Netscape Navigator's inability to execute it.) In other words, ASP offers *browser independence* .

Of course, it can be argued that, even if an Active Server Page only outputs HTML, it really isn't browser independent, since different browsers support different implementations of HTML. Any nontrivial web page that's generated by an Active Server will almost certainly be unable to run on at least a handful of browsers. However, ASP has a solution for this: one of the standard server components that you can use with VBScript and ASP is the Browser Capabilities component, which allows you to maintain a list of which browsers support frames, scripting, etc. You can then access this list from within your ASP script to determine how a page should be constructed to optimize the experience for the user of a particular browser.

Although you can use ASP to produce single web pages, you can also use ASP to craft a single web site that is more than a collection of individual documents.

With ASP, a web site—that is, a collection of HTML pages within a common root or virtual domain—is called an *application*. This is because, unlike those in the normal HTML server, documents within an ASP application can be interrelated; you can share data, objects, and variables across all files. You also know when a new user has entered the ASP application. In fact, with ASP, you should think of your web site in the same terms as you would a Windows application—as a collection of interrelated forms or modules within a common executable.

An ASP application is driven from a single file called *GLOBAL.ASA*, which is never actually seen by the user. When you first create an ASP application using Visual Interdev, a *GLOBAL.ASA* file with a sample script template is created for you, as shown in Example E-3. As you can see, the *GLOBAL.ASA* file is all script, and nothing but script. This is where you create global variables and define global event handlers that can be accessed by every page in the application.

*Example E-3. A Sample GLOBAL.ASA File*

```
<SCRIPT LANGUAGE="VBScript" RUNAT="Server">

'You can add special event handlers in this file that will be run
'automatically when special Active Server Pages events
'occur.  To create these handlers, just create a subroutine with a name
'from the list below that corresponds to the event
'you want to use.  For example, to create an event handler for Session_
'OnStart, you would put the following code into this
'file (without the comments):
'Sub Session_OnStart
'**Put your code here **
'End Sub

'EventName                 Description
'Session_OnStart           Runs the first time a user runs any page in your
                           'application
'Session_OnEnd             Runs when a user's session times out or quits your
                           'application
'Application_OnStart       Runs once when the first page of your application is
                           'run for the first time by any user
'Application_OnEnd         Runs once when the web server shuts down

</SCRIPT>
```

# Scripting for the Active Server

So far, we've looked at Active Server Pages at a rather abstract level. Let's take a concrete look at how you actually include scripts in an Active Server page.

## *The <% %> and <%= %> Tags*

There are two sets of ASP tags that you can use to surround short snippets of code within your ASP page. Both are recognized by the ASP server as delimiting a script that requires processing:

- <% %>. This tag is used to surround any script that is to be executed at the server. At no time does the client see the contents of the code within these tags. The ASP <% %> tags can be used for complete scripts or for single expressions.

- <%= %>. This tag is used to transmit data to the client in the HTML stream at the point at which the tag appears within the document. <%= is really short-hand for *Response.Write*, the method used to write data to the output buffer.

For example, the following line assigns the value 10 to the variable *iMyNumber*:

```
<% iMyNumber = 10 %>
```

The following line is shorthand for "send the value of *iMyNumber* to the browser":

```
<%= iMyNumber %>
```

which translates to:

```
<% Response.Write iMyNumber %>
```

Whichever tag is used, the client will be unaware of the contents of the script. The client will only see any output that the scripts have inserted into the output stream. In the case of the last two scripts, for instance, the client will see only the string "10."

## *The <SCRIPT> Tag*

The other way you can execute a script at the server is to include your code within a <SCRIPT> tag, just as you would when writing client-side scripts. But server-side scripting does not preclude using client-side scripts in a web page. So how does the server know which <SCRIPT> tags should be sent intact to the browser for client-side processing, and which should be parsed, compiled, and executed, with only their resulting data being sent to the browser?

The Active server is able to differentiate between scripts intended for the client and those to be executed at the server by the <SCRIPT> tag's RUNAT attribute. The RUNAT attribute informs the server where the code within the script tag is to be executed. If its value is "server," the Active server knows that it is to parse, compile, and execute the script. Otherwise, the script is simply to be transmitted to the client.

You write the complete tag like this:

```
<SCRIPT LANGUAGE="vbscript" RUNAT="server">
```

Actually, the default scripting language for ASP is VBScript. This contrasts with client-side scripts running under Microsoft Internet Explorer, where JScript is the default. So you could get away without specifying the language attribute.

There is one proviso to using the `<SCRIPT>` tag within an ASP page: the code between the `<SCRIPT>` and `</SCRIPT>` tags must form complete procedures. This means that you can't include code in a `<SCRIPT>` tag that is outside of a subroutine, function, or event handler. The script-level code that is permissible in client-side VBScript is not permitted in ASP. In addition, for procedures other than event handlers, you must therefore call the subroutine or function from within `<% %>` tags, as shown earlier Example E-1.

## Included Files

You can also include external files that are parsed with the rest of the ASP document as though they were an integral part of the document. This allows you to create a shared set or library of scripts and procedures that can be used over and over again by different pages within your ASP application. They need only be written once and stored in one file. As a result, should you later need to amend or maintain the procedure, you have only one file to alter, thus reducing the chance of a bug being introduced.

To create an include file, write the file and save it with the extension .INC. In fact, there's no strict requirement for this extension, but it allows you to easily distinguish an include file. To include the file in your ASP document, simply use the ASP `<!--#include FILE/VIRTUAL=`*filename*` -->` preprocessor directive. As you can see, the include file in Example E-4 contains a single, simple procedure used to create a footer for the application's pages.

Example E-4 shows a sample include file. It's a plaintext file stored in the same virtual directory on the server as the ASP file or files that will use it.

*Example E-4. A Sample Include File*

```
<SCRIPT LANGUAGE="vbscript" RUNAT="server">
  Sub PageFooter
    Response.Write "<P><CENTER><FONT SIZE=1><B>"
    Response.Write "Designed and Maintained by Paul Lomax<BR>"
    Response.Write "Document parsed in "
    Response.Write Timer - tTime
    Response.Write " seconds"
    Response.Write "</B></FONT></CENTER></P>"
  End Sub
</SCRIPT>
```

Example E-5 shows an ASP file that uses the include file shown in Example E-4. Note, first of all, that the `#include` preprocessor directive is placed within HTML comment tags. Second, note the use of the `#include` directive's `File` keyword, which informs the Active Server that this filename is relative to the current document.

*Example E-5. Using the #include Directive*

```
<%@ LANGUAGE="VBSCRIPT" %>
<% tTime = Timer %>
<HTML>
<HEAD>
<META NAME="GENERATOR" Content="Microsoft Visual InterDev 1.0">
<META HTTP-EQUIV="Content-Type" content="text/html; charset=iso-8859-1">
<TITLE>Example of Include</TITLE>
</HEAD>
<BODY BGCOLOR="white"><FONT FACE="arial">
<CENTER>
<H2>This is a sample of an Include</H2>

<!-- #include file="myinclude.inc" -->

<% PageFooter %>
</BODY>
</HTML>
```

When the preprocessor encounters the `#include` directive, it simply inserts the include file at the point where it encounters the `#include` directive, which it then replaces. From this point (where the scripts are processed by ASP) onward, the two documents are merged into one. This is apparent from examining Example E-6, which contains the HTML source for the page that the server actually sends to a client when the client requests the URL of the document shown in Example E-5. First, the ASP file in Example E-5 contains a call to a subroutine, *PageFooter*, which doesn't exist in Example E-5 before the file in Example E-4 is included. Second, the include file in Example E-4 uses a variable, *tTime*, which is defined and initialized in the ASP document in Example E-5, but not in the include file itself. Both of these approaches are possible only because included files are incorporated into the ASP document before any scripts are processed.

*Example E-6. HTML Document Produced by Example E-5*

```
<HTML>
<HEAD>
<META NAME="GENERATOR" Content="Microsoft Visual InterDev 1.0">
<META HTTP-EQUIV="Content-Type" content="text/html; charset=iso-8859-1">
<TITLE>Example of Include</TITLE>
</HEAD>
<BODY BGCOLOR="white"><FONT FACE="arial">
<CENTER>
<H2>This is a sample of an Include</H2>
```

*Example E-6. HTML Document Produced by Example E-5 (continued)*

```
<P><CENTER><FONT SIZE=1><B>Designed and Maintained by Paul Lomax<BR>
Document parsed in 0.329834 seconds</B></FONT></CENTER></P>
</BODY>
</HTML>
```

There's no limit to the number of included files you can use in an ASP document. You can even include files in the included file. What you can't do, though, is to create a circular reference. For example, assume that Document A includes Document B, and that Document B includes Document C. If Document C tried to include Document A, an error would be generated.

# Creating ASP Documents and Applications

So far in our overview of server-side scripting with Active Server Pages, we've seen how to include server-side scripts in our ASP documents by using the necessary tags along with VBScript language elements. However, very much as client-side VBScript would be underpowered without its ability to access and control HTML intrinsic controls, ActiveX controls, and the MSIE object model, ASP would be of little significance if it consisted only of VBScript language elements and some tags to mark their position within a document. Instead, the real power of ASP comes from its ability to access ActiveX components, as well as from its ability to interface with the server through the Active Server object model.

## Server-Side Components

Server-side components are OLE automation objects that you can include in your ASP application to extend your application's functionality. You can create your own OLE automation server components using either C++ or Visual Basic. In addition, ASP includes a number of built-in components:

- **Ad Rotator**. The *Ad Rotator* allows you to rotate advertisements that appear in your web pages. Advertisements can be rotated randomly, or you can assign a weighting to each ad in your list. Through redirection, the Ad Rotator can also log the rate and frequency of user clicks on each ad.

- **Browser Capabilities**. Despite the supposed "browser independence" of ASP, we all know that, unless you plan for the lowest common denominator, someone, somewhere, isn't going to see your page as it was intended to be seen. To make sure that your web pages look as good as possible on your users' browsers, Active servers include the *Browser Capabilities* component, which allows your scripts to access information about the client browser's capabilities. By using the Browser Capabilities component, you can create an almost infinite variety of the same web page and be sure that the appropriate one is being displayed on a particular browser.

- **Content Linker**. The *Content Linker* component maintains a list of your site's URLs, which allows you to automatically generate tables of contents and navigational links to previous and subsequent web pages.

- **Database Access**. Arguably the most important Active Server component is the Active Data Object (ADO). Whether you are creating a small-scale application to interface Access with the Personal Web Server on Windows 95, or a complex real-time web application running on NT4 using SQL Server, the Database Access component allows you to link to the database with the minimum of fuss and work. Your ASP script can send SQL queries to the database and handle the resulting record set. Because the query is built and executed exclusively on the server, the speed of retrieval is very fast.

  Database access is achieved using *Open Database Connectivity* (ODBC), and the *ODBC Data* object is usually created in the *GLOBAL.ASA* file as the current session commences. The benefits of this are twofold. First, the *GLOBAL.ASA* file cannot be accessed from the client, so any password information that is held within the data object creation string is hidden. Secondly, the overhead in terms of processing time that is associated with creating the link to the database is only experienced once, at the beginning of the session; all subsequent processing occurs through the now open data connection.

- **File Access**. The *File Access* component allows you to create, open, read from, and write to an ASCII text file in the local file system.

## The Active Server Object Model

In very much the same way that client-side VBScript has access to the browser's objects via the MSIE object model, when used at the server, VBScript can access and manipulate the Active Server object model through the following five built-in server objects:

- **Application object**. The *Application* object—which is instantiated in the *GLOBAL.ASA* file—can be used to share data across the ASP application, because it allows you to store values within the object as user-defined properties. Because many different users may be using your ASP application at the same time, the Application object allows you to lock and unlock the user-defined properties when you are updating them, an essential part of a multiuser environment. For example, the following code fragment shows how to store a value in the Application object:

```
<% Application("MyBackColor") = "green" %>
```

It does this by creating a new user-defined property, *MyBackColor*, and assigning it a value of "Green." Once the property is defined, it can then be accessed by all the files that make up the application. To continue with our example, you could then create a uniform <BODY> tag for each page of the application as follows:

```
<BODY BGCOLOR=<%=Application("MyBackColor")%> >
```

- **Request object**. This object contains the values passed to the server as part of an HTTP request. The values are held in the Request object in five collections, as shown in Table E-1.

*Table E-1. Collections of the Request Object*

| Collection | Description |
| --- | --- |
| ClientCertificate | Contains the values requested from the client by the server in an SSL protocol connection. |
| Cookies | Contains the values of any cookies transmitted as part of the HTTP request. |
| Forms | Contains the values passed to the server by a Form submission using a POST method. For instance, the value of an HTTP intrinsic text box control named EmailAddr can be retrieved with a code fragment like the following:<br>`<% sEmail = Request.Form("EMailAddr")%>` |
| QueryString | Contains the values passed to the server by a Form submission using the GET method. The values are passed in the HTTP query string, which, if it is present, follows the ? in the URL. |
| ServerVariables | Contains a range of environment variables, such as `HTTP_USER_AGENT`. |

- **Response object**. The *Response* object is used to send information and output back to the client. This can be done in either of two ways: by sending cookies back to the browser to be stored for use at a later time, or by calling the Response object's *Write* method to place a string in the HTML output stream. Example E-4, for instance, used the *Response.Write* method to create a footer on multiple web pages.

- **Server object**. By exposing a property and several utility methods, all of which are listed in Table E-2, the Server object allows your script to interact with the server.

*Table E-2. Properties and Methods of the Server Object*

| Name | Type | Description |
| --- | --- | --- |
| ScriptTimeout | Property | Sets the time that a script is allowed to execute before it times out. For example:<br>`<% Server.ScriptTimeout = 30 %>` |
| CreateObject | Method | Creates an instance of a server component |

*Table E-2. Properties and Methods of the Server Object (continued)*

| Name | Type | Description |
|------|------|-------------|
| HTMLEncode | Method | Applies HTML encoding to a specified string |
| MapPath | Method | Maps a virtual path (like the relative path to the current page) to a physical path |
| URLEncode | Method | Applies URL encoding to a specified string |

- **Session object**. The *Session* object stores information about a user session. A user session is created when a particular user downloads a page from the ASP application for the first time (i.e., the user does not already have a session), and it remains in existence until there is no activity from the user for the number of minutes set by the *Session Timeout* property. By using the *Abandon* method, you can also programmatically end the current user session. During the session, the values stored by the *Session* object are available throughout the application. The *Session* object is only available to clients that support and accept cookies. Along with the application-defined properties that can be stored to it, the *Session* object supports the properties and methods shown in Table E-3.

*Table E-3. Properties and Methods of the Session Object*

| Name | Type | Description |
|------|------|-------------|
| SessionID | Property | Returns the session identifier, a unique long integer assigned to the current user's session |
| Timeout | Property | Sets or returns the timeout period for this application session, in minutes |
| Abandon | Method | Destroys the current *Session* object and releases its resources |

# Dynamic Client-Side Scripts

Typically, client-side scripting and server-side scripting are seen as two distinct, almost unrelated, technologies. However, a really neat feature of ASP is that it gives a server-side script the ability to create a client-side script dynamically as the script executes on the server. You create your client-side scripts in the normal way, leaving out the `RUNAT` attribute of the `<SCRIPT>` tag. However, you place the dynamic parts of your script within the ASP `<% %>` tags, as Example E-7 shows. Example E-8 shows how the web page in Example E-7 appears to the browser.

*Example E-7. A Dynamic Server-Side Script*

```
<%@ LANGUAGE="VBSCRIPT" %>
<% sLinkPage = "anotherpage.asp"%>
<% sDescription = "Go to another page" %>
```

*Example E-7. A Dynamic Server-Side Script (continued)*

```
<% sLinkName = "newlink" %>
<HTML>
<HEAD>
<META NAME="GENERATOR" Content="Microsoft Visual InterDev 1.0">
<META HTTP-EQUIV="Content-Type" content="text/html; charset=iso-8859-1">
<TITLE>Document Title</TITLE>
<SCRIPT LANGUAGE="vbscript">
  Sub <%=sLinkName%>_MouseMove(s,b,x,y)
     Status = "<%=sDescription%>"
     tID = SetTimeout("Status=''",4000)
  End Sub
</SCRIPT>
</HEAD>
<BODY BGCOLOR="white"><FONT FACE="arial"><CENTER>
<H2>A Dynamically Created Script</H2>
<P>
Click to go to
<A NAME="<%=sLinkName%>" HREF="<%=sLinkPage%>"><%=sLinkPage%></A>

</BODY>
</HTML>
```

*Example E-8 . HTML Source Provided by Example E-7*

```
<HTML>
<HEAD>
<META NAME="GENERATOR" Content="Microsoft Visual InterDev 1.0">
<META HTTP-EQUIV="Content-Type" content="text/html; charset=iso-8859-1">
<TITLE>Document Title</TITLE>
<SCRIPT LANGUAGE="vbscript">
  Sub newlink_MouseMove(s,b,x,y)
     Status = "Go to another page"
     tID = SetTimeout("Status=''",4000)
  End Sub
</SCRIPT>
</HEAD>
<BODY BGCOLOR="white"><FONT FACE="arial"><CENTER>
<H2>A Dynamically Created Script</H2>
<P>
Click to go to
<A NAME="newlink" HREF="anotherpage.asp">anotherpage.asp</A>

</BODY>
</HTML>
```

# F

# *The Learning VBScript CD-ROM*

The CD-ROM accompanying *Learning VBScript* contains all the source code for the examples used in this book (over 170 full working examples in all!). In the root of the CD-ROM, you'll find a web page named *index.htm*; this is the CD-ROM's "home page" and contains the index for all the source code. When you load the *index.htm* file into your MSIE browser (make sure you have VBScript Version 2 first), you are presented with two options for viewing the examples:

- Browse by Chapter
- List by Topic

---

## *Getting VBScript 2.0*

You can determine which version of VBScript is installed on your system by loading the web page *AppendixB\scriptengine.htm* from the CD-ROM and clicking the Button button. If the resulting dialog reports no version number, you have VBScript Version 1 and need to upgrade.

The latest version of VBScript is available for free download from Microsoft's web site. Check *http://www.microsoft.com/vbscript* for details.

If you've installed VBScript Version 2 and are having difficulty getting the programs to run because some VBScript 2 features (like support for the Dictionary object, which is used to create the browsing framework for the CD-ROM) are not recognized, consult the *readme.htm* file found in the root directory of the CD-ROM.

---

The index is in fact quite a complex client side VBScript program (you can view the VBScript source in *title.htm*) which builds a memory-resident referential database of all the examples, the topics the example covers, the filenames of the examples, and the chapter in which each example appears.

## Browsing Examples by Chapter

When you click the "Browse by Chapter" hyperlink, the middle of the screen lists all the chapters and their titles. When you click the hyperlink for the chapter in which you are interested, a list of that chapter's examples are then displayed in the right side of the screen, as shown in Figure F-1. Clicking the example's hyperlink will load the file or files required to run the example in a new browser window. You can inspect the HTML and VBScript source for each example by selecting the Source option from the MSIE View menu. If this main web page consists of a <FRAMESET> tag, you can view the HTML and VBScript source for each frame by right-clicking on the frame and selecting the View Source option from the context menu.

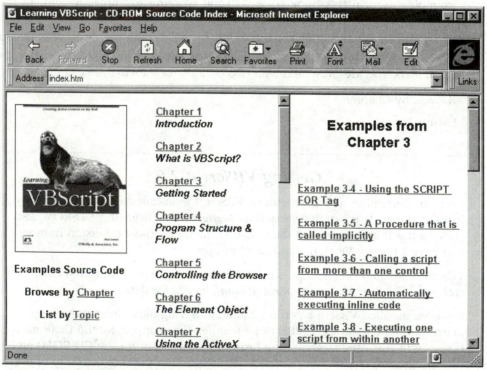

*Figure F-1. Browsing examples by chapter*

The CD-ROM contains all complete examples from the book. In most cases, these correspond to particular labeled examples. In Figure F-1, for instance, you can see a hyperlink for "Example 3-4 - Using the SCRIPT FOR Tag". However, a number of examples for which source code was not provided in *Learning VBScript* (most of which are found in Chapter 1) are included in the accompanying CD-ROM. Finally, there is a single hyperlink for the VBScript Shopping Cart application found in Chapter 16, *The VBScript Shopping Cart*, although it corresponds to multiple labeled examples.

## Finding Examples by Topic

Frequently, you want to look at a piece of sample script because you need to do something in your own script, but can't quite remember how it's done. You know there's an example in the book that covers what you're looking for, but you're not sure where to find it. This is where the List by Topic feature comes in. When you click the "List by Topic" hyperlink, the center of the page displays a drop-down list containing all the major subjects and topics covered in the book. When you select a topic and click the "Find Examples" button, all the examples from the book that are relevant to that particular topic are displayed in the right portion of the page, as shown in Figure F-2. Once again, you merely have to click the hyperlink to load the example in a new browser window.

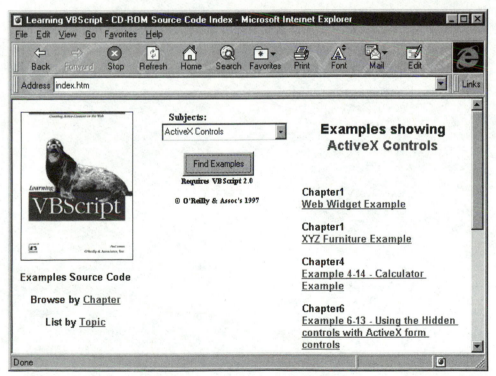

*Figure F-2. Listing the examples by topic*

## *The Format of the CD-ROM*

The CD-ROM accompanying *Learning VBScript* is formatted in an extended version of ISO 9660, which supports long filenames and is not strictly compatible with the DOS/Windows 3.x 16-bit file system, and particularly with its 8.3 file-naming convention. This means that the CD-ROM requires that it be run under either Windows 95 or Windows NT *with a 32-bit CD-ROM driver*.

If you are running the Windows 3.x version of Microsoft Internet Explorer, or if you are using Win95 with a 16-bit CD-ROM driver, you can download a copy of the sample files from our web site *ftp://www.ora.com/published/oreilly/windows/vbscript.learn/examples.zip*.

# *Index*

# About the Author

Paul Lomax is Technical Director of Mentorweb (*http://www.mentorweb.net/*), a leading web design and hosting company. Over the past two years, Paul has created and maintained over 60 commercial web sites for Mentorweb's clients. He is also the driving force behind ShopAssistant, a new NT/ASP based high-end shopping cart/web commerce server (*http://www.shopassistant.com/*). He has been a programmer for over 12 years and has been a dedicated fan of Visual Basic since Version 1. Paul has written systems for financial derivatives forecasting, satellite TV broadcasting, and the life insurance industry, and he's written a major materials tracking system for the oil and gas industry. He is also responsible for the concept, design, and programming of the successful "Contact" series of national business databases. Paul has also created a web resource dedicated to VBScript at *http://www.vbscripts.com/*. When not sitting in front of a keyboard, Paul can usually be found behind the wheel of a racing car competing in events around the UK. Paul and his family—wife Deborah and children Russel and Victoria—have recently returned to their home in England after several years spent living in the Arabian Gulf.

# Colophon

The animal featured on the cover of Learning VBScript is an eared seal. There are 18 living species of seal, grouped into 13 genera. Of these, 14 species, in 6 genera, are eared seals, family Otariidae. Eared seals are widely distributed throughout the world, especially in the southern hemisphere. The diet of this marine mammal consists mainly of fish. Some seals can dive as deep as 600 feet in search of food.

Aside from the existence of external ears, eared seals differ from earless seals in that they can bring their rear flippers forward under their bodies. This makes them more mobile on land than earless seals. In the water, both eared and earless seals move with a rowing motion of the front flippers, not using their rear flippers at all.

Eared seals fall into one of two categories—fur seals or sea lions. Fur seals grow a thick undercoat of fur, used as insulation. In one species of fur seal, over 50,000 hairs were counted in one square centimeter of skin. This thick undercoat of fur has made the fur seal very appealing to hunters.

Of the five species of sea lion, the California sea lion is the best known. Because they are relatively small, and the most graceful on land of all the seals, California sea lions are the seals most likely to be used in circus acts or kept in zoos.

Edie Freedman designed the cover of this book, using a 19th-century engraving from the Dover Pictorial Archive. The cover layout was produced with Quark XPress 3.32 using the ITC Garamond font.

The inside layout was designed by Nancy Priest and implemented in FrameMaker 5.0 by Mike Sierra. The text and heading fonts are ITC Garamond Light and Garamond Book. The CD design was created by Hanna Dyer. The illustrations that appear in the book were created in Macromedia Freehand 5.0 by Robert Romano. This colophon was written by Clairemarie Fisher O'Leary.

Whenever possible, our books use RepKover™, a durable and flexible lay-flat binding. If the page count exceeds RepKover's limit, perfect binding is used.

# *More Titles from O'Reilly*

## Visual Basic Programming

### Developing Visual Basic Add-ins

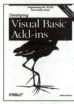

By Steven Roman
1st Edition December 1998
186 pages, ISBN 1-56592-527-0

A tutorial and reference guide in one, this short book covers all the basics of creating customized VB add-ins to extend the IDE, allowing developers to work more productively with Visual Basic. Readers with even a modest acquaintance with VB will be developing add-ins in no time. Includes numerous simple code examples.

### VB & VBA in a Nutshell: The Language

By Paul Lomax
1st Edition October 1998
656 pages, ISBN 1-56592-358-8

For Visual Basic and VBA programmers, this book boils down the essentials of the VB and VBA languages into a single volume, including undocumented and little-documented areas essential to everyday programming. The convenient alphabetical reference to all functions, procedures, statements, and keywords allows programmers to use this book both as a standard reference guide and as a tool for troubleshooting and identifying programming problems.

### Access & DAO Object Models: The Definitive Reference

By Helen Feddema
1st Edition December 1999 (est.)
550 pages (est.), Includes CD-ROM
ISBN 1-56592-435-5

This book, for advanced Access users or keen intermediate users, details the two Access object models, with code samples to use in VBA and/or VBScript. It will be *the* reference guide VB developers reach for when working with data in Access tables or when manipulating components of the Access interface from other Office applications.

### Learning Word Programming

By Steven Roman
1st Edition October 1998
408 pages, ISBN 1-56592-524-6

This no-nonsense book delves into VBA programming and tells how you can use VBA to automate all the tedious, repetitive jobs you never thought you could do in Microsoft Word. It takes the reader step-by-step through writing VBA macros and programs, illustrating how to generate tables of a particular format, manage shortcut keys, create fax cover sheets, and reformat documents.

### Visual Basic Controls in a Nutshell

By Evan S. Dictor
1st Edition July 1999
762 pages, ISBN 1-56592-294-8

To create professional applications, developers need extensive knowledge of Visual Basic controls and their numerous properties, methods, and events. This quick reference documents the steps involved in using each major VB control, the order in which their events are fired, and the unexpected ways in which their properties, methods, and events interact.

### ADO: The Definitive Guide

By Jason T. Roff
1st Edition February 2000 (est.)
450 pages (est.), ISBN 1-56592-415-0

The architecture of ADO, Microsoft's newest form of database communication, is simple, concise, and efficient. This indispensable reference takes a comprehensive look at every object, collection, method, and property of ADO for developers who want to get a leg up on this exciting new technology.

## O'REILLY®

TO ORDER: **800-998-9938** • *order@oreilly.com* • *http://www.oreilly.com/*
*OUR PRODUCTS ARE AVAILABLE AT A BOOKSTORE OR SOFTWARE STORE NEAR YOU.*
FOR INFORMATION: **800-998-9938** • **707-829-0515** • *info@oreilly.com*

# Visual Basic Programming

## ASP in a Nutshell

By A. Keyton Weissinger
1st Edition February 1999
426 pages, ISBN 1-56592-490-8

This detailed reference contains all
the information Web developers need to
create effective Active Server Pages (ASP)
applications. It focuses on how features
are used in a real application and highlights
little-known or undocumented aspects,
enabling even experienced developers to advance their ASP
applications to new levels.

## Developing ASP Components

By Shelley Powers
1st Edition April 1999
510 pages, ISBN 1-56592-446-0

Developing add-on controls and components
is emerging as a multibillion dollar industry
that is increasingly attracting the attention of
developers. This book provides developers
with the information and real-world examples
they need to create custom ASP components using any of the three
major development tools: Visual Basic, Visual C++, and J++.

## Learning DCOM

By Thuan L. Thai
1st Edition April 1999
502 pages, ISBN 1-56592-581-5

This book introduces C++ programmers
to DCOM and gives them the basic tools
they need to write secure, maintainable
programs. It clearly describes the C++ code
needed to create distributed components
and the communications exchanged between systems and objects,
providing background, a guide to Visual C++ development tools
and wizards, and insight for performance tuning, debugging, and
understanding what the system is doing with your code.

## Writing Excel Macros

By Steven Roman
1st Edition May 1999
552 pages, ISBN 1-56592-587-4

*Writing Excel Macros* offers a solid
introduction to writing VBA macros and
programs in Excel and shows you how
to get more power out of Excel at the
programming level. Learn how to get
the most out of this formidable application as you focus on
programming languages, the Visual Basic Editor, handling
code, and the Excel object model.

## Win32 API Programming with Visual Basic

By Steve Roman
1st Edition November 1999 (est.)
500 pages (est.), Includes CD-ROM
ISBN 1-56592-631-5

This book provides the missing documentation
for VB programmers who want to harness
the power of accessing the Win32 API within
Visual Basic. It shows how to create powerful
and unique applications without needing a background in Visual
C++ or Win32 API programming.

## Learning Perl on Win32 Systems

By Randal L. Schwartz,
Erik Olson & Tom Christiansen
1st Edition August 1997
306 pages, ISBN 1-56592-324-3

In this carefully paced course, leading Perl
trainers and a Windows NT practitioner teach
you to program in the language that promises
to emerge as the scripting language of choice
on NT. Based on the "llama" book, this book features tips for PC
users and new NT-specific examples, along with a foreword by
Larry Wall, the creator of Perl, and Dick Hardt, the creator of
Perl for Win32.

# O'REILLY®

TO ORDER: **800-998-9938** • *order@oreilly.com* • *http://www.oreilly.com/*
*OUR PRODUCTS ARE AVAILABLE AT A BOOKSTORE OR SOFTWARE STORE NEAR YOU.*
*FOR INFORMATION:* **800-998-9938** • **707-829-0515** • *info@oreilly.com*

# Windows Programming

## Inside the Windows 95 File System

By Stan Mitchell
1st Edition May 1997
378 pages, Includes diskette
ISBN 1-56592-200-X

In this book, Stan Mitchell describes the Windows 95 File System, as well as the opportunities and challenges it brings for developers. Its "hands-on" approach will help developers become better equipped to make design decisions using the new Win95 File System features. Includes a diskette containing MULTIMON, a general-purpose monitor for examining Windows internals.

## Inside the Windows 95 Registry

By Ron Petrusha
1st Edition August 1996
594 pages, Includes diskette
ISBN 1-56592-170-4

An in-depth examination of remote registry access, differences between the Win95 and NT registries, registry backup, undocumented registry services, and the role the registry plays in OLE. This book shows programmers how to access the Win95 registry from Win32, Win16, and DOS programs in C and Visual Basic. It includes VxD sample code and comes with a diskette that contains registry tools.

## Developing Windows Error Messages

By Ben Ezzell
1st Edition March 1998
254 pages, Includes CD-ROM
ISBN 1-56592-356-1

This book teaches C, C++, and Visual Basic programmers how to write effective error messages that notify the user of an error, clearly explain the error, and most important, offer a solution. The book also discusses methods for preventing and trapping errors before they occur and tells how to create flexible input and response routines to keep unnecessary errors from happening.

## Win32 Multithreaded Programming

By Aaron Cohen & Mike Woodring
1st Edition December 1997
724 pages, Includes CD-ROM
ISBN 1-56592-296-4

This book clearly explains the concepts of multithreaded programs and shows developers how to construct efficient and complex applications. An important book for any developer, it illustrates all aspects of Win32 multithreaded programming, including what has previously been undocumented or poorly explained.

## Windows NT File System Internals

By Rajeev Nagar
1st Edition September 1997
794 pages, Includes diskette
ISBN 1-56592-249-2

*Windows NT File System Internals* presents the details of the NT I/O Manager, the Cache Manager, and the Memory Manager from the perspective of a software developer writing a file system driver or implementing a kernel-mode filter driver. The book provides numerous code examples included on diskette, as well as the source for a complete, usable filter driver.

## Windows NT SNMP

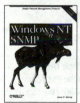

By James D. Murray
1st Edition January 1998
464 pages, Includes CD-ROM
ISBN 1-56592-338-3

This book describes the implementation of SNMP (the Simple Network Management Protocol) on Windows NT 3.51 and 4.0 (with a look ahead to NT 5.0) and Windows 95 systems. It covers SNMP and network basics and provides detailed information on developing SNMP management applications and extension agents. The book comes with a CD-ROM containing a wealth of additional information: standards documents, sample code from the book, and many third-party, SNMP-related software tools, libraries, and demos.

# Windows Programming

### Transact-SQL Programming

By Kevin Kline, Lee Gould & Andrew Zanevsky
1st Edition March 1999
836 pages, Includes CD-ROM
ISBN 1-56592-401-0

Full of examples, best practices, and real-world advice, this book thoroughly explores Transact-SQL, a full-featured procedural language that extends the power of SQL on both Microsoft SQL Server 6.5/7.0 and Sybase version 11.5. Comes with a CD-ROM containing extensive examples.

### Python Programming on Win32

By Mark Hammond & Andy Robinson
1st Edition December 1999 (est.)
450 pages (est.), ISBN 1-56592-621-8

Despite Python's increasing popularity on Windows, *Python Programming on Win32* is the first book to demonstrate how to use it as a serious Windows development and administration tool. This book addresses all the basic technologies for common integration tasks on Windows, explaining both the Windows issues and the Python code you need to glue things together.

# Web Programming

### Webmaster in a Nutshell, 2nd Edition

By Stephen Spainhour & Robert Eckstein
2nd Edition June 1999
540 pages, ISBN 1-56592-325-1

This indispensable books takes all the essential reference information for the Web and pulls it together into one volume. It covers HTML 4.0, CSS, XML, CGI, SSI, JavaScript 1.2, PHP, HTTP 1.1, and administration for the Apache server.

### Practical Internet Groupware

By Jon Udell
1st Edition October 1999 (est.)
384 pages (est.), ISBN 1-56592-537-8

This revolutionary book tells users, programmers, IS managers, and system administrators how to build Internet groupware applications that organize the casual and chaotic transmission of online information into useful, disciplined, and documented data.

### DocBook: The Definitive Guide

By Norman Walsh & Leonard Muellner
1st Edition October 1999
652 pages, Includes CD-ROM
ISBN 1-56592-580-7

DocBook is a Document Type Definition (DTD) for use with XML (the Extensible Markup Language) and SGML (the Standard Generalized Markup Language). DocBook lets authors in technical groups exchange and reuse technical information. This book contains an introduction to SGML, XML, and the DocBook DTD, plus the complete reference information for DocBook.

### Java Servlet Programming

By Jason Hunter with William Crawford
1st Edition November 1998
528 pages, ISBN 1-56592-391-X

Java servlets offer a fast, powerful, portable replacement for CGI scripts. *Java Servlet Programming* covers everything you need to know to write effective servlets. Topics include: serving dynamic Web content, maintaining state information, session tracking, database connectivity using JDBC, and applet-servlet communication.

# Web Programming

## CGI Programming with Perl, 2nd Edition

By Shishir Gundavaram
2nd Edition June 2000 (est.)
450 pages (est.), ISBN 1-56592-419-3

Completely rewritten, this comprehensive
explanation of CGI for those who want to
provide their own Web servers features Perl 5
techniques and shows how to use two popular
Perl modules, CGI.pm and CGI_lite. It also
covers speed-up techniques, such as FastCGI and mod_perl, and
new material on searching and indexing, security, generating
graphics through ImageMagick, database access through DBI,
Apache configuration, and combining CGI with JavaScript.

## Dynamic HTML: The Definitive Reference

By Danny Goodman
1st Edition July 1998
1088 pages, ISBN 1-56592-494-0

*Dynamic HTML: The Definitive Reference* is an
indispensable compendium for Web content
developers. It contains complete reference
material for all of the HTML tags, CSS style
attributes, browser document objects, and
JavaScript objects supported by the various standards and the latest
versions of Netscape Navigator and Microsoft Internet Explorer.

## Frontier: The Definitive Guide

By Matt Neuburg
1st Edition February 1998
616 pages, ISBN 1-56592-383-9

This definitive guide is the first book devoted
exclusively to teaching and documenting
Userland Frontier, a powerful scripting
environment for Web site management and
system level scripting. Packed with examples,
advice, tricks, and tips, *Frontier: The Definitive Guide* teaches you
Frontier from the ground up. Learn how to automate repetitive
processes, control remote computers across a network, beef
up your Web site by generating hundreds of related Web pages
automatically, and more. Covers Frontier 4.2.3 for the Macintosh.

## JavaScript: The Definitive Guide, 3rd Edition

By David Flanagan
3rd Edition June 1998
800 pages, ISBN 1-56592-392-8

This third edition of the definitive reference
to JavaScript covers the latest version of the
language, JavaScript 1.2, as supported by
Netscape Navigator 4 and Internet Explorer
4. JavaScript, which is being standardized
under the name ECMAScript, is a scripting language that can be
embedded directly in HTML to give Web pages programming-
language capabilities.

## Learning VBScript

By Paul Lomax
1st Edition July 1997
616 pages, Includes CD-ROM
ISBN 1-56592-247-6,

This definitive guide shows Web developers
how to take full advantage of client-side
scripting with the VBScript language. In
addition to basic language features, it covers
the Internet Explorer object model and discusses techniques for
client-side scripting, like adding ActiveX controls to a Web page
or validating data before sending it to the server. Includes CD-ROM
with over 170 code samples.

## JavaScript Application Cookbook

By Jerry Bradenbaugh
1st Edition September 1999
478 pages, ISBN 1-56592-577-7

*JavaScript Application Cookbook* literally
hands the Webmaster a set of ready-to-go,
client-side JavaScript applications with
thorough documentation to help them
understand and extend the applications.
By providing such a set of applications, *JavaScript Application
Cookbook* allows Webmasters to immediately add extra
functionality to their Web sites.

# O'REILLY®

TO ORDER: **800-998-9938** • **order@oreilly.com** • **http://www.oreilly.com/**
OUR PRODUCTS ARE AVAILABLE AT A BOOKSTORE OR SOFTWARE STORE NEAR YOU.
FOR INFORMATION: **800-998-9938** • **707-829-0515** • **info@oreilly.com**

# How to stay in touch with O'Reilly

## 1. Visit Our Award-Winning Web Site

### http://www.oreilly.com/

★ "Top 100 Sites on the Web" —*PC Magazine*
★ "Top 5% Web sites" —*Point Communications*
★ "3-Star site" —*The McKinley Group*

Our web site contains a library of comprehensive product information (including book excerpts and tables of contents), downloadable software, background articles, interviews with technology leaders, links to relevant sites, book cover art, and more. File us in your Bookmarks or Hotlist!

## 2. Join Our Email Mailing Lists

### New Product Releases

To receive automatic email with brief descriptions of all new O'Reilly products as they are released, send email to:
**listproc@online.oreilly.com**
Put the following information in the first line of your message (*not* in the Subject field):
**subscribe oreilly-news**

### O'Reilly Events

If you'd also like us to send information about trade show events, special promotions, and other O'Reilly events, send email to:
**listproc@online.oreilly.com**
Put the following information in the first line of your message (*not* in the Subject field):
**subscribe oreilly-events**

## 3. Get Examples from Our Books via FTP

There are two ways to access an archive of example files from our books:

### Regular FTP

- ftp to:
  **ftp.oreilly.com**
  (login: anonymous
  password: your email address)
- Point your web browser to:
  **ftp://ftp.oreilly.com/**

### FTPMAIL

- Send an email message to:
  **ftpmail@online.oreilly.com**
  (Write "help" in the message body)

## 4. Contact Us via Email

**order@oreilly.com**
To place a book or software order online. Good for North American and international customers.

**subscriptions@oreilly.com**
To place an order for any of our newsletters or periodicals.

**books@oreilly.com**
General questions about any of our books.

**software@oreilly.com**
For general questions and product information about our software. Check out O'Reilly Software Online at **http://software.oreilly.com/** for software and technical support information. Registered O'Reilly software users send your questions to: **website-support@oreilly.com**

**cs@oreilly.com**
For answers to problems regarding your order or our products.

**booktech@oreilly.com**
For book content technical questions or corrections.

**proposals@oreilly.com**
To submit new book or software proposals to our editors and product managers.

**international@oreilly.com**
For information about our international distributors or translation queries. For a list of our distributors outside of North America check out:
**http://www.oreilly.com/www/order/country.html**

O'Reilly & Associates, Inc.
101 Morris Street, Sebastopol, CA 95472 USA
TEL 707-829-0515 or 800-998-9938
(6am to 5pm PST)
FAX 707-829-0104

# International Distributors

## UK, EUROPE, MIDDLE EAST AND AFRICA (EXCEPT FRANCE, GERMANY, AUSTRIA, SWITZERLAND, LUXEMBOURG, LIECHTENSTEIN, AND EASTERN EUROPE)

### INQUIRIES
O'Reilly UK Limited
4 Castle Street
Farnham
Surrey, GU9 7HS
United Kingdom
Telephone: 44-1252-711776
Fax: 44-1252-734211
Email: josette@oreilly.com

### ORDERS
Wiley Distribution Services Ltd.
1 Oldlands Way
Bognor Regis
West Sussex PO22 9SA
United Kingdom
Telephone: 44-1243-779777
Fax: 44-1243-820250
Email: cs-books@wiley.co.uk

## FRANCE

### ORDERS
GEODIF
61, Bd Saint-Germain
75240 Paris Cedex 05, France
Tel: 33-1-44-41-46-16 (French books)
Tel: 33-1-44-41-11-87 (English books)
Fax: 33-1-44-41-11-44
Email: distribution@eyrolles.com

### INQUIRIES
Éditions O'Reilly
18 rue Séguier
75006 Paris, France
Tel: 33-1-40-51-52-30
Fax: 33-1-40-51-52-31
Email: france@editions-oreilly.fr

## GERMANY, SWITZERLAND, AUSTRIA, EASTERN EUROPE, LUXEMBOURG, AND LIECHTENSTEIN

### INQUIRIES & ORDERS
O'Reilly Verlag
Balthasarstr. 81
D-50670 Köln
Germany
Telephone: 49-221-973160-91
Fax: 49-221-973160-8
Email: anfragen@oreilly.de (inquiries)
Email: order@oreilly.de (orders)

## CANADA (FRENCH LANGUAGE BOOKS)
Les Éditions Flammarion ltée
375, Avenue Laurier Ouest
Montréal (Québec) H2V 2K3
Tel: 00-1-514-277-8807
Fax: 00-1-514-278-2085
Email: info@flammarion.qc.ca

## HONG KONG
City Discount Subscription Service, Ltd.
Unit D, 3rd Floor, Yan's Tower
27 Wong Chuk Hang Road
Aberdeen, Hong Kong
Tel: 852-2580-3539
Fax: 852-2580-6463
Email: citydis@ppn.com.hk

## KOREA
Hanbit Media, Inc.
Sonyoung Bldg. 202
Yeksam-dong 736-36
Kangnam-ku
Seoul, Korea
Tel: 822-554-9610
Fax: 822-556-0363
Email: hant93@chollian.dacom.co.kr

## PHILIPPINES
Mutual Books, Inc.
429-D Shaw Boulevard
Mandaluyong City, Metro
Manila, Philippines
Tel: 632-725-7538
Fax: 632-721-3056
Email: mbikikog@mnl.sequel.net

## TAIWAN
O'Reilly Taiwan
No. 3, Lane 131
Hang-Chow South Road
Section 1, Taipei, Taiwan
Tel: 886-2-23968990
Fax: 886-2-23968916
Email: taiwan@oreilly.com

## CHINA
O'Reilly Beijing
Room 2410
160, FuXingMenNeiDaJie
XiCheng District
Beijing, China PR 100031
Tel: 86-10-86631006
Fax: 86-10-86631007
Email: beijing@oreilly.com

## INDIA
Computer Bookshop (India) Pvt. Ltd.
190 Dr. D.N. Road, Fort
Bombay 400 001 India
Tel: 91-22-207-0989
Fax: 91-22-262-3551
Email: cbsbom@giasbm01.vsnl.net.in

## JAPAN
O'Reilly Japan, Inc.
Kiyoshige Building 2F
12-Bancho, Sanei-cho
Shinjuku-ku
Tokyo 160-0008 Japan
Tel: 81-3-3356-5227
Fax: 81-3-3356-5261
Email: japan@oreilly.com

## ALL OTHER ASIAN COUNTRIES
O'Reilly & Associates, Inc.
101 Morris Street
Sebastopol, CA 95472 USA
Tel: 707-829-0515
Fax: 707-829-0104
Email: order@oreilly.com

## AUSTRALIA
WoodsLane Pty., Ltd.
7/5 Vuko Place
Warriewood NSW 2102
Australia
Tel: 61-2-9970-5111
Fax: 61-2-9970-5002
Email: info@woodslane.com.au

## NEW ZEALAND
Woodslane New Zealand, Ltd.
21 Cooks Street (P.O. Box 575)
Waganui, New Zealand
Tel: 64-6-347-6543
Fax: 64-6-345-4840
Email: info@woodslane.com.au

## LATIN AMERICA
McGraw-Hill Interamericana
Editores, S.A. de C.V.
Cedro No. 512
Col. Atlampa
06450, Mexico, D.F.
Tel: 52-5-547-6777
Fax: 52-5-547-3336
Email: mcgraw-hill@infosel.net.mx